NEW DIRECTIONS
FOR LAW IN AUSTRALIA
ESSAYS IN CONTEMPORARY LAW REFORM

NEW DIRECTIONS
FOR LAW IN AUSTRALIA
ESSAYS IN CONTEMPORARY LAW REFORM

EDITED BY RON LEVY, MOLLY O'BRIEN, SIMON RICE,
PAULINE RIDGE AND MARGARET THORNTON

Australian
National
University

PRESS

ANU PRESS

Published by ANU Press
The Australian National University
Acton ACT 2601, Australia
Email: anupress@anu.edu.au
This title is also available online at press.anu.edu.au

National Library of Australia Cataloguing-in-Publication entry

Title: New directions for law in Australia : essays in
             contemporary law reform / edited by Ron
             Levy, Molly O'Brien, Simon Rice,
             Pauline Ridge, Margaret Thornton.

ISBN: 9781760461416 (paperback) 9781760461423 (ebook)

Subjects: Law reform--Australia.
           Law--Australia.
           Essays.

Other Creators/Contributors:
           Levy, Ron, editor.
           O'Brien, Molly Townes, editor.
           Rice, Simon, editor.
           Ridge, Pauline, editor.
           Thornton, Margaret (Margaret Rose), editor.

Cover design and layout by ANU Press. Cover photograph by Kate Ogg.

Contents

Part II. Criminal Law and Evidence

Part III. Environmental Law

Part VI. Legal Practice and Legal Education

Foreword

The Hon Michael Kirby AC CMG[1]

Academic lawyers in Australia have long played a vital role in the national project of law reform. They thought about it; they wrote about it; they worried about its haphazard ways; and they taught their students, and others who would listen, about the need for a more systematic and effective approach to the challenge.

As I discovered, soon after my appointment as inaugural Chairman (as the office was then styled) of the Australian Law Reform Commission (ALRC), many members of the judiciary and practising branches of the legal profession were hostile to, or apathetic about, law reform.[2] It was substantially left to academic scholars and civil society organisations and individual politicians to stimulate the demand for reform and to propose the directions that it should take.

In part, this impasse came about because judges and practitioners were distracted by the daily tasks of resolving, according to the law, the large and often mundane problems presented for the application of the existing law. Although that task frequently revealed imperfections, uncertainties, antiquities and inconsistencies in the law, there was a great deal of complacency. Where injustice was revealed, this was ascribed to the inevitable deficiencies of law since ancient times, against which victims might protest but would rarely prevail.

---

1   Chairman of the Australian Law Reform Commission (1975–1984); President of the New South Wales Court of Appeal (1984–1996); Justice of the High Court of Australia (1996–2009).
2   See, for example, P A Jacobs, 'A Plea for Law Reform' (1940) 13 *Australian Law Journal* 398.

Whereas many judges and practitioners retained this attitude well into the life of the ALRC, academics were much more ready to challenge the law and to urge changes that would bring it into line with contemporary social attitudes, perceptions of justice, technology and needs for rationalisation and simplification.

The ALRC quickly became a vehicle by which Australia's academic lawyers were brought into a more active contact with the formal law reform process in Australia. They were appointed commissioners (full-time and part-time), consultants and staff members of the ALRC. They were consulted, listened to, engaged with and involved in the development of the program of law reform and with its fulfilment. Many of them found the opportunity to serve for a short time stimulating to their careers and their interests in legal doctrine and useful to their professional tasks of teaching, analysing and writing about the law. This was one of the useful consequences of establishing full-time institutional law reform commissions in Australia, after the model established in England by Sir Leslie Scarman in 1965.

By the 1970s and 1980s, such full-time bodies had been created in Australia in the federal sphere and in New South Wales, Victoria, Queensland and Western Australia. Commissions or Committees with part-time members were created in the Australian Capital Territory, South Australia and Tasmania. In addition to these bodies, particular statutes created advisory bodies to perform specialised law reform work.[3] Academic lawyers continued, of course, in their lectures and publications to propose both small and large projects of law reform. These supplemented their engagements with law reform commissions. But the latter enhanced the role and function of Australia's legal academics in contributing to actual improvements in the legal system. It gave many of them a direct voice to government. It also encouraged them to think more systematically about law reform and to view it more emphatically, as part of their duties as legal scholars. This meant not only chronicling and describing the law as it existed, but also critiquing its provisions and identifying faults and deficiencies so as to make the legal system work more efficiently and fairly for the people governed by it.

---

3   Such as the Administrative Review Council, the Family Law Council and the Australian Institute of Criminology.

The manifest inefficiencies of the traditional part-time model for institutional law reform gave rise to full-time law reform commissions in India, the United Kingdom and Australia. Unfortunately, hostility towards the resulting bodies in Australia did not disappear with the established efficiencies and successes of the agencies. Right into the present time, a number of members of the Australian judiciary and practising legal profession have exhibited animosity towards institutional law reform. Such critics never comprised a majority of the practising profession. But their voices were loud and influential. They tended to undermine the credibility of, and respect for, the law reform institutions in circles where this mattered. They played into the hands of bureaucratic opponents who viewed full-time law reform agencies as a challenge to the power and control they had held over the emergence of law and public policy, which they desired to centralise in their own hands. Ostensibly, their antagonism was justified by reference to cost saving and such noble causes as the protection of ministers, the government and the Westminster system itself.

An instance of the hostility to which I refer was given a voice in the recent retirement speech of a distinguished and capable judge in New South Wales. Surveying the perceived defects in the law that had emerged during his lifetime, astonishingly he included amongst the worst offenders institutional law reform. He revealed that they were, with journalists, amongst his 'pet hates'. According to a whimsical description by one such journalist of these retirement remarks, the judge described law reformers as people who have an 'unwholesome ambition for personal power and aggrandisement, or people who, to speak frankly, are ... unstable'.[4]

Perhaps the judge on this occasion was speaking with tongue in cheek. His own subsequent engagement with academic life suggests that this might have been the case. But his words were seen by the journalist as 'blowing a gasket'.[5] However, if so, he was not the only one to react to institutional law reform in this way.

In the years after the ALRC was created in 1975, we witnessed in Australia the rise and ascendency of institutional law reform. However, this was quickly followed by a decline and fall. From a thriving body – usually with

4   Richard Ackland, 'A Sully Serve for Sullied Media, Law Reformers', *The Sydney Morning Herald*, 30 March 2017, www.smh.com.au/news/opinion/a-sully-serve-for-sullied-media-law-reformers/2007/03/29/1174761664005.html.
5   Ibid.

three or four full-time commissioners (many academics) and five or more part-time commissioners (many judges, academics and practitioners) – the Commission shrank in the number of its members; the recruitment of consultants; the engagement of staff; and the enlistment of social scientists, whose empirical research capacity was designed to support the quality of the Commission's reports.

At the time of the blown judicial 'gasket' over institutional law reformers, the ALRC had but one full-time commissioner and two part-time (judicial) commissioners. Its budget had been slashed from former times. Its work program limped along but without a substantial program. No longer could it be described as a thriving, busy assistant to the Federal Parliament in diverse tasks necessary for the reform, modernisation and simplification of the law. Instead, it was crippled by the lack of multiple references from the Attorney-General; resources suitable to viability and effectiveness; and personnel essential to be taken seriously if it were to fulfil the function envisaged for it under its statute.[6] Describing such a body as ambitious for 'personal power and aggrandisement' could only be viewed as absurd, unless the near demolition worked upon it was itself a consequence of a similar view held by the successive ministers and officials who had brought the body to this fate.

For small mercies one must be grateful in recounting this chronicle. The Law Reform Commission of Canada was abolished not once but twice. State law reform commissions in Australia have also been abolished on the suggested ground that they were 'expensive luxuries'.[7] As one writer, after describing the successes of institutional law reform in England and South Africa, laments: 'When we turn to Australia, the sky becomes much more cloudy, and in places extremely dark and gloomy – a far cry from the confident days of the early 1980s'.[8]

It is distressing to write in this way, and in this book, about the institutional law reform scene in Australia today. It has lacked political engagement from a new generation of champions who see a need for a proper system of auditing and modernising the legal system of the nation.

---

6   *Law Reform Commission Act 1973* (Cth) s 6; now *Australian Law Reform Commission Act 1996* (Cth) s 21.

7   Michael Tilbury, Simon N M Young and Ludwig Ng, 'Law Reform Today', in Michael Tilbury, Simon N M Young and Ludwig Ng (eds), *Reforming Law Reform: Perspectives from Hong Kong and Beyond* (Hong Kong University Press, 2014) 5.

8   John Hannaford, 'The Changing Face of Law Reform' (1999) 73 *Australian Law Journal* 503, 511.

It lacks advocates who can point to the economic and financial case for constantly and systematically reforming the law in a country pretending to adherence to the rule of law. It ignores the generally good strike rate of the full-time commissions in the conversion of their law reform recommendations into enacted law and implemented policy. It overlooks the capacity of such independent bodies to consult the community in ways that politicians and the public service could not do, and thereby to defuse unsettling controversy in society. It removes the academic and the private legal profession's talent and inclination for independent thinking and criticism of the law. It lacks reform derived from conceptual thinking and empirical data. It returns the landscape of law reform in Australia to a thing of shreds and patches, of band aids and political fixes: something to be done in tiny projects by overworked part-time volunteers at the fag-end of the week, over a glass of whisky or two.

When, as is occasionally the case, I am invited to return to the Attorney-General's Department in Canberra, I remember the very different place it presented on my first visit in 1975. There I found a small, highly talented, expert cadre of excellent federal lawyers enthusiastic for institutional law reform. Now it is a huge undertaking, greatly expanded by the addition of larger operational functions of federal police, security and anti-terrorism. Whilst these tasks are surely essential features of a modern society that protects the rule of law, so also is institutional law reform. Withdrawal or radical reduction of the budget subventions for institutional law reform represents a shift from an optimistic and liberal view of the role of the law in Australian society to a controlling and pessimistic view which should not be allowed to predominate. At least it should not be allowed to eviscerate the regular institutional improvement of the law by the use of expert, well resourced and full-time machinery to that end. If we ran a large corporation without incorporating institutional means of examining, updating, simplifying and reforming its processes, we would soon run into trouble from the shareholders.

One of the saddest consequences of the decline and fall of institutional law reform in Australia has been the substantial withdrawal of the engagement of Australia's distinguished legal academics in law reform, which was a hallmark of the splendid work, in federal, state and territory jurisdictions, that was performed in decades gone by. This book shows that the involvement of Australia's legal scholars in issues of law reform continues. It is most valuable. I praise and honour it. However, engagement in the processes of government has been substantially lost or certainly radically reduced. This is a tragedy for the conversion of bold ideas for law reform into action and implementation.

I hope that the former state of affairs will be restored. And that the legal scholars of Australia will raise their voices to complain about the institutional breakdown we have witnessed. This is not a partisan political appeal. Each of the major political groupings in Australia has contributed to where we have now ended up. Each of them needs to reconsider the simple proposition that the rule of law in our nation requires more than rules. It requires rules that are just, modern, efficient and in harmony with the values of a free and democratic people. And that means a revival of the confident days of the past and the restoration of well-funded public institutions of law reform, appropriate to a period of rapid social, economic and global change.

Michael Kirby
Sydney
14 September 2017

Introduction

Ron Levy, Molly O'Brien, Simon Rice,
Pauline Ridge and Margaret Thornton[1]

This volume emerges from the inaugural National Law Reform Conference held in April 2016 at The Australian National University. The conference's animating idea was that, for reasons of effectiveness, efficiency and equity, directions in the development of the law should be planned carefully, and that academics can and should take the lead in this process. The conference organisers' intention was to provide an opportunity for academic experts to incubate considered proposals for contemporary law reform in Australia. The 60-plus academics in attendance were invited to focus on future directions that the law ought to take in their areas of expertise. They addressed these central questions:

> To what challenges should [your area of law] be geared in the near-to-medium term future; what should be the legal and policy responses, and why?

The conference deliberations were broad in scope and organised into six streams: commercial activities, criminal law and evidence, environmental law, private law, public law, and legal practice and legal education. Indigenous perspectives on law reform were encouraged across all streams. An informed group of 160 conference participants, drawn from government, practice and the academy, discussed, evaluated and helped to improve the resulting papers.

The conference opened with an address from the Honourable Michael Kirby AC CMG, former Justice of the High Court of Australia. In his historical survey of law reform in Australia, Mr Kirby reminded us

---

1   All of ANU College of Law, The Australian National University.

that at the same venue 40 years earlier, as President of the Australian Law Reform Commission, he had addressed the second Australasian Law Reform Agencies Conference. It is fitting that the foreword to this book is by him. The keynote address, which now appears in revised form at the outset of this book, was delivered by Professor Margaret Davies. She advocated for a sophisticated and nuanced approach to law reform, and urged participants to challenge accepted meanings of both 'law' and 'law reform' – a challenge which some took up in their contributions. A selection of conference papers was revised, edited and double-blind peer reviewed to produce the remaining 50-plus chapters of the book.

Like the conference itself, this book provides a national focal point for legal innovation. The chapters provide a bird's-eye view of the current state and the future of law reform in Australia. The book's six main parts mirror the six subject streams of the conference; each part contains a set of reform ideas, drawing on theoretical, sociolegal and doctrinal work, and encapsulated in short, digestible 3,000-word essays. We hope that the book will be of value to policymakers, media, law reform agencies, academics, practitioners and the judiciary. The proposition that academic research serves the public interest in Australia is strongly supported by efforts such as these, especially in an era of reduced public resourcing of law reform agencies.[2]

We would like to thank the ANU College of Law and the Dean, Professor Stephen Bottomley, for providing financial support for the conference and publication of this collection of essays. We are also grateful to John Mahony, Isabella Wildsmith and Harry McLaurin for editorial assistance.

Keynote: Reforming Law

In the opening chapter, Margaret Davies provides a provocation to the conventional understanding of law reform. Although legal positivism remains the dominant legal theory that underpins both law and law reform, Davies encourages us to transcend a narrow conceptualisation. Feminist, sociolegal and pluralist legal scholars have shown that law comprises far more than that found in the statute books for, as Sarat says, it is in fact

---

2   One notable previous effort in Australia – albeit one focused primarily on the *process* of institutional law reform – is Brian Opeskin and David Weisbrot (eds), *The Promise of Law Reform* (Federation Press, 2005).

'all over'. Accordingly, we need to think about meta-legal reform, that is, new concepts of law that transcend the realm of legal experts. Alternative ways of thinking about law reform have the potential to effect a shift in legal consciousness so that we can imagine justice in new ways.

Part I: Commercial and Corporate Law

The chapters in this Part, organised thematically, propose new directions for law to address challenging issues in commercial and corporate activity. The first three chapters address corporations, consumers and taxation. Ross Grantham argues that 'an increasingly self-executing, enclosed system' of corporate activity has significant implications for the form of the *Corporations Act*. Further, his research shows that this shift to corporate self-regulation significantly reduces the supervisory role of the court. Grantham argues that the exercise of corporate power is now largely unaccountable, creating 'a significant democratic deficit'. Russell Miller puts his account of reforming the anti-competition provision (s 46) of the *Australian Consumer Law* in the context of consumer protection reforms in Australia since the 1990s. He describes the difficult journey of the Harper Panel's proposed reforms which negotiated 'vigorous debate' over two approaches to the same end, neither of which 'could be said to be entirely right or entirely wrong'. John Passant discusses the role of taxation in addressing social inequality. He argues that taxation can ameliorate 'the fundamental inequality between capital and labour', and canvasses two possible tax reforms: a net wealth tax; and a minimum threshold, or 'Buffett rule', for individuals and companies. Passant makes the argument to direct policymakers towards measures that can 'address growing inequality and the threat that poses to our democracy and economy'.

The next three chapters move to specific issues of employer regulation and home lending. Joellen Riley proposes a way of regulating the new, shared economy. Riley focuses on the current inadequacy of the protection of the rights, pay and conditions of workers in the new economy, and suggests that existing small business regulation in Australia offers models for regulating unconventional work arrangements. With similar attention to protecting workers' pay and conditions, Tess Hardy examines the measures for holding 'lead firms' liable for employment contraventions in their supply chain, corporate group or franchise network. Drawing on existing models of third party liability, she reviews proposals for statutory measures to reconceptualise legal responsibility for employment contraventions.

Gill North notes the large proportion of household debt represented by residential property mortgage debt in Australia, and proposes three policy reforms that protect against possible future consumer losses and hardship should the housing market decline sharply.

This Part closes with two chapters addressing our understanding of corporate whistleblowers. Kath Hall and Heather Cork challenge two limiting assumptions about whistleblowing – that whistleblowers act alone, and that reporting involves a single disclosure – and propose definitional reforms to broaden the reach and protection of whistleblowing laws. Suzanne Le Mire and Christine Parker also promote a broader understanding of whistleblowing, focusing on lawyers and their potential as 'gatekeepers for justice'. Le Mire and Parker propose a reexamination of lawyers' ethical duties to enable lawyers to disclose information that they hold of corporate wrongdoing.

Part II: Criminal Law and Evidence

The first chapter in this Part, by Lorana Bartels, explores the need for reform in criminal law and critiques Australia's 'addiction to prison'. She posits a new future in which all public policy proposals must hold the promise of decreasing the imprisonment rate. She points to the recent increase in the incarceration rate, its cost, the unfairness of the over-incarceration of Indigenous people, and the fact that prison is not an effective crime reduction tool. Both victims and offenders could be better served, she argues, by reallocating resources away from prison. In the second chapter, Simon Bronitt reviews the past few decades' practice in law reform commissions in the United Kingdom and Australia, especially in relation to criminal law. He asks whether, as in the past, our aspirations for criminal law reform should extend no further than the 'liberal promise' of a more 'principled and codified' criminal law. Next, Wendy Larcombe advocates a new approach to rape law, arguing that the law should better support the needs of sexual violence victims. Larcombe contends that, in spite of 40 years of law reform, the system does not provide accessible and effective resolutions for the vast majority of victims. She argues that trials for sexual offences should be heard by a judge alone, and that innovative and restorative justice alternatives to criminal prosecution should be provided to give victims of sexual assault more options. In another chapter that focuses on sexual assault cases, John Anderson argues that the dichotomy between tendency and context evidence is false: relationship or context evidence must be presumed prejudicial and inadmissible unless the prosecution can show its probative value outweighs its prejudicial effect. Jonathan Clough takes a broader reform scope in his chapter which proposes improving the mechanisms for prosecuting transnational corporate crime. He argues that corporate criminal liability continues to evolve, and that Australia must make sure it has appropriate structures in place so that large transnational corporations can be effectively prosecuted.

Several chapters place the focus of reform on jury activity. Blake McKimmie examines the influence of stereotypes on jurors, and argues that changes should be made in the manner of presenting expert evidence and in the appearance and positioning of defendants in the courtroom. Diane Sivasubramaniam suggests that the potential divergence between the deliberative legal and the retributive community notions of justice may not be reduced by restorative justice and preventative detention reforms. She argues that the retributive impulse is a strong human response and must not be ignored in the process of implementing legal reforms. In another chapter that relates to jury decision-making, Helen Fraser reviews a case in which the jury listens to a covertly made recording of a conversation between police and the accused. In accord with standard practice, the jury read a transcript of the conversation written by a detective acting as an ad hoc expert. Fraser examines the recording and concludes that the transcript is inaccurate. Because the process of involving the police in making a transcript is flawed and invites injustice, Fraser advocates designing a system that will produce reliable transcripts. In the final chapter in this Part, Anne Wallace looks at criminal courtroom processes and finds that they are in transition toward a more efficient system that makes use of online resources and is more user-centric. She points to reforms that she sees leading the courts into the 21st century.

Part III: Environmental Law

Irene Watson begins this Part with the provocative proposition that ecocide of First Nation territories parallels the genocide committed against First Nation peoples. She rejects conventional law reform because of its unlawful colonial foundation associated with *terra nullius*, and argues for a re-emergence and acknowledgement of the ancient laws of the land which, she avers, would be truly mainstream. Virginia Marshall's chapter also addresses the impact of the postcolonial legacy on the environmental interests of Indigenous peoples, with particular regard to water to overturn *aqua nullius*. She is critical of the characterisation of Indigenous peoples as a minority interest, and argues for a focus on international human rights principles as expressed in the UN Declaration on the Rights of Indigenous Peoples (UNDRIP), which would more effectively give expression to the exercise and enjoyment of Indigenous communities' rights to water. In her chapter, Natalie Stoianoff describes Australia's slow progress towards recognising Indigenous ecological knowledge (IEK) in conserving biological diversity and managing natural resources. She reports on the development of an Indigenous governance framework for environmental management, the 2014 NSW Office of Environment and Heritage White Paper, *Recognising and Protecting Aboriginal Knowledge Associated with Natural Resource Management*.

Beginning with the idea that the earth's life support systems are experiencing profound and potentially devastating change, Jan McDonald takes on the task of reforming environmental law to make it more responsive. She identifies a reform agenda for environmental law, comprising techniques and tools for building in flexibility to environmental decisions and environmental law-making processes more generally. She argues that law reform must be part of a broader shift towards polycentric and adaptive governance that recognises system complexity.

Cameron Holley's chapter considers one of Australia's central environmental challenges: sustaining the supply of water. He considers a suite of reforms to improve upon past initiatives in the area. In the final chapter, Paul Martin, Amanda Kennedy and Jacqueline Williams provide one of several 'meta-reform' perspectives in this book. They examine the proliferation of laws on rural biodiversity and, finding past efforts wanting, suggest changes to the process of reform: future law-making should take a 'whole-of-landscape, socioeconomically realistic' approach.

Part IV: Private Law

The first group of chapters on private law exposes the perils of statutory law reform in areas traditionally governed by judge-made law. Darryn Jensen provides a simple illustration: a perceived flaw in the common law concerning receipt of misapplied trust assets was corrected by legislation in some states. But these 'piecemeal' reforms have proved to be problematic and redundant. Matthew Harding and Joachim Dietrich expose serious problems that may arise from the interaction of legislation and common law in a federal system. Harding explains how the proliferation of statutory definitions of 'charity' has created complexity, inconsistency and, in some instances, rule of law concerns. Dietrich criticises the extraordinarily complex package of tort law, contract law and legislation concerning liability for personal injuries sustained during performance of a contract for recreational services. He illustrates his theme by reference to the differing tort defences under different regimes, the failure of legislatures to further the objective of a uniform national consumer law, and the uncertainty surrounding contractual exclusion of liability. Elise Bant and Jeannie Paterson consider the challenges of 'meta-legislation' such as the *Australian Consumer Law (ACL)*. Using the remedial provisions that respond to misleading conduct and unconscionable conduct, the authors consider how coherent development of the law can be achieved and how to ensure that the *ACL*'s density and complexity do not undermine its efficacy. They recommend, among other measures, soft law practice notes for consumers and decision-makers. Finally, in the first group of chapters, Robyn Carroll and Catherine Graville explain the potency of alternative remedies to damages for defamation, and evaluate the efficacy of alternative remedial schemes in the current uniform defamation laws. They argue for inclusion of a 'reasonable apology' requirement in an offer to make amends.

The second group of chapters uses private law theory to inform regulatory design. Simone Degeling and Kit Barker argue that corrective justice provides the most morally and ethically appropriate framework for reparative schemes to redress grave historical injustices. They make important recommendations for the improvement of existing reparation schemes, such as the scheme established to redress abuse within the Australian Defence Force, and for the design of new schemes, such as that proposed to redress institutional child sexual abuse. Prue Vines also focuses on corrective justice. She argues that the law of negligence for personal injury responds inadequately to the parties' symbolic, emotional and monetary needs and that an apology may better meet the corrective justice objectives of tort law.

The third group of chapters identifies two areas where fundamental reform is required. Robyn Honey argues for a more nuanced understanding of capacity and consent in property and contract law. She proposes a set of reform principles that will avoid paternalism and appropriately promote autonomy. Ian Murray's chapter concerns the point in time at which a charity should be expected to produce a public benefit from currently held resources. He argues on theoretical and practical grounds that more attention should be paid by charities to intergenerational balance in accumulating or applying charity funds, and he spells out how this might be done.

Part V: Public Law

The chapters on public law offer 10 proposals, including blueprints for dramatic legal change. Initial chapters argue for meta-reforms: ways to reform the process of law reform itself. Graeme Orr's chapter takes on the vexed question of compulsory voting in constitutional referendums. Orr argues that, given the distinctive nature of constitutional law and reform, voting at constitutional referendums should be voluntary. Scott Stephenson's chapter also rethinks constitutional referendums. His solution to the problem of Australia's stalled process of constitutional change is the use of citizens' assemblies – randomly selected, rigorously informed and demographically representative bodies empowered to draft referendum questions. As dramatic as Orr and Stephenson's reforms would be, the next two meta-reforms arguably would be even more fundamental. Lael Weis compares the culture of constitutional reform in Australia to that of the United States, where a 'popular constitutional culture' sees many or even most Americans deliberate about the meanings and directions of their founding document. Weis advocates approaches to help 'cultivate' an Australian popular constitutional culture. Gabrielle Appleby and Anna Olijnyk in turn consider an important set of cases where the constitutionality of a legislative Bill is uncertain. Their proposed reforms aim to enhance parliamentary constitutional deliberations.

The first four chapters described share a common focus on deliberation – a dominant concern in academic studies of politics, and an emergent concern for public law scholars. Two more chapters also consider deliberation, in particular in relation to human rights. Dominique Dalla-Pozza's chapter assesses the Commonwealth's Parliamentary Joint Committee on Intelligence and Security, while Julie Debeljak's examines the first decade of judicial decisions – and legislative reactions – under the Victorian *Charter of Human Rights and Responsibilities*. Both models leave parliaments ultimately sovereign, yet both seek to increase the scrutiny of legislation against rights standards. Before recommending key reforms, each author recounts the recent histories of the respective rights models.

The next chapter, by Andrew Henderson and Kim Rubenstein, reflects some of the themes Debeljak raises. But Henderson and Rubenstein invert these themes by considering how courts can constitute an historical record of key Australian debates and events.

Three final chapters rethink particular subjects in public law. Andrew Kenyon's chapter charts expanding notions of free speech in jurisdictions including Germany. Kenyon lays out a case for speech interests to be understood not only in classical negative terms (i.e. anti-censorship), but also as a positive and collective interest requiring, for example, the airing of diverse points of view. Melissa Castan and Paula Gerber explore the profound personal and social significance of a seemingly innocuous document: the Australian birth certificate. Noting how the certificate's absence is both a consequence and a cause of social disadvantage (e.g. among immigrant and Indigenous communities), they suggest specific reforms. Daniel Stewart closes this Part by bringing to light problems in government secrecy laws. He considers law reforms that would better manage disclosure and privacy interests in relation, for instance, to immigration detention centres and public servants' uses of social media.

Part VI: Legal Practice and Legal Education

In this final Part of the book, six chapters are devoted to the reform of legal practice and three to legal education. The first three chapters address the perennially vexed issue of ethics in legal practice. The *Legal Profession Uniform Law* (*LPUL*) (so far enacted only in NSW and Victoria) represents an important step towards uniformity, but Vivien Holmes, Stephen Tang, Tony Foley and Margie Rowe argue that the *LPUL* adopts a retrograde stance in regard to ethics. They advocate a return to the proactive model of ethics management devised in NSW only a few years earlier. In evincing concern about the complicity of lawyers in the unethical conduct of their clients, Adrian Evans identifies numerous weak points in lawyer education and training. Rather than institutional reform, he argues for a heightened awareness on the part of individual practitioners. In contrast, Justine Rogers advocates that the ethical focus should be on the team, the typical organisational unit within firms. She recommends that attention be accorded to 'teamthink' in legal education, professional regulation and scholarship.

The next three chapters offer reformist perspectives on discrete aspects of legal practice. First, Bronwen Morgan, Joanne McNeill and Isobel Blomfield consider the legal ambiguity confronting sustainable economic initiatives in response to environmental challenges. As this type of entrepreneurialism falls between for-profit and not-for-profit models, Morgan et al recommend that attention be paid to creating a dedicated professional network for legal practitioners and service providers. Second, Mary Anne Noone addresses the challenges that arise when lawyers act as mediators, as required by courts and tribunals, because the lawyer then becomes both an officer of the court and third party neutral. Noone suggests that the tension be minimised by making parties aware of their rights, reporting systemic issues and placing a prohibition on immunity from liability. Third, Liz Curran articulates her concern that the voices of the marginalised are rarely heard in the law reform process. She argues that, with imagination and little cost, it is possible to empower marginalised people, a proposition she illustrates with examples.

The final trio of chapters is concerned with the reform of legal education. The first, by Craig Collins, draws attention to the Renaissance movement of Ramism that harnessed the power of printing, and to the textbook, which became central to legal education. As technological change is effecting the end of Ramism, Collins argues that less weight be paid to academic requirements and more to practical legal education. Paul Maharg addresses the complexity of the increasingly onerous regulation requirements of legal education, which are subject not only to mediation and intermediation, but also to the disruptive process of disintermediation. Maharg argues for a neutral space where regulators and others can meet and deliberate, a process likely to improve the quality of regulation. Finally, Margaret Thornton highlights the disjuncture between the standardised curriculum and the reality that most law graduates no longer enter traditional private practice. She argues that the Priestley 11 should cease to be mandatory, enabling law schools to develop diverse curricula that would better equip graduates for a range of destinations.

Keynote: Reforming Law – The Role of Theory

Margaret Davies[1]

I. Introduction

The anarchist Peter Kropotkin began his 1886 pamphlet *Law and Authority* by describing the tendency of law to proliferate so that it takes over every aspect of social life:[2]

> when ignorance reigns in society and disorder in the minds of men, laws are multiplied, legislation is expected to do everything, and each fresh law, being a fresh miscalculation, men are continually led to demand from it what can proceed only from their own education and their own morality.

Kropotkin continues by noting that, because of this demand for law to fix things, laws continue to multiply, to the point that there is 'a law everywhere and about everything.' As an anarchist, Kropotkin thought that the desire for law to rectify society's problems stemmed from a learned reliance on others rather than reliance on the intrinsic resources of the self and the immediate community. He argued that law achieves its power by weaving together two elements: longstanding and useful customs which society is committed to, and mechanisms allowing the privileged classes to maintain their power. It was not an entirely simplistic view of law as an instrument of dominance. However, he saw the socially accepted parts of law as a foil, which were there to conceal the fact that law essentially operates to strengthen the power of the privileged.

---

1   Matthew Flinders Distinguished Professor of Law, Flinders University.
2   Peter Kropotkin, *Law and Authority: An Anarchist Essay* (Open Socialist Publishing, 2006) 6.

If there was too much law for Kropotkin in 19th century Europe I don't like to imagine what he would have made of modern nation states and the legal effects of globalisation. (Indeed the phenomenon of 'juridification' has been much analysed in the later 20th and early 21st centuries.[3]) In some ways Kropotkin's underlying image of law was not completely unlike the image held by 19th and 20th century liberal thinkers. This image was of a law with its own sphere, a law with a conceptual limit beyond which people could organise their lives as they saw fit. Beyond law's sphere of regulation lay freedom and the private sphere. Kropotkin's agenda was to reduce and eventually eliminate law – he concludes his pamphlet with the words 'no more laws! No more judges!'[4] The more moderate concern of many other writers who also adopt the image of a limited law and an outside or non-regulated area of freedom and privacy has been and continues to be where to draw the line of legal intervention, and how to improve the limited law to make it more efficient and consistent, less obscure, and in tune with current social values.

The idea of a limited sphere of law and a non-legal sphere of freedom was tested repeatedly throughout the 20th century, often in conjunction with an appreciation of the disseminated nature of power. The image of a limited law was, for instance, revealed to be incoherent in the 1980s by feminist writers such as Frances Olsen and Katherine O'Donovan who pointed to the many ways in which law shapes the conditions for social life and structures legal subjects and their relationships.[5] Law is not neutral as regards social order, but rather creates, normalises and replicates social life. At the same time, by perpetuating the idea that abstract individualism is gender-neutral and race-neutral, and that the person is a natural rather than constructed feature of social life, law obscures its own role in producing social relations. As feminists argued, beyond law was not freedom but, rather, a pervasively normalised and legally inflected social and private life. As Margaret Thornton wrote in the 1990s, 'For women, neither the polity nor the market have been realms of freedom or self-realisation, but realms of hostility'.[6]

---

3   See, in particular, Jurgen Habermas, *Theory of Communicative Action* Vol 2 (Beacon Press, 1987) 356–73.
4   Kropotkin, above n 2, 34.
5   Frances Olsen, 'The Family and the Market: A Study of Ideology and Legal Reform' (1983) 96 *Harvard Law Review* 1497; Katherine O'Donovan, *Sexual Divisions in Law* (Weidenfeld and Nicholson, 1985).
6   Margaret Thornton, 'The Cartography of Public and Private' in Margaret Thornton (ed), *Public and Private: Feminist Legal Debates* (Oxford University Press, 1995).

Sociolegal scholars also pointed to the unlimited nature of law. In 1990 Austin Sarat wrote an influential article about the legal experiences of welfare recipients in New England.[7] One of his respondents claimed that the 'law is all over' – in other words it is pervasive and unavoidable. This was not so much a view of formal law as having expanded uncontrollably in the way that Kropotkin envisaged – rather, it was a realistic assessment of the fact that law is a different thing for people in different social situations. The welfare recipient had a constant need to engage with law and so felt its presence immediately and materially. Such necessity leads to an experience of law which is, as Sarat says, 'embodied in a particular set of lived conditions: ... a law of practices, not promises, of material transactions, not abstract ideals'.[8] Understood from the bottom up, law is everywhere and has an oppressive weight – it doesn't liberate but sets the conditions for survival and demands constant engagement.

Legal pluralists have also challenged the limited view of law, and I would broadly divide this scholarship into two different types. One rather dominant strand of pluralism has examined forms of law outside the state, from Indigenous and religious law to semi-formalised systems of non-legal governance. Such approaches, like legal positivism, tend to view law as an objectifiable and self-contained thing. A second type of pluralism, which has grown in part out of the first, looks at law as emerging from human interactions and narratives, making it fluid and local, and often leading to hybrid forms where people combine norms from different sources in order to create a kind of social law.

Clearly the writers of recent decades did not mean (or perhaps did not only mean) that the nightmare implied by Kropotkin had come to pass – that doctrinal law has reached further and further into the interstices it creates so that no corner of life is left unlegislated and unregulated. It would perhaps be plausible to hold this view, but feminist, sociolegal and many pluralist theorists start with a different view of law, where it is always embedded in social life. Rather than think of law as an additive or an intervention which expands from a small space to occupy almost everything but which still has its own identity and autonomy, law is seen

---

7   Austin Sarat, '"The Law is All Over": Power, Resistance, and the Legal Consciousness of the Welfare Poor' (1990) 2 *Yale Journal of Law and the Humanities* 343.
8   Ibid. 378.

as more pervasive and less cohesive, a dispersed set of practices and values, not necessarily emanating from a single place, and experienced and performed differently by different groups of people.

Where does law reform sit in an image of law which is 'all over', as Sarat's respondent said, and where different groups of people have quite different views of what law is and how it operates? I'd like to address this question in three parts. First, by reference to the familiar notion that law reform is about changing doctrinal law so that it better suits the social conditions of the times. Second, by thinking about the idea that law reform can equally address a changing concept of law. Third, by looking at changes in the social and cultural conditions which underpin law.

II. Reforming Law

First, then, to the familiar notion that law reform essentially concerns improvements to the positive law to make it more coherent, to deal with new social, economic and technological conditions, or to address social problems. In 1949,[9] Lord Denning compared a national society to a river and the law to the 'conservator' who keeps the river in good shape. He argued that once the law is stable and developed, the conservator only has to do occasional maintenance – cutting the weeds and repairing the banks, for instance. 'The river flows peacefully and slowly' he said.[10]

> But in ... days of great social changes ... the law ha[s] to develop apace so as to meet the needs of the time. The greater the social revolution, the greater the need of law reform. The river is turbulent and restless and is in danger of getting out of control. The hatches have to be opened. New channels have to be cut. It requires legal statesmanship of the highest order to keep the law abreast of the social changes. If it does not do so, the rule of law itself may be engulfed and flooded out.

In this image, society usually goes along within the constraints set in place by the law. Social life is the water which flows through the form preserved by law. There is no sense in this image that the characteristics of the river as a whole have been formed by the flow of water; rather, the flow is determined by the solid surfaces maintained by the law. Law reform

---

9   Alfred Thomson Denning (Baron), 'The Universities and Law Reform' (1949) 1 *Journal of the Society of Public Teachers of Law* 258.
10   Ibid. 258.

is about tidying up the banks and eliminating obstructions, and, in times of dangerous social upheaval, undertaking more substantial changes to the size, depth and direction of flow. It is an extremely benign view of law – law is basically fine and has a pre-given form, but needs to be tidied up from time to time.

Denning's river is a variation on the idea of a limited sphere of law outside which there is freedom. The image does imply that law provides rather total conditions and shape for social life, but it nonetheless promotes a largely contained view of law. Law provides a neutral form for social existence and, within the confines of the river banks, the individual water molecules can do largely as they please.

There was of course dispute throughout the 20th century about whether both parliament *and* judges are the appropriate agents of reform in the law. The debate has many layers which I will not go into here, but primarily it counterposes the common law tradition and the newer theory of legal realism, against the more rationalist positivism of Austin and Bentham.[11] The common law tradition gave judges a prime role in identifying and developing the law, and realists took the view that judges, as human actors, necessarily interpret and apply law in the light of social values. By contrast, Austin and Bentham were adamant about the need to distinguish sharply the question of what law is from what it ought to be. They saw the inquiry into what law is as a matter for those who identify and apply the law, while the question of what law ought to be is determined by parliament and law reformers. Keeping a clear view of the separation of these things was essential for law reform to operate properly and, indeed, in their view much law reform by way of clarification and, ideally, codification was needed in order to make it possible.

As foreshadowed at the beginning of my chapter, the success of the positivist view of law also poses real dilemmas for broad change. For instance, in gender relations, because the underlying idea of law is so doctrinally focused, positivism enforces a pernicious choice between engaging or not engaging with law, between standing inside or outside the law.[12] Because this idea of law is so invested with a view of its own

---

11   John Gava, 'The Rise of the Hero Judge' (2001) 24 *UNSW Law Review* 747; J D Heydon, 'Judicial Activism and the Death of the Rule of Law' (2004) 10 *Otago Law Review* 493; Michael Kirby '"Judicial Activism"? A Riposte to the Counter-Reformation' (2005) 11 *Otago Law Review* 1.
12   See Mari Matsuda, 'When the First Quail Calls: Multiple Consciousness as Jurisprudential Method' (1988) 11 *Women's Rights Law Reporter* 7, 8.

neutrality vis-à-vis social power, engaging from a position that does not accept its neutrality has been very difficult. This has led to a good deal of caution among all critics of state law about whether and how to engage with law and law reform: What can be expected of law reform? Does engaging with law simply legitimate its exclusion of alternative knowledges? How can values of care be imported into doctrinal law? How can the experiences of marginalised others be incorporated into the assumed knowledge of law? How can legal subjects be reconstructed as relational rather than atomistic? How can entrenched biases in the operation of law be addressed? How can we even commence the 'horizontal dialogue' that Irene Watson has spoken of between modern Australian colonial law and the first, original, law of this country?[13] The very form of positivist law seems to prevent anything but ad hoc change which may, of course, accumulate into something larger over time, but it is a very slow process.

III. Reforming Concepts of Law

It has always been extremely interesting to me to think that Austin and Bentham were themselves engaged not only in law reform but in a meta-legal reform – the reform of the concept of law. The theory of legal positivism, much criticised throughout the 20th century but also completely ingrained in legal pedagogy and ideology, was itself the product of a strategic conceptual change and emerged as part of a reformist agenda. Theory is not only about describing and understanding the world; rather, it both responds to *and makes* the world. Legal positivism is an extremely successful example of what might be termed conceptual reform.[14] It made, and continues to make, the concept of law as something separate from society while also purporting to describe what it has itself made. The point has been made by Wayne Morrison in relation to Austin:[15]

> knowledge claims are part of, and not antecedent to, [Austin's] overall project. Austin is not a simple positivist in the sense that his knowledge claim has no pretence to anything other than the 'thing-in-itself', for his

---

13   Irene Watson, 'What is the Mainstream? The Laws of First Nations Peoples', see Ch 18, this collection.

14   See, in particular, Frederick Schauer, 'The Path-Dependence of Legal Positivism' (2015) 101 *Virginia Law Review* 957, 960–69.

15   W Morrison, *Jurisprudence: From the Greeks to Post-modernism* (Cavendish, 1997) 227; see also, discussing Bentham, Schauer, above n 14, 960–69; Tom Campbell, *The Legal Theory of Ethical Positivism* (Dartmouth, 1996).

image of positive law is one element of an overall project. ... Austin's claims for jurisprudence are pragmatic in the sense that the demand for a clear jurisprudence arises to get something done, and that something is to create an image of law suitable for law to become a powerful and rational image of modernity.

HLA Hart also described Austin and Bentham's project in terms of conceptual reform – to construct a workable concept of law which would enable the doctrinal law to be improved. He described them as 'the vanguard of a movement which labored with passionate intensity and much success' and also insisted that their 'prime reason' for insisting on the separation of law and morality 'was to enable [people] to see steadily the precise issues posed by the existence of morally bad laws'.[16] In other words, separating is from ought was not a description of a reality, but rather an *act of theory construction* which was part of an overall agenda of rationalisation in the law. They made what they wanted to describe and it obviously resonated more broadly – in time it became true because people acted as if it were true. However, as I have indicated, the problem with the success of positivism was that it seemed to leave the only option for legal change as change in the content of law – its doctrines and procedures.

I have laboured this point, because for some years I have taken inspiration from Austin and Bentham on this issue and regarded theory to be not only about analysing and describing, but also constructing alternative concepts of law which are future-oriented. That this is possible is reinforced in social theory and critical philosophy. Drawing out aspects of the present which appear to provide direction for the future, and intensifying them theoretically, prefigures a world that is commensurable with the present and past, but which perhaps adds additional emphasis to those elements of it worth promoting. Theory can therefore be seen as an imaginative response to present circumstances, in which theorists actively choose their abstractions from a complex world. This is true of all theory, not only of theory based on an explicit normative vision.

This broader need for law reform to encompass not only reform in doctrinal law but also new concepts of law was explicitly recognised in the now disbanded Law Commission of Canada. As well as more recognisable law reform objectives, it had a statutory mandate to 'work towards the

---

16   H L A Hart, 'Positivism and the Separation of Law and Morality' (1958) 71 *Harvard Law Review* 593, 596.

development of new concepts of law and new approaches to law'.[17] The Law Commission stated that it 'interprets this legislative purpose as directing it to examine critically even the most fundamental principles of the Canadian legal system'.[18]

Over the past half century there have been some efforts to develop alternative concepts of law and I think it would be correct to say that some paradigm shifting is underway. This was true when I began my career as a legal scholar, though 25 years ago I hoped things would have become more certain by now. That was a misplaced hope, and legal theory remains in an uncertain but very interesting situation. No alternative concept has at this stage reached the prominence of legal positivism which, as I have said, has attained its status because of its widespread adoption. But some themes can perhaps be observed.

First, as I indicated above, there is an appreciation of law as distributed or networked across social life as opposed to existing in its own limited sphere. Understanding law as distributed, or perhaps diffused, means several things: it means, as many scholars have observed, that law shapes and leaves imprints across all social relationships, even or especially those that were once regarded as intrinsically private;[19] it means that law has a spatial and material presence and not just an abstract one;[20] and it means that doctrinal law is a conceptually crystallised form of human normative relationships but is never self-contained or self-generating, because of its reliance on human intervention in the form of interpretations and applications of law.

These observations are connected to a second theme of the newer approaches to law, which is that law is not simply a top-down imposition, but also in many forms has to be regarded as emerging from subjective and material human experiences.[21] In a sense, this has involved two or possibly three shifts. First, there is an appreciation that law is not a thing in itself that can be reflected or represented in theory but, rather, is the product

---

17   *Law Commission of Canada Act 1996* s 3(a).

18   Records of Law Commission of Canada held on the website of the Library and Archives of Canada: epe.lac-bac.gc.ca/100/206/301/law_commission_of_canada-ef/2006-12-06/www.lcc.gc.ca/about/mandate-en.asp.

19   O'Donovan, above n 5.

20   See, for example, David Delaney, *The Spatial, the Legal and the Pragmatics of World-Making: Nomospheric Investigations* (Routledge, 2010).

21   For further elaboration, see Margaret Davies, *Law Unlimited: Materialism, Pluralism, and Legal Theory* (Routledge, 2017).

of active knowing, active performance and active construal. Second there is an appreciation that those who 'know' and perform law are not just legal experts and judges, and that legal knowledge is formed also in the situated and narrative positions of a far more diverse range of identities; in other words, that knowledge of law is produced and it can be produced by people other than experts in law. Third, and increasingly, we are also seeing materialist ideas of law emerge, which place all normativity in the relationships formed between human society and our physical environments.

This is not to say that legal expert knowledge does not have its own specific role and technical purpose; rather, that the theoretical questions 'What is law?', 'Where is law?', 'Who is law for?' and so on cannot be answered simply by reference to this perspective. Thus feminists and pluralists have made efforts to replace the 'embodied imagining' of an idealised masculine subject with diverse and relational subjectivities, situated in gendered social contexts.[22] Legal consciousness scholars have studied the everyday knowledge about law, decentring official knowledge of law in favour of everyday knowledge.[23] And Robert Cover famously argued for norm-construction or jurisgenesis at the level of religious communities, an insight which has since been extended to the processes of norm construction across all cultural groups.[24] In all of these contributions, we see an image where the traditional view of state law is only one narrow and exclusive form distilled from the widespread circulation and construction of norms throughout society. But we also see a different image of state law emerging – instead of being a mirror image of the autonomous person with *his* boundaries and rationality, the law constructed in the image of (gender and otherwise) diverse subjects is more relational, more embedded in social practices, and less cohesive.

What does such change in the concept of law have to do with law reform? Or, to return to my original question, if law is distributed or 'all over', how can we conceptualise change in legal doctrine? Who is in control of it, how is change generated?

---

22   On 'embodied imagining', see Judith Grbich 'The Body in Legal Theory' (1992) 11 *University of Tasmania Law Review* 26.
23   Patricia Ewick and Susan Silbey, 'Conformity, Contestation, and Resistance: An Account of Legal Consciousness' (1992) 26 *New England Law Review* 731.
24   Robert Cover, 'Nomos and Narrative' (1983) 97 *Harvard Law Review* 4; see also Robert Post, 'Who's Afraid of Jurispathic Courts: Violence and Public Reason in Nomos and Narrative' (2005) 17 *Yale Law Journal of Law and the Humanities* 9.

I don't have a very clear answer to these questions, but my sense is that the more traditional attitudes to law reform have substantially changed and are now more in keeping with an expansive and even experimental view of what law is. I would make a couple of observations.

First, critical and sociolegal approaches add support to using an evidence-based approach to reform rather than an approach based on abstract rationality. Empirical sociolegal evidence is very significant in this context, as are efforts (discussed below) to read or interpret legal doctrine in ways which accommodate both diversity of values and diversity of life experiences. Second, a more disseminated image of law is perhaps more receptive to efforts to test successor legalities in and around the edges of state law. In some contexts, state law itself can become an experimental space for new ideas about law. One could cite, for example, so-called 'alternative' practices of law, such as non-court-based dispute resolution or Indigenous sentencing courts which introduce values of negotiation, accommodation, recognition of the other, and legal plurality into the practice and meaning of law. At the margins of or beyond state law, examples might include truth and reconciliation commissions and efforts to mobilise civil society in justice initiatives, such as the Women's International War Crimes Tribunal and other people's tribunals.[25] These instances draw on state legality but also deliberately eschew it in the interests of (in part) taking law beyond its self-defined boundaries. They are of course indicative of a two-way process or oscillation between practice and theory:[26] new practices help to generate new theory, which in turn widens the possibilities for further new practices.

IV. Changing Culture

The problem with deliberately choosing or trying to shape a concept of law is that it is not possible to predict the consequences of such a change. And therefore it is also necessary to pay attention to the surrounding culture and the ways in which it informs what is even thinkable. Around the same time as Denning was speaking about the river of society with its conservator – the

---

25   Ustinia Dolgopol, 'Redressing Partial Justice – A Possible Role for Civil Society' in Ustina Dolgopol and Judith Gardam (eds), *The Challenge of Conflict: International Law Responds* (Martinus Nihjoff, 2006); Christine Chinkin, 'Women's International Tribunal on Japanese Military Sexual Slavery' (2001) 95 *American Journal of International Law* 335.
26   Davina Cooper, *Everyday Utopias: The Conceptual Life of Promising Spaces* (Duke University Press, 2014).

law reformer – keeping it in order, Ludwig Wittgenstein also wrote about a river in his collection of notes, subsequently published as *On Certainty*.[27] Wittgenstein's river differentiates between things we know to be true, and the inherited mythologies and shared cultural background which we need to support this knowledge. His writing is ambiguous, but essentially he differentiates between the riverbed on the one hand, which is the substratum of knowledge or the shared ideas we have that make knowledge possible, and on the other hand the river flow itself, which consists of everyday claims and propositions made possible by the background to our knowledge. The image is very similar to Denning's, except that in Wittgenstein's case there is no reformer to keep the river clear and flowing. It changes itself and, over time, parts of the riverbed become dislodged:[28]

> The mythology may change back into a state of flux, the river-bed of thoughts may shift. But I distinguish between the movement of the waters on the river-bed and the shift of the bed itself; though there is not a sharp division of the one from the other.

Wittgenstein does not explicitly place law in his metaphor, but it might be supposed that everyday knowledge about law is part of the flow, while shared and presumed cultural knowledge is part of the riverbed – the presupposed cultural knowledge would include the liberal and colonial views of law as discrete, and as disconnected from social identity.

Philosopher Susan Hekman notes that philosophical theories that differentiate between an epistemological background and everyday truths are often extremely conservative, because they do not acknowledge that cultural assumptions may change, and do not offer any ideas about how to encourage such change.[29] They simply rely on cultural background as pre-given and immutable. She argues that Wittgenstein's image holds more potential for theorising and promoting change than most theories of the background because it acknowledges that the riverbed may shift and that it is not sharply divided from the everyday truths which it supports.

So how can cultural change be promoted? Cultural change does not occur because people are presented with a logical argument as to why something ought to be the case. It is much more incremental, and depends as much

---

27   Ludwig Wittgenstein, *On Certainty*, trans G E M Anscombe (Blackwell, 1969).
28   Ibid. s 97.
29   Susan Hekman, 'Backgrounds and Riverbeds: Feminist Reflections' (1999) 25 *Feminist Studies* 427. I would like to thank Sami Alrashidi for drawing my attention to this article and for his persuasive arguments as to its significance.

on what are understood to be the criteria for truth within the cultural background as it does on any new claim. As Hekman says, 'feminist truth does not make sense in the discourse of abstract masculinity', and 'we must first alter the criteria of what it makes sense to say before we can proclaim another "truth" and expect it to be heard'.[30] To take a historical example, claims for gender and racial equality could not be heard until presupposed knowledge had shifted sufficiently for women and those of non-Caucasian heritage to be regarded as people and equal citizens. Many cultural norms still exist which make the resulting formal equality inadequate. Claims to marriage equality still do not make sense to some people who see marriage as necessarily heterosexual. There is no logic in this view but there is a foundation – the foundation provided by a heteronormative cultural background that still divides people into two sexes. In a quite different sphere, it is still almost impossible for those educated within a Eurocentric legal paradigm, with its obsessive taxonomies and entrenched distinctions, to comprehend the relationality and connectedness of First Nations' approaches to law. It seems almost beyond impossible for us to move past human exceptionalism and separation to a view where people are seen as fully part of the physical and natural world.

Hekman argues that changes in the cultural background essentially occur by the emergence of new narratives and perspectives which decentre, defamiliarise and eventually alter accepted knowledge.[31] The trends I have alluded to above, in relation to bringing different perspectives into doctrinal law and understanding law itself in a more disseminated and less hierarchical way, are themselves part of such a cultural change, as is the extensive scholarship which challenges the accepted nature and limits of law.

One partial illustration of a contestation of the doctrine, concept and cultural presuppositions of law is evident in the feminist judgments projects, which have an English and Australian iteration, as well as several others to come.[32] The feminist judgments projects asked academic and activist writers to provide an alternative feminist judgment to a case chosen by the writer. Although all of the judgments were feminist, there are of course many varieties of feminism, and also many ways in which feminism can be brought to bear on particular issues. The objective in

---

30   Ibid. 438.
31   Ibid.
32   Rosemary Hunter, Clare McGlynn and Erika Rackley (eds), *Feminist Judgments: From Theory to Practice* (Hart, 2010); Heather Douglas, Francesca Bartlett, Trish Luker and Rosemary Hunter (eds), *Australian Feminist Judgments: Righting and Rewriting Law* (Hart, 2014).

the English project was to leave 'a female-gendered mark on the law'.[33] This was achieved not in any simplistic translation of feminist theory into practice: feminism is far too diverse for that, and what a theory requires in a practical sense is not always evident. Rather, the impact of the feminist judgments projects lies in the amassing of feminist readings of cases, which collectively illustrate a potential shift in legal consciousness. That is, the feminist judgments show how law *is* gendered and how it *could* be different, how the resources for a different understanding of law are to be found in the law itself in combination with the interpretations made by (academic or real) judges.[34] The judgments remained within the narrowly circumscribed horizon of mainstream colonial law.[35] But the academic performance of this law did bring different voices to that law and push it towards being a different thing.

In this way, changes in law may be promoted by foregrounding changes in the cultural background. Like the alternative or experimental legal forms mentioned above, feminist judgments also test the boundaries of the present with an eye on the future. As I have said elsewhere, such 'prefigurative practices cross the divide between the legal present and our legal futures: they enact possible futures in the present and leave indelible traces of what is to come on the here and now'.[36]

* * *

In this chapter I have very artificially distinguished between the law understood as substance, the law understood as concept, and the cultural presuppositions which constitute the conditions for thinking and talking about law and its concept. But of course – and as I hope will be clear by now – these are artificial distinctions. Changing the content of law over time may also change its shape and contours, and such changes are also connected to shifts in cultural presuppositions. The riverbed is not distinct from the river, and more importantly, the flow of the river is as important as the banks and bed in influencing its overall shape and form.

---

33   Hunter et al, ibid, 8.
34   See generally Margaret Davies, 'The Law Becomes Us: Rediscovering Judgment' (2012) 20 *Feminist Legal Studies* 167.
35   Irene Watson, 'First Nations Stories, Grandmother's Law: Too Many Stories to Tell' in Douglas et al, above n 32.
36   Davies, above n 21, 17.

Part I. Commercial and Corporate Law

1

The Privatisation of Australian Corporate Law

Ross Grantham[1]

Anyone looking at the *Corporations Act 2001* (Cth) would be justified in thinking that company law in Australia was both wholly statutory and an instrument of public regulation. Although Anglo-Australian company law may have originally grown out of the law of partnership and been built, largely by the courts, from the material of the private law, the growth over the last 30 years in the complexity, range of matters covered and sheer volume of the *Corporations Act* would seem to confirm the intuition that Australia's company law is now both statutory and public. However, while there is no denying the shift in the source of company law, the particular form corporate regulation now takes is actually making Australian company law more, rather than less, private.

This trend has at least two important implications for the future of Australian company law and the *Corporations Act* in particular. First, the primary audience of the law must now be understood to be those who are involved in the operation of companies – business people rather than lawyers and the courts. If that is the case, then the form, language and complexity of the *Corporations Act* seems wholly ill-suited to that task. Second, privatisation brings to the fore the issues of the legitimacy of corporate power, and the purposes for which as a matter of policy we

---

1   Professor of Commercial Law, T C Beirne School of Law, University of Queensland.

should recognise the corporate form. These two factors combine to suggest that the *Corporations Act* is no longer fit for purpose and must be reformed and reconceived from the ground up.

I. The Privatisation of Australian Company Law

The privatisation of company law is, in large measure, a consequence of a 'proceduralised' approach to regulation.[2] Broadly, this means that instead of directly prescribing the policy goals or desired outcomes, the legislature seeks to achieve the substantive policy goals by creating a self-balancing system that creates and relies upon incentives designed to induce those being regulated to bring about the desired conduct or outcomes. The policy goals remain public-regarding, but the mechanisms no longer rely on a direct prescription backed by sanctions and imposed by external regulators such as the courts. Instead, the mechanisms now used to implement corporate regulation focus on the process of decision-making and the creation of largely internal governance procedures as the means of regulating the behaviour of the participants in the corporate enterprise.

By prescribing the way in which a company might achieve its goals – through restructuring its decision-making processes such that the 'right' people are involved and that the decision-making process itself is conducted in a way that is permeable to the state's social-economic policies – the overall regulatory goals for the company are achieved. Thus, corporate regulation increasingly reflects an ideal model of decision-making that embodies the essential features of procedural correctness. These features are broadly that the decision-makers are impartial, that they are informed, and that the decision is rational or reasonable.

Evidence of proceduralisation may now be found in most parts of the *Corporations Act*, but two examples will suffice.[3] One example is the procedure established to deal with directors' conflicts of interest. Traditionally, this was dealt with by a common law rule which prohibited a director from acting while conflicted and was enforced by claims brought

---

2   J Black, 'Proceduralizing Regulation: Part I' (2000) 20 *Oxford Journal of Legal Studies* 597 and 'Proceduralizing Regulation: Part II' (2001) 21 *Oxford Journal of Legal Studies* 33.

3   The case for a proceduralised approach now being a defining characteristic of Australian company law is made fully in R Grantham, 'The Proceduralisation of Australian Corporate Law' (2015) 43 *Federal Law Review* 233.

in the courts by those aggrieved by a breach of the rule. The solution to this issue that is now found in ss 191 to 196 of the *Corporations Act* requires that a conflicted director disclose the conflict, in a prescribed form, to designated groups. The procedure vests in those designated groups power to approve the conflicted director's continuing involvement and to validate tainted transactions, and then provides an escape valve through a delegation to ASIC to make exemptions.

A second example is in relation to changes to the company's capital structure – reductions in capital, companies buying their own shares, and providing financial assistance. Historically, there was an absolute prohibition on such activity. The law then moved to allow such changes with external regulatory supervision (court approval). Now we have a situation where the regulatory approval is given by shareholders. The likely incentives of the shareholders are such that their approval (or not) will secure the underlying policy goals.

The important consequence for present purposes is that whether by design or consequence, a proceduralised approach is making company law more, rather than less, private. The use of internal governance procedures to address many of the perennial issues of company law, in place of external supervision by regulators or the courts, is making company law an increasingly self-executing, enclosed system. The state may have prescribed how things must be done, but the application of these processes is increasingly vested in the participants in the corporate enterprise.

The second and closely related factor contributing to privatisation is the sharp decline in recent decades in the volume, and type, of matters reaching the courts. Some sense of the magnitude of the change is provided by a survey of the cases reported in Australia's two specialist sets of corporate law reports.[4] In the period from 1991, before the reforms of the Corporate Law Simplification Program and Corporate Law Economic Reform Program were introduced, to 2013, there was a decline in the number of cases being reported of 37 per cent. The change is even more marked when one focuses on core company law issues – matters that define and reflect the essential characteristics of the corporate form and the minimum content of corporate law – where the rate of decline in cases is well over 50 per cent in the same period.

---

4   See Grantham, n 3 above.

It is also clear from this survey that the role of the court has changed. Whereas in 1991 the majority of cases saw the courts fulfilling the traditional judicial role of interpreting statutory provisions and corporate constitutions, and applying common law doctrines, to determine the rights and duties of the litigants, by 2013 the courts were hearing only a handful of core corporate law issues and in the vast majority of those the court's role was merely a regulatory one of supervising a decision-making process prescribed by the *Corporations Act* or the company's constitution.

Whether the decline in court cases is a consequence of proceduralisation or part of the worldwide decline in civil litigation in favour of private dispute resolution,[5] the result is that issues and practices that would hitherto have been aired publicly in court are now dealt with within the company behind closed doors. While it is true that there are now more cases of directors' personal liability, it is important to recognise that the basis of liability is not the substance of corporate decisions but rather how the directors went about making the decision. The directors of James Hardie were not held liable for abandoning the victims of asbestos, but for the way in which they announced this to the market. Where previously litigation between private disputants brought issues of substance about what companies were doing into the public forum, this is no longer the case.

II. The Implications of Privatisation

The somewhat paradoxical effect of the regulatory approach leading to a privatisation of company law has many potential implications. Two merit comment.

A. The manner and form of the *Corporations Act*

An important implication of privatisation concerns the manner and form of Australian company law and the *Corporations Act* in particular. If the intention is to internalise much of the regulation of the company within the company's own governance structures – where the focus of the legislation is to set out the processes and procedures those involved in the corporate enterprise must follow – then the question arises as to whom the Act

---

5   See H Genn, *Judging Civil Justice* (Hamlyn Lectures 2008, CUP, 2009) Ch 2.

is primarily addressed. Historically, all legislation, including companies legislation, was addressed to lawyers and the courts. The language of legislation, its layout, its presuppositions as to background knowledge and context, and even its accessibility, were all tailored by and for lawyers. If, however, the intention now is to directly address those involved in the corporate enterprise – to set out what they must do and how they must do it – then the *Corporations Act* seems ill-suited to that role. Some idea of what a user-oriented corporate statute would look like can be had by looking at the companies legislation of Canada and New Zealand: it is concise, principles-based and expressed in genuinely plain language.

In contrast, to use Cally Jordan's phrase, the *Corporations Act* is 'unlovely and unloved'.[6] It is extraordinarily dense, complex, unclear, poorly organised and, in many respects, rather outdated. At over 2,600 substantive sections, few people if any can claim to know the Act in its entirety. Although the Simplification program in the 1990s tried to 'make it capable of being understood so that users can act on their rights and carry out their responsibilities',[7] the large number of amendments made to the Act over the years has effectively deprived it of any rational or conceptual organisation – any statute that needs sections numbered to four capital letters has a problem.[8] The result is that as a user guide or statement of first recourse for those involved in the corporate enterprise, the Act may as well be written Sanskrit.[9] What is needed, therefore, is a root and branch review and rewriting of the Act. This endeavour, however, faces a number of significant challenges.

First, there will be an understandable reluctance to reopen the constitutional settlement underpinning the Act. The gestation of the federal legislation was long and painful and it may be thought better not to reopen old wounds. On the other hand, however, there may be advantages in reassessing the merits of federal corporate legislation. Although the advantages of federalising company law were presented during the federal takeover of corporate law in the 1990s as being

---

6   C Jordan, 'Unlovely and Unloved: Corporate Law Reform's Progeny' (2009) 33 *Melbourne University Law Review* 626.

7   Corporations Law Simplification Program, *Task Force – Plan of Action* (Attorney-General's Department, December 1993) 1.

8   Section 601SCAA, *Corporations Act 2001* (Cth).

9   The inaccessibility of the Act may in part explain the rise of 'soft law' guides and codes of best practice.

obvious,[10] there were in fact other models and what is arguably the most successful corporate economy, the US, has a state-based model with significant, productive diversity. One of the insights of the Public Choice theory is that law is a product and that there is a market for this product.[11] The federalisation of corporate law created in substance a single supplier of corporate law (the Commonwealth Parliament) and thus an effective monopoly for the supply of company law in Australia, with all of the downsides entailed by such monopolies.[12]

Second, Australian company law is a one-size-fits-all model. This builds complexity into the law as it seeks to carve out exceptions to adapt a model originally designed to meet the needs of large-scale enterprises in the 19th century to micro-firms and small family businesses in the 21st century. Again, this is not the only model. Most notably, both Europe and the US have created a range of special purpose entities tailored to the specific needs of the business or activity.[13] If the ultimate aim of Australian company law is to provide an efficient and simple vehicle to conduct business, then Australia must at least consider more tailored structures.

Third, and perhaps most importantly, any reform of the *Corporations Act* to make it more user-friendly faces the challenge presented by Australia's current predilection for large, highly prescriptive and prolix legislation. Whatever the reasons for the explosion in legislation in the 1980s,[14] and the prescriptive drafting style now in vogue, this approach clearly stands in the way of Australia adopting the sort of plain-language, principles-based, user-oriented companies legislation adopted by the likes of New

---

10   M Whincop, 'The Political Economy of Corporate Law Reform in Australia' (1999) 27 *Federal Law Review* 77.

11   Generally, see G Tullock, 'Public Choice' in S Durlauf and L Blume (eds), *The New Palgrave Dictionary of Economics* (London, Palgrave Macmillan, 2nd edn, 1987).

12   A monopolistic market is one characterised by barriers to entry to the market by other suppliers, the imposition of higher prices, a reduction in consumer surplus and a limiting of consumer choice. In relation to corporate law in Australia, see Whincop (n 10) and I Ramsay, 'Company Law and the Economics of Federalism' (1990) 19 *Federal Law Review* 169.

13   In the US, for example, the Limited Liability Company (LLC) is a vehicle tailored to the specific needs of small businesses and quasi-partnerships, while the Professional Limited Liability Company (PLLC) is a vehicle tailored to the needs of those conducting a profession, such as medical services. A 'benefit corporation' is a particular type of for-profit entity but which includes in its defined goals consideration of social and environmental impact. Europe has always provided for quite separate forms for closely held companies and publicly held companies (designated in Germany, for example, as 'GmbH' and 'AG' respectively).

14   C Berg, *Policy without Parliament: The Growth of Regulation in Australia* (Institute of Public Affairs, IPA Backgrounder, November 2007, Vol 19/3) 3. Berg's analysis shows a sudden and massive leap in legislative production starting in the late 1980s.

Zealand and Canada. However, if the primary audience of company law in Australia is to be those involved in the corporate enterprise, then the expression and accessibility of the law must be massively simplified.

B. Privatisation and the legitimacy of the corporate form

The second fundamental implication of the privatising trend in Australia relates to the legitimacy of the corporate form and its social and economic power. Companies have always been repositories of wealth and power and it is a fundamental premise of modern Western liberal society that power must be legitimated.[15] Where that power is subject to public oversight and control, corporate power is legitimated on fundamentally the same basis as the power of the state. However, to the extent that companies are or have become more private, questions arise as to whether, and how, the aggregation of economic, political, social and cultural power in the hands of ostensibly private entities that are legally accountable to only a small group of shareholders and in practice are accountable to no one may be justified.

This is obviously a deep and complex issue that cannot be addressed properly here. However, it is worth noting that changes over the last 20 years in the *nature* of corporate power have changed how this question must be understood.[16] Historically, the most widely accepted basis of legitimacy of corporate power was the instrumental value of the company as a creator of wealth. The efficient utilisation of scarce resources and the maximisation of the wealth of society is a good thing, both as a means to other substantive goals and as an end in itself. The pursuit of the maximisation of social wealth is, therefore, in the public interest and, being in the public interest, serves to legitimate those institutions that bring about that goal. The modern company has proven itself to be a highly efficient means of producing wealth and, although it is not perfect and the power that is inevitably vested in the company may generate costs, those costs are more than justified by the gains. Thus, the power that arises from placing the means of production in private hands is legitimated by its superiority in maximising social wealth.

---

15   J W Hurst, *The Legitimacy of the Business Corporation* (Charlottesville, University Press of Virginia, 1970) 58.
16   See R Grantham, 'The Legitimacy of the Company as a Source of (Private) Power' in K Barker et al (eds), *Private Law and Power* (Oxford, Hart, 2016) Ch 10.

The real difficulty now, however, lies in the rising social and cultural power of the company. The last 20 years have seen the rise of social media, social networking, and 'Big Data', and the ability of companies such as Google, Facebook, Apple, and Microsoft to shape our social interactions, what we know of the world, and even our identities as individuals.[17] As Richards and King have said:

> With even the most basic access to a combination of big data pools like phone records, surfing history, buying history, social networking posts, and others, 'I am' and 'I like' risk becoming 'you are' and 'you will like.' Every Google user is already influenced by big-data-fed feedback loops from Google's tailored search results, which risk producing individual and collective echo chambers of thought.[18]

In respect of the costs arising from this social and cultural power, the argument for the legitimacy of the company as a generator of material wealth simply does not hold. The benefits to society of the survival of a small town or the rural way of life, or the reduction in greenhouse gas emissions, or the right of the individual to be forgotten,[19] and the increases in profitability of moving a major source of employment off-shore or the invasion of our privacy to more precisely target marketing, seem to be expressed in fundamentally different currencies. The increase in one cannot bear upon or make up for losses in the other. Therefore, while as a purely economic institution the company's preeminent capacity to generate material wealth seems to more than justify the economic power it has come to hold, these economic benefits cannot justify or legitimate the social power and impact of the company. To that extent, the privatisation of Australian company law exposes a significant democratic deficit and the issue of how that deficit is to be accounted for is, arguably, the most significant challenge facing company law.

17　The rise and extent of this power is described more fully in Grantham, above n 16.

18　N Richards and J King, 'Three Paradoxes of Big Data' (2013) 66 *Stanford Law Review Online* 41, 43–44.

19　The proposed European Union General Data Protection Regulation would allow an individual to request their erasure from metadata held by companies such as Google: European Commission, 'Agreement on Commission's EU Data Protection Reform Will Boost Digital Single Market', Press Release, 15 December 2015 (IP/15/6321).

III. Conclusion

In its fundamentals, the *Corporations Act* embodies a model that was created in 1844. That model is now overlaid with decades of amendments that reflect the ebb and flow of socioeconomic policy from laissez-faire to interventionist, and the knee-jerk reactions to a succession of scandals. The *Corporations Act* has thus been built up through an accretion of ideas and events whose features continue to cast a confusing shadow long after those ideas were discarded and we have forgotten the events which gave rise to them. As a practical guide and user manual for those who are actually involved in the corporate enterprise, the Act is not only wholly unsuited, but its complexity, prolixity and incoherence represent the single largest obstacle to addressing the central issues facing companies and company law in the coming decades.

2

On the Road to Improved Social and Economic Welfare: The Contribution to Australian Competition and Consumer Law and Policy Law Reform

Russell Miller AM[1]

The Australian Law Reform Commission's role is to review Australia's laws to ensure they provide improved access to justice for all Australians by making laws and related processes more equitable, modern, fair and efficient.[2] While the Commission has an excellent record in addressing access to justice issues, in their many guises, access to justice is only one aspect to law reform.

The essential focus of law reform is on contributing to an Australian society that is more equitable, modern, fair and efficient. Or, to put it in the language of economists, to improve both consumer welfare and producer welfare through competition and consumer protection laws that are fair, open, efficient and effective. This is no easy task in any area of law reform and the economic area is no exception.

---

1   Member, Minter Ellison Australasian Competition Group; Fellow, Centre for Strategy and Governance; Fellow of the Australian Academy of Law.
2   *Australian Law Reform Commission Act 1996* (Cth) s 21.

Nevertheless, Australia has come a long way with competition and consumer protection law reform in the past 25 years, and that journey continues. I will demonstrate this by reference to three examples: a competition law example from the past, a more recent consumer law example, and a new horizon competition law example.

Before I do so I should observe that, while we all accept as self-evident the contribution consumer protection law makes to goals of equity, transparency and fairness, the same may not be said for competition law.

We value competition not for its own sake, but because it provides a flexible set of rules to promote efficiency and fair business dealings, thereby enhancing the welfare of all Australians.[3] While competition rules do not always work in the way some would like, every modern market economy sees benefit in a set of equitable rules intended to ensure that competitive processes are not undermined by anticompetitive behaviour. In short, we value competition because it fosters opportunity, innovation, productivity and growth, thereby creating national wealth.[4]

For the purposes of this chapter, our journey on the road to improved social and economic welfare in Australia through competition and consumer law reform starts with a competition example drawn from the 1990s.[5] At that time Australia had fallen behind other developed countries, in part because our economy was, as the then Chair of the Productivity Commission, Professor Gary Banks, explained,[6] 'highly regulated, anti-competitive and redistributive: captured nicely by the expression "protection all round" – a policy that for much of the last century had bi-partisan support and wide community acceptance'.

As Professor Banks pointed out,[7] Australia had the highest per capita income in the world at the start of the 20th century, but this had steadily declined. There were many causes for that decline, but for the purposes of this chapter I will concentrate on one – the limited reach of

---

3   The object of the *Competition and Consumer Act 2010* (as with the *Trade Practices Act 1974* before it) is to 'enhance the welfare of Australians through the promotion of competition and fair trading and provision for consumer protection', s 2.

4   See, for example, Nick Godfrey, *Why is Competition Important for Growth and Poverty Reduction?*, OECD Global Forum on Investment, March 2008, 3.

5   In fact it started in the early 1900s. See *Miller's Australian Competition Law and Policy* (Thomson Reuters 2nd edn, 2012) 1.

6   Gary Banks, *Structural Reform Australian-Style: Lessons for Others?* Presentation to the IMF and World Bank (Washington DC, 26–27 May 2005) and OECD (Paris, 31 May 2005) 2.

7   Ibid. 2.

competition law.[8] By 1993, although competition laws had applied to Australian businesses for almost 20 years, the competition law did not apply to federal and state statutory authorities that provided public utility and other services, sometimes on a monopoly basis and sometimes in competition to others.[9] They did so, Professor Banks said, by and large on the basis that their 'fair' prices incorporated the cost of poor management and labour practices.[10]

In October 1992 the then Prime Minister, with the agreement of the states and territories, commissioned a panel, led by Professor Fred Hilmer, to review national competition policy and law, giving effect to principles including:

- No participant in the market should be able to engage in anticompetitive conduct against the public interest.
- As far as possible, universal and uniformly applied rules of market conduct should apply to all market participants regardless of the form of business ownership.
- Any changes to the coverage or nature of competition policy should be consistent with, and support, the general thrust of reforms:
  - to develop an open, integrated domestic market for goods and services by removing unnecessary barriers to trade and competition; and
  - in recognition of the increasingly national operation of markets, to reduce complexity and eliminate administrative duplication.

In August 1993, the panel's report recommended what was then regarded as very radical law reform across a spectrum of competition policy areas. For the purposes of this example I will focus on a few. First, the report recommended that the exemption from competition laws that then applied to government businesses should be removed, and that competition law should extend to sectors of the economy, such as professions, not then

---

8   Australia had had statutes addressing competition law since 1906, but modern competition law in Australia has its origins in the *Trade Practices Act 1974*.
9   The Industry Commission (now the Productivity Commission) undertook major studies of rail transport (1991), energy generation and distribution (1991) and water resources (1992), concluding that, in those industries alone, efficiencies could increase gross domestic product by $8 billion per annum: *National Competition Policy: Report by the Independent Committee of Inquiry*, 23 August 1993 (the 'Hilmer Report'), 129.
10   Banks, above n 6.

covered by the law.[11] Second, it recommended pro-competitive structural reform of public utilities, with the separation of regulatory and business functions, and vertical separation of integrated utilities.

Both recommendations were based on the firm conviction that, by increasing competition, including by removing regulatory restrictions, restructuring public monopolies and applying competition law to sectors of the economy not then subject to the law, Australia would be a more equitable, modern, fair and efficient society. As the Hilmer Report stated:[12]

> if Australia is to prosper as a nation, and maintain and improve living standards and opportunities for its people, it has no choice but to improve the productivity and international competitiveness of its firms and institutions. Australian organisations, irrespective of their size, location or ownership, must become more efficient, more innovative and more flexible.

The Hilmer Report's recommendations were accepted by all Australian governments and implemented through law reform projects that saw significant changes to the national competition law. Complementary state and territory laws[13] were introduced to apply competition law to areas of the economy where the Commonwealth lacked constitutional competence. Unprecedented reform of state and territory statutory utility regulation was implemented, leading in some cases to privatisation and in others to corporatisation, assisted by compensation payments by the Commonwealth.

One measure of the success of this law reform initiative, and all the other initiatives that surrounded it, was that Australia's economic ranking internationally had risen from 15th in 1990 to 8th in 2002.[14] But, far more importantly, this law reform initiative and the policies that accompanied it radically and permanently improved the welfare of all Australians.

---

11 The Hilmer Report, ibid. 124–39.
12 Ibid. 1.
13 Uniform Competition Policy Reform Acts; for example, *Competition Policy Reform (New South Wales) Act 1995*.
14 Banks, above n 6, 9. According to Banks, Australia had been number 5 in 1950. Australia's ranking in per capita incomes had slipped by the late 1980s from 12th to 16th.

In 2004 the then federal treasurer requested the Productivity Commission to review the results of Hilmer reforms. In its report, released in February 2005,[15] the Commission reported that:[16]

National Competition Policy (NCP) has delivered substantial benefits to the Australian community which, overall, have greatly outweighed the costs. It has:

- contributed to the productivity surge that has underpinned 13 years of continuous economic growth, and associated strong growth in household incomes;
- directly reduced the prices of goods and services such as electricity and milk;
- stimulated business innovation, customer responsiveness and choice; and
- helped meet some environmental goals, including the more efficient use of water.

The second example of improved social and economic welfare in Australia through competition and consumer law reform is in the consumer law field.

Australia has a strong tradition in consumer protection but, until the introduction of the *Trade Practices Act* in 1974, consumer protection had been the sole province of state and territory governments. While the *Trade Practices Act* made an important contribution to consumer protection and fair trading, constitutional limitations meant that it could not cover the field. The result was a patchwork of state and territory laws. While the Trade Practices Commission[17] pursued consumer complaints vigorously[18] within the limits of its authority, a range of consumer affairs departments and agencies administered the rest with varying degrees of success.

In December 2006, the then treasurer requested the Productivity Commission to undertake an inquiry into Australia's consumer policy framework. The terms of reference included:[19]

---

15   Productivity Commission, *Review of National Competition Policy Reforms*, No 33, 28 February 2005.
16   Ibid. xii.
17   Now the Australian Competition and Consumer Commission.
18   See, for example, the cases brought by the ACCC under ss 52 and 53 of the *Trade Practices Act* up to 2010 digested in Miller's *Annotated Trade Practices Act – Australian Competition and Consumer Law* (Thomson Reuters 31ˢᵗ edn, 2010).
19   Productivity Commission Inquiry Report No 45, 2008: *Review of Australia's Consumer Policy Framework*, vi.

- ways to improve the consumer policy framework so as to assist and empower consumers, including disadvantaged and vulnerable consumers, to meet current and future challenges, including the information and other challenges posed by an increasing variety of more complex product offerings and methods of transacting;

- any barriers to, and ways to improve, the harmonisation and coordination of consumer policy and its development and administration across jurisdictions in Australia, including ways to improve institutional arrangements and to avoid duplication of effort;

- any areas of consumer regulation which are unlikely to provide net benefits to Australia and which could be revised or repealed.

The law reform objective in this, as in other areas of the law, was to advise on improvements that would benefit the community as a whole. That means, in the context of consumer protection, improving protections for consumers but only where the improvements produce a net benefit when weighed against the cost regulation imposes on society.

The Productivity Commission reported in 2008, concluding that:[20]

> While Australia's consumer policy framework has considerable strengths, parts of it require an overhaul.
>
> - The current division of responsibility for the framework between the Australian and State and Territory Governments leads to variable outcomes for consumers, added costs for businesses and a lack of responsiveness in policy making.
> - There are gaps and inconsistencies in the policy and enforcement tool kit and weaknesses in redress mechanisms for consumers.
> - These problems will make it increasingly difficult to respond to rapidly changing consumer markets, meaning that the associated costs for consumers and the community will continue to grow.
>
> Addressing these problems will have significant direct benefits for consumers. Also, by better engaging and empowering consumers and furthering the development of nationally competitive markets, reform will enhance productivity and innovation.

The result was the most comprehensive law reform initiative in the consumer protection field that Australia had ever seen. The Productivity Commission's report was so persuasive that the federal, state and territory

---

20   Ibid. 2.

governments all agreed to embark on the creation of a national consumer law. The result was the *Australian Consumer Law*, introduced in an innovative way as a Schedule to the renamed *Trade Practices Act* – the *Competition and Consumer Act* – as a free-standing code,[21] then applied in each state and territory by complementary legislation.[22]

In addition to repeating the provisions of the old *Trade Practices Act* in relation to misleading and deceptive conduct and false representations – provisions that had in any event been largely duplicated in state and territory law[23] – the *Australian Consumer Law* expanded and upgraded coverage. This includes a nationally consistent law on unfair contract terms[24] and on unconscionable conduct,[25] an upgrade of statutory implied warranties to consumer guarantees,[26] stronger product safety laws,[27] and detailed laws on door-to-door, internet and over-the-phone selling.[28]

This law reform measure produced a more equitable, modern, fair and efficient commercial and trading environment for consumers and traders alike: the Productivity Commission assessed the net benefit to Australia in monetary terms and concluded that the economic gain to the community by implementing its recommendations would be between $1.5 billion and $4.5 billion each year.[29] But there is little doubt that the contribution to a fairer, more equitable Australian society was the major benefit.

A third example of improved social and economic welfare through competition and consumer law reform – the 'new horizon' competition law example – is law reform in the making. Although I will briefly describe what has been proposed and has subsequently been enacted, my primary reason for raising this example is to highlight the difficulties often encountered in the law reform process.

21　Schedule 2 to the *Competition and Consumer Act 2010*, applied as a law of the Commonwealth under Pt XI of that Act.
22　For a list, see *Miller's Australian Competition and Consumer Law Annotated* (Thomson Reuters 38th edn, 2016) 1470.
23　See, for example, *Fair Trading Act 1985* (Victoria), *Fair Trading Act 1987* (NSW).
24　Originally introduced in Victoria and now Pt 2-3 of the *Australian Consumer Law*. This law is to be extended to small business contracts from 12 November 2016.
25　Now Pt 2-2 of the *Australian Consumer Law*.
26　Part 3-2, Div 1 of the *Australian Consumer Law*.
27　Part 3-3, Div 1 of the *Australian Consumer Law*.
28　Part 3-2, Div 2 of the *Australian Consumer Law*.
29　Productivity Commission Inquiry Report No 45, 2008, 3.

On 27 March 2014 the then Minister for Small Business commissioned Professor Ian Harper to lead a panel to undertake a broad ranging review of competition policy,[30] the first such review since the Hilmer Report.[31]

The panel reported on 31 March 2015,[32] providing the government with wide-ranging recommendations covering all areas of competition policy and administration. The sections on access and choice in high-quality health, education and community services – areas not often seen at the forefront of competition policy reform – had the potential to be a real game changer, but they are not the areas I am focusing on here.

The following summary of a cross-section of recommendations demonstrates the scope of the law reforms the Harper Panel recommended:

- legislative frameworks and government policies and regulations that bind the public and private sectors should not restrict competition;[33]
- cost-reflective road pricing, with independent oversight;[34]
- an overarching review of intellectual property law, including the contentious competition law exemption;[35]
- removal of restrictions on competition in state and territory planning and zoning laws unless they result in a net benefit;[36]
- removal of remaining restrictions on retail trading hours;[37]
- removal of restrictions on parallel imports unless the restrictions produce benefits that outweigh the costs and those benefits cannot be achieved in less restrictive ways;[38] and

---

30   Media Release by the Hon Bruce Billson MP, 27 March 2014, bfb.ministers.treasury.gov.au/media-release/014-2014/.

31   Sir Darryl Dawson had led a more limited review in 2003: see *Review of the Competition Provisions of the Trade Practices Act* (The Dawson Review), tpareview.treasury.gov.au/content/report.asp.

32   *Competition Policy Review Final Report*, March 2015, competitionpolicyreview.gov.au/final-report/.

33   Ibid. Recommendation 1. The government supported this recommendation.

34   Ibid. Recommendation 3. The government supported this recommendation.

35   Ibid. Recommendations 6 and 7. On 18 August 2005 the then treasurer instructed the Productivity Commission to conduct such a review 'to ensure that the intellectual property system provides appropriate incentives for innovation, investment and the production of creative works while ensuring it does not unreasonably impede further innovation, competition, investment and access to goods and services': www.pc.gov.au/inquiries/current/intellectual-property/terms-of-reference.

36   Ibid. Recommendation 9. The government supported this recommendation but noted that it is a state and territory responsibility.

37   Ibid. Recommendation 12. The government supported this recommendation but noted that it is a state and territory responsibility.

38   Ibid. Recommendation 13. The government supported this recommendation in part.

- removal of current legal restrictions on pharmacy ownership and location in the long term interests of consumers.[39]

The Harper Panel reaffirmed that, if Australia is to improve economic performance, there is much that can and should be done in relation to competition policy, and therefore law reform in this area. Indeed, a concerted effort on law reform in the competition policy area is crucial if Australia is to achieve the outcomes foreshadowed in its G20 Comprehensive Growth Plan: to 'raise Australia's economic growth potential, create one million new jobs over the next five years … and support continued improvements in national living standards'.

It is trite to observe that law reform is never easy. When reforms are proposed there are inevitably winners and losers. There is a fine balance to be struck by governments, weighing the benefits likely to be achieved against the costs to be imposed on those who enjoy the protections of the law as it currently stands. Nowhere is this more apparent than in relation to the law reform proposals the Harper Panel recommended. One example stands out.

Notwithstanding the breadth of the Harper recommendations, almost all of which were accepted in principle by the government and most of which are controversial, the recommendation that drew the most public comment was for changes to the law on misuse of market power.[40] The battle over this law provides an interesting example of the challenges in delivering law reform.

The Harper Panel's consideration of the current misuse of market power law reenlivened a debate Australia has been having, on and off, for over 40 years. The current provision, introduced in 1974,[41] prohibits firms with market power using that power for the purpose[42] of damaging competitors, preventing competitors entering a market, or deterring competitors from engaging in competitive conduct.

---

39   Ibid. Recommendation 14. The government noted the recommendation.
40   *Competition and Consumer Act 2010* s 46.
41   Section 46. The provision originally appeared in the *Trade Practices Act 1974*. Although amendments were made in 1986, 2007 and 2008, they did not affect the essential features relevant to this chapter.
42   For the meaning of 'purpose', in this context, see *Melway Publishing Pty Ltd v Robert Hicks Pty Ltd* [2001] HCA13; (2001) 205 CLR 1 at [31]; *Universal Music Australia Pty Ltd v ACCC* [2003] FCAFC 193; (2003) ATPR 41-947 at [256].

Those who supported changing s 46 argue that the provision is wrongly directed at competitors rather than protecting the competitive process, and that it is out of step with modern competition law in other countries which focuses on the effect of market power on the competitive process, not on a firm's subjective purpose.[43] Further, they argued that the current law results in under-capture of exclusionary conduct, because it requires a court to determine whether a firm is using its market power (and not any other power it may have), by considering whether a firm that does not have market power would likely behave as the firm under investigation has acted.[44] Those who argued for the status quo asserted that the provision, particularly the requirement to establish that the firm had taken advantage of its power, appropriately distinguished between pro-competitive and anticompetitive conduct, and that the changes proposed would have unintended adverse consequences for consumers.

The Harper Panel supported change. They recommended that the prohibition should focus on protecting the competitive process – on conduct by firms with market power that has the purpose, effect or likely effect of substantially lessening competition.[45] The Harper Panel also recommended that the courts should be required to mitigate against inadvertently capturing pro-competitive conduct, by having regard to the extent to which the conduct has the purpose, effect or likely effect of both increasing competition (including by enhancing efficiency, innovation, product quality or price competitiveness) and lessening competition (including by preventing, restricting or deterring the potential for competitive conduct or new entry).

However, the recommendation that the prohibition should focus on protecting the competitive process brought strident and vocal opposition from some within the business community. Objections were so strong that the government deferred a decision on the recommendation, deciding instead to undertake further consultations before making a decision. On 11 December 2015 the treasurer issued a discussion paper with six

---

43 See *ACCC v Pfizer Australia Pty Ltd* [2015] FCA 113.

44 See *Rural Press Ltd v ACCC* [2003] HCA 75; 216 CLR 53 and *Competition and Consumer Act 2010* s 46(6A)(c).

45 *Competition Policy Review*, above n 31. Recommendation 30, 348. For an explanation of the phrase 'substantially lessen competition', see *Miller's Australian Competition and Consumer Law Annotated* (Thomson Reuters, 38th edn, 2016) [1.45.60].

options for change, including that recommended by the Harper Panel.[46] Submissions on the options were called for and the assistant treasurer convened two roundtable sessions attended by representatives of small and large business and the Law Council of Australia. In all, 86 written submissions were received, arguing strongly for or against change.[47] As one submission correctly put it:[48] 'There are two deeply entrenched, vigorous and irreconcilable positions being taken on the Harper Review's recommendation to amend Section 46'.

Although there was a sharp divide, neither point of view could be said to be entirely right or entirely wrong. The concerns of some of those opposing change were overstated, and the expectations of many who supported change were overly optimistic. The fact is that this is a very complex area of economic regulation. There is no bright line rule for determining what is, and what is not, exclusionary conduct that adversely affects the competitive process.[49] However, international experience shows that a law that focuses on conduct that adversely affects the competitive process presents the best approach in this vexed area.

In the end the government decided to accept the Harper recommendation, in what would seem to be a triumph for good public policy because the focus of the law should be on exclusionary conduct that adversely affects the competitive process. On 16 March 2016 the Prime Minister announced that the government would proceed with an exposure draft of legislation to fully implement the Harper Panel's recommendation, stating that:[50]

> The Government is committed to fixing Australia's competition policy and the amendment of Section 46 to deal with unilateral anti-competitive conduct is an important step to ensure Australia has the best possible competition framework to support innovation and boost economic growth and jobs.

---

46   The options paper is accessible at www.treasury.gov.au/-/media/Treasury/Consultations%20 and%20Reviews/Consultations/2015/Options%20to%20strengthen%20the%20misuse%20of%20 market%20power%20law/Key%20Documents/PDF/dpoptions_marketpowerlaw.ashx.

47   The public submissions are available at www.treasury.gov.au/ConsultationsandReviews/ Consultations/2015/Options-to-strengthen-the-misuse-of-market-power-law/Submissions.

48   Submission by John Dahlsen, JC Dahlsen Pty Ltd, 28.

49   See, for example, *Novel Inc v Microsoft Corporation* [2013-2] Trade Cases 78,523 at 128,271.

50   Prime Minister's media release 16 March 2016 at www.pm.gov.au/media/2016-03-16/joint-media-statement-fixing-competition-policy-drive-economic-growth-and-jobs.

Few would disagree with those objectives – but the vigorous debate over s 46 illustrates that there is no single right or wrong way to reform this law to achieve them.

Finally, on 1 December 2016, the government introduced legislation[51] to replace s 46 in accordance with the Harper Panel recommendation. The Senate Economics Legislation Committee considered the Bill and reported in February 2017,[52] with members divided on party lines on whether or not to support the initiative. The majority agreed that s 46 is unfit for purpose because it has not provided adequate protection for non-dominant firms.[53] The minority, while welcoming 'strong competition policy', thought that the change would add a 'new layer of red tape' deterring job-creating investment in Australia.[54] However, the Bill was passed on 23 August 2017 to come into effect later in 2017.[55]

To conclude the journey by returning to consumer law reform, on 31 March 2016 the Minister for Small Business and assistant treasurer published a review of the *Australian Consumer Law*.[56] That review, briefed by the minister[57] to consider whether or not 'the law is operating as intended and addresses the risk of consumer detriment without imposing unnecessary red tape',[58] recommended 18 changes to the *Australian Consumer Law*, including a significant increase in penalties for contravention.

With that report and the pending legislation to implement the Harper Panel recommendations, we continue on the road to improving Australian society through law reform in the areas of competition and consumer law and policy.

---

51   Competition and Consumer Amendment (Misuse of Market Power) Bill 2016. A second Bill was introduced on 30 March 2017 to implement other Harper Panel recommendations supported by the government: Competition and Consumer Amendment (Competition Policy Review) Bill 2017.
52   The Senate Economics Legislation Committee, *Competition and Consumer Amendment (Misuse of Market Power) Bill 2016 Report*, February 2017, www.aph.gov.au/Parliamentary_Business/ Committees/Senate/Economics/Misuseofmarketpower16/Report.
53   Report, paras 2.74, 2.75.
54   Report, paras 1.27, 1.28.
55   *Competition and Consumer Amendment (Misuse of Market Power) Act 2017* (Cth).
56   consumerlaw.gov.au/review-of-the-australian-consumer-law/final-report/.
57   Media Release by the Hon Kelly O'Dwyer MP, 31 March 2016, kmo.ministers.treasury.gov.au/ media-release/029-2016/.
58   'Australian Consumer Law Fact Sheet 2', consumerlaw.gov.au/files/2016/03/ACL_Review _FS2.pdf.

3

Tax, Inequality and Challenges for the Future

John Passant[1]

I. Introduction

As in most countries in the developed world, inequality in Australia has been growing for more than three decades.[2] In part this is due to systemic issues associated with the relative power of capital and labour and the decline in the share of national factor income going to labour.[3] In part it has to do with deliberate government policy. In a nutshell, growing inequality undermines the meritocracy on which democracy depends. It creates a sense of unfairness and disillusionment with society, both politically and economically, concentrating more wealth and power in the hands of already powerful and wealthy people. It corrupts or can corrupt institutions and, as the past 30 or so years have shown, can undermine

---

1   Lecturer, Business School, Charles Darwin University; PhD candidate, School of Politics and International Relations, ANU. This research is supported by an Australian Government Research Training Program (RTP) Scholarship.

2   Australian Council of Social Service (ACOSS), *Inequality in Australia 2015: A Nation Divided* (Sydney, 2015) 8, www.acoss.org.au/wp-content/uploads/2015/06/Inequality_in_Australia_FINAL.pdf (viewed 24 April 2016).

3   Factor income is the income arising from the factors of production – land, labour and capital. For the changes in shares over time, see Australian Bureau of Statistics (ABS), 'Income at Current Prices, December Quarter 2015' in ABS, 5206.0 – Australian National Accounts: National Income, Expenditure and Product, Dec 2015, www.abs.gov.au/ausstats/abs@.nsf/Latestproducts/5206.0Main%20Features4Dec%202015?opendocument&tabname=Summary&prodno=5206.0&issue=Dec%202015&num=&view= (viewed 26 April 2016).

both directly and indirectly those institutions and policies aimed at redistributing wealth from the rich to the less well off. In addition, growing inequality creates economic instability because it undermines the capacity of those in lower income brackets to consume the products of the top income earners and wealth holders. As Sheil and Stilwell say: 'The deep-seated economic inequalities also have major social and political consequences. They fracture social cohesion and create power imbalances that can undermine the nominally democratic institutions.'[4]

Tax reform – or what I have elsewhere described as neoliberal tax reform[5] – has contributed to that increasing inequality.[6] Australia's tax system has become less and less progressive over time.[7] The tax base has shifted to some extent from income to consumption, and the income tax system itself is less progressive. Over time, tax rates have decreased, for individuals and for companies. In addition, the creation of tax expenditures such as a range of superannuation-related taxation concessions and the capital gains tax concessions, among others, favour and benefit those in the richer and wealthier strata of society.[8]

While income inequality has grown in Australia, wealth remains concentrated in the hands of those at the top. As ACOSS puts it: 'The top 10% of households own 45% of all wealth, most of the remainder

---

4   Christopher Sheil and Frank Stilwell, *The Wealth of the Nation: Current Data on the Distribution of Wealth in Australia* (Evatt Foundation 2016), evatt.org.au/files/files/The%20Wealth%20of%20 the%20Nation.pdf (viewed 16 July 2016).

5   John Passant, 'Neoliberalism in Australia and the Henry Tax Review' (2013) 8(1) *The Journal of the Australasian Tax Teachers Association* 117, www.business.unsw.edu.au/About-Site/Schools-Site/Taxation-Business-Law-Site/Journal%20of%20The%20Australasian%20Tax%20Teachers%20 Associati/JATTA_8-1_2014.pdf (viewed 28 April 2016).

6   See, for example, Bob Douglas, Sharon Friel, Richard Denniss and David Morawetz, *Advance Australia Fair? What to Do About Growing Inequality in Australia* (Australia21, 2014) 17, gallery. mailchimp.com/d2331cf87fedd353f6dada8de/files/1b2c7f48-928f-4298-81db-cf053a224320.pdf (viewed 3 May 2016).

7   Organisation for Economic Cooperation and Development (OECD), *Divided We Stand: Why Inequality Keeps Rising – Country Note: Australia* (Paris 2011) 1, www.oecd.org/australia/49177643. pdf (viewed 3 May 2016); Andrew Leigh, *Battlers and Billionaires: The Story of Inequality in Australia* (Redback Press, 2013) 77; Neil Brooks, 'Taxing the Wealthy' in Chris Evans, Richard Krever and Peter Mellor (eds), *Australia's Future Tax System: The Prospects After Henry* (Thomson Reuters, Sydney 2010) 197, 202.

8   The superannuation concessions and the capital gains discount tax expenditures, together with rental property negative gearing, total according to the Treasury about $40 billion in revenue forgone annually, of which the superannuation concessions make up about $30 billion. For a compilation of the more than $100 billion worth of tax expenditures (i.e. disguised grants through the tax system), see The Treasury, 'Tax Expenditure Statement 2015' (Canberra, January 2016), www.treasury.gov.au/ PublicationsAndMedia/Publications/2016/TES-2015 (viewed 4 May 2016).

of wealth is owned by the next 50% of households, while the bottom 40% of households own just 5% of all wealth'.[9] More recent analysis suggests the top 10 per cent of households own more than 50 per cent of all wealth.[10] Writing for the Evatt Foundation, Sheil and Stilwell argue that increasing inequality is deepening two rifts within society. They say:

> This affluent elite – the Top 10% and especially the Top 1% – is getting cumulatively richer, not only relative to poor households but also, significantly, in relation to the next 50% of households. Two fault lines are widening – between the bottom 40% and the rest, and between the Top 10% and the 50% in the middle.

They are not alone in their disquiet. Thomas Piketty, Joseph Stiglitz, Richard Wilkinson and Kate Pickett, Neil Brooks, Andrew Leigh and ACOSS have all, among many others, raised concerns that this growing disparity of income and wealth threatens social stability and economic performance, and is even a threat to democracy.[11]

Tax won't address the fundamental inequality between capital and labour, but it can ameliorate that inequality. The suggestions in this chapter of a net wealth tax and minimum taxes on wealthy individuals and big business are made in light of the fact that by OECD standards Australia is a low tax country,[12] and understanding that about 2.99 million citizens in 2013–14 lived in poverty, including 731,300 children.[13] These proposals have the capacity to contribute to the lessening of inequality and poverty.

Reintroducing equity into the tax debate means considering, among other things, wealth taxes, ways to make the current income tax system more progressive (including higher tax rates at higher income levels and addressing tax expenditures that favour well-off taxpayers), and revisiting taxes on *all* economic rent (that is, not limiting tax to resource rents).

---

9   ACOSS, above n 2, 31.
10   Sheil and Stilwell, above n 4, in the Overview, not page numbered.
11   Thomas Piketty, *Capital in the Twenty-First Century* (The Belknap Press of Harvard University Press, Cambridge, Massachusetts, 2014); Joseph E Stiglitz, *The Price of Inequality* (Penguin Books Ltd, London, 2012); Richard Wilkinson and Kate Pickett, *The Spirit Level: Why Greater Equality Makes Societies Stronger* (2009, Bloomsbury Press, New York); Neil Brooks, 'Taxing the Wealthy' in Chris Evans, Richard Krever and Peter Mellor, *Australia's Future Tax System: The Prospects After Henry* (Thomson Reuters, Sydney 2010) 197; Andrew Leigh, *Battlers and Billionaires: The Story of Inequality in Australia* (Black Inc, Collingwood, 2013), ACOSS above n 2, 8.
12   OECD Centre for Tax Policy and Administration, *Revenue Statistics 2015 – Australia* (OECD, 2015), www.oecd.org/tax/revenue-statistics-australia.pdf (viewed 2 May 2016).
13   Social Policy Research Centre and ACOSS, *Poverty in Australia 2016* (Strawberry Hills, 2014) 5, www.acoss.org.au/wp-content/uploads/2016/10/Poverty-in-Australia-2016.pdf (viewed 6 April 2017).

Rethinking ways to deal with the low tax burdens of big business could be part of that discussion. Pollution and financial transaction taxes could also be part of any wide ranging tax reform discussion and debate.

These are just a few reform proposals we could investigate. We are limited only by our own imaginations and the power of capital and the rich. Given space constraints, this chapter deals with just two of the proposals. The first is a Buffett rule for individuals and companies. The second is a wealth tax.

II. A Buffet Rule for Individuals and Companies?

A. Individuals

Warren Buffett was shocked to learn that his average tax rate was lower than that of his secretary.[14] This was because, for example, his business deductions, exemptions, offsets (credits), concessional taxation of some activities and deferral of liability reduced his taxable income. Many of these are deviations from accounting norms and the benchmark tax base. Such deviations from the tax benchmark are known as tax expenditures.[15] The Treasury explains this benchmark against which to judge income tax expenditures in this way:

> The tax base for the income tax benchmark is based on the Schanz–Haig–Simons definition of income. An entity's income is defined as the increase in the entity's economic wealth (stock of assets) between two points in time, plus the entity's consumption in that period. Consumption includes all expenditures except those incurred in earning or producing income.

In other words, a buck is a buck is a buck and should be taxed in the same way irrespective of the nature of the gain or who made it.

---

14   The National Economic Council, *The Buffett Rule: A Basic Principle of Tax Fairness* (Washington, April 2012), obamawhitehouse.archives.gov/blog/2012/04/10/white-house-report-buffett-rule-basic-principle-tax-fairness (viewed 2 May 2016).
15   The Treasury, *Tax Expenditure Statement 2015* (Canberra 2016) 3, www.treasury.gov.au/-/media/Treasury/Publications%20and%20Media/Publications/2016/Tax%20Expenditures%20Statement%202015/Downloads/PDF/2015_TES.ashx (viewed 2 May 2016).

The Buffett rule attempts to recoup some of those tax expenditures by imposing a tax liability based on gross income, not taxable income. For example, in 2012 it was reported that President Obama 'proposed the Buffett Rule as a basic rule of tax fairness that should be met in tax reform. To achieve this principle, the President … proposed that no millionaire pay less than 30% of their income in taxes.'[16]

The President is not alone. The Greens in Australia have suggested a Buffett rule of 35 per cent of the gross income of those individuals whose gross income is $300,000 or more, while the Labor Party Opposition appears split on the issue.[17] The Greens' proposed $300,000 threshold covers the top 1 per cent of income earners;[18] they use as an example the case of 56 millionaires with gross income in total of $129 million who, through deductions, reduced their taxable income to below the tax-free threshold of $18,200 and hence paid no income tax.[19] Among the deductions claimed by the 56 was $47 million for tax advice.[20] A Buffett rule at the level the Greens propose would recoup 35 per cent of their $129 million gross revenue or $45.15 million. There will be many more well off taxpayers caught by such a rule and yielding much more revenue for the Commonwealth.

A Buffett rule conflicts with general tax principles. Under such principles, taxable income equals assessable income less allowable deductions. The appropriate tax rate is then applied to this net amount. The tax to be paid can then be reduced by any offsets (such as franking credits and foreign tax credits). In part, what a Buffett rule does is recoup the tax expenditures (in the Greens' example, the deductibility of tax advice) built into the tax system. Even if the tax reduction occurs not because of tax expenditures but, for example, as a result of 'legitimate' benchmark appropriate deductions, the Buffett rule accepts that such a large gross revenue requires some contribution back to society because it arises from society, and that people with incomes of $300,000 or more a year have a capacity to pay (or borrow to pay) despite their non-taxable or low tax status for the income year in question.

---

16   The National Economic Council, above n 14, 1.

17   The Greens, 'Buffett Rule: A High-Income Tax Guarantee', greens.org.au/buffett-rule (viewed 3 May 2016); Katherine Murphy, 'Labor Faces Internal Wrangle Over "Buffett rule" to Stop Wealthy Avoiding Tax', *The Guardian Australia* 4 April 2017, www.theguardian.com/australia-news/2017/apr/04/labor-faces-internal-wrangle-over-buffett-rule-to-stop-wealthy-avoiding-tax (viewed 6 April 2017).

18   The Greens, above n 17, 1.

19   Ibid.

20   Ibid.

B. A Buffett rule for big business?

The same arguments apply to big business. In December 2016 the Commissioner of Taxation released the *Corporate Tax Transparency Report for the 2014–15 Income Year*. It covers public companies with a turnover of more than $100 million and $200 million for private companies. The report shows that 679, or 36 per cent, of the 1,904 entities in the target group paid no income tax in the 2014/2015 income year.[21] There are, as the report points out, a range of reasons why the big businesses in question paid no income tax, including market conditions, use of previous year tax losses, offsets and the like. Tax expenditures and tax avoidance are only part of the explanation.

However, we can look at this from another angle. A Buffett rule for companies can be seen as the Australian Government, on behalf of the Australian people, imposing an operating fee on big business to allow it to pursue its profit-seeking activity in Australia. The fee would be a ground rent imposed on business for the ability or potential to derive profit from Australian workers and consumers. Such a fee or tax could apply not just to companies who paid no income tax but also to those with a low effective tax rate.[22] On top of the non-taxable companies, there are many 'low tax' companies; a Tax Justice Network/United Voice study of the ASX top 200 companies, for example, found that one-third of those companies have an effective tax rate of less than 10 per cent.[23]

It is a valid criticism that a Buffett rule for companies would undermine the intent and actuality of the tax expenditures that allow deductions, offsets or exemptions outside the benchmark. However, the equitable and socially responsible response must be that those with very large gross

---

21   Australian Taxation Office, *Corporate Tax Transparency Report for the 2014–15 Income Year* (Canberra, 2017), www.ato.gov.au/business/large-business/in-detail/tax-transparency/corporate-tax-transparency-report-for-the-2014-15-income-year/?page=5#Net_losses_and_nil_tax_payable (viewed 6 April 2017).

22   For an argument in favour of royalties on resource companies as a substitute for this, see John Passant, 'Taxing Resource Rents in Australia – What a Capital Idea'. A draft is available here: www.researchgate.net/publication/292149294_Taxing_resource_rents_in_Australia_-_what_a_capital_idea (viewed 5 May 2016). A company's effective tax rate is the amount of tax actually paid as a percentage of accounting (not taxable) income. A revised version of this article will be published in 2017 in the *Journal of Australian Political Economy*.

23   United Voice and the Tax Justice Network, *Who Pays for Our Common Wealth? Tax Practices of the ASX 200* (Melbourne, 2014) 21, www.unitedvoice.org.au/news/who-pays-our-common-wealth (viewed 4 May 2016).

incomes can afford to contribute to Australian society and the winding back of such tax expenditures is a limit on those expenditures, not their abolition.

The fee or tax could, for example, be a percentage of a company's gross revenue from Australian sources, reducing as the company's effective tax rate approaches the company tax rate of 30 per cent. Estimates are that the untaxed gross income of big public companies and foreign private entities revealed by the Commissioner of Taxation's Corporate Tax Transparency Report is $462 billion.[24] A 3 per cent tax on that gross income would yield over $13 billion in income from those 679 companies.[25] The same fee-based ground rent approach could apply to those big businesses with an effective tax rate of 10 per cent or less, at the rate say of 2 per cent of the gross revenue, and similarly a rate of 1 per cent for those big businesses with effective tax rates between 10 and say 20 per cent.

Let's now turn to wealth taxes.

III. Wealth Taxes

In *Capital in the Twenty-First Century*,[26] Thomas Piketty – to use the words of a roundtable on inequality in Australia – suggested 'that the most powerful force pushing in the direction of growing inequality is the tendency of the rate of return on capital "r" to exceed the rate of growth of output "g".'[27] For the reasons mentioned in the first paragraph of this

24   Richard O'Brien, 'Turnbull & Morrison Tax Consultants', The Australian Independent Media Network, 11 December 2016, theaimn.com/turnbull-morrison-tax-consultants/ (viewed 6 April 2017); for the 2013–14 Report issued December 2015, the estimate was $405.9 billion of gross revenue that was untaxed for public companies alone. See Nassim Khadem and Craig Butt, 'Which of Australia's Biggest Companies Are Not Paying Tax', *The Sydney Morning Herald* 17 December 2015, www.smh.com.au/business/the-economy/which-of-australias-biggest-companies-are-not-paying-tax-20151216-glpl3a.html (viewed 4 May 2016).

25   The figure does not include the 30 per cent of private Australian companies in the target group who paid no income tax. ATO, *Corporate Tax Transparency Report for the 2013–14 Income Year* (Canberra 2016), www.ato.gov.au/Business/Large-business/In-detail/Tax-transparency/Corporate-tax-transparency-report-for-the-2013-14-income-year/ (viewed 4 May 2016).

26   Thomas Piketty, *Capital in the Twenty-First Century* (The Belknap Press of Harvard University Press, Cambridge, Massachusetts, 2014).

27   Bob Douglas et al, above n 6, 21. In my view Piketty misunderstands the nature of capitalism in that he fails to differentiate between the means of production (and ownership of such) and other assets. At page 52 he dismisses Marx's law of the tendency of the rate of profit to fall as 'quite wrong'. The law is based on the labour theory of value, and in my view is an excellent way of understanding the shift in wealth and income from labour to capital as one countervailing tendency to address the law.

chapter, this systemic and increasing inequality of income and wealth threatens both growth and democracy.[28] To address this, Piketty argues for a progressive global tax on capital[29] in conjunction with financial transparency.[30] He sees a global wealth tax as both a counterweight to increasing concentrations of wealth (and, as a consequence, declining democracy) and as a spur for greater fiscal openness and transparency.[31] By 'capital' Piketty essentially means assets, irrespective of whether they are productive or not. Specifically, Piketty suggests 0 per cent tax for net assets below €1 million, 1 per cent between €1 million and €5 million and 2 per cent above that.[32] He also suggests consideration of much higher rates – in the order of 5 per cent or 10 per cent – for the super wealthy, those with assets greater than €1 billion.[33]

While Piketty recognises that the global cooperation needed for this tax renders the proposal utopian, he argues it is nevertheless useful as both a benchmark and to help countries and regions (such as the European Union) to move incrementally towards this goal.[34] Let's be utopian *and* incremental. Australia could begin the taxation of wealth process that other countries could then follow. Since the top 10 per cent own 45 per cent of Australia's wealth,[35] and given that Australia's net wealth is about $10 trillion,[36] the top 10 per cent own about $4.5 trillion. A 1 per cent annual wealth tax on that group would yield about $45 billion annually. Further, the minimum net worth of the top 1 per cent is over $5 million each.[37] As there are 90,000 people in the top 1 per cent, a net wealth tax of 2 per cent would raise as a minimum well over $9 billion. The amount is likely to be much higher: using the Evatt Foundation figures mentioned above, the top 1 per cent of households own more than 15 per cent of Australia's wealth, which means in concrete terms they own more than

---

28 Ibid.
29 Thomas Piketty, above n 26, 515.
30 Ibid. 518.
31 Ibid. 527.
32 Ibid. 517.
33 Ibid.
34 Ibid. 515.
35 ACOSS, above n 2, 31.
36 Philip Lowe, 'National Wealth, Land Values and Monetary Policy', address by Philip Lowe, Deputy Governor of the Reserve Bank of Australia, to the 54th Shann Memorial Lecture, Perth, 12 August 2015, 3, www.bis.org/review/r150812f.pdf (viewed 4 May 2016).
37 Douglas et al, above n 6, 14.

$1.5 trillion of assets here. On those figures a 1 per cent wealth tax on the wealth of the top 1 per cent would yield $15 billion annually and a 2 per cent tax would bring in about $30 billion.

One argument Piketty uses for net wealth taxes is that, apart from helping to reclaim democracy and citizen participation in society through redistributive policies, wealth is a better indicator of capacity to pay than income.[38] Further, net wealth taxes will see an increase in productive investment into assets capable of producing adequate income returns to pay the tax.[39] In addition, a global wealth tax can exist only in an environment of fiscal transparency, and such transparency would clear up the opaque nature of wealth ownership and allow a more rational debate about, for example, the social state, addressing climate change, and global poverty.[40]

An alternative to an annual net wealth tax is, as the Henry Tax Review, Neil Brooks and the Australia Institute suggest, a tax on net wealth transfers on death.[41] Inter-state tax competition, driven by then Queensland Premier Joh Bjelke-Petersen, destroyed estate and gift duties in Australia in the 1970s when Queensland abolished such taxes and the other states and the Commonwealth responded quickly by also abolishing theirs. The reintroduction of such duties on, for example, the top 1 per cent of wealth holders (that is, those with estates greater than $5 million), at rates which recognise that such intergenerational transfers occur only once, would tax the 'undeserving rich'.[42] It could be structured so as to provide the equivalent, over time, of an annual net wealth tax,[43] thereby providing funds to help address to some extent further growth in inequality through, for example, increases in social welfare payments and establishing new or strengthening existing institutions of governance that restrain the market and empower the less powerful.[44] However, as Piketty argues, a progressive

---

38 Piketty, above n 26, 526.
39 Ibid.
40 Ibid. 519.
41 Australian Government, *Australia's Future Tax System: Report to the Treasurer, Part Two: Detailed Analysis, Vol 1* (AGPS, Canberra December 2009), 137; Neil Brooks, 'Taxing the Wealthy' in Chris Evans, Richard Krever and Peter Mellor, *Australia's Future Tax System: The Prospects After Henry* (Thomson Reuters, Sydney 2010) 197, 223ff; David Richardson, *Surprise Me When I'm Dead: Revisiting the Case for Estate Duties* (The Australia Institute, February 2016), www.tai.org.au/sites/defualt/files/Revisiting%20the%20Case%20for%20Estate%20Duties.pdf (viewed 9 May 2017).
42 Neil Brooks, 'Taxing the Wealthy' in Chris Evans, Richard Krever and Peter Mellor, *Australia's Future Tax System: The Prospects After Henry* (Thomson Reuters, Sydney 2010) 197, 206.
43 Thomas Piketty, above n 26, 374.
44 Neil Brooks, above n 42, 223ff.

annual global tax on wealth is but one of a suite of progressive taxes to achieve this aim and other aims.[45] For Piketty, the tax is not so much about financing the social state on its own as about addressing growing inequality and, to avoid future economic crisis, regulating the financial and banking systems; it is about regulating capitalism.[46]

IV. Conclusion

A Buffett rule for individuals and companies, and a wealth tax, are but two reforms among many that would make the overall tax system more equitable. Powerful, very wealthy forces and the democratic institutions they dominate are, as the history of the last 40 years or so globally shows, pushing in the direction of greater and greater freedom for market forces, resulting in greater and greater inequality. This means that at the present juncture in human history the two proposals I have proffered will not be taken up. Nevertheless these two measures, among a range of other tax and non-tax prescriptions, would help policymakers address growing inequality and the threat that poses to our democracy and economy.

---

45   Thomas Piketty, above n 26, 518.
46   Ibid.

4

Brand New 'Sharing' or Plain Old 'Sweating'? A Proposal for Regulating the New 'Gig Economy'

Joellen Riley[1]

I. Enter the 'Collaborative Economy'

Politicians on both sides of the political spectrum in Australia have been embracing what they are calling the 'sharing', or 'collaborative' economy, typified by new app-enabled business enterprises linking up consumers with service providers of many kinds. Examples include Uber and Lyft in the passenger transport business; Airtasker and TaskRabbit in the market for odd-job services; Deliveroo and Foodora in takeaway food delivery; and Airbnb in short-term accommodation letting. The notion that these businesses involve 'sharing' or 'collaboration' depends on seeing them as means by which those who have surplus energy or assets can make money from sharing their skills or assets with others – and the app-based intermediary takes a commission from making the introduction. In New South Wales, a November 2015 position paper stated: 'The NSW government welcomes the positive impact of the collaborative economy

---

1   Professor of Labour Law, Sydney Law School, University of Sydney. For an extended argument of this proposal, see Joellen Riley, 'Regulating Work in the "Gig" Economy' in Mia Ronnmar and Jenny Julen Votinius, *Festskrift Till Ann Numhauser-Henning* (Jurisforlaget I Lund, Sweden, 2017) 669–83.

for consumer choice, employment and productivity'.[2] This same paper stated that at the end of 2015 the collaborative economy in NSW was valued at about $504 million a year, and approximately 45,000 people earned income from it – though this income was described as 'additional' or 'supplementary'.

Both sides of politics appear to recognise the need for some regulation of this new sector of the economy, although all are concerned that new regulation should not strangle innovation and forfeit all these coveted economic benefits. To date, most regulatory initiatives have focused on consumer protection, and the risks of unfair competition with existing services. So, for example, the *Road Transport (Public Passenger Services) (Taxi Industry Innovation) Amendment Act 2015* (ACT) introduces amendments to the *Road Transport (Public Passenger Services) Act 2001* (ACT) to ensure that the new passenger transport services provided by the likes of Uber and Lyft are regulated alongside the taxi hire car industries in the interests of passenger safety, by ensuring the registration and accreditation of drivers. With the possible exception of regulation of 'maximum driving times and minimum rest times'[3] (matters which may be made subject to regulations, but had not been at the time of writing[4]), this legislation manifests no particular concern with the labour standards observed by these new 'ridesharing' services.

There are, however, real risks to labour standards in the operation of those businesses in the so-called sharing economy that depend on the engagement of workers. These risks have become apparent in recent news stories in Australia about Uber drivers being 'blocked' (a new word for 'sacked') in apparently unfair circumstances.[5] And in the United States there have been stories of driver protests against Uber for cutting fares without warning by 25 per cent.[6] Workers in the 'gig'[7] economy are as

---

2   State of NSW Department of Finance, Services and Innovation, 'The Collaborative Economy in NSW – A Position Paper', November 2015, www.finance.nsw.gov.au/publication-and-resources/collaborative-economy.

3   See *Road Transport (Public Passenger Services) Act 2001* (ACT) s 60I(d).

4   The Regulations were consulted on 4 April 2017.

5   See Georgia Wilkins, 'Driver Sues Uber after termination', *Australian Financial Review*, 19 May 2016, 9.

6   See Adrian Chen 'An Uber Labor Movement born in a LaGuardia Parking Lot', *New Yorker*, 8 February 2016, www.newyorker.com/business/currency/an-uber-labor-movement-born-in-a-laguardia-parking-lot (viewed 13 May 2016).

7   The 'gig' is well-known in the music industry as the one-off performance of a job of work, with no expectation of continuing engagement.

much in need of basic labour market protections as are other kinds of workers.[8] The question for law reform is: What kind of regulation best accommodates this kind of work? Should these workers be treated as employees, and enjoy all the protections available in the *Fair Work Act 2009* (Cth)?[9] This chapter recommends that a better solution would be the introduction of a special scheme providing protections similar to those available to other small business workers in special kinds of commercial relationships.

Two current regulatory schemes spring to mind: legislation protecting owner-drivers in the transport industry, and the Franchising Code of Conduct (FCC) dealing with the rights of the small businesses who operate in franchised business networks.[10] A particular provision, typical in statutory schemes for protecting small business operators from exploitation, is protection from capricious termination of work contracts. A 'gig' worker who has invested heavily in a car or other equipment to perform the job is extremely vulnerable if they are working under a contract which can be terminated immediately and without sufficient justification. Another important protection is the right to form associations for the purpose of collective bargaining. Before explaining this proposal, it is worth reflecting on the realities of work for the 'gig' economy labourer.

II. Who Profits From the 'Gig' Economy?

Businesses such as Uber (in the 'ridesharing' market), and Airtasker (in the odd-job business) have become multimillion dollar enterprises (multibillion dollar in the case of Uber), by creating and managing phone 'apps' that connect customers with services. They derive their revenue by deducting a commission from the automatic electronic payment made for every ride or gig arranged on their apps. In the case of Airtasker the

---

8   See the special issue on 'Crowdsourcing, the Gig-Economy and the Law' in (2016) 37(3) *Comparative Labor Law and Policy Journal*, for a number of academic studies on the need for labour protection in a proliferating world of digitally-sourced work.

9   In the United Kingdom, an Employment Tribunal has held that Uber drivers are 'workers' (but not necessarily 'employees') for the purposes of the *Employment Rights Act 1996* s 230(3)(b): see *Aslam, Farrer v Uber BV, Uber London and Uber Britannia Ltd*, Case Nos 2202551/2015, decided on 12 October 2016.

10   The FCC was made under the *Competition and Consumer (Industry Codes – Franchising) Regulation 2014* and is enforceable as a consequence of the *Competition and Consumer Act 2010* (Cth) s 51AD.

commission is 15 per cent of the agreed fee for the work.[11] Airtasker claims to have around 480,000 users on its platform, and turned over $13 million in tasks in the year to April 2016.[12]

These organisations emphatically disavow any suggestion that they are employers of the workers. They describe what they do as 'facilitating sharing', in ways that unlock and exploit the unused potential in underused assets – such as cars that might otherwise be sitting in garages. In reality, there is very little 'sharing' involved in these relationships, notwithstanding that Uber has been successful in persuading the ACT legislature to adopt the terminology of the 'rideshare' service in its newly enacted provisions in the *Road Transport (Public Passenger Services) Act*.

The true nature of these relationships is that Uber and others are intermediaries profiting from the sale of labour. Some may say that they are 'commodifying' labour[13] in a way abhorrent to a fundamental principle of the International Labour Organization, that 'labour is not a commodity'.[14] They do not provide any tools of trade for the worker, apart from maintaining the app that connects supply and demand in the market for the work. The workers bear the costs of maintaining their tools and equipment. In the case of Uber drivers, that may mean covering the loan or finance lease repayments on an expensive, late model motor vehicle.[15] The intermediary also forswears any entitlement to control the worker, and so avoids characterisation as an employer under the common law definition of employment.[16] Workers decide themselves how much time to spend on the job, and which tasks to accept. The intermediary does not need to monitor performance as an employer would, because

---

11 Ewin Hannan 'Old School, New School', *AFR Boss*, April 2016, Vol 17, 23.

12 Cara Waters 'Outsourcing Jobs Frees Up Entrepreneurs', *The Sydney Morning Herald*, 4 April 2016, 24.

13 See Antonio Aloisi, 'Commoditized Workers: Case Study Research on Labour Law Issues Arising from a Set of "On-demand/Gig Economy" Platforms' (2016) 37(3) *Comparative Labor Law and Policy Journal* 653.

14 See Paul O'Higgins, '"Labour is not a Commodity"– an Irish Contribution to International Labour Law' (1997) 26 *Industrial Law Journal* 225–34.

15 It is a condition of driving for Uber that the driver maintains an unblemished late model vehicle.

16 For a recent analysis of the concept of 'employment', see Joellen Riley, 'The Definition of the Contract of Employment and its Differentiation from Other Contracts and Other Work Relations' in Mark Freedland, Alan Bogg, David Cabrelli et al (eds), *The Contract of Employment* (Oxford University Press, United Kingdom, 2016) 321–40. Note that some commentators have suggested that Uber's arrangements in Australia may constitute an employment relationship between Uber and the drivers. See, for example, Josh Bornstein's blog: joshbornstein.com.au/writing/the-great-uber-fairness-fallacy-as-a-driver-how-do-you-bargain-with-an-app/ (viewed 5 April 2017). See also *Aslam, Farrer v Uber BV, Uber London and Uber Britannia Ltd*, above n 9.

the app itself contains a rating tool to gather the views of customers. The worker is 'blocked' from using the app if ratings drop below an acceptable standard, so drivers have a big incentive to remain upbeat and cheery. (This could be why Uber users regularly report that Uber drivers love chauffeuring them around: nobody 'likes' a depressed and grumpy servant.) If the allegations in the press surrounding the 'blocking' of drivers are true, Uber drivers have no opportunity to contest poor ratings, and so are at the mercy of mean-spirited or possibly discriminatory assessments by customers.[17] Some apps – such as Airtasker – allow the worker to propose their own rate of pay, so workers bid competitively for tasks. As there is no minimum wage for a gig worker, rates can be low. According to a study conducted by the International Labour Organisation of online clerical workers engaged by Amazon Mechanical Turk, the mean hourly pay for a worker in the United States was $US5.55.[18]

Low prices for work mean that the other beneficiaries of this kind of work are the customers who are able to source labour more cheaply than by direct employment. We know that many young people use Uber because it is cheaper than hiring a taxi, but it is not only individual domestic customers who are attracted by lower prices. At the university I work for it has been suggested that we switch from Cabcharge to Uber accounts to save on transport costs. Airtasker has reported that about a third of its turnover is driven by small businesses, not householders. According to an enthusiast for these kinds of services, 'This is a new wave of outsourcing micro tasks when you don't need to hire someone for a day, you just need them for an hour'.[19] This kind of micro outsourcing by businesses may not be all that new at all. It looks very like the labour engagement practices of a hundred or more years ago, before the establishment of the standard weekly wage, when impecunious wharf labourers had to bid each day for work loading and unloading ships on the Hungry Mile at the Sydney wharves. Over the course of the past century we have regulated the engagement of labour to protect workers from the risks of highly precarious work. Past regulation has generally accepted that those who profit from the exploitation of labour ought to bear some of the cost of protective

---

17   See the story of Mr Mike Oze-Igiehon in Georgia Wilkins, 'Driver Sues Uber after Termination', *Australian Financial Review*, 19 May 2016, 9. Similar stories are collected in Janine Berg, 'Income Security in the On-demand Economy: Findings and Policy Lessons for a Survey of Crowdworkers' (2016) 37(3) *Comparative Labor Law and Policy Journal* 543–76.

18   See Janine Berg, above n 17.

19   Author Rachel Botsman, cited in Waters, above n 12.

regulation. After all, how much of Uber's billion-dollar value is down to the creation of the app, and how much depends upon the availability of the drivers, with their shiny new vehicles and perpetual smiles?

III. What Kind of Regulation?

In designing regulation for this new-old form of labour engagement it would be wise to resist squeezing these inventive app intermediaries into employment regulation – bearing in mind that employment is itself a relatively new concept, historically speaking,[20] and the strictures of employment regulation have sometimes created the incentives to invent new forms of labour engagement. The Uber driver agreement[21] is itself insistent that the company operating the Uber app is 'a technology service provider that does not provide transportation services … nor operate as an agent for the transportation of passengers'. It also explicitly forswears the existence of any employment relationship with drivers, and devises its terms to avoid any appearance of controlling when, where or whether drivers agree to pick up passengers. The only thing the company does control (rigidly) is maximum fares, and its own commission, which is withheld before drivers are paid.

If we accept that the drivers are not employees of Uber (as seems sensible, given that the terms of the arrangement do thrust a great deal of responsibility and discretion on the drivers), how else might they access some worker rights? Are there innovative ways of regulating these kinds of labour market exchanges without stifling innovation, but also without risking a return to the Hungry Mile?

We can look to existing small business regulation in Australia to see some models for reducing the harshest effects of precarity for gig economy workers. If we focus particularly on the rideshare drivers, we may find a potential model of regulation in aspects of state-based regulation in the road transport industry.[22] This state legislation remains enforceable,

---

20   See John Howe and Richard Mitchell, 'The Evolution of the Contract of Employment in Australia: A Discussion' (1999) 12 *Australian Journal of Labour Law* 113.
21   The author obtained a copy of the Rasier Pacific VOF Services Agreement, last updated on 23 December 2015, under which drivers agree to provide transportation services to Uber users. Copy on file with the author.
22   Such as *Industrial Relations Act 1996* (NSW) Ch 6, which provides for regulation of work in the taxi and owner driver transport industries.

notwithstanding the enactment of the federal *Independent Contractors Act 2006* (Cth) (*IC Act*), because s 7(2) of the *IC Act* specifically preserves the operation of these statutes.

The Victorian *Owner Drivers and Forestry Contractors Act 2005* (Vic) (*ODFC Act*), provides a useful illustration of the kinds of provisions that might also be enacted to protect rideshare drivers. As outlined below, these include provisions seeking to promote decent levels of remuneration, protection from capricious termination of working arrangements, and access to affordable and fair dispute resolution mechanisms to enable drivers to secure these entitlements. The legislation also accommodates a pragmatic application of the right to freedom of association, so that drivers can join together to agitate for fair treatment.

The standard Uber driver contract permits Uber to determine maximum fares, and to vary fares without consultation with drivers.[23] There is no provision for fares to be set taking into account any of the drivers' costs for motor vehicle expenses, or for a telecommunications provider's charges to a driver for accessing the large amounts of data required to operate the app. Under the *ODFC Act*, rates and cost schedules for truck drivers can be reviewed by the minister, in consultation with the Transport Industry Council and Forestry Industry Council, with a view to ensuring that owner drivers can earn similar remuneration to employees engaged to do the same work.[24] Hirers must include these rates schedules in written information provided to drivers.[25] A hirer who fails to provide this information takes the risk that the Victorian Civil and Administrative Tribunal (VCAT) will exercise a power to order that the contractor be paid what VCAT determines is a 'fair and reasonable rate', notwithstanding the terms of the contract.[26] The establishment of an administrative body to provide similar review of fares and costs for rideshare drivers would help them to secure fair remuneration for their work.

Truck drivers can also complain to VCAT if they believe they have been subjected to 'unconscionable conduct',[27] the definition of which includes 'whether or not the regulated contract allows for the payment of any increases in fixed and variable overhead costs on a regular and

---

23   Clause 4 of the contract, see n 21.
24   *ODFC Act* s 14(2)(b).
25   *ODFC Act* s 16.
26   *ODFC Act* s 45.
27   Defined in *ODFC Act* s 31.

systematic basis'.[28] The available remedies include a 'contract variation order'.[29] The special danger of a 'contract variation order' is that it may be extended generally, to other contracts of a specified class. A trade union has standing to apply for a contract variation order made in one case to be extended to cover other contracts.

Rights to collective negotiation should also be supported for rideshare drivers. Uber drivers with grievances about things like Uber's sudden reduction of fares have already demonstrated a propensity to protest collectively, and to form associations.[30] Under the *ODFC Act*, drivers are permitted to bargain collectively through 'negotiating agents',[31] and such conduct is expressly exempted from any sanction under the *Competition and Consumer Act 2010* (Cth).[32]

Protection from capricious loss of one's job is also a key entitlement for workers, whether they are employees or contractors. According to the Uber driver contract, drivers can be given seven days' notice of termination for any reason or no reason at all,[33] and they can lose access to the app without notice if their ratings drop below an acceptable level.[34] By way of contrast, under the *ODFC Act* heavy vehicle drivers must be given a minimum of three months' notice,[35] recognising that these drivers have invested in job-specific, expensive rigs. Although a shorter period may be warranted for Uber drivers who have invested in ordinary passenger vehicles which are more readily sold, there ought to be some recognition of drivers' sunk costs in acquiring a vehicle when determining a fair and appropriate notice period for terminating driving contracts.

---

28   *ODFC Act* s 31(2)(k).

29   *ODFC Act* s 44(1)(g) and 47(2).

30   See Adrian Chen, 'An Uber Labor Movement born in a LaGuardia Parking Lot', *New Yorker*, 8 February 2016, www.newyorker.com/business/currency/an-uber-labor-movement-born-in-a-laguardia-parking-lot (viewed 13 May 2016).

31   *ODFC Act* ss 25–26.

32   *ODFC Act* s 64(1)(c)–(e). In Australia, the anti-trust provisions in the *Competition and Consumer Act 2010* (Cth) operate to limit, if not curtail entirely, the scope for independent contractors to engage in collective industrial action. See Shae McCrystal, 'Organising Independent Contractors: The Impact of Competition Law' in Judy Fudge, Shae McCrystal and Kamala Sankaran, *Challenging the Legal Boundaries of Work Regulation* (Hart, Oxford, 2012) 139.

33   Clause 12.2.

34   Clause 2.5.2.

35   *ODFC Act* s 21.

Two other provisions in the *ODFC Act* might be included in a specific scheme to protect rideshare drivers. One is similar to the general protection provisions in the *Fair Work Act* Pt 3-1, which prohibits threatening a person with detriment if they claim any of their rights under the Act.[36] Another is access to a Small Business Commissioner for mediation or other dispute resolution processes, before resorting to VCAT with a complaint;[37] any regulatory scheme designed to assist small business people needs to provide access to quick and inexpensive dispute resolution services.

IV. General 'Fair Trading' Protections

A special scheme for rideshare drivers, designed to provide similar protections to those enjoyed by owner truck drivers, is one solution to providing satisfactory worker protection for one part of the 'gig' economy. More general protections may be needed for the freelancers working on other platforms, such as Airtasker. The *Competition and Consumer Act 2010* (Cth) already includes protections for small businesses against predatory practices of larger ones in its provisions prohibiting unconscionable dealing.[38] Perhaps these provisions need to be supplemented by a special industry code of conduct, similar to the Franchising Code of Conduct (FCC), which also deals with matters such as adequate disclosure of contract terms, and protections from capricious termination of contracts.[39]

The policymakers who framed the original FCC were responding to a number of reports and enquiries that had uncovered widespread exploitative practices in the franchising industry.[40] The typical franchise

---

36   *ODFC Act* s 61.
37   *ODFC Act* s 35.
38   See *Competition and Consumer Act 2010* (Cth) ss 51AA–51AC.
39   See *Competition and Consumer (Industry Codes – Franchising) Regulation* 2014, and the *Competition and Consumer Act 2010* (Cth) s 51AD.
40   See the Swanson Trade Practices Act Review Committee, *Report to the Minister for Business and Consumer Affairs* (Commonwealth of Australia, Canberra, 1976); Trade Practices Consultative Committee, *Small Business and the Trade Practices Act* Vol 1 (Commonwealth of Australia, Canberra, 1979) (Blunt Committee); House of Representatives Standing Committee on Industry Science and Technology, *Small Business in Australia: Challenges, Problems and Opportunities* (Commonwealth of Australia, Canberra, 1990) (Beddall Committee); R Gardini, *Review of the Franchising Code of Practice: Report to the Minister for Small Business, Customs and Construction* (Commonwealth of Australia, Canberra, 1994); Reid Committee Report, *Finding a Balance towards Fair Trading in Australia. Report by the House of Representatives Standing Committee on Industry, Science and Technology* (Commonwealth of Australia, Canberra, 1997).

agreement requires considerable investment by the franchisee in a business heavily controlled by someone else. Franchisees are especially vulnerable to the risk of losing their investment if the franchise is terminated, much in the same way as a gig economy worker is at considerable financial risk if she or he sets up a business in reliance on a clientele sourced through the app, but is subsequently 'blocked' from using the app. The FCC deals with this risk by including provisions protecting franchisees from capricious termination of the franchise. Even if a franchisee has committed some breach of the franchise agreement, a franchisor may not summarily terminate the franchise, but must notify the franchisee of the alleged breach and the proposal to terminate, and give the franchisee a reasonable time (not exceeding 30 days) to remedy the breach. If the franchisee remedies the breach, the franchisor is not permitted to terminate on account of that breach.[41] If gig economy workers had this kind of right, it would go some way to protecting any investment they have made in their 'micro enterprises' by ensuring they could not have their capacity to earn withdrawn without warning.

Like owner truck drivers, franchisees also enjoy a freedom to form associations, and they are protected from any conduct of the franchisor to restrict or impair that right by a 300 penalty unit fine.[42] The FCC does not, however, clarify whether this freedom extends to engaging in collective negotiations or boycotts.

Like the *ODFC Act*, the FCC also encourages parties to use mediation to resolve disputes (though parties retain their rights to litigate), and the *Competition and Consumer Act 2010* (Cth) empowers a third party watchdog – the Australian Competition and Consumer Commission – to take action on behalf of franchisees, and seek a range of flexible remedies, including orders for the variation of contracts.[43]

V. Conclusion

Workers in the 'gig' economy, like all others who rely on their own labour for a livelihood, need the security of decent incomes and protection from capricious termination of jobs. We have laws protecting these kinds

---

41   FCC cl 27(4).
42   FCC cl 33.
43   See *Competition and Consumer Act 2010* (Cth) s 87.

of interests for other workers outside the boundaries of employment legislation, in all manner of special schemes designed to promote fair dealing for small enterprise operators. Politicians across the spectrum in Australia ought to be looking at these models with a view to designing suitable regulation to protect the growing armies of workers in the 'gig' economy. Key elements of new regulation need to be a suitably empowered watchdog (similar to the ACCC, or the Fair Work Ombudsman), and an easily accessible dispute resolution forum.

5

Good Call: Extending Liability for Employment Contraventions Beyond the Direct Employer

Tess Hardy[1]

I. Introduction

A raft of recent inquiries and investigations have revealed that non-compliance with employment standards regulation[2] is a pressing problem in Australia.[3] While there are many factors which may have contributed to a lack of employer compliance, including the growing vulnerability of segments of the workforce and a decline in unionisation, this chapter will focus on some of the most critical limits of the *Fair Work Act 2009* (Cth) (*FW Act*). The inquiry into the 7-Eleven franchise network undertaken by the Office of the Fair Work Ombudsman (FWO) in 2016 will be

---

1   Senior Lecturer, Melbourne Law School.
2   Unless otherwise specified, the terms 'employment standards' or 'workplace standards' are used to refer to the regulation governing minimum rates of pay, hours of work, and leave and termination entitlements, including by way of the *Fair Work Act 2009* (Cth), modern awards and enterprise agreements.
3   See, for example, Senate Education and Employment References Committee, Inquiry into the Impact of Australia's Temporary Work Visa Programs on the Australian Labour Market and on the Temporary Work Visa Holders (Final Report, 17 March 2016); Caro Meldrum-Hanna and Ali Russell, 'Slaving Away', *Four Corners*, 4 May 2015; Adele Ferguson and Klaus Toft, '7-Eleven: The Price of Convenience', *Four Corners*, 31 August 2015.

used to illustrate some of the key regulatory challenges.[4] In exploring possible reform options, this chapter will consider whether, and in what circumstances, liability for employment standards contraventions should extend beyond the direct employer. In particular, this chapter is especially focused on the extent to which so-called 'lead firms' should be held liable for employment contraventions taking place in their supply chain, corporate group or franchise network.[5] The paper will conclude with some preliminary observations regarding the merits (or otherwise) of the Fair Work Amendment (Protecting Vulnerable Workers) Bill 2017 (Cth) ('Vulnerable Workers Bill') which was introduced into federal parliament on 1 March 2017.

II. Limitations of the Current Regulatory Regime

The *FW Act* largely continues to reflect the unitary conception of the 'employer' – the idea that there is only one person or entity responsible for setting and complying with employment conditions.[6] However, there is growing evidence to suggest that key conditions of employment – such as recruitment, pay, working hours, supervision and termination – may be determined by a number of organisations outside and beyond the direct employer as a result of outsourcing, subcontracting, labour hire or franchising.

While these various commercial arrangements are all legitimate business strategies, the fragmentation of corporate structures and working arrangements into loosely connected networks has blurred the lines of responsibility for ensuring workplace compliance. It has also made the enforcement of employment standards regulation undoubtedly more complex and potentially less effective.[7] Civil remedy litigation is increasingly foiled by the fact that the putative employer entity may

---

4   Office of the Fair Work Ombudsman, 'A Report of the Fair Work Ombudsman's Inquiry into 7-Eleven' (Australian Government, April 2016) (*7-Eleven Inquiry*).

5   The term 'lead firm' is used in a broad sense to capture those companies which sit at the top of a supply chain, the head of a corporate group or at the apex of a franchise network. In reality, identifying only one lead firm may not be straightforward, particularly where the putative lead firm is part of a larger corporate group. For further discussion of this issue, see Tess Hardy, 'Who Should Be Held Liable for Workplace Contraventions and on What Basis?' (2016) 29 *Australian Journal of Labour Law* 78.

6   See generally Jeremias Prassl, *The Concept of the Employer* (Oxford University Press, 2015).

7   David Weil, *The Fissured Workplace: Why Work Became So Bad for So Many and What Can Be Done to Improve It* (Harvard University Press, 2014).

elect to liquidate or deregister the relevant employing corporation. This not only has the effect of rendering the employer immune from the legal consequences of its non-compliance, it may mean that underpayments are never fully recovered.[8] Moreover, targeting the direct employer may not be effective in addressing some of the systemic drivers of employer non-compliance, which may be determined by more powerful firms positioned higher in the supply chain, the corporate group or the franchise network.

It seems that the laws which were originally intended to protect workers from exploitation may now perpetuate such problems 'by focusing regulatory attention on the wrong parties'.[9] By positioning the direct employer entity as the primary wrongdoer, the civil remedy regime established under the *FW Act* does not fully account for the disaggregation of employer functions described above. Rather, the existing legal framework appears to permit lead firms to 'have it both ways'[10] – that is, firms positioned at the top of a supply chain, at the head of a corporate group, or at the apex of a franchise network, may exercise high levels of control over the performance of work, and yet remain legally insulated from the problems this may create. This particular issue was highlighted in the FWO's recent public inquiry into allegations of widespread underpayment of workers in the 7-Eleven franchise network.

III. The FWO's Inquiry into the 7-Eleven Franchise Network

A significant component of the FWO's current compliance and enforcement strategy is the conduct of formal, public inquiries. These in-depth inquiries are generally prompted by allegations or concerns about systemic employer non-compliance in an industry, region, supply chain or labour market. They normally entail the regulator undertaking a detailed examination of the drivers of compliance behaviour through site visits, interviews and payroll audits. Specific focus is placed on the role of lead firms. At the conclusion of an inquiry, a written report is made publicly available which sets out the key findings, the regulator's recommendations, and any actions taken including whether the regulator has (or is likely to) initiate enforcement litigation against one or more persons.[11]

---

8   See, for example, *Fair Work Ombudsman v Haider Pty Ltd* [2015] FCCA 2113 (30 July 2015).
9   Weil, above n 7, 4.
10   Ibid. 14.
11   Fair Work Ombudsman, *Annual Report 2014–15*, 31.

The FWO's inquiry into the 7-Eleven franchise network sought to better understand the regulatory role played by head office of the 7-Eleven franchise, namely 7-Eleven Stores Pty Ltd ('7-Eleven Stores'), as well as its franchisees and their employees. The FWO's report makes clear that 7-Eleven Stores 'had a reasonable basis on which to inquire and act'[12] into allegations of franchisee non-compliance with employment standards. In particular, the regulator noted that, for at least five years prior to the public airing of these issues, 7-Eleven Stores was aware that multiple outlets within its network had deliberately sought to evade employment regulation through the falsification of employment and payroll records.

Notwithstanding the mounting evidence of widespread workplace contraventions in this period, the FWO found that 7-Eleven head office largely failed to take any substantive steps to curb employer non-compliance. In particular, the FWO noted that while 7-Eleven Stores exercised a high degree of control over its franchisees, it did not implement any significant changes to its franchise model, its existing monitoring mechanisms or its payroll systems. Indeed, despite the pattern of poor compliance behaviour across its network, 7-Eleven Stores expressly declined to participate in the FWO's voluntary franchise program which was specifically designed to leverage the franchise relationship in a way that enhanced employment standards compliance amongst franchisees.[13] In short, the FWO found that while 7-Eleven Stores ostensibly promoted compliance with workplace standards, it 'did not adequately detect or address deliberate non-compliance and as a consequence compounded it'.[14]

Notwithstanding this finding, the FWO ultimately determined that 7-Eleven Stores' failure to do more or act earlier did not give rise to any legal liability. In particular, the FWO concluded that it did not have sufficient probative evidence to pursue 7-Eleven Stores under the accessorial liability provisions of the *FW Act*.[15] Accordingly, the regulator decided not to initiate civil remedy litigation against the lead firm in this instance.

---

12   *7-Eleven Inquiry*, above n 4, 67.

13   Ibid. 10. See also Tess Hardy, 'Brandishing the Brand: Enhancing Employer Compliance through the Regulatory Enrolment of Franchisors' (Paper presented at the Labour Law Research Network Conference, Amsterdam, 25–27 June 2015).

14   *7-Eleven Inquiry*, above n 4, 4.

15   *FW Act* s 550.

Initially, the conclusion reached by the FWO in this inquiry – that 7-Eleven Stores was not liable for the employment contraventions which had taken place in its network – was not especially concerning from a regulatory perspective given that the 7-Eleven head office had already taken a range of far-reaching compliance measures in the intervening period, including:

a. reviewing key aspects of the franchise model;

b. setting up an independent panel to receive and process wage claims; and

c. introducing more rigorous and accountable monitoring and payroll systems.[16]

While these types of voluntary measures are valuable, it is somewhat telling that these proactive steps were only taken by 7-Eleven Stores after the media story broke and the brand had suffered a significant public bruising. Indeed, it seems that ongoing media pressure and intense public scrutiny were critical to the finalisation of a proactive compliance deed with the FWO.[17] This deed, which formalised many of the compliance commitments the franchisor had already adopted, was concluded only after extensive negotiation and continuing controversy about the way in which head office was handling claims following its surprise decision to dismantle the independent panel previously led by Professor Fels.[18] Another factor which may have further amplified the pressure being placed on 7-Eleven Stores was the Coalition Government's announcement in May 2016 of its intention to introduce new civil remedy provisions 'that capture franchisors ... who fail to deal with exploitation by their franchisees'.[19]

Since then, the Coalition Government has moved to implement this policy by way of the Vulnerable Workers Bill. This Bill is explicitly designed to respond to some of the problems identified by the FWO in the 7-Eleven Inquiry and elsewhere, including the fact that some franchisors may 'operate on a business model based on underpaying workers'[20] and 'have

---

16 *7-Eleven Inquiry*, above n 4, 52–65.

17 See Proactive Compliance Deed between the Commonwealth of Australia (as represented by the Office of the Fair Work Ombudsman) and 7-Eleven Stores Pty Ltd (6 December 2016).

18 Adele Ferguson and Sarah Danckert, '7-Eleven Kills Independent Wage Panel', *The Sydney Morning Herald*, 11 May 2016.

19 Liberal Party of Australia, 'The Coalition's Policy to Protect Vulnerable Workers', 19 May 2016.

20 Explanatory Memorandum, Vulnerable Workers Bill, 6.

either been blind to the problem or not taken sufficient action to deal with it once it was brought to their attention'.[21] In particular, in a submission regarding the Bill, the FWO noted that:

> franchisors can be reluctant to proactively engage with the FWO before issues are uncovered, either by the FWO or through the media. Reputational leverage works as a 'push' factor for franchisors to act, but has had limited effect as a general deterrence measure to encourage other franchisors to take reasonable steps to detect non-compliance and support franchisees to be compliant.[22]

These observations reflect the existing sociolegal literature which similarly suggests that, without compelling incentives or coercive sanctions, it is difficult for a regulator to leverage lead firms to genuinely and sustainably engage with softer, voluntary initiatives.[23] Indeed, the 7-Eleven case summarised above not only illustrates some of the problems of relying on methods of self-regulation, but also underlines a number of the limits of the existing legal framework in making lead firms accountable for conduct taking place in their business networks.

IV. Limitations of Accessorial Liability Provisions

Under existing law, the principal statutory mechanism for extending liability beyond the direct employer – and holding lead firms to account with respect to employment standards compliance – are the accessorial liability provisions of the *FW Act*. Essentially, these provisions provide that persons found to be 'involved in' a contravention of the *FW Act* may be liable under a civil remedy provision, even where they are not the actual employer of the worker whose rights have been breached. Broadly speaking, a person will be taken to be 'involved in' a contravention if the person has:

---

21   Ibid.

22   Fair Work Ombudsman, Submission to the Senate Education and Employment Legislation Committee Inquiry into the Fair Work Amendment (Protecting Vulnerable Workers) Bill 2017, 6 April 2017.

23   Guy Davidov, 'The Enforcement Crisis in Labour Law and the Fallacy of Voluntarist Solutions' (2010) 26 *International Journal of Comparative Labour Law and Industrial Relations* 61. See also David Weil, 'Improving Workplace Conditions through Strategic Enforcement' (Report to the Wage and Hour Division, United States Department of Labor, 2010) 87.

a. aided, abetted, counselled or procured the contravention;

b. induced the contravention (whether by threats or promises or otherwise);

c. been in any way, by act or omission, 'knowingly concerned' in the contravention; or

d. conspired with others to effect the contravention.[24]

The third limb of this definition is arguably the most critical given that it is this subclause which is routinely relied upon by the FWO and other regulators. However, a series of recent cases have set a high bar in relation to satisfying the 'requisite knowledge' requirement under s 550(2)(c) of the *FW Act*, particularly with respect to contraventions of modern awards.[25] One of the challenges with using s 550(2)(c) is the need to establish that the accessory had 'actual knowledge' of the essential elements of the contravention. Actual knowledge is said to include 'wilful blindness' but does not generally encompass 'recklessness or negligence'.[26] Further, constructive knowledge is not sufficient.[27]

The way in which the requisite knowledge requirement has been interpreted and applied by the courts may make it difficult to pin liability on the alleged accessory, especially in complex supply chains, where the lead firm may be more removed from the affected employees and less aware of the precise employment arrangements (e.g. the employment status of the employee, the duties performed, the hours worked etc.). Further, it is not yet clear to what extent it is possible to aggregate the knowledge of multiple officers in larger companies, franchise networks or corporate groups.[28] Questions arise as to when, and in what circumstances, an accessory's omission to act is likely to 'support the inference of actual knowledge'.[29]

---

24 *FW Act* s 550(2).

25 *FW Act* s 45. See, for example, *FWO v Devine Marine* [2015] FCA 370; and *Potter v Fair Work Ombudsman* [2014] FCA 187.

26 *Keller v LED Technologies Pty Ltd* [2010] FCAFC 55.

27 *Giorgianni v The Queen* (1985) 156 CLR 473; *Young Investments Group Pty Ltd v Mann* (2012) 293 ALR 537, 541.

28 Ingmar Taylor and Larissa Andelman, 'Accessorial Liability under the *Fair Work Act*' (Paper presented at the Australian Labour Law Association, Sydney, 14–15 November 2014).

29 *Fair Work Ombudsman v South Jin Pty Ltd* [2015] FCA 1456 [49]. See also *Fair Work Ombudsman v Liquid Fuel Pty Ltd* [2015] FCCA 2694.

In the view of the FWO, previous cases suggest that '[m]ere knowledge of general non-compliance or suspicions about compliance will not be sufficient to meet the test of section 550(2)(c)'.[30] This appeared to present a real problem for a finding of liability in the 7-Eleven case. The FWO found that a number of individuals employed or engaged by 7-Eleven Stores may have had knowledge of, or capacity to access, essential facts relating to the contraventions committed by the franchisees. However, many of these individuals were unwilling to provide evidence to the FWO about their own conduct or the conduct of others.[31] The lack of relevant evidence meant that the FWO believed that it was not in a position to prove that 7-Eleven Stores had been 'knowingly concerned' in the contraventions of its franchisees and therefore unable to institute proceedings against 7-Eleven Stores on this basis.

In order to better address these evidentiary issues, the FWO has called for the power to require a person to answer questions on the record in relation to alleged contraventions of the *FW Act*.[32] The Vulnerable Workers Bill contains provisions to this effect.[33] While this may tackle part of the problem, it does not necessarily address some of the more fundamental questions raised by the 7-Eleven case – that is, whether the existing accessorial liability provisions are 'fit for purpose' in terms of achieving the broader policy objective of ensuring employers duly comply with the law, employees are properly paid, and lead firms adopt the necessary measures to make certain this occurs.

In particular, when liability continues to turn on whether a lead firm was 'knowingly concerned' in a contravention committed by another (e.g. an employer entity), the regulatory framework may not properly address the risk of 'counterproductive liability avoidance'.[34] This is where firms seek to rework their contractual relationships to avoid being held liable for employment contraventions. This may involve reducing (rather than expanding) the extent to which they monitor and direct their contractors' or franchisees' compliance practices.

---

30   *7-Eleven Inquiry*, above n 4, 71.

31   Ibid. 72.

32   Ibid. An alternative way in which to address some of the evidentiary problems facing the FWO – particularly where employment records are absent or inaccurate – is to shift the onus of proof to the alleged wrongdoer. For further discussion, see Hardy, above n 5.

33   Vulnerable Workers Bill Pt 4.

34   Cynthia Estlund, 'Who Mops the Floor at the Fortune 500? Corporate Self-Regulation and the Low Wage Workplace' (2008) 12(3) *Lewis & Clark Law Review* 671, 692.

V. Possible Reform

In a separate article, I have surveyed some alternative statutory mechanisms for extending liability for employment contraventions beyond the direct employer entity to other individuals or entities.[35] These third-party liability regimes have often been principally designed, or primarily used, to tactically target lead firms and combat some of the compliance problems raised by fragmented work structures, such as outsourcing, subcontracting and franchising. In comparison to some of the inherent limits of the accessorial liability provisions of the *FW Act*, these legislative alternatives are potentially more flexible, and more effective, in achieving the core policy objective of promoting and sustaining widespread workplace relations compliance.

While there are obvious practical advantages and efficiency arguments which support the legal pursuit of lead firms, especially where the direct employer entity is judgment-proof,[36] the ascription of liability to such firms can be normatively justified on a number of other grounds. For instance, some of the existing literature suggests that making lead firms liable for employment contraventions is defensible where:

a. the lead firm has *caused* the direct employer to contravene the law;

b. the lead firm has, directly or indirectly, *benefited* from the contraventions;

c. the lead firm has power to *prevent* or *deter* workplace contraventions taking place; and/or

d. the behaviour of the lead firm increases social costs and invites *moral sanction* – this is especially relevant where the lead firm has made public representations that it is committed to ensuring workplace relations compliance throughout its business, supply chain or franchise network.[37]

The FWO's findings in the 7-Eleven Inquiry lend weight to many of these normative justifications. For example, 7-Eleven Stores has vigorously denied that the viability of the 7-Eleven franchise system is (or was) dependent

---

35 Hardy, above n 5.
36 Brishen Rogers, 'Toward Third-Party Liability for Wage Theft' (2010) *Berkeley Journal of Employment and Labour Law* 1.
37 See generally Guy Davidov, 'Indirect Employment: Should Lead Companies Be Liable?' (2015)
37 *Comparative Labor Law & Policy Journal* 5.

on franchisees underpaying their staff. The FWO also acknowledged that 7-Eleven Stores 'does not directly benefit when a franchisee underpays their workers'.[38] However, the regulator went on to observe that the franchisor gains an indirect benefit from the (often misguided) perception of store profitability in so far as it allows the store to continue to trade and to generate revenue and other fees for 7-Eleven Stores.[39]

In addition, the FWO noted, as part of its Inquiry, that 7-Eleven Stores was in a position to prevent workplace contraventions amongst its franchisees, given that it 'controlled the settings of the system in which the franchisee employers operated'[40] and had the resources and capacity to detect and deter franchisee non-compliance. Indeed, the various changes adopted by 7-Eleven Stores in response to public scrutiny, including modifying its business model, enhancing its monitoring and payroll systems and terminating franchise agreements, highlight the regulatory power wielded by the franchisor in this context.

In circumstances where lead firm liability is normatively appropriate, the next key question is an instrumental one: which legal mechanism can and should be used to ascribe liability to lead firms? A key challenge in devising a new model of liability is how best to ensure that it not only achieves the relevant policy objective, but that it remains workable in practice. Drawing on the disparate and distinctive liability models surveyed in my separate article,[41] it seems that one of the most straightforward and promising ways to extend liability is to expand the current statutory definition of what it means to be 'involved in' a contravention under s 550 of the *FW Act*. For instance, a new limb could be added to the existing statutory provision which does not pivot on knowledge or control – rather, a person (including a lead firm) could be taken to be 'involved in' a contravention under s 550 if:

a. the person was in a position to prevent or deter the contravention; and

b. that person has failed to take all reasonably practicable steps to prevent or deter the contravention.

---

38 *7-Eleven Inquiry*, above n 4, 38.
39 Ibid. 39.
40 Ibid. 67.
41 Hardy, above n 5.

In assessing the firm's capacity for prevention and deterrence, the court could be required to have regard to the resources, market position and bureaucratic power held by the lead firm, as well as the nature and duration of the relationship between the lead firm and the direct employer.

In determining whether the lead firm has satisfied the relevant statutory duty, the court may be required to take into account a non-exhaustive range of factors, such as whether the alleged accessory has:

a. adopted rigorous and accountable monitoring practices;

b. engaged only reliable and well-capitalised contractors;

c. ensured that the relevant supply contract, labour hire agreement and/ or franchise model is financially viable;

d. otherwise facilitated or encouraged compliance through tailored financial incentives and commercial sanctions.

While I have used the 7-Eleven example to illustrate some of the regulatory challenges in this context, the proposal for reform outlined above is presented as more than a simple statutory fix for discrete issues raised in the public consciousness. Rather, it is aimed at regulating the foreseeable (and unforeseen) problems that may arise in a range of business networks.[42] Indeed, one of the most significant gaps in the Vulnerable Workers Bill is that it extends liability for employment contraventions only in franchise networks and corporate groups. Other organisational forms, such as labour hire arrangements and supply chains, are not captured by these provisions.

While this Bill is not without some substantial weaknesses, it represents, and remains, a momentous step forward in enhancing compliance with employment standards regulation in this country.[43] To a large extent, it addresses key points raised in this article and elsewhere. For example, the proposed provisions allow the court to take into account not only what the responsible franchisor entity (or one of its officers) 'knew' about the contravention of the franchisee entity, but also what it (or the officer) 'could reasonably be expected to have known'.[44] In short, the provisions

---

42   Hugh Collins, 'Introduction' in Gunter Teubner, *Networks as Connected Contracts* (Hart, 2011).
43   For example, one critical issue identified in the submissions to the ongoing inquiry is the definition of 'responsible franchisor entity'. See, for example, Tess Hardy and Joo-Cheong Tham, Submission to the Senate Education and Employment Legislation Committee Inquiry into the Fair Work Amendment (Protecting Vulnerable Workers) Bill 2017, 10 April 2017.
44   Vulnerable Workers Bill s 558B(1)(d)(i) and (ii).

encompass both actual knowledge and constructive knowledge and, in doing so, potentially address one of the most challenging aspects of the accessorial liability provisions as they currently apply to fragmented work arrangements.

Another critical feature of the Vulnerable Workers Bill is the statutory defence which is embedded in Pt 2. In brief, the Bill provides that the person (i.e. a franchisor, a holding company or a relevant officer) will not contravene the extended liability provisions if, at the time the contravention took place, the 'person had taken reasonable steps to prevent a contravention by the franchisee entity or subsidiary of the same of similar character.'[45] In determining whether a person has taken such 'reasonable steps', the court is directed to have regard to a range of relevant matters, including the size and resources of the franchise or body corporate, any action the person took to inform the employer of the relevant workplace laws and obligations, and any arrangements the person had in place for assessing the employer's ensuing compliance with workplace obligations. Imposing reasonable standards of diligence not only allows the court to undertake a fact-sensitive analysis which takes into account the full range of circumstances, but also seeks to promote the right type of liability avoidance on the part of lead firms – that is, by encouraging franchisors and holding companies to do more (not less) to enhance compliance with workplace laws across their respective business networks.

VI. Conclusion

The various practical and legal issues identified in the 7-Eleven case suggest that self-regulatory mechanisms are not sufficient, and the current accessorial liability provisions of the FW Act may be inadequate, in addressing some of the most profound problems raised by complex and integrated economic organisations. In seeking to ensure that employees are fully and properly paid in Australia, and in trying to promote lead firms to do more in this respect, it seems that the conception of legal responsibility for employment contraventions may need to be statutorily recalibrated. The Vulnerable Workers Bill represents the first (but, it is hoped, not the last) step in such a direction.

---

45   Vulnerable Workers Bill s 558B(3).

6

The Australian House Party Has Been Glorious – But the Hangover May Be Severe: Reforms to Mitigate Some of the Risks

Gill North[1]

I. Introduction

The scope and efficacy of regulation around mortgage lending in Australia is critical, not just for the health of financial institutions and financial stability, but also for the financial position and wellbeing of Australian households. The biggest risk presently is complacency. Lending secured to residential properties (including to owner occupiers and investors) constitutes more than 65 per cent of the total lending of Australian financial institutions.[2] Hence, the exposure of the finance sector to housing markets is large, both on an historical basis and relative to other jurisdictions.[3] Similarly, levels of household debt to disposable income are now at record levels in Australia and residential property mortgage debt makes up more than 50 per cent of total household debt.[4]

---

1   Professor, Law School, Deakin University; Adjunct Associate Professor, Law School, University of Western Australia.
2   W Byres, 'Sound Lending Standards and Adequate Capital: Preconditions for Long Term Success' (Speech presented at COBA and CEO & Director Forum, 13 May 2015) 1.
3   These exposures have arisen largely because of the low default rates and high returns on residential property over the last 20 years.
4   AMP.NATSEM, *Buy Now Pay Later: Household Debt in Australia* (Income and Wealth Report, Issue 38, December 2015) 8.

Two-thirds of Australian households own a residential property, approximately half of these households have a residential property mortgage,[5] and around 35 per cent of these mortgages are to investors.[6] Accordingly, it is vital that Australians fully comprehend the nature and risks of acquiring residential property, the risks of leveraging these assets, and the regulatory protection afforded when taking on credit and receiving credit assistance. The primary lesson from the global financial crisis is that housing cycles, like all asset classes, move downwards as well as upwards, and sometimes this movement is sudden and sharp. So any assumptions by households that the purchase of residential property funded by a mortgage secured on a residential property does not involve market exposure are flawed and dangerous for the nation.

The housing party in Australia is likely to continue under existing policy settings, but like all asset cycles founded largely on credit, this party will eventually end and the subsequent hangover may be severe. The further house prices move beyond economic fundamentals and normal price trends, the more severe the likely corrections and adverse consequences, especially for highly indebted households that have minimal asset and income buffers. Policy intervention is needed to mitigate the growing exposures of households, financial institutions and the nation. Specific reforms are proposed in relation to the remuneration of mortgage intermediaries, responsible lending assessments and negative gearing concessions.

The chapter is organised into five parts. Part 2 provides essential background on the macro risks around residential housing in Australia. Part 3 summarises the existing policy settings and potential exposures. Part 4 outlines proposed reforms to mitigate possible consumer losses and hardship. Part 5 concludes.

---

5   Australian Bureau of Statistics, *Residential Property Price Indexes: Eight Capital Cities* (December 2015); Australian Prudential Regulation Authority (APRA), *Prudential Practice Guide APG 223 – Residential Mortgage Lending* (5 November 2014) 7.

6   Reserve Bank of Australia (RBA), *Financial Aggregates* (March 2016, released 29 April 2016).

II. Background

Growth in residential property prices and mortgage lending in Australia has run at well above GDP growth levels over the last two decades, at around 7 per cent per annum.[7] Moreover, the level of average household debt (including mortgage loans) to disposable income is at record levels, this ratio has almost tripled from 64 per cent in 1988 to 185 per cent in 2015, the most leveraged Australia households (the top 10 per cent) have a debt to disposable income ratio of 6 times, and the top 10 per cent of the most indebted low-income households have a debt to income ratio of 10 times with debt repayments taking 60 per cent of their disposable income.[8] Credit growth in Australia (including mortgage and other forms of credit) well above levels of economic growth and increases in household disposable income cannot continue indefinitely.[9] A major factor driving higher levels of housing-related debt in Australia has been decreasing interest rates, which have made debt repayments appear more manageable. Nonetheless, more than 25 per cent of Australian households are already in some form of financial distress or stress,[10] and should interest rates rise again these levels may escalate rapidly.

The poorly diversified portfolios of Australian lenders as a whole, combined with the highly concentrated nature of the finance sector,[11] a heavy reliance on housing construction as a driver of economic activity,[12] a concentration of household wealth in residential property,[13] and strong links between housing wealth and business and consumer confidence and spending,[14] leave Australia highly vulnerable to any significant downturn

---

7   RBA, *Monthly D2 Lending and Credit Aggregates* (March 2016, released 29 April 2016).

8   AMP.NATSEM, above n 4, 4, 13.

9   W Willits, 'Australia Vulnerable to Debt Crisis, Says Forbes', *SMH.com* (28 March 2016), www.smh.com.au/business/the-economy/australia-vulnerable-to-debt-crisis-says-forbes-20160328-gns1jn.html. M Phillips, 'The World's Debt is Alarmingly High. But is it Contagious?', *SMH.com* (25 February 2016), www.smh.com.au/business/the-economy/the-worlds-debt-is-alarmingly-high-but-is-it-contagious-20160224-gn2baj.html.

10   Digital Finance Analytics, *The Stressed Finance Landscape Data Analysis* (October 2015); AMP. NATSEM, above n 4, 15.

11   Financial Service Inquiry Interim Report (July 2014) ('Interim Report') xvii. See also S Rose and J Eyers, 'Australia's Banks Are "Too Big to Get Sick": APRA', *SMH.com* 4 April 2016, www.smh.com. au/business/banking-and-finance/australias-banks-are-too-big-to-get-sick-apra-20160403-gnwztl. html#ixzz44ndw9ZLl.

12   RBA, *Statement on Monetary Policy* (May 2016) 44.

13   Jonathan Shapiro, 'Exploring Australia's "Wealth Effect"', *The Sydney Morning Herald*, 19 November 2014. Shapiro notes that 55 per cent of gross household assets in Australia are invested in housing while 27 per cent are in shares.

14   RBA, above n 12, 28.

in the housing markets. Stress tests are carried out regularly by Australian lenders and the major banks suggest any concerns are unwarranted.[15] However, in an environment of record low interest rates and relatively stable unemployment levels in Australia, the financial positions of residential property lenders and borrowers have not yet been fully tested. The true position and exposure of individual banks, households, and the nation will only be revealed during the next financial crisis or economic recession. And, as noted in the Financial Sector Inquiry reports, adverse effects from high levels of interconnectedness across a finance sector and contagion are often underestimated.[16]

Some housing-related policy adjustments have been made over the last year, but further action is called for.

III. Policy Settings and Exposures

Australian households with a residential mortgage have various protections under law. The most important of these are the responsible lending obligations in the *National Consumer Credit Protection Act 2009* (Cth) (*NCCP*) which are intended to limit lending to amounts that borrowers can afford.[17] These provisions are supported by additional protections within the *National Credit Code* (*NCC*) in Sch 1 of the *NCCP*, including default notice requirements and hardship provisions. ASIC is responsible for administering both the *NCCP* and the *NCC*.[18]

In an industry survey in 2014, the Australian Prudential Regulation Authority (APRA) found there were wide differences in how lenders assessed the risk of a given borrower.[19] Significant factors leading to these differences included the assessments of borrower's living expenses,

---

15 Byres, above n 2, 2.

16 Interim Report, above n 11, 2–57; Financial System Inquiry Final Report (November 2014) 43–44, 47. See also Reserve Bank of New Zealand, *Bulletin* Vol 79, No 12 (July 2016).

17 Parts 3.1 and 3.2 of the *National Consumer Credit Protection Act 2009* (Cth) impose responsible lending obligations on all participants involved in the provision of housing credit, including licensees that provide credit assistance in relation to credit contracts and credit providers. The responsible lending obligations apply to existing consumer credit contracts when consumers apply for an increase in a credit limit, and to the provision of new credit to consumers. These obligations are intended to introduce standards of conduct to encourage prudent lending; curtail undesirable market practices, particularly where intermediaries are involved in lending; and impose sanctions for irresponsible lending and leasing.

18 *Consumer Credit and Corporations Legislation Amendment (Enhancements) Act 2012* (Cth).

19 Byres, above n 2, 3.

the treatment of 'other income sources', the discount applied to declared rental income, the size of interest rate buffers allowed, and the service period allowed for repayment of the loan principal on interest only loans.[20] In a letter to lenders, it highlighted the high growth rate of mortgage lending to investors and 'encouraged' them to limit the amount of new lending to this segment to 10 per cent per annum. It also recommended they apply an interest rate buffer of at least 2 per cent and a minimum rate of at least 7 per cent to the mortgage serviceability assessments.[21]

Further, at the end of 2014, ASIC indicated that demand for interest only loans had grown 80 per cent since 2012 and the average value of these loans was substantially higher than principal and interest home loans.[22] ASIC conducted a survey of lenders of these loans (including the big four banks) to assess their compliance with the responsible lending laws, and concluded that lending standards required lifting to meet important consumer protection laws.[23] It found that many lenders were failing to consider whether this type of loan satisfied consumer needs, particularly in the medium to longer term. Specific issues included the time period allowed for repayment of the principal of the loan, a lack of evidence about the borrower's requirements and a failure to consider the borrower's actual living expenses. ASIC also expressed concerns about the ability of borrowers to afford the loans if interest rates were to rise.[24]

There is some evidence that Australian lenders have tightened their mortgage serviceability criteria over the last year.[25] However, mortgages with a loan-to-valuation ratio (LVR) of 95 per cent are still available from mainstream lenders, and borrowers can find mortgages with LVRs above this level if parents or family members are willing to be guarantors and offer their own property as security if the original owner defaults on their loan.[26]

---

20   Ibid. 2–5.
21   APRA, 'APRA Outlines Further Steps to Reinforce Sound Residential Mortgage Lending Practices' (Media Release, 9 December 2014).
22   The Australian and Securities Investment Commission (ASIC) noted the vulnerability of these loans to credit losses.
23   ASIC, 'Lenders to Improve Standards Following Interest-Only Loan Review' (Media release 15-220MR, 20 August 2015).
24   Ibid. See also ASIC, Report 445: *Interest-Only Home Loan Review* (August 2015).
25   APRA, *Insight*, Issue One, 2016.
26   See, for example, Finder.com, '100% Home Loans: Borrow 100% of the Property Value', at www.finder.com.au/100-percent-home-loans.

Lenders naturally seek to protect their commercial position. A mortgage on residential property allows the institution to ultimately sell the property and use the proceeds to repay debts owing if the borrower defaults. Additionally, borrowers seeking a mortgage with an LVR above 80 per cent are generally required to purchase lenders mortgage insurance. These policies are used when a borrower fails to repay the mortgage and the combined proceeds from sale of the mortgaged property and other personal assets of the borrower are insufficient to cover debts owing.

Australian households are now highly exposed to the housing cycle. Many Australians may see housing as a 'safe haven' given the strong performance of house prices over the last 20 years, but this is a fallacy with potentially catastrophic consequences. Should the housing market decline sharply, some borrower households will likely fall into a negative equity position on mortgaged residential property, even though they can repay their mortgages. Some of these borrowers may be forced to sell the property while house prices remain depressed and may lose any personal equity invested. In extreme circumstances, where the sale of a residential property or shares does not cover the full extent of the mortgage or margin loan and accrued interest, individuals may be personally liable for any outstanding debts. Consequently, all consumers who purchase residential property, especially those who borrow heavily to purchase a property, should understand that this involves significant risks, including possible temporary or permanent capital losses, foreclosure, and loss of the property. Household borrowers that present with one or more of the following characteristics are most exposed: borrowings on one or more residential properties with high loan-to-valuation levels, minimal or nil net equity in the properties, and significant changes in the personal circumstances of the borrower.

IV. Proposed Reforms

The family home is the most important asset of most Australians and a mortgage on residential property is the most significant credit product in Australia; hence the need for sound housing-related policy and consumer protection are difficult to overstate. Policy reforms to mitigate possible future consumer losses and hardship are proposed across three areas: the remuneration of mortgage intermediaries, responsible lending assessments, and restrictions on negative gearing.

A. The remuneration of mortgage intermediaries

For credit assistance and advice to be trustworthy and competitive in Australia, the legal frameworks need to include remuneration structures for mortgage providers and intermediaries with appropriate incentives.[27] Close to 48 per cent of all mortgages in Australia are arranged through intermediaries, while the remainder are sought directly from credit entities that provide home loans.[28] Yet current rules concerning the remuneration received by credit providers or assisters are limited to a general disclosure obligation.[29] Under existing law, mortgage intermediaries may recommend or provide a mortgage that is most lucrative for the provider or assister, provided the recommended credit product is 'not unsuitable' and it satisfies the consumer's objectives and requirements.[30]

Notably, the customer suitability, client duties, and remuneration provisions across the credit and financial advisory schemes differ significantly. A person who provides personal financial advice to a retail client and recommends investment in a financial product using borrowed money is bound by the best interest provisions in Pt 7.7A of the *Corporations Act 2001* (Cth) and is prohibited from receiving commissions on the borrowed amount. However, reasonable consumers are unlikely to understand the legal distinction between credit and financial products, would likely assume credit products are financial in nature, and would expect mortgage brokers to recommend a mortgage product that is suitable for their needs and serves their best interests (rather than a product that is most profitable for the intermediary).

B. Responsible lending assessments

Credit providers and assisters must comply with the responsible lending provisions under the *NCCP* when consumers purchase residential properties funded by a mortgage for leasing purposes. Additional protection is also afforded under the *NCC* (including through default

---

27   See C Yeates, 'Mortgage Brokers to Remain in Spotlight after ASIC Review', *SMH.com*, 8 May 2016, www.smh.com.au/business/banking-and-finance/mortgage-brokers-to-remain-in-spotlight-after-asic-review-20160506-goo666.

28   APRA, *Quarterly Authorised Deposit-taking Institution Property Exposures – December 2015* (issued 23 February 2016).

29   *NCCP* s 121(2).

30   For further details, see G North, 'Regulation Governing the Provision of Credit Assistance and Financial Advice in Australia: A Consumer's Perspective' (2015) 43 *Federal Law Review* 369, 382–83.

notices and hardship provisions). These provisions are sound, but empirical evidence from APRA and ASIC suggests there are significant practical issues and additional consumer protection is required given the high levels of exposure to residential property by Australian financial institutions and households.

There is some international evidence suggesting mortgages to investors are higher risk than loans to owner occupiers.[31] However, there is no legal requirement in Australia for credit providers and assisters to adjust their assessment of a borrower's ability to repay a mortgage when it is used for investment rather than residential purposes. More critically, there is no APRA or ASIC guidance suggesting a consumer's ability or willingness to bear temporary or permanent capital losses during periods of significant house price declines and/or economic weakness should be considered by lenders, and discussed with borrowers.

The author's proposed reforms include:

- Regulatory guidance from APRA and ASIC to mortgage lenders suggesting the responsible lending assessments should be scalable and should take into account: i) the state of the economy and housing and credit markets; ii) the potential impact on borrowers should interest rates rise or the price of residential property decline; and iii) the impact on borrowers should their personal circumstances change. Lenders should allow pro-cyclical buffers depending on the levels of risk in the economy, housing and credit markets, and should consider a consumer's ability to repay a mortgage over the long term, including during periods of cyclical change.

- Mortgage lenders and intermediaries should provide: i) online warnings that interest rates may rise and housing prices may decline significantly; and ii) online sensitivity calculators that enable consumers to assess the impacts of adverse economic, housing and personal factors (including the cumulative effect of a number of changes) on the ability to repay the mortgage.

---

31   See Reserve Bank of New Zealand, *Summary of Submissions and Final Policy Position on the Review of the Asset Class Treatment of Residential Property Investment Loans in BS2A and BS2B* (29 May 2015).

C. Restrictions on negative gearing concessions

Some policy restrictions on the form and level of concessionary negative gearing would mitigate the increasingly significant housing and debt-related risks in Australia, would allow housing demand to moderate earlier than otherwise, and may shift capital to more productive uses. While the existing policy settings remain, many Australians will likely continue to invest (or speculate) in housing, without sufficient regard to the pending risks involved. And given tight federal budgetary constraints and high levels of personal indebtedness, our ability as a nation to respond to future adverse events will be limited.

V. Conclusion: Everybody is at the Party

APRA acknowledges the increasing proportion of lending attributable to housing over the last decade[32] and suggests that 'if all our eggs are increasingly being placed in one basket, we need to make sure the basket isn't dropped'.[33] Further, its chairman stated in 2015 that:

> the current economic environment for housing lenders is characterised by heightened levels of risk, reflecting a combination of historically low interest rates, high household debt, subdued income growth, unemployment that has drifted higher, significant house price growth, and strong competitive pressures.

Notably, though, APRA suggests that house prices and the levels of household debt are beyond its mandate.[34] The RBA is also aware of the risks but nonetheless suggests housing credit growth of 7 per cent per annum is likely to continue.[35] The Coalition Government concedes that Australia's economy is heavily reliant on housing-related activity and prefers not to dampen this activity and consumer confidence in the near term.

In the marketplace, banks are likely to continue to lend to residential property owners because the existing capital rules and returns to date encourage it. Similarly, Australians are likely to continue to invest in housing, with tax incentives to do so and a dearth of other savings

---

32   Ibid. 1–2, 5–6.
33   Ibid. 8.
34   Ibid. 2.
35   RBA, above n 6, 2.

opportunities that provide a reasonable return. However, the housing party in Australia will inevitably end at some point and the severity of the hangover will depend on the nature and scale of advance action taken by lawmakers and regulators. The further house prices rise above normal trend lines and economic fundamentals, the more severe the potential corrections and adverse consequences are likely to be, particularly on highly indebted households.

7

Back to Basics: Reforming Australia's Private Sector Whistleblowing Laws

Kath Hall and Heather Cork[1]

I. Introduction

The important role that whistleblowers play in exposing corporate misconduct in Australia has been highlighted by a number of recent scandals. Whistleblowers have been central to uncovering impropriety in leading Australian companies including the Reserve Bank of Australia, Note Printing Australia, Leighton Holdings, Tabcorp, the Commonwealth Bank, the NAB, CommInsure and 7-Eleven.[2] Many of the whistleblowers involved in these cases experienced retaliation, redundancy, dismissal, workplace ostracism and negative publicity as a result. Regrettably these consequences are not unusual, and have led to pressure for reform of Australia's private sector whistleblowing laws, contained in Pt 9.4AAA of

---

1   Dr Kath Hall is an Associate Professor at The Australian National University College of Law and Heather Cork is a graduate lawyer with the Department of Employment Canberra.
2   Other examples include the Amcor and Visy Industry's cardboard box price-fixing racket (unveiled in an earlier iteration by an aggrieved Visy executive); and the personal misbehaviour allegations that led to the resignation of David Jones CEO Mark McInnes.

the *Corporations Act 2001* (Cth).[3] While most of the calls for reform have focused on the narrow definitions of 'discloser' and 'wrongdoing', the lack of protection for anonymous disclosures and disclosures to third parties, and the lack of incentives or compensation for reporting in the Act, no-one has so far asked: do we have the basic framework right for regulating whistleblowing?

This chapter answers that question by focusing on two fundamental assumptions underlying the research and the regulation of whistleblowing: that whistleblowing involves *a person* making *an identifiable disclosure* of wrongdoing. These assumptions – that whistleblowers act alone and that reporting involves one identifiable act of disclosure – remain largely unchallenged in the dominant narrative on whistleblowing. As a result, the reality that whistleblowing often involves more than one person engaged in multiple acts of disclosure is not reflected in the current policy or legislative suggestions for reform.

Embracing the factual complexity of whistleblowing could improve corporate and regulatory responses in a number of ways. First, debunking the myth that whistleblowing involves one person reporting misconduct could improve the way that corporate whistleblowing systems and policies are framed and implemented. Psychological research confirms that group membership is important, particularly in the work context; encouraging employees to discuss wrongdoing concerns with others and make group reports could increase the rate of reporting and reduce the likelihood and/ or severity of retaliation.[4] Second, expanding the legislative definition of a 'disclosure' could result in employees qualifying for protection earlier and enable different types of discussions on wrongdoing (including seeking advice). Finally, challenging the dominant narrative that whistleblowers act alone in making formal reports on wrongdoing could lead to new research questions and better answers on how to encourage, manage and support whistleblowing.

---

3   In 2016 this pressure increased significantly as a result of the passage of the *Registered Organisations (Fair Work) Amendment Act 2016*. Two government inquiries were established; the Parliamentary Joint Committee on Corporations and Financial Services *Inquiry into Whistleblower Protections in the Corporate, Public and Not-For-Profit Sectors* for reporting by 30 June 2017 and the Treasury Review of Tax and Corporate Whistleblower Protections in Australia.

4   See generally Solomon Asch, 'Studies of Independence and Conformity: A Minority of One Against a Unanimous Majority' (1956) 70 *Psychological Monographs* 1; Maureen Scully and Mary Rowe, 'Bystander Training Within Organizations' (2009) 2 *Journal of the International Ombudsman Association* 1; Frances J Milliken, Elizabeth W Morrison and Patricia F Hewlin, 'An Exploratory Study of Employee Silence: Issues that Employees don't Communicate Upward and Why' (2003) 40 *Journal of Management Studies* 1453.

II. The Importance of Whistleblowing

It is widely understood that employees play a key role in detecting and reporting corporate misconduct. In the private sector, wrongdoing is often difficult to uncover because it occurs away from the public eye, and can involve multiple actors and events over an extended period of time.[5] Given employees' access to information and knowledge on organisational behaviour, they are best placed to detect and report misconduct.[6] As Pascoe and Welsh note, 'providing a workable framework to encourage and protect whistleblowers is a vital aspect of companies' corporate governance and risk management strategies' and provides 'assistance to regulators in the detection and enforcement of corporate crimes'.[7]

Numerous surveys have qualitatively demonstrated the value of whistleblowing. In a 2008 Australian public sector survey, managers rated employee reporting as the most important means of bringing wrongdoing to light.[8] The survey confirmed that 'the unique position of employees within organisations gives them a strategic role as quality information sources'.[9] Similarly, PricewaterhouseCoopers' 2010 report on public sector fraud found that 31 per cent of cases detected in the previous 12 months were reported internally by employees,[10] and 5 per cent were reported using formal internal whistleblowing systems.[11] In the private sector, PricewaterhouseCoopers' 2016 Global Economic Crime Survey reported that 54 per cent of respondents used management reporting to ensure compliance with their programs and that 42 per cent had whistleblowing hotlines.[12]

International support for protecting and supporting whistleblowers has also grown significantly. Since 2012, the OECD has published five guides to assist governments and corporates to facilitate whistleblowing. In 2015, the UN published a comprehensive *Resource Guide on Good Practices in*

---

5   Janine Pascoe and Michelle Welsh 'Whistleblowing, Ethics and Corporate Culture: Theory and Practice in Australia' (2011) 40 *Common Law World Review* 144, 146 (footnotes omitted).

6   Sulette Lombard and Vivienne Brand, 'Corporate Whistleblowing: Public Lessons for Private Disclosure' (2014) 42 *Australian Business Law Review* 351, 352.

7   Pascoe and Welsh, above n 5, 148.

8   A J Brown, Evalynn Mazurski and Jane Olsen, 'The Incidence and Significance of Whistleblowing' in A J Brown (ed), *Whistleblowing in the Public Sector* (ANU E Press, 2008) 25, 44–45.

9   Ibid. 44.

10   PricewaterhouseCoopers, *Fighting Fraud in the Public Sector* (Research Report, 2010) 13.

11   Ibid.

12   Ibid. 36.

the Protection of Reporting Persons.[13] Furthermore, the 2013–14 G20 *Anti-Corruption Action Plan* now requires G20 countries that do not already have whistleblower protections to enact and implement whistleblower protection rules and to take specific actions 'to ensure that those reporting on corruption can exercise their function without fear of any harassment or threat or of private or government legal action'.[14]

III. Challenging the 'One Whistleblower' Narrative

Despite these developments, almost every discussion of whistleblowing, whether by government, academics, the media or corporates, assumes that whistleblowers act alone. In Australia, the main provisions dealing with private sector whistleblowing contained in the *Corporations Act 2001* (Cth) contemplate a single 'discloser' of information.[15] Similarly, the US *Sarbanes-Oxley Act* of 2002 protects 'an employee' of a private company who reports suspected violations of federal law,[16] and the UK *Public Interest Disclosure Act 1998* entitles 'a worker' to make a protected disclosure.[17]

The assumption that whistleblowers are alone in raising concerns within organisations is also prevalent in social science research. Vandekerckhove, one of the leading researchers on whistleblowing, uncritically comments that 'what is common to all possible definitions … is that whistleblowing is always about individuals disclosing information'.[18] Similarly, Gundlach, Douglas and Martinko note that 'there are two primary parties involved in whistle-blowing: the wrongdoer and the whistle-blower'.[19] Miceli and Near, in their famous 1992 book *Blowing the Whistle*, asked research questions such as: Who is the whistleblower? What are their individual

---

13   *The United Nations Convention against Corruption, Resource Guide on Good Practices in the Protection of Reporting Persons*, United Nations, August 2015, www.unodc.org/documents/corruption/Publications/2015/15-04741_Person_Guide_eBook.pdf.

14   G20, *Anti-Corruption Action Plan (2013–2014)* 2, www.oecd.org/g20/topics/anti-corruption/G20_Anti-Corruption_Action_Plan_%282013-2014%29.pdf. The G20 acknowledges that corruption increases business costs and is responsible for billions of dollars of losses annually and that whistleblowing is one of the most effective means of exposing it.

15   Part 9.4AAA s 1317AA.

16   S 806 18 U.S. Code § 1514A.

17   Part IVA s 43A.

18   Wim Vandekerckhove and David Crowther, *Whistleblowing and Organisational Social Responsibility* (Ashgate e-Books, 2006) 92.

19   M J Gundlach, S C Douglas and M J Martinko, 'The Decision to Blow the Whistle: A Social Information Processing Framework' (2003) 28 *Academy of Management Review* 107-23, 108.

characteristics? What are the costs and benefits to the whistleblower? And is motive relevant?[20] Since then, behavioural research has continued to focus on the effect of personal factors such as gender, age, education, religiosity and ethics on a person's likelihood to report.[21] None of this research, however, has considered the possibility of groups of persons blowing the whistle.

Basic research, however, reveals that many famous whistleblowers were not alone in raising concerns within their organisations. For example, in the Enron collapse, Sherron Watkins, Vice President of Corporate Development, is credited with having blown the whistle when she wrote a letter to senior management warning of improper accounting practices.[22] Watkins later assisted investigators, testified before Congressional Committees, and in 2008 was named one of *Time Magazine*'s Persons of the Year.[23] However, evidence shows that other Enron employees also took steps to raise their concerns: Cliff Baxter, a senior Enron employee, complained to Enron's President and CEO and 'all who would listen' about the company's inappropriate transactions;[24] Margaret Ceconi, an employee of Enron Energy Services, wrote a 10-page letter to the board warning of excessive spending and the prospect of customer lawsuits;[25] and Vince Kaminski, head of Enron's Research Group, raised concerns about corporate dealings.[26] Yet subsequent discussions of Enron's collapse rarely acknowledge the actions of these individuals, and focus almost exclusively on Watkins.

Similarly, in the famous Challenger Shuttle Disaster, Roger Boisjoly, a mechanical engineer, is credited with being 'the whistleblower' after he tried to alert NASA executives of design faults in the Shuttle the day

---

20   Marcia Miceli and Janet Near, *Blowing the Whistle: The Organizational and Legal Implications for Companies and Employees* (Lexington Press, 1992).

21   Muel Kaptein, 'From Inaction to External Whistleblowing: The Influence of the Ethical Culture of Organizations on Employee Responses to Observed Wrongdoing' (2011) 98 *Journal of Business Ethics* 513; Janet Near and Marcia Miceli, 'Effective Whistleblowing' (1995) 20 *Academy of Management Review* 679; Tim Barnett, Ken Bass and Gene Brown, 'Religiosity, Ethical Ideology, and Intentions to Report a Peer's Wrongdoing' (1996) 15 *Journal of Business Ethics* 1161.

22   Lesley Curwen, 'The Corporate Conscience', *The Guardian* (online) 21 June 2003, www.theguardian.com/business/2003/jun/21/corporatefraud.enron.

23   Dan Ackman, 'Sherron Watkins Had Whistle, But Blew it', *Forbes* (online), 14 February 2002, www.forbes.com/2002/02/14/0214watkins.html.

24   Bethany McLean and Peter Elkind, *The Smartest Guys in the Room* (Penguin Books, 2004) 356.

25   Ibid. 358–59.

26   Ibid. 192, 305.

before the launch took place.[27] However, again, Boisjoly was not the only employee who voiced such concerns: Joe Kilminster, Vice President of the Space Booster Program, and George Hardy, a NASA employee, both recommended that the launch not go ahead, and another engineer, Arnie Thompson, tried to explain the structural defects.[28] Allan MacDonald, who was at the Kennedy Space Center, argued for delay even after the decision was made, saying that if the mission failed he would not know how to explain to a board of inquiry the decision to launch. Yet only Boisjoly was awarded the Prize for Scientific Freedom and Responsibility by the American Association for the Advancement of Science.[29] Only he is was recognised as 'the whistleblower' in this case.

Closer to home, in 2013, three senior Australian employees exposed serious misconduct in the financial planning unit of the Commonwealth Bank.[30] These employees used the pseudonym 'The Three Ferrets';[31] however, only one, Jeff Morris, is consistently identified as the whistleblower in this case.[32]

These cases echo psychological research that suggests that people prefer to act as part of a group than alone, and that unethical conduct rarely goes unnoticed. Research indicates that even when a majority of people acquiesce to misconduct, there will still be a minority who are concerned enough to complain or question the behaviour.[33] Research on whistleblowing also shows that co-workers' opinions are paramount in a whistleblower's decision to report. According to Noelle-Neumann,

---

27 See generally Barbara Romzek and Melvin Dubnick, 'Accountability in the Public Sector: Lessons from the Challenger Tragedy' (1987) 47 *Public Administration Review* 227.

28 Roger Boisjoly, 'Telecon Meeting' in *Ethical Decisions – Morton Thiokol and the Challenger Disaster*, 15 May 2006, www.onlineethics.org/Topics/ProfPractice/PPEssays/thiokolshuttle/shuttle_telecon.aspx.

29 Douglas Martin, 'Roger Boisjoly, 73, Dies; Warned of Shuttle Danger', *The New York Times* (online), 3 February 2012, www.nytimes.com/2012/02/04/us/roger-boisjoly-73-dies-warned-of-shuttle -danger.html?_r=0.

30 See generally James Eyers, 'The Man Who Blew the Whistle on CBA', *Financial Review* (online), 28 June 2014, www.afr.com/business/banking-and-finance/financial-services/the-man-who-blew-the-whistle-on-cba-20140627-je1mp; Jeffrey Morris, Submission No 421 to the Senate Economics Reference Inquiry, *The Performance of the Australian Securities and Investments Commission*.

31 Jeffrey Morris, Submission No 421 to the Senate Economics Reference Inquiry, *The Performance of the Australian Securities and Investments Commission*.

32 Possibly because he was the only member of the group willing to be named. The other Ferrets' names are redacted from Morris's publicly available submission to the Senate Enquiry into the performance of ASIC.

33 See, for example, Milgram, Stanley 'Behavioral Study of Obedience' (1963) 67 *Journal of Abnormal and Social Psychology* 371 and subsequent research.

employees test their interpretation of the situation against others' and, if theirs is not met with approval, often remain silent.[34] Milliken et al suggest that employees mentally 'test out' certain behaviours by either imagining their co-workers' responses or discussing courses of action with colleagues.[35] Yet corporate or regulatory policies on whistleblowing fail to recognise that employees may feel more confident in acting as part of a group in speaking up than acting alone.

IV. Challenging the 'One Disclosure' Narrative

The idea that there is a single act of disclosure by a whistleblower is also included in most legislative and scholarly discussions on whistleblowing. Section 1317AA of the *Corporations Act* confers protection on an individual who makes 'a disclosure'. Similarly, s 10 of the *Public Interest Disclosure Act 2013* (Cth) protects employees who make 'a public interest disclosure', while s 337A of the *Fair Work (Registered Organisations) Act 2009* (Cth) protects an officer, member or employee of a trade union who makes 'a disclosure of information'.

The dominant narrative surrounding whistleblowing also contains the language of one disclosure. Jubb characterises whistleblowing as 'a dissenting act of public accusation'[36] and 'a deliberate, non-obligatory act of disclosure'.[37] Miceli and Near consider whistleblowing involves 'the disclosure … of illegal, immoral or illegitimate practices',[38] while Vandekerckhove suggests that a key element of whistleblowing is always 'the act of … disclosure'.[39]

---

34   Elisabeth Noelle-Neumann, 'The Spiral of Silence: A Theory of Public Opinion' (1974) 24 *Journal of Communication* 24.

35   Frances Milliken, Elizabeth Morrison and Patricia Hewlin, 'An Exploratory Study of Employee Silence: Issues that Employees don't Communicate Upward and Why' (2003) 40 *Journal of Management Studies* 1453.

36   Peter Jubb, 'Whistleblowing: A Restrictive Definition and Interpretation' (1999) 21 *Journal of Business Ethics* 77, 77.

37   Ibid. 78.

38   Janet Near and Marcia Miceli, 'Organizational Dissidence: The Case of Whistle-Blowing' (1985) 4 *Journal of Business Ethics* 1, 4.

39   Wim Vandekerckhove, *Whistleblowing and Organizational Social Responsibility: A Global Assessment* (Ashgate Publishing, 2006) 23.

However, case studies reveal that whistleblowers often make multiple disclosures. Brian Hood, who publicly exposed improper payments made to foreign agents by subsidiaries of the Reserve Bank of Australia (RBA) stated that, '[w]hile there were one or two key events, lots of things happened over quite a period of time'.[40] Hood reported his concerns about the payments at least five times, including to one of the subsidiary's boards, the Deputy Governor of the RBA, the media and ASIC. Similarly, in the Commonwealth Bank case referred to above, the 'Three Ferrets' made six disclosures to the media, the regulator and the company.

These cases are consistent with research that suggests that employees frequently raise concerns internally before reporting externally.[41] Moreover, they accord with an emerging body of research that suggests that reporting wrongdoing involves an ongoing decision-making process, with whistleblowers often vacillating between action and inaction. As Blenkinsopp and Edwards note, deciding to report requires 'an iterative process shaped by multiple factors, including events unfolding in real-time' in a complex and ever changing employment environment.[42]

The process of reporting may be protracted, as evidence is often obtained over a period of time. Employees can face challenges determining whether they have actually observed wrongdoing,[43] and cultural attitudes may conflict with an employee's sense of what amounts to impropriety.[44] Further, misconduct that is seemingly endorsed by management can become 'normalised' as standard organisational practice, challenging a whistleblower's perception that something is wrong.[45] Research also indicates that employees' responses to wrongdoing are influenced by their perception of the causal link between the wrongdoer and the outcome

---

40   Evidence to Parliamentary Joint Committee on the Australian Commission for Law Enforcement Integrity: Integrity of Overseas Commonwealth Law Enforcement Operations, Senate, Sydney, 4 October 2012, 10 (Brian Hood).

41   Marcia Miceli and Janet Near, *Blowing the Whistle: The Organizational and Legal Implications for Companies and Employees* (Lexington Books, 1992) 13.

42   Jon Blenkinsopp and Marissa Edwards, 'On Not Blowing the Whistle: Quiescent Silence as an Emotion Episode' in Neal Ashkanasy, Wilfred Zerbe and Charmine Härtel (eds), *Emotions, Ethics and Decision-Making* (Emerald Publishing, 2008) 186.

43   For example, witnesses of sexual harassment sometimes harbour concerns that they are reading too much into the situation. Ibid. 184.

44   Wim Vandekerckhove, 'The Perception of Whistleblowing Worldwide' in Richard Calland and Guy Dehn (eds), *Whistleblowing Around the World: Law, Culture and Practice* (ODAC and PCaW in partnership with the British Council, 2004).

45   Vikas Anand, Blake Ashforth and Mahendra Joshi, 'Business as Usual: The Acceptance and Perpetuation of Corruption in Organizations' (2004) 18 *Academy of Management Executive* 39.

of the wrongdoing.[46] It usually takes time for a whistleblower to gather sufficient information to properly evaluate blame attributions, which explains why whistleblowers often act gradually.

V. Where to from Here

There is currently considerable momentum, both nationally and globally, to improve processes and protection for people who report corporate misconduct. Acknowledging the reality that there may often be more than one employee willing to raise concerns within an organisation can influence both the narrative about, and the strategies that support, whistleblowing. Because individuals experience safety in numbers, encouraging employees to work with others, and ensuring they are protected when they do, may increase rates of whistleblowing and reduce negative consequences, including isolation and retaliation. Express recognition that group reporting may make the process easier can also encourage and improve corporate reporting.

Further, legislative reform can remove the need to identify a single disclosure, and ensure that protection is available from the start of the reporting process. A broader definition of 'reporting' in the *Corporations Act* is required to cover both disclosure to a supervisor and reporting to the media. The Act should also provide protection for whistleblowers who seek advice from the regulator, regardless of whether a formal disclosure of information is subsequently made. Currently, to qualify for protection, a person must make an official report to ASIC. However, employees should be able to contact ASIC for advice on the strength of their information, and protection from retaliation should be available from that point.

This chapter argues that the dominant narrative on whistleblowing is currently limiting the discussion and research on reform. There is value in getting back to basics when it comes to designing improvements to law and practices in this context, and making sure that we appreciate that the process of whistleblowing is not as simple as is often assumed.

---

46   See, for example, Linn Van Dyne, Soon Ang and Isabel Botero, 'Conceptualizing Employee Silence and Employee Voice as Multidimensional Constructs' (2003) 40 *Journal of Management Studies* 1359, 1374.

8

Lawyers as Whistleblowers: The Need for a Gatekeeper of Justice Whistleblowing Obligation/Exception

Suzanne Le Mire and Christine Parker[1]

In 2006 Christopher Dale, a partner in large Australian commercial law firm Clayton Utz, leaked internal law firm documents. He believed those documents showed that his own firm had assisted its tobacco company client to commit a 'fraud on justice'[2] while defending a prominent case brought by Rolah McCabe, who was suffering from terminal cancer.[3] The Dale case brought the possibility of lawyer whistleblowing to

---

1   University of Adelaide and University of Melbourne, respectively. We are grateful to Anita Mackay for her very helpful research assistance in this project. A more detailed exposition of this argument can be found in a forthcoming article: Christine Parker, Suzanne Le Mire and Anita Mackay, 'Lawyers, Confidentiality and Whistleblowing: Lessons from the McCabe Tobacco Litigation' (2017) 40(3) *Melbourne University Law Review* 999.
2   Dale used the term 'miscarriage of justice' and stated that he was motivated by the belief that 'there may have been a fraud committed on the Supreme Court of Victoria and that a full investigation was required': quoted in William Birnbauer, 'Lawyer Revealed as Smoking Source', *The Age* (online), 28 January 2007. In later litigation, it was argued that his whistleblowing fell into the 'fraud on justice' exception to lawyer–client privilege: *British American Tobacco Australia Services Limited v Slater & Gordon Ltd and Roxanne Joy Cowell* [2009] VSC 619 [158].
3   McCabe took action against British American Tobacco for personal injury arising from her smoking of cigarettes manufactured and sold by that company and its predecessors. The facts are described in a case Dale brought against Clayton Utz; see *Christopher Anthony Dale v Clayton Utz (No 2)* [2013] VSC 54, [101].

our front pages, but the appropriateness of Dale's leak has remained unresolved since emerging into the public sphere. More recently, another whistleblower has exposed the way Mossack Fonseca, a Panama law firm, aided aggressive tax planning.[4] It is not known whether the anonymous 'Panama papers' whistleblower is a lawyer with the firm but, like Dale, he or she had access to confidential lawyer–client information and blew the whistle with the intention of exposing a series of global injustices perpetrated by lawyers helping clients abuse the legal system.[5]

Under professional conduct rules and conventional codes of ethics, the breach of client confidence by a lawyer is prohibited unless it falls within certain limited exceptions. These exceptions apply in situations where a client is about to commit a serious criminal offence or is in imminent danger of serious physical harm to him or herself or another person.[6]

In this chapter we argue that lawyers should be permitted to whistleblow where they have information about clients or other lawyers using legal services to subvert the administration of justice in circumstances where there is misconduct analogous to situations where courts or regulatory authorities would refuse to uphold client legal privilege on the basis of the crime/fraud exception.[7]

First, we briefly illustrate the potential significance of lawyer whistleblowing in the justice system by describing the Dale case. Second, we argue that there is a strong ethical need for lawyers to be allowed to whistleblow in order to fulfil their obligations to act as 'gatekeepers' of the justice system when they are privy to wrongdoing that is likely to harm the justice system. The lawyer's role as gatekeeper builds on the conventional view that lawyers' duties to the court, the law and the administration of justice override their duties to clients, colleagues and third parties, and that lawyers' professional reputation is based on the assumption that they

---

4   Luke Harding, 'Panama Papers Source Breaks Silence over "Scale of Injustices"', Saturday 7 May 2016, *The Guardian* (online), www.theguardian.com/news/2016/may/06/panama-papers-source-breaks-silence-over-scale-of-injustices.

5   Ibid.

6   See *Australian Solicitors Conduct Rules* 9.2.4 and 9.2.5; and Christine Parker and Adrian Evans, *Inside Lawyers Ethics* (Cambridge University Press, 2nd edn, 2014) 110–30.

7   For examples of this exception to privilege, see *Attorney-General (NT) v Kearney* (1985) 158 CLR 510, 514 (Gibbs CJ); *R v Bell; Ex parte Lees* (1980) 146 CLR 141, 156 (Stephen J). The iniquity rule defence to breach of confidentiality would also apply in such situations: see Kaaren Koomen, 'Breach of Confidence and the Public Interest Defence: Is it in the Public Interest? A Review of the English Public Interest Defence and the Options for Australia' (1994) 10 *Queensland University of Technology Law Journal* 56.

will not assist clients to breach the law or breach their duties to the court to serve clients' or colleagues' interests.[8] We go on to suggest three guiding principles for appropriate lawyer whistleblowing relating to the nature of the relationship between the lawyer and the wrongdoer, the nature of the wrongdoing itself, and the process used to disclose the wrongdoing. The chapter suggests reforms to the law to permit and encourage appropriate lawyer whistleblowing in line with these principles.

I. The Dale Case

It is now well known that tobacco products kill up to one half of all their users, around 6 million people per year. The harm is seriously compounded by the highly addictive nature of cigarette smoking and the fact that many users start young.[9] Serious global efforts are underway to restrict the marketing and sale of cigarettes, especially to children; to avoid others being exposed to second-hand smoke; and to implement various other measures under the auspices of the World Health Organization Framework Convention on Tobacco Control, a treaty that has been signed by 180 parties representing 90 per cent of the world's population.[10]

Yet there is a long history of lawyers assisting tobacco companies to avoid public and legal scrutiny of their responsibility and culpability in relation to the marketing of cigarettes, their addictiveness and harm. In the 1990s, it was revealed that tobacco companies in the UK and US had, with the help of their lawyers, hidden or destroyed many relevant documents about the health effects of smoking.[11] In 2006, the NSW Dust Diseases Tribunal heard evidence from Mr Gulston, former Company Secretary and in-house solicitor for British American Tobacco Australia Services Limited (BATAS), and a whistleblower. His evidence was that as early as 1985 Australian law firm Clayton Utz was 'warehousing'[12] 230,000 documents

---

8   The paramount duty to the court is set out in the *Australian Solicitors Conduct Rules*, r 3. See also John C Coffee Jr, *Gatekeepers: The Professions and Corporate Governance* (Oxford University Press, 2006) 2; John C Coffee Jr, 'Can Lawyers Wear Blinders? Gatekeepers and Third Party Opinions' (2005) 84 *Texas Law Review* 59, 67–68. See *ASIC v Somerville* [2009] NSWSC 934 for a case where a lawyer was sanctioned for being involved in his client's strategy to avoid paying tax debts.

9   See World Health Organization, *Tobacco Fact Sheet No. 339*, 6 July 2015.

10   Ibid.

11   Stanton Glantz et al (eds), *The Cigarette Papers* (University of California Press, 1998).

12   'Warehousing' is a term describing the transfer of the custody of documents to third parties, in order to avoid the disclosure under discovery: *McCabe* [328]; Camille Cameron, 'Case Note. Hired Guns and Smoking Guns: McCabe v British American Tobacco Australia Ltd' (2002) 25(3) *UNSW*

and claiming privilege over them, thus avoiding its exposure in any legal proceedings.[13] The copies had been given to Clayton Utz ostensibly for legal advice and the originals at BATAS destroyed.[14]

The McCabe case brought the ethics of tobacco company litigation tactics to a head in Australia. Rolah McCabe sued BATAS for her terminal lung cancer on the basis that she had become addicted to cigarettes as a young teenager.[15] Documentary evidence showing what the tobacco company knew about the harm of its products, and how they were marketed, was clearly critical to the case. Yet few internal documents were uncovered in the usual processes of discovery because of their destruction or 'warehousing'. In 2002 Justice Eames struck out BATAS's defence on the basis that the tobacco company had 'followed a strategy designed to deny to any litigant access to documents to which the litigant would have been entitled and which would be of importance to the outcome of such proceedings'.[16]

Some eight months later the Victorian Court of Appeal reversed a number of Eames J's findings, restored the defence's pleadings and remitted the case for trial.[17] Rolah McCabe died before the appeal decision was handed down and the full case was never heard.

The litigation tactics of BATAS and its lawyers were controversial, and were the subject of internal review by Clayton Utz and investigations by the Australian Competition and Consumer Commission, legal profession regulators and the Victorian Department of Public Prosecutions.[18] New legislation that criminalised the destruction of material relevant to litigation was also created in direct response to the case.[19]

Christopher Dale had been involved in an internal Clayton Utz review of the lawyers' conduct in the case. He believed that this review had shown that senior Clayton Utz lawyers had assisted BATAS in misleading

Law Journal 768, 784.

13   *Re Mowbray: Brambles Australia Ltd v British American Tobacco Australia Services Ltd* [2006] NSWDDT 15, [19]. See also, Cameron, above n 12, 781–83.

14   Susannah Moran, 'Cloaks of Privilege and Smoking Guns', *The Australian Financial Review* (Sydney) 19 May 2006, 57.

15   *McCabe v British American Tobacco Australia Services Limited* [2002] VSC 73, [7] ('*McCabe*').

16   *McCabe* [13].

17   *British American Tobacco Australia Services Limited v Cowell* [2002] VSCA 197, [191].

18   See Parker and Evans, *Inside Lawyers Ethics*, above n 6, 119–20.

19   *Crimes (Document Destruction) Act 2006* (Vic); *Evidence (Document Unavailability) Act 2006* (Vic). See Suzanne Le Mire, 'Document Destruction and Corporate Culture: A Victorian Initiative' (2006) 19 *Australian Journal of Corporate Law* 304, 308.

the court and perverting the course of justice by destroying scientific documents that would have been relevant to litigation, hiding the extent and purpose of the destruction, and avoiding discovery of certain documents without adequate grounds.[20] In late 2006, after his partnership had been terminated by the firm, Mr Dale leaked documents from the review to the McCabe family's lawyer, Peter Gordon, and through him to William Birnbauer, a journalist.[21] Birnbauer published a series of newspaper articles in *The Sunday Age* alleging that the internal review had found evidence of lawyer misconduct.[22]

BATAS claimed confidentiality over the leaked documents and initiated a number of legal actions to prevent their further use.[23] Dale was subjected to considerable pressure: Clayton Utz made a disciplinary complaint about him[24] and BATAS sued under the general law of confidentiality.[25] Despite these events, there has been no legal decision as to the appropriateness or otherwise of Dale's leak.[26]

---

20 *Dale v Clayton Utz* [93]–[95].

21 Ibid. [110].

22 William Birnbauer, 'Cheated by the Law. Exclusive – Exposed: Dirty Tricks Behind Top Lawyers' Plot to Deny Justice to Cancer Victims' and 'Justice Denied: How Lawyers Set Out to Defeat a Dying Woman', *The Age* (online), 29 October 2006; William Birnbauer, 'Lawyer Revealed as Smoking Source', *The Age* (online), 28 January 2007.

23 See n 24 below.

24 Reportedly Clayton Utz made a complaint about breach of confidence to the professional disciplinary authority, although no outcome has been reported. See William Birnbauer, 'Thrust, Parry as Law Firm Slams Ex-partner', *The Age* (Victoria), 4 February 2007.

25 Between November 2006 and March 2007 two British American Tobacco companies in Australia sought restraining orders and injunctions against further use of the leaked material against Fairfax Publications, Slater and Gordon and Peter Gordon (the McCabe lawyers), Mrs Cowell (McCabe's executor) and Christopher Dale. These proceedings all settled with a number of restraining orders made by consent. Mrs Cowell was (reportedly) the last to settle in March 2011: see Richard Ackland, 'McCabe Litigation Took 10 Years in Two States', *Justinian*, 2 April 2011. See *British American Tobacco Australia Ltd v Peter Gordon* [2009] VSC 619; *British American Tobacco Australia Services Ltd v John Fairfax Publications* [2006] NSWSC 1197; *British American Tobacco Australia Services Ltd v John Fairfax Publications* [2006] NSWSC 1175; *British American Tobacco Australia Ltd v Fairfax* [2006] NSWSC 1328; *British American Tobacco Australia Ltd v Peter Gordon* [2006] NSWSC 1473; *British American Tobacco Australia Ltd v Peter Gordon* [2007] NSWSC 109; *British American Tobacco Australia Ltd v Peter Gordon* [2007] NSWSC 230; *British American Tobacco Australia Ltd v Peter Gordon* [2007] NSWSC 292; *McCabe v British American Tobacco Australia Services Ltd* [2007] VSC 216; *Cowell v British American Tobacco Australia Services Ltd* [2007] VSCA 301; *British American Tobacco Australia Ltd v Peter Gordon* [2009] VSC 77; *British American Tobacco Australia Ltd v Peter Gordon* [2009] VSC 619.

26 The possibility that Dale's leak might be justified under rules of professional conduct or general laws of confidentiality was considered by the Victorian Supreme Court in interlocutory proceedings concerning an action brought by BATAS against Mrs Cowell (McCabe's executor) to restrain her from further disclosing the internal Clayton Utz documents Dale had leaked: ibid. The case was settled before any final authoritative determination of the issues was made. See above n 25.

While the work of lawyers can ensure 'law is still the most powerful instrument for creating and maintaining a world that is free, rational and just',[27] it can also have a dark side. Global tobacco companies, with the help of their lawyers, continue their fight against tobacco control measures such as bans on advertising and plain packaging. Indeed, a recent decision by the Permanent Court of Arbitration found Philip Morris Asia's challenge to Australia's plain packaging laws to be an 'abuse of rights', essentially because it amounted to impermissible forum shopping.[28] Other revelations, such as the Panama Papers leak, show that there is also a broader need to examine, debate and change the way in which lawyers work with powerful and rich clients to avoid legal scrutiny, undermine the purposes of law and regulation and thus inhibit justice.

II. Whistleblowing

Lawyers have explicit duties to the law, the court and the administration of justice, which are considered to be paramount over duties to clients, colleagues and the firm.[29] As John Coffee Jr explains in his influential book on professionals as gatekeepers, lawyers and other professionals lend their corporate clients their 'reputational capital' and thus encourage investors, the market, other parties and indeed courts to rely on the clients' disclosures and assurances in a way that they might not if the lawyer was not involved.[30] It follows that the market, the justice system, and all the parties who take part in them, rely on lawyers to act as gatekeepers and not use their reputation to assist clients who act dishonestly or illegally. Moreover it is in lawyers' own interests, as individuals and as a whole profession, to preserve their own reputation for ensuring duties to the court, the law and the administration of justice are upheld. It is therefore well established that a lawyer should be neither an instigator of, nor a party to, any breach of the law, duty to the court or abuse of justice

---

27 Sir Daryl Dawson, 'Legal Services Market' (1996) 5 *Journal of Judicial Administration* 147, 153.
28 *Philip Morris Asia v Australia PCA* Case no. 2012-12, Award on Jurisdiction and Admissibility, 17 December 2015.
29 *Australian Solicitors' Conduct Rules*, r 3.
30 John C Coffee Jr, *Gatekeepers: The Professions and Corporate Governance* (Oxford University Press, 2006) 2.

by his or her clients or colleagues, and that they should act as gatekeeper at least in the sense of actively advising clients and colleagues against such breaches.[31]

We suggest that this 'gatekeeper of justice' role should extend to justify lawyer whistleblowing in certain circumstances (outlined in the sections below). The literature on gatekeeping generally stops short of advocating whistleblowing. Yet the gatekeeper of justice obligation is meaningless without the possibility of whistleblowing. Without that the lawyer gatekeeper is constrained to persuasion or withdrawal of services, neither of which may be effective. In effect these actions may simply defer the problem, and even render it less likely that it will be resolved in a satisfactory way. As Waters suggests, '[a]ll a silent withdrawal does is pass the problem along to another securities lawyer, possibly one who is not as concerned with ethics and professional responsibility'.[32]

Currently lawyer whistleblowing is strongly discouraged by lawyers' confidentiality obligations. These are enshrined in the professional conduct rules enforced by the disciplinary system, implied into the terms of every lawyer–client contract, and enforceable under equitable principles of confidentiality.[33] Client legal privilege, which protects lawyer–client confidentiality from enforced disclosure by courts and various enforcement authorities, has been recognised as a fundamental common law principle.[34] This privilege covers information communicated from the client to the lawyer for the purposes of legal advice, and information communicated to the lawyer by third party experts for the purposes of preparation for litigation. There are even obligations of confidentiality, akin to the privilege, owed to opposing parties for material disclosed for the purposes of litigation, and equity can enforce confidentiality in any situation where information was communicated confidentially with

---

31   See, for example, 'Law Society of NSW v Dennis' (1981) 7 *Family Law Review* 417; *ACCC v Real Estate Institute of Western Australia Inc* [1999] FCA 18. See also Gino Dal Pont, *Lawyers' Professional Responsibility* (Thomson Reuters, 5th edn, 2012) 615 (citations omitted): 'Lawyers must not engage in conduct that is dishonest, illegal, unprofessional, that may otherwise bring the profession into disrepute or that is prejudicial to the administration of justice. Lawyers must not therefore seek to advance their client's causes by unfair or dishonest means.'

32   David Waters, 'The Wisdom of Whistleblowing: The Sarbanes-Oxley Act of 2002 and the "Noisy Withdrawal" Provision' (2010) 34 *Journal of the Legal Profession* 411, 423.

33   See Parker and Evans, *Inside Lawyers' Ethics*, above n 6, 110–13.

34   *Baker v Campbell* (1983) 153 CLR 52.

NEW DIRECTIONS FOR LAW IN AUSTRALIA

an expectation that confidentiality would be maintained.[35] The justice system would not operate effectively if parties could not freely disclose information in litigation without the understanding that it will not be used for purposes other than the resolution of the dispute.[36]

If lawyer whistleblowing were over-encouraged, clients might lose faith in lawyer confidentiality, undermining frankness between lawyer and client and thus detracting from the administration of justice. However, the justice system is not just if lawyers see wrongdoing by clients or colleagues that amounts to a fraud on justice, are unable to prevent it via confidential advice, and have only the option of silent withdrawal or resignation in response. We argue that it is crucial to the administration of justice that professional conduct regulation sets out clear guidance and protection for appropriate whistleblowing by lawyers. This is only likely to be necessary and appropriate in certain circumstances, and there are three elements that must be considered:

- the *relationship* between the lawyer whistleblower and the wrongdoer – whistleblowing protection is necessary for some relationships more than others;
- only certain types of *wrongdoing* are serious enough to be disclosed; and
- a lawyer whistleblower faced with misconduct must use an appropriate *process* to seek to prevent the wrongdoing before blowing the whistle and to blow the whistle as quietly as possible consistent with effectively addressing the wrongdoing.

The remainder of the chapter discusses these three elements.

A. Relationship

The potential for lawyers to whistleblow and their vulnerability to reprisals will vary depending on the relationship between the lawyer and the wrongdoer. We canvas four possible situations below. We suggest

---

35   Matthew Groves, 'The Implied Undertaking Restricting the Use of Material Obtained during Legal Proceedings' (2003) 23(3) *Australian Bar Review* 314–44.

36   See discussion of the implied undertaking in *British American Tobacco Australia Services Ltd v Cowell (as representing the estate of Rolah Ann McCabe, deceased)* [2003] VSCA 43, [19–20].

that lawyers in each of the situations should be permitted to blow the whistle and given protection from retaliation if they do so via changes to professional conduct rules and legal profession regulation.

Lawyers in an internal or employment relationship with the wrongdoer are most likely to hold information 'worthy of disclosure' (the criteria for what should be disclosed are addressed in the next subsection).[37] External lawyers directly briefed by the wrongdoing organisation may also identify wrongdoing, although in such a case the client can tailor information to obscure it. Lawyers in both these situations may be able to prevent wrongdoing through their advice to the client. However, if that advice is ignored and the client persists with the wrongdoing, then the lawyer should whistleblow. In such a situation, the strength of the duty of confidentiality and loyalty to the client, and the vulnerability to retaliation through loss of employment, disciplinary complaint or lawsuit, is currently high. Professional conduct rules should set out when whistleblowing should be allowed and provide protection from retaliation similar to that provided to public sector employees under the *Public Interest Disclosure Act*.

Lawyers may also discover wrongdoing involving their colleagues in the firm and the clients of their colleagues. All partners in a firm have an obligation to ensure ethical conduct in the firm.[38] But there are significant disincentives for whistleblowing within a law firm if and when counselling and persuasion fail. If one lawyer in a firm owes obligations of confidentiality to a client or in relation to information communicated by a third party, then all lawyers in the firm will be bound. Thus, in the Dale case, even though Dale did not himself act for the tobacco company, as a partner in the firm he owed obligations of confidentiality to all his firm's clients as if he was their own lawyer. He would also have owed obligations of confidentiality in equity and contract to his fellow partners in his firm about internal operations of the firm. This situation should also be covered by whistleblowing exceptions to confidentiality and protection of the lawyer whistleblower.

Lawyers might discover the wrongdoing of those on the other side in a transaction or in litigation. For these lawyers, their duty and vulnerability to retaliation and discipline will depend in part on the attitude of their

---

37 Paul Latimer and A J Brown, 'Whistleblower Laws: International Best Practice' (2008) 31 *University of New South Wales Law Journal* 766, 775.

38 This flows from the vicarious liability of partners: for example, *Partnership Act 1891* (SA) s 10. See also, for example, obligations to supervise, *Australian Solicitors' Conduct Rules* (ACSR) r 37.

own client to the disclosure. So, for example, clients may retaliate if the disclosure is not in their interests by lodging a complaint (which may or may not be successful), or curtailing work. A second layer of confidentiality may exist if the lawyer has come across the information in a context where there has been an undertaking to preserve confidence, such as in a due diligence or discovery process.[39]

The final relationship within which a lawyer could be a whistleblower concerns those lawyers who discover wrongdoing through their personal or professional networks. The lawyer's power to intervene is less obvious in this context, and the whistleblowing might simply take the form of a disciplinary complaint about the wrongdoer.

It is plausible that reforms to support whistleblowing explicitly would assist those considering their response to wrongdoing. So, for example, changes to the professional conduct rules and other legislative whistleblower protections (including, for example, Pt 9.4AAA of the *Corporations Act* and the Commonwealth *Public Interest Disclosure Act*) could assist in building a culture of permission for appropriate lawyer whistleblowing, while also addressing the possibility of reprisals.

B. Wrongdoing

We suggest that where misconduct is analogous to conduct that would fall within the crime/fraud exception to lawyer client privilege, then gatekeeper of justice obligations are triggered and external whistleblowing may be permitted if other measures to address the misconduct fail (as discussed in the next section). The crime/fraud exception to privilege covers information about the commission of a crime, fraud or civil offence,[40] and extends to 'communications made with the intention of frustrating the processes of law, and which may be described as a "fraud on justice"'.[41] The courts already recognise that the privilege should not apply in such circumstances because clients should not be able to rely on lawyer confidentiality where that would conflict with the lawyers' role as an officer of the court. The 'iniquity rule' defence to breach of confidence

---

39   See, for example, *The Solicitor-General v Miss Alice* [2007] 2 NZLR 783.

40   *R v Cox & Railton* (1884) 10 QBD 153 [158].

41   *Attorney-General (NT) v Kearney* (1985) 158 CLR 510, 514 (Gibbs CJ); *R v Bell; Ex parte Lees* (1980) 146 CLR 141, 156 (Stephen J); *British American Tobacco Australia Limited v Peter Gordon* [2009] VSC 619 [158].

at equity would also apply in such situations.[42] Professional conduct rules should also be changed to recognise that whistleblowing can be appropriate where the crime/fraud exception would apply (provided an appropriate process is followed).

Examples of the kind of wrongdoing that could justify whistleblowing on the part of the lawyer under this exception include situations where the courts or other regulatory authorities have been misled or deceived by either the lawyer's own client or a lawyer or client on the other side, or indeed anyone else. This is the situation alleged by Dale. Dale stated that he was motivated by the belief that 'there may have been a fraud committed on the Supreme Court of Victoria and that a full investigation was required.'[43] His leaks were aimed at providing further evidence that the client and the law firm acted in violation of the applicable norms by concealing evidence of the intentionally manipulative or negligent marketing of a product known to be harmful, and subverting the judicial process to avoid scrutiny and liability for its own harmful conduct.

Another example would be the Australian Wheat Board's subversion of the UN's 'Oil for Food' program to illegally channel funds to Saddam Hussein's regime.[44] In such a situation the lawyer would have a clear duty not to counsel or assist in illegal conduct.[45] However, should the client persist with the wrongdoing, the pressure on the lawyer to conceal the wrongdoing is likely to be high. Moreover the client may embroil the lawyer in its illegal purpose by expecting the lawyer to defend and even further the client's purpose. This type of wrongdoing furthers the organisation's purpose, yet falls within the crime/fraud exception, and

---

42   The iniquity rule defence to breach of confidence at general law covers 'crimes, frauds and misdeeds' including civil wrongs: *Initial Services v Putterill* [1968] 1 QB 396; see also Kaaren Koomen, 'Breach of Confidence and the Public Interest Defence: Is it in the Public Interest? A Review of the English Public Interest Defence and the Options for Australia' (1994) 10 *Queensland University of Technology Law Journal* 56, 58.

43   William Birnbauer, 'Lawyer Revealed as Smoking Source', *The Sunday Age* 28 January 2007. Quoted in *Dale v Clayton Utz* [101]. Dale repeated the substance of this account in his evidence to the court in *Dale v Clayton Utz*: see [101].

44   Caroline Overington, *Kickback: Inside the Australian Wheat Board Scandal* (Allen and Unwin, 2007).

45   See, for example, 'Law Society of NSW v Dennis' (1981) 7 *Family Law Review* 417; *ACCC v Real Estate Institute of Western Australia Inc* [1999] FCA 18. See also Gino Dal Pont, *Lawyers' Professional Responsibility* (Thomson Reuters, 5th edn, 2012) 615 (citations omitted): 'Lawyers must not engage in conduct that is dishonest, illegal, unprofessional, that may otherwise bring the profession into disrepute or that is prejudicial to the administration of justice. Lawyers must not therefore seek to advance their client's causes by unfair or dishonest means.'

thus it is desirable to make the conduct rules clear about when and how lawyers can whistleblow externally in such a situation and provide them with protection from retaliation if they do so.

C. The process

Whistleblowing is ethically problematic because it breaches shared understandings of loyalty and confidentiality within a relationship or organisation.[46] It is, therefore, important that lawyer whistleblowers leak confidential information only when it is ethically justified to do so and do not unnecessarily breach other ethical obligations in the process.[47] In order to encourage appropriate use of a whistleblowing exception, the conduct rules should set out the circumstances when whistleblowing is permissible and the process that should be followed.

First, the conduct rules should require lawyer whistleblowers to use judgment and ensure they are accurate in their assessment of any wrongdoing. That is, they should verify that they have accurate and sufficient evidence to at least prompt a further investigation by a regulatory authority before whistleblowing.

Second, the rules should ensure the breach of loyalty is minimised by directing lawyer whistleblowers to explore appropriate alternative options for preventing wrongdoing (such as strong advice and persuasion) before sounding the alarm. Other reasonable options for addressing the wrongdoing should be exhausted before whistleblowing. This also means that any disclosure should be as narrow as possible and directed to the appropriate party who can rectify or prevent the wrong – usually, first, an authoritative figure within the firm or company, and then a regulatory authority or court. Public disclosure, such as via the media in the Dale case, should generally be a last resort as it carries with it a complete loss of control over the information in ways that do not necessarily occur when information is disclosed to regulators or courts.

Third, the rules should encourage lawyer whistleblowers to disclose sufficient information but only that which is necessary to address the wrongdoing. They should not, for example, disclose extraneous personal

---

46   Sissela Bok, *Secrets: On the Ethics of Concealment and Revelation* (Vintage Books, 1989) 120.
47   Based on Bok, ibid, 219ff.

matters or hide what evidence they have. Rather, the whistleblowing should put matters of significance to an appropriate forum for investigation and accountability.

Changes such as these to the professional conduct rules, coupled with education by legal profession regulators and appropriate protections for lawyer whistleblowers in legislation, would provide guidance to potential whistleblowers faced with difficult choices. Once appropriate changes are made to the professional conduct rules, lawyers could draw on existing ethical guidance hotlines for advice about the appropriateness and process for whistleblowing, and should be protected from disciplinary action if they seek and follow such advice. Ultimately this could enhance the possibility that wrongdoing that impacts the justice system would be confidentially investigated and, where appropriate, brought into public discussion and accountability.

III. Concluding Remarks

Lawyer whistleblowing has the potential to address specific occasions of harm to the administration of justice. It has barely, however, been addressed by professional conduct rules and professional regulators. Our chapter suggests how to begin to address this issue in the legal profession. The changes we have proposed could assist practitioners as well as provide a welcome demonstration of the profession's commitment to justice.

Part II. Criminal Law and Evidence

9

Criminal Justice Law Reform Challenges for the Future: It's Time to Curb Australia's Prison Addiction

Lorana Bartels[1]

I. Introduction

This chapter will examine Australia's addiction to prison. It will commence by examining where we have arrived at in relation to our use of imprisonment, and why we must turn this around. In particular, it will consider the monetary and non-monetary costs of imprisonment, and the evidence on the crime prevention effects of prison. It will then posit what a new future in criminal justice might look like, drawing inspiration from recent development in the United States (US) and United Kingdom (UK). The role of the media, research on sentencing and public opinion, impact on victims, and the emerging case for justice reinvestment will also be considered.

The chapter concludes by arguing that all policy should henceforth be focused around the central issue of whether any proposed reform will increase or decrease our prison population. If it appears that the former

---

1   Associate Professor and Head, School of Law and Justice, University of Canberra; Adjunct Associate Professor, University of Tasmania.

is likely to occur, then the proposal should not proceed. In making this shift, it is acknowledged that the imprisonment rate is influenced by both substantive laws, such as the creation of new offences, and changes to procedure, such as reforms to bail, as well as reforms in other contexts, such as housing. All initiatives should be immediately off the policy-making table if they are likely to significantly increase our prison population. There must be particular scrutiny if the proposed initiative is likely to impact disproportionately on Indigenous people. If it appears that the proposal will reduce the prison population (e.g. by making sentencing laws less punitive), then this should in the first instance be licence to proceed, but the inquiry must not be left there. All initiatives must be subject to adequately funded independent evaluation to determine if they have actually had this desired impact. Adopting this approach would require courage and commitment from politicians, policymakers, the media and the public. The chapter ends by demonstrating what law reform might look like if we went down this path.

II. Australia's Prison Addiction

The chapter will commence with figures that contextualise the debate and make the case that Australia has become addicted to prison.[2] As of December 2016, we had 39,568 people in our prisons.[3] Only three years earlier, the prison population was less than 30,000,[4] but at the current rate of increase – exceeding 7 per cent a year[5] – we will reach 40,000 prisoners in 2017. Our imprisonment rate is now just over 200 per 100,000.[6] It should be noted that this masks some significant variation, with Tasmania and the Australian Capital Territory (ACT) the lowest imprisoning jurisdictions, at around 141 per 100,000, while the Northern Territory now incarcerates

---

2   This section draws on the data and rhetoric respectively of the following recent papers: Don Weatherburn, '"Rack 'Em, Pack 'Em and Stack 'Em": Decarceration in an Age of Zero Tolerance' (2016) 28 *Current Issues in Criminal Justice* 137; Andrew Leigh, 'Prisons Dilemma: An Economist's Perspective on Incarceration', Paper presented at the Justice Connections 4 Symposium, November 2015, Canberra. Discussions with Don Weatherburn in particular have informed the development of this chapter.
3   Australian Bureau of Statistics (ABS), 'Corrective Services, Australia – December 2016 Quarter' (Cat No 4512.0, ABS, 2017).
4   ABS, 'Corrective Services, Australia – December 2013 Quarter' (Cat No 4512.0, ABS, 2014).
5   ABS (2017), above n 3.
6   Ibid.

a staggering 891 people per 100,000 in December 2016, although this had fallen from a peak of 968 in January 2016.[7] However, all jurisdictions have increased their imprisonment rates over the last 15 years.

Interestingly, and perhaps surprisingly, our high imprisonment rate is a relatively recent phenomenon.[8] As set out in Figure 9.1, the imprisonment rate fell steadily from 1900 to 1920, from 126 to 52 per 100,000. It generally stayed around this level for the next 30 years, before starting to climb, from 52 in 1950 to 81 in 1970. It then fell again, to 62–66 in 1975 to 1985. Since then, it has risen steadily between 1950 and 1980. It then climbed, but only fairly gradually, increasing to 66 in 1985. Over the 30 years that followed, however, it increased by nearly 300 per cent, to 196 in 2015 and 211 by December 2016.

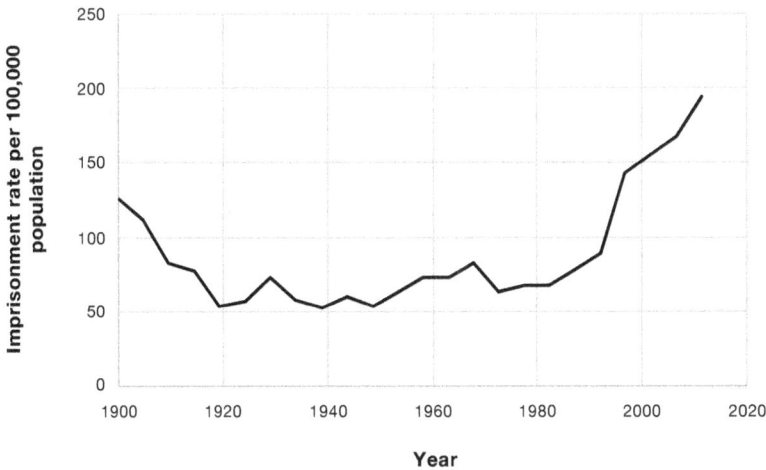

Figure 9.1: Australia's imprisonment rate (per 100,000), 1900–2015
Source: Adapted from Graycar (2001); ABS (various years)

---

7   Ibid.
8   See Adam Graycar, 'Crime in Twentieth Century Australia' (Cat No 1301.1, ABS, 2001); ABS 'Corrective Services, Australia – December 2001 Quarter' (Cat No 4512.0, ABS, 2002); ABS 'Corrective Services, Australia – December 2005 Quarter' (Cat No 4512.0, ABS, 2006); ABS 'Corrective Services, Australia – December 2010 Quarter' (Cat No 4512.0, ABS, 2011); ABS, ibid.

To place this in an international context, Canada's imprisonment rate is 106.[9] The imprisonment rate in England and Wales, the highest in Western Europe, is 147.[10] A number of European countries have rates well under 100 per 100,000, while Iceland's is only 45.[11] Of course, we're not doing as badly as the US, where the rate is just under 700 per 100,000,[12] but their rate is declining slowly,[13] while ours is on a steady upwards trajectory.

When we examine the situation for Indigenous people, it is obviously much worse. In spite of only accounting for 3 per cent of the Australian population, Indigenous people make up 27 per cent of the national prison population, and reached 10,000 prisoners for the first time in the December 2015 quarter.[14] Worse still, a third of the adult female population[15] and over half of the juvenile detention population are Indigenous.[16] The imprisonment rate[17] tells the story in more detail. Overall, the Indigenous imprisonment rate in Australia in December 2016 was 2,409 per 100,000. For men, it was 4,370. An oft-cited figure is that an Indigenous man is more likely to go to prison than university. For men in Western Australia, the imprisonment rate is 7,002 per 100,000. In other words, seven out of every 100 Indigenous men in Western Australia are in prison at any given time. This is the most imprisoned group of people in the world. Suddenly, the imprisonment rate in the US doesn't look so bad.

A. The costs of prison

One context in which the US actually does better than Australia, if it can be termed such, is in relation to the cost of prison. Now, that itself comes at a price. For example, the US has much lower staff to inmate ratios than in Australia, and are generally far more punitive in their prison

---

9   Ibid. It should be noted that the Institute of Criminal Policy Research (ICPR) places our imprisonment rate at 151 per 100,000, compared with the ABS figure of 196: Roy Walmsley, *World Prison Population List* (ICPR, 11th edn, 2016). The reasons for this discrepancy are not entirely clear, but should be borne in mind in the context of international comparisons.

10   Ibid.

11   Ibid.

12   Ibid.

13   Lauren Glaze et al, *Correctional Populations in the United States*, 2014 (NCJ 249513, US Bureau of Justice Statistics, 2015).

14   ABS, above n 3.

15   Ibid.

16   Australian Institute of Health and Welfare (AIHW), *Youth Detention Population in Australia* 2016 (AIHW, 2016).

17   ABS, above n 3.

administration. Nevertheless, imprisonment costs around $45,000 per prisoner, per year in the US.[18] In Australia, that figure is over $110,000, including capital costs.[19] In the ACT, which hosts Australia's first 'human rights prison',[20] the price tag exceeds $160,000 per year. Australia now spends more than $3.8 billion on prisons every year.[21]

Then there are the non-monetary costs. In the recent guideline judgment of *Boulton*,[22] the Victorian Court of Appeal acknowledged the limitations of prison, including loss of personal autonomy and privacy, the risk of violence, institutionalisation and exposure to more serious criminals. The impact on prisoners' families is also a major concern, although poor data collection hampers our understanding in this context. In 2005, Quilty[23] estimated that 5 per cent of all Australian children are affected by parental incarceration in any given year and this rose to 20 per cent for Indigenous children. Both of these figures are likely to have increased significantly in line with increased imprisonment rates. Parental incarceration has in turn been linked with adverse effects on children.[24]

B. But don't we need prison to keep us safe?

So, prison costs us a lot in a variety of ways. But don't we need it to prevent crime? Well, the good news there is that crime is already well down. In fact, over the last 15 years, the national homicide rate has fallen by 32 per cent, and robbery and burglary rates have fallen by 66 per cent and 67 per cent respectively. In addition, motor vehicle theft has fallen by 71 per cent, while other forms of theft have fallen by a still impressive 43 per cent.[25]

---

18   Vera Institute of Justice, *The Price of Prisons: What Incarceration Costs Taxpayers* (2012).
19   Productivity Commission, *Report on Government Services 2016* (2016).
20   For comment, see Lorana Bartels, 'The State of Imprisonment in Australia: Can the ACT Achieve a "Human Rights" Prison?', *The Conversation*, 17 April 2015, theconversation.com/state-of-imprisonment-can-act-achieve-a-human-rights-prison-39119; Lorana Bartels, 'The ACT Prison: Human Rights Rhetoric Versus Crowded and Bored Reality' (2015) 9 *Court of Conscience* 21; Lorana Bartels and Jeremy Boland, 'Human rights and Prison: A Case Study from the Australian Capital Territory', in Elaine Fishwick, Marinella Marmo and Leanne Weber (eds), *Routledge International Handbook of Criminology and Human Rights* (Routledge, 2016), 556–67.
21   Productivity Commission, above n 19.
22   *Boulton v The Queen* [2014] VSCA 342. For discussion, see Lorana Bartels, 'Sentencing Review 2014–15' (2015) 39 *Criminal Law Journal* 326.
23   Simon Quilty, 'The Magnitude of Experience of Parental Incarceration in Australia' (2005) *Psychiatry, Psychology and Law* 12(1), 256–57.
24   Weatherburn, above n 2.
25   Ibid.

It may then be argued that our increased use of prison achieved these results. However, Australian data indicate little correlation between each jurisdiction's crime and imprisonment rates.[26] The international data tell a similar story.[27] In any event, US[28] and Australian[29] research suggests that you would need to increase the prison population by 10 per cent to get a 1 to 2 per cent decrease, with changes in sentence length having no impact. That would generally be regarded as a pretty poor return on investment.

Other research indicates that once a community gets past a certain point, rather than preventing crime, prison actually *causes* crime.[30] Todd Clear's[31] hypothesis for why this occurs is that rising prison rates take more and more people out of certain highly disadvantaged neighbourhoods. Past a certain point, he argues, this leaves the community weakened, fragmented and unable to defend itself against crime. As Weatherburn[32] recently observed in the Australian context, this may well be what is happening with some Indigenous communities.

III. A New Future?

The foregoing is well known to criminologists, who do not need to be further convinced of the need for a different approach.[33] What is required, however, is for this message to permeate through to politicians, in the first instance, and the media and public. What we need is support from

---

26   For discussion, see Rick Sarre, 'Social Innovation, Law and Justice' (Paper presented at the History and Future of Social Innovation Conference, Adelaide, June 2008).

27   See Bronwyn Naylor, 'The Evidence Is In: You Can't Link Imprisonment to Crime Rates', *The Conversation*, 23 April 2015, theconversation.com/the-evidence-is-in-you-cant-link-imprisonment-to-crime-rates-40074.

28   John Donahue, 'Assessing the Relative Benefits of Incarceration: Overall Changes and the Benefits on the Margin' in Steven Raphael and Michael Stoll (eds), *Do Prisons Make Us Safer? The Benefits and Costs of the Prison Boom* (Russell Sage Federation Press, 2009) 269–342.

29   Wai-Yin Wan et al, 'The Effect of Arrest and Imprisonment on Crime' (Crime and Justice Bulletin No 158, NSW Bureau of Crime Statistics and Research (BOCSAR), 2012). See also Don Weatherburn, Jiuzhao Hua and Steve Moffatt, 'How Much Crime Does Prison Stop? The Incapacitation Effect of Prison on Burglary' (Crime and Justice Bulletin No 93, BOCSAR, 2006).

30   See Weatherburn, above n 2, for discussion.

31   Todd Clear, *Imprisoning Communities: How Mass Incarceration Makes Disadvantaged Neighborhoods Worse* (Oxford University Press, 2007), as summarised in Weatherburn, ibid. See also Mark Kleiman, *When Brute Force Fails: How to Have Less Crime and Less Punishment* (Princeton University Press, 2009).

32   Weatherburn, ibid.

33   See, for example, Weatherburn, ibid; Sarre, above n 26; Mirko Bagaric, 'Prisons Policy Is Turning Australia into the Second Nation of Captives', *The Conversation*, 10 April 2015, theconversation.com/prisons-policy-is-turning-australia-into-the-second-nation-of-captives-38842.

across the political spectrum to stop doing things the way we've been doing them for the last generation, and try a new way. That might sound laughable in a world of tabloid newspapers and talkback radio, but it is happening now in the US, which has seen small prison population reductions each year since 2012.[34] In October 2015, over 130 senior police officers, prosecutors and sheriffs formed a group called 'Law Enforcement Leaders to Reduce Crime and Incarceration', which 'represents an abrupt public shift in philosophy for dozens of law enforcement officials who have sustained careers based upon tough-on-crime strategies'.[35] In January this year, a bipartisan task force appointed by Congress to suggest ways to reduce the federal prison population provided its final recommendations to the White House. The recommendations included sending fewer low-level drug offenders to prison and imposing shorter sentences.[36] In March 2016, then President Barack Obama also asserted that drug addiction is a health issue, not a criminal justice problem, and committed over $150 million to drug treatment.[37]

In the UK, David Cameron recently became the first prime minister to give a speech on prison reform in over 20 years, in which he acknowledged that 'politicians from all sides of the political spectrum are starting to realise the diminishing returns from ever higher levels of incarceration'.[38] He spoke of the need for wholesale reform and explained that 'the truth is that simply warehousing ever more prisoners is not financially sustainable, nor is it necessarily the most cost-effective way of cutting crime'.[39] Furthermore, he recognised that prisons are 'often miserable,

---

34   Erica Good, 'US Prison Populations Decline, Reflecting New Approach to Crime', *New York Times*, 25 July 2013, www.nytimes.com/2013/07/26/us/us-prison-populations-decline-reflecting-new-approach-to-crime.html; Lauren Carroll, 'Federal Prison Population Drops for First Time in 3 Decades, Eric Holder Says', *Politifact*, 23 February 2015, www.politifact.com/truth-o-meter/statements/2015/feb/23/eric-holder/federal-prison-population-drops-first-time-3-decad/.

35   Timothy Williams, 'Police Leaders Join Call to Cut Prison Rosters', *New York Times*, 20 October 2015, www.nytimes.com/2015/10/21/us/police-leaders-join-call-to-cut-prison-rosters.html.

36   Charles Colson Taskforce on Corrections, *Transforming Prisons, Restoring Lives: Final Recommendations of the Charles Colson Task Force on Federal Corrections* (Urban Institute, 2016). For comment, see Eric Tucker, 'A Bipartisan Task Force Is Suggesting a Policy Shift That Could Save the Federal Government $5 Billion', *Business Insider*, 26 January 2016, www.businessinsider.com/ap-task-force-recommends-how-to-cut-us-prisoner-count-by-60000-2016-1?IR=T.

37   Timothy Pratt, 'Obama: "Drug Addiction Is a Health Problem, Not a Criminal Problem"', *The Guardian*, 30 March 2016, www.theguardian.com/us-news/2016/mar/29/barack-obama-drug-addiction-health-problem-not-criminal-problem.

38   David Cameron, 'Cameron Prison Reform Speech in Full', 8 February 2016, www.politics.co.uk/comment-analysis/2016/02/08/cameron-prison-reform-speech-in-full.

39   Ibid.

painful environments. Isolation. Mental anguish. Idleness. Bullying. Self-harm. Violence. Suicide … These establishments are full of damaged individuals'.[40]

If the US and UK – with respectively higher and lower imprisonment rates than Australia – can show signs of shifting their rhetoric, surely we can too. But it won't be easy. A few years ago, the NSW Liberal Attorney-General, Greg Smith SC, was very open, both before and after his election, about his commitment to reducing the prison population.[41] Under his watch, the NSW prison population started falling. In 2012, he ordered three prisons to be closed. Unfortunately, this was all a bit too sensible for the rest of his party or the NSW shock jocks, and he lost his portfolio in 2014, having been lampooned in the tabloid media as 'Marshmallow Smith' for being soft on crime.[42] Since then, the NSW prison population has been on the rise, hitting 12,000 for the first time recently.[43]

The ACT recently had in Simon Corbell an Attorney-General who consistently refused to play the law and order game and pushed back against calls for mandatory sentences.[44] The early indications about his successor, Gordon Ramsay, suggest he is no more likely to embrace the tough-on-crime rhetoric.[45] We obviously need more politicians of courage, regardless of their political affiliation. At the federal level, Labor's Shadow Assistant Treasurer, Andrew Leigh,[46] has spoken about the need to reduce imprisonment rates. The Australian Greens' justice policy aims include, *inter alia*:

---

40 Ibid.

41 Robert Milliken, 'Ending Sydney's Law-and-Order Auction', *Inside Story*, 3 April 2012, insidestory.org.au/ending-sydneys-law-and-order-auction.

42 For comment, see Milliken, ibid; David Brown, 'Is Rational Law Reform Still Possible in a Shock-jock Tabloid World?', *The Conversation*, 15 August 2014, theconversation.com/is-rational-law-reform-still-possible-in-a-shock-jock-tabloid-world-30416; for comment, see David Brown, 'State of Imprisonment: Prisoners of NSW Politics and Perceptions', *The Conversation*, 21 April 2015, theconversation.com/state-of-imprisonment-prisoners-of-nsw-politics-and-perceptions-38985; Jonathon Green, 'Back to Prison', *ABC Background Briefing*, 18 May 2014, www.abc.net.au/radionational/programs/backgroundbriefing/2014-05-18/5452044.

43 ABS, above n 3.

44 Michael Inman, 'No One Punch Laws in ACT, Says Corbell', *Canberra Times*, 4 February 2014, www.canberratimes.com.au/act-news/no-onepunch-laws-in-act-says-corbell-20140203-31xpn.html; Alexandra Back, 'Attorney-General Simon Corbell Stands Firm On One-punch Laws', *Canberra Times*, 1 February 2016, www.canberratimes.com.au/act-news/attorneygeneral-simon-corbell-stands-firm-on-onepunch-laws-20160131-gmieeu.html.

45 Megan Gorrey, 'Attorney-General Gordon Ramsay Says Legal Aid Critical to "Inclusive" Judiciary', *Canberra Times*, 4 February 2017, www.canberratimes.com.au/act-news/attorneygeneral-gordon-ramsay-says-legal-aid-critical-to-inclusive-judiciary-20170131-gu2d8j.html.

46 Leigh, above n 2.

- an end to politically-motivated law and order campaigns that exploit and fuel public anxieties;
- a comprehensive, multidisciplinary and evidence-based approach to reduce crime by addressing the underlying causes of crime and recidivism;
- the implementation of alternatives to imprisonment where appropriate, including restorative justice, diversionary programs and justice reinvestment strategies;
- action to address the continued overrepresentation of Aboriginal and Torres Strait Islander Peoples in the justice system.[47]

As others have repeatedly argued,[48] we also need a sensible media. Again, we are quite lucky in the ACT, which, for the most part, has well-informed journalists willing to listen to evidence, and generally more willing to inform than inflame. It is refreshing to see stories where the facts are allowed to speak for themselves.[49] Other media outlets need to do this, too.

Sarre has called on the public to 'challenge populism, and to tell governments that they *can* build long term social investment into criminal justice policy-making without risking electoral backlash'.[50] For this to occur, we need to communicate honestly and effectively with the public. We need to get people to understand that prison is not a particularly effective crime reduction tool. People also need to understand that crime is decreasing, and has been doing so for some time.[51] We need to ensure

---

47   Australian Greens, *Justice Policy*, greens.org.au/policies/justice (viewed 16 April 2016).

48   See, for example, Russell Hogg and David Brown, *Rethinking Law and Order* (Pluto Press, 1998); Nicholas Cowdery QC, *Getting Justice Wrong: Myths, Media and Crime* (Allen and Unwin, 2001); Sarre, above n 26.

49   See, for example, Michael Inman, 'Suspended Sentence For Shoe Store Manager Who Stole More Than $70,000', *Canberra Times*, 12 November 2015, www.canberratimes.com.au/act-news/suspended-sentence-for-shoe-store-manager-who-stole-more-than-70000-20151112-gkx06r.html; Michael Inman, 'Devout Christian Brenton Honeyman Gets Suspended Jail Sentence For Child Porn Possession', *Canberra Times*, 6 January 2016, www.canberratimes.com.au/act-news/devout-christian-gets-suspended-jail-sentence-for-child-porn-possession-20160106-gm08h1.html.

50   Sarre, above n 26, 11–12.

51   See, for example, Don Weatherburn and David Indermaur, 'Public Perceptions of Crime Trends in New South Wales and Western Australia' (Crime and Justice Bulletin No 80, BOCSAR, 2004); Brent Davis and Kym Dossetor, '(Mis)perceptions of Crime in Australia' (Trends and Issues in Crime and Criminal Justice No 396, Australian Institute of Criminology, 2010).

the public is well-informed. Research from both Australia[52] and overseas[53] demonstrates that the more educated people are about crime, the less punitive they become. In addition, a national Australian study[54] found that there were equal levels of satisfaction about sentencing across the country, even though we obviously have widely disparate sentencing patterns. Given people are not likely to become any more satisfied with sentencing if we increase penalties, we might as well cut them. They are certainly not likely to be any less pleased with the outcome.

What about the victims? Research[55] indicates that victims are no more punitive than others. Nevertheless, the media are often keen to sell the story that supposedly lenient penalties disadvantage victims.[56] Again, the ACT provides something of an unusual case study, with a Victims of Crime Commissioner, John Hinchey, who readily acknowledges the crime prevention role of a range of strategies. For example, in the context of recent debate on one-punch assaults in the ACT, he pointed to the need for increased police powers and 'reforms aimed at promoting long-term cultural change related to alcohol consumption, acceptability of violence and substance misuse'.[57] He is to be commended for recognising that we can't imprison our way out of crime, and it is of no benefit to victims to attempt to do so.

Victims – including the many offenders who are themselves victims[58] – have legitimate physical, financial, emotional and psychological needs, and we need to attend to them. But tougher sentencing isn't the answer.

---

52   Kate Warner et al, 'Public Judgement on Sentencing: Final Results from the Tasmanian Jury Sentencing Study' (Trends and Issues in Crime and Criminal Justice No 407, Australian Institute of Criminology, 2011).

53   See, for example, Tony Doob and Julian Roberts, *An Analysis of the Public's View of Sentencing: A Report to the Department of Justice, Canada* (1983). See also Karen Gelb, *More Myths and Misconceptions* (Victorian Sentencing Advisory Council, 2008) for an overview.

54   Lynne Roberts et al, 'A Country Not Divided: A Comparison of Public Punitiveness and Confidence in Sentencing across Australia (2011) 44 *Australian and New Zealand Journal of Criminology* 370.

55   Gelb, above n 53.

56   See, for example, Lisa Morrison, 'Twenty-year Domestic Violence Victim Attacks "Lenient" Sentence for Ex-Partner', *The West Australian*, 31 July 2015, au.news.yahoo.com/thewest/regional/great-southern/a/29150713/twenty-year-domestic-violence-victim-attacks-lenient-sentence-for-ex-partner/.

57   Megan Gorrey and Alexandra Back, 'Man Charged Over Alleged One-punch Attack in Civic', *Canberra Times*, 8 January 2016, www.canberratimes.com.au/act-news/canberra-victim-of-new-years-onepunch-attack-in-civic-surprised-hes-alive-20160108-gm1x8e.html.

58   Russell Marks, 'Taking Victims Seriously', *The Monthly*, 14 March 2015, www.themonthly.com.au/blog/russell-marks/2015/14/2015/1426288245/taking-victims-seriously.

In fact, saving money on prisons will enable us to reallocate resources towards things that will help victims, such as counselling and financial support. If we cut our imprisonment rate in half, we'll have an extra $1.7 billion per year to support victims, with money left over for a range of effective crime prevention measures.[59]

IV. Conclusion

This chapter has argued that the challenge to which our criminal laws and our legal system more generally must be geared is curbing our addiction to prison. One means of doing so would be significant review of our sentencing laws; for example, the use of mandatory sentences.[60] However, the issue is much broader and deeper than this. From now on, every time a proposal is put forward, policymakers, politicians, the media and members of the public should have to ask themselves and each other one simple question: 'Will this proposal drive the prison population up or down?' It is conceded that it may at times be difficult to determine the ultimate impact of particular law reforms. There may also be good reasons for creating new offences; for example, where there is an identified gap, especially in the context of technological developments. However, it should equally be noted that there is a tendency to legislate in circumstances where there is a perceived gap, but existing laws could be used instead and the new offence may end up being only rarely prosecuted.[61] In light of the far-reaching implications of policy in a range of portfolios outside of the criminal justice system and the inefficiency and ineffectiveness of current

---

59   It is beyond the scope of this chapter to explore the concept of justice reinvestment in detail, but this seeks to allocate money that would have been spent on prisons on community-based initiatives that seek to address the causes of crime. For discussion, see, for example, Senate Standing Committee on Legal and Constitutional Affairs, *Value of a Justice Reinvestment Approach to Criminal Justice in Australia* (Commonwealth of Australia, 2013); Sarah Hopkins, 'Justice Reinvestment Saves Huge Costs of Law-and-Order Auctions', *The Conversation*, 20 October 2014, theconversation.com/justice-reinvestment-saves-huge-costs-of-law-and-order-auctions-33018. A pilot project is currently underway in Cowra, NSW: 'Justice Reinvestment Program Reaches New Milestone', *Cowra Guardian*, 8 January 2016, www.cowraguardian.com.au/story/3649006/justice-reinvestment-program-reaches-new-milestone/?cs=593. The ACT Government has also committed to 'the development of a whole of government justice reinvestment approach aimed at reducing recidivism and diverting offenders, and those at risk of becoming offenders, from the justice system': ACT Justice and Community Safety Directorate, *Justice Reinvestment Strategy* (2015). The author is a member of the advisory group for this strategy.

60   For discussion, see, for example, Lorana Bartels and Rick Sarre, 'Law Reform Targeting Crime and Disorder', in Rick Sarre and Antje Deckert (eds), *Australian and New Zealand Handbook of Criminology, Crime and Justice* (Palgrave, forthcoming).

61   For discussion, see Arlie Loughnan, 'Drink Spiking and Rock Throwing: The Creation and Construction of Criminal Offences in the Current Era' (2010) 35 *Alternative Law Journal* 18.

practices, it is further argued that this approach should apply not only to criminal justice, but *all* relevant policy; for example, housing, education, health and transport. If the answer is likely to be 'up', then that should be the end of that initiative.

For the reasons also set out above, particular scrutiny should be required as to the potential impact of any policy on Indigenous people. In addition, ongoing consultation and collaboration with Indigenous stakeholders is required to reduce the shameful rates of overrepresentation in our prisons.[62] Opposition Leader Bill Shorten has committed to reinstating a justice target to achieve this,[63] while the federal government has described such an approach as 'foolish', arguing that it had 'no control' over justice policy.[64] The Red Cross[65] recently recommended that *all* Australian governments commit to reducing Indigenous imprisonment rates by 50 per cent over the next five years. This recommendation is sensible, given the overrepresentation of Indigenous people in the criminal justice system in all Australian jurisdictions, and the practical and normative impact of federal policy on state and territory criminal justice practices. The current inquiry by the Australian Law Reform Commission on the incarceration rates of Indigenous peoples[66] may provide some impetus for change in this regard.

Even if a proposal appears to pass muster, the inquiry must not end there. Resources need to be allocated to ensure the initiative is independently evaluated for its outcomes, to determine whether it has actually had the desired results. If not, it must be determined why not and, in due course, that approach should also be abandoned in favour of one with a more

---

62   See, for example, Michael Gordon, 'Patrick Dodson Makes Impassioned Plea for "a Smarter Form of Justice"', *The Sydney Morning Herald*, 13 April 2016, www.smh.com.au/federal-politics/political-news/patrick-dodson-makes-emotional-plea-for-action-on-aboriginal-incarceration-20160413-go52vi.html.

63   Anna Henderson, 'Bill Shorten Pledges to End "National Shame" By Reviving Indigenous Imprisonment Reduction Targets', *ABC News*, 19 November 2015, www.abc.net.au/news/2015-11-19/labor-pledges-to-revive-indigenous-justice-targets/6953032.

64   Calla Wahlquist, 'Nigel Scullion Scoffs at Proposed National Target on Indigenous Jail Rates', *The Guardian*, 12 February 2016, www.theguardian.com/australia-news/2016/feb/12/nigel-scullion-scoffs-at-proposed-national-target-on-indigenous-jail-rates.

65   Australian Red Cross, *Vulnerability Report 2016: Rethinking Justice* (2016), www.redcross.org.au/files/VulnerabilityReport2016.pdf.

66   Australian Law Reform Commission, *Incarceration Rates of Aboriginal and Torres Strait Islander Peoples*, www.alrc.gov.au/inquiries/indigenous-incarceration. Australian Law Reform Commission, *Incarceration Rates of Aboriginal and Torres Strait Islander Peoples*, Discussion Paper No 84 (2017).

beneficial outcome. A genuine commitment to evidence-based practice is paramount in this endeavour, and all stakeholders must have the courage to constantly reevaluate their preconceptions about 'what works'.

Others have likewise made this clarion call. Bagaric has called on Australian governments to 'develop a strategy to reduce incarceration numbers to about 100 per 100,000'.[67] Weatherburn recently pressed the case for a 'complete overhaul of the way crime and imprisonment is addressed in NSW'.[68] As noted above, the Red Cross has called for a 50 per cent reduction in Indigenous imprisonment rates over the next five years. In addition, it recommended a 10 per cent reduction in overall imprisonment rates over this timeframe.[69]

Adopting this approach would clearly require a fundamental shift. It would require the courage to abandon decades of tough on crime rhetoric. Political parties would no longer be able to criticise each other for being soft on crime, although being 'stupid' on crime would perhaps become a greater political risk. Over a decade ago, Weatherburn suggested that many politicians 'would welcome an opportunity to stop beating the law and order drum, if one were provided that did not come at too high a political price'.[70] Politicians who dare to speak the truth should not have to risk their political careers as Greg Smith did.[71]

Fortunately, we have a model of what law-making might look like if there were the political will to adopt this approach. Sarre[72] helpfully prepared the following hypothetical transcript:

> THE PREMIER: Thank you Mr Speaker. I rise to announce a new goal that this government intends to meet in the next twelve months, that is, to reduce the imprisonment rate by 20 per cent ... We do this because we recognise that higher rates of imprisonment have not made any difference to rates of violent crime over the last decade. We note the

---

67 Bagaric, above n 33.
68 Rachel Olding, 'BOCSAR Crime Stats Boss Don Weatherburn Calls for Lighter Prison Sentences', *The Sydney Morning Herald*, 17 February 2016, www.smh.com.au/nsw/weatherburn-comes-out-swinging-20160216-gmvavn.html.
69 Australian Red Cross, above n 65. Somewhat remarkably, the Federal Justice Minister, Michael Keenan, responded to the Red Cross report by asserting that '[t]he idea that locking up bad people doesn't work is not true. It does, we know that for a fact': Sam Tomlin, 'Locking Bad People Up "Works": Minister for Justice Rejects Calls for Prison Overhaul', *ABC News*, 31 March 2016, www.abc.net.au/news/2016-03-31/federal-justice-minister-rejects-prison-criticism/7289038.
70 Don Weatherburn, *Law and Order in Australia: Rhetoric and Reality* (Federation Press, 2004) 47.
71 For comment, see Brown (2014) and Brown (2015), above n 42.
72 Sarre, above n 26, 1.

wildly disproportionate way in which Indigenous Australians are over-represented ... in prison in this state, and the drain on state resources ... We plan to make these reductions on the basis of the research evidence ...

THE SPEAKER: I recognise the Honourable the Leader of the Opposition.

THE LEADER OF THE OPPOSITION: Thank you Mr Speaker. I applaud the Premier's zeal on this matter but I argue that he is setting his sights far too low. The electorate deserves better than that. If elected, our party will drop imprisonment rates even further, to 50 per cent ... We also plan to spend the money we save on custodial corrections on victim support services. The evidence, I might add, points to victims being far less vindictive than we might otherwise assume. Finally, we will also commission more research into the evaluation of existing and new initiatives to ensure that we get the best outcomes for the dollars we spend.

Hopefully, it is not too far-fetched to dream that we might one day see this in an Australian parliament.

10

Is Criminal Law Reform a Lost Cause?

Simon Bronitt[1]

I. Introduction: The Agendas of Criminal Law Reform in the 1990s

In the 1990s, criminal law reform in Australia, as in the United Kingdom, was foremost a technical exercise in rationalising legal doctrine (found in common law and statutes) in order to resolve ambiguity and modernise the law.[2] More progressively, law reform commissions, in ongoing partnership with the legal academy, set about devising new templates for the criminal law founded on codification. In the United Kingdom, this work by The Law Commission resulted in the Draft Criminal Code for England and Wales in 1989.[3] In Australia, criminal law reform followed a similar path, beginning with a review of federal criminal law in 1989, subsequently spawning a program of national harmonisation in the Model Criminal Code (MCC) project, and the enactment of *Criminal Code Act 1995* (Cth).

---

1   TC Beirne School of Law, University of Queensland. I would like to thank Michael Potts and Zoe Brereton for research assistance.

2   Under its parent Act, The Law Commission (England and Wales) was tasked with keeping the law under review 'with a view to its systematic development and reform, including in particular the codification of law': *Law Commissions Act 1965* (UK) c 22, s 3.

3   The Law Commission, *A Criminal Code for England and Wales*, Consultation Paper No 177 (1989) Vols 1 and 2.

The reform programs in the United Kingdom and Australia adhered to similar formats. The normative resources for criminal law reform were limited to a narrow set of guiding principles promoting the liberal values of certainty, coherence, and fairness. Little, if any, thought was given to the criminal law as a tool of public policy or regulation, or even how criminal laws operated *in practice*; namely, how legal definitions, defences or rules of evidence and procedure were mediated, and sometimes even subverted, by police culture, prosecutorial and trial practice, or jury directions. Empirical perspectives on the operation of the law were gleaned only incidentally through the public submission processes, which solicited 'real world' experiences from professional experts and interest groups.

Institutional law reform in the 1990s, reflecting the professional backgrounds and skills of the judges and legal academics involved, tended to focus narrowly on 'lawyers' law', disregarding broader issues of empiricism which had animated the legal realism and sociolegal studies movement a century earlier: the questions of why, when and how the 'law in books' diverged from the 'law in action'.[4] Without addressing such critical contextual questions, insights from social science, psychology or criminology rarely informed recommendations about the proper direction of reform. As a result, key questions related to regulatory effectiveness were rarely addressed, namely whether criminalisation would produce the aims of policymakers, or conversely result in unintended (even counterproductive) consequences.

For the purposes of institutional law reform, the guiding normative resources were based on three perspectives or sub-disciplines:

- *Comparative law*, for reflecting on progress made in similar 'advanced' common law jurisdictions;[5]
- *Legal history*, for tracing the genealogy of common law doctrine, legislative reform and learned academic writings in a particular field;[6]

---

4   A gap first identified by Roscoe Pound in his influential article, 'Law in Books and Law in Action' (1910) 44 *American Law Reports* 12.

5   In the UK, comparative research rarely ventured beyond surveys of other comparable 'developed' common law systems of Australia, Canada and New Zealand.

6   Legal history rarely ventured beyond examining formal sources of law, ignoring the wider sociocultural, political and economic influences shaping legal development. Cf A Norrie, *Crime, Reason and History: A Critical Introduction to Criminal Law* (Cambridge University Press, 2nd edn, 2001); L Farmer, *Criminal Law, Tradition and Legal Order* (Cambridge University Press, 1997).

- *Legal theory*, for invoking philosophical ideas, values and principles (with primacy accorded to liberal values) to underpin or undermine specific reform proposals.[7]

This failure to engage with external, contextual perspectives on the criminal law – to move beyond what Nicola Lacey has termed the 'immanent' or internal critiques of legal doctrine[8] – severely limited the capacity of law reform commissions to drive significant legal change.[9]

There are some notable exceptions where law reform inquiries did venture beyond its disciplinary boundaries. For example, in its review of homicide law, The Law Commission of England and Wales funded an empirical study investigating public opinion relating to homicide severity. This groundbreaking research revealed the extent to which moral intuitions about offence seriousness in the general public did not always match the view of criminal law theorists, or indeed law reformers, especially in relation to felony murder.[10] But fundamentally, criminal law reform remained a liberal enterprise, a technical job for legal scholars and academically-minded judges committed to rationalising, simplifying and modernising the tangled mess of common law and ad hoc statutes.

In his millennial essay, the distinguished legal scholar Professor Andrew Ashworth posed the question whether 'criminal law is a lost cause'.[11] His conclusion then, as now, is that the quest for a more principled criminal law, one achieving better conformity between principles and legal doctrine, has proven highly elusive. Ashworth's assessment would equally apply to Australia, and to the impact of law reform. But this essay poses the question in a different form – whether criminal law *reform* is a lost cause – and, more significantly, draws different conclusions. The essay asks whether the 'liberal promise' of a more principled and codified criminal law should be exhaustive of our aspirations for criminal law reform.

---

7   See, for example, The Law Commission, *Consent in the Criminal Law: A Consultation Paper*, Consultation Paper No 139 (1995), app C.

8   N Lacey, 'Legal Constructions of Crime', in M Maguire, R Morgan and R Reiner (eds), *The Oxford Handbook of Criminology* (Oxford University Press, 4th edn, 2007) 192.

9   See discussion in S Bronitt and McSherry, *Principles of Criminal Law* (Lawbook Co, 4th edn, 2017), [1.185]ff.

10   B Mitchell, 'Public Perceptions of Homicide and Criminal Justice' (1998) 38(3) *British Journal of Criminology* 453, 459; see also B Mitchell, 'Further Evidence of the Relationship between Legal and Public Opinion on the Law of Homicide' [2000] *Criminal Law Review* 814.

11   A Ashworth, 'Is the Criminal Law a Lost Cause?' (2000) 116 *Law Quarterly Review* 225, 232.

Part II provides a reflection on the impact of institutional law reform over the past quarter-century upon the criminal law in Australia, assessing the reasons for the prevailing 'parochial codiphobia' which resists codification, uniformity or even harmonisation at the national level.[12] Freed from the present obsession with general principles and codification,[13] criminal law reform needs to be *re*-formed, drawing upon a broader array of resources – disciplinary and methodological as well as financial – than are typically available to existing institutional law reform bodies. Part III provides an overview of the ad hoc bodies also engaged in law reform, examining the reform agenda of the current Royal Commission into Institutional Child Sexual Abuse. The essay assesses whether these new agents of law reform, although not without limitations, are better positioned to tackle reform in a more systemic, holistic and contextual manner, harnessing relevant disciplinary and empirical knowledge to produce better policy outcomes.

II. Model Criminal Laws and the False Promise of Codification?

As noted above, the approach to criminal law reform in Australia in the 1980s and 1990s was not dissimilar to that in the United Kingdom, codification being the main priority in both jurisdictions. In the United Kingdom, The Law Commission, assisted by a 'Dream Team' of leading criminal law scholars,[14] was tasked to prepare a draft Criminal Code for England and Wales. Contemporaneously in Australia, the federal Attorney-General commissioned former High Court Justice Sir Harry Gibbs to lead the Review of Commonwealth Criminal Law, with a view to codifying its general principles.[15] While the Gibbs Review laid the foundations for the *Criminal Code Act 1995* (Cth), the proposal for codification in the United Kingdom encountered stronger opposition when published

---

12 The term 'codiphobia' was first coined in the 1850s by Professor Amos to describe the legislative hostility to codification: discussed in A Hemming, 'When Is a Code a Code?' (2010) 15(1) *Deakin Law Review* 65, fn 9. My adaptation of this neologism is offered in the spirit of Jeremy Bentham, who first coined the term 'codification'. See discussion in S Bronitt, 'Towards a Universal Theory of Criminal Law: Rethinking the Comparative and International Project' (2008) 27 *Criminal Justice Ethics* 53.

13 See L Farmer, 'The Obsession with Definition: The Nature of Crime and Critical Legal Theory' (1996) 5 *Social and Legal Studies* 57.

14 The team comprised Sir John Smith, Edward Griew and Ian Dennis: P Roberts, 'Philosophy, Feinberg, Codification, and Consent: A Progress Report on English Experiences of Criminal Law Reform' (2001) 5 *Buffalo Criminal Law Review* 173, 194.

15 H Gibbs, R Watson and A Menzies, *Review of Commonwealth Criminal Law: Final Report* (1991).

in 1989. Ultimately the draft was shelved as a legislative project, doomed to gather dust and haunt the footnotes of academic textbooks. Australia, by contrast, was more receptive to codification. This was unsurprising in light of the success of codification a century earlier, when Sir Samuel Griffith embarked on the modernisation of Queensland's criminal law that led to the passage of the highly influential *Criminal Code 1899* (Qld).[16]

Building on the momentum following the completion of the Gibbs Review in 1988, the Standing Committee of Attorneys-General (SCAG) established an intergovernmental Model Criminal Code Officers Committee (MCCOC) to draft a Model Criminal Code (MCC) for Australia. The lack of uniformity in Australia's criminal law in the late 1980s became a focus of concern of these senior officials working in the Attorneys-Generals' Departments of the Commonwealth, states and territories. Extending the federal ambition for codification of general principles to a national level was never going to be easy. The selling point for the MCC was framed in terms of traditional liberal rationale for codification: as one member of the MCCOC noted, codification would make the criminal law 'easy to discover, easy to understand, cheap to buy, and democratically made and amended'.[17]

Implementation, however, has proved to be a stumbling block, with selective and piecemeal uptake of the MCC.[18] Even regarding the Commonwealth, Australian Capital Territory and Northern Territory, the degree of uniformity achieved has been partial and approximate, focused primarily on implementation of the 'general part' of the MCC dealing with principles of responsibility. Notwithstanding the significant time, effort and costs devoted to the MCC project,[19] as one commentator noted, 'the political impetus to advance the unification of criminal law through a common code appears to have waned for the time being, and a profound divide between the two major worlds – the Griffith-based codes and the "common law states" – remains'.[20]

---

16 See R S O'Regan, 'Sir Samuel Griffith's Criminal Code' (1991) 7(2) *Australian Bar Review* 141 and D Wells, '"The Griffith Code" – Then and Now' (1994) 3(2) *Griffith Law Review* 205.

17 M Goode, 'Codification of the Australian Criminal Law' (1992) 16 *Criminal Law Journal* 5, 8.

18 Ibid. 226, 234.

19 M Goode, 'Constructing Criminal Law Reform and the Model Criminal Code' (2002) 26 *Criminal Law Journal* 152.

20 S Tarrant, 'Building Bridges in Australian Criminal Law: Codification and the Common Law' (2013) 39(3) *Monash University Law Review* 838, 840 (footnote omitted); see also S Bronitt and M Gani, 'Criminal Codes in the 21ˢᵗ Century: The Paradox of the Liberal Promise', in B McSherry, A Norrie and S Bronitt (eds), *Regulating Deviance: The Redirection of Criminalisation and the Futures of Criminal Law* (Hart Publishing, 2009) 235–60.

Reform of Australia's criminal law should neither be defined nor limited by the dual aims of codification and uniformity, which have proved elusive not only because of the 'code' and 'non-code' divide, but also because of the prevailing political discourse of sovereign states' rights in the field of 'law and order'. This has meant that, across many significant fields of the criminal law, law reform has occurred at variable speeds, sometimes separated by decades. For example, the 'marital rape immunity' was repealed by the New South Wales Parliament on 15 May 1981 through the enactment of the *Crimes (Sexual Assault) Amendment Act 1981* (NSW), 11 years before its repeal in South Australia by way of the *Criminal Law Consolidation (Rape) Amendment Act 1992* (SA). Similarly, the decriminalisation of same sex intercourse was first addressed by South Australia through *The Criminal Law (Sexual Offences) Amendment Act 1975* (SA), while Tasmania was the last jurisdiction to enact amending legislation in 1997.[21]

What causes 'variable speed' law reform? One cause undoubtedly relates to the fact that federal parliament does not possess plenary power vis-a-vis criminal law, only having the power to enact offences 'incidental' to other heads of power under the Constitution. Consequently, criminal law remains the primary responsibility of each state and territory, rendering it especially vulnerable to local 'law and order' politics.[22] Commonly heard claims of jurisdictional uniqueness, especially at election time, undoubtedly impede national consensus about the necessity, direction and pace of law reform. While in other fields 'cooperative federalism' has operated to forge national consensus and policy convergence between jurisdictions, a condition of 'uncooperative federalism' has prevailed.

Having identified the structural limitations facing institutional criminal law reform at national and local levels, I turn in Part III to whether ad hoc public inquiries – such as Royal Commissions – would be better equipped for this purpose.

---

21   *Criminal Code Amendment Act 1997* (Tas).
22   R Hogg and D Brown, *Rethinking Law and Order* (Pluto Press, 1998), Ch 1; see also D Weatherburn, *Law and Order in Australia: Rhetoric and Reality* (Federation Press, 2004).

III. Ad Hoc Law Reform: Royal Commissions and Other Public Inquiries

The Australian Law Reform Commission undertook an inquiry into the roles and functions of Royal Commissions and other public inquiries in 2009.[23] While the use of ad hoc public inquiries is longstanding, their purposes have changed over time. In the 19th century, for example, various criminal law commissions were established in the United Kingdom and its colonies to consider reform. Heavily influenced by Benthamite ideals,[24] ad hoc commissions can be viewed as the embodiment of liberal modernity, aspiring to rationalise, consolidate, and, where possible, codify the tangled mess of common law and statutory modifications.

The advent of more investigative Royal Commissions in the 20th century had little in common with these earlier commissions. Beyond exercising wide inquisitorial fact-finding powers, these bodies were empowered to make recommendations for reform. Royal Commissions, however, have a somewhat mixed track-record in term of law reform. For example, the Royal Commission into Aboriginal Deaths in Custody (1987–1991) placed a spotlight on the issue, and developed an ambitious program of national reform, though implementation over the subsequent decades has been painfully slow.[25] More recently, the Royal Commission into Institutional Child Sexual Abuse (2013–present) has been highly successful in drawing attention to historic and ongoing abuse within institutional settings, with an investigative function matched by a significant agenda of national policy development and law reform.[26] The merits of ad hoc commissions are that they are constituted for a *specific* purpose, undertake extensive fact-finding, garner expertise from wherever it exists, and demand more public and political attention than standing law reform bodies, which in the field of criminal law tend to generate reports that sit on shelves gathering dust.

---

23   Australian Law Reform Commission, *Making Inquiries – A New Statutory Framework*, Report No 111 (2009).

24   See W Holdsworth, *A History of English Law* (Sweet & Maxwell, 7th edn, 1971) Vol 13, 272.

25   See T Sansbury, 'State and Territory Implementation of the Recommendations of the Royal Commission' (2001) 5(8) *Indigenous Law Bulletin* 6.

26   See Royal Commission into Institutional Responses to Child Sexual Abuse, *Terms of Reference* (13 November 2014), www.childabuseroyalcommission.gov.au/about-us/terms-of-reference.

A strong contrary view has been put forward by the distinguished judge and jurist, Ron Sackville. Reviewing the relative merits of standing law reform bodies over ad hoc commissions or inquiries, Sackville pointed to the high degree of functional overlap, since both bodies: invite or seek input on policy through public consultation; maintain a degree of independence from the executive; confer democratic legitimacy since both are constituted by statute, and recommendations, if implemented, are done so by an elected parliament;[27] and receive terms of reference from the executive, ensuring accountability to government.[28] According to Sackville, the key difference between these two bodies relates to longevity: Royal Commissions are ad hoc and time-limited processes, while law reform bodies are permanent.[29] The former are not dominated by lawyers, and often frequently inquire into areas that would not be viewed as within the remit of law reform, even in its broadest sense. Citing the Fitzgerald Inquiry (1987–1989) as an example, Sackville concluded that far-reaching reform in electoral matters and governmental transparency in Queensland would probably never have been addressed by a law reform agency. That said, he concluded the differences may not be as great as they first appear, with significant overlap in terms of the range of matters reviewed and recommendations made.[30]

From a systemic perspective, Sackville concluded this functional overlap was duplicative and wasteful. Also, many of the issues tackled were ongoing, leading some ad hoc commissions to call for the establishment of standing bodies to govern the subject matter into which they are inquiring. Sackville concluded that standing law reform agencies, given their relative low cost and specialisation in undertaking inquiries, should assume (at least in part) the law reform functions of Royal Commissions.[31]

I do not share Sackville's assessment of comparative advantage for the following reasons. First, in terms of 'value for money', law reform agencies look much less impressive when implementation records are compared. Secondly, Sackville's view of enhanced 'specialisation' within

---

27   R Sackville, 'Law Reform Agencies and Royal Commissions: Toiling in the Same Field?' in B Opeskin and D Weisbrot (eds), *The Promise of Law Reform* (Federation Press, 2005) 274, 281.
28   This makes the timing and tailoring of such inquiries inherently political and vulnerable to misuse: ibid. 284.
29   That said, Royal Commissions often examine matters not initially contemplated by the governments that established them: ibid. 281.
30   Ibid. 283.
31   For a similar viewpoint, see D Weisbrot, 'The Future for Institutional Law Reform', in B Opeskin and D Weisbrot (eds), *The Promise of Law Reform* (Federation Press, 2005) 18, 22.

standing law reform agencies is restricted to legal knowledge and research methods, overlooking broader interdisciplinary capabilities and resources potentially available to ad hoc bodies. Regarding the latter, ad hoc commissions are better placed to harness and coordinate a wider diversity of expertise and inputs into the policy change and law reform processes, and to approach the 'problem' in a more systemic, holistic and contextual manner. Importantly, ad hoc bodies are not limited to recommending *legal* solutions, but can examine a much wider range of policy options including, but not limited to, law reform. Another advantage is that the ad hoc model tends to attract more public and political attention than the work of standing agencies, which, though independent from government, receive less attention when their reports are released. Even with the advent of executive summaries and media releases, a technical law reform commission final report on the law of complicity, for example, is unlikely to attract much interest beyond a small group of practitioners, judges and academics. Finally, like a jury, which commands great power for only a brief moment in time, the ad hoc body may achieve a higher degree of practical independence than a standing body, whose organisational culture and independence may ultimately be negatively affected by governmental clientelism and budgetary insecurity.[32]

IV. Conclusion

For much of the past two decades, criminal law reform has focused on the dual related agendas of codification and harmonisation, though the realisation of the liberal promise for the criminal law has been hampered by 'parochial codiphobia' and an 'uncivil' politics of law and order. As a consequence, many carefully researched and considered recommendations of standing law reform bodies remain unimplemented. The precise extent of this 'implementation deficit' is unknown, which is surprising in the modern era of new public management with its emphasis on impact and performance measurement in the public sector.

---

32   The erosion of funding and government support for institutional law reform is outlined in a Submission by former ALRC President, David Weisbrot, to the Senate Legal and Constitutional Committee, 28 January 2011: www.aph.gov.au/Parliamentary_Business/Committees/Senate/Legal_ and_Constitutional_Affairs/Completed_inquiries/2010-13/lawreformcommission/submissions.

Perhaps it is time to return to investigate more fully the relationship between ad hoc and standing law reform bodies, and how the beneficial aspects these various bodies and processes can be harnessed and better coordinated. In my view, the benchmark for 'good' or 'better' criminal law reform should be the same that applies to public policy generally: is reform based on the best available evidence, and informed by expert opinion? Expertise in this context should not be limited to the judiciary, profession and legal academy. My contextual approach to reform requires a stronger commitment to empiricism, but also proactive engagement with the wider community. This will provide a better understanding of the complexity of the problem, as well as enhance the legitimacy of the reform process. The ad hoc model ultimately favoured in this essay does carry some risk of increased cost, delay and political misuse – though in this respect, the model is no different from those risks associated with the current 'mixed' system.

11

Rethinking Rape Law Reform: Challenges and Possibilities

Wendy Larcombe[1]

I. Rape Law Reform

Having been involved with rape law reform in different roles and capacities over the past 25 years, it is disappointing to be arguing that the main challenge to be addressed in this field of law in the future is the same as it was 25 and more years ago. That challenge is: the legal system, and in particular the criminal justice system, must better support the justice needs of sexual violence survivors.

I want to make this argument with some care because Australian jurisdictions have now experienced more than 40 years of rape law reforms intended to:

- redress gender bias in the criminal law's definition of and response to rape;
- make the law more reflective of the 'reality' of sexual violence – who perpetrates it, against whom, in what circumstances and contexts; and
- improve the experience for complainants participating in criminal prosecutions.

---

1   Associate Professor, Law School, University of Melbourne.

Those legislative reforms – to the substantive criminal law, to evidence law and court procedures – have been driven by the immense determination and intelligence of feminist activists and victim/survivor advocates. Every change has been hard-fought and hard-won.

And much has been achieved. As a feminist and queer scholar, I view it as a significant achievement that rape and other forms of sexual offending against male, trans and intersex people are now recognised, while only non-consensual (and not consensual) sexual activity within lesbian, gay, bisexual and queer communities is now prosecuted. Prior to the statutory reforms of recent decades this was not the case.

It is also highly significant that there is no longer legal immunity for husbands who rape their wives. Although the High Court told us in 2012 that there was no such immunity under the common law in Australia during the 20th century,[2] as no one had known that that was the case, the legislative reforms to criminalise rape in marriage from the mid-1980s onward were critically important.

Other significant advances include:

- that complainants can no longer be routinely cross-examined about their general sexual history;

- that a rape complaint is no longer disqualified if the victim/survivor cannot be sure whether it was a penis or a finger or an object that was inserted into their vagina or anus;

- that judges can no longer give routine warnings about the unreliability of the evidence that women and children provide in sexual matters and, hence, the need for corroboration;

- the development of affirmative, statutory definitions of consent as 'free agreement' and codification of circumstances that preclude consent;

- restrictions on the defence use of a complainant's confidential counselling records;

- provisions for vulnerable witnesses to give evidence remotely and/or have a support person sit with them; and

---

2   *PGA v The Queen* [2012] 245 CLR 355. See Wendy Larcombe and Mary Heath, 'Developing the Common Law and Rewriting the History of Rape in Marriage in Australia: PGA v The Queen' (2012) 34 *Sydney Law Review* 785.

- specialist police units and specialist court lists for sexual offences in which investigators, judges, prosecutors and court personnel have undertaken training in the needs and experiences of sexual violence victims/survivors.

The list of positive reforms goes on. *Much has been achieved.* Yet, frustratingly, the primary challenge for law reform remains the same. To better support the justice needs of sexual violence survivors, two core problems must be addressed.

A. Problem 1: The criminal justice system does not provide an accessible, effective resolution to sexual offending for the vast majority of victims/survivors

The Australian Bureau of Statistics[3] reports that 17 per cent of women and 4 per cent of men have experienced sexual assault since the age of 15 years. In addition, 12 per cent of women and 4.5 per cent of men experienced sexual assault before the age of 15 years. It is estimated that fewer than one in five sexual assaults is reported to the police and that figure has not increased in response to reforms.[4] Of those reported assaults, fewer than one in five will be prosecuted and approximately 10–15 per cent will register a conviction on any charge. This means that the overall conviction rate for sexual assaults in Australia is less than 5 per cent and, in some jurisdictions, less than 1 per cent.

Paradoxically, conviction rates for rape have fallen across the 40 years of feminist-inspired law reform. The (widely known) low conviction rate now contributes to low reporting. It also confirms the public perception that rape survivors are treated poorly and their claims not taken seriously

---

3   Australian Bureau of Statistics (ABS) (2012). *Personal Safety Survey: 4906.0* (Canberra: Australian Bureau of Statistics).
4   Statistics on rape case attrition are reviewed at length in Wendy Larcombe, 'Sex Offender Risk Assessment: The Need to Place Recidivism Research in the Context of Attrition in the Criminal Justice System' (2012) 18(4) *Violence Against Women* 482; W Larcombe, 'Falling Rape Conviction Rates: (Some) Feminist Aims and Measures for Rape Law' (2011) 19(1) *Feminist Legal Studies* 27; Kathleen Daly and Brigitte Bouhours, 'Rape and Attrition in the Legal Process: A Comparative Analysis of Five Countries', in M Tonry (ed), *Crime and Justice: An Annual Review of Research* (University of Chicago Press, 2010) Vol 39, 485–565.

in the criminal justice process.[5] As a result, more than 80 per cent of people who experience sexual violence do not engage with the criminal justice system.

B. Problem 2: Those convictions that are secured for sexual assault are unrepresentative of the most common forms of sexual violence experienced by women and children

Most sexual assaults are committed against women and children by known male family members, friends or acquaintances, in private homes, and in circumstances where force or violence are not necessary to effect the assault. In many instances, women and children are subjected to repeated offences by the same offender.[6] ABS and police data show that young women aged 16 to 24, Indigenous and Torres Strait Islander women, and people with cognitive impairments or intellectual disabilities are particularly vulnerable to sexual assault. It is this offending that victim advocates and feminist reformers have wanted recognised and criminalised through legislative amendments. That is why the focus has been on removing requirements for force and resistance, abolishing spousal immunity, and requiring free and voluntary consent (from a person who has the capacity at the time to provide such consent).

However, if we look at the outcomes of criminal prosecutions, rather than the statutory provisions, it is evident that the criminal justice process continues to reproduce what Susan Estrich called the 'real rape' stereotype.[7] The cases that secure, and those that fail to secure, criminal convictions tell us that it is still very difficult to successfully prosecute rape or sexual assault when:

- the offender is a current or former intimate partner;
- no weapon or threats of physical violence were used;
- the victim did not sustain physical injury;

---

5   See especially Denise Lievore, *Non-reporting and Hidden Recording of Sexual Assault: An International Literature Review* (Australian Institute of Criminology for the Commonwealth Office of the Status of Women, 2003); Haley Clark, 'What is the Justice System Willing to Offer?': Understanding Sexual Assault Victim/Survivors' Criminal Justice Needs', *Family Matters* No 85 (Australian Institute of Family Studies, 2010).

6   ABS, above n 3; Lievore, above n 5.

7   Susan Estrich, *Real Rape* (Harvard University Press, 1987).

- the victim did not resist or protest;
- the victim was heavily intoxicated (by drugs or alcohol) but not unconscious;
- the victim has a history of mental health difficulties, has previously experienced or reported sexual assault, or has a criminal conviction.

In short, the stereotype of 'real rape' continues to disqualify the majority of women and many members of highly vulnerable groups who experience sexual assault from securing legal redress. Victims/survivors with particular attributes and capacities are still preferred in the criminal justice process.[8] Just as problematic, rape case attrition is highly skewed in favour of prosecuting a small class of offenders. As I've argued elsewhere, those convicted of sex offences are not representative of those who commit sex offences, nor are they always representative of those who pose the most 'danger' to women and children.[9]

A distorted idea of the sex offender who merits criminal punishment has only been exacerbated in recent years by (non-feminist) criminal law reform that has introduced measures such as post-sentence detention, ongoing supervision and registration of 'serious' sex offenders. These provisions perpetuate (false) beliefs that sexual offenders are a small group of deviant psychopaths, with unique characteristics who pose a distinct risk to the community. This 'myth' undermines attempts to criminalise commonplace sexual offending.

In sum, the criminal law, in practice, is not providing an effective, accessible justice option for victims/survivors and, by not being able to prosecute the most common forms of sexual offending practised in the community, it is actively contributing to the minimisation and normalisation of such violence, while reproducing a distorted idea of 'real rape' and deviant 'sexual offenders'.

---

8   Wendy Larcombe, 'The Ideal Victim v Successful Rape Complainants: Not What You Might Expect' (2002) 10(2) *Feminist Legal Studies* 131.
9   Larcombe, 'Sex Offender Risk Assessment', above n 4.

II. What Should the Legal and Policy Responses Be, and Why?

The following three proposals are my priorities for further law reform. Note that these are in the 'blue sky' domain of what is needed, not necessarily the domain of 'what is immediately feasible', or 'politically realistic'.

A. Proposal 1: Judge-alone trials

In line with practice in Canada, and with calls from commentators and service providers in New Zealand and England and Wales, I would advocate that *trials for sexual offences should be heard by judge alone*. I know this proposal will be contentious, but I believe that removing the jury is the single measure most likely to improve criminal prosecutions and outcomes for sexual offences. More particularly, I believe it is a necessary step for rebuilding victims/survivors' confidence in the criminal justice system, and ensuring convictions in 'ordinary' cases of sexual offending.

The jury is currently perceived by various stakeholders as the 'weakest link' in the criminal prosecution of sexual offences.[10] Much of the attrition that marks sexual cases in the criminal process is attributable to the fact that decision-makers at each stage anticipate (correctly) that at least some jurors on any panel will endorse so-called 'rape myths' and 'victim-blaming attitudes'. Such beliefs and attitudes are known to be widely held *and* to predetermine interpretations of evidence and fact-finding in rape cases. This is why we have already created specialised courts (or court lists) for sexual offences in which judges, prosecutors and other court personnel have received training in the distinct features and diverse forms of sexual offending. The average person simply does not have a sound understanding of when or how sexual offending occurs, how it is effected by perpetrators, and how survivors may respond. This makes sexual offending ill-suited to jury determination.

A range of measures have been developed or proposed in recent years to try to educate criminal juries about sexual assault and to correct common misconceptions. Why is jury education not preferable to judge-only trials? First, we cannot know whether jury education works to remediate

---

10 Wendy Larcombe et al, "'I Think It's Rape and I Think He Would Be Found Not Guilty': Focus Group Perceptions of (un)Reasonable Belief in Consent in Rape Law' (2016) 25(5) *Social & Legal Studies* 611–629.

misconceptions and flawed decision-making (decision-making based on false assumptions and stereotypes). We cannot eavesdrop on jury deliberations and the verdict does not reveal the reasoning. In any event, jury education cannot be done efficiently. If an expert has to be sworn in for every sexual offence trial in the county or district courts, experts will be spending most of their time in court speaking to juries about sexual offending. It is simply more efficient to educate the judiciary and allow them to determine the questions of fact as well as those of law.

Other potential benefits of judge-alone trials discussed in the literature include that they:

- ensure decision-making based on legally relevant factors and evidence;
- mean that published reasons are available – everyone can know where or why a prosecution or defence failed (or succeeded);
- solve problems with jury understanding of the proper uses (and limitations) of tendency or context evidence, forensic evidence and expert witness testimony;
- eliminate appeals based on inadequate or inaccurate jury directions;
- may be fairer to defendants who fit negative stereotypes or who are charged with highly stigmatised offences;
- afford the court greater flexibility in management of trials;
- may enable prosecutors and defence to focus more on testing of evidence and less on jury understanding and persuasion;
- may assist to secure community and professional confidence in criminal prosecutions and outcomes – undermined currently by the expectation that criminal prosecutions will be determined by jury members' beliefs and attitudes.

Note that I do not imagine that judge-alone trials will be a silver bullet that solves all the issues that have been identified with rape trials. And I do not for a minute think that all judges, even if they have been selected and trained to sit on sexual offences lists, will have a sensitive understanding of sexual offending and survivor responses. But we would be able to identify ongoing issues and problems through the published reasons. And wrongful acquittals will be potentially correctable by an appeal court.[11] Jury education does not enable such review.

---

11 See, for example, the decision of the Court of Appeal of Alberta on an appeal against acquittal in *R v Wagar*, 2015 ABCA 327 (CanLII).

B. Proposal 2: Promote alternative justice options utilising civil law and civil society

While it is essential that the criminal justice response to sexual offending is improved, in order to offer effective forms of redress to all survivors of sexual violence, the criminal law's monopoly on sexual assault must be broken. Rape and sexual assault cannot always, and perhaps should not always, be criminally prosecuted. Depending on the context and the victim/survivor's wishes, it may be more appropriate to respond to sexual assault as a tortious wrong, or through the frameworks providing protection against sexual harassment and discrimination, or through family violence protection orders, or through family conferencing or mediation, or through 'restorative justice' conferencing – via public funded or private services.

Until relatively recently, the criminal law's monopoly on rape and sexual assault has been supported by feminist efforts to ensure that sexual violence is formally treated as criminal conduct, not merely as 'bad' or 'unwanted sex'. However, the rise and rise of 'tough on crime' politics and, with it, the increasing stigma associated with sexual offending have changed the politics of this field. Those changes have not been positive – especially considering that many victims/survivors do not want to bring the shame and stigma of identifying a 'sex offender' in their immediate social or family circle. As a result, 'ordinary' forms of sexual assault may now be more readily acknowledged and redressed if they are not prosecuted as a crime.

And we may do less harm to complainants in the process. Sexual assault is a violation of a person's autonomy and integrity. That injury has been compounded in traditional criminal justice processes by the victim/survivor being re-placed in a powerless position as a witness for the prosecution, often feeling that they are again being used instrumentally to advance others' interests (society's this time), while their choices and needs are disregarded or belittled. This positioning of the survivor echoes and triggers elements of the original assault, generating distress and often prolonging recovery.[12]

---

12   Clark, above n 5.

These shortcomings of 'conventional criminal' processes have led to a recent wave of interest and investment in 'innovative' and 'restorative' justice alternatives for sexual violence. It is critical that, as alternative justice processes or pathways are promoted and hopefully better coordinated, victim/survivors are given greater say about what they would like to happen, as well as information and advice about which justice pathways or options may best suit their needs. Indeed, affording the survivor some agency in decisions about processes and forms of redress will be critical to these being genuine 'alternatives' to the criminal justice response.

C. Proposal 3: A national legal response

Sexual violence is a pervasive and wicked social problem. It is not caused by, but it is not helped by, divergent legal provisions and inconsistent legal enforcement across the different Australian jurisdictions. There has been a strong degree of convergence in the criminal provisions governing sexual offences in the various Australian jurisdictions over the past 10–20 years, so the call for consistency may seem less urgent now than it was when model criminal codes were being developed in the 1990s. But there are still problems at the borders (literally) in terms of different investigation and charging practices on either side of state lines, problems for the public in understanding the different terms used to label offences in different jurisdictions, and problems in the differential treatment of offenders and victims depending on the prosecuting jurisdiction. For victims *and* offenders, a postcode lottery should not determine the services, programs and choices available.

To address similar problems in relation to family violence, the Australian Law Reform Commission[13] has called for development of 'a common interpretative framework', to be applied across relevant state, territory and Commonwealth legislation, that establishes a shared understanding of: the nature, features and dynamics of family violence; core purposes of legislative schemes; and guiding principles for equality of treatment of family violence victims, with coordinated responses administered (for all intents and purposes) through a 'single court'. Hopefully, the current pressure to integrate (or at least coordinate) family violence and sexual assault responses – which have historically been handled within civil and criminal frameworks respectively – will mean that sexual assault is also

13   ALRC, *Family Violence: A National Legal Response* (Report 114, 2010).

understood to require a consistent national response. If the justice needs of victims/survivors are to be appropriately supported, strategies, services and responses to sexual violence must be consistent and coordinated, nationally.

III. Conclusion

To ensure that the law provides and supports effective redress for sexual violence victims/survivors, law reform should:

- institute judge-alone trials for common sexual offences;
- promote civil law and civil-society 'alternatives' to criminal prosecution;
- develop a national legal response that promotes consistency in approach, and equality in treatment and service access, across the jurisdictions.

I hope it will not take another 25 years to see these proposals realised.

12

The Fraught Dichotomy between Context and Tendency Evidence in Sexual Assault Cases – Suggestions for Reform

John Anderson[1]

These distinctions [between tendency and relationship/context evidence] – somewhat fine – are productive of much uncertainty, and therefore much difficulty for trial judges. In a trial for a sexual offence, where many of these concepts may intersect, the task of a trial judge in explaining coherently the use (and non-misuse) of evidence falling within the different categories is an unenviable one, as is the task of a jury of lay persons in comprehending and faithfully applying the required directions. In my opinion, relationship evidence – including context evidence – should be seen for what it is. It is tendency evidence.[2]

---

1   Associate Professor, Newcastle Law School, University of Newcastle.
2   *Murdoch v The Queen* [2013] VSCA 272, [92]–[93] (Priest JA).

I. Background: Characterisation of Evidence as Tendency or Relationship/Context

Evidence to establish a relationship between the defendant and complainant in a trial involving allegations of sexual assault or to provide a contextual background to those allegations has been held to be relevant for a variety of reasons,[3] although they can be summed up as going to the credibility of the complainant by assisting to explain what the tribunal of fact often perceives to be their counterintuitive behaviours. Relevance will depend on the nature of the defence case, as relationship evidence can place the complainant's account of events in its realistic context, thus providing the capacity to answer questions which 'may fairly be expected to arise in the minds of the jury were they limited to a consideration of evidence of the offences charged'.[4] Accordingly, on those bases such evidence will ordinarily reach the threshold of a minimal logical connection to 'the probability of the existence of a fact in issue in the proceeding',[5] usually whether the sexual conduct took place at all. As Howie J usefully observed, it is evidence that 'may allow the jury to infer some aspect of the complainant's conduct but it does not give rise to any inference about the accused's conduct'.[6]

Importantly, context evidence cannot be used for a tendency purpose, that is, to establish that any of the charged offences occurred or as tending to show the defendant had wrongful sexual feelings towards the complainant and it was more likely they committed those offences.[7] In practice, the nature of context evidence is finely distinguished from tendency evidence particularly where it involves uncharged sexual acts of the same general nature as the sexual assault charges in the indictment. There is clear potential for overlap, which results in significant complexity in properly categorising the evidence. Priest JA was driven to the conclusion that 'relationship evidence – including context evidence – should be seen for

---

3   For example, it may be relevant to explain why a complainant feared the defendant (*R v AH* (1997) 42 NSWLR 702; *R v WJT* [2001] NSWCCA 405), or why there was a failure to show distress or complain: *KTR v The Queen* [2010] NSWCCA 271, [99]–[101]; *FH v The Queen* [2014] NSWCCA 231, [49]–[50].

4   *HML v The Queen* (2008) 235 CLR 334, 397 (Kiefel J). See also *Steadman v The Queen (No 2)* [2013] NSWCCA 56, [13].

5   *Evidence Act 1995* (Cth) s 55. The Evidence Acts in NSW, Victoria, Tasmania, ACT and NT are modelled on the Commonwealth Act and are substantially uniform in their construction.

6   *Qualtieri v The Queen* (2006) 171 A Crim R 463, 494.

7   *Rodden v The Queen* [2008] NSWCCA 53, [48].

what it is ... tendency evidence'. [8] Although the other two judges didn't join in this opinion, [9] the correct characterisation of the 'true relevance' of the evidence is a most important concern of the courts as they must ensure that relationship evidence is not simply 'tendency evidence admitted by the back door'. [10] In the interests of a fair trial, the existence of this complex dichotomy is such that the court must either exclude relationship/context evidence entirely or properly limit its use through precise guidance. Specific examples of evidence that may not be admissible if relationship/context evidence was treated as if it were tendency evidence include: multiple huggings by an adult of a child by bringing their whole bodies into contact for an extended period, [11] being very 'touchy feely' with a young child by having an arm constantly around her and kissing her on the cheek, [12] and multiple acts of a sexual nature such as being naked and masturbating in the presence of a child, walking in while the child is showering, trying to get into the child's bed and demanding she take off her clothes. [13]

There are important procedural distinctions in the admissibility of these two subtly different types of evidence. Relationship/context evidence doesn't fall within the s 97 exclusionary rule or the further admissibility restriction in s 101(2). After meeting the relevance threshold, it becomes subject only to judicial exclusion through ss 135 or 137. As such evidence is invariably adduced by the prosecution in sexual assault cases, the defendant seeking exclusion under s 137 must persuade [14] the court that the 'probative value' [15] is outweighed by the danger of unfair prejudice to the defendant'. [16] This onus is directly opposed to ss 97 and 101(2) which makes tendency evidence inadmissible unless the prosecution

---

8   *Murdoch v The Queen*, above n 2.

9   Observing at [11] it was 'not the occasion ... to explore context or relationship evidence' in the specific circumstances of the case.

10   *RWC v The Queen* [2010] NSWCCA 332, [115]; *Steadman v The Queen (No 2)* [2013] NSWCCA 56, [11]–[18].

11   See *R v Landmeter* [2015] SASCFC 3.

12   See *R v Zappavigna* [2015] SASCFC 8.

13   *Steadman v The Queen [No 1]* [2013] NSWCCA 55 and *Steadman v The Queen [No 2]* [2013] NSWCCA 56.

14   *R v DG* [2010] VSCA 173, [54].

15   Probative value is taken 'at its highest': see *IMM v The Queen* [2016] HCA 14, [44]–[58].

16   That is, a real risk that the evidence will be misused in some unfair way: see *R v Lisoff* [1999] NSWCCA 364.

persuades the court that the evidence is of 'significant probative value'[17] and it substantially outweighs any prejudicial effect it may have on the defendant.

Therefore, rather than relationship/context evidence being excluded under s 137, it is often admitted as relevant subject to the need for careful judicial directions about its limited use in jury deliberations, particularly that 'the relationship evidence cannot be regarded as a substitute for the evidence that the accused committed the charged sexual acts, or for the purpose of showing that the accused is "the kind of person" likely to have committed that offence'.[18] As Priest JA observed, this is an 'unenviable task',[19] which assumes juror comprehension of using the evidence for a purpose that has been otherwise described as 'contrary to ordinary human experience'[20] and counterintuitive to the ordinary reasoning processes of lay fact-finders about human behaviour. The directions are supposed to be capable of ameliorating the potential prejudicial effect to the defendant; however, various jury studies indicate the assumption of courts that directions are effective may be misplaced in certain circumstances.[21]

---

17   The divergent Victorian and NSW judicial approaches to the interpretation of the phrase 'significant probative value' in s 97 evident when comparing *Velkoski v The Queen* [2014] VSCA 121 with *Hughes v The Queen* [2015] NSWCCA 330 were resolved by a 4:3 majority decision of the High Court in *Hughes v The Queen* [2017] HCA 20. The broader NSW approach was adopted by the High Court in holding that similarity between the tendency evidence and facts in issue of the charged offence is not a pre-requisite to a finding of 'significant probative value'. The tendency evidence should make more likely, to a significant extent, the facts that make up the elements of the offence charged either by itself or together with other evidence adduced or to be adduced in the case. This does not include a requirement for 'similarity or … of "underlying unity", "pattern of conduct" or "modus operandi"'(per Kiefel CJ, Bell, Keane and Edelman JJ at [34]).

18   *Benson v The Queen* [2014] VSCA 51, [30] (Neave JA).

19   *Murdoch v The Queen*, above n 2.

20   *DJV v The Queen* [2008] NSWCCA 272, [31]. See also *Qualtieri v The Queen* (2006) 171 A Crim R 463 where the court referred to the NSW Judicial Commission *Criminal Trial Courts Bench Book* model direction on relationship evidence ([4-215]) with approval.

21   See, for example, Wissler and Saks, 'On the Inefficacy of Limiting Instructions' (1985) 9 *Law and Human Behaviour* 37; Lloyd-Bostock, 'The Effects on Juries of Hearing about the Defendant's Previous Criminal Record: A Simulation Study' (2000) *Criminal Law Review* 734; Schaefer and Hansen, 'Similar Fact Evidence and Limited Use Instructions: An Empirical Investigation' (1990) 14 *Criminal Law Journal* 157; Cush and Goodman-Delahunty, 'The Influence of Limiting Instructions on Processing and Judgments of Emotionally Evocative Evidence' (2006) 13(1) *Psychiatry, Psychology and Law* 110. Compare Trimboli, 'Juror Understanding of Judicial Instructions in Criminal Trials' (2008) NSW BOCSAR Crime and Justice Bulletin No 119.

II. The Problem

The upshot of experiences in criminal trials and appeals involving sexual assault offences is a fraught dichotomy between relationship/context and tendency evidence. The essential problem is whether priority should be given to admitting all probative evidence or to minimising the risk of wrongful convictions.

Policy arguments to accommodate admissibility of relationship/context evidence focus on facilitating the successful prosecution of sexual assault charges, particularly cases where the perceived counterintuitive behaviours revealed in testimony requiring some form of explanation may be most evident. Arguments include that the entire law enforcement and court process makes it difficult for complainants, particularly children, to be encouraged to report sexual assaults and then give evidence in court, the low rate of convictions where such cases proceed to trial, and the serious nature of the problem in society where it is perceived as abhorrent but that most perpetrators 'get away with it'. The arguments for more liberal admissibility of 'discreditable' forms of evidence extend to lowering the threshold of admissibility of tendency evidence because of courts 'placing unwarranted obstacles in the path of efforts to prosecute child sexual offenders'.[22] The trial spotlight is on the 'battle of credibility between the complainant and the defendant' where the presumption of innocence and the standard of proof beyond reasonable doubt are viewed as strongly favouring the defendant such that the stringent operation of the exclusionary rule is challenged and it is contended that other probative misconduct evidence should be more readily admissible.[23]

Contrary to these arguments, the overriding requirement of a fair trial for a defendant who is presumed innocent and the highly prejudicial nature of most relationship/context evidence, particularly uncharged sexual acts, raises counter-arguments that there must be closer analysis of the relevance of context evidence and a transparent balancing of the important factors in deciding its admissibility to ensure a conviction is not on the basis of suspicion and unfair preconceptions of a defendant's

---

22 Hamer, 'Proof of Serial Child Sexual Abuse: Case-law Developments and Recidivism Data' in Crofts and Loughnan (eds), *Criminalisation and Criminal Responsibility in Australia* (2015), 247, 250–51. See also Cossins, 'The Behaviour of Serial Child Sex Offenders; Implications for the Prosecution of Child Sex Offences in Joint Trials' (2011) 35(3) *Melbourne University Law Review* 821.
23 Hamer, above n 22, 244, 260.

'character'. The frequency and likeness of the 'discreditable' conduct can ultimately lead to a blurring of the incidents and preemptive judgment of guilt without the ordinary procedural safeguards that apply to proof of a criminal offence. That does not necessarily mean there will be fewer convictions in these cases; rather, due process and fairness are placed at the forefront of procedural and evidentiary considerations.

III. Suggestions for Reform

The Australian Law Reform Commission (ALRC) considered a proposal for broadening the scope of s 101 to encompass all evidence that tends to reveal the past disreputable conduct of a defendant.[24] There were strongly opposing views: concern that such dangerous evidence was currently too readily admitted into evidence against the concern that important probative evidence would be excluded leading to inconsistent outcomes.[25] The three procedural safeguards which apply to tendency evidence in relation to the party bearing the onus of proof, the heightened barrier for admissibility requiring significant probative value, and the evidence having 'any prejudicial effect' as opposed to a 'danger of unfair prejudice' were examined for extension to context evidence. Ultimately, though, the ALRC view was that the prosecution would be likely in practice to 'disavow any attempt to use the evidence for a propensity purpose and concede the need for a warning that the evidence not be used for that purpose'[26] thereby providing a strong argument that the probative value for a context purpose substantially outweighs any prejudicial effect on the defendant. This approach takes advantage of the court's firm assumption that limiting directions are capable of alleviating prejudice, making it difficult for the defence to challenge admissibility on the basis that directions would be inadequate. Overall, the benefits were found to be inconclusive and, as extending the scope of s 101 was unlikely to have a practical impact, it was better not to do so. This reasoning was largely speculative and not persuasive.

---

24 Australian Law Reform Commission (ALRC), *Uniform Evidence Law*, Report 102 (2005), [11.76].
25 Ibid. [11.80]–[11.81].
26 Ibid. [11.87].

South Australia, a common law jurisdiction, inserted s 34P into their *Evidence Act 1929*,[27] which makes evidence of all 'discreditable conduct', including uncharged sexual acts, presumptively inadmissible. The prosecution must persuade the judge that the probative value of such evidence, which relies on a particular disposition of the defendant as circumstantial evidence of a fact in issue, is strong having regard to the particular issue/s arising at trial and must substantially outweigh any prejudicial effect it may have on the defendant before it is admissible. When determining the balance between probative value and prejudicial effect the judge must consider whether the permissible use of the discreditable conduct evidence can be kept sufficiently separate and distinct so as to remove any appreciable risk of it being used impermissibly to prove that the defendant is more likely to have committed the offence. The legislative intention is to ensure that the trial judge engages in a transparent balancing task to reflect the more burdensome threshold for admissibility of this potentially dangerous evidence. Further, s 34R requires the trial judge to identify and explain to the jury the purposes for which the discreditable conduct evidence may and may not be used. This is to compel judges to carefully consider the nature and utility of directions. The genuine effectiveness of such directions is not directly addressed by the legislation and can only be urged in defence arguments using relevant studies and empirical evidence.

The practical effect of these provisions can be gauged through their interpretation and application in the cases. Largely, the ALRC prediction in relation to extending the scope of s 101 has been realised through the practical operation of s 34P. Judges continue to rely heavily on the utility of directions to ameliorate the prejudicial effect of relationship/ context evidence and have continued to admit such evidence as relevant and probative[28] or have characterised it as forming part of the proof of elements of generalised charges, such as 'persistent sexual exploitation of a child'.[29] If the courts continue to make the assumption that directions are effective in restricting prejudice, the legislative efforts through the transparent balancing test with the prosecution onus to persuade the

---

27   *Evidence (Discreditable Conduct) Amendment Act 2011* (SA) commenced 1 June 2012. An important catalyst was the confusing aftermath of the High Court decision in *HML v The Queen* (2008) 235 CLR 334.

28   See, for example, *R v Maiolo (No 2)* (2013) 117 SASR 1; *R v C, CN* [2013] SASCFC 44; *R v Zappavigna* [2015] SASCFC 8, [34]–[60]; *R v F, AD* [2015] SASCFC 130, [21]–[41].

29   See *R v Landmeter* [2015] SASCFC 3, [27] (Vanstone and Bampton JJ), [113]–[114] (Peek J dissenting).

court that the 'discreditable evidence' should be admitted will come to nought. Arguably the intent and spirit of the legislation would support a more exacting application of the admissibility threshold with directions only available where they can effectively remove any appreciable risk of the evidence being used for the impermissible purpose.

If it is largely about maintaining the credibility of complainants because they appear to have behaved in a counterintuitive manner, then more liberal use of expert evidence to explain this behaviour may be preferable to the possibility of creating another statutory exclusionary rule. Alternatively, these reforms could operate to complement each other in practical operation and effect. The credibility of a complainant may be tainted to varying degrees by having to narrate isolated incidents, as the jury may find such a disjointed account to be 'astonishing, and almost unbelievable'.[30] This reform suggestion raises the issue of whether expert evidence is an effective and less prejudicial alternative to the use of relationship/context evidence as a means of dispelling common misconceptions about how sexual assault complainants behave, both before and after sexual abuse, particularly where it has been systematic and sustained.

Sections 79(2) and 108C(2) specifically provide for the use of expert evidence in child sexual assault cases, allowing persons with specialised knowledge to testify on matters concerning child development and behaviour as an exception to the opinion and credibility rules.[31] In *MA v The Queen* the prosecution led expert evidence at trial 'with respect to the behavioural framework within which the evidence of the complainant's reactions to the alleged abuse should be assessed and understood'. On appeal this was argued to be irrelevant and unfairly prejudicial, but the Court of Appeal ruled it was relevant and not so unfairly prejudicial that exclusion was warranted as it 'could establish that the counter-intuitive behaviour complained of was of neutral significance ... [and] could not demonstrate that the behaviour rendered it more or less likely that offending had occurred as alleged'.[32] This case deals with the very situation contemplated by legislators and shows its successful use in practice to explain the counterintuitive behaviours of a complainant in a

---

30   *R v Beserick* (1993) 30 NSWLR 510, 515.
31   These provisions commenced 1 January 2009 to curb the judicial reluctance to allow such expert evidence because it wasn't considered to be outside the ordinary experience of jurors – ALRC, above n 24, [9.156].
32   (2013) 226 A Crim R 575, [22]–[34].

child sexual assault case. Overall, though, prosecutors don't appear to have regularly invoked these provisions to evidence that psychological research doesn't support many of the existing misconceptions.[33]

One concern is the 'white coat effect': that undue weight will be given to this evidence because of the aura of scientific certainty surrounding expert testimony.[34] Therefore, it is important to situate the role of this evidence and consider directions about its use. The court is 'simply offered an alternative explanation for specific behaviour', without being offered an opinion on the specific credibility of the complainant, so the jury is assisted not supplanted by the expert.[35] Arguably an increased use of expert testimony in sexual assault cases would reduce the need for a complainant to recount a history of 'grooming' conduct by a defendant. This approach won't be successful for all forms of relationship/context evidence but it may represent a more objective way of maintaining the complainant's credibility without causing undue prejudice to the defendant. To obviate appeals about judicial directions it is contended that a standardised direction about psychological research into child development and behaviour during and following sexual abuse should be developed. This could be incorporated into legislation[36] and Law Reform Commissions have recommended the development of model directions drawing on the expertise of relevant professional and research bodies.[37]

IV. Conclusion

The dichotomy between tendency and relationship/context evidence in sexual assault cases cannot be logically sustained when the real relevance of relationship/context evidence is realised. First, given the prejudicial nature of most relationship/context evidence, it should be presumptively

---

33   Arguably such experts are material witnesses and should be called by the prosecution: *R v Apostilides* (1984) 154 CLR 563. These provisions may also be used by the defence so there may be prosecutorial reluctance based on an expectation that the defence will counter with expert evidence to reinstate the misconceptions. Experience in practice, however, shows that such defence tactics are likely to meet with judicial resistance: see *R v WR (No 3)* [2010] ACTSC 89, [32].

34   Ward, 'Usurping the Role of the Jury? Expert Evidence and Witness Credibility in English Trials' (2009) 13 *International Journal of Evidence and Proof* 83, 88.

35   Ellison, 'Closing the Credibility Gap: The Prosecutorial Use of Expert Witness Testimony in Sexual Assault Cases' (2005) 9 *International Journal of Evidence and Proof* 239, 258.

36   See *Jury Directions Act 2015* (Vic) ss 27, 29; and *Evidence Regulation 2007* (NZ) cl 49.

37   Cossins for the National Child Sexual Assault Reform Committee, 'Alternative Models for Prosecuting Child Sex Offences in Australia' (2010), 233–35; ALRC, *Family Violence*, Report 114 (2009) [27-11]–[27-12]; NSW Law Reform Commission, *Jury Directions*, Report 136 (2012) [5.5].

inadmissible. The prosecution must persuade the court it is admissible through a transparent balancing of probative value and prejudicial effect. Judges must not simply rely on the outmoded notion that jury directions will ameliorate any prejudice to defendants. Second, the courts should move towards increased use of expert evidence to explain counterintuitive behaviours of complainants so that the prosecution can still present its case fairly and thoroughly but with decreased reliance on highly prejudicial relationship/context evidence.

13

Improving the Effectiveness of Corporate Criminal Liability: Old Challenges in a Transnational World

Jonathan Clough[1]

I. Introduction

In 1842, in the middle of the Industrial Revolution, the Birmingham & Gloucester Railway Co was convicted of failing to obey an order requiring it to construct arches over land severed by the railway.[2] In 2008, the Industrial Revolution long overtaken by the digital revolution, German company Siemens AG pleaded guilty to breaches of the US *Foreign Corrupt Practices Act* (*FCPA*), and was ordered to pay a combined total of more than US$1.6 billion in fines, penalties and disgorgement of profits.[3]

Separated by over 160 years, these cases provide convenient bookends to the multivolume history of corporate criminal liability. While historically many countries, particularly civil law jurisdictions, did not recognise the

---

1   Professor, Faculty of Law, Monash University.
2   *R v Birmingham & Gloucester Railway Co* (1842) 3 QB 223.
3   US Department of Justice, 'Siemens AG and Three Subsidiaries Plead Guilty to Foreign Corrupt Practices Act Violations and Agree to Pay $450 Million in Combined Criminal Fines' (Press Release, 15 December 2008).

criminal liability of legal persons, the idea that a corporation could be criminally liable came to be widely accepted in common law countries. Today, driven in part by the need to comply with a number of international instruments, corporate criminal liability is widely accepted in a range of jurisdictions and legal systems.[4]

Recognition of corporate criminal liability and the effective prosecution of corporations are, however, quite distinct issues. While the United States has a history of successful corporate prosecutions, particularly for foreign corruption, this is not reflective of the wider story. Corporate prosecutions, where they occur, tend to be for relatively minor 'regulatory offences'. Allegations of misconduct in the financial sector are, more commonly, dealt with by way of 'civil penalties', while the prosecution of corporations for homicide in relation to workplace deaths has been largely unsuccessful.[5] Attempts to bring multinational corporations to account for alleged human rights violations typically result in protracted civil ligation.[6] There is, understandably, a perception that if corporations are in fact subject to the threat of prosecution, it is an idle threat.

This is not to suggest that these are simple matters. The regulation of corporations is a complex issue requiring a range of responses. However, corporate regulation is not advanced if a crucial component of the regulatory response is ineffective. For corporate criminal liability to be a real possibility, it must be underpinned by legal structures that allow the culpability of a legal person to be determined and effective sanctions imposed. Further, given the ability of corporations to act transnationally, enforcement must be supported by mechanisms that allow for effective international cooperation.

Using bribery of foreign officials as an example,[7] this chapter provides a snapshot of corporate criminal liability in Australia, and its capacity to operate effectively in a transnational world.[8] It begins with a summary of the models of liability which may be applied to corporations, followed by a discussion of corporate sanctions, and finally measures which must

---

4   For example, United Nations Convention against Corruption, A/58/422 (31 October 2003) UNTS Vol 2349, Art 26.
5   See, for example, *R v AC Hatrick Chemicals Pty Ltd* (1995) 140 IR 243.
6   See, for example, *Doe v Unocal*, 395 F3d 932 (9th Cir, 2002).
7   *Criminal Code Act 1995* (Cth) s 70.2 (*Criminal Code*).
8   Although the focus of this chapter is on corporations, there are of course many other types of legal persons, including unincorporated associations, trusts, partnerships and trade unions.

be adopted in order to enforce the criminal law against transnational corporations. It is argued that law reform is not only desirable, it can in most cases be easily implemented. Obstacles to transnational prosecutions are not insurmountable. This leaves the more challenging question of whether there are the resources to investigate and the will to prosecute.

II. Models of Liability

Even for those jurisdictions willing to recognise that a corporation may be a criminal, a fundamental challenge is to develop a model of liability that finds culpability in an artificial entity. This challenge has occupied courts and legislatures for over a century, with broadly speaking two models emerging.

The first is a 'nominalist' or 'derivative' theory of liability, where the liability of the legal person is 'derived' from the liability of an individual. For example, a company may be made liable for a criminal offence committed by an officer or employee of the corporation. The simplest form of derivative liability is 'vicarious liability' whereby a corporation is liable for the conduct of an individual employee or agent acting within the course or scope of his or her employment/agency, and at least in part for the benefit of the organisation. Although a simple form of liability, it does not necessarily reflect organisational fault. Nonetheless, it is applied in US federal law, including the *Foreign Corrupt Practices Act*,[9] which may go some way to explaining the relative success of US officials in prosecuting corporations for foreign bribery.

Another form of derivative liability is the so-called 'attribution' or 'identification' doctrine. In contrast to vicarious liability, the individual on whom liability is based must be of sufficient standing that they may be said to represent the entity; for example, the Board of Directors and other senior officers of a company such as the CEO, managing director, and the like. Because this person is said to *be* the company for these purposes, the company is said to be liable in its own right.[10]

---

9 US Department of Justice and the US Securities and Exchange Commission, *A Resource Guide to the US Foreign Corrupt Practices Act* (2012) 27.
10 *Tesco Supermarkets Ltd v Nattrass* [1972] AC 153.

Although applied in a number of common law countries, the identification doctrine has proved to be hopelessly inadequate in prosecuting medium to large corporations for serious crimes, particularly in the context of workplace deaths.[11] In modern decentralised organisations senior officers may be removed from the relevant conduct, with considerable authority often vested in 'middle-managers'. For this reason, some jurisdictions have defined the relevant person more broadly. For example, in Australia the Commonwealth *Criminal Code* provides for a form of attribution based on the conduct of a 'high managerial agent', defined as 'an employee, agent or officer of the body corporate with duties of such responsibility that his or her conduct may fairly be assumed to represent the body corporate's policy'.[12]

Even if the scope of derivative liability is expanded, it is still dependent on individual liability. This is particularly problematic in large organisations where it may be difficult to prove individual responsibility. In contrast, 'realist' or 'organisational' models of liability seek to reflect the culpability of the organisation itself; for example, by its policies and the way in which it is structured.

A particularly clear example is found in Pt 2.5 of the *Criminal Code* which applies to federal offences including bribery of foreign officials under s 70.2. In addition to liability based on attribution, it imposes liability on corporations based on the concept of 'corporate culture', defined to mean 'an attitude, policy, rule, course of conduct or practice existing within the body corporate generally or in the part of the body corporate in which the relevant activities takes place'.[13] Although an ambitious example of organisational liability, it has yet to be applied in practice. It may be that prosecutors are wary of basing prosecutions on such a novel and nebulous concept,[14] and it is notable that there have been no successful prosecutions for foreign bribery in the 15 years since the current laws were enacted.[15]

---

11   See generally, Jonathan Clough, 'A Glaring Omission? Corporate Liability for Negligent Manslaughter' (2007) 20 *Australian Journal of Labour Law* 29, 32–33.

12   *Criminal Code* s 12.3(6).

13   Ibid.

14   Jonathan Clough and Carmel Mulhern, *The Prosecution of Corporations* (Oxford University Press, 2002) 144.

15   Law Council of Australia, Submission to the Senate Economics Reference Committee Inquiry into Foreign Bribery, 24 August 2015.

In contrast, one of the simplest and potentially most effective forms of organisational liability is liability for omissions. That is, where a legal person is under a legal obligation to act, its failure to discharge that obligation can be established without finding fault in an individual. This may then be combined with a fault element such as negligence, or a defence of due diligence to reflect organisational fault. For example, under s 7 of the *Bribery Act 2010* (UK), where an associated person engages in bribery, the organisation is liable for failing to prevent it. However, this liability is subject to a defence where the company can prove that it had in place adequate procedures designed to prevent such conduct.

The above discussion provides only a brief summary of the various ways in which criminal liability may be imposed on corporations. From a reform perspective, the challenge is not so much finding new models of liability, it is applying those models consistently and appropriately. For example, although Pt 2.5 of the *Criminal Code* provides a default model of liability for federal offences, no such state provision exists, leaving them to rely on the demonstrably inadequate common law.[16] If a particular model is found to be ineffective, it may be amended. Pt 2.5, for example, is excluded from some competition law provisions in favour of other models of liability.[17]

III. Sanctions

Although criminal liability without an effective sanction is largely a symbolic gesture, the sentencing of corporations has typically been neglected in law reform. While a corporation cannot be rehabilitated or deterred in the same way as a person, it does not mean that these concepts do not apply to corporations.[18] For example, an emphasis on organisational fault provides a means by which change can be brought about at an organisational level.

However, in all Australian jurisdictions the sentencing options that may be imposed on a corporate defendant are determined by the relevant offence, typically a fine. While a financial penalty may be an appropriate sanction in many cases, the sentencing judge has limited ability to tailor

---

16   See, for example, *ABC Developmental Learning Centres Pty Ltd v Wallace* [2007] VSCA 138.
17   *Competition and Consumer Act 2010* (Cth) s 6AA.
18   Clough and Mulhern, above n 14, 186–87.

the penalty to achieve sentencing outcomes. In this respect, Australian legislation falls behind some international examples. The French Penal Code, for example, makes provision for a range of sanctions applicable to legal persons.[19] Similarly, the United States Sentencing Guidelines contain sophisticated guidance for trial judges in sentencing organisations.[20] While it is beyond the scope of this chapter to discuss them in detail, it is important to give some sense of the range of sanctions that may be applied to legal persons.

A. Monetary penalties

Fines are a common form of sanction against legal persons, and may provide an effective deterrent. In many cases the fine to be imposed is set as a multiple of that applicable to a natural person. Although in some cases a fine may simply be absorbed as a business cost, the impact of a monetary penalty may also be felt by 'innocent' third parties such as employees, shareholders and consumers. A challenge is therefore to set the appropriate level of penalty to be applied. For example, s 70.2 of the *Criminal Code* provides that where a body corporate is found guilty of bribing a foreign official, the maximum penalty to be imposed is the greatest of 100,000 penalty units, three times the value of the benefit obtained, or 10 per cent of the annual turnover of the body corporate during the relevant period.

B. Adverse publicity

For corporations with a significant reputation, publicising its offending may have a significant deterrent impact both on the organisation itself and others. It may also have an important educative effect, making other entities, stakeholders and the community aware of the illegality of the relevant conduct.

C. Probation

As part of its sentence, a corporation may agree to comply with certain undertakings and to be subject to a period of supervision. Such conditions may be remedial, aimed at making good the harm caused by the

---

19   Articles 131–39.
20   United States Sentencing Commission, *Federal Sentencing Guidelines Manual,* Ch 8.

commission of the offence, or rehabilitative; that is, requiring steps to be taken in order to ensure organisational change. As such conditions would generally be subject to the supervision of the court or regulator, they are potentially a powerful mechanism for achieving organisational change.

D. Disqualification or disestablishment

A legal person that has committed an offence can be disqualified from engaging in certain activities, or can be disqualified from government contracts or funding. At the most extreme end, a corporation may be disestablished; the equivalent of capital punishment. Given the serious secondary impacts of such a sanction, it is likely to be applied rarely; for example, to organisations with no legitimate purpose.

As with models of liability, the reform challenge in relation to corporate sanctions is less to do with available options, and more to do with consistency and availability. Many of the sanctions outlined above are found in various pieces of legislation, but their availability is limited to contraventions of those acts.[21]

IV. Transnational Crime

A crucial feature of the success of modern corporations is their ability to operate transnationally, with companies in one jurisdiction operating in other jurisdictions through subsidiaries or other related entities. Combined with the doctrine of separate legal personality, this has allowed corporations to derive global profits while distributing corporate risk. For example, in 2016 German company Siemens AG employed approximately 351,000 people, in over 200 countries, generating revenues of €79.6 billion.[22] Imposing criminal liability on such corporations presents considerable legal challenges. In addition to ensuring that local corporations may be prosecuted for conduct occurring outside the jurisdiction, it is also important that law enforcement agencies are able to cooperate effectively to investigate and prosecute transnational corporate crime. Three particular issues that should be considered are jurisdiction, the liability of corporate groups, and mutual assistance.

---

21   See, for example, *Crimes Act 1900* (ACT) s 49E; *Competition and Consumer Act 2010* (Cth) s 86C.
22   Siemens AG, *About Siemens*, www.siemens.com/about/en/.

A. Jurisdiction

Although criminal law is typically local in operation, extraterritorial liability may be imposed on corporations for conduct occurring outside the jurisdiction. Typically this is based on the 'nationality principle' where liability is imposed on a corporation incorporated in the jurisdiction for conduct occurring anywhere in the world. For example, an Australian corporation may be convicted of bribery even if the conduct constituting the offence occurred wholly outside Australia.[23]

B. Corporate groups

In many cases, legal persons will act through subsidiaries or other related entities. It may therefore be necessary to consider whether one organisation may be made liable for the conduct of other organisations. For example, a parent company may be made liable for bribery by a subsidiary incorporated in another jurisdiction.

In some cases it may be possible to impose liability on the parent for being an accessory to the offence, or for conspiring to commit the offence. Alternatively, liability may be imposed where a corporation can be shown to have exercised control over another entity,[24] or for failing to prevent the commission of an offence by an associated entity.[25]

C. Mutual legal assistance

Effective prosecution of transnational crime often requires significant international cooperation. However, challenges may arise where, for example, a country does not recognise the criminal liability of corporations, but chooses to impose administrative liability. In such cases, a request for assistance may be refused in the absence of dual criminality. It is therefore important for countries to consider the extent to which they are able to provide assistance in relation to civil and administrative proceedings where this is consistent with their domestic legal system.[26]

---

23 *Criminal Code* s 70.5. See also *Bribery Act 2010* (UK) s 7(5).
24 For example, US *Age Discrimination in Employment Act* (29 USC § 623(h)).
25 For example, *Bribery Act 2010* (UK) s 7(5).
26 UN General Assembly, United Nations Convention against Corruption, A/58/422 (31 October 2003) UNTS Vol 2349, Art 43(1).

V. Conclusion

This chapter began with two events illustrating the arc of corporate criminal liability over the past century and a half. The use of bookends as a metaphor was, to some extent, inapposite if it suggests that the evolution of corporate criminal liability is over. Such liability will continue to evolve, particularly in its application to transnational criminal activity. In other respects the metaphor is apt as the prosecution of Siemens, and others like it, illustrate that with appropriate structures in place even large transnational corporations can be effectively prosecuted.

Law reform should focus on ensuring that these mechanisms are in place across the range of corporate activity, including transnational operations, so that the focus can move from whether it can happen, to whether it should. In the Australian context, there is a need for a review of models of corporate criminal liability. The corporate liability provisions of Pt 2.5 of the *Criminal Code* provide a sophisticated default model of liability that is rarely used. This would be an ideal starting point for considering the impediments to its use, and whether alternative forms of liability should be imposed in specific areas of corporate activity. Such a review could also consider whether extraterritorial legislation is appropriate in certain cases, and the mechanisms by which liability could be imposed on corporate groups. The importance of such reforms is equally applicable to the states, where corporate criminal liability is often dependent on the inadequacies of the common law. In the context of sentencing reform, a simple and potentially highly effective reform would be for each jurisdiction to provide for a separate section of their sentencing legislation dedicated to corporate offenders, outlining the sanctions available and principles to be applied.

Not surprisingly, political interest in corporate criminal liability ebbs and flows as a result of specific concerns such as workplace deaths,[27] cartel behaviour[28] and, most recently, foreign corruption.[29] While this can produce important reform outcomes, there is the danger of a piecemeal approach and a missed opportunity to look at corporations as a class of

---

27 *Crimes (Industrial Manslaughter) Amendment Act 2003* (ACT).
28 Trade Practices Act Review Committee, *Review of the Competition Provisions of the Trade Practices Act* (January 2003).
29 Attorney-General's Department, *Proposed Amendments to the Foreign Bribery Offence in the Criminal Code Act 1995* (Public Consultation Paper, April 2017).

offender across a range of offences. Ensuring that all corporate offences are supported by an effective model of liability, backed by appropriate sanctions, would provide the essential foundation for effective prosecutions, and clarity for business as to the basis on which they are to be held liable. Australia has been a leader in this field in the past. Reform of corporate criminal liability would not only improve the quality of corporate regulation domestically, it would allow Australia to play a leading role in international efforts to tackle the use of legal persons in the commission of transnational crimes.

14

Stereotypes in the Courtroom

Blake M McKimmie[1]

Stereotypes have a functional, relatively automatic, and pervasive influence on how we form impressions of other people. As an extra-legal factor, stereotypes are an undesirable influence on decisions, but their use does not represent a failing on the part of jurors. This chapter explores how stereotypes influence jurors in a number of domains – expert testimony, sexual assault, and perceptions of dangerousness of criminal defendants. By understanding how and why jurors are influenced by stereotypes, we are better placed to identify strategies to reduce the effect of stereotypes on jurors' decisions. The possible avenues for law reform include changes to the way expert evidence is admitted, changes to how evidence is presented, changes to the design of the courtroom, and changes to how jurors are instructed by judges.

One useful way to think about a criminal trial is as a series of persuasive messages directed at the jury. The research on persuasion generally agrees that there are two ways in which persuasive messages can influence. These processes are described in the dual process models, specifically the heuristic systematic[2] and the elaboration likelihood[3] models. According to these models there are two modes of thinking. The central or systematic

---

1   Associate Professor, School of Psychology, University of Queensland.
2   Shelly Chaiken, 'Heuristic Versus Systematic Information Processing and the Use of Source Versus Message Cues in Persuasion' (1980) 39(5) *Journal of Personality and Social Psychology* 752.
3   Richard E Petty and John T Cacioppo, 'The Elaboration Likelihood Model of Persuasion' (1986) 19 *Advances in Experimental Social Psychology* 123.

route involves more careful deliberative thought while the peripheral or heuristic route relies more on short cuts and pre-existing knowledge such as schemas and stereotypes. For example, if we are using the central route, we might think carefully about the prosecution's case against the defendant, weighing the strengths and weaknesses of the evidence. If we are using the peripheral route, we might decide that we do not like the look of the defendant, or decide that a witness seems credible because they have an honest face. While the central systematic route sounds like the best way of making decisions, perceivers can only engage in effortful thinking when they have the motivation and ability to do so. When information becomes too complex or ambiguous, it is not possible for perceivers to successfully evaluate a persuasive message using central or systematic processing.

I. Stereotypes and Expert Evidence

Research has shown, despite jurors' claims that they understand complex testimony,[4] jurors are influenced by an expert's characteristics and behaviour in addition to what that expert says. A good illustration of this is in a study[5] in which participants watched a video of a trial recreation. The plaintiff's expert was presented as having either weak or strong credentials, and gave evidence using either simple or complex language. Consistent with the dual process models of persuasion, the expert's credentials affected how much participants were influenced by the expert, but only when the testimony was complex and difficult to understand.

Some of our research suggests that there are similar effects for expert gender.[6] In our research we presented participants with a price-fixing case involving either a male or female expert. The businesses alleged to have been price-fixing were either involved in a male-oriented business domain or a female-oriented domain. We found that participants were more

---

4   Brian H Bornstein and Edie Greene, 'Jury Decision Making: Implications for and from Psychology' (2011) 20(1) *Current Directions in Psychological Science* 63.

5   Joel Cooper, Elizabeth A Bennett, and Holly L Sukel, 'Complex Scientific Testimony: How Do Jurors Make Decisions?' (1996) 20(4) *Law & Human Behavior* 379.

6   Blake M McKimmie et al, 'Jurors' Responses to Expert Witness Testimony: The Effects of Gender Stereotypes' (2004) 7(2) *Group Processes and Intergroup Relations* 131; Regina A Schuller, Deborah J Terry, and Blake M McKimmie, 'The Impact of an Expert's Gender on Jurors' Decisions' (2001) 25 *Law and Psychology Review* 59; Regina A Schuller, Deborah J Terry, and Blake M McKimmie, 'The Impact of Expert Testimony on Jurors' Decisions: Gender of the Expert and Testimony Complexity' (2005) 35(6) *Journal of Applied Social Psychology* 1266.

influenced by the expert when the expert's gender matched the domain of the case, and that this effect was more pronounced when the expert's testimony was complex compared to simple. This latter finding suggests that expert gender is used as a heuristic cue.

To find out whether jurors are aware of the influence of these factors, my colleagues and I surveyed jurors, judges, lawyers, and experts about expert testimony in 55 criminal trials in Queensland, New South Wales, and Victoria.[7] We found that while the vast majority of jurors thought that they understood the expert testimony, participants still identified a number of barriers to their complete comprehension of that testimony. These barriers were: overuse of technical language; the complexity of DNA evidence; the presentation style of the expert; and presentations of evidence that were too lengthy. Jurors in this study were still influenced by a range of features associated with the expert testimony beyond the content of that testimony. The results even suggested that jurors were using the complexity of the testimony as a cue to its correctness, even though complexity was seen as a barrier to comprehension. This may have occurred because expert testimony is stereotypically expected to be complex (this is, after all, the definition of expert testimony).

II. Stereotypes and Sexual Assault

Another area in which stereotypes influence jurors is in relation to victim blaming in cases of sexual assault. Reporting, prosecution and conviction rates for sexual assault remain disproportionately low in Australia,[8] and around the world.[9] Convictions for sexual assault are often dependent on circumstantial evidence, as there is typically little corroborating evidence.[10]

---

7   Ian Freckelton, Jane Delahunty, Jacqueline Horan, and Blake M McKimmie, *Expert Evidence and Criminal Jury Trials* (Oxford University Press, 2016).

8   Australian Bureau of Statistics (ABS), 2005.

9   Kathleen Daly and Brigitte Bouhours, 'Rape and Attrition in the Legal Process: A Comparative Analysis of Five Countries' (2010) 39 *Crime and Justice* 565.

10   Mark R Kebbell and Nina J Westera, 'Promoting Pre-recorded Complainant Evidence in Rape Trials: Psychology and Practice Perspectives' (2011) 35 *Criminal Law Journal* 376.

Because of this, jurors in rape or sexual assault cases are likely to draw on their existing knowledge or cognitive schemas and stereotypes to interpret what happened and how blame should be apportioned.[11]

Our research suggests that if an assault is judged as stereotypical (for example, when the perpetrator and victim are strangers to each other), then perceivers are more likely to believe the victim, blame her less, and convict the defendant. When the offence is not stereotypical, however, perceivers turn to other stereotypes to give meaning to the events presented to them.[12] In particular, perceivers are influenced by whether the victim appears to act in ways that are inconsistent with the consent script. For example, does she physically and verbally resist the assault? Or, does she behave in ways that are stereotypically consistent with being a genuine victim, such as being emotional? If she does, then again she is seen as more credible and less to blame for the assault, and consequently the defendant is seen as being more likely to be guilty.

Our most recent data indicates that there are a small number of central cues that are seen as prototypical of consent, and which allow perceivers to infer the presence of a range of other features associated with sexual assault. Typically, events preceding an acquaintance assault (the most common type of sexual assault) match the consent script reasonably well as they often involve a certain degree of social interaction between the victim and the alleged perpetrator. If, however, the victim's account begins with the assault itself, there is little opportunity for jurors to form a story about the events based on the consent script, and so they appear more likely to interpret events as being sexual assault.

---

11   Louise Ellison and Vanessa E Munro, 'A Stranger in the Bushes, or an Elephant in the Room? Critical Reflections upon Received Rape Myth Wisdom in the Context of a Mock Jury Study' (2010) 13(4) *New Criminal Law Review: An International and Interdisciplinary Journal* 781; Nancy Pennington and Reid Hastie, 'Explaining the Evidence: Tests of the Story Model for Juror Decision Making' (1992) 62(2) *Journal of Personality and Social Psychology* 189.
12   Blake M McKimmie, Barbara M Masser and Renata Bongiorno, 'What Counts as Rape? The Effect of Offence Prototypes, Victim Stereotypes and Participant Gender on How the Complainant and Defendant Are Perceived' (2014) 29(1) *Journal of Interpersonal Violence* 2273.

III. Stereotypes and Defendants

There is a reasonable amount of evidence that jurors are often influenced by the characteristics of defendants, such as their attractiveness,[13] race,[14] and socioeconomic status.[15] Defendants are seen as being more likely to be guilty when they come from social categories that are stereotypically linked to the features of the particular crime they are alleged to have committed.[16]

However, are stereotypes just a decision cue? One assumption is that perceivers use the least mental effort possible and so use stereotypes to reduce the amount of effort required.[17] However, there is some evidence that perceivers think more carefully about unexpected, or stereotype inconsistent, information.[18] Our research[19] suggests that stereotypes can be used to maximise the amount of information that can be evaluated under taxing conditions. Stereotypes help us encode some of the information in an efficient manner, thus freeing up our capacity to attend to other parts of the evidence to extract the maximum amount of information.[20]

In one study, participants read a 12-page summary describing an armed robbery case. In this summary, the defendant was either a man or a woman, and the strength of the forensic evidence against the defendant was either weak or strong. Consistent with a cognitive optimiser perspective, the

---

13 R L Michelini and S R Snodgrass, 'Defendant Characteristics and Juridic Decisions' (1980) 14(3) *Journal of Research in Personality* 340.

14 R Mazzella and A Feingold, 'The Effects of Physical Attractiveness, Race, Socioeconomic Status, and Gender of Defendants and Victims on Judgments of Mock Jurors: A Meta-Analysis' (1994) 24(15) *Journal of Applied Social Psychology* 1315.

15 C W Esqueda, R K E Espinoza and S E Culhane, 'The Effects of Ethnicity, SES, and Crime Status on Juror Decision Making: A Cross-Cultural Examination of European American and Mexican American Mock Jurors' (2008) 30(2) *Hispanic Journal of Behavioral Sciences* 181.

16 R A Gordon et al, 'Perceptions of Blue-Collar and White-Collar Crime: The Effect of Defendant Race on Simulated Juror Decisions' (1988) 128(2) *The Journal of Social Psychology* 191.

17 S T Fiske and S E Taylor, *Social Cognition: Topics in Social Psychology* (New York: Random House, 1984); D T Gilbert, and J G Hixon, 'The Trouble of Thinking: Activation and Application of Stereotypic Beliefs' (1991) 60(4) *Journal of Personality and Social Psychology* 509.

18 L D Stern et al, 'Processing Time and the Recall of Inconsistent and Consistent Behaviors of Individuals and Groups' (1984) 47(2) *Journal of Personality and Social Psychology* 253.

19 Blake M McKimmie et al, 'Stereotypical and Counterstereotypical Defendants: Who Is He and What Was the Case Against Her?' (2013) 19(3) *Psychology, Public Policy and Law* 343.

20 C N Macrae, A B Milne, and G V Bodenhausen, 'Stereotypes as Energy-Saving Devices: A Peek Inside the Cognitive Toolbox' (1994) 66(1) *Journal of Personality and Social Psychology* 37; J W Sherman, F R Conrey, and C J Groom, 'Encoding Flexibility Revisited: Evidence for Enhanced Encoding of Stereotype-Inconsistent Information Under Cognitive Load' (2004) 22(2) *Social Cognition* 214.

strength of the evidence only influenced mock jurors' verdicts when the defendant was male and therefore consistent with the stereotypical offender for this type of offence. When the defendant was a woman, the verdicts returned did not differ as a function of the strength of the case presented.

A second study, this time using a summary of a case involving the murder of a child, showed that participants remembered more of the case-related evidence when the defendant was male compared to female. However, participants were more accurate in identifying who the defendant was when the defendant was female compared to male. Both of these findings are consistent with the idea that a stereotypical defendant frees up the perceivers' attention to allow more thorough encoding of the evidence (at the expense of the defendant's characteristics), whereas a counter-stereotypical defendant is attention-grabbing and so the evidence is not processed as thoroughly.

IV. Stereotypes and Courtroom Design

In contrast to person-centred stereotypes that are associated with the attributes and behaviours of those people and are therefore less open to direct manipulation, one cue that is relatively easily changeable and appears to have an effect on how jurors rely on stereotypes is the design of the courtroom. My colleagues and I[21] have conducted a series of studies on how courtroom design influences jurors.

Our initial study[22] asked 275 community members to look at one of four images featuring a defendant in a criminal trial sitting at the bar table, in an open dock, in an open dock with a correctional officer nearby, or in a glass dock. These latter three images are more representative of courtrooms in Australia. We found that participants were more likely to say the defendant had committed a crime involving violence when the defendant was depicted as sitting inside a glass dock compared to the other courtroom configurations.

---

21   David Tait et al, *Towards a Distributed Courtroom* (Western Sydney University, 2015).
22   Blake M McKimmie, Jillian M Hays and David Tait, 'Just Spaces: Does Courtroom Design Affect How the Defendant is Perceived? (2016) *Psychiatry, Psychology and Law*, dx.doi.org/10.1080/1 3218719.2016.1174054.

Another as yet unpublished study involved 215 community members in a series of trial recreations held in an active courtroom with professional actors. The trial involved allegations that the defendant was involved in a plot to commit a terrorist act. For some of the recreations, the defendant sat at the bar table with his lawyer; in others he sat either in an open dock or a glass dock at the side of the courtroom. Participants then deliberated as a group to arrive at a verdict. The initial findings of this study suggest that there was no difference in verdicts for both of the dock conditions, but that participants were more likely to acquit in the bar table condition compared to the two dock conditions.

V. Conclusions

The research reviewed highlights a variety of ways that stereotypes influence how jurors make decisions. However, we have not argued that jurors are inherently biased and should be replaced with another fact finder. Attempting to replace jurors with another fact finder serves only to displace the challenge posed by stereotypes, and research suggests that even highly trained legal decision-makers, such as judges, are just as vulnerable to the effects of stereotypes.[23]

So if we accept that stereotypes exert a pervasive influence on fact finders, what changes can we make to reduce the negative effects of stereotypes? One possibility is to set up the juror's task so that they have less need to rely on stereotypes in their role. As we have seen, two of the factors that increase the use of stereotypes by jurors are ambiguity and complexity. If the juror's task is changed from a single decision about guilt or innocence into a series of discrete factual questions about the events at issue, then jurors will be more able to think carefully about each smaller decision. This is the approach of using question trails to instruct jurors rather than traditional verbal instructions[24] and it has the potential to reduce the use of stereotypes by jurors. However, more research is needed to establish whether this is in fact the case.

---

23 A J Wistrich, C Guthrie, and J J Rachlinski, 'Can Judges Ignore Inadmissible Information? The Difficulty of Deliberately Disregarding' (2005) 153(4) *University of Pennsylvania Law Review* 1251; J J Rachlinski et al, 'Does Unconscious Racial Bias Affect Trial Judges?' (2008) 84 *Notre Dame Law Review* 1195.

24 J Clough, 'The Role of Question Trails in Assisting Juror Comprehension' (Presentation at the 10th Annual Jury Research and Practice Conference, The Australian National University, 8 February 2013).

Another possible avenue for intervention is to redesign courtrooms to minimise jurors' awareness of negative stereotypes about the defendant. While having the defendant seated at the bar table is common in some jurisdictions, there may be security concerns with this configuration. An alternative is to use technology to reconfigure the courtroom, a possibility recently piloted by David Tait and his colleagues.[25]

In terms of stereotypes that influence how expert testimony is perceived, one possibility is to ensure that the task of evaluating the quality of the expert's evidence is carried out before the evidence is admitted. For example, decisions about admissibility could be based more clearly on the underlying scientific merit or accuracy of that type of testimony in general, rather than this specific expert's credentials or evidence.[26]

Finally, advocates can alter the order in which they present the evidence to reduce the negative effect of stereotypes about victims. For example, in a case involving allegations of sexual assault, rather than starting with a chronological presentation of evidence, it might be more effective for the prosecution to start with the victim's retelling of the assault itself, before moving to the context around the assault. This may help to reduce the ambiguity in how the events are defined in jurors' minds.

By understanding when and how stereotypes influence fact finders, we are able to suggest a number of different ways in which the effect of stereotypes can be reduced. Some of these strategies can be used without any changes to existing practices. Although there is good empirical evidence for many of these suggestions, more research is needed to fully test their effectiveness. Using empirical behavioural science research to inform law reform increases the chances that any particular reform will improve the fairness of the criminal justice system.

---

25   See above n 21.
26   See above n 6.

15

The Justice Motive: Psychological Research on Perceptions of Justice in Criminal Law

Diane Sivasubramaniam[1]

Psychological research demonstrates that people's intuitive judgments of justice differ from legal notions of justice. While several principles guide the determination of just outcomes in criminal law, psychological research indicates the existence of a retributive impulse that can dominate people's justice reasoning. To what extent will this mismatch between legal and human notions of justice affect the acceptability of criminal law reforms in the community and, ultimately, the viability of those reforms? In this chapter, I address this question in relation to restorative justice (RJ) and preventive detention. The psychological literature sheds light on the fundamental motivations driving people's decision-making about RJ and preventive detention. Understanding the factors driving community perceptions of justice is crucial in managing the long-term viability of criminal law reform.

---

1   Senior Lecturer, Department of Psychological Sciences, Swinburne University.

I. Divergence of Legal and Community Notions of Justice

The production of a 'just outcome' in a criminal case, according to the process of the law, is a complex and deliberative event. When judges determine a sentence in response to a criminal offence, they are guided by several sentencing principles.[2] Judges may be advised or required to consider aggravating and mitigating factors, and must also consider the common law as developed by appellate courts. Judges then engage in what the High Court terms an 'intuitive synthesis' – an exercise in which all relevant considerations are simultaneously unified and weighed, and translated into an appropriate sentence. In addition, judges must balance individualised justice (ensuring a sentence is appropriate for the individual case) and consistency across similar types of cases.[3] Moreover, judges are highly specialised individuals, capable of complex cognitive undertakings, and accustomed to the particular synthesis required in sentencing according to the law.

These characteristics of judicial reasoning contrast with laypeople's decision-making about 'just outcomes'. To understand how just outcomes are conceptualised in the broader community, we can turn to recent psychological research on distributive justice, which divides the human response to justice-related events into two channels: heuristic and systematic processing.[4]

When a person considers an emotionally engaging and serious injustice, like a criminal offence, this prompts the heuristic response. The heuristic response is quick to occur, automatic and intuitive. Once a person becomes aware of an injustice, the heuristic response basically consists of an appraisal of who or what is to blame, and an underlying imperative to re-establish justice, with little or no further consideration of circumstances.

---

2   'Sentencing Bench Book' ([2-200] Purposes of Sentencing), www.judcom.nsw.gov.au/publications/benchbks/sentencing/purposes_of_sentencing.html; 'Victorian Sentencing Manual' (7.1 Sentencing purposes generally), www.judicialcollege.vic.edu.au/eManuals/VSM/index.htm#15298.htm.

3   Sarah Krasnostein and Arie Freiberg, 'Pursuing Consistency in an Individualistic Sentencing Framework: If You Know Where You're Going, How Do You Know When You've Got There' (2013) 76 Law & Contemporary Problems 265.

4   Shelly Chaiken and Yaacov Trope, Dual-process Theories in Social Psychology (Guilford Press, 1999); Daniel Kahneman, Thinking, Fast and Slow (Macmillan, 2011); Melvin J Lerner, 'The Justice Motive: Where Social Psychologists Found It, How They Lost It, and Why They May Not Find It Again' (2003) 7(4) Personality and Social Psychology Review 388.

When the observer is seeing harm done to one person by another, this immediate motivation to restore justice equates to a desire for retribution: the bad person, the offender, deserves punishment. Effectively, cognitions and emotions in the heuristic response appear as a scripted package typically involving anger and the desire to punish. It often consists of simple associations of outcomes, personal characteristics, emotions, and restorative acts (e.g. bad people deserve bad outcomes). Over time, the emotions of the heuristic response dissipate to make way for a second type of processing.

The systematic response follows thoughtful consideration of the relevant circumstances of an event. This consideration is slower to occur, and includes assessments of what a person deserves, attributions of the person's responsibility and the culpability of various possible agents of the injustice, and consideration of various courses of action. The systematic response is deliberative, so it requires cognitive resources. However, cognitive resources can be limited by the situation (e.g. a person may not have the time or cognitive capacity to consider all of the circumstances), or they can be limited by the disposition of the observer in question (e.g. preference for intuitive versus deliberative reasoning is a personality dimension that varies across individuals, and shapes the degree to which people voluntarily engage in deliberative reasoning about an event).[5]

While judges therefore engage in a careful synthesis of factors, ensuring the systematic response supersedes the heuristic response in the determination of a just outcome in the law, the conditions to support the systematic response are by no means guaranteed when laypeople consider a just outcome outside the structures of judicial reasoning. To the extent that people do not have the time, opportunity, preference, or capacity for deliberation (or to the extent that avenues of popular discourse, such as press reporting, promote quick, emotive processing of information), the heuristic response (the initial, retributive impulse) will dominate people's decisions about just outcomes, prompting a divergence between legal and lay notions of justice.

---

5   Juliette Richetin et al, 'The Moderator Role of Intuitive Versus Deliberative Decision Making For the Predictive Validity of Implicit and Explicit Measures' (2007) 21(4) *European Journal of Personality* 529.

There is certainly evidence that community sentiment about crime is dominated by retributive notions, with public demands for harsher sentences common in many parts of the world[6] (though the use, effects and acceptability of various forms of punishment may vary across cultures[7]). Research shows that we feel an emotional impulse to punish an offender when we witness an injustice,[8] even when doing so will be costly to us.[9] This retributive impulse fulfils several important social needs; for example, it levels the power imbalance caused by a transgression.[10] Punishment also serves an instrumental purpose – people are concerned about becoming victims of crime in future and look to punishment to reduce the likelihood of future harm[11] – but research shows that retribution, not behaviour control, is the dominant motivation underlying people's calls for sanctions,[12] and people choose to administer punishment even when they know it has limited ability to prevent future offences.[13]

Thus, there is often a discrepancy between the deliberative, legal notions of just outcomes formed through judicial reasoning, and the more often heuristic, retributive notions of just outcomes that dominate in the community. Whether or not we endorse it, widespread punitive sentiment can shape the design of crime control policy and the operation

6   Monica M Gerber and Jonathan Jackson, 'Authority and Punishment: On the Ideological Basis of Punitive Attitudes towards Criminals' (2016) 23(1) *Psychiatry, Psychology and Law* 113.

7   Huesmann and Podolski, 'Punishment: A Psychological Perspective' in McConville and Devon (eds), *The Use of Punishment* (Willan Publishing, 2003) 55–88.

8   Kevin M Carlsmith and John M Darley, 'Psychological Aspects of Retributive Justice' (2008) 40 *Advances in Experimental Social Psychology* 193; John Darley, 'Just Punishments: Research on Retributional Justice' in M Ross and D T Miller (eds), *The Justice Motive in Everyday Life* (Cambridge University Press, 2002) 314; Norman T Feather, *Values, Achievement, and Justice: Studies in the Psychology of Deservingness* (Springer Science & Business Media, 2006); Neil Vidmar and Dale T Miller, 'Social Psychological Processes Underlying Attitudes toward Legal Punishment' (1980) *Law and Society Review* 565.

9   Ernst Fehr and Urs Fischbacher, 'Third-party Punishment and Social Norms' (Pt Elsevier Science) (2004) 25(2) *Evolution and Human Behavior* 63; Ernst Fehr and Simon Gächter, 'Altruistic Punishment in Humans' (Pt Nature Publishing Group) (2002) 415(6868) *Nature* 137.

10   Jeffrie G Murphy and Jean Hampton, *Forgiveness and Mercy* (Cambridge University Press, 1990); Vidmar and Miller, above n 8, 571.

11   Gerber and Jackson, above n 6.

12   Kevin M Carlsmith, John M Darley And Paul H Robinson, 'Why Do We Punish?: Deterrence And Just Deserts As Motives For Punishment' (2002) 83(2) *Journal Of Personality And Social Psychology* 284; John M Darley, Kevin M Carlsmith And Paul H Robinson, 'Incapacitation And Just Deserts As Motives For Punishment' (2000) 24(6) *Law And Human Behavior* 659; Robert M Mcfatter, 'Purposes Of Punishment: Effects of Utilities of Criminal Sanctions on Perceived Appropriateness' (1982) 67(3) *Journal of Applied Psychology* 255.

13   Robert J MacCoun, 'Drugs and the Law: A Psychological Analysis of Drug Prohibition' (1993) 113(3) *Psychological Bulletin* 497; Tom R Tyler, *Why People Obey the Law* (Princeton University Press, 2006).

of legal institutions.[14] In this chapter, I consider this divergence of legal and community notions of justice in light of two recent legal reforms: restorative justice and preventive detention. While each of these new paradigms changes the way in which a just outcome is determined in the law, they may not actually reduce the divergence between legal and community notions of justice.

II. Restorative Justice (RJ)

RJ is an alternative response to crime, now integral in several legal systems worldwide.[15] RJ scholars assert that the traditional criminal justice system is primarily retributive, in that its central objective is to assess culpability for a crime and, if necessary, apply proportional punishment.[16] This justice model has been critiqued by RJ theorists for failing to address a broader range of concerns following a crime – in particular, restoration of harmed parties. RJ is fundamentally concerned with harm reparation,[17] and challenges the assumption underlying the traditional criminal justice system that punishment is necessary to restore justice after a crime has occurred.[18]

RJ is typically enacted by involving the affected parties (victims, offenders and supporters) in an interactive process. Restorative outcomes to address the harm can include compensation to the victim or sanctions that are meaningful to the offender and also benefit the victim, community or offender.[19] While punishing the offender can be part of a RJ outcome, it is not fundamental. Rather, what is central to RJ is the interactive process emphasising healing of stakeholders.[20]

---

14   David Garland, *Punishment and Modern Society: A Study in Social Theory* (Oxford University Press, 1990); David Garland, *Mass Imprisonment: Social Causes and Consequences* (Sage, 2001); David Garland, 'The Culture of Control: Crime and Social Order in Contemporary Society' (2001); Nicola Lacey, *The Prisoners' Dilemma: Political Economy and Punishment in Contemporary Democracies* (Cambridge University Press, 2008).
15   Alana Saulnier and Diane Sivasubramaniam, 'Restorative Justice: Underlying Mechanisms and Future Directions' (2015) 18(4) *New Criminal Law Review* 510.
16   Howard Zehr, Harry Mika and Mark Umbreit, 'Restorative Justice: The Concept' (1997) 59 *Corrections Today* 68.
17   Saulnier and Sivasubramaniam, above n 15.
18   Michael Wenzel et al, 'Retributive and Restorative Justice' (2008) 32(5) *Law and Human Behavior* 375.
19   Gordon Bazemore, 'Restorative Justice and Earned Redemption: Communities, Victims, and Offender Reintegration' (1998) 41(6) *American Behavioral Scientist* 768.
20   John Braithwaite, *Restorative Justice and Responsive Regulation* (Oxford University Press, 2002).

The RJ approach poses an interesting challenge: as noted above, the research indicates that punishment is a prime mechanism for justice restoration in response to transgressions.[21] In designating punishment as a (potentially) unnecessary goal of the restorative outcome, RJ clearly deviates even further from the retributive impulse than the traditional justice system, which recognises punishment as one of several core goals to be balanced in sentencing.

We may question how RJ can serve a sense of justice if it does not centralise the imposition of punishment on the offender. Overall, the research suggests that support for RJ results from a complex array of factors: the existence of some motivation to punish an offender does not necessarily preclude people's endorsements of restorative procedures[22] (though people view RJ as a more appropriate response to serious crime when it involves the possibility of retributive sanctions).[23] There are several aspects of RJ that generate strong support for the approach; for example, the opportunity for stakeholders, especially victims, to voice their concerns.[24] Overall, it is likely that the interactive process undertaken by participants will itself engage systematic, deliberative reasoning that will temper the retributive response.

A problem arises, however, if an individual's retributive impulse is not tempered by systematic processing, and is left unaddressed and unacknowledged; if this occurs, the retributive impulse may impact particular RJ processes as well as the broader viability of RJ as a legal reform. If the individual in question is a stakeholder in a conference (e.g. a victim or their supporter), then the person's retributive impulse may play a subtle, implicit role in the outcomes they advocate to resolve the RJ process, or in some cases may even lead to an unsuccessful process (in which an outcome cannot be agreed by all parties). If the individual in question is a community member considering the suitability of RJ as a response to crime, the retributive impulse, untempered by systematic reasoning, could lead to scepticism, reducing the likelihood that the person will participate in RJ if invited in future, as well as reducing overall support for the restorative approach in the community.

---

21   Carlsmith, Darley and Robinson, above n 12.
22   Saulnier and Sivasubramaniam, above n 15; Wenzel et al, above n 18.
23   Dena M Gromet and John M Darley, 'Restoration and Retribution: How Including Retributive Components Affects the Acceptability of Restorative Justice Procedures' (2006) 19(4) *Social Justice Research* 395.
24   Elizabeth Moore, *Crime and Justice Statistics: Bureau Brief,* No 77 (BOCSAR, February, 2012).

III. Preventive Detention

Preventive detention schemes targeting sex offenders have operated in Australia since 2003, with legislation allowing community supervision or ongoing detention of offenders following the completion of their original sentences.[25] Generally a court decides whether to impose conditions for the supervision or detention of the offender, though there is some variation in the exact mechanisms by which this is accomplished across jurisdictions.

The primary goal of preventive detention is utilitarian: it is justified in terms of the broader interests of the community and the long-term interests of the offender. This is specifically articulated; for example, the Victorian Act states that its aim is to enhance the protection of the community and facilitate offender rehabilitation.[26] However, some scholars have raised concerns that imposing supervision or detention on an offender (without a fresh conviction) amounts to additional punishment.[27] In a case in the United States addressing civil commitment, the mechanism of preventive detention is referred to as 'a thinly veiled attempt to seek an additional term of incarceration'.[28] The key question, therefore, turns on the motivations driving preventive detention decisions in practice – is preventive detention actually based on utilitarian motives (community protection and offender rehabilitation) or retributive motives (additional punishment)?

Psychological research supports these concerns, indicating that the retributive impulse impacts decision-making in preventive detention. In one study on civil commitment in the United States,[29] researchers presented participants with a case study describing a serious sex offender, and varied two factors in the description. The first factor, risk of recidivism, was manipulated by telling participants that an expert assessed the offender's risk of reoffence as either high or low. (Note that this is a

---

25 Mickael N Bojczenko and Diane Sivasubramaniam, 'A Psychological Perspective on Preventive Detention Decisions' (2016) *Psychiatry, Psychology and Law* 1.

26 *Serious Sex Offenders (Detention and Supervision) Act 2009* (Victoria).

27 Bernadette McSherry, *Managing Fear: The Law and Ethics of Preventive Detention and Risk Assessment* (Routledge, 2013).

28 *Kansas v Hendricks* (US, 1997) 117 S. Ct. 2072, Brief for Respondent and Cross Petitioner at 21–22.

29 Kevin M Carlsmith, John Monahan and Alison Evans, 'The Function of Punishment in the "Civil" Commitment of Sexually Violent Predators' (2007) 25(4) *Behavioral Sciences & the Law* 437.

criterion on which preventive detention should be administered – when risk to the community is high, preventive detention is warranted under the legislation.) The second factor manipulated was the original sentence – participants were told that the offender had already served either a short or long sentence for his original offence. (This is not a criterion on which preventive detention should be administered – when the previous sanction is insufficient, preventive detention is not justified as a means of administering additional punishment.) After reading the description, participants were asked whether they would support civil commitment for the perpetrator. A higher risk of recidivism increased support for civil commitment; this is warranted, and aligns with the utilitarian principle that should drive preventive detention. Disturbingly, however, previous punishment also affected support for civil commitment: when the previous punishment was insufficient (a short, rather than long, sentence), support for civil commitment increased. The authors suggest that participants used civil commitment as a mechanism to correct the injustice, administering additional punishment via ongoing detention. This is not justified under the utilitarian principles of preventive detention, and appears to reflect a retributive impulse.

The conditions of Carlsmith et al's study do not replicate judicial decision-making; judges would undertake far more systematic, deliberative processing than participants in this study. But this study illuminates how people in the broader community might determine their support for preventive detention. These findings suggest the operation of a retributive impulse, and, in conjunction with the justice literature reviewed earlier, we could conclude that the less systematic processing people engage in, the more that retributive impulse will shape support for preventive detention. To the extent that retribution operates in people's reasoning about preventive detention, support for the legislation deviates from its intended, utilitarian purpose.

IV. Conclusions

Neither RJ nor preventive detention acknowledges the retributive notions of justice people can hold. While both legal reforms uphold worthy justice goals (restoration of harmed parties in RJ and utilitarian motives to protect communities in preventive detention), failure to recognise an intuitive, retributive impulse means that this impulse may play a subtle and insidious role in the implementation of these reforms. Whether or not it should be indulged, the retributive impulse is a human response we must study and acknowledge to ensure it is managed and tempered by deliberative reasoning, not only among legal decision-makers, but in the broader community. Contextual cues impact people's reasoning about specific situations,[30] suggesting that when laypeople do engage systematic reasoning to process accurate information about a particular case, their assessment of justice outcomes align more closely with those of judges; however, as noted above, the conditions to support the systematic response are by no means guaranteed when laypeople consider a just outcome outside the structures of judicial reasoning. While we need not advocate retribution in the content of legal reforms, we must recognise the retributive impulse in the process of implementing legal reforms and communicating them to the public. Failure to address this would undermine legal reforms that deviate from retributive notions.

---

30   N Finkel, *Commonsense Justice: Jurors' Notions of the Law* (Cambridge, MA: Harvard University Press, 2001).

16

How Interpretation of Indistinct Covert Recordings Can Lead to Wrongful Conviction: A Case Study and Recommendations for Reform

Helen Fraser[1]

I. Introduction and Overview

Covert recording ('bugging') is now authorised in almost every major police investigation. Unfortunately, because the need for secrecy compromises control over recording conditions, the audio is often indistinct. Legal practice regarding the use of indistinct covert recordings in trials has evolved haphazardly over the past 30 years, with no consultation of phonetic science. This has resulted in a number of anomalies, notably the fact that detectives are allowed (as 'ad hoc experts') to present their own transcripts of indistinct audio to 'assist' the jury in interpreting the audio evidence.

---

1   Forensic Phonetics Australia, forensicphonetics.com.au.

This chapter[2] highlights problems with this practice via a case study of a murder conviction obtained on the basis of a demonstrably inaccurate police transcript, then suggests directions for reform.

II. What Are Covert Recordings?

Covert recordings are conversations recorded secretly, without the knowledge of one or more of the speakers, via telephone intercept, hidden listening device or similar means. Legally obtained covert recordings can provide powerful evidence in criminal cases, capturing speakers giving information or making admissions they might not be willing to reveal openly in court.

While covert recordings are highly useful, they have a major drawback. Since it is difficult to control the recording conditions, the audio is frequently of extremely poor quality, to the extent it is impossible to make out what is said on one hearing. Several examples are given at forensictranscription. com.au, including an excerpt from a recording used in a murder trial that forms the basis of an extensive case study summarised briefly here.

This excerpt features a whispered conversation evidently about a pact related to the murder. The issue to be resolved by the trial was whether this was a pact to conceal the murder (making the speaker an accessory after the fact, a crime to which the defendant admitted) or a pact to commit the murder (making the speaker an accessory before the fact, which he denied).

This recording was the only direct evidence bearing on this issue, all the other evidence being described by the judge as circumstantial. The problem is that, on one or even several hearings, the audio is indecipherable. This is a common occurrence, that the law has had to deal with since covert recordings started to be used routinely by police in the 1980s.

---

2   This chapter summarises material from several previous publications. The following in particular contains extensive background references: H Fraser, 'Transcription of Indistinct Covert Recordings Used as Evidence in Criminal Trials' in H Selby and I Freckelton (eds), *Expert Evidence* (Thomson Reuters, 2015).

III. Standard Practice

Following *Butera* (1987),[3] a range of practices have been standardised in relation to indistinct covert recordings.

First, since it is clearly not convenient to play audio repeatedly in court, the judge can allow a transcript to assist the jury in making out what is said in the recording. Second, the transcript can be prepared by detectives working on the case. Many citizens are surprised or even alarmed to find that police transcripts are used in this way. However, when the reasons are explained, they are found to have a certain logic.

Indistinct audio is too hard for regular transcription agencies. However, since most covert recordings are obtained on behalf of police, detectives create their own transcripts as part of their investigations. When lawyers listen to an indistinct recording with the aid of a police transcript, it seems evident that the transcript is at least largely accurate. It appears that police transcribers, by listening many times to the indistinct audio, have been able to make out the words, and that their transcript is able to help listeners, saving them the trouble of repeated listening.

Of course it is clear that there are some risks in allowing police transcripts to assist in this way. In legal contexts, transcripts are often used as a convenient replacement for the audio itself. This makes some sense for reliable transcripts of overt recordings, such as court proceedings or police interviews, but it is essential that a jury should not be allowed simply to read a (possibly misleading) police transcript as a factual representation of audio used in evidence.

To avoid this, legal practice has developed a number of checks and balances. First, the defence is expected to scrutinise police transcripts thoroughly. In the event of disagreement over particular words or sections, the judge is expected to listen personally and make a ruling. Most commonly, this results in the decision being deemed 'a matter for the jury' – though it is open for the judge to exclude the police transcript, and there are precedents for this.

---

3   *Butera v DPP* (1987) 164 CLR 180.

In addition, the law insists the judge should carefully instruct the jury that the evidence is the audio, not the transcript. The transcript is provided only to assist them in hearing the recording, not as a replacement for it. After the audio has been played once in open court, it is given to the jury, who are encouraged to listen carefully in their own time, and form their own opinion as to what is said.

In essence, the transcript is provided, not as a factual representation of the recording, but as an opinion about its contents, for evaluation by the jury. In order to be allowed to offer an opinion (as opposed to factual evidence) in court, detectives provide transcripts in the role of so-called 'ad hoc expert'.[4] An 'ad hoc expert' is someone who, though lacking genuine expertise in a particular discipline, is deemed to have 'specialised knowledge'[5] in relation to a particular trial. With indistinct covert recordings, the specialised knowledge is understood to emerge from repeated listening to the audio.

IV. Spurious Reasoning

This explanation usually eases the qualms of those who are initially uncomfortable with the concept of police transcripts being used to assist with the interpretation of indistinct audio. However, although its logic may seem plausible on the basis of common knowledge, from the point of view of phonetic science it is entirely spurious. Indeed the potential for injustice is far greater than recognised by those with general unease regarding use of police transcripts.

Phonetics (the science of speech) is a little known and much misunderstood subject, even among scientists from other disciplines. Many assume it simply adds technical detail to facts already widely known through general education. The reality is that the findings of phonetic science overturn many apparent truisms of everyday knowledge. In particular, ideas underpinning the legal practice just described, widely accepted as self-evidently true, turn out to be fallacies.

---

4   G Edmond and M San Roque, 'Quasi-Justice: Ad Hoc Expertise and Identification Evidence' (2009) 33 *Criminal Law Journal* 8.

5   *Evidence Act 1995* (Cth) s 79.

A. Fallacy: Transcription is a mere 'secretarial skill'

Transcripts are used frequently in legal contexts, where transcription is deemed a simple process of writing down what was said, the main requirement being an ability to spell. This view has limited validity for transcription of clear, overt recordings. However, in relation to covert recordings it is straightforwardly fallacious. Both determining what was said, and rendering it in an appropriate format, require complex, high-level skills. As is well known in the language sciences, a transcript is never 'the' transcript. It can only ever be 'a' transcript.[6]

B. Fallacy: The more you listen the more accurately you hear

Listening many times is essential for creating a reliable transcript of indistinct audio. However, it is far from being sufficient. It is quite possible to listen many times and be wrong every time. Indeed, depending on the circumstances, listening repeatedly is more likely to entrench inaccurate perception than correct it.

C. Fallacy: It is easy to pick up errors by checking the transcript against the audio

When we listen to audio first without a transcript and then with a transcript, it seems that the transcript is aiding our perception. In fact it is creating our perception (as explained further below). Surprising as it may seem, the easiest way to change listeners' perception of indistinct audio is not to tamper with the audio itself, but simply to provide a different transcript. It is impossible to convey this effect adequately on paper (see examples at forensictranscription.com.au) but what it means is that errors are unlikely to be detected through normal 'checking'.

---

6   H Fraser, 'Transcription of Indistinct Forensic Recordings: Problems and Solutions from the Perspective of Phonetic Science' (2014) 1 *Language and Law/Linguagem e Direito* 5, ler.letras.up.pt/site/default.aspx?qry=id05id1444id2692&sum=sim.

V. The Fascinating Role of Expectation in Speech Perception

Demonstrations of these fallacies, though well known in phonetic science, are generally found 'amazing' and 'fascinating' by those who first encounter them. 'Common knowledge' asserts that hearing is a straightforward process of picking up 'what is there to be heard'. However, the reality is that listeners' unconscious *expectations* play an enormous role in shaping speech perception. This is similar to the general phenomenon of cognitive bias, or suggestibility,[7] but plays out rather differently with speech than with other kinds of perception.

In fact, the ability of expectation to mislead speech perception is not unknown in everyday life. It forms the basis of entertainment based on misheard song lyrics and other kinds of humour. However, it has a darker side in criminal law. In particular, it means all the checks and balances intended to ensure that a police transcript assists, rather than misleads, the jury are ineffective.

The 'pact' case study discussed earlier makes a good example. Experimental studies[8] show that listeners who are given the excerpt 'cold' never hear anything about a pact. Only when they are led by context to understand that the conversation relates to some kind of pact, do they hear the word 'pact', and even then no one hears the exact words of the police transcript ('at the start we made a pact'). However, once the police transcript is shown, the interpretation 'at the start we made a pact' is readily accepted by a majority of listeners – who are then willing to offer an opinion as to whether the covert recording suggests the pact was to commit or conceal murder.

This could be interpreted, and indeed is often experienced by those going through the perceptual stages just described, as the transcript 'assisting' perception. This interpretation, however, is contradicted by the fact that phonetic analysis demonstrates 'at the start we made a pact' is an inaccurate transcription. Unfortunately, it is not so easy to state with

---

7   A M Ridley, F Gabbert and D J La Rooy, *Suggestibility in Legal Contexts* (Wiley-Blackwell, 2013) 254.

8   H Fraser and B Stevenson, 'The Power and Persistence of Contextual Priming: More Risks in Using Police Transcripts to Aid Jurors' Perception of Poor Quality Covert Recordings' (2014) 18 *International Journal of Evidence and Proof* 205.

certainty exactly what was said, but it is something with the rhythmic structure of 'it's fucking payback' – quite different from that of 'at the start we made a pact'.

This demonstrates how expectations created by viewing a transcript can influence perception even when the transcript is manifestly wrong. The experience of being assisted by a reliable transcript is indistinguishable from the experience of being misled by an unreliable one.

As discussed above, this is a major problem for the standard legal concept that inaccuracies in a police transcript will be detected by ensuring it is checked against the audio by the defence, the judge, and the jury. A further finding of phonetic science creates even bigger problems for that concept. When participants are told that expert analysis reveals a transcript to be inaccurate, many still prefer the version they now seem to 'hear with their own ears', forgetting that it was only after being 'assisted' by the transcript that 'their own ears' heard anything remotely like the words it contains.

In considering the relevance of findings like these, it is worth recalling that juries evaluate police transcripts under conditions far less favourable for detection of inaccuracy than do participants in these experiments. Among other factors, participants hear the audio in short, carefully prepared sections, which they play repeatedly under a range of conditions deliberately constructed to reduce the influence of the transcript. Juries have neither the means nor the time to experience this.

Most importantly, participants first hear the audio 'cold', while a jury knows the content of the transcript in advance. This means a jury never has the experience of being 'unable to hear a word' before the transcript is presented, an important (though not always effective) factor in raising awareness that the transcript has influenced perception.

VI. A Flawed Process

All this means the likelihood of misleading errors or omissions in police transcripts being detected is very low, as first prosecutors, then defence, then the judge, and ultimately the jury, are deeply but unwittingly influenced by what they see on the page.

It also means the likelihood of police transcripts containing misleading errors or omissions is very high. What helps police hear indistinct audio that is opaque to others is not their repeated listening. It is their knowledge and assumptions about the context of the recording. To the extent such knowledge and assumptions are valid, they can indeed give valuable insight into the content of an indistinct recording. However, they are a double edged sword, which can mislead as easily as help.[9]

The potential for injustice is evident, and I am personally aware of an alarming number of cases where demonstrably inaccurate and misleading transcripts have been admitted as 'assistance' to the court. The case study described earlier recounts one of the most troubling.

In this trial, the defendant was found guilty of murder and sentenced to 30 years in prison, largely on the basis that a covert recording revealed him saying 'at the start we made a pact'. However, as discussed above, phonetic analysis makes clear that these words were not actually spoken.

In considering the import of this finding, it is useful to know that the murder was actually committed by this man's son (who confessed and was convicted and sentenced in a separate trial), at a time when the father had a solid alibi. The whole idea that the father was involved in any way arose through a detective erroneously believing he heard words which he interpreted as an admission that the father had masterminded the murder. Of course, once this idea had arisen, a good deal of 'circumstantial' evidence was able to be accumulated to support it. However, it is an open question how much might or might not have been made of that evidence without the (inaccurate) transcript to filter the interpretation of, first, investigators, and finally the jury. Recent demonstration in a very thorough, large-scale study[10] of the role of 'tunnel vision' as a factor increasing the risk of wrongful conviction is surely relevant.

Unfortunately, expert analysis of the audio in this case occurred only after the defence had exhausted all avenues of appeal (none related to the transcript). The only recourse was to seek to have the case reopened via an application to review the conviction. This application has recently been

---

9   H Fraser, 'Issues in Transcription: Factors Affecting the Reliability of Transcripts as Evidence in Legal Cases' (2003) 10 *International Journal of Speech Language and the Law* 203.

10   J B Gould et al, *Predicting Erroneous Convictions: A Social Science Approach to Miscarriages of Justice* (National Institute of Justice, 2012).

rejected in a ruling that disappointingly upholds fallacious ideas about speech and speech perception such as those discussed above (see case study at forensictranscription.com.au).

VII. The Problem and the Solution

The law's aim of maximising the assistance juries can derive from police insights about the content of covert recordings, while minimising the effect of transcript inaccuracies, is entirely reasonable, and one that phonetic science can assist with. Unfortunately, the practices the law has so far developed to achieve this aim are ineffective. Essentially they bring back 'verballing'[11] on a grand scale, without requiring conscious intention on the part of police,[12] creating substantial problems of actual and potential injustice.

The most important step in solving any problem is to a gain good understanding of its causes. Otherwise attempted solutions simply create new problems.

Here, it is clear that the problems are caused by the law taking phonetic science into its own hands, unaware of how many ideas about speech and speech perception, still accepted as 'common knowledge', have been shown to be false. Equally clearly, then, a good solution is unlikely to be found by continuing the process of developing practice for handling speech evidence by creating and applying legal precedents. Even if the original judgment is valid, its application in subsequent cases may not be, as seen in the less-than-optimal response in the UK to a useful judgment[13] criticising 'ad hoc expert' speaker identification evidence.

---

11 'Verballing' is claiming someone said something when in fact they didn't, notably in fabricated confessions. Evidence of verballing being used to obtain convictions was an important element in findings of police corruption in the 1990s (e.g. Wood, J R T (1997), *Royal Commission into the New South Wales Police Service, Volume 1: Corruption* (Sydney: Government of NSW).

12 H Fraser, 'Covert Recordings as Evidence in Court: The Return of Police "Verballing"?' [2013] *The Conversation,* theconversation.com/covert-recordings-as-evidence-in-court-the-return-of-police-verballing-14072.

13 See *R v Flynn* [2008] 2 Cr App R 266.

What is needed is wholesale reform[14] of legal practice around the handling and admission of indistinct covert recordings. To quickly forestall a common kneejerk excuse for avoiding the issue, such a system would certainly not involve having every covert recording transcribed by an expert in phonetic science.

Rather it would involve designing a system that ensures transcripts are reliable before covert recordings enter the legal process. Deciding the exact nature of such a system requires discussion and research conducted in close collaboration between phonetic science and the law. However, once the will is in place, it need not be overly difficult. An excellent precedent is seen in the highly practical and universally appreciated system for creating and using recorded police interviews, implemented to prevent police 'verballing'.

---

14   Perhaps more accurately undoing of the unfortunate effects of reforms introduced by *Butera*.

17

Australia's Lower-level Criminal Courts: Tackling 21st Century Problems in a 19th Century Paradigm?

Anne Wallace[1]

I. Introduction

Australia's courts have been significantly impacted by change over the past 30 years. They have, to some extent, modernised their procedures and practices, but are caught very much in a period of transition: between approaches to dealing with criminal cases that would be familiar to 19th century lawyers, and are focused on efficiency and volume, to those that require greater engagement with the needs of court users. This is particularly the case in the high-volume magistrates' courts that deal with most of the criminal caseload.

Magistrates' courts are characterised by high judicial workloads. They have accounted for most of the rise in criminal caseload over the past five years[2] and, in 2014–15, accounted for nearly 97 per cent of all matters finalised.[3]

---

1   Professor, La Trobe University Law School.
2   Productivity Commission, *Report on Government Services 2016* (Commonwealth of Australia, 2016) Table 7A.1.
3   Ibid. 7.16.

In a 2007 survey of Australian magistrates, three-quarters of respondents agreed that 'The volume of cases is unrelenting'.[4] Notwithstanding, most of these courts have maintained positive clearance rates,[5] with the same, or, in some cases, fewer, magistrates,[6] and backlogs have remained relatively constant.[7]

A 2004 National Court Observation Study found that the average time taken to dispose of a criminal matter in magistrates' courts was 4 minutes and 13 seconds.[8] Recent research commissioned by the Victorian Royal Commission into Family Violence (VRCFV) found that the average duration of family violence matters observed across eight court locations varied from 3 minutes 34 seconds to 10 minutes 17 seconds.[9] However, there are no established benchmarks for disposals of matters in any Australian criminal court.

II. Current Practice

The only measures for assessing the institutional performance of Australian criminal courts are those used by the Commonwealth Government Productivity Commission's annual 'Report on Government Services' (RoGS) – on backlogs and clearance rates, and judicial officers per finalisation.[10] These have been the focus of much debate,[11] and the absence of any more sophisticated methods of performance measurement arguably disadvantages courts in making the case for additional resources.

It is also arguable that focusing limited court resources on collecting RoGS data impedes courts' ability to collect and analyse data that assist their workforce planning. Research into caseload allocation found very few lower courts keep records of allocations, so that while all aim to equalise

---

4   Kathy Mack, Anne Wallace and Sharyn Roach Anleu, *Judicial Workload: Time, Tasks and Work Organisation* (Australasian Institute of Judicial Administration, 2013) 31–32.

5   That is, an excess of finalisations over lodgements: Productivity Commission, above n 2, 7.36.

6   Ibid. Table 7A.28.

7   Ibid. Table 7A.19; Table 7A.21.

8   Mack, Wallace and Roach Anleu, above n 4, 52–53.

9   Karen Gelb, *Understanding Family Violence Court Proceedings: The Impact of Family Violence on the Magistrates Court of Victoria* (March 2016) 54.

10   Productivity Commission, above n 2.

11   Brian Opeskin, 'The State of the Judicature: A Statistical Profile of Australian Courts and Judges' (2013) 35(3) *Sydney Law Review* 489, 491–92; J J Spigelman, 'Measuring Court Performance' (2006) 16(2) *Journal of Judicial Administration* 69.

the volume of judicial workload over time, and to deploy specialist judicial skills most effectively, they are unable to track whether or not these outcomes are achieved.[12]

The focus on RoGS data has also not assisted courts to identify and service the needs of court users, first identified as a pressing issue in 1998.[13] For example, despite widespread perceptions of an increase in numbers of unrepresented persons appearing before them in recent decades, most courts do not collect data about this, or do so only minimally or sporadically.[14]

An 'increasing diversity amongst court users, especially in terms of ethnic and cultural background and capacity to understand the language and procedures of courts'[15] was also identified in 1998. There are ongoing attempts, including Indigenous sentencing courts[16] and cultural awareness training for judicial officers,[17] to improve court outcomes for Aboriginal and Torres Strait Islander (ATSI) Australians and their communities. However, there is little data available on ATSI populations in courts, or the cultural and linguistic background of any court users.

In 2015, the newly-formed Judicial Council on Cultural Diversity (JCCD) conducted consultations to assess the capacity of the courts to provide access to justice for women from both groups. The subsequent reports identified a number of issues that impede effective communication with and participation at court by these vulnerable groups.[18] Previously

---

12   Mack, Wallace and Roach Anleu, above n 4, 9, 66, 73–74, 95–96, 99–100.

13   Stephen Parker, *Courts and the Public* (Australian Institute of Judicial Administration, 1998) 159–60.

14   Tania Sourdin, Elizabeth Richardson and Nerida Wallace, *Self-represented Litigants: Literature Review* (Monash University, 2012) 23.

15   Parker, above n 13, 159.

16   Michael King et al, *Non-Adversarial Justice* (The Federation Press, 2nd edn, 2014) 207–15.

17   Anne Wallace, *Australia's Indigenous People – A Curriculum Framework for Professional Development Programs for Australian Judicial Officers* (National Judicial College of Australia, 2013).

18   Judicial Council on Cultural Diversity, *The Path to Justice: Migrant and Refugee Women's Experience of the Courts: A Report Prepared for the Judicial Council on Cultural Diversity* (2016, Judicial Council on Cultural Diversity) 7 ('*JCCD Migrant Refugee Report*').

documented language and communication issues for ATSI populations[19] were confirmed as ongoing problems.[20] The reports also documented serious concerns about the provision of interpreters in courts.[21]

The JCCD and the VRCFV reported a range of other concerns about the court experience of vulnerable women:

- inadequate, out of date and unsafe court buildings;[22]
- lack of safe waiting spaces;
- lengthy, and indeterminate, waiting periods;[23]
- lack of understanding of court processes;[24]
- difficulty understanding forms, charges, orders, or judgments;[25] and
- courtroom dynamics, including the impact of actions and attitudes of judicial officers.[26]

The JCCD and VRCFV's emphasis on user-focused court services is a key feature of therapeutic and restorative theories of justice that have informed the development of new approaches to criminal cases over recent decades. These approaches feature direct engagement with offenders by judicial officers, multidisciplinary collaborative processes between the courts and service providers, less-adversarial paradigms, and outcomes that address community needs as well as those of victims.[27]

---

19   See, for example, Diana Eades, 'Judicial Understandings of Aboriginality and Language Use in Criminal Cases' in Peter Toner (ed), *Strings of Connectedness: Essays in Honour of Ian Keen* (ANU Press, 2015) 27–51.

20   Judicial Council on Cultural Diversity, *The Path to Justice: Aboriginal and Torres Strait Islander Women's Experience of the Courts: A Report Prepared for the Judicial Council on Cultural Diversity* (2016, Judicial Council on Cultural Diversity) 23–24 ('*JCCD ATSI Report*').

21   *JCCD ATSI Report*, above n 20, 24–25; *JCCD Migrant Refugee Report*, above n 18, 16, 29.

22   Victoria, Royal Commission into Family Violence, *Report and Recommendations Volume III* (March 2016) 130–32, 138; *JCCD ATSI Report*, above n 20, 28; *JCCD Migrant Refugee Report*, above n 18, 37–39.

23   Ibid.

24   Victoria, above n 22, 129–30; *JCCD ATSI Report*, above n 20, 28–29; *JCCD Migrant Refugee Report*, above n 18, 39.

25   Victoria, above n 22, 137; *JCCD ATSI Report*, above n 20, 29; *JCCD Migrant Refugee Report*, above n 18, 39.

26   Victoria, above n 22, 132–33; *JCCD ATSI Report*, above n 20, 30–32; *JCCD Migrant Refugee Report*, above n 18, 40–44.

27   King et al, above n 16, 241–45.

In contrast to the development of more engaged and therapeutic styles of judging, modern magistrates' courts also feature increasing use of audio-visual (video) links. Prison videolinks are now the presumed form of court appearance for defendants in custody in less formal court proceedings (variously categorised) across most jurisdictions.[28] Although the exact extent of their use is difficult to quantify,[29] well over half (57 per cent) of all court appearances by defendants in custody in New South Wales during 2013–14 were made by audio-visual link. [30]

Videolinks are thought to provide a more cost-effective and efficient, safer and less disruptive means of bringing prisoners to the court than physically transporting them.[31] There has also been a trend to provide interpreting services by telephone or videolink in the interests of saving costs.[32] Videolinks or CCTV are now used extensively to take evidence from vulnerable witnesses,[33] and the JCCD and the VRCFV recommended expanding this use.[34] Overseas, a recent review of efficiency in the criminal courts of England and Wales also recommended giving priority to audio and videolink hearings.[35]

Yet, while vulnerable witnesses generally experience a technology-mediated court appearance favourably, there has been little research about its impact on defendants,[36] including those who are unrepresented, or on interpreting. Research has found that the way that videolinks are used can impact on the ability to achieve effective engagement.[37]

---

28   Emma Rowden et al, *Gateways to Justice: Design and Operational Guidelines for Remote Participation in Court Proceedings* (2013, University of Western Sydney) 27, 95–102.
29   Ibid. 22–23.
30   Department of Police and Justice, Government of New South Wales, *Department of Police and Justice 2013–14 Annual Report* (2014) 82, www.justice.nsw.gov.au/Documents/Annual%20 Reports/2013-14_Annual_Report.pdf.
31   Rowden et al, above n 28, 21.
32   See, for example, Department of the Attorney-General, Government of Western Australia, *Videolinks*, www.courts.dotag.wa.gov.au/V/video_link.aspx?uid=3226-3984-5962-8567.
33   Rowden et al, above n 28.
34   Victoria, above n 22, 173; *JCCD ATSI Report,* above n 20, 40; *JCCD Migrant Refugee Report,* above n 18, 53.
35   Sir Brian Leveson, *Review of Efficiency in Criminal Proceedings* (Judiciary of England and Wales, January 2015) 17.
36   Carolyn McKay, 'Video Links from Prison: Permeability and the Carceral World' (2016) 5(1) *International Journal for Crime, Justice and Social Democracy* 21, 22–23.
37   Rowden et al, above n 28, 68–73.

III. The Future

The only recent systematic attention given to the operation of lower-level criminal courts in Australia has been as part of the VRCFV's investigation, and the increasing impact of family violence on the workload of these courts[38] also suggests that its findings bear close examination. The JCCD recommendations and academic research also identify ways in which these courts can complete their transition to a 21st century operating paradigm.

First, there is a need to recognise that the skills required for judicial work in these courts have changed. While magistrates have always needed to communicate effectively with self-represented parties, increasingly they need to be able to engage with individuals from diverse cultural and linguistic backgrounds and to work effectively with interpreters.[39] They also need to engage effectively with increasing numbers of people who will appear before them 'virtually' rather than physically.

There is also an increasing need for specialisation: in therapeutic courts, which require particular types of judicial skills, and to manage particular lists where other special expertise and knowledge is required.[40] Those allocating caseload to judicial officers already take into account a range of special skills and differential expertise.[41] However, in most of the courts studied in the research, there are no formal mechanisms available for identifying and developing specialist skills and expertise.[42] There would be merit in courts making more transparent the process by which the qualities and skills required for specialist judicial work are identified, fostered, and supported.[43]

The VRCFV called for investigation into which matters need to come before a court, and which do not, and, of those that do, which need to be dealt with by a judicial officer. It noted that the time taken to deal with 'straightforward or procedural matters'[44] including 'adjudication

---

38   Victoria, above n 22, 148.
39   *JCCD ATSI Report*, above n 20, 9; *JCCD Migrant Refugee Report*, above n 18, 9.
40   Anne Wallace, Kathy Mack and Sharyn Roach Anleu, 'Judicial Caseload Allocation and Specialisation: Finding the "Right Judge"?' (December 2012) *International Journal for Court Administration* 68, 69.
41   Mack, Wallace and Roach Anleu, above n 4, 102.
42   Wallace, Mack and Roach Anleu, above n 40, 79.
43   Ibid. 79–80.
44   Victoria, above n 22, 148.

and administration of traffic matters, including low-level offences such as driving a vehicle in a toll zone without registration'[45] can constitute 'a significant proportion of court business'. [46]

The VRCFV and the JCCD focused on the need for courts to develop the role of court staff, to encourage and deploy specialist skills. To free up resources and improve services to court users, the VRCFV recommended that courts move away from inefficient manual and paper-based processes towards electronic and online processes, to enable the use of staff such as registrars as 'highly skilled and proactive … case and list managers'.[47] The JCCD called for the introduction of Court Cultural Liaison and Indigenous Court Liaison officers in all courts.[48]

The VRCFV drew attention to the current system of case-listing which requires parties to turn up at fixed times (usually 10 am) to wait for an indeterminate period for their matter to be dealt with.[49] This system was also highlighted in a recent review of efficiency in UK criminal courts, which called for a review of court opening hours.[50]

The VRCFV recommended staggered listings and benchmarking waiting time to provide greater guidance to parties as to when their cases would be heard and how long they should have to wait.[51] It noted that 'Effective use of benchmarks necessitates data-collection practices that allow courts to reliably measure performance'. It recommended capping family violence lists 'at a level that allows magistrates sufficient time to hear each matter',[52] an exercise that also requires attention to benchmarking.

The JCCD and the VRCFV recommended improvements to court buildings, including waiting areas, security, support services and signage.[53] The VRCFV noted the importance of courts working in therapeutic mode being able to work in partnership with relevant court-based professionals and services.[54] The JCCD reports emphasised the importance of building relationships between courts and the community more broadly, including

---

45   Ibid.
46   Ibid.
47   Ibid.
48   *JCCD ATSI Report*, above n 20, 9; *JCCD Migrant Refugee Repo*rt, above n 18, 9.
49   Victoria, above n 22, 167.
50   Leveson, above n 35, 42 [146].
51   Victoria, above n 22, 167–68.
52   Ibid. 168.
53   Ibid. 172; *JCCD ATSI Report*, above n 20, 39; *JCCD Migrant Refugee Report*, above n 18, 53.
54   Victoria, above n 22, 181.

collaborative efforts to educate and improve understanding of court processes.[55] They also recommended clear court policies in relation to identifying the need for, engaging with and using interpreters.[56]

The VRCFV found the information technology (IT) infrastructure in Victoria's magistrates' courts was inadequate and that: 'An upgraded, fit-for-purpose IT system is an essential precursor to change'.[57] It recommended freeing-up resources by creating an online electronic court registry to allow registry-related inquiries to be centralised and carried out by a specialist workforce[58] and IT upgrades to enable the court to better receive and share information. The JCCD called for improved data collection by courts about the cultural, linguistic and gender diversity of their users.[59] Research suggests that diary and calendaring systems also require updating from the manual and stand-alone systems used in most courts.[60]

The VRCFV also noted the potential for newer smart, agile, technology solutions to craft user-centric services, such as a case management system using 'a real-time airport-style electronic display of listed matters, and alerts transmitted to parties' mobile phones, [to enable] parties ... to observe their place in the order of matters being heard on a given day',[61] alleviate the anxieties of indeterminate waiting and enable those attending court to more effectively structure their time.[62]

A further step might be the development of guided online resolution systems for minor or quasi-criminal offences, such as traffic matters. In addition to saving costs, this might appeal to a newer generation who are familiar with online dispute resolution systems in contexts such as eBay. The resource savings could be used to provide support to court users who are not digitally empowered and whose matters are more serious or complex.

---

55 *JCCD ATSI Report*, above n 20, 38; *JCCD Migrant Refugee Report*, above n 18, 8.
56 *JCCD ATSI Report*, above n 20, 39; *JCCD Migrant Refugee Report*, above n 18, 53.
57 Victoria, above n 22, 162.
58 Ibid. 163.
59 *JCCD ATSI Report*, above n 20, 9; *JCCD Migrant Refugee Report*, above n 18, 9.
60 Mack, Wallace and Roach Anleu, above n 4, 66–67.
61 Victoria, above n 22, 168.
62 Ibid.

Courts can improve their use of existing technology. Research has shown that court videolinks could be considerably enhanced by greater attention to configuration, supporting environment, protocols, procedures, and training.[63]

It is clear from the JCCD and VRCFV reports that assessment of court performance needs to move beyond the focus of the RoGS data to a greater emphasis on assessing whether courts are meeting the needs of their users. Both JCCD reports call for the establishment of key performance indicators to measure progress against their recommendations,[64] and, as noted, a number of the VRCFV's recommendations require benchmarking.

The JCCD now provides resources and support to courts to deliver services to a culturally diverse community.[65] As it has noted, the International Court Excellence Framework, to which a number of Australian courts subscribe, could also serve as a forum for standard-setting and performance measurement with a focus on client perspectives and access to justice.[66] It has already been used, for example, by the Victorian courts to establish key performance indicators for use in the budgeting process.[67]

IV. Conclusion

Australia's first-instance criminal courts are moving from an outdated paradigm – an operational environment focused on the convenience of the court and the professional participants – to one that is user-centric and places greater value on engagement with court users. But progress has been slow. Solutions designed to increase efficiency still often focus on 'throughput' and cost-savings for executive government. Many staff still operate largely in a transactional mindset, with the imperative of the yearly RoGS data collection hanging over them.

There have been significant pulls in the other direction – the development of therapeutic and problem solving approaches, methods of taking evidence to reduce trauma for children and victim witnesses, and greater awareness

---

63   Rowden et al, above n 28, 45–79.
64   *JCCD ATSI Report*, above n 20, 41; *JCCD Migrant Refugee Report*, above n 18, 55.
65   Judicial Council on Cultural Diversity, *Cultural Diversity within the Judicial Context: Existing Court Resources* (15 February 2016, Judicial Council on Cultural Diversity), www.jccd.org.au/publications/.
66   Ibid. 7.
67   Court Services Victoria, *Court Services Victoria Annual Report 2015–16*, 22 (November 2016, Court Services Victoria).

of the needs of unrepresented parties, of Indigenous Australians and those from migrant and refugee backgrounds. There has been strong judicial leadership for these developments, including the recent establishment of the JCCD. The current priority given to family violence at government level and the attention to court reform given by the VRCFV may provide the best opportunity yet to move the lower criminal courts fully into the 21st century.

Part III.
Environmental Law

18

What is the Mainstream? The Laws of First Nations Peoples

Irene Watson[1]

I. Introduction

The business of colonialism is not yet finished; it rolls on relentlessly. This fact presents us with certain challenges. For Australia, the legal limit in dealing with the fact of First Nations Peoples' existence was reiterated by the High Court in *Mabo (No 2)*.[2] It determined that the extent of recognition of First Nations cannot move beyond the 'skeletal' principle which is the foundation of the colonial state.[3]

As a result of this position taken by the High Court, one that has been restricted even further by the Australian state,[4] the genocide of First Nations is able to continue.[5] As a parallel, but as part of the same project,

1   Research Professor of Law, University of South Australia. I acknowledge the support of an ARC Indigenous Discovery Award which enabled me to work on the project Indigenous Knowledges: Law, Society and the State. I also acknowledge the research assistance of Jo Bird and Emily Collins.
2   *Mabo v Queensland (No 2)* (1992) 175 CLR 1.
3   Ibid. 30.
4   *Native Title Act 1993* (Cth). For a discussion of the limitations of this Act, see Irene Watson, 'Sovereign Spaces, Caring for Country and the Homeless Position of Aboriginal Peoples' (2009) 108 *South Atlantic Quarterly* 27; Irene Watson, *Aboriginal Peoples, Colonialism and International Law: Raw Law* (Routledge, 2015).
5   On genocide, see Watson, *Aboriginal Peoples*, above n 4, 109–44.

Australia still holds records for animal and plant extinctions and our territories are threatened with ecocide with each new and damaging development proposal.[6]

While this chapter sits within an environment stream, which includes resources, Indigenous relationships to the environment and property, my call for reform crosses all areas of the law, so the cast of the chapter is much broader. Western legal systems are segmented and categorised into property, contract, torts and so on; First Nations' legal systems are relational. This chapter will embrace the complexity of First Nations' legal systems and the problem of having to fit Aboriginal laws within colonial foundations. In the near future the challenges will be immense and those formulating the legal and policy responses should be aware of those complexities. So where to begin?

II. Where to Begin

We need to move beyond the politics of recognition: politics which are limited by the colonial foundations of the state.[7] These foundations pass as law, but it is military power and colonial violence that are the foundations of the colonising project called Australia, a project which continues to this day. The urgency of our time calls for law, certainly, but my argument is not so much for the reform of Euro-centric law, because its colonial foundation is unlawful, but instead for the re-emergence of the ancient laws of this continent now called Australia.[8]

---

6   For example, Australia has the highest rate of mammal extinction in the world. Globally, over the past 400 years, one in three mammal extinctions have occurred in Australia. A 2015 review of the literature indicates that since 1788, 28 species of Australian land mammals have become extinct. Compare this with post-invasion North America, in which only one mammal species has become extinct over more than 400 years. See John Woinarski, Andrew Burbidge and Peter Harrison, 'Ongoing Unravelling of a Continental Fauna: Decline and Extinction of Australian Mammals since European Settlement' (2015) 112 *Proceedings of the National Academy of Sciences* 4531. For information on flora both extinct and threatened, see Department of the Environment and Energy, *EPBC Act List of Threatened Flora*, www.environment.gov.au/cgi-bin/sprat/public/publicthreatenedlist. pl?wanted=flora; and, for a comparison with international data, see 'Fact Check: Does Australia Have One of the "Highest Loss of Species Anywhere in the World"?', *ABC News*, 4 March 2016, www.abc. net.au/news/2015-08-19/fact-check-does-australia-have-one-of-the-highest-extinction/6691026.
7   I discuss the politics of recognition in Watson, *Aboriginal Peoples*, above n 4, 18.
8   For further discussion see ibid.

The Australian state continues to run on an unlawful foundation; the opportunity to review this position was presented in *Mabo (No 2)*, but the High Court decided there was no possibility other than to retain the skeleton principle of colonial Australia's foundation. So are we stuck with this, an unlawful foundation that, regardless of *Mabo (No 2)*'s rejection of *terra nullius*, also rejects the continuity of Aboriginal laws? We now have affirmed the unlawfulness of the *terra nullius* state, but with no alternative in its place.

I propose another truth, another way of knowing law, a way which was the 'mainstream law' for this continent for millennia, since the first sunrise, a way which still lives as the laws of the land to this day. The laws of the land are ancient and as old as the continent itself; they continue to exist. The laws of the land cannot be finished, other than perhaps in the minds of those humans who proclaim their ending. But law continues, just as the natural world continues, regardless of how it may be denied by humans. For that is the law.

The reform I advocate is that the colonial settler society should better see and know this law, so that it becomes visible to those who cannot see it beneath the continuing cover of *terra nullius*. It is a radical call, one which calls for us to begin again. It may be an impossible call, but not to respond to it and to do nothing presages an impossible future, not only for humans, but for all life on earth.

At this stage some readers may be thinking 'Can't we have our cake and eat it?', but we can't do that anymore. The dire consequences if we do have been pointed out many times.

III. Beyond the Politics of Recognition

Kombu-Merri and Waka Waka elder and philosopher Mary Graham has argued that First Nations have managed this country forever and that we still have the authority to do so today.[9] Clearly we do not have the power beyond the 'recognition' politics of the colonial state but we do still hold the lawful authority to carry out ancient obligations to care for country.

---

9   Mary Graham, 'Some Thoughts about the Philosophical Underpinnings of Aboriginal Worldviews' (2008) 45 *Australian Humanities Review* 181, www.australianhumanitiesreview.org/archive/Issue-November-2008/graham.html.

Many First Nations share the obligation to care for country; it is in our laws to ensure that future generations – not only human but all species, including our ngaitji[10] relations – have a sustainable future. Many First Nations understand that this is law which is core to our being and hold this core even in the face of the colonial assimilation policies that were intended to destroy our connections to law.

The challenge for non-Indigenous Australians is to see First Nations Peoples and the laws of the land from another horizon, one of law outside and beyond the continuing *terra nullius* cover of the colonial project. That is to see beyond the commodification of land and the constructions of Aboriginality as backward and savage.

The dialogue we need to have must move beyond the current trajectory emanating from a politics of recognition to become one which listens to the laws of the land and acts lawfully in response. We need to move beyond pragmatism, short-term solutions, and political and economic gains and embrace the truth of the natural world and its ancient laws.

IV. International Law

International law concepts such as self-determination, territorial integrity, and free, prior and informed consent have all been considered possible tools to transform coloniality. From within a critical First Nations' lens, concepts of self-determination, territorial integrity, and free, prior and informed consent have been considered for the possibility of coexistence beyond the current assimilationist framework we are subjected to.

Across my work I have considered the limitations of Euro-centred international and domestic laws on 'Indigenous recognition'. I have considered the illusion of recognition and have advocated for the real possibility of an ongoing existence based on Aboriginal laws and their inherent philosophy of relationality.

To continue the current 'progress and development' agenda is to ensure the decline of life on earth, and the death of many species. The possibility of our survival is enmeshed in relationships with all life forms and requires respect for Aboriginal laws and their core philosophies of relationality.

---

10   Our ngaitji represents the relationship or kinship we share with our surrounding natural world. It is a relationship that teaches us about the unity we share with all natural things.

As I oppose the fracking and other developments of ancestral lands which I am related to and obliged to care for, the greater part of humanity is also tied to the matrix of like connections.[11] We are all dependent upon air and water, and our airs and waters flow together and are connected.

The maintenance and centring of First Nations epistemologies is essential to survival. Is it then possible to reconstruct international law so that it is liberated from its colonial origins, and is replaced with or at least inclusive of First Nations laws, philosophies and knowledges?

V. First Nations Epistemologies

If First Nations are not positioned to reframe the dialogue (as we are not currently), then coloniality will continue and with it the same old destructive development agenda. A horizontal dialogue between colonialist interests and First Nations-centred epistemologies is essential to human survival. We must put the discussion of Indigenous rights at the centre of the debate, moving beyond the literature on colonially constructed identities. Current human-rights frameworks ignore our core role as carers for the land for future generations; the fullness of Indigenous epistemologies is misunderstood and also ignored. Our inherent connectedness to the natural world is ignored and remains largely unfathomable to the non-Indigenous world. The critical need for another way of being law-full is not known or is currently incapable of being seen. Opening our eyes widely and seeing and knowing law is critical.

VI. Recognition: The Mainstream Context

Aboriginal law has run and continues to run across Aboriginal lands; it remains the invisible mainstream law. But it continues to be rendered invisible by the colonial project, which continues today even though its existence is denied.

---

11   Irene Watson and Kungari Aboriginal Heritage Association, Submission No 103 to Parliament of South Australia Natural Resources Committee, *Inquiry into Unconventional Gas (Fracking) in the South East of South Australia*, 29 January 2015; Irene Watson and Kungari Aboriginal Heritage Association, submission in response to *Nora Creina Golf Course and Tourism Resort: Major Project Public Environmental Report*, January 2016.

The law is the law is the law. It just is, and no amount of violence and no colonial system established by force and constructing itself as 'law' will override or extinguish it. While the colonial legal system has constructed myths which emanate from *terra nullius*, they are just that – myths of non-existence constructed for the purpose of enabling an unlawful foundation. Aboriginal laws remain the mainstream and, while First Nations are deemed peoples without law and merely objects of the colonial law, this is not the truth.

The colonial project posits and constructs rules which overlay the law of the land, rules which reject First Nations' laws as Aboriginal oral stories, and represent their reliance upon the memory of elders as mere myth and fable. While science is only now catching up with many of our stories and songs (as noted in a recent example concerning the rising waters which resulted in the Great Barrier Reef[12]), they are too often fobbed off as childlike, and their ancient coded knowledge of the codependence between humans and their environments remains unexamined.

Eurocentric law postures as being secular, and holds that the central position of spirituality and relationality in First Nations' laws means that they are not real law. But this position denies that the origins of Western Eurocentric legal systems were and remain founded upon religious law. Christianity both annihilated and excluded the 'heathen' because they were not Christians.

VII. Possibilities for Common Ground: What will Happen if We do Nothing?

Critical sociologist and legal theorist Boaventura de Sousa Santos reminds us of our obligations beyond critical discourse and of the need for talk about the unspeakable when he warns of the risk of an epistemicide, the murder of knowledge, if the exclusion of 'different' voices continues.[13] Although as I have said above the law is the law – it just is and it cannot be extinguished – the potential for juricide also looms if Aboriginal

---

12   Nick Reid and Patrick Nunn, 'Aboriginal Memories of Inundation of the Australian Coast Dating from More than 7000 Years Ago' (2016) 47 *Australian Geographer* 11.
13   Boaventura de Sousa Santos, *Epistemologies of the South: Justice against Epistemicide* (Paradigm Publishers, 2014).

legal systems continue to be ignored. Perhaps it is more accurate to say that there is the potential for a death of knowledge of the law and its connection to the First Nations carriers of law.

Is there a possibility for common ground, or even a dialogue on these concerns, beyond the dominance of a Western-centric universalism and incommensurability between cultures?[14] An equality of power relations, that is, relations of shared authority which could fit the purposes of intercultural translations, is the necessary precursor, since only then can reciprocity among social groups or movements be obtained.[15]

In thinking through this terrain, First Nations' critical approaches to vague and loaded concepts such as 'equality' remain essential. They are essential to the possibility of First Nations' voices being heard and not suppressed so as not even to register.[16]

I consider that the following questions and comments raised by Santos contribute to the possibility of our voices being heard by dominant colonial states:

- How do the power relations between First Nations and states translate into Western law?
- What place or space is there to speak of coloniality, for where is the world free of colonialism?
- Opening up the space is more than an intellectual process.
- Inter-cultural translation is an instrument for mediation and negotiation and can only flourish where there is a commitment to decolonising power relations.

What are the possibilities for First Nations' laws? How can we re-centre them and the natural world? First Nations' perspectives on authority and power should be central to any intercultural dialogue.

In understanding that the natural world holds authority, it would follow then that all places and spaces are open to being contact zones. We need to listen about climate change. We need to listen about coal mining and fracking, and to all events which affect our natural ecosystems.

---

14   Ibid. 212.
15   Ibid. 214.
16   Miranda Fricker, *Epistemic Injustice: Power and the Ethics of Knowing* (Oxford University Press, 2007).

Our natural world is in crisis which makes the need for translation ever more urgent.[17] The West has reached the end point of project progress, and does not have the solutions to the crisis. It has no other lands to invade and colonise beyond leaving our mother Earth and searching for other planets. Current regimes of recognition and protection do not work. We are on the brink of sacrificing our waters, our oceans and our lands which provide for an overpopulated planet. Recognition laws in respect of First Nations come in the form of native title laws[18] and Aboriginal heritage protection,[19] and they are accompanied by named environmental laws,[20] but none of them have the capacity to protect the environments which are vital to our survival. We are on a trajectory which it appears could sacrifice all life forms, but we still have the capacity for ongoing life. Cycles do return, to begin again. Aboriginal law is an ongoing cycle; it is the law.

---

17 Santos, above n 13, 233.
18 *Native Title Act 1993* (Cth); *Native Title Amendment Act 1998* (Cth).
19 *Aboriginal and Torres Strait Islander Heritage Protection Act 1984* (Cth).
20 *Environment Protection and Biodiversity Conservation Act 1999* (Cth), among other Australian state and Commonwealth laws.

19

Overturning *Aqua Nullius*: Pathways to National Law Reform

Virginia Marshall[1]

I. Background and Introduction

The purpose of this chapter is to identify and propose new pathways to reform legal issues affecting Indigenous people in the exercise of their traditional and revitalised rights and interests in water within national and state water regimes. I argue that the exercise of traditional and revitalised laws as expressed in Art 11 of the UN Declaration on the Rights of Indigenous Peoples (UNDRIP) should be incorporated into Australia's water laws and policies, in addition to other articles of the Declaration, for example Art 20, for Indigenous peoples to develop economic opportunities in water. These and other relevant international instruments incorporated into Australian law would give expression to the exercise and enjoyment of traditional and revitalised rights to water, economic and cultural property rights and interests, to create substantive pathways for Indigenous First Peoples of Australia.

The colonisation of Australia into existing states and territories was staggered over temporal phases, and the nation state progressively excluded, controlled and marginalised Indigenous communities' cultural

---

1   Principal Solicitor, Triple BL Legal.

and economic water rights and interests. Pathways to water reform must acknowledge that there have been few opportunities for Indigenous communities in Australia to advance and strengthen their own economy:

> The boundaries to the ownership and control of water and other resources inherent to Indigenous peoples have been defined by the Crown. The Commonwealth water legislation has clearly defined the parameters of the rights and interests of Indigenous peoples' water resources. The exercise of water rights in Australia by Aboriginal communities historically turns on 'government political will' to include Aboriginal peoples in policy and legislative development.[2]

Private property rights lie at the heart of Western market-based economies such as Australia, where alienable freehold land and tradeable water rights generate wealth, and prevail over native title rights and interests. Although the concept of private property rights in water is not new, as 'the Romans legislated individual property rights to regulate water use',[3] it is new for Indigenous peoples of Australia.

There is a need to create new concepts of water tenure and property models which do not leave Indigenous communities vulnerable to forfeit on default in failing to meet their legal obligations. Any proposed reform to the Australian Government's water policy and laws requires the full review of the National Water Initiative which should be subject to the scrutiny of human rights principles such as UNDRIP. The Organisation for Economic Co-operation and Development (OECD) baseline projection is that 3.9 billion people will be subject to severe water stress by 2050.[4] The OECD Taskforce on Water Security and Sustainable Growth states that:

> the goal of improving material wealth of societies must be negotiated within the boundaries imposed by the availability and sustainability of the water resource, and balanced with the cultural and spiritual values of water.[5]

---

2   Virginia Marshall, *A Web of Aboriginal Water Rights: Examining the Competing Aboriginal Claim for Water Property Rights and Interests in Australia* (PhD Thesis, Macquarie University, 2014) 225.
3   Joshua Getzler, *A History of Water Rights at Common Law* (Oxford University Press, 2006) 11.
4   C W Saddoff et al, 'Securing Water, Sustaining Growth: Report of the GWP/OECD Task Force on Water Security and Sustainable Growth' (2015) 30.
5   Ibid. 39.

The creation of Australian property rights in water was enacted by the statutory separation of water from land. National Water Reform was 'intended to create effective water management and certainty for business and industry' including 'investment in water trading'.[6] Indigenous peoples were afforded the incorporation of discretionary Indigenous Clauses in the 'blueprint for national water reform' under the National Water Initiative, which relegated the status of Indigenous peoples to one of many minority interests in water. The recent progress for Aboriginal peoples' water interests in the Murray–Darling Basin was a result of the parliament's amendment of s 202(5)(c) of the *Water Act 2007* (Cth) to include 'at least 2 Indigenous persons with expertise in Indigenous matters relevant to the Basin's water resources'.[7] Such amendments are inadequate.

The background to the exploration of an Indigenous water discourse should acknowledge that water resources are framed by a Western postcolonial legacy which 'built' Australia's wealth by fortifying control through state and federal constitutions to secure rights to water and land tenure. Observations by settlers and the establishment were cognisant of the presence of Indigenous peoples, their laws, customs and practices, often tolerating coexisting water use in the expectation that it would not impede Western modes of economic development. Australian governments have 'historically given water entitlements to farmers for free and encouraged them to utilize available water'.[8]

On the one hand Australian water management by the colonial founders estranged Indigenous communities from continuing to participate in their historic Indigenous economies. On the other hand those same colonial constructs were apparent during the government's national water reform process with the lack of inclusion of Indigenous rights and interests and offering limited scope in this process to address repugnant historical water policies such as the treatment of Indigenous water rights as *aqua nullius* and 'belonging to no one'.[9]

---

6   Marshall, above n 2, 323. Citing the National Water Commission, 'Australian Water Reform 2009: Second Biennial Assessment of Progress in Implementation of the National Water Initiative' ('Report', Australian Government, 2010) 104. See also Dr Virginia Marshall, Submission No 21 to Australian Government, Productivity Commission, *National Water Reform*, 18 April 2017.

7   See Virginia Marshall, 'The Progress of Aboriginal Water Rights in the Murray–Darling Basin in NSW: An Essential Element of Culture' (2015) *Australian Environment Review* 158.

8   Seamus Parker and Robert Speed, 'Agricultural Water Pricing: Australia' (Background Report, to the OECD Study 'Sustainable Management of Water Resources', 2010) 7.

9   Dr Virginia Marshall, *Overturning Aqua Nullius: Securing Aboriginal Water Rights* (Aboriginal Studies Press, 2017).

II. Indigenous Water Rights as 'First Rights'

National water reforms have failed to recognise Indigenous peoples 'first rights' in Australia's water use timeline. The concept of first rights is to clearly express that Indigenous people of Australia were, and continue to be, the 'first right' water users; a concept drawn from water concepts recognised for native peoples in the US as either 'prior appropriation' for beneficial water use or 'first in time' use for riparian water right use.[10] Indigenous peoples of Australia seek to exercise their legal and cultural rights for economic development as well as a *sui generis* use of water resources; for example, through native title, water trading, cultural heritage protection and cultural activities; in conjunction with the exercise of other statutory and common law land rights regimes established for Indigenous peoples.

The Crown's treatment of any purported continuing existence of Aboriginal people's rights to land and waters, prior to the High Court decision in *Mabo v Queensland (No 2)*,[11] concurred that such rights did not survive annexation, based upon the doctrine of *terra nullius*. Similarly the concept of *aqua nullius*, that is, 'water that belongs to no other', raises important questions that align equally with discourse on Indigenous land rights and are generally ignored in the broader discussion on property rights in water. Pre-colonial Indigenous tenure is expressed in *Mabo (No 2)* as 'special collective rights vested in an Aboriginal group by virtue of its long residence and communal use of land or its resources'.[12]

The *Mabo (No 2)* decision highlights the importance of incorporating international law into Australia's water law. The majority in the High Court *Mabo (No 2)* decision concluded that s 9 of the *Racial Discrimination Act 1975* (Cth) (*RDA*) referred to 'the enjoyment or exercise of fundamental freedoms' from Art 5 of the International Convention on the Elimination of All Forms of Racial Discrimination (CERD) but found it did not

---

10   See Michael C Blumm, 'Federal Reserved Water Rights as a Rule of Law' (2016) 52 *Idaho Law Review* 369. See also Robert T Anderson, 'Water Rights, Water Quality, and Regulatory Jurisdiction in Indian Country' (2015) 34(2) *Stanford Environmental Law Journal* 195.
11   (1992) 175 CLR 1.
12   Ibid. 33, *Mabo v Queensland (No 2)* HC judgement.

contravene 'the enjoyment of the applicant's traditional title'.[13] The court then turned its mind to *RDA* s 10 which referred to Art 5 that 'the right to be immune from arbitrary deprivation of property is a human right'.[14]

The incorporation of CERD and UNDRIP into Australia's water policies and laws would enshrine water as a human right and, as in *Mabo (No 2)*, 'draw upon international law and concepts of equality and social justice' to consider whether Australia has met its legal obligations. First Peoples' rights in water should be exercised as human rights. The Australian Law Reform Commission (ALRC) identified that the UNDRIP principles represent a 'principled way of moving forward' in the recognition and protection of Indigenous peoples' rights and interests.[15]

The ALRC proposes the concept of 'moving forward' as a 'platform for engagement on Indigenous issues'.[16] However, in relation to Indigenous water rights and interests, there is a conceptual national framework for Australia's water resources which should have prioritised Indigenous peoples as First Peoples in the hierarchy of water users, and not as a stakeholder. It is a matter of urgency that Indigenous water rights and interests require governments and other sector interests in water to recognise Indigenous communities as 'first use' rights and not a minority interest stakeholder in the consumptive and non-consumptive pools. The centrality of First Nation water use, ownership and management of water operates under the Indigenous rule of laws,[17] and the framework to understanding the use, management and ownership of water, collectively or otherwise.

---

13   *Mabo (No 2) v Queensland* 175 CLR 1.

14   Ibid.

15   Australian Law Reform Commission, *Connection to Country: Review of the Native Title Act 1993* (Cth), Final Report No 126 (2015) 82–85.

16   Ibid. 85.

17   The Indigenous ontological understanding of the Indigenous rule of laws is not singular. See Dr Virginia Marshall, 'Deconstructing Aqua Nullius: Reclaiming Aboriginal Water Rights and Communal Identity in Australia' (2016) 8/26 *Indigenous Law Bulletin*.

III. The Indigenous Rule of Law and Rights to Water

The communal nature of Indigenous water rights, or land rights, as a property right is not a contested concept among Indigenous communities in Australia; for example, the permission or denial of entering 'country' underpinned by Indigenous laws has clear consequences far more severe than Australia's breach of trespass law. Unlike Western property rights, Indigenous property rights are connected to 'country and place' by birth and death in familial connection,[18] in a gendered environment[19] and defined by ancient boundaries.[20] The 'territorial association and ceremonial relationships' to country *is* tenure, and Indigenous laws that provide for the rules of succession enable the Indigenous rule of law to survive.

Michael Kirby noted in his paper 'The Rule of Law beyond the Law of Rules' that 'compliance with the letter of the law is an idea that lies at the very heart of the purpose of law in every society'.[21] Further, Kirby argues that we should be 'concerned with the content of the rule of law and procedures' to mitigate against 'prejudice and unequal treatment'.[22] Indigenous laws '*are* at the heart' of Indigenous culture, its communities and social order.

In Australian society Western interpretations of Indigenous laws were poorly conceptualised, for example, into categories of culture, spirituality, mythology, knowledge and heritage, wherein the treatment of Indigenous language, painting, ceremony, sites and familial relationships are considered somehow divisible parts of Indigenous laws. The Indigenous rule of law over water rights 'lies within an Aboriginal concept where Aboriginal laws determine that water is inseparable from the land'.[23]

---

18 Marshall, above n 2, 163–64.
19 Ibid. 165.
20 Ibid. 187.
21 Michael Kirby, 'The Rule of Law beyond the Law of Rules' (2010) 33(3) *Australian Bar Review* 197.
22 Ibid. 210.
23 Dr Virginia Marshall, 'The Progress of Aboriginal Water Rights and Interests in the Murray–Darling Basin in NSW: An Essential Element of Culture' (2015) *Australian Environment Review* 158.

Indigenous water knowledge and the laws which connect to the creation story establish the permissible use of water, the types of activities and purposes for water use and the obligations to maintain the health and quality of water, among other things.[24] Article 34 of the UNDRIP expresses the 'rights to promote, develop and maintain their institutional structures, customs, procedures, among other things'. The recognition of the Indigenous rule of law into Australian water laws and policies elevates the status of Indigenous peoples as 'First Peoples' and not stakeholders.

IV. Northern Australian Development and the Tenure Reform

The Australian Government's proposal to develop northern Australia 'as a trade gateway'[25] set out in 'Our North, Our Future: White Paper on Developing Northern Australia' (2015) raises significant issues in regards to water, and land use. The development proposal is based upon 'five pillars' to realise growth: food and agribusiness, resources and energy, tourism and hospitality, international education, healthcare, medical research and aged care.[26] All of the government's 'five pillars' require access to water and high abstraction levels, with the highest water abstractions sought by food, agribusiness, resources and energy. The government points out that 'without secure, tradeable titles to land and water'[27] it flounders, as the majority of land is held under 'pastoral leases and exclusive native title'.[28] The government requires unlimited 'groundwater and surface water' to 'attract investors to build water infrastructure' and 'access'.[29] Such plans include amending the definition of native title rights to include 'commercial use where exclusive native title rights are held'.[30]

To date, native title rights have been deemed solely for traditional non-economic purposes; however, the recent High Court decision in *Akiba v Commonwealth* [2013] HCA 33 recognised 'commercial purposes'. The Australian Government recognises that any development of northern

---

24 Ibid. 12, citing Walmajarri Senior Lawman Joe Brown describing laws for water.
25 Australian Government, 'Our North, Our Future: White Paper on Developing Northern Australia' (White Paper, Australian Government, 2015) 2.
26 Ibid. 3.
27 Ibid. 5.
28 Ibid. 5–6.
29 Ibid. 6.
30 Ibid. 11.

Australia 'needs to be done in full partnership with Indigenous peoples'[31] and 'access to water is a key constraint to develop the north',[32] where northern lands and waters are largely exclusive rights held by Indigenous native title holders. The Australian Law Reform Commission inquiry into a review of the *Native Title Act 1993* (Cth) highlighted that Australia has not met its international obligations for Indigenous peoples of Australia; the United Nations International Covenant on Economic, Social and Cultural Rights (ICESCR) Committee noted concerns on the 'high cost, complexity and strict rules regulating native title claims and the inadequate protection of Indigenous cultural and intellectual property'. However, the government's proposal to 'streamline the process' and 'remove red tape' to provide 'long term water security for farmers and investors'[33] is highly problematic because of the absence of independent evidence on the long-term impacts for Aboriginal water use and upon Aboriginal lands, waters and resources, as well as the cultural and heritage impact.

The consideration of the Australian Government reforms would create a substantive move away from the narrow *sui generis* interpretation of the *Native Title Act 1993* (Cth) as expressed in s 223(1) which defines native title and the rights and interests comprised in s 223(2). The key aspects of the Australian Government's 'White Paper' directly affect the security of Indigenous water rights and it will have direct implications for Indigenous communities across Australia, including the impact of water reform.

V. Expanding the Concept of Cultural Water Use

In terms of Western policy concepts these 'customs and practices' are often couched in expressions of culture such as 'cultural flows'[34] and 'cultural licences' that extend to beneficial water use. The complex legal interpretation of native title rights to water under s 211 of the *Native Title*

---

31 Ibid. 4.
32 Ibid. 50.
33 Ibid. 11–12.
34 Cultural flows are by application for approval for water supply works, and/or water use under s 92 of the *Water Management Act 2000* (NSW).

Act 1993 (Cth) for usufructuary rights and the type of activities that are permitted in personal, domestic and non-economic use[35] limit the full expression of Indigenous water rights and interests.

The Aboriginal concept of cultural water use is 'bound to Aboriginal peoples' relationship with the Aboriginal environment (lands and waters of Australia) based upon the founding Aboriginal principle of the inseparability of land from water'.[36] The Commonwealth water legislation such as the *Water Act 2007* (Cth)[37] 'decouples Aboriginal ontological water concepts (Aboriginal norms) from its statutory provisions'.[38] Aboriginal water values, law and cultural expressions are not separate from environmental water flows; in fact, Aboriginal cultural flows and Aboriginal cultural activities in water inform on maintaining the health of Australia's Aboriginal environment.

The statutory cultural flows for communal and cultural activities are restrictive and conditional; for example, for a specific purpose water access licence (WAL) up to 10 megalitres per year under s 61(1)(a) of the *Water Management Act 2000* (NSW), subject to the *Water Management (General) Regulation 2004*, the licence can be made under the water sharing plan. However, if there are low or no flows identified in the water sharing plan, a WAL will not be granted.[39] These types of licences provide limited opportunities for Indigenous peoples to exercise their laws, customs and practices.

A study undertaken by the UN Permanent Forum on Indigenous Issues in 2016, in relation to Indigenous peoples of the Pacific, sought that policy and legislative measures be implemented to protect and maintain the traditional knowledge of Indigenous peoples and their relationships

---

35   *Native Title Act 1993* (Cth) s 211.

36   Dr Virginia Marshall, *Overturning Aqua Nullius: Securing Aboriginal Water Rights* (Aboriginal Studies Press, 2017) 145.

37   Ibid. Marshall raises the inconsistency in s 20(b) of the *Water Act 2007* (Cth) which refers to the 'purpose of the Murray–Darling Basin Plan' to set 'environmental limits' to 'protect land and waters valued by Aboriginal peoples'. However, the water legislation does not elaborate on what compliance mechanisms could enforce the protection of Aboriginal cultural water values or the role of engagement for Aboriginal communities in the Murray–Darling Basin region and to inform governments on the 'environmental sustainability' through Aboriginal water knowledge.

38   Ibid.

39   NSW Office of Water, www.water.nsw.gov.au/water-management/water-sharing; www.water.nsw.gov.au/water-licensing/about-licences/new-access-licences.

within their constitutions.[40] The Australian Constitution does not include provisions to protect and maintain traditional knowledge regimes of Indigenous peoples and this should be considered in any review of issues relating to water, land and resources. It has been suggested that the current Australian debate on Indigenous Constitutional Recognition should include the Aboriginal recognition in water law.[41]

This national dialogue has failed to include substantive issues to address Indigenous water rights and interests such as perpetual water allocations outside the consumptive pool, a Reserved Indigenous Water Rights[42] regime on a 'first rights user' basis, the exclusion of caps on native title water rights and an Aboriginal Water Holder model to facilitate intergenerational equity for Indigenous peoples. Defining the parameters of Indigenous water rights and interests as either cultural or economic concepts applies a rigidity which narrows future opportunities for Indigenous communities to adapt to the challenges of changing climatic conditions and global water scarcity.

VI. Conclusion

The principles of human rights are instrumental in achieving the full participation of Indigenous water rights and interests in Australia, and the language of UNDRIP provides formative instruments to incorporate into Australia's domestic law and policy on water. Australia's water policy has advantaged sectional stakeholders and disadvantaged First Peoples, securing a tranche of water reform for themselves and merely discretionary provisions for Indigenous peoples. While Australia delays the legal recognition of equitable water reforms, the potential prospects for Indigenous ownership continue to diminish.

---

40   V Toki, *Study on the Relationship between Indigenous Peoples and the Pacific Ocean*, UN ESC, Permanent Forum on Indigenous Issues, Agenda Item 3, E/C.19/2016/3 (19 February 2016) 6.

41   Environmental Justice Australia, 'Aboriginal Water Rights: Legal analysis of Submissions to the Review of the Commonwealth Water Act' (Submission, Environmental Justice Australia, 20 November 2014) 7.

42   See the recommendations proposed by the author in *Overturning Aqua Nullius: Securing Aboriginal Water Rights* (Aboriginal Studies Press, 2017) 216–24.

20

A Governance Framework for Indigenous Ecological Knowledge Protection and Use

Natalie P Stoianoff[1]

I. Introduction

Indigenous communities hold knowledge critical to the conservation of biological diversity and natural resource management. This Indigenous ecological knowledge (IEK) is increasingly recognised as a more effective means of managing the Australian landscape given the holistic approach of understanding the seasons, biodiversity, land and water.[2] The threat of intergenerational loss of such knowledge about Country is a well-recognised issue creating cause for concern for the knowledge holders, their communities and the whole of humanity. Protecting IEK benefits not only Indigenous Australian and local communities but also the long-term economic security and sustainable development of Australia.

Despite numerous consultations, reports, landmark cases, suggested protocols, models and draft legislation, Australia has been slow to meet international expectations in providing an effective mechanism for

---

1   Professor Stoianoff is the Director of the Intellectual Property Program in the Faculty of Law at the University of Technology Sydney and Chair of the Indigenous Knowledge Forum Committee.
2   Commonwealth of Australia, *Caring for Our Country – Outcomes 2008–2013* (2013), 21, 31, 36–37, 39.

recognising and protecting Indigenous knowledge and culture.[3] Confusion as to whether intellectual property law (federal law) or environmental law (state law) provides the appropriate mechanism for such protection is a contributing factor.

The legislative solution proposed by the 2014 White Paper, *Recognising and Protecting Aboriginal Knowledge associated with Natural Resource Management*, prepared for the Office of Environment and Heritage New South Wales (NSW) (the NSW White Paper)[4], provides a solution that may operate at state level or be adopted federally. It establishes a competent authority and governance framework to administer a protection, access and benefit sharing regime. It recognises concerns that community consultation has raised about the form such an authority would take, its independence from government, how it would be funded and wound up, local Aboriginal representation and engagement. This chapter reports on the making of such a governance framework.

II. Theoretical Framework

The theoretical framework for this chapter is drawn from the principles established in the Convention on Biological Diversity (1992) (CBD)[5], expanded in the Nagoya Protocol (2011)[6], and reinforced in the United Nations Declaration on the Rights of Indigenous Peoples (2007) (UNDRIP)[7]. These principles provide Indigenous knowledge holders with a right to share in the benefits obtained from the use of their knowledge, emphasising the need for free prior informed consent to be given by the knowledge holders prior to access and use of that knowledge on mutually agreed terms. Action research and Indigenous research

---

3   Natalie Stoianoff and Alpana Roy, 'Indigenous Knowledge and Culture in Australia – The Case For Sui Generis Legislation', *Monash University Law Review* (Vol 41, No 3) 745–46.

4   UTS Indigenous Knowledge Forum and North West Local Land Services (2014), *Recognising and Protecting Aboriginal Knowledge Associated with Natural Resource Management*, White Paper for the Office of Environment and Heritage NSW, indigenousknowledgeforum.org/components/com_content/models/forms/white_paper.pdf.

5   Convention on Biological Diversity, opened for signature 5 June 1992, 1760 UNTS 79 (entered into force 29 December 1993) ('CBD').

6   Nagoya Protocol on Access to Genetic Resources and the Fair and Equitable Sharing of Benefits Arising from their Utilization to the Convention on Biological Diversity, opened for signature 2 February 2011 (entered into force 12 October 2014) ('Nagoya Protocol').

7   United Nations Declaration on the Rights of Indigenous People, GA Res 61/295, UN GAOR, 61st sess, 107th plen mtg, Agenda Item 68, Supp No 49, UN Doc A/RES/61/295 (13 September 2007).

paradigm methodologies were utilised by the author and her research team in developing the legal framework for a regime that encapsulates these principles.

The focus was on the Aboriginal communities of Northwest NSW and accordingly reflects the concerns and interests of those communities while incorporating the international law principles described above. This was achieved through an initial comparative analysis of regimes existing in other nations, the establishment of a highly skilled and multidisciplinary Working Party of Indigenous and non-Indigenous individuals and stakeholders, and finally through Aboriginal community consultation.

III. Principles for a Governance Framework of Recognition and Protection

Several international instruments recognise the significance of traditional and Indigenous knowledge and cultural expressions, and emphasise the need to respect, preserve and maintain knowledge, innovations and practices of Indigenous and local communities.[8] For example, the CBD provides member nations with the opportunity to establish regimes that regulate foreign and domestic access to valuable genetic resources and traditional and Indigenous knowledge while enabling benefit-sharing mechanisms for such access.[9]

This has led to significant international debate on the interrelationship between IEK and intellectual property rights, particularly patents and plant breeders' rights developed from genetic resources. The role of IEK in this context is significant as it brings into the equation the broader cultural property of Indigenous and local communities. Meanwhile, Art 11 of UNDRIP recognises the right of Indigenous people 'to practise and revitalize their cultural traditions and customs' and extends to 'the right to maintain, protect and develop the past, present and future manifestations of their cultures'. The state is expected to develop with Indigenous peoples effective compensation mechanisms 'with respect to their cultural, intellectual, religious and spiritual property taken without their free, prior and informed consent or in violation of their laws, traditions and customs'.[10]

---

8   See Stoianoff and Roy, above n 3, 753–68.
9   CBD, Arts 8j, 10(c) and 18(4).
10   UNDRIP, Art 11.

Many nations and regions have adopted legal instruments covering such rights. Nations utilising *sui generis* legislation[11] to do so include Brazil,[12] Peru,[13] Panama[14] and the Philippines,[15] requiring the establishment of registers or databases and a representative authority. Some of these legal instruments are based on the *WIPO-UNESCO Model Provisions*,[16] containing intellectual property type provisions. At the same time, the *Pacific Regional Framework for the Protection of Traditional Knowledge and Expressions of Culture* (2002) provides the *Model Law for the Protection of Traditional Knowledge and Expressions of Culture 2002* which sets out cultural rights and moral rights over traditional knowledge and expressions, the need for prior informed consent, a mechanism establishing applications for use and identifying the traditional owners, authorised user agreements, civil and criminal enforcement including defences, and a cultural authority to oversee the regime. Other regional solutions are found in Africa,[17] the Andean Community of Nations,[18] and ASEAN.[19]

The CBD provides that alternative mechanisms (guidelines, *sui generis* systems or ethical codes of conduct) can be utilised for respecting, preserving and maintaining Indigenous or traditional knowledge.[20] Some Australian jurisdictions have their own approach to dealing with

11   Intergovernmental Committee on Intellectual Property and Genetic Resources, Traditional Knowledge and Folklore (2012), *Glossary of Key Terms Related to Intellectual Property and Genetic Resources, Traditional Knowledge and Traditional Cultural Expressions*, Twenty-Second Session, Geneva (July 9 to 13, 2012).

12   Law No 13.123 of May 20, 2015 (*Access and Benefits Sharing of Genetic Resources and Associated Traditional Knowledge*) (Brazil).

13   Law No 27,811 of 2002 *Introducing a Protection Regime for the Collective Knowledge of Indigenous People Derived from Biological Resources* (Peru).

14   Law No 20 of June 26, 2000, on *Special System for the Collective Intellectual Property Rights of Indigenous Peoples for the Protection and Defense of their Cultural Identity and their Traditional Knowledge* (Panama).

15   *Indigenous Peoples Rights Act* of 1997 (Philippines).

16   *Model Provisions for National Laws on the Protection of Expressions of Folklore Against Illicit Exploitation and Other Prejudicial Action* (UNESCO and WIPO, 1982).

17   See the Organisation of African Unity, *Model Legislation for the Protection of the Rights of Local Communities, Farmers and Breeders, and for the Regulation of Access to Biological Resources*, 2000; and the African Regional Intellectual Property Organization, *Swakopmund Protocol on the Protection of Traditional Knowledge and Expressions of Folklore* (2010).

18   *Common Regime on Access to Genetic Resources*, Decision 391, 2 July 1996, Official Gazette 17 July 1996.

19   *ASEAN Framework Agreement on Access to Biological and Genetic Resources, 24 February 2000* (draft).

20   See COP 5 Decision V/16, www.cbd.int/decision/cop/default.shtml?id=7158.

IEK using voluntary protocols rather than mandatory obligations,[21] with varying degrees of success. The Australian Government has said that its domestic measures are consistent with the Nagoya Protocol.[22] This may be true of protecting Australia's genetic resources but is questionable in the case of associated IEK. The Nagoya Protocol requires that where 'Indigenous traditional knowledge [is utilised] countries have to make sure that the knowledge was acquired in accordance with the rules of the country where those Indigenous people live'.[23] This requires the prior informed consent of the Indigenous community that is providing the knowledge, on mutually agreed terms, an element that some Australian jurisdictions fail to include in their access and benefit-sharing legislation for genetic resources.[24]

Collaboration between the United Nations Environment Programme (UNEP), responsible for the introduction of the CBD, and the World Intellectual Property Organization (WIPO) resulted in the WIPO General Assembly establishing the Intergovernmental Committee on Intellectual Property and Genetic Resources, Traditional Knowledge and Folklore (IGC) in 2000.[25] This committee has been negotiating international instruments for the protection of traditional or Indigenous knowledge and culture from an intellectual property perspective, and has produced three draft international instruments.

Adjei and Stoianoff point out that there are eight key elements to a framework of protection for traditional knowledge:

1. The meaning of traditional knowledge and its scope.
2. The identification of beneficiaries.

---

21   See, for example, the *Queensland Code of Ethical Practice for Biotechnology 2001* superseded by the *Queensland Biotechnology Code of Ethics (updated 2006)* which applies to organisations conducting biotechnology research with Queensland Government funding, www.qld.gov.au/dsiti/assets/documents/qld-biotechnology-code-of-ethics.pdf. See also the *Indigenous Ecological Knowledge Manual* by Territory Natural Resource Management, media.wix.com/ugd/da28f0_624bf834d6ef4672b98820bac2b77283.pdf. For a more local example, see the draft *Blue Mountains City Council's Aboriginal Cultural Protocols 2010* which applies to councillors and council staff.

22   Australian Government, 'The Nagoya Protocol in Australia' (2015), www.environment.gov.au/system/files/pages/9fc06ac0-f5af-4b47-a80f-d9378088d743/files/nagoya-factsheet_1.pdf.

23   Ibid.

24   For example, *Biodiscovery Act 2004* (Qld).

25   UNEP and WIPO jointly commissioned a study on the issue of how intellectual property rights can support the objectives of the CBD, in particular, what role such rights can play in the process of benefit sharing: WO/GA/26/6, WIPO General Assembly, Twenty-Sixth (12th Extraordinary) Session, Geneva, September 25 to October 3, 2000, *Matters Concerning Intellectual Property and Genetic Resources, Traditional Knowledge and Folklore*, 2.

3. The scope of protection: elements of confidentiality and moral rights, protecting against misappropriation and misuse.

4. Sanctions and remedies emulating those used in intellectual property law.

5. The need for disclosure in existing patent and plant variety rights regimes.

6. The establishment of a competent authority to manage the data, rights conferred, enforcement, dispute resolution and national treatment.

7. The creation of databases.

8. Accommodating trans-boundary cooperations where knowledge and biodiversity extend across national borders.[26]

The IGC is exploring a *sui generis* (stand alone) model for the protection of traditional knowledge, recognising that protecting such knowledge does not fit into the existing intellectual property paradigm due to the need for protection in perpetuity in accordance with cultural norms, the difficulty of identifying the 'author' or 'creator' of the knowledge, and the failure of conventional intellectual property to recognise communal rights over that knowledge. Consequently, the IGC embarked on a process of developing a protection model that will accommodate the peculiarities of Indigenous knowledge. The NSW White Paper[27] took a similar approach and developed such a *sui generis* model law.

The arguments for and against a *sui generis* law were acknowledged.[28] International support for a *sui generis* regime was evident from WIPO, UNEP and the Conference of the Parties for the CBD.[29] Customary laws could be incorporated into such a regime taking 'into account needs and expectations of Indigenous and local Communities, [enabling] protect[ion of the] integrity of traditional knowledge and [punishing] use that offends Indigenous and local Communities while encouraging acceptable use by third parties'.[30] If IEK is to be recognised as part of a living culture that requires access to Country for it be preserved, maintained, respected and developed in accordance with customary laws, crossing the thresholds of

---

26 Patricia Adjei and Natalie P Stoianoff (2013), 'The World Intellectual Property Organisation (WIPO) and the Intergovernmental Committee: Developments on Traditional Knowledge and Cultural Expressions', *Intellectual Property Forum*, Issue 92, March 2013, 37–48.

27 UTS (2014), above n 4.

28 Ibid

29 Ibid

30 Ibid. 15.

intellectual property type rights and environmental responsibilities, then the legal framework must be inevitably unique, hence the need for a *sui generis* law.[31]

IV. Method and Methodology

The inaugural Indigenous Knowledge Forum held at the University of Technology, Sydney, (UTS) in August 2012 inspired the design of the NSW White Paper project which engaged the Namoi Catchment Aboriginal Community in developing a model of involvement in natural resource management and access to Country.[32] The project was funded by the Aboriginal Communities Funding Scheme of the Namoi Catchment Management Authority (now North West Local Land Services (NWLLS)) with the advice of the Aboriginal Officer and the Namoi Aboriginal Advisory Committee (NAAC). It was carried out in three stages, commencing with development of a comparative framework, followed by drafting of the *sui generis* regime, and Aboriginal community consultation to refine the regime. The first stage involved a doctrinal comparative study, analysing legislative and policy regimes operating around the world. Key criteria in each regime were identified and then compared to international obligations. This comparative analysis provided the framework on which a model could be developed to ensure the recognition and protection of IEK.

In stage two, a working party was formed to assist in developing a *sui generis* regime, comprising Indigenous and non-Indigenous members from the UTS Indigenous Knowledge Forum committees,[33] participants from the 2012 Indigenous Knowledge Forum, and key personnel from the NWLLS and the NAAC.

A Discussion Paper incorporating the Comparative Study Report and Draft Regime was prepared, and in stage three it was distributed through the NWLLS to the Namoi Catchment Aboriginal Communities and other interested parties. Consultation sessions were conducted on Country according to relevant cultural norms and protocols in key locations in

---

31   Chidi Oguamanam, *International Law and Indigenous Knowledge: Intellectual Property, Plant Biodiversity and Traditional Medicine* (University of Toronto Press, Toronto, 2006) 217–19.
32   *Indigenous Knowledge Forum Report* (2012), indigenousknowledgeforum.org/images/ikf-report.pdf.
33   The Organising Committee and the Advisory Board.

the region. The consultations tested the draft legal framework against Aboriginal community concerns and expectations, thereby enabling it to be refined into a culturally acceptable model which was set out in the NSW White Paper and presented to the Office of Environment and Heritage.

The project addressed the need for recognition and protection of IEK by engaging the local, grassroots level, employing variations of an action research methodology coupled with an Indigenous research paradigm at both stages two and three of the project. Indigenous Australians were given an opportunity to actively participate in the process of formulating legislation for their benefit. The action research methodology emphasises cooperative or collaborative inquiry[34] whereby all active participants, Indigenous and non-Indigenous, are fully involved in research decisions as co-researchers.[35] Through the internet, the project provided all interested parties with access to analysis of current models for, and outcomes of implementing, similar legislation in other countries. This assisted in the process of identifying how best to accommodate unique aspects of IEK and culture as they relate to the interests of Indigenous Australians.

Participation assisted in generating Indigenous ownership of the outcomes, understanding of any resulting legislation and its intent, and an opportunity to deliver robust legislation that meets Australia's international obligations and effectively protects the interests of an important sector of the Australian community. During stage two the Indigenous research paradigm was important in engaging all participants in the collection of research data through the method of storytelling by Indigenous Elders in the group, exploring meaning and working through issues together to ensure accurate interpretation of language.[36] This process was then adopted during consultations on Country, being mindful of the culture of place and the privilege of sharing in the flow of cultural knowledge.

34   John Heron, *Co-operative Inquiry: Research into the Human Condition* (Sage, London, 1996).
35   Peter Reason and Hilary Bradbury, *Handbook of Action Research* (Sage, London, 2nd edn, 2007).
36   Ewa Czaykowska-Higgins, 'Research Models, Community Engagement, and Linguistic Fieldwork: Reflections on Working within Canadian Indigenous Communities', *Language Documentation & Conservation* 3(1), June 2009.

V. Results and Conclusions

The key outcome of this project was the development of a legislative regime that facilitates the recognition, preservation and protection of IEK, enabling its custodians to share in the benefits of its use. The resulting draft legislation, explained in the NSW White Paper,[37] sets out key principles rather than detailed prescriptive provisions which are left to regulations that would need to be implemented.

The preamble of the draft legislation recognises the impact of European arrival on IEK and connection to Country of Aboriginal peoples, and sets out the aims of the legislation. Section 1 establishes the rights of Aboriginal communities over their knowledge. Key terms are defined in s 2 and the beneficiaries under the legislation are identified in s 3. The process of access to the knowledge is described in s 4, and guidelines for benefit-sharing are set out in s 5. Sanctions and remedies for breaches of the legislation are provided for in s 6, emulating remedies available for infringement of intellectual property rights with penalties ranging from fines to imprisonment. Section 7 requires the establishment of a Competent Authority to administer this regime including managing databases to enable the access process to operate. Section 8 provides for dispute resolution where there are multiple communities claiming 'ownership' of the same or similar knowledge. Every regime requires a set of express exceptions and s 9 provides for that eventuality. The nature of the three types of databases and the obligations regarding disclosure are dealt with in s 10. The remaining three provisions are general in nature, dealing with interaction between existing laws (s 11), mutual recognition of rights and compliance (s 12), and transitional provisions (s 13).

Although the NSW White Paper[38] provides a fictitious case study to demonstrate the operation of the draft regime, it does not claim to provide a complete solution for recognition and protection of IEK. Shortcomings include the need to clarify the form and nature of the Competent Authority and governance processes; the way the databases are to be formed, funded and managed from community level to state and national levels; and the administration processes for access and benefit-sharing, including guidance on mutually beneficial terms, model agreements and processes for negotiation.

---

37   UTS, above n 4, Ch 7.
38   Ibid. Ch 8.

Introducing such a regime has beneficial flow-on effects including:

a. Recognition that IEK is part of a living culture that requires access to Country for it to be preserved, maintained respected and developed;

b. A mechanism for documenting, recording and recovering IEK for future generations of Indigenous Australians;

c. A response to intergenerational loss of knowledge about Country (land and water) by encouraging younger generations to spend time on Country with their Elders to regain their traditional language and oral tradition through which culture and knowledge are maintained;

d. Improved natural resource management by facilitating access to Country, aimed at both Indigenous engagement and sustainable use of IEK; and

e. Recognition that IEK is to be valued and utilised in accordance with Indigenous protocols that govern use and dissemination of this knowledge, including the need for prior informed consent and the establishment of an appropriate benefit sharing arrangement on mutually agreed terms.

IEK is of significant spiritual, cultural and economic value not only to Aboriginal and Torres Strait Islander communities but also to society at large, including governments, research institutions and commercial interests.[39] As Australia moves towards ratification of the Nagoya Protocol, two main measures require implementation: ensuring (i) that prior informed consent of Indigenous communities is obtained for access to their traditional knowledge, and (ii) that fair and equitable benefit-sharing mechanisms are agreed on for the use of that knowledge, consistent with community laws and procedures as well as customary use and exchange.[40] The governance framework espoused in the NSW White Paper addresses these expectations. The journey continues towards the goal of determining the nature of the Competent Authority required to administer the framework. The author and her research team has been awarded an ARC Linkage grant for the project, *Garuwanga: Forming a Competent Authority to Protect Indigenous Knowledge*, and will work towards achieving that goal over the next three years.

---

39 Susette Biber-Klemm and Danuta Szymura Berglas, 'Problems and Goals' in Susette Biber-Klemm, Thomas Cottier and Danuta Szymura Berglas (eds), *Rights to Plant Genetic Resources and Traditional Knowledge: Basic Issues and Perspectives* (CAB International, 2006) 3, 21.

40 Nagoya Protocol, Arts 7 and 12.

While New South Wales has made little progress on implementing a regime along the lines recommended by the White Paper, the State of Victoria has recently amended its Aboriginal Heritage legislation to establish a database system to protect Aboriginal intangible heritage,[41] which is another way of describing Indigenous knowledge or IEK. Further, IP Australia invited the submission of the NSW White Paper to the Indigenous Knowledge Consultation which is about to move to the next stage of preparing a discussion paper. We are hopeful that the model provided by the NSW White Paper may encourage the creation of a national scheme of protection of IEK.

---

41 *Aboriginal Heritage Amendment Act 2016.*

21

Reforming Environmental Law for Responsiveness to Change

Jan McDonald[1]

I. Introduction

Law reform is about change. This contribution argues that such change needs to be about change itself. The earth's life support systems are experiencing profound and potentially devastating change.[2] Anthropogenic interference with the earth's atmosphere, nitrogen cycle, biodiversity, and water resources fundamentally challenge the adequacy of current environmental laws,[3] but the forces of change in environmental law are not limited to environmental or climatic conditions. They are also influenced by the ways humans react to change, through large-scale demographic shifts as well as through altering behaviour. Other significant changes either militate or facilitate environmental law reform. These include developments in our understanding of the environmental impacts of human activities and interactions and alterations to the impacts of particular activities when they are modified. Societal values relating to environmental and other priorities are also in a state of constant evolution. Public interest in issues such as climate change is cyclical, but there are also

---

1   Professor, Faculty of Law, Centre for Marine Socioecology and Institute for the Study of Social Change, University of Tasmania.
2   J Rockström et al, 'Planetary Boundaries: Exploring the Safe Operating Space for Humanity' (2009) 14(2) *Ecology and Society* 32.
3   Ibid.

slower, multi-decadal trends in public attitudes towards environmental protection. Lastly, technological innovation is occurring at an increasingly rapid rate, offering the potential for cheaper and improved monitoring of environmental performance and indicators and more nuanced and targeted regulatory measures.

The institutions of Western legal systems provide stability and predictability in the face of this pervasive and increasingly rapid change. The typical approach of environmental, planning, and more recently, climate law, is to endorse and protect existing rights.[4] This takes the form of existing use rights in planning law that permit the continuation of activities that are inconsistent with new zoning requirements. Similarly, the grandfathering of environmental licences into new regulatory regimes or provisions that limit the application of new requirements to activities commenced after a certain date also allows existing operations to continue on the same terms. They represent another common way of insulating past activities from the influence of change. Providing legal rights of compensation when existing land uses are constrained by new environmental or planning regulation make it hard for the law to innovate and adapt as new circumstances demand.[5]

These constraints are also reflected in the organisational culture and practices of agencies charged with administering environmental laws. In an increasingly corporatised and risk-averse public service, experimentation is not encouraged. Tight agency budgets are likely to adopt fiscally conservative strategies that entrench current practices and punish efforts at adaptive management that are perceived to have 'failed'.[6]

Far from equipping us to manage the impacts or seize the opportunities of future change, then, our current approach to environmental law and its governance institutions entrench maladaptive practices and increase

---

4   A Macintosh, A Foerster and J McDonald (2014), 'Policy Design, Spatial Planning and Climate Change Adaptation: A Case Study from Australia', *Journal of Environmental Planning and Management* 57, 1–22.

5   A Foerster, A Macintosh and J McDonald, 'Trade-offs in Adaptation Planning: Protecting Public Interest Environmental Values' (2015) 17 *Journal of Environmental Law* 1.

6   A Wiersema, 'A Train without Tracks: Rethinking the Place of Law and Goals in Environmental Law and Natural Resources Law' (2008) 38 *Environmental Law Journal* 1239, 1250–52.

our vulnerability.[7] In the context of unprecedented and sustained rates of environmental and social change, it would be overly simplistic to suggest that there is a single suite of environmental law reforms that can improve conditions into the future.[8] A new approach is needed that places system dynamism and ongoing change at the centre of law reform efforts.[9] This chapter therefore argues that Australian environmental law requires ongoing reform in order to manage change itself.

II. A Resilience Framing for Environmental Law Reform

Resilience thinking provides a useful framing for a more change-oriented environmental law regime.[10] Rather than a theory, resilience thinking consists of a broad set of principles that are aimed at enhancing the capacity of social-ecological systems to withstand change without losing system function.[11] Resilience thinking is premised upon social and ecological systems being complex and interconnected and in a process of constant adaptation.[12] The value of resilience thinking lies in its recognition that systems are constantly changing, and that this change occurs through so-called adaptive cycles involving periods of growth or exploitation, conservation or consolidation, release or collapse, and reorganisation.

---

7   H Doremus, 'Adapting to Climate Change with Law that Bends without Breaking' (2010) 2 *San Diego Journal of Climate Energy Law* 45; R K Craig, 'Stationarity is Dead – Long Live Transformation: Five Principles for Climate Change Adaptation Law' (2010) 34 *Harvard Environmental Law Review* 9; J B Ruhl, 'Climate Change Adaptation and the Structural Transformation of Environmental Law' (2010) 40 *Environmental Law* 363.

8   Craig 2010, above n 7; Ruhl 2010, above n 7; C Arnold and L Gunderson, 'Adaptive Law and Resilience' (2013) 43 *Environmental Law Reporter* 10436–443; A Garmestani and C Allen, *Social-ecological Resilience and Law* (Columbia University Press, 2013); O Odom Green et al, 'Barriers and Bridges to the Integration of Social-Ecological Resilience and Law' (2015) 13:6 *Frontiers in Ecology and Environment* 332–37.

9   J Adler, 'Dynamic Environmentalism and Adaptive Management: Legal Obstacles and Opportunities' (2015) 11 *Journal of Law, Economics & Policy* 133.

10   R K Craig and M Benson, 'Replacing Sustainability' (2013) 46 *Akron Law Review* 841–80; Odom Green et al, above n 8, Arnold and Gunderson, above n 8, Garmestani and Allen, above n 8.

11   F Berkes, J Colding and C Folke (eds), *Navigating Social Ecological Systems: Building Resilience for Complexity and Change* (Cambridge University Press, 2003); C Folke, 'Resilience: The Emergence of a Perspective for Social-Ecological Systems' (2006) 16:3 *Global Environmental Change* 2253–267; D Nelson, N Adger and K Brown, 'Adaptation to Environmental Change: Contributions of a Resilience Framework' (2009) 32 *Annual Review of Environment & Resources* 395–419.

12   L Gunderson, C Allen and C S Holling (eds), *Foundations of Ecological Resilience* (Island Press, 2009).

These adaptive cycles occur within nested hierarchies of temporal, spatial and geopolitical subsystems, with each cycle influencing or influenced by those above and below it.[13]

By placing change and multi-scalar system dynamism at the centre of its approach, resilience thinking represents a radical departure from traditional resource management approaches.[14] It also fundamentally challenges legal arrangements that are aimed at providing certainty, predictability and stability. Resilience thinking calls for the promotion of diversity and redundancy to enable system components to withstand shocks; the management of slow variables and feedback; ongoing learning; public participation and polycentric governance models. The focus of the following discussion is on how best to make environmental law responsive to change and promote learning.

III. Improving Responsiveness to Change

The precise modes by which environmental law might be reformed depend on the types of activities the law is intended to govern or manage. Activities occurring, or with impacts manifesting, over shorter timescales must account for different scenarios of future change than those with decisions that endure over decades or more. Governance arrangements for decision-making over the location of major public infrastructure, for example, must consider climate projections beyond 2100, whereas the development of a five or 10 year protected area management plan can afford to consider a narrower range of possible influences.[15]

The ways in which flexibility and responsiveness are built into new laws and legal instruments depend, not surprisingly, on their scope and purpose. The following section discusses the ways in which such reforms can be advanced in laws and regulations, management plans, operational decision-making, and environmental approvals and licensing.

---

13 L Gunderson and C S Holling (eds), *Panarchy: Understanding Transformations in Human and Natural Systems* (Island Press, 2002).

14 Craig and Benson, above n 10; B Cosens, L Gunderson and B Chaffin, 'The Adaptive Water Governance Project: Assessing Law, Resilience and Governance in Regional Socio-Ecological Water Systems Facing a Changing Climate' (2014) 51 *Idaho Law Review* 1.

15 M Stafford Smith et al, 'Rethinking Adaptation for a 4 Degree Centigrade World' (2011) 369 *Philosophical Transactions of the Royal Society* 196.

A. Laws and regulations

Legislation itself should contain mechanisms by which to respond to change. These could take several forms.[16] First, legislation and regulations themselves need mechanisms for review. The simplest approach would be to insert sunset clauses that set a predetermined date on which the legislative regime must be reviewed. Time-bound provisions of this sort, however, can come either too soon or too late. They may trigger review before it is required, and run the risk or of governments preferring to abandon a legislative regime rather than engage in costly review. Alternatively, they may set the review date too late to address changing conditions before damage is done. The preferable approach is to identify predefined thresholds of environmental or other change that will trigger either legislative review or the transition to a new predetermined regulatory phase. Event triggers are more nuanced and responsive, but also require that such triggers are capable of upfront identification and clear articulation. They may perform poorly in conditions of radical and volatile change and require political commitment to follow through on the shift when they are triggered, but nonetheless offer a preferable alternative to current static approaches.

The second way in which responsiveness to change might be built in to laws and regulations is the inclusion of adaptation to future changes in the statutory objectives of environmental laws.[17] A related mechanism is to require decision-makers to take the impacts of future environmental or climate change into account. For specific regimes, the objectives may be modified in more subject-specific ways. For example, in light of strong evidence that climate change will dramatically alter the range and habitat of many species, it may be necessary to modify our conservation objectives regarding *in situ* conservation or protection of species 'in the wild'.[18]

---

16   J McDonald and M Styles, 'Legal Strategies for Adaptive Management under Climate Change' (2014) 17 *Journal of Environmental Law* 1.
17   Ibid.
18   J McDonald et al, 'Rethinking Legal Objectives for Climate-Adaptive Conservation' (2016) *Ecology and Society* np.

B. Management planning

With greater flexibility in legislative design, modification of statutory instruments should become easier. For example, the identification and designation of protected areas could become more agile, as existing areas become less valuable and sites currently outside the reserve network become more valuable. The management plans governing such areas also need to include adaptation and responsiveness to change as key objectives. The nascent application of dynamic ocean management techniques is worthy of further consideration. Currently used principally to manage by-catch and reduce conflict with fishers, dynamic ocean management uses new monitoring and detection technologies and short-term spatial closures to protect pelagic or migratory species as their location shifts.[19] The transferability of such approaches to a terrestrial context is yet to be fully explored. While there is a pressing need for resource, species and protected area management plans to adopt adaptive management, great care must be taken to ensure that adaptive management is not used to justify the lowering of standards or a random trial and error approach that could have irreversible impacts.[20]

C. Environmental approvals and EIA

A critical aspect of environmental regulation in need of reform is the environmental approvals and associated environmental impact assessment (EIA) processes.[21] Recognition that both project plans and environmental conditions will change demands a fundamental shift away from the current front-end approach to environmental regulation. Existing EIA processes award approvals or licences with limited or no capacity to modify conditions should they prove to be inadequate. They assume that the environmental impact assessment process has adequately and accurately identified all potential impacts from a proposed development. This approach is theoretically flawed because it assumes that all future scenarios are capable of being anticipated and prepared for at the initial approval stage. In practice, the proponent-driven nature of EIA compromises its ability to provide an impartial and wide-ranging assessment of the risks.

---

19   A Hobday et al, 'Dynamic Ocean Management: Integrating Scientific and Technological Capacity with Law, Policy, and Management' (2014) 33 *Stanford Environmental Law Journal*, 122.
20   J B Ruhl, 'Regulation by Adaptive Management – Is It Possible?' (2005–6) 7 *Minnesota Journal of Law, Science, & Technology* 72.
21   Ruhl 2010, above n 7.

Changing the nature of development approvals so that they are either time-bound or limited by compliance with specified environmental performance measures would fundamentally alter this process.[22] An adaptive management approach to approvals and licensing would enable projects and developments to proceed subject to stages or on the basis that approval could be modified or withdrawn if conditions changed. If proponents knew that their approval was only as good as the project's subsequent environmental performance, they might be more willing to invest in high-quality assessment processes, and weigh more carefully the costs and benefits of investing in environmentally-risky projects. For example, the widespread practice of securing offset sites to compensate for unavoidable impacts on biodiversity offsetting may be far less attractive if there is the chance that additional sites will have to be acquired or restored in future should the initial offsets package fail to achieve a 'no net loss' target.

Like legislative triggers, adaptive management approaches of this kind require clear agreement about, and articulation of, overarching environmental standards/performance measures to be maintained.[23] This in turn requires more baseline information about environmental conditions and assumes we know or can know what standards must be met. It also requires monitoring and evaluation of both compliance with *and* effectiveness of requirements, and enforcement of the requirement that operations be modified or potentially discontinued when monitoring and evaluation shows that environmental standards cannot be maintained.

IV. Risks, Constraints and Design Considerations

Reforming environmental laws so that managing for change is a key objective carries with it risks and constraints. The main risk associated with more adaptive approaches is that they may result in a gradual weakening of environmental standards over time, especially if adaptive approaches are not adequately funded. In some cases, agility may demand that choices be made between environmental values. In such cases, careful

---

22 E Biber and J B Ruhl, 'The Permit Power Revisited: The Theory and Practice of Regulatory Permits in the Administrative State' (2014) 64 *Duke Law Journal* 133.
23 Macintosh, Foerster and McDonald (2013), above n 4.

and transparent prioritisation of ecological values, safeguards regarding the maintenance of particular standards or performance-based measures, and a clearly articulated goal of 'trading up' will be required.

While most of these risks can be overcome through appropriate design, there are also some circumstances in which adaptive approaches are simply inappropriate. There is little scope, for example, for approving projects that have the potential for irreversible impacts using an adaptive management approach. Where a major project is an 'all-or-nothing' proposition, there is little scope for responsiveness.[24] The need for laws to respond to change is not intended to supplant the precautionary principle. Rather, it should complement it, by providing options for enhancing the adaptiveness of law, either where circumstances mean that the option of not proceeding is simply unavailable, or where there is minimal risk of serious or irreversible harm.

Adaptive laws face other constraints. As has been noted, they are likely to be expensive to implement because of the requirements for monitoring and evaluation, and the processes of modification. These costs may be reduced by technological advances in monitoring, and better citizen and stakeholder engagement at key phases of environmental regulation and management. The benefits of better environmental management should also offset the increased costs, though these benefits – both economically and ecologically valuable – are seldom accounted for in the same way as the economic costs. Responsive approaches require long-term institutional commitments to monitoring and evaluation programs which extend beyond political cycles. Given that increasing rates of change will impose their own costs on the administration of environmental laws and force the development of long-term goals and implementation plans, this constraint is not necessarily onerous.

The most common objection to more responsive and agile law-making is that it will undermine investor confidence by removing some of the law's predictability and eroding the value of development 'rights'. A key premise of this chapter, however, is that environmental degradation will make many current activities untenable in the future, and that better accounting for that prospect now is likely to enhance the long-term stability of development activity. A related objection is that such measures

---

24   J McDonald, 'The Role of Law in Adapting to Climate Change' (2011) 2(2) *WIREs: Climate Change* 283; McDonald and Styles, above n 16; Cosens, Gunderson and Chaffin, above n 14.

and decisions may be ruled invalid on grounds of uncertainty. These concerns can be allayed by ensuring that the environmental standards to be achieved are predetermined, with clearly defined parameters.

Built-in triggers and staged approaches to regulation may limit some aspects of public participation. There may not be the same opportunity for consultation and input to approval conditions or alterations to management plans where activities follow the built-in trigger and staged approach. It may also be necessary to limit judicial review of adaptive management decision-making to ensure that responsiveness is not lost by protracted litigation. Curtailing public participating runs counter to the principles of ecologically sustainable development and environmental good governance, as well as the key elements of Resilience Thinking. But this risk can be offset by facilitating meaningful public engagement at critical junctures.[25]

For the most part, these risks and constraints can be overcome with appropriate levels of funding and commitment. Indeed, they reduce significantly when compared to the risks of retaining the suite of inflexible, unresponsive laws, plans and processes that currently comprise the environmental law toolkit.

V. Conclusions

The legal and governance framework for environmental protection and biodiversity conservation that we have established over decades is poorly equipped to respond to changing conditions. Designed to offer legal certainty and stability, most regulatory frameworks are premised on notions of system stasis. This contribution has identified a reform agenda for environmental law, comprising techniques and tools for building-in flexibility to environmental decisions and environmental law-making processes more generally. Adoption of such approaches would go far, but there will be limits to what law can achieve. To meet future challenges, law reform must be part of a broader shift towards polycentric and adaptive governance[26] that recognises system complexity and embraces an array of novel governance arrangements.

---

25   R K Craig and J B Ruhl, 'Designing Administrative Law for Adaptive Management' (2014) 67 *Vanderbilt Law Review* 1.
26   C Folke et al, 'Adaptive Governance of Social-Ecological Systems' (2005) 30 *Annual Review Environment & Resources* 441; E Ostrom, *Governing the Commons: The Evolution of Institutions for Collective Action* (Cambridge University Press, 1990).

Future Water: Improving Planning, Markets, Enforcement and Learning

Cameron Holley[1]

I. Introduction

Water is indispensable to our life, our economy, our food security and our environment.[2] Ensuring its protection and sustainable use requires effective and efficient law and policy. Over the last 120 years, our water laws have been on a prolonged reform journey. Spurred by Australia's water-scarce environment and ongoing overallocation challenges,[3] Australia's water law system has progressed from common law rights, to state regulation, to intergovernmental action under the Council of Australian Governments (COAG) led National Competition Policy reforms and the National Water Initiative (NWI). The latter agreement, which embraced statutory-based collaborative water planning, cap and

1 Associate Professor, UNSW Faculty of Law. This research was funded by an Australian Research Council Discovery Early Career Researcher Award (DE140101216) and an Australian Research Council Discovery Project (DP170100281). I am gratefully for the research assistance of Genevieve Wilks, Antonia Ross and Bonnie Perris, and the excellent suggestions made by Darren Sinclair, Ron Levy and the anonymous reviewer of this chapter.
2 UN Sustainable Development Goals, Goal 6, www.un.org/sustainabledevelopment/water-and-sanitation.
3 National Water Commission (NWC), *Sustainable Levels of Extraction: National Water Commission Position* (NWC, 2010).

trade markets, regulation and accounting, monitoring and review, has demarcated Australia as a leading laboratory of water governance.[4] Even so, after such a long reform journey, fatigue and apathy are increasingly palpable in water policy.[5] Notwithstanding recent emphasis on northern water resource development,[6] this equivocation about continued national reforms is jeopardising Australia's long-term water sustainability.[7]

This chapter argues that entrenching and extending national reforms is vital to Australia's future water security. It argues for four key broad reforms. The context and justification for each reform is given by briefly evaluating the performance of NWI planning, markets, regulation and monitoring. The discussion focuses particularly on non-urban water management. This is because agriculture is the largest consumer of Australia's water, making it the area where some of the biggest gains can be made in securing sustainable water management.[8]

II. Four Fundamental Water Law and Policy Reforms

A. Prioritise integration and engagement in water planning

Australia's rivers and aquifers have different local ecologies and are used by many different agricultural communities. Collaborative water plans are the core mechanism for incorporating and managing these diverse contexts and users. While there has been substantial experimentation in

---

4   Lee Godden and Anita Foerster 'Introduction: Institutional Transitions and Water Law Governance' (2011) 22(2/3) *The Journal of Water Law* 53–57.

5   Cameron Holley and Darren Sinclair 'Rethinking Australian Water Governance: Successes, Challenges and Future Directions' (2016) 33(4) *Environmental and Planning Law Journal* 275; National Water Commission (NWC), *Australia's Water Blueprint: National Reform Assessment 2014* (NWC 2014); Wentworth Group of Concerned Scientists, *Blueprint for a Healthy Environment and a Productive Economy* (Wentworth Group, 2014).

6   Australian Government, *Our North Our Future: White Paper on Developing Northern Australia* (2015), northernaustralia.gov.au/files/files/NAWP-FullReport.pdf.

7   NWC, above n 5, 4; Holley and Sinclair, above n 5. See also Productivity Commission (PC), *Inquiry into Progress with the Reform of Australia's Water Resources Sector* (PC, April 2017), www.pc.gov. au/inquiries/current/water-reform.

8   In a paper of this size, the analysis is inevitably selective in its coverage. It does not cover for example, the *Water Act 2007* (Cth) and the Basin Plan 2012 (Cth) in detail. Australian Bureau of Statistics (ABS), *Water Account Australia 2012–13* (ABS, 2014); Wentworth Group, above n 5.

water planning across states and territories,[9] most plans set environmental outcomes, rules for the allocation and trading of water for consumption, and monitoring and reporting requirements. Despite a slow start, there have been noted improvements in the quality and extent of planning across Australia, with some 170 finalised water plans now managing over 80 per cent of Australia's water use.[10] Despite this progress, water plans continue to suffer from fragmented coverage of uses and a history of poor community engagement.

One of the most prominent examples of fragmentation is the water use of the mineral and petroleum sectors. Recognised as facing 'special circumstances' (e.g. short durations, isolation and difficulties accounting for water extraction), mineral and petroleum developments like coal seam gas were to be addressed outside of the NWI and its plans.[11] However, these non-NWI regimes have not achieved the level of integration necessary to attend to the interdependencies between these developments and their impacts on water,[12] not least reduced water availability and altered flows. Significant public concern about these failures[13] led to a recent patchwork of federal and state reforms (e.g. the Commonwealth's water trigger, bioregional assessments and NSW's Aquifer Interference Policy). However, most of these remain ad hoc or partial, with industries' water use not always well integrated with broader regional water planning processes, and various states continuing to allow industries to sit outside of NWI water plans (e.g. Queensland).[14]

In terms of community engagement, there are many instrumental reasons why community consultation in planning is pursued, including encouraging trust and buy-in,[15] and developing effective responses to local

---

9   Poh-Ling Tan, Kathleen Bowmer and John Mackenzie, 'Deliberative Tools for Meeting the Challenges of Water Planning in Australia' (2012) 474 *Journal of Hydrology* 2; NWC above n 5, 26.
10   National Water Commission (NWC), *The National Water Planning Report Card 2013* (NWC, 2013); NWC, above n 5, 26, 351.
11   *NWI 2004*, cl 34.
12   Karen Hussey, Jamie Pittock and Stephen Dovers, 'Justifying, Extending and Applying 'Nexus' Thinking in the Quest for Sustainable Development' in J Pittock, K Hussey and S Dovers (eds), *Climate, Energy and Water* (CUP, 2015); NWC above n 5.
13   National Water Commission, 'Coal Seam Gas and Water Position Statement' (NWC, 2012); National Water Commission (NWC), *Water for Mining and Unconventional Gas under the National Water Initiative* (NWC, 2014) (hereinafter NWC, *Water for Mining*).
14   NWC, *Water for Mining*, above n 13, 10; John Williams, Tim Stubbs and Ann Milligan, *An Analysis of Coal Seam Gas Production and NRM in Australia* (JWSS, 2012).
15   Tom Tyler, *Readings in Procedural Justice* (Ashgate, 2005).

problems (e.g. water cutbacks).[16] However, government designed planning processes have tended to focus on traditional, quick and easy consultation methods (e.g. community meetings or panels), leading to Indigenous and many other interests (e.g. environmental and local farmers) being poorly engaged.[17] While there are signs of improving consultation in more recent plans,[18] these advances were arguably slow in coming and have produced profound legitimacy shortfalls and mistrust across affected communities.[19] As a recent survey revealed, the majority of respondents disagreed that their views about the Basin Plan (58 per cent, n 4,719) and coal seam gas (65 per cent, n 1,272) would be listened to.[20]

To successfully resolve the above shortcomings, planning processes must prioritise integration and commitments to deeper stakeholder engagement. This will require new obligations to identify all beneficiaries and interests affected by planning up front (so as to ensure more widespread engagement and avoid sectoral fragmentation causing difficulties during implementation);[21] joining up currently separate water planning processes and mining and gas development approval processes;[22] and legislating commitments to create, sustain and fund deeper deliberative engagement across a broader range of interests.[23] Pursuing such reforms will enhance opportunities for greater community 'buy-in' and produce more innovative, integrated and effective responses to local water problems.

---

16   Tan, Bowmer and Mackenzie, above n 9; Po-Ling Tan, Kathleen Bowmer and Claudia Baldwin, 'Continued Challenges in the Policy and Legal Framework for Collaborative Water Planning' (2012) 474 *Journal of Hydrology* 84; *NWI 2004* cl 97.

17   Sue Jackson et al, 'Meeting Indigenous peoples' Objectives in Environmental Flow Assessments: Case Studies from an Australian Multi-Jurisdictional Water Sharing Initiative' (2015) 522 *Journal of Hydrology* 141; Tan, Bowmer and Baldwin, above n 16.

18   NWC, above n 5, 27.

19   Bruce Lindsay, 'Public Participation, Litigation and Adjudicative Procedure in Water Resources Management' (2016) 33(4) *Environmental and Planning Law Journal* 325; National Water Commission, *The NWI – Securing Australia's Water Future: 2011 Assessment* (NWC 2011).

20   NWC, above n 5, 408–9.

21   Claudia Baldwin and Mark Hamstead, *Integrated Water Resource Planning* (Earthscan, 2015) 218.

22   NWC, *Water for Mining*, above n 13, 6; Poh-Ling Tan, David George and Maria Comino, 'Cumulative Risk Management, Coal Seam Gas, Sustainable Water, and Agriculture in Australia' (2015) 31(4) *International Journal of Water Resources Development* 682.

23   See Cameron Holley and Darren Sinclair, 'Deliberative Participation, Environmental Law and Collaborative Governance: Insights from Surface and Groundwater Studies' (2013) 30(1) *Environmental and Planning Law Journal* 32; Mark Hamstead, Claudia Baldwin and Vanessa O'Keefe, 'Water Allocation Planning in Australia', *Waterlines (6)* (NWC, 2008); Baldwin and Hamstead, above n 21.

B. Embrace regulatory pluralism to address market failures

A cornerstone of Australia's water reforms has been a cap and trade market-based system. Like market-based approaches in climate, pollution, biodiversity and fisheries contexts,[24] Australia's water market scheme is underpinned by a belief that environmental degradation occurs because of a failure to properly value environmental resources.[25] By setting a cap on acceptable resource use levels, assigning rights to extractors and enabling those rights to be traded, governments seek to facilitate rational, self-maximising individuals to promote 'public interests' by relocating natural resources to those who value them most highly in both the long and the short term.[26] Over the last 20 years this approach has delivered important benefits, at least in the Murray Darling Basin where significant surface water trading is occurring. Trading has facilitated flexible responses to droughts,[27] and produced economic benefits for individual farmers and regional communities (albeit selectively and relatively), by providing new sources of income, securities for loans and reinvestment on farms.[28] Moreover, these benefits appear likely to intensify, as there are encouraging signs that Australia's water market is increasingly functioning at a more optimal and efficient level, as a result of ongoing facilitation of trade and diffusion of information.[29]

Despite these benefits, Australia's water markets confront many ongoing challenges, including limited trading outside of the Murray Darling Basin and perhaps most significantly the lack of universality of environmental impacts in the context of groundwater trades. The use of market trading as an environmental tool works best when there is universality of the environmental impact; however, in the case of discrete groundwater

---

24   See Cameron Holley and Darren Sinclair 'Governing Water Markets – Achievements, Limitations and the Need for Regulatory Reform' (2016) 33(4) *Environmental and Planning Law Journal* 301.

25   Ronald Coase, 'The Problem of Social Cost' (1960) 3 *Journal of Law and Economics* 1; Antonio Roma, 'Energy, Money and Pollution' (2006) 56 *Ecological Economics* 534.

26   Bradley Karkkainen, Archon Fung and Charles Sabel, 'After Backyard Environmentalism' (2000) 44 *American Behavioural Scientist* 692, 693; National Water Commission (NWC), *Water Markets in Australia: A Short History* (NWC, 2011) 8; Holley and Sinclair, above n 24, 302.

27   Sarah Wheeler et al, 'Reviewing the Adoption and Impact of Water Markets in the Murray–Darling Basin, Australia' (2014) 518 *Journal of Hydrology* 28, 37.

28   NWC, above n 5, 358–59.

29   Sarah Wheeler, Alec Zuo and Neal Hughes, 'The Impact of Water Ownership and Water Market Trade Strategy on Australian Irrigators' Farm Viability' (2014) 129 *Agricultural Systems* 81; Holley and Sinclair, above n 24, 321.

aquifers, it is both environmentally undesirable to trade water in or out, and virtually physically impossible. To the extent that such situations prevail, the policy of water trading may be compromised. Indeed, despite making up around 21 per cent by volume of entitlements on issue in Australia, trading of groundwater entitlements is quite limited in most jurisdictions, accounting for around 12 per cent of total entitlement trading and only around 1 per cent of allocation trading (in NSW and Vic).[30] The limited trading of groundwater means that the consequential economic efficiencies will likely be undermined.[31] In light of this challenge, other complementary policy approaches are arguably needed to plug the gaps in market operation for groundwater.

As legal pluralist theories suggest, complementary mixes of instruments can often produce better outcomes than a reliance on a single instrument approach.[32] To address the limitations of the market regarding groundwater, reforms should accordingly focus on utilising a more comprehensive and complementary suite of innovative regulatory approaches, such as prescription standards (e.g. requirements that regulated actors adopt particular technologies or best practice or equivalence provisions), process standards (e.g. regulated entities establish target, auditing and reporting processes particular to their circumstances)[33] and perhaps more credibly the model of Audited Self-Management (ASM). I have argued elsewhere (with Sinclair) that the ASM model, which uses a mix of prescription, process and performance standards (e.g. setting and allocating an allowable water extraction or setting a particular level of pollutant), offers an innovative way to harness the benefits of flexibility (inherent to markets), while re-engaging and building trust with the agricultural community (an important issue given the weaknesses in planning discussed above).[34] Implementing ASM would involve establishing policy to support six

---

30   Holley and Sinclair, above n 24, 316–17; National Water Commission, *Australian Water Markets: Trends and Drivers 2007–08 to 2012–13* (Australian Government, 2011), 5, 37, www.nwc. gov.au/publications/topic/water-industry/trends-and-drivers-2012-13.

31   GHD, Hamstead Consulting and Vanessa O'Keefe, *A Framework for Managing and Developing Groundwater Trading* (NWC, 2011) xii; Holley and Sinclair, above n 24, 316–17.

32   Neil Gunningham, Peter Grabosky and Darren Sinclair, *Smart Regulation* (Oxford University Press, 1998).

33   For further discussion of these and other regulatory approaches, see Neil Gunningham and Cameron Holley, 'Next Generation Environmental Regulation' (2016) 12 *Annual Review of Law and Social Science* 273; Cameron Holley and Darren Sinclair, 'A New Water Policy Option for Australia? Collaborative Water Governance, Compliance and Enforcement and Audited Self-Management' (2014) 17(2) *Australasian Journal of National Resources Law and Policy* 189, 195.

34   Holley and Sinclair, above n 24, 322–23.

core ASM features, namely: enabling water users to form a legal entity or collective capable of managing the ASM program; allocating to the entity a collective water right (in effect, a bubble licence) covering all the ASM participating members; enabling participants to determine individual annual extractions as they see fit (effectively trading within the bubble licence); ensuring members have in place accurate metering that uses telemetry to generate real-time water extraction data; making the extraction data available to all participants (disaggregated to the individual level) and the government regulator (aggregated to the collective level); and putting in place, under the ASM program, appropriate integrity (e.g. auditor) and enforcement mechanisms to ensure compliance, including, if necessary, the capacity to draw on the support of the external government regulator.[35]

C. Support and implement water regulation

A core element of Australia's water governance approach is traditional regulation, conducted primarily by state-based regulatory agencies. Effective regulation, compliance and enforcement is vital to the NWI. The entire edifice of the market can be undermined if caps set in collaborative water allocation plans are exceeded due to illegal water extraction; if the various licences, approvals and tradeable water rights (essential to efficient markets) are not adhered to; and if stakeholders lack confidence that there is an equitable sharing of water resources (particularly in periods of drought).[36] While traditional regulatory arrangements vary between each state and territory, there are reasons to conclude that they remain less than ideal. In part this is because traditional regulation in the agricultural sector has proven complex and lagged other industries,[37] but also because NWI policy attention has naturally focused on establishing plans, entitlements and markets, rather than their enforcement. In view of these challenges, significant federal government investment was committed to improve state water regulation across Australia.[38] While NSW and a number of other

---

35   Holley and Sinclair, above n 24, 323.

36   NSW Office of Water, 'Compliance Policy' (NSW DPI, May 2015), www.water.nsw.gov.au/__data/assets/pdf_file/0005/560192/compliance_policy_2015.pdf; Cameron Holley and Darren Sinclair, 'Compliance and Enforcement of Water Licences in NSW: Limitations in Law, Policy and Institutions' (2013) 15 *Australasian Journal of National Resources Law and Policy* 149, 151–52.

37   Holley and Sinclair, above n 36.

38   Australian Government Department of Sustainability, Environment, Water, Population and Communities (DSEWPC), *National Framework for Compliance and Enforcement Systems for Water Resource Management* (Australian Government, 2012).

states have demonstrated progress in meeting many of the framework's milestones, completion rates across a number of issues (e.g. stakeholder education and monitoring) lag across many states, and federal funding is coming to an end.[39]

More generally, a recent survey on water compliance and enforcement in NSW suggest that water regulation still requires substantial improvement. The findings indicate that only around 49 per cent of respondents (n 604) were confident that water users in their region complied with their licence conditions, with an almost equal amount (45 per cent) unsure.[40] These less than optimal levels of perceived compliance and high levels of uncertainty[41] are causes for concern, as people who are regulated are less likely to comply with rules where norms of compliance are not widespread in practice.[42] The risk of non-compliance only appears to be compounded by related results that suggest that very few respondents agreed that compliance officers regularly worked in their region (26 per cent, n 533) or that people illegally taking water will be caught (33 per cent, n 611).[43]

To the extent that such problems are reflected across Australia, fixing these challenges and enhancing compliance and enforcement will require increased and continued investment. Such investment will be vital to implementing fundamental regulatory activities, including enhancing public communication of government enforcement; increasing and publicising compliance officer activities (e.g. education and periodic targeting of regions/sectors); leveraging peers and third parties in promoting compliance; and utilising a more responsive regulatory regime that maintains the support of water users.

---

39   NWC, above n 5, 353.

40   Cameron Holley and Darren Sinclair, *Water Extraction in NSW: Stakeholder Views and Experience of Compliance and Enforcement* (UNSW CWI, Feb 2015), www.connectedwaters.unsw.edu.au/sites/all/files/Water-extraction-in-NSW-stakeholder-views-of-compliance-and-enforcement-survey-report.pdf; Holley and Sinclair, n 24, 315.

41   Moreover, 51 per cent (n 504) wanted more information about compliance and enforcement activities of the regulator. Holley and Sinclair, above n 40.

42   Ibid.

43   Ibid.; Holley and Sinclair, n 24, 315.

D. Rebuild and intensify system-wide monitoring and benchmarking

Arguably one of the most successful features of the NWI is its system of monitoring and continuous improvement. Significant government funding was committed to monitoring, oversight and continual 'learning by doing' activities, including major investment in the Bureau of Meteorology (which gathered significant national water information); and financial backing for an independent National Water Commission (NWC) – a skills-based body whose tasks included conducting periodic assessments of the reforms and producing a series of related products, research studies, performance indicators and position statements.

Nevertheless, there are a number of shortfalls in the NWI's monitoring and continuous improvement systems. While monitoring of water plan outcomes is still impoverished,[44] perhaps the biggest shortfall relates to oversight of the NWI system itself. As a tool for improving and progressing the NWI, the NWC assessments were arguably its most important product, helping to facilitate benchmarking of performance. The assessments also shed light on gaps in the agenda, and publicly 'prodded' governments when they were dragging the chain on water reform.[45] This success is worth noting given that, subsequent to the National Competition Reforms and their incentive arrangements, there has been little funding to encourage state commitment to implementation (other than those tied to specific programs or places like the National Framework for Compliance and Enforcement and the Murray Darling Basin national partnership agreement payments).

Despite the success of the NWC, it was abolished in 2015. This decision was based on the view that progress in implementing the NWI was such that monitoring of national reforms was no longer needed, with statutory functions to be transferred to existing Commonwealth agencies.[46] With the government left to self-assess progress (albeit alongside ad hoc senate and independent inquiries), the disciplinary drivers that arose from the NWC's public transparency and comparisons are likely to fall away. As the

---

44 National Water Commission (NWC), *Monitoring and Evaluation for Adaptive Water Management: Issues Paper* (NWC 2013); NWC above n 5, 404.

45 David Rosalky, *COAG Review of the National Water Commission* (COAG, 2011) iii–iv.

46 P Hannam, 'Parched NSW Seeks Help as National Water Commission Axed', *The Sydney Morning Herald*, 13 May 2015, www.smh.com.au/environment/parched-nsw-seeks-help-as-national-water-commission-axed-20150513-gh0ork.html.

Commission itself noted before being disbanded, there is 'little assurance against backsliding on previous gains'.[47] This is particularly worrying given the substantial amount of work still to be completed on water, including recent federal proposals to develop Australia's northern water resources, as well as addressing challenges of coal seam gas, mining, community engagement, regulation and monitoring (noted above).

At a minimum, improving the NWI's commitment to monitoring and improvement goals requires increasing monitoring budgets (e.g. for water plans) and re-embracing an independent oversight body like the NWC. A more fundamental change would extend the NWI monitoring and improvement model so as to mirror the so-called experimentalist learning architecture,[48] replete with new obligations for localised benchmarking of water plans, greater horizontal diffusion of information between water catchments (facilitated by an oversight body like the NWC), and setting and ratcheting up minimal standards of good performance and process. Doing so would enhance opportunities for sharing more detailed learning and innovation (such as how best to integrate gas and mining in water planning, or manage environmental assets) across contexts, as well as enhancing opportunities for peer-to-peer accountability.

III. Conclusion

Continuing to improve Australia's national water law and policy will be central to future water security in an age of climate change. This chapter has surveyed non-urban water governance, identifying successes and several lingering shortfalls, including weak community engagement, gaps in integration, regulation and market trading, and limitations in continuous improvement caused by a dismantling of the NWC. Overcoming these weaknesses will require concerted efforts to continue the evolution and implementation of the NWI goals, such as the efforts canvassed in this chapter.

---

47 NWC, above n 5, 108.
48 Karkkainen, Fung and Sabel, above n 26.

23

Effective Law for Rural Environmental Governance: Meta-Governance Reform and Farm Stewardship

Paul Martin, Amanda Kennedy and Jacqueline Williams[1]

I. Introduction

Protection of biodiversity is principally concerned with the governance of rural lands and surface waters. This is because intact biodiversity is most likely to be found in rural areas that have not been converted to industry or urbanisation. But Australia's biodiversity performance is not heartening, despite the existence of many legal and other instruments and programs.[2] Threatened species in particular have suffered, with 50 animal species and 48 plant species listed as extinct since the passage of the *Environment*

---

1   Australian Centre for Agriculture and Law, University of New England.
2   Department of the Environment, 'Australia's Fifth National Report under the Convention on Biological Diversity' (Australian Government, 2014); Department of the Environment, 'State of the Environment Report 2011' (Australian Government, 2011); IISD Reporting Services, *OAS, UNEP Increase Cooperation on Environmental Rule of Law* (19 November 2014), sd.iisd.org/news/oas-unep-increase-cooperation-on-environmental-rule-of-law/.

Protection and Biodiversity Conservation Act 1999 (*EPBC Act*).[3] Public funding for biodiversity protection is also insufficient and under threat,[4] while the complexity of the biodiversity challenge is increasing.

Biodiversity decline has continued despite the proliferation of governance programs and laws, suggesting a failure of implementation.[5] There is support for this hypothesis.[6] The Secretary General of the Chief of Staff of the Organization of American States has joined a growing cohort highlighting the implementation failings of environmental governance, calling the implementation of environmental law 'the greatest challenge of our century'.[7] Traditional legal instruments for rural environmental governance, and scholarly discussions of the issues, tend to emphasise individual stewardship by private landholders. They also tend to focus on specific governance instruments, rather than the determinants of the performance of the governance system as a whole. Many fundamental strategic challenges are overlooked. Current approaches do not generate the whole-of-landscape, socioeconomically realistic responses that are needed for increasingly complex systemic problems. This complexity stems from factors including diverse land uses and ownership; fundamental disagreements about the objectives and methods of protection and restoration; the proliferation of governance interventions; and the insufficient economic capacity of farmers and other rural people to implement law, compared to their urban counterparts.

In this chapter we consider some less obvious systemic challenges and opportunities to overcome issues that limit conventional environmental governance approaches. We then propose some approaches to reform *meta-governance* processes – that is, to the governance of governance

---

3   Australian Bureau of Statistics, *1301.0 – Year Book Australia, 2009–10: Australia's Biodiversity* (ABS, 2010), www.abs.gov.au/ausstats/abs@.nsf/Previousproducts/1301.0Feature%20Article12009 %E2%80%9310?opendocument&tabname=Summary&prodno=1301.0&issue=2009%9610& num=&view=.
4   The Australian budget released in May 2014 included significant cuts of funding to Landcare and Cooperative Research Centres, and the abolishment of the National Water Commission and the Biodiversity Fund. This was after significant cuts in 2013 to biodiversity and carbon farming futures programs for rural landholders.
5   Euan Ritchie et al, 'Continental-Scale Governance Failure Will Hasten Loss of Australia's Biodiversity' (2013) 27(6) *Conservation Biology* 1133; Department of the Environment, 'Australia's Fifth National Report under the Convention on Biological Diversity' (Australian Government, 2014).
6   Ibid.
7   Organization of American States Secretary General Hugo De Zela, on the signing of the Agreement on Environmental Rule of Law and Sustainable Development, 19 November 2014, Washington DC; see IISD Reporting Services, above n 2.

frameworks themselves.[8] These proposals concern the arrangements used to create, review, reform and implement governance instruments, rather than the content of legal instruments. It is at this level that the greatest challenges to legal effectiveness exist, and the most significant innovations are needed. The major innovation we propose is not a new instrument, though this will also be needed. Rather, we suggest reforms to meta-governance processes. These changes will be needed to ensure that instrumental innovations (i) can be effectively implemented by the people who are required to take action, (ii) are efficient in how they operate at the front line, and (iii) fairly allocate the costs and benefits of protecting biodiversity and of the governance system itself.

II. Conditions for Effective Environmental Law

We begin with a simple question: what are the conditions under which an environmental law is likely to be effective? For the past decade our research team has concentrated on rural legal governance as a systems issue. Our research suggests that there are three necessary conditions for the success of governance instruments:

1. *Reliable policy concepts* allow governance interventions precisely to address the problem. A misguided or incomplete understanding of the problem will increase the risk of failure.[9]

2. *Efficient and effective instrument design* creates effective interventions with a feasible strategy for implementation. This involves choosing the most appropriate instrument – regulation, market or social intervention – to encourage the behavioural change required, depending upon the characteristics of those being regulated, and the available resources and commitment to implementation.[10]

---

8   See Jan Kooiman and Svein Jentoft, 'Meta-governance: Values, Norms and Principles, and the Making of Hard Choices' (2009) 87(4) *Public Administration* 818; Stephen Bell and Alex Park, 'The Problematic Metagovernance of Networks: Water Reform in New South Wales' (2006) 26(1) *Journal of Public Policy* 63; Bob Jessop, 'The Rise of Governance and the Risk of Failure: The Case of Economic Development' (1998) 50(155) *International Social Science Journal* 29; Michael Lockwood et al, 'Multi-level Environmental Governance: Lessons from Australian Natural Resource Management' (2009) 40(2) *Australian Geographer* 169; Louis Meuleman, *Public Management and the Metagovernance of Hierarchies, Networks and Markets: The Feasibility of Designing and Managing Governance Style Combinations* (Springer Science & Business Media, 2008).

9   Paul Martin and Jacqueline Williams, 'Policy Risk Assessment' (CRC for Irrigation Futures Technical Report Series No 03/10, 2010).

10   Paul Martin and Jacqueline Williams, 'Next Generation Rural Natural Resource Governance: A Careful Diagnosis' in Volker Mauerhofer (ed), *Legal Aspects of Sustainable Development* (Springer International Publishing, 2016) 607.

3. *Community support* makes the success of environmental law more likely. The intervention (the law) must reasonably align with self-interest to encourage desired action (or at least not generate negative reaction). There should also be a social perception that the intervention is justified and fair, and that the implementing body has integrity. A perception that an intervention is impractical or unfair can legitimate non-compliance and deprive the intervention of its social supports.[11]

There are many aspects of the current system that do not adequately satisfy these preconditions for performance. Our research suggests that while positive farmer attitudes are always important, new challenges and socioeconomic and natural resource management realities mean that many conventional governance solutions face serious challenges of feasibility, and risk undesirable spillovers. We argue that significant change in how we approach the design and implementation of rural governance is needed if we are to improve biodiversity outcomes. Australia needs a far more systematic approach to creating, implementing and evaluating the instruments and strategies of rural governance.

III. Challenges to Achieving Effective Rural Environmental Governance

Environmental governance involves instruments to control, direct, and motivate behaviour to achieve public goals for the ever-changing state of the environment. Success requires a good 'fit' between the instruments, the context, resources and the capabilities and commitment of those charged with implementation.[12] There are many aspects of the current system that do not adequately satisfy the necessary conditions for governance success.

Many conventional approaches to rural governance reflect a view of land use being principally agricultural, mainly broad-acre cropping and animal production. Readily identifiable on-farm environmental problems include soil erosion, land-clearing, wasteful use of water, excessive

---

11   Paul Martin, Jacqueline Williams and Christopher Stone, 'Transaction Costs and Water Reform: The Devils Hiding in the Details' (Cooperative Research Centre for Irrigation Futures Technical Report No 08/08, 2008).

12   Paul Martin and Donna Craig, 'Accelerating the Evolution of Environmental Law through Continuous Learning from Applied Experience' in Paul Martin and Amanda Kennedy (eds), *Implementing Environmental Law* (Edward Elgar, 2015) 27.

chemical use and habitat destruction. The natural focus of governance is, therefore, on farmer stewardship within individual estates. Examples of egregious irresponsibility prosecuted or reported in the media lead many in society to associate stewardship failure with *mala fides*; however, this assumption overlooks the contextual socioeconomic factors that underlie environmental problems.[13]

As many farmers argue, farm financial vulnerability and volatility, limited human resources and the relatively poor socioeconomic status of rural communities create conditions in which it is not feasible for them to meet the stewardship expectations that the law and (urban-based) public opinion place upon them. As a percentage of total population, Australia's rural population is a little over 10 per cent, and spread thinly over an extensive landscape.[14] Physical distance – both between citizens within rural communities, and between rural communities and (usually urban) centres of power and decision-making – creates spatial isolation which increases the transaction costs of governance. While rural and remote communities are not homogenous, the economic capacity of rural communities is also typically constrained in comparison to urban areas.[15]

Systemic issues, such as issues concerning biodiversity caused by climate change, and the need for habitat connectivity and control of invasive species to protect biodiversity, require coordinated action by landholders who operate diverse enterprises (with different incentives and concerns) and whose capacities vary. In general, coordinated action is impeded by fragmentation due to land titles and land use diversity. Homogenous farming landscapes are declining due to subdivision (including lifestyle farms) and ownership diversification (including Indigenous lands, corporate and international ownership). Coordinated action is further confounded by institutional fragmentation through an increasing number of private and public governance 'silos', and many laws and programs.[16]

---

13   Martin and Williams (2016), above n 10.
14   Bill Pritchard, *Land of Discontent: The Dynamics of Change in Rural And Regional Australia* (UNSW Press, 2000).
15   Vaughan Higgins and Stewart Lockie, 'Re-discovering the Social: Neo-Liberalism and Hybrid Practices of Governing in Rural Natural Resource Management' (2002) 18(4) *Journal of Rural Studies* 419.
16   Martin and Williams (2010), above n 9.

The reality of conditions faced by those living in rural areas raises difficult policy questions including:

1. To what degree is it reasonable or fair to expect landholders to privately fund public-good investment where there is no private benefit, without a public contribution to that work? This is a particularly difficult question when episodic factors like drought prevent otherwise responsible landholders from carrying out essential environmental works.

2. To what degree is it sensible and in the public interest to impose economically or physically infeasible requirements? This problem is particularly pronounced when farmlands are marginal, where abandonment or chronic incapacity will lead to no environmental work being conducted (other than at the full cost to the public purse).

'Public/private' allocation approaches to social problems, which may make sense when both public and private resources are available,[17] do not work well when the public or private purse is empty. Nor do approaches work when they oblige farmers to take stewardship actions beyond their traditional obligations. Rural governance arrangements must find ways that transcend private boundaries to share the load of biodiversity protection, and to provide resources and incentives to encourage action.

IV. Changing Meta-Governance

The discussion above suggests that Australia's strategy for making and implementing legal arrangements must become far more nuanced. We propose four meta-governance reforms, which combine different governance mechanisms to achieve a more coordinated and effective rural environmental governance regime.[18] The degree of change we recommend is radical, but if the present system is not working then radical change must be entertained.

---

17   For example, David Pannell, *Pannell Discussions No. 80: Public Benefits, Private Benefits: The Final Framework* (Pannell Discussions, 19 June 2006), www.pannelldiscussions.net/2006/06/80-public-benefits-private-benefits-the-final-framework/.
18   Louis Meuleman and Ingeborg Niestroy, 'Common but Differentiated Governance: A Metagovernance Approach to Make the SDGs Work' (2015) 7(9) *Sustainability* 12295–321.

1. *A more systemic approach.* Many rural natural resource governance problems are systemic in nature and laws need to reflect this to be more effective. This approach has three levels:[19]

   a. A more sophisticated national approach to rural biodiversity protection and restoration that provides a comprehensive framework for governance. The approach needs to interweave biophysical and socioeconomic factors to address the implementation challenges. The approach should be coupled with ongoing performance reviews of governance to provide a 'roadmap' for continuing improvement in rural environmental governance including law reform.

   b. Legal instruments need to more effectively address system protection and should have explicit implementation strategies, notably for whole-of-landscape action beyond individual farm boundaries. Often this will require interventions to align the socioeconomic context with the legal strategy in order to support change.

   c. Governance is becoming less government centred, as citizen organisations and industry take an increasing role and as the limits to government power and capacity become more pronounced.[20] Industry self-regulation and co-regulation are already significant in farming, in the form of buyer-chain environmental and other requirements, industry standards and codes, and market-based standards.[21] Still lacking are a strategy to harness this potential, and integrity mechanisms to ensure that such schemes are not *de facto* unjustifiable deregulation.

2. *Rural regulatory design and review processes.*[22] Current regulatory review is minimal and focused only on business cost. It does not address risks of implementation failure, nor of social spillovers. A more comprehensive approach is needed to:

---

19   For further details, see Paul Martin and Neil Gunningham, 'Improving Regulatory Arrangements for Sustainable Agriculture: Groundwater as an Illustration' (2014) 1(1) *Australian Journal of Environmental Law* 5; Mark Burgman et al, 'Designing Regulation for Conservation and Biosecurity' (2009) 13(1) *Australasian Journal of Natural Resources Law and Policy* 93.

20   C E Wilson, T H Morrison and J-A Everingham, 'Linking the "Meta-Governance" Imperative to Regional Governance in Resource Communities' (2017) 50 *Journal of Rural Studies* 188–97.

21   See Andrew Lawson, *Farmers, Voluntary Stewardship Programs, and Collaborative Natural Resource Governance in Rural Australia* (PhD thesis, University of New England, 2016).

22   Paul Martin et al, *Developing a Good Regulatory Practice Model for Environmental Regulations Impacting on Farmers* (Australian Farm Institute and Land and Water Australia, 2007).

   a. objectively review plans for implementation, including consideration of commitments from government to funding and other implementation requirements for the laws that they propose to create;

   b. consider the likely outcome effectiveness and distributional effects of proposed laws, and canvass how possible inadequacies and perverse impacts will be addressed.

3. An investment model is needed for the rural environment. This in turn has two levels:[23]

   a. Our estimate is that landscape protection and restoration requires approximately 2 per cent of GDP,[24] and others would argue that far more is needed.[25] After extensive research we have been unable to identify how much is actually being invested and by whom. There is no institutional mechanism to coordinate potential streams of investment, nor to maximise that investment. Economic feasibility is fundamental to legal effectiveness, and the lack of an investment strategy for the environment suggests a fundamental weakness in Australia's governance efforts.

   b. Investment is needed to support coordinated action by landholders, particularly when action goes beyond their site-specific legal responsibilities, if stewardship is to be effective. New project-specific funding streams are possible, but legal and institutional arrangements are needed to maximise and organise these opportunities. Organisational structures, and issues of contract and securitisation, are representative of issues where better legal arrangements are needed. Other law reforms such as changes to taxation may be needed to encourage private collective investment.

---

23   Paul Martin and Kip Werren, 'The Use of Taxation Incentives to Create New Eco-Service Markets: Critical Issues' in Lin-Heng Lye and Janet E Milne (eds), *Critical Issues in Environmental Taxation* (Oxford University Press, 2009) Vol 7, 511; Paul Martin and Kip Werren, 'Discussion Paper: An Industry Plan for the Victorian Environment?' (Department of Sustainability and Environment, State Government of Victoria, 2009); Kip Werren, *Utilising Taxation Incentives to Promote Private Sector Funded Conservation* (PhD Thesis, University of Western Sydney, 2015).

24   Martin and Werren, above n 23.

25   Marty Sammon and Mark Thomson, *Land Stewardship: Private Investor Needs For Land Stewardship Investment* (Department of Sustainability and Environment, State Government of Victoria, 2003); The Virtual Consulting Group and Griffin NRM Pty Ltd, 'National Investment in Rural Landscapes: An Investment Scenario for NFF and ACF with the Assistance of LWRRDC' (Australian Conservation Foundation and National Farmers Federation with assistance from Land & Water Resources Research & Development Corporation, 2000).

4. *Negotiated regionalism.* Bioregional planning is possible under the *Environment Protection and Biodiversity Conservation Act*, and could make a substantial contribution to improved biodiversity outcomes. From a socioeconomic perspective, this presents the opportunity to marry a science-based approach to a more community-based approach.

V. Conclusion

Australia has a national biodiversity strategy,[26] and provides a national assessment of its performance under that strategy when reporting on implementation of its international commitments to biodiversity protection.[27] On a regular basis, independent scientists publish the Australian State of Environment Report, a review of the biophysical status of the environment. Australia also has institutional arrangements to ensure that the welfare of rural communities and the sustainability of rural landscapes are protected. What Australia has not yet done is tie these elements together in a process of continuous improvement in the effectiveness of our legal arrangements for rural biodiversity protection. Similarly, Australia has a tradition of regulatory review, but it has not extended that process to properly take into account the implementation requirements and social justice implications of laws.

These are gaps in meta-governance which could be filled by an extension of existing rules and structures, potentially forming a basis for disciplined continuous improvement, based on sound empirical evidence of governance performance. Well-focused attention on the actual performance of legal arrangements, and the reasons for that performance, would be most likely to highlight the other issues we have discussed in this chapter, including the need for a viable investment base for sustainability, and the challenges of social justice embedded in the pursuit of this goal. Of all the possible changes that could improve the rural biodiversity outcomes for Australia, the most powerful would be reforming meta-governance in order to embed a process of empirically-based improvement in laws, other rules and institutions for implementation.

---

26   It is updated periodically; for the current strategy, see National Biodiversity Strategy Review Task Group, 'Australia's Biodiversity Conservation Strategy 2010–2030' (Natural Resource Management Ministerial Council, 2010).

27   Department of the Environment, 'Australia's Fifth National Report under the Convention on Biological Diversity' (Australian Government, 2014).

Part IV. Private Law

24

Pitfalls of Statutory Reform in Private Law: Recipient Liability for Breach of Trust

Darryn Jensen[1]

I. Introduction

Statutory law reform in relation to private law obligations has, historically, been mostly a matter of piecemeal adjustment rather than radical reconstruction. The piecemeal approach recognises the value in structures that have emerged gradually from case law. It seeks to resolve ambiguities or address concerns which arise in localised areas of the larger structure. Nevertheless, piecemeal statutory reform involves two risks. First, if there is inadequate reflection upon how the localised area of concern fits into the larger structure, the result may be to create a disjuncture between adjoining parts of the structure. Second, subsequent developments in the case law may render what was enshrined in statute redundant or nonsensical. Statute law in Western Australia and Queensland that was enacted primarily to remedy certain problems raised by the *Diplock* litigation[2] has turned out to be a mixed blessing. It will be argued that the rules about the order of enforcement of claims against the trustee and

---

1   ANU College of Law.
2   *Re Diplock* [1948] Ch 465; *Ministry of Health v Simpson* [1951] AC 251.

recipients should be discarded and that case law developments in relation to the common law claim for money paid by mistake have resolved the central problem in the *Diplock* litigation.

II. Recipient Liability for Breach of Trust

Where someone receives a distribution of trust property and was not entitled to receive it, there are three types of equitable claim which the 'true' beneficiaries of the trust may bring against the recipient. First, if misappropriated trust funds can be traced into an asset, the beneficiaries may claim the asset or a share of the asset which is proportionate to the trust fund's contribution thereto. Whether the asset is legally owned by the trustee or a third party is irrelevant, except that a third party may be able to rely upon a defence of bona fide purchaser for value without notice. In *Foskett v McKeown*,[3] Lord Millett observed that, in such a claim, the claimants 'seek to vindicate their property rights, not to reverse unjust enrichment'.[4] This stance has been rationalised on the basis that, if a trustee has the power to make an effective transfer of trust assets, then 'any assets received in exchange are made subject to the same equitable interests as bound the original trust assets'.[5]

Second, if a trustee conveys trust assets to, or confers an interest in trust assets on, a third party and the third party receives those assets or that interest knowing of the breach of trust, the third party will be liable in every way that the trustee would have been liable had the trustee been sued.[6] Knowing receipt opens up the possibility that the recipient will be personally liable to restore the trust estate, so is potentially a more exacting

---

3   [2001] 1 AC 102.
4   [2001] 1 AC 102, 129. See also similar comments at 108 (Lord Browne-Wilkinson) and 115 (Lord Hoffmann).
5   R B Grantham and C E F Rickett, 'Property Rights as a Legally Significant Event' (2003) 62 *Cambridge Law Journal* 717, 747. Contrast *Scott v Scott* (1963) 109 CLR 649, 660 in which it was said that the proprietary order made at first instance (and ultimately upheld by the High Court) was based on the liability of the trustee 'to make good a breach of trust' and 'to account for a profit which accrued to him'. In *Evans v European Bank Ltd* (2004) 61 NSWLR 75, 103, the New South Wales Court of Appeal declined to clarify the basis for proprietary claims because it was not necessary to do so in order to decide the case before it.
6   The traditional formulation is that the recipient becomes a 'constructive trustee' (*Barnes v Addy* (1874) LR 9 Ch App 244, 252). In *Selangor United Rubber Estates Limited v Cradock (No 3)* [1968] 1 WLR 1555, 1582, Ungoed-Thomas J explained that the defendant is liable in equity 'as though he were a trustee'. See also Lionel Smith, 'Constructive Trusts and Constructive Trustees' (1999) 58 *Cambridge Law Journal* 294, 300.

form of recipient liability than that which results from a proprietary claim. Where a traceable asset in the recipient's hands does not represent the full value of the misappropriated trust assets, the recipient merely has to transfer the asset. There is no liability to compensate the trust estate for any shortfall arising from a depreciation of the traceable asset.[7] Knowing receipt liability, on the other hand, is a true substitute for the beneficiaries' claim against the trustee.

Finally, it is conceivable that, where a trustee incorrectly distributes trust funds, a beneficiary or other person claiming through the trustee (such as a creditor of the trustee) ought to be able to recover from an *innocent* recipient the amount that the recipient received but should not have received. Equity is said to intervene in such a case because the recipient 'has received some share of the estate to which he was not entitled'.[8] *Re Diplock* was a case about a deceased estate. The House of Lords, in dismissing an appeal, reasoned on the basis that this equitable claim was available against persons who had received distributions from deceased estates.[9] Accordingly, it has been uncertain whether distributees of funds from *inter vivos* trusts are similarly liable. Lord Nicholls (writing extra-judicially) has suggested that a restriction to deceased estates, although explicable in historical terms, is irrational.[10] In his Lordship's opinion, a claim should be available against a recipient from either type of trust estate 'to prevent what would otherwise be an unjust enrichment'.[11] The recipient's liability is to make restitution of what it received and nothing more. This is a significant limitation because the loss suffered by the trust estate by reason of an unauthorised distribution will often be greater than the amount received by the unauthorised recipient.[12]

---

7   Where, in relation to a particular transaction in breach of trust, the plaintiffs elect to take the traceable asset rather than make a personal claim against the trustee for restoration of the trust estate, the traceable asset will be 'the full measure of relief available to them' (*Scott v Scott* (1963) 109 CLR 649, 660).

8   [1948] Ch 465, 503.

9   *Ministry of Health v Simpson* [1951] AC 251, 265. Lord Simonds remarked that 'the particular branch of the jurisdiction of the Court of Chancery with which [the case was] concerned relates to the administration of assets of a deceased person'.

10   Lord Nicholls, 'Knowing Receipt: The Need for a New Landmark' in W R Cornish, Richard Nolan, Janet O'Sullivan and Graham Virgo (eds), *Restitution Past, Present and Future: Essays in Honour of Gareth Jones* (Hart Publishing, 1998) 240–41.

11   Ibid. 237.

12   For example, as in *Re Dawson* [1966] 2 NSWR 211. See generally Jamie Glister, 'Breach of trust and consequential loss' (2014) 8 *Journal of Equity* 235.

In *Re Diplock*, it was said that the amount recoverable was limited to the amount which could not be recovered from the trustee.[13] In other words, the beneficiaries must recover what they can from the trustee before recovering any amount from the recipient. This restriction was supposed to be related to the equitable nature of the claim. The 'absence or exhaustion' of the beneficiaries' claim against the trustee was taken to be 'the justification for calling for equity to come to the aid of the law'.[14] In *Re Diplock*, where the trustee had made the payments under a mistaken belief that a will provision was legally enforceable, there was no common law claim for money had and received, but the rule is clearly not concerned with the absence or exhaustion of that claim. It is concerned with the exhaustion of the claim *against the trustee* for restoration of the trust estate, which is an equitable claim. As Lord Nicholls remarked, the problem is 'internal to equity'.[15]

III. Statutory Reform

The Western Australian and Queensland statutory provisions do three things. First, they provide that a personal restitutionary claim of the *Re Diplock* type is available in *all* cases of incorrect distribution of trust property.[16] Second, they create statutory change of position defences under which a recipient could, under certain conditions, be relieved of liability to repay the whole or part of what it received.[17] These reforms were justified. There is nothing in the rationale of the personal restitutionary claim that demands that it be confined to cases involving deceased estates. The change of position defence is welcome because recipients who have disbursed the funds that they received may suffer hardship if required to repay.

Third, and more contentiously, the statutes set down rules about the order of enforcement of claims against the trustee and claims against recipients. The Western Australian legislation reverses the *Re Diplock* order of enforcement. No remedy may be enforced against the trustee until the beneficiary has exhausted 'all other remedies available to him, whether

---

13   [1948] Ch 465, 503.
14   [1948] Ch 465, 503–4; see also *Ministry of Health v Simpson* [1951] AC 251, 266.
15   Lord Nicholls, above n 10, 241.
16   *Trustees Act 1962* (WA) s 65(1); *Trusts Act 1973* (Qld) s 113(1).
17   *Trustees Act 1962* (WA) s 65(8); *Trusts Act 1973* (Qld) s 113(3).

under this section or in equity or otherwise'.[18] This language clearly encompasses claims to traceable assets held by recipients, knowing receipt or assistance claims and personal restitutionary claims against recipients.[19] The Queensland Law Reform Commission took the view that there was 'no virtue whatever in placing the primary responsibility for a wrongful distribution on the distributee'.[20] Accordingly, the Queensland legislation affirms the rule stated in *Re Diplock*,[21] so that the personal restitutionary claim against the recipient cannot be enforced until all remedies, personal and proprietary, against the trustee have been exhausted.[22]

IV. The Pitfalls of Reform

A. Order of enforcement of claims

The Queensland provision emphasises the trustee's culpability in respect of the incorrect distribution. The trustee should be primarily responsible for putting things right. This premise is open to challenge. Certainly, the culpability of the executor in *Re Diplock* was of the slightest variety. The executor had acted in accordance with the terms of the will. The executor's mistake was simply to assume that the relevant clause of the will was legally enforceable when it was not. A conclusion that such a trustee should always bear the burden of restoring the trust estate ahead of a recipient who has made a windfall gain is questionable.

The greater difficulty is that recipients, unless they are *knowing* recipients, are not liable to restore the trust estate. Their liability is limited to the value of what they have received. Under the Queensland provision, the recipient is liable to give back only so much of what it received as is necessary to make up for the trustee's inability to restore the trust estate in full. If, on the other hand, Lord Nicholls is correct is saying that the *Re Diplock* claim 'presupposes that the recipient was enriched by a windfall

---

18   *Trustees Act 1962* (WA) s 65(7)(b).
19   *Corporate Systems Publishing v Lingard (No 4)* [2008] WASC 21, [184]. Beech J described the prerequisite to enforcement of a judgment against a trustee as 'any judgment against the recipients or assisters is satisfied'. See also Peter Creighton and Elise Bant, 'Recipient Liability in Western Australia' (2000) 29 *Western Australian Law Review* 205, 229.
20   Queensland Law Reform Commission, *Report on the Law relating to Trusts, Trustees, Settled Land and Charities* (QLRC 8) (1971) 74.
21   *Trusts Act 1973* (Qld) s 113(2).
22   *Ron Kingham Real Estate Pty Ltd v Edgar* [1999] 2 QdR 439, 445 (McPherson JA).

gain',[23] a requirement that claims against the trustee be exhausted first does not harmonise with the rationale for making the recipient liable. The recipient should be liable to give back what it received regardless of the trustee's means to restore the trust estate. The rule that claims against the trustee must be exhausted first protects a recipient on the basis of the happy circumstance that the trustee has the resources to restore the trust estate.

Equally, it is not clear that a trustee should be relieved of liability to the extent that the trust estate can be restored by recovering what has passed into the hands of third parties or, where there is a knowing recipient, by making the recipient personally liable to restore the trust estate. Under the Western Australian legislation, the difference between cases in which remedies can be enforced against trustees and those in which they cannot be is the happy circumstance that third parties have either traceable assets or sufficient monetary resources to pay back the amounts that they received. Where a third party is a knowing recipient, that third party is jointly and severally liable to restore the trust estate on account of the third party's culpability in respect of the breach of trust being as great as that of the trustee, but the third party is not necessarily any more culpable than the trustee. Of course, it *may* be convenient for a plaintiff to enforce first any of the remedies against third party recipients on the basis that it is easy to do so compared to requiring the trustees to restore the trust estate using their own resources, but it is difficult to see any principled justification for *requiring* plaintiffs to do so. Creighton and Bant have remarked that it would be 'preferable simply to eliminate any requirement for exhaustion of remedies'.[24]

B. Redundancy

In *Re Diplock*, the beneficiaries had to rely upon equity to found their restitutionary claim against the recipients because a common law claim would not have been available. At the time, it was generally believed that a common law action for money had and received was not available where the payer's mistake was a mistake as to the law. The 'mistake' in *Re Diplock*

---

23 Lord Nicholls, above n 10, 241.

24 Creighton and Bant, above n 19, 230. In 2013, the Queensland Law Reform Commission recommended that the requirement that remedies against the trustee should be exhausted before enforcing remedies against recipients should be removed (Queensland Law Reform Commission, *Review of the Trusts Act 1973* (QLRC 71) (2013) 129). At the time of writing, subs 113(2) remained unamended.

was an assumption that the provision of the will under which the payments were made was legally enforceable. The provision was unenforceable because the trustee's discretion to choose recipients encompassed entities that did not have charitable purposes. This was a mistake as to law.

By the end of the 1990s, in both England and Australia, it had been recognised that money paid under a mistake of law is recoverable by way of a common law action.[25] In so far as situations involving receipt of funds from trustees fall within the scope of a general common law rule that demands the restitution of mistaken payments, then the equitable claim would be redundant. Equity operates on the basis that the common law is inadequate to do justice, rather than on the basis that the payer is a trustee. The common law claim applies to all recipients. It is not restricted to funds received from deceased estates. A plaintiff who relies on the common law claim would not have to exhaust any remedies that are available against the trustee before enforcing the claim. It has become clear that a defendant recipient would, in appropriate cases, be able to invoke a *common law* change of position defence.[26]

The proper plaintiff in a claim for money had and received against the recipient of trust funds is the payer of the funds – that is, the trustee. A beneficiary is not normally entitled to bring an action in place of the trustee, but it is clear that a beneficiary could bring a derivative action against a debtor of the trustee if the action 'is needed to avoid injustice'.[27] It has been argued that a beneficiary may bring a derivative action where the trustee 'unjustifiably fails to bring an action to protect the trust'.[28] The trustee would be obliged to recover the incorrect distribution from the recipient. This would be an aspect of the trustee's duty to restore the trust estate. Beneficiaries could compel the trustee to bring the action, so the derivative action simply aggregates the beneficiary's action to compel the trustees to recover the debt and the trustee's action against the recipient.[29] The cumulative effect of the abrogation of the fact/law

---

25 *David Securities Pty Ltd v Commonwealth Bank of Australia* (1992) 175 CLR 353; *Kleinwort Benson Ltd v Lincoln City Council* [1999] 2 AC 349.

26 *Port of Brisbane Corporation v ANZ Securities Limited* [2002] QCA 158, [27]; *Alpha Wealth Financial Services Pty Ltd v Frankland River Olive Company Limited* [2008] WASC 119, [196]–[211]; *Australian Financial Services and Leasing Pty Limited v Hills Industries Limited* [2014] HCA 14.

27 *Roberts v Gill & Co* [2010] UKSC 22, [110] (Lord Collins).

28 Emma Hargreaves, 'The Nature of Beneficiaries' Rights under Trusts' (2011) 25 *Trust Law International* 163, 178.

29 H A J Ford and W A Lee, *Principles of the Law of Trusts* (Thomson Reuters, Sydney, 4th edn, 2010) [17.4110].

distinction and the availability of derivative actions is that beneficiaries can bring *common law* claims to recover the funds incorrectly distributed. Therefore, statutory provisions which entrench the *Re Diplock* claim as part of the law and set down prerequisites to its enforcement might be seen to be redundant.[30]

V. Conclusion

To preserve the Western Australian and Queensland statutory provisions on recipient liability in their current form is to retain unnecessary complication and to invite confusion. It is time for the content and form of these provisions to be reconsidered. There should be a shift from prescribing the order of enforcement to allowing plaintiffs to choose the order in which remedies are enforced, subject to a provision that the total amount recovered by way of *personal* claims against the trustees and recipients should not exceed the total amount required to restore the trust estate.

---

30   Ibid. [17.7010]. Ford and Lee observed that 'these provisions, while they still may be of some procedural value, are no longer needed'.

Recent Reforms to Australian Charity Law

Matthew Harding[1]

I. Introduction

In Australia, until recently, the definition of charity for all legal purposes was drawn almost exclusively from judge-made law.[2] Thus, whether the setting was an inquiry into the validity of a purpose trust or eligibility for a Commonwealth, state or territory tax concession available to charities, judge-made law typically supplied a complete answer to the definitional question. As a result of recent legislative reforms, this is no longer the case. The legal landscape in Australia is now one in which judge-made law supplies the definition of charity for some legal purposes, Commonwealth statutory law supplies it for others, and state and territory legislation supplies it for others still. The current picture is thus one of definitional proliferation.

---

1 Melbourne Law School. My thanks to Ian Murray for characteristically perceptive comments on a draft.

2 There were, however, exceptions: see, for example, *Extension of Charitable Purposes Act 2004* (Cth).

II. Commonwealth Reforms

At the Commonwealth level, the key reform is the *Charities Act 2013*. This Act defines charity for the purposes of Commonwealth law including, crucially, the purposes of Div 50 of the *Income Tax Assessment Act 1997* (which makes provision for income tax exemptions for charities). The *Charities Act 2013* is not designed to operate as a code, departing radically from the judge-made law that preceded it; rather, the preamble to the Act states that it will 'ensur[e] continuity by utilising familiar concepts from the common law'. However, many of the concepts in the Act, and much of the language in which the statutory text is expressed, are in fact foreign to judge-made charity law. Thus, for example, s 12 identifies as charitable 'the purpose of promoting reconciliation, mutual respect and tolerance between groups of individuals that are in Australia' and 'the purpose of promoting or protecting human rights'; one struggles to find statements in judge-made charity law to the effect that either type of purpose is charitable.[3] And s 7 seems not only to reflect the judicial strategy of presuming the benefit of certain types of purpose; it seems also to presume that those types of purpose are public in character, a strategy that has never been deployed in judge-made charity law.[4] The precise relation of the *Charities Act 2013*, and the judge-made charity law onto which it has been overlain, is thus unclear.

To what extent should decision-makers interpret the *Charities Act 2013* by drawing on antecedent judge-made law, and to what extent should they apply principles of statutory interpretation that demand departure from that judge-made law? This sort of question is not new in the history of charity law. It has arisen in cases where judges have been asked to interpret the term 'charity' (or one of its cognates) in the context of a tax statute. In *Commissioners for Special Purposes of Income Tax v Pemsel* itself, the House of Lords had to determine whether references to 'charitable' purposes in the *Income Tax Act 1842* were to be given the 'technical legal' meaning developed over centuries by judges in equity or some other meaning more in accord with contemporary understandings.[5] And the High Court of Australia was asked, in *Chesterman v Federal Commissioner of Taxation*,

---

3   Indeed, the judge-made law points the other way: *McGovern v Attorney-General* [1982] 1 Ch 321 (Slade J).

4   For further analysis of the approach in judge-made law, see Matthew Harding, *Charity Law and the Liberal State* (Cambridge University Press, 2014) 25–29.

5   See [1891] AC 531 at 534–39 for a summary of counsel's arguments.

to rule on the question whether the word 'charitable' in the *Estate Duty Assessment Act 1914–1916* (Cth) was to be given a meaning drawn from judge-made law, or whether principles of statutory interpretation demanded that some different meaning be recognised.[6]

In both *Pemsel* and *Chesterman*, courts ultimately preferred interpretations that drew on antecedent judge-made law. But in neither case was this preference uncontested.[7] And the basis for the preference, at least as expressed in *Pemsel* and *Chesterman*, is open to question in light of contemporary understandings of statutory interpretation. In *Pemsel*, Lord Macnaghten stated that '[i]n construing Acts of Parliament, it is a general rule … that words must be taken in their legal sense unless a contrary intention appears'.[8] This principle has been endorsed by Australian cases of the highest authority.[9] However, it seems, at least to some degree, at odds with other principles of statutory interpretation that have also been approved by the High Court of Australia, according to which interpreters must look to the ordinary meaning of the statutory text in context, and to relevant legislative purposes.[10] This tension in the law of statutory interpretation, as it applies to the legal definition of charity, will not be manifested in a post–*Charities Act 2013* world in quite the same way as it was in cases like *Pemsel* and *Chesterman*. Decision-makers called on to interpret references to 'charity' in Commonwealth tax statutes must now look to the *Charities Act 2013* for guidance and to that extent need not make interpretive decisions. But in ascertaining the meaning of the *Charities Act 2013* itself, so as to apply the definition of charity that the Act sets out, decision-makers may find that they are confronted with interpretive challenges of the type experienced in *Pemsel* and *Chesterman*, challenges that surround the interpretation of statutory terms with judge-made histories. In the *Charities Act 2013*, these include key terms like 'advancing education', 'advancing religion' and 'public benefit'.[11]

---

6   (1923) 32 CLR 362.

7   *Pemsel* was a 3:2 decision. And in *Chesterman*, a majority of the High Court of Australia actually rejected an interpretation drawing on antecedent judge-made law; the case was subsequently appealed to the Privy Council, which overturned the decision of the High Court. I discuss the two cases in detail in Matthew Harding, 'Equity and Statute in Charity Law' (2015) 9 *Journal of Equity* 167, 173–75.

8   [1891] AC 534 at 580.

9   See the authorities discussed in D C Pearce and R S Geddes, *Statutory Interpretation in Australia* (LexisNexis, 8th edn, 2014) [4.13].

10   See *Project Blue Sky Inc v Australian Broadcasting Authority* (1998) 194 CLR 355; *Lacey v Attorney-General (QLD)* (2011) 242 CLR 573. And note the judgment of Kirby J in *Central Bayside General Practice Association Ltd v Commissioner of State Revenue* (2006) 228 CLR 168 [91]–[119].

11   *Charities Act 2013* (Cth) ss 12(1)(b), 12(1)(d) and 6.

Further interpretive challenges arise in relation to the numerous terms in the *Charities Act 2013* that do not originate in judge-made law. For example, s 12(1)(c) of the Act refers to 'the purpose of advancing social or public welfare', a phrase that is not known to judge-made charity law. And s 12(1)(h) refers to 'the purpose of advancing the security and safety of Australia or the Australian public'; the closest that judge-made law comes to this phrase is 'the promotion of public defence and security'.[12] When it comes to provisions like these, the principle that words 'must be taken in their legal sense unless a contrary intention appears' cannot be applied because there is no legal sense in which to take them. Without that principle to guide them, decision-makers are likely to fall back on other principles of statutory interpretation, such that the definition of charity under the *Charities Act 2013* may, over time, come to diverge in substantial ways from the definition of charity in antecedent judge-made law. This is hardly surprising; it seems a natural consequence of enacting a statute that is to a non-trivial degree couched in terms unknown to the judge-made charity law that preceded it. But it may nonetheless be a matter for concern, at least while the extent to which it is desirable for the *Charities Act 2013* to innovate in relation to the definition of charity in Commonwealth law remains unclear.

III. State and Territory Reforms

Reforms in state and territory law have taken a different path. In 2012, the Western Australian State Administrative Tribunal determined that the Chamber of Commerce and Industry of Western Australia was a charitable organisation for the purposes of that state's *Pay-Roll Tax Assessment Act 2002*, notwithstanding that it was, to some degree, an organisation committed to serving members.[13] Where judges have found that an organisation's dominant purpose is to benefit members, they have refused to extend charity status to that organisation;[14] in contrast, judges have recognised as charities organisations with a purpose of serving members, so long as their

---

12 *Downing v Federal Commissioner of Taxation* (1971) 125 CLR 185 at 198 (Walsh J).

13 *Chamber of Commerce and Industry of Western Australia Inc v Commissioner of State Revenue* [2012] WASAT 146 (Justice J A Cheney).

14 See, for example, *Inland Revenue Commissioners v City of Glasgow Police Athletics Association* [1953] AC 380 (HL); and, perhaps more controversially, *Law Institute of Victoria v Commissioner of State Revenue* [2015] VSC 604 (Digby J).

dominant purpose is to generate public benefit.[15] The Western Australian Tribunal decision, when read in that light, is unremarkable. That is not, however, how it was read by the Western Australian legislature. In 2015, by the *Taxation Legislation Amendment Act (No 2)*, that legislature sought to narrow the definition of charity for certain purposes of Western Australian law.

According to the Western Australian reforms, a range of member-serving organisations cannot be charities for the purposes of Western Australian tax law. And, crucially, the Western Australian reforms exclude from the definition of charity, for the purposes of Western Australian tax law, a 'professional association'. 'Professional association' is, in turn, defined to mean an organisation 'having *as one of its objects or activities* the promotion of the interests of its members in any profession'.[16] That definition encompasses organisations with a dominant purpose of generating public benefit, and a subsidiary purpose or even a practice of benefiting a membership drawn from a particular profession. And the Western Australian reforms tighten the definition of charity for the purposes of Western Australian tax law in another way as well, by excluding from tax concessions an organisation that 'promotes trade, industry or commerce'.[17] The promotion of trade, industry or commerce has long been recognised as a type of charitable purpose in judge-made law,[18] and to the extent that the Western Australian reforms mean that for the purposes of Western Australian tax law this recognition has been withdrawn, the Western Australian reforms represent a significant departure from antecedent law.

The Western Australian reforms make provision for a professional member-serving or commerce-promoting organisation to apply to the Minister for Finance for a determination that the organisation is not in fact excluded from tax concessions despite the other provisions that the Western Australian reforms have brought into effect. The minister is empowered under the Western Australian reforms to make such a determination, with the concurrence of the state treasurer, and also to

---

15   See, for example, *Royal College of Surgeons of England v National Provincial Bank Ltd* [1952] AC 681 (HL).

16   *Duties Act 2008* (WA) ss 3, 95, 96A; *Land Tax Assessment Act 2002* (WA) ss 37, 38AA, Sch 1, Glossary; *Pay-Roll Tax Assessment Act 2002* (WA) ss 41, 42A, Sch 1, Glossary. Emphasis added.

17   Ibid.

18   See *Crystal Palace Trustees v Minister of Town and Country Planning* [1950] 2 Ch 857 (Danckwerts J); *Tasmanian Electronic Commerce Centre Pty Ltd v Federal Commissioner of Taxation* (2005) 142 FCR 371 (Heerey J).

revoke or amend the determination, again with the concurrence of the treasurer. The minister may make, revoke or amend a determination 'only if the Minister is of the opinion that it is in the public interest to do so and after considering any information that the Minister considers relevant'.[19] No action may be brought in a court to compel the minister to make a determination, and the minister's determination may not be reviewed or appealed in any way.[20]

The Western Australian reforms have been taken up elsewhere. In the Australian Capital Territory, by the *Revenue (Charitable Organisations) Legislation Amendment Act 2015*, the legislature has withdrawn charity status, for the purposes of tax law, from professional member-serving and commerce-promoting organisations.[21] Like the Western Australian reforms, the ACT reforms enable excluded organisations to apply for a determination that they ought not to be excluded; but unlike the Western Australian reforms, the ACT reforms empower the Commissioner for ACT Revenue, rather than the relevant government minister, to make such a determination, and they spell out more clearly than the Western Australian reforms the grounds on which the determination may be made.[22] Moreover, the ACT reforms provide that the Commissioner's determinations and revocations of determinations are reviewable.[23]

In the Northern Territory, the *Revenue and Other Legislation Amendment Act 2015* effects changes to that territory's *Payroll Tax Act* similar to the Western Australian and ACT reforms. The Northern Territory reforms withdraw payroll tax exemptions from professional member-serving and commerce-promoting organisations;[24] at the same time the Northern Territory reforms empower the Commissioner of Territory Revenue, presumably following an application in the ordinary case, to make a determination that a member-serving or commerce-promoting organisation ought not to be excluded. The Northern Territory reforms make reference to considerations to which the Commissioner 'may' have regard when deciding whether to make such a determination, and

---

19   *Duties Act 2008* (WA) ss 95, 96B, 96C; *Land Tax Assessment Act 2002* (WA) ss 37, 38AB, 38AC; *Pay-Roll Tax Assessment Act 2002* (WA) ss 41, 42B, 42C, Sch 1.
20   *Taxation Administration Act 2003* (WA) s 34A.
21   *Taxation Administration Act 1999* (ACT) ss 18B and 18C.
22   Ibid. ss 18E, 18F and 18G.
23   Ibid. Sch 1, ss 1.2(b) and (c).
24   *Payroll Tax Act* (NT) ss 48, 48A and 48B.

these considerations are similar to those set out in the ACT reforms.[25] Determinations of the Commissioner are reviewable under the *Taxation Administration Act*.[26]

These state and territory law reforms bring with them at least two challenges. The first challenge is in identifying a sound basis for excluding from the definition of charity, for certain purposes of state or territory law, organisations whose dominant purpose is to generate public benefit. One legacy of the great case of *Morice v Bishop of Durham* is that not all public benefit purposes are recognised in law as charitable;[27] thus, a state or territory legislature that withdraws charitable status from organisations with certain public benefit purposes is not, to that extent, engaging in heterodoxy. Moreover, recent state and territory reforms to the legal definition of charity have been enacted in order to preserve government revenues against perceived threats. This is an entirely appropriate policy objective for the legislatures in those jurisdictions to form and pursue.[28] Perhaps more difficult to defend is the legislative choice to seek to preserve government revenues by modifying the legal definition of charity when different conceptual architecture could have been used. Recent state and territory reforms have created legislation that relies largely on traditional charity law criteria – the *Pemsel* taxonomy and a public benefit test – but at the same time denies charity status to certain purposes that meet those criteria, on the basis of considerations external to charity law as it has developed over the centuries. Should the legal definition of charity be affected by such external considerations, or are those considerations best reflected in legal rules that do not bear on the definition of charity but nonetheless affect the operation of charities?[29] This is a large and fundamental question which requires careful consideration in light of the state and territory reforms of recent years.

A second challenge generated by state and territory law reforms is in keeping the operation of Australian charity law consistent with rule of law ideals. In each of the three reforming jurisdictions, charity status has been

---

25 Ibid. s 48E.
26 *Taxation Administration Act* (NT) ss 107–15.
27 (1804) 9 Ves Jun 399 at 405 (Sir William Grant MR); (1805) 10 Ves Jun 522 at 541 (Lord Eldon). See also Joshua Getzler, '*Morice v Bishop of Durham* (1805)' in Charles Mitchell and Paul Mitchell (eds), *Landmark Cases in Equity* (Hart, 2012) 157 at 196–97.
28 Whether or not it is a sound objective for courts to pursue is another matter: see generally *AYSA Amateur Youth Soccer Association v Canada (Revenue Agency)* [2007] 3 SCR 217.
29 For one view on this question, see Adam Parachin, 'Legal Privilege as a Defining Characteristic of Charity' (2009) 48 *Canadian Business Law Journal* 36.

withdrawn from professional member-serving and commerce-promoting organisations, and such organisations have been enabled to apply to an officer of the executive branch of government for a determination that they ought not to be excluded. In antecedent law, a professional member-serving or commerce-promoting organisation could rely on a tax official applying rules and principles of law in determining whether or not it was a charity; moreover, such an organisation could seek review of the tax official's decision in a tribunal or court. Following the reforms, organisations must rely to a much greater extent on relatively unfettered executive discretion. This is clearest in the case of the Western Australian reforms, where determinations are to be made by the Minister of Finance taking into account vague criteria of 'public interest' and relevance, and where there is no right of review. But executive discretion is also pronounced in the ACT and Northern Territory reforms, notwithstanding that legislation in those jurisdictions articulates criteria that may be taken into account in the exercise of executive discretion and notwithstanding that determinations may be reviewed. If Australian charity law is to live up to rule of law ideals, this reliance on executive discretion as a means to determining charity status should be extended no further than is currently the case, and indeed should be abandoned in the jurisdictions in which it is now embedded.

IV. Conclusion

The reforms to Australian charity law that have been effected recently are of interest insofar as they alter a legal landscape formed and reformed over hundreds of years. However, they represent just the beginning of an even more interesting journey, as judges and other decision-makers work with the statute law that has brought about the reforms in question, interpreting that statute law and fashioning it with an eye to social, political and economic circumstances. In this regard, notwithstanding recent reforms, the future of Australian charity law may be viewed as the continuation of a tradition that began with early interpretations of the preamble to the Statute of Elizabeth.

26

Consumer Protection, Recreational Activities and Personal Injury Compensation: Inconsistency in Need of Reform

Joachim Dietrich[1]

I. Introduction

Participation in sport and recreation is one of the most significant causes of personal injury in Australia, including many injuries of a serious nature. The relevant liability rules pursuant to contract, tort and statute therefore constitute a practically important area of law. Despite their importance, however, those rules are not uniform. They are also in parts complex and uncertain. This chapter highlights some of the key difficulties and suggests areas that are in need of reform.

This chapter is mainly concerned with injuries resulting from activities undertaken pursuant to a *contract* for recreational services (e.g. a paid-for activity such as trampolining). A person negligently injured in the course of the performance of a services contract may sue the defendant supplier of the services for failure to comply with statutory guarantees imposed by the *Australian Consumer Law* (*ACL*), among other possible

1   My thanks to Iain Field and Pauline Ridge for their helpful comments on earlier drafts. Any remaining errors are solely mine.

claims in contract or negligence. In the *absence* of a contract, an injured party may proceed only in negligence, against possible defendants such as supervisors of activities, occupiers of premises, etc. Different legal rules may apply accordingly.

Three sources of legal difficulties are highlighted in this chapter:

1. The lack of uniformity as to the available defences under the state and territory ('state') Civil Liability Acts (CLAs), dealing particularly with recreational activities.

2. The interaction between state CLAs laws on negligence and the *ACL* statutory guarantees in relation to services; and the fact that those *different* state negligence laws continue to operate despite the 'uniform' *ACL*.

3. The uncertain legal effect of contract clauses that purport to exclude liability for negligently supplied recreational services.

II. Defences Relevant to Recreational Activities

As a result of the passage of the various, non-uniform, state CLAs,[2] we now have eight separate tort law regimes in Australia. There are many differences between the laws in each jurisdiction, but one area in which those regimes differ markedly is in their respective approaches to defences concerning recreational activities.

In four states, plaintiffs engaged in a 'dangerous recreational activity' (DRA) are disentitled from bringing action for harm caused by the 'materialisation' of an obvious risk of that activity.[3] One focus of litigation has been on the meaning of the qualifying terms 'dangerous recreational activity' (e.g. s 5L *CLA* (NSW)). A recreational activity is dangerous if it involves a significant risk of harm (s 5K). Importantly, all of 'the particular circumstances in which the activity was being undertaken' are relevant in

---

2   The titles of the various Acts, like their content, are not uniform. See, for example, *Civil Liability Act 2002* (NSW); *Wrongs Act 1958* (Vic).

3   See s 5L *CLA* (NSW), s 19 *CLA* (Qld), s 20 *CLA* (Tas), s 5H *CLA* (WA).

determining its inherent dangerousness.[4] It has been held that diving into water of uncertain depth is a DRA;[5] as is riding a bike on a skate park;[6] but playing touch football[7] and calm water cruising[8] are not.

The term 'obvious risk' is defined broadly in the various provisions as any risks that in the circumstances would have been obvious to a 'reasonable person in the position of' the plaintiff.[9] There are, however, some differences in the details between jurisdictions. Although the test is objective, the issue is one of whether 'the probability of [the risk's] occurrence is or is not readily apparent to the reasonable person in the position of the plaintiff'.[10] The degree of precision or generality with which one states the 'risk' in question will impact on the conclusion.[11] For example, what needs to be obvious is more than the end result of an activity – such as falling off a horse – but the manner in which the risk materialised, such as falling off a horse as a result of the saddle slipping.[12] The courts have drawn subtle distinctions in the interpretation and application of the concepts of 'obvious' risks and 'materialisation' of such risk and the law is complex.

Two jurisdictions only, NSW and WA, have provisions that excuse defendants for any liability arising from risks of recreational activities in respect of which the defendant has given a 'risk warning'. Sections 5M *CLA* (NSW) and 5I *CLA* (WA) (which are not identical) are fairly complex and long. Attempts by defendants to rely on them have met with mixed success.[13] One reason why it may be difficult to rely successfully on these provisions is that a risk warning must be 'given in a manner that is reasonably likely to result in people being warned of the risk before engaging in the recreational activity': s 5M(3) *CLA* (NSW); s 5I(4) *CLA* (WA).

---

4   *Smith v Perese* [2006] NSWSC 288 [86].
5   *Jaber v Rockdale City Council* (2008) Aust Tort Reps 81-952 (*Jaber*).
6   *Vreman and Morris v Albury City Council* [2011] NSWSC 39 (*Vreman*).
7   *Falvo v Australian Oztag Sports Association* (2006) Aust Torts Reps 81-831.
8   *Lormine Pty Ltd v Xuereb* [2006] NSWCA 200.
9   See s 5F *CLA* (NSW), s 13 *CLA* (Qld), s 15 *CLA* (Tas), s 5F *CLA* (WA).
10   *Jaber* (2008) Aust Tort Reps 81-952 [35] (Tobias JA).
11   *C G Maloney Pty Ltd v Hutton-Potts* [2006] NSWCA 136 [174] (Bryson JA, McColl JA agreeing).
12   Compare *Mikronis v Adams* [2004] 1 DCLR (NSW) 369; see s 13(5) *CLA* (Qld) and s 53 *Wrongs Act* (1958) (Vic), clarifying this point specifically.
13   See, for example, *Vreman* [2011] NSWSC 39 [107]–[114].

The upshot of this is that the law that governs claims by persons injured in recreational activities in one jurisdiction will differ to that which applies to persons injured in another and will depend on difficult statutory interpretation issues in some jurisdictions.

But what of the situation where a person is injured as a result of a negligently performed contract of recreational *services*, or indeed, services more generally, and therefore the *ACL* applies?

III. *ACL* and Inconsistent Consumer Protection

The new *ACL* came into effect on 1 January 2011. Its stated aim was to 'create a single national consumer law'.[14] There are, however, exceptions to this uniformity. The *ACL* is the result of a complex exercise of cooperative federalism, with the *Competition and Consumer Act 2010* (Cth) (*CCA*) inserting the *ACL* as Sch 2 of the *CCA*. Part XIAA of the *CCA* provides for the application of the *ACL* as a law of the states and territories.[15]

Commonwealth jurisdiction applies (s 131 *CCA*) where a consumer enters into a contract with a '*corporation*', as defined in s 4 and as extended by s 6 to natural persons in certain defined contexts.[16] Hence, if a 'corporation' (in its extended sense) supplies services in trade and commerce to a consumer, it is bound by the *ACL* as a law of the Commonwealth via s 131 and Pt XI of the *CCA*. In relation to natural persons, the applicable law is that of the relevant state jurisdiction in which the services were supplied. State provisions also apply to corporations, of course, so long as they are not inconsistent with Commonwealth law. If the *ACL* were truly uniform, it would not matter which jurisdiction, Commonwealth or state, applied or, in the latter case, *which* state law applied. However, the *ACL* is not uniform. Importantly, the *ACL*'s uniformity is seriously undermined in the context of a failure to comply with the guarantee that *services* are supplied with due care and skill, where such failure results in personal injury or property damage.

---

14 Commonwealth, *Explanatory Memorandum to Trade Practices Amendment (Australian Consumer Law) Bill No 2* (2010) 3.

15 All jurisdictions have applied the *ACL* under their relevant Fair Trading Acts. See, for example, *Fair Trading Act 1987* (NSW) Pt 3, Div 2, inserted by the *Fair Trading Amendment (Australian Consumer Law) Act 2010* (NSW).

16 See para 6(2)(c).

Section 60 of the *ACL* provides: 'If a person supplies, in trade or commerce, services to a consumer, there is a guarantee that the services will be rendered with due care and skill'. A consumer who suffers 'reasonably foreseeable' personal injury or property damage as a result of a careless supply of services can seek damages under s 267. For example, if a climbing instructor fails properly to instruct the client on the use of safety gear so that the client falls and suffers injury or (to take a non-recreational example) a mechanic carelessly repairs a car, causing brake failure, the client has a potential claim for damages under s 267.

Where a claim is brought under the *ACL*, the state CLAs continue to apply in relation to establishing the legal requirements for liability, any applicable defences, and the applicable principles for calculating damages (including the various limits contained in the CLAs). This is because, first, the CLAs set out general principles applying to claims arising *from a failure to take reasonable care*, irrespective of whether such claims are brought in tort, contract *or under statute*;[17] and second, and importantly, s 275 *ACL* allows for the continued operation of state laws that apply to the careless supply of services under a contract.

Section 275 is a complex section, and all of the difficulties that it raises cannot be explored here. To simplify, the effect of the section appears to be to engage any law, of the state that is the relevant 'proper law of the contract',[18] which law 'applies to limit or preclude liability' under a claim on the contract. Consequently, provisions of the various CLAs that *directly* limit or preclude liability for careless conduct will be effective and applicable. According to the High Court in *Insight Vacations Pty Ltd v Young*,[19] a case concerning the (almost identically worded)[20] equivalent s 74(2a) under the previous *Trade Practices Act* (*TPA*), s 74(2A) operated to pick up and apply 'as surrogate federal law'[21] a state law that *of itself*

---

17   See, for example, *CLA* (NSW) s 5A; *CLA* (Qld) Ch 2, Pt 1 (most sections apply to 'breach of duty of care', defined to include claims in contract or under statute, though Div 4 on dangerous recreational activities applies only to 'negligence', suggesting that breaches of contractual duties of care *are not within the scope* of the Division: see R J Douglas, G R Mullins and S R Grant, *The Annotated Civil Liability Act 2003 (Qld)* (LexisNexis, 3rd edn, 2012) [19.5]).

18   One difficulty is that the proper law of the contract may not be the same as the place where the services are provided, but it is unlikely that the CLAs have extra-territorial operation: cf *Insight Vacations Pty Ltd v Young* (2011) 243 CLR 149 [35].

19   (2011) 243 CLR 149 (*Insight*).

20   This is apart from seemingly minor changes to the wording to reflect the change from implied terms to statutory guarantees.

21   *Insight* (2011) 243 CLR 149 [12].

applies to limit or preclude liability.[22] In other words, s 74(2A) allowed state laws to directly limit rights of consumers via the CLAs; that is, it picked up, for example, sections in some states that deal with DRAs.[23]

Assuming that s 275 *ACL* has a similar effect as s 74(2A) *TPA*, then important consequences follow for the overall scheme of the *ACL*. As a result of s 275, some differing state provisions that determine liability for personal injury suffered as a result of carelessness continue to operate in each jurisdiction. These would apply equally to corporate (defendant) suppliers. Some of the key inconsistencies arising between jurisdictions include:

1. Different state laws place different limitations on various heads of personal injury damages. This is a complex patchwork of rules that applies where state jurisdiction is activated; where Commonwealth jurisdiction applies, Pt VIB *CCA* has *similar* limitations.

2. *Some* specific defences adopted in some jurisdictions, including perhaps those dealing with recreational activities, continue to operate via s 275,[24] as noted above. For example, if a consumer of a supplier of services is injured while engaged in a DRA, the supplier of such services can potentially defend such a claim on that basis in NSW, even where such a supplier was negligent,[25] whereas a supplier in Victoria could not.

3. Apart from defences concerning recreation, other defences have been adopted in some jurisdictions and not others, such as those dealing with intoxicated plaintiffs.

The consistent treatment *within* states of all claims for carelessly caused injuries leads to *inconsistency* and lack of uniformity *between* different states. This lack of uniformity arises for some provisions even if Commonwealth

---

22 Ibid. [12], [35]–[36] (French CJ, Gummow, Hayne, Kiefel and Bell JJ).

23 See for more detailed discussion of these issues, see J Dietrich, 'Liability for Personal Injuries from Recreational Services and the New Australian Consumer Law' (2011) 19 *Torts Law Journal* 55; and 'Service Guarantees and Consequential Loss under the ACL: The illusion of uniformity' (2012) 20 *Competition & Consumer Law Journal* 43.

24 Admittedly, however, restrictions on liability that are picked up by s 275 include even general defences, such as contributory negligence and voluntary assumption of risk, which are probably only effective as a result of s 275.

25 The DRA defences are picked up because the provisions 'limit' liability. However, s 5M *CLA* (NSW) is not picked up, as it states that no duty arises at all (rather than limits liability for a duty that has been breached): see *Motorcycling Events Group Australia Pty Ltd v Kelly* [2013] NSWCA 361 [87]–[96] (*Motorcycling*). This case also highlights numerous other complex issues, not herein considered, that arise from the interaction between state and Commonwealth law.

jurisdiction applies. Why the legislatures have not considered uniformity to be desirable given such potentially serious consequences is puzzling. Ultimately, that lack of uniformity is a result of politics and the failure of the states to agree on a uniform *CLA* regime, and that was and remains a regrettable state of affairs.

IV. Exclusion of Liability

A further area in which reform is needed concerns the law on exclusion of liability for failure to comply with the statutory guarantees. The statutory guarantees cannot *generally*[26] be excluded by a supplier of services as a result of s 64 *ACL*: such a term is void if it seeks to exclude, restrict or modify the rights conferred and liabilities imposed under the consumer guarantees. Critically, however, it is possible under the *CCA* for a supplier to exclude liability for failure to comply with the guarantees in the supply of recreational services. Section 139A *CCA* replicates the previous s 68B *TPA*, which aimed to 'permit self-assumption of risk by individuals who choose to participate in inherently risky activities'.[27] A term excluding liability for breach of s 60 *ACL* guarantee is not void under s 64 if it 'excludes, restricts or modifies' such a statutory guarantee (s 139A(1)), for death or physical or mental injury (and not for property damage, for example). The definition of recreational services is broad (and not identical to that in various state CLAs).

Importantly, s 139A(4) does not allow for the exclusion of liability for reckless conduct, defined in subs (5). If an exclusion clause *effectively* excludes liability for conduct contravening s 60, it will almost certainly also exclude liability for any negligence claims in *tort* as between the parties to the contract. If an exclusion clause is not effective in excluding liability for contravention of s 60, then a claim for damages for loss arising from contravention of s 60 (and presumably also in tort) will be available against a defendant service-provider.

Although the purpose of s 139A is clear enough, for a lawyer advising a client as to whether a clause effectively operates to exclude a claim the question is fraught with legal difficulties including:

---

26 Note, however, s 64A(2) *ACL*.
27 Explanatory Memorandum provided with the *Trade Practices Amendment (Liability for Recreational Services) Bill 2002*.

1. Section 139A does not set out how an exclusion clause is to be effectively worded and incorporated into a service contract. This means that the important question of the effectiveness of an attempted exclusion of liability is determined by the vagaries of the labyrinthine common law contract principles on the incorporation of terms and their interpretation.

2. An exclusion clause that purports to exclude liability in broader terms than is permitted under s 139A (e.g. for recklessness) *may* be void,[28] even if the injury sustained comes within the permitted exclusions (e.g. if caused by ordinary negligence).

3. Adding to the complexity, s 139A *CCA* introduces a new distinction, between ordinary negligence, which can be excluded, and 'recklessness', which cannot. Obviously, this restriction has merit, in that it precludes the most serious carelessness from going unremedied; but it adds a new complication to the law by creating *degrees* of negligence.

4. An exclusion clause that purports to exclude liability in wider terms than is permitted is void, but the presence of such a void clause may mislead consumers into thinking that their rights are more limited, and may thus amount to misleading conduct under s 18 *ACL*.[29]

5. Section 139A raises a nuanced question of possible inconsistency between state and Commonwealth law, since Victoria has legislated to allow for the exclusion of liability for non-compliance with the statutory guarantees[30] in narrower terms, that is, that are more onerous in setting out *how* a supplier can exclude liability. Does s 275 *ACL* pick up the Victorian legislation or is there an inconsistency such that s 139A will prevail?[31]

6. The legal effect of exclusion clauses that purport to bind minors is not adverted to in s 139A, yet the law on this is uncertain and in a confused state.[32] This is so despite the widespread use of such clauses. The confusion arises because of the fundamental common law principle that minors do not have contractual capacity, such

---

28 Under the previous and differently worded s 68B *TPA*, such clause was void if it exceeded the permitted exclusions: see *Motorcycling* [2013] NSWCA 361. The different wording of s 139A *CCA* leaves the question in doubt.
29 And see s 29(1)(m) and (n) *ACL*.
30 See Dietrich, above n 23.
31 *Insight* (2011) 243 CLR 149 does not deal with this because it deals with the indirect exclusion of liability in *broader* circumstances than permitted by Commonwealth law.
32 See generally, J Dietrich, 'Minors and the Exclusion of Liability for Negligence' (2007) 15 *Torts Law Journal* 87.

that contracts entered into by minors, except for 'necessaries', are unenforceable against them; and nor do guardians have a general power to contract on minors' behalf.

V. Reform

The hope of a simplified and uniform regime of liability for personal injuries sustained during performance of a service contract has not been achieved. Obviously, the best solution to this problem would be for the states to reach agreement on a uniform civil liability regime, but the likelihood of this occurring in the medium-term future appears remote given that the *ACL* process itself has not resulted in uniform solutions. At the very least, we need to reopen debate about our consumer protection laws and consider the competing policies that are at stake here. Key issues in this debate include: whether the desirability of uniformity is trumped by the desire (of some state legislatures) to enhance the assumption of 'self-responsibility'; the value of having a national injury compensation law; the need for clarity for consumers as to their rights (e.g. as to how and when exclusion clauses are effective); and, particularly, the need to protect minors from unfair and one-sided contractual provisions.

27

Statutory Interpretation and the Critical Role of Soft Law Guidelines in Developing a Coherent Law of Remedies in Australia

Elise Bant[1] and Jeannie Paterson[2]

I. Introduction

This chapter considers three particular challenges faced by meta-legislation such as the *Australian Consumer Law* (*ACL*).[3] The first is to ensure coherent development of the law both within the legislative regime and also between that regime and the common law context in which it is squarely situated. The second, related challenge is to promote the principled and coherent development of an important legal regime in a context where its beneficiaries are unlikely to pursue their rights in court. This requires the regime effectively to be self-enforcing; directing parties to the appropriate standards of conduct and assisting them to resolve any

---

1 Professor of Law, University of Melbourne.
2 Associate Professor of Law, University of Melbourne.
3 *Australian Consumer Law* (*ACL*) contained in Sch 2 of the *Competition and Consumer Act 2010* (*CCA*, formerly the *Trade Practices Act 1974* (Cth) (*TPA*)). See also the equivalent provisions in the *Australian Securities and Investments Commission Act 2001* (Cth) Div 2, *Corporations Act 2001* (Cth) and the Torrens Statutes.

disputes that develop. A third challenge, which underpins the previous two, is the density and complexity of the legislation. This complexity impedes access to justice objectives and constitutes a significant hurdle to the statute being self-executing to any degree.

The chapter considers these challenges in regard to the remedial provisions responding to misleading conduct and unconscionable conduct under the *ACL*. It proposes two possible responses and also makes a law reform suggestion. First, it models an approach to statutory interpretation that both promotes the protective purpose of the statute and encourages coherent evolution of consumer law within and outside of the statutory context. Second, the chapter considers the potential value of problem-based practice notes that model the application of key provisions against standard problem scenarios. Finally, the chapter suggests that an understanding of both the influence of the general context in which the legislation is sited, and the way in which consumers use the legislation to protect their rights, should influence statutory design and drafting.

II. The Principle of Coherence and Remedies under the *ACL*

The High Court has recently and repeatedly emphasised the principle of coherence as an overriding criterion in the application and development of the law.[4] While its precise requirements are yet to be fully charted, the principle likely demands an integrated approach to the analysis and application of statutory and judge-made law.[5] In the context of consumer protection law, which pervades most commercial and consumer disputes and overlaps considerably with the private law of contract, tort and equity, a major challenge is how to move beyond the traditional 'oil and water'[6] approach to the relationship between general and statutory law. In this context, the principle of coherence entails an enquiry into the extent to

---

4   *Miller v Miller* (2002) 242 CLR 446, 454 [15] (French CJ, Gummow, Hayne, Crennan, Keifel and Bell JJ); *Equuscorp Pty Ltd v Haxton* (2012) 246 CLR 498, 518 [34], 520 [38], 523 [35] (French CJ, Crennan and Kiefel JJ).

5   For example, Mark Leeming, 'Theories and Principles Underlying the Development of the Common Law – The Statutory Elephant in the Room' (2013) 36(3) *UNSW Law Journal* 1002; Paul Finn, 'Statutes and the Common Law' (1992) 22 *University of Western Australia Law Review* 7; Paul Finn, 'Statutes and the Common Law: The Continuing Story' in Suzanne Corcoran and Stephen Bottomley (eds), *Interpreting Statutes* (Federation Press, 2005) 52.

6   Jack Beatson, 'Has the Common Law a Future?' (1997) 56 *Cambridge Law Journal* 300.

which cognate principles of general law remedies properly influence the interpretation and operation of remedial consumer protection provisions of the *ACL* and, conversely, whether the *ACL* itself exerts a 'gravitational force' on the continuing evolution of those general law principles.[7]

In approaching interpretation and application of the *ACL*, the starting point is that '[a]nalogy ... is a servant not a master'.[8] Primacy must be given to the words and purpose of the statute. On the other hand, while common law analogies 'are not controlling ... they represent an accumulation of valuable insight and experience which may be useful in applying the Act'.[9] This chapter accordingly proposes a model of reasoning that starts with the words of the statute, interpreted in light of its purpose. However, common law and equitable principles and doctrines may then properly be drawn upon where they reflect and promote the aims of the statutory orders and are consistent with the statutory scheme as a whole. The chapter illustrates how this approach may promote a more coherent law of consumer remedies, using as examples the debated nature of loss under s 236 of the *ACL* and the award of rescission-like relief using a combination of s 243(a)(c) and (d).

A. Section 236: Actions for damages

The *ACL* does not define the meaning of 'loss or damage' that may be compensated through statutory damages. By contrast, the general law has developed highly sophisticated understandings of the roles and rationales of different conceptions of loss and damage. It seems highly unlikely that parliament chose these words intending that they should reflect entirely novel meanings, in the absence of any legislative definition. Courts have accordingly turned to the general law concepts of loss and damage for guidance. In that context, '[t]he task is to select a measure of damages which conforms to the remedial purpose of the statute and to the justice and equity of the case'.[10] However, courts have vacillated over the relevant analogical source.[11]

---

7   Elise Bant, 'Statute and Common Law: Interaction and Influence in Light of the Principle of Coherence' (2015) 38(1) *UNSW Law Journal* 362.
8   *Marks v GIO Holdings Ltd* (1998) 196 CLR 494, 529 [103] (Gummow J).
9   *Henville v Walker* (2001) 206 CLR 459, 470 [18] (Gleeson CJ).
10   Ibid.
11   Compare *Marks v GIO Holdings Ltd* (1998) 196 CLR 494 and *Murphy v Overton Investments Pty Ltd* (2004) 216 CLR 388.

The critical point is to draw upon common law concepts that are consistent with and promote the particular statutory words and their protective purpose. Not all common law conceptions of loss are, on that approach, relevant or appropriate sources of analogy. For example, it is well understood in the law of contract that expectation damages are a form of normative, not factual, loss.[12] Expectation damages make sense in a context where the normative legal order demands contracts must be performed[13] and a contract has been breached. A plaintiff's dashed expectation of gain caused by proscribed conduct constitutes 'loss' because the plaintiff not only expected the profit but was entitled to it.

By contrast, s 18 *ACL* does not require defendants to perform their promises or make true their representations. Rather, it requires that defendants do not engage in misleading or deceptive conduct. It follows that expectation damages are not an appropriate measure of loss in cases of misleading or deceptive conduct.

A more appropriate analogical source for s 236 damages, and one consistently identified by the courts, is the concept of reliance loss familiar from, for example, the tort of deceit.[14] This measure supports and promotes the language of the statute, which directs courts to consider loss caused by misleading or deceptive conduct. This may require us to examine the plaintiff's changes of position made in reliance on that conduct.[15] Identifying loss flowing from or caused by acts of reliance is therefore a logical starting point for the statutory enquiry and makes deceit an apt analogical source. Likewise the law of negligent misstatement offers an appropriate source of guidance, a point perhaps under-appreciated in the statutory case law to date.[16] On this approach, the disappointment of shattered hopes may be compensated as a type of distress damage.[17]

---

12   L Fuller and R Perdue, 'The Reliance Interest in Contract Damages: 1' (1936) 46 *Yale Law Journal* 52, 53.

13   *Clark v Macourt* (2013) 88 ALJR 190, 194 [11] (Hayne J).

14   See *Kizbeau Pty Ltd v WG & B Pty Ltd* (1995) 184 CLR 281, 291 (Brennan, Deane, Dawson, Gaudron and McHugh JJ); *Kenny & Good Pty Ltd v MGICA (1992) Ltd* (1999) 199 CLR 413, 460–61 [129] (Kirby and Callinan JJ).

15   Note *Caffey v Leatt-hayter [No 3]* [2013] WASC 348 (20 September 2013) [466]–[476] (Beech J).

16   Elise Bant and Jeannie Paterson, 'Limitations on Defendant Liability for Misleading or Deceptive Conduct under Statute: Some Insights from Negligent Misstatement' in Kit Barker, Ross Grantham and Warren Swan (eds), *The Law of Misstatements: 50 Years on from Hedley Byrne v Heller* (Bloomsbury, 2015) Ch 7.

17   *New South Wales Lotteries Corporation Pty Ltd v Kuzmanovski* (2011) 195 FCR 234. Cf *Competition and Consumer Act 2010* (Cth) s 137C.

B. Sections 237–39 and 243: Compensation orders etc.

Sections 237–239 provide courts with the discretion to make a wide range of creative orders, illustrations of which are set out in s 243,[18] in response to contraventions of the *ACL*. None of the orders listed in s 243 adopt the language of rescission, nor do they refer to other related general law concepts such as counter-restitution or the requirement of *restitutio in integrum*. Further, s 237(2) of the *ACL* makes explicit that the remedial aim of the provisions is compensatory, not restitutionary.

Nonetheless, courts have repeatedly held that these provisions empower them to award rescission-like remedies which require restitution and counter-restitution of benefits transferred pursuant to the impugned transaction. In this context, the equitable remedy of rescission has been a powerful albeit not binding guide to the relevant considerations that inform the making of analogous orders under the provision.[19]

Courts have married the restitutionary nature of rescission with the compensatory purpose of the statutory scheme by emphasising that the conception of loss under s 87 *TPA*, the precursor to s 237 *ACL*, is much broader than the traditional characterisations of loss the subject of compensation orders in tort and, indeed, those covered by the compensatory provisions in s 82 *TPA* (now s 236 *ACL*). In *Demagogue Pty Ltd v Ramensky*, Black CJ explained, 'the loss or damage contemplated by s 87(1A) is not limited to loss or damage in the s 82 [s 236 *ACL*] sense but was intended to include the detriment suffered by being bound to a contract unconscionably induced'.[20] The language and structure of the statute taken as a whole 'emphasises that the phrase "the loss or damage", at least in s 87, may be concerned with more than pecuniary recovery as understood in the law of damages in tort' and may extend to entry into contractual obligations as a result of misleading or deceptive conduct.[21]

---

18 For similar provisions to which this discussion can be extended, see, for example, *Australian Securities and Investments Commission Act 2001* (Cth) ss 12GM, 12GNC; *Corporations Act 2001* (Cth) s 1325; *Contracts Review Act 1980* (NSW) s 7; *National Consumer Credit Protection Act 2009* (Cth) ss 179–80.

19 *Marks v GIO Australia Holdings Ltd* (1998) 196 CLR 494, 535 (Gummow J). See also *Tenji v Henneberry & Associates Pty Ltd* (2000) 98 FCR 324, 329–30 [12] (French J).

20 *Demagogue Pty Ltd v Ramensky* (1992) 39 FCR 31, 33.

21 Ibid. 43 (Gummow J).

This broad, policy-driven conception of 'loss or damage' under the statute is evident in the orders made by courts effecting statutory rescission. Courts adopt a broad conception of detriment that considers whether the plaintiff would suffer detriment in the absence of, or indeed as a result of, the award. [22] The focus of the enquiry, as for equitable rescission, seems to be whether it is possible to return the parties to the status quo ante. To that end, courts routinely apply change of position–style considerations to protect rescinding plaintiffs from being placed in a worse position than they occupied prior to the impugned transaction. [23]

This approach strongly echoes the evolving approach taken at general law to the change of position defence in claims for restitution of mistaken payments. [24] The statute in this context provides a model of analogous principles that can and arguably should be drawn upon by courts seeking to further develop that defence, as well as when exercising the equitable doctrine of rescission. On this approach, the statutory jurisprudence would exert a 'gravitational force' on contested issues such as the proper treatment of non-reliance-based changes of position that may promote more coherent and integrated common law, equitable and statutory principles governing restitutionary liability. [25]

III. The Potential Role of 'Soft Law' Practice Notes

There is relatively little case law developing the more nuanced aspects of the remedial regime discussed above. What authority does exist rarely involves consumer–trader disputes, and almost none deals with the remedial responses to unconscionable conduct. This is because relatively few private litigants' claims for relief from proscribed conduct under the *ACL* reach courts. Many disputes covered by the regime involve modest sums, and the value of the claim will not justify the expense of litigation. Many consumers, and some traders, will lack the resources, confidence or

---

22   See, for example, *Munchies Management Pty Ltd v Belperio* (1988) 58 FCR 274, 287–89; *Akron Securities Ltd v Iliffe* (1997) 41 NSWLR 353, in particular the judgment of Mason P.

23   *Munchies Management Pty Ltd v Belperio* (1988) 58 FCR 274, 287–89; *Akron Securities Ltd v Iliffe* (1997) 41 NSWLR 353.

24   *Australian Financial Services and Leasing Pty Ltd v Hills Industries Ltd* (2014) 253 CLR 560.

25   Cf *Vadasz v Pioneer Concrete* (1995) 184 CLR 102, 115–16. See further E Bant, 'Rescission, Restitution and Compensation' in S Degeling and J Varuhas (eds), *Equitable Compensation and Disgorgement* (Hart Publishing, 2017) Ch 13.

expertise to pursue such claims. Most disputes will be resolved informally, without input by lawyers or judges. If not resolved informally or through mediation, consumer–trader disputes under the *ACL* will usually be heard in small claims courts and consumer tribunals.

There is a delicate balance to maintain here. While consumers need access to low cost informal mechanisms to help them resolve disputes, if access to justice is not to be illusory, it is critically important that those disputes are resolved in accordance with the rights and responsibilities granted by the statutory regime. It is impossible for the regime to evolve and adapt to new conditions if the complex points of interpretation and principle it raises are not given an opportunity to be considered, analysed and debated as in a manner appropriate to any serious body of law.

In this context, the potential role of soft law guidance is significant.[26] The style of soft law practice notes envisioned would seek to encapsulate key legal principles in a straightforward and accessible format and then illustrate their operation by reference to a series of simple but realistic examples.[27] The notes need not be exhaustive: the aim is to provide general guidance on the main rights and liabilities that arise under relevant provisions, accepting that exceptions and distinctions can arise which warrant different outcomes.

The potential attractions of this form of guidance include facilitating access to justice under the statute by enabling consumers and traders to better understand their rights and obligations under the law, and providing guidance to courts, tribunals and other decision-makers so as to promote a coherent, consistent rule of law. Practice notes can readily engage in important remedial enquiries that generally fall outside the enforcement action by a regulator and could serve to support and enforce broader legislative objectives beyond those held by the regulator. Practice notes potentially represent an objective snapshot of the law, drawing on a consensus of the views of invested and disinterested stakeholders alike, reflecting the body of case law and reality of common dispute patterns, to produce a guide to consistent dispute resolution that is not aligned to any particular stakeholder perspective. Courts would retain an important

---

26 See generally R E Megarry, 'Administrative Quasi-Legislation' (1944) 60 *Law Quarterly Review* 125; Greg Weeks, 'The Use and Enforcement of Soft Law by Australian Public Authorities' (2014) 42 *Federal Law Review* 181.

27 For good examples of this style of guide, see 'Guidance on the Consumer Protection (Amendment) Regulations' (UK Department for Business Innovation and Skills, 2014).

role in this context by both drawing on the notes as a source of shared conceptions of the operation of the regime and also feeding back into the process, by correcting and rationalising the examples given in the practice notes as required and in light of the broader legal landscape.

IV. Statutory Design and Drafting

The foregoing discussion demonstrates that the way in which decision-makers interpret legislation is very much influenced by its structure and terms. We have seen that where the *ACL* uses language such as 'loss or damage' that echoes general law concepts, courts are encouraged to draw upon those concepts to interpret the legislation. Further, positioning that same phrase within separate sections can allow courts to distinguish its meaning and operation, enabling remedial diversity that promotes the statutory purpose. These are positive outcomes of statutory drafting and design.

However, the complex, convoluted and confusing structure of the *ACL* presents a major impediment to the orderly development of the law, the expressive role of the *ACL* and the access to justice objectives referred to above. For example, the *ACL* often requires users to connect provisions located in quite different sections of the same legislation (e.g. the statutory prohibition against misleading conduct in s 18 with the remedial options in ss 236–38 and 243 of the *ACL*) or within different legislation (e.g. the apportionment provisions found in s 137B *CCA*, relevant to liability under the *ACL*).[28] These isolated but connected provisions are challenging to navigate for the legally trained, let alone for the lay stakeholders to whom the legislation is addressed. In this context, shorter and simpler legislation that deliberately invites the sort of interpretive process modelled earlier may be more effective in promoting the statutory purposes than a regime that attempts to be comprehensive.

---

28   See also *Wingecarribee Shire Council v Lehman Brothers Australia Ltd* (in liq) [2012] FCA 1028 [947]–[949] (Rares J).

V. Conclusion

This chapter has suggested a method for ensuring a dialogue between the legislative regime and the common law context in which it exists with the aim of promoting the consistent and coherent development of both bodies of law. It has also posited the use of soft law practice notes as a way of promulgating this type of development and thereby promoting access to justice. Finally, it has noted the value of simple statutory design in a context where the statute largely needs to be self-enforcing. These are considerations to bear in mind through the ongoing process of legislative revision and reform.

28

Meeting the Potential of Alternative Remedies in Australian Defamation Law

Robyn Carroll[1] and Catherine Graville[2]

I. Introduction

The primacy of damages as the remedial response to breaches of civil obligations sometimes obscures the role in law of other responses to wrongdoing, including corrections and apologies. In defamation law, the case for alternative remedies is particularly strong and has been the subject of judicial, academic and law reform urgings over the years. At the same time, efforts to achieve fair and effective remedies without the inevitable delays of litigation have resulted in developments in dispute resolution processes and defences aimed at quicker resolution of defamation disputes. There are a number of ways in which the law affects the extent to which alternative processes and remedies achieve the remedial objects of defamation law.

This chapter reviews the recommendations for alternative remedies made in law reform processes in Australia since the 1970s. We refer, in particular, to the offer to make amends provisions introduced by state and territory defamation laws that encourage non-litigious and prompt resolution of

---

1   Professor of Law, University of Western Australia.
2   BA, LLB (Hons), University of Western Australia.

defamation disputes and create a defence when a reasonable offer by the publisher is rejected by an aggrieved person. We conclude that alternative remedies and the offer to make amends defence play an important role in Australian defamation law. We recommend, in particular, that the offer to make amends provisions should require a 'sufficient apology' as a term of an offer as well as a 'reasonable correction'.

II. The Potential of Alternative Remedies and Processes for Defamation

The effectiveness of damages as a remedy for defamation has long been doubted.[3] There is evidence that the primary interest of most plaintiffs, immediately after a defamatory publication, is the effective restoration of their reputation, rather than damages.[4] Law reform commissions report that corrections and sometimes apologies are what most plaintiffs seek, initially at least.[5] It can take years for a claim to be heard and it is doubtful whether the result becomes generally known to readers of the original defamatory statement. As a result, to a successful plaintiff an award of damages 'is not a restoration of his reputation but a money reparation for his loss'.[6]

There have been numerous proposals emanating from law reform bodies and government reports aimed at encouraging defendants to take prompt steps to respond to a complaint by a person that they have defamed, and for plaintiffs to settle on fair and reasonable terms. These include a defence of prompt and adequate correction,[7] giving defendants an option of either paying damages or publishing a correction,[8] provision of an opportunity

---

3   Australian Law Reform Commission, *Unfair Publication: Defamation and Privacy*, Report No 11 (Australian Government Printing Service) [253] ('ALRC, *Unfair Publication*').
4   Randall P Benzanson, 'The Libel Suit in Retrospect: What Plaintiffs Want and What Plaintiffs Get' (1986) 74 *California Law Review* 789, 791.
5   For example, New South Wales Law Reform Commission, *Defamation*, Report 75 (1995), [8.1] ('NSWLRC, *Defamation*').
6   ALRC, *Unfair Publication*, [253].
7   NSWLRC, *Defamation*, Ch 8.
8   Standing Committee of Attorneys-General Working Group of State and Territory Officers, *Proposal for Uniform Defamation Laws* (July 2004) 29 ('SCAG Proposal').

for reply[9] and the defence of offer to make amends.[10] Other proposals provide for court orders in the form of correction orders,[11] including a correction order as an alternative to damages,[12] vindication orders,[13] declarations of falsity,[14] and retraction and apology orders[15] in addition to damages, declarations and injunctions. There have also been calls for a right of reply in certain circumstances.[16]

Further proposals note the importance, and increased use, of mediation and case management of litigated matters, the availability of strike-out proceedings,[17] and less costly proceedings to dispose of unmeritorious defamation claims.[18]

III. The Legislative Response to the Call for Alternative Remedies and Processes

A. Reform under the uniform defamation laws

Between 2005 and 2006, uniform defamation laws were enacted across all Australian jurisdictions.[19] The objects of the *Defamation Act 2005* (NSW) (the Act), stated in s 3, include:

---

9   ALRC, *Unfair Publication*, [294].

10   New South Wales Law Reform Commission, *Defamation*, Report No 11 (1971) [40]; New South Wales Law Reform Commission, *Defamation*, Report 75 (1995) [8.21]–[8.24]; Australian Capital Territory Community Law Reform Committee, *Defamation Report*, Report No 10 (1995) 18–19; Attorney-General's Task Force for Defamation Law Reform (NSW), *Defamation Law Proposals for Reform in NSW* (September 2002) 6–7.

11   ALRC, *Unfair Publication*, [258]; Australian Government, Attorney-General's Department, *Revised Outline of a Possible National Defamation Law*, July 2004, 34 ('A-G's *Revised Outline*').

12   SCAG Proposal, 29.

13   Attorney-General (ACT), *Defamation Report in the ACT* (September 1998) 6–8.

14   NSWLRC, *Defamation*, 103.

15   ALRC, *Unfair Publication*, [257]; see also Dario Milo, *Defamation and Freedom of Speech* (Oxford University Press, 2008) 273.

16   ALRC, *Unfair Publication*, [156], [178], [294]; A-G's *Revised Outline*, 32; see also John Fleming, 'Retraction and Reply: Alternative Remedies for Defamation' (1978) 12 *University of British Columbia Law Review* 15; Dario Milo, *Defamation and Freedom of Speech* (Oxford University Press, 2008) Ch VIII.D.2; Patrick George, *Defamation Law in Australia* (LexisNexis Butterworths, 2nd edn, 2012) Ch 40; David Rolph, *Defamation Law* (Lawbook Co, 2016) Ch 17.

17   A-G's *Revised Outline*, 29–30.

18   Ibid. 31.

19   The *Defamation Act 2005* (NSW) is representative of the uniform defamation laws enacted in each of the Australian states and territories. The national laws are enacted by the: *Defamation Act 2005* (Qld); *Defamation Act 2005* (SA); *Defamation Act 2005* (Tas); *Defamation Act 2005* (Vic); *Defamation Act 2005* (WA); *Civil Law (Wrongs) Act 2002* (ACT) and the *Defamation Act 2006* (NT).

(c) to provide effective and fair remedies for persons whose reputations are harmed by the publication of defamatory matter, and

(d) to promote speedy and non-litigious methods of resolving disputes about the publication of defamatory matter.

Consistent with s 3(c), there were significant amendments aimed at encouraging vindicatory responses to defamatory publications other than damages.[20] Subsections 38(1)(a)–(b) respectively provide for evidence of published apologies and corrections to be admitted in mitigation of damages. Section 20 provides that an apology is not an express or implied admission of liability or admissible as evidence of fault or liability. This section 'is designed to encourage defendants to say sorry'[21] and is consistent with the Commonwealth Attorney-General Department's conclusion that defendants are more likely to apologise for, or retract, defamatory statements if their apology or retraction is not taken to be an admission of liability.[22] There were also significant amendments introduced by the Act to the damages remedy, which created a cap on defamation damages for non-economic loss and abolished exemplary or punitive damages.[23] There appears to be strong support for uniform defamation laws in Australia although differing views remain as to the appropriate liability rules, defences and damages available.[24]

B. Alternative remedies (remedies other than damages)

Despite the proposals outlined above, no provisions were introduced under the uniform defamation laws to confer power on the courts to order or to recommend alternative remedies. Plaintiffs need therefore to rely on negotiated outcomes and offers of compromise to achieve these outcomes, or use the offer to make amends provisions.

---

20 *Defamation Act 2005* (NSW) ss 20, 38(1)(b).
21 NSW Hansard, Defamation Bill, 18 October 2005, the Hon Henry Tsang, Parliamentary Secretary, referred to in *Hunt v Radio 2SM Pty Ltd* (No. 2) [2010] NSWDC 43, [36] (Gibson DCJ) ('*Hunt*').
22 A-G's *Revised Outline*, 33.
23 Part 4, Div 3, 'Remedies'.
24 See submissions to NSW Department of Attorney-General and Justice Review of the *Defamation Act 2005* ('NSW Review'). This five year review is required by s 49 of the Act. The submissions are available at www.justice.nsw.gov.au/justicepolicy/Pages/lpclrd/lpclrd_consultation/lpclrd_stat_reviews.aspx#ReviewofDefamationAct2005.

C. The offer to make amends

The offer to make amends provisions in Pt 3 Div 1 of the Act create a mechanism that aims to encourage parties to settle a defamation claim quickly without a trial and on terms that recognise the value of remedial responses other than the payment of damages, seemingly consistent with the objects in s 3(c)–(d). Broadly speaking, these provisions allow a publisher (referred to here as 'defendant') to offer to the aggrieved person (referred to here as 'plaintiff') to publish a correction and pay expenses, and, optionally, to publish an apology and to pay compensation. If the plaintiff accepts the offer to make amends, they are barred from commencing or continuing an action in defamation.[25] If the plaintiff does not accept the offer, then in subsequent proceedings the defendant may rely on the fact of having made a reasonable offer as a complete defence.[26] If the defendant is successful at trial, the plaintiff may also have to pay indemnity costs for having unreasonably failed to accept a reasonable offer to make amends.[27] If the plaintiff is successful, the defendant may have to pay indemnity costs for unreasonably failing to make a settlement offer.[28]

It is difficult to calculate how often the offer to make amends provisions are being used because of the private nature of settlement. The volume of reported cases considering offer to make amends provisions to date is small but there are indications that the provisions are being used more than under previous legislation. The provisions have been described as a 'simpler and more streamlined process of offer to make amends'[29] and as a 'revolution' in defamation law.[30] Suggestions have been made to address uncertainties in their operation.[31] It has also been commented judicially that the provisions operate to the disadvantage of plaintiffs over defendants.[32]

---

25   *Defamation Act 2005* (NSW) s 17(1).

26   Ibid. s 18(1).

27   *Defamation Act 2005* (NSW) ss 40(2)(b), (3). This is the same inquiry as to whether an offer is 'reasonable' for the purposes of the defence under s 18(1): *Sleeman v Tuloch Pty Ltd (No 4)* [2013] NSWDC 111 (19 July 2013) 10 [25] (Gibson DCJ) ('*Sleeman*').

28   *Defamation Act 2005* (NSW) s 40(2)(a). A 'settlement offer' includes a reasonable offer to make amends: s 40(3).

29   *Hunt*, n 18 [36].

30   Andrew Kenyon, 'Six Years of Australian Uniform Defamation Law: Damages, Opinion and Defence Meanings' (2012) 35 *University of New South Wales Law Journal* 31, 35.

31   See, for example, NSW Bar Association, 'Submission to the New South Wales Department of Attorney-General and Justice, *Review of Defamation Act 2005*', undated, 19; Matthew Collins, 'Five Years On: A Report Card on Australia's National Scheme Defamation Laws' (2011) 16 *Media and Arts Law Review* 317, 322–23.

32   *Pingel v Toowoomba Newspapers Pty Ltd* [2010] QCA 175 (16 July 2010) 21 [62]–[63] ('*Pingel*'); *Pedavoli v Fairfax Media Publications Pty Ltd* (2014) 324 ALR 166, 173) ('*Pedavoli*').

IV. Meeting the Potential of Alternative Remedies and Processes in Australian Defamation Laws

Based on past experience and concerns it seems unlikely that consensus will be reached easily across governments on an expansion of remedial alternatives. Instead, the offer to make amends provisions continue the Anglo-American preference for attaining desirable objectives by 'rewards rather than force';[33] that is, by creating a defence to a defamation claim when a reasonable offer has been made to a plaintiff, rather than compelling, for example, a right of reply. These provisions seek to balance the objective of effective and fair remedies with promoting speedy and non-litigious resolution of disputes.

A. The potential for further development of alternative remedies

There is merit in ongoing consideration of the remedies of retractions and apologies, corrections, rights of reply and declarations of falsity.[34] Realistically, legislation for a right of reply and for corrections and apologies is unlikely as the legislatures have made it clear they prefer to encourage and not compel these remedial actions. In the absence of legislation expressly conferring power on the court to make these orders, courts are unlikely to grant them as common law remedies, in part due to concerns about interference with a publisher's freedom of expression.[35]

B. Correction and apology as required components

Given the unlikelihood that more extensive remedial powers will be enacted in the near future, the offer to make amends provisions need to strike a fair balance between the s 3(c)–(d) objects. At present, s 15(1)(d) of the Act mandates the inclusion of a 'reasonable correction' in an offer to make amends. If the defendant does not include an offer to publish

---

33 Fleming, n 16, 24.
34 For support, see Rolph, n 16, [17.110]–[17.1.30]; Milo, n 16, 269–78.
35 *Summertime Holdings Pty Ltd v Environmental Defender's Office Ltd* (1998) 45 NSWLR 291, 297; Robyn Carroll, 'Beyond Compensation: Apology as a Private Law Remedy' in Jeffrey Berryman and Rick Bigwood (eds), *The Law of Remedies: New Directions in the Common Law* (Irwin Law, 2010) 323, 370–71.

a reasonable correction, then the purported offer to make amends will be invalid.[36] By contrast, the absence of an offer to publish an apology will only be relevant to the 'reasonableness' of the offer in determining whether a defence exists if the offer is rejected and for the purposes of awarding indemnity costs (s 40). The plaintiff can only obtain an offer of apology by negotiation with the defendant. If the plaintiff proceeds with litigation, the defendant can rely on alternative defences, not just their offer to make amends.[37]

Section 38(1)(a) of the Act recognises the ability of an apology about the publication of a defamatory matter, as well as a published correction, to mitigate damage to a plaintiff's reputation and injured feelings. The Act makes a distinction in s 15 between 'corrections' and 'apologies' (though neither term is defined) notwithstanding that these terms are often used interchangeably and correction sometimes is incorporated within apology.[38] George notes that, '[i]n practice, apologies are usually related to the meaning of the words, corrections usually relate to misstatements of facts'.[39] Making amends for publication of a matter that 'is or may be defamatory' (s 13(1)) must surely involve more than correction of a misstatement of fact. In *Szanto v Melville*, Kaye J reasoned that a correction for s 15(1)(e) requires at the very least a 'plain acknowledgement that the defendant defamed the plaintiff'.[40] The line between correction and apology in this context is not clear, as acknowledgement that a publication is defamatory is more than a correction of fact.

The offer to make amends defences in the UK and Ireland, which have similar purposes, require a 'suitable correction' and a 'sufficient apology'.[41] In the absence of a broad statutory definition of 'correction' in the Act

---

36 *Szanto v Melville* [2011] VSC 574 (4 November 2011) 57 [169] (Kaye J).

37 Contrast the operation of the offer to make amends defence in the UK and Ireland where reliance on the offer to make amends defence precludes reliance on alternative defences.

38 See, for example, *Pedavoli*, n 32, 180. The A-G's *Revised Outline*, n 11, equates correction with apology and proposed that 'apologies' be defined to include retractions and voluntary corrections: 33. Contrast the NSWLRC, *Defamation*, n 5, which defines a 'correction' as a 'collective term for retractions, apologies and replies ... [which] recognises that the purpose of all three forms of expression is to correct public misconceptions as to the plaintiff's reputation, and as to the true facts': 14 [2.14].

39 George, n 16, 419, who concludes that the usefulness, therefore, of correction orders may in practice be limited.

40 [2011] VSC 618, 7–8.

41 *Defamation Act 1996* (UK) c 31, s (2)(1); *Defamation Act 2009* (Ire) s 22(5)(a). This also reflects the fact that reliance on the defence created by these provisions necessarily involves conceding that the publication was defamatory: *Nail v News Group Newspapers Ltd* [2004] EMLR 362 paras 34–36; [2005] 1 All ER 1040, [19] CA.

in Australia that incorporates apology, we submit that s 15 similarly should require both a 'reasonable correction' and a 'sufficient' apology or an apology that is 'reasonable' in the circumstances.[42] What constitutes a sufficient apology and what will be a reasonable offer for purposes of s 18(1) of the Act in each case will be highly fact sensitive and judged in light of all of the circumstances. Depending on the circumstances, it may be sufficient to apologise for any offence caused by the publication.[43] In more serious cases, acknowledgement of the falsity of the defamatory statement may be necessary.[44] The defence that arises by making a reasonable offer to make amends, after all, is based on an offer to make amends for harm caused by publication of matter that is incorrect. Further, ss 19[45] and 20 are intended to address concerns that an offer of apology will be used adversely as evidence of an admission of fault.

Finally, if there is a concern that this amendment would be tantamount to compelling a publisher of matter that 'is or may be defamatory' to apologise, this is countered by the fact that a defendant is not under any compulsion to offer an apology (or a correction for that matter). Use of these provisions is optional. The choice not to use them may detract from the 'speedy and non-litigious' object in the Act but that needs to be balanced against the 'effective and fair remedies' object.

C. Less costly proceedings for minor matters

Concerns remain about the high cost of proceedings to resolve some matters relating to offer to make amends proceedings.[46] Suggestions that merit attention include that the Act be amended to provide for lower cost court options[47] and consideration be given to conferring jurisdiction on

---

42   See also Robyn Carroll and Jeffrey Berryman, 'Making Amends by Apologising for Defamatory Publications – Developments in the 21st Century', in Kit Barker, Ross Grantham and Karen Fairweather (eds), *Private Law in the 21st Century* (Hart Publishing, 2017) Ch 24.

43   For example, *Sleeman*, n 27. It was also considered reasonable in this case to offer the apology without an offer to pay compensation. The text of the apology is available at *Sleeman v Tuloch Pty Ltd (No 4)* [2013] NSWDC 111.

44   For example, *Ell v Milne (No 9)* [2014] NSWSC 489 (11 April 2014) 10 (McCallum J).

45   See *Pingel*, n 32, [24]–[25] (Fraser JA), 41–42 [165]–[166], [169]–[170] (Applegarth J).

46   Bridgette Styles, 'The Power of a Timely Apology' (2013) 51(7) *Law Society Journal* 24.

47   See *Hunt*, n 21, [56].

low cost tribunals.[48] The outcomes of a review of the Act conducted by the NSW Department of Attorney-General and Justice may well provide other recommendations relating to the offer to make amends defence.[49]

V. Conclusion

Through common law principles and now a number of provisions of the Act, the law attaches importance to prompt, fair and effective remedial responses to defamatory publications. The private nature of settlement, however, makes it difficult to calculate the rate of use and satisfaction with the laws and provisions that result in matters not coming to court. The primary aim of this chapter is to draw attention to aspects of the Pt 3 Div 1 provisions that will promote object 3(c) more coherently and consistently.

---

48   NSW Review, n 24, NSW Bar Association Submission.
49   This five year review is required by s 49 of the Act. The submissions to the Review are available at: www.justice.nsw.gov.au/justicepolicy/Pages/lpclrd/lpclrd_consultation/lpclrd_stat_reviews.aspx# ReviewofDefamationAct2005. At the time of writing, the call for submission was closed and no information is publicly available as to when the report can be expected.

29

Designing Reparation: Lessons from Private Law

Simone Degeling[1] and Kit Barker[2]

I. Introduction

This chapter is concerned with reparations schemes in domestic law which are intended to repair grave historical injustice. Recent examples include the Defence Abuse Reparations Scheme (DART) established to deal with institutionalised abuse within the Australian Defence Force (ADF)[3] and the model of redress proposed by the Commonwealth Royal Commission into Institutional Responses to Child Sexual Abuse ('Royal Commission Model'),[4] discussed here with particular reference to clergy abuse in the Australian Catholic Church. We argue that such schemes – precisely because they are being proffered by the institutions bearing moral and legal responsibility for the wrongs done – ought more closely to map the ethical commitments and remedial lessons of private law.[5] Although private law

---

1   Professor, UNSW Law.
2   Professor, TC Beirne School of Law, University of Queensland.
3   Australian Government, *Defence Abuse Response Taskforce: Amended Terms of Reference* (November 2015), www.defenceabusetaskforce.gov.au/Aboutus/Documents/Amended-Terms-of-Reference.pdf ('DART Terms of Reference'). DART comprises reparations payments, restorative engagement and an extensive counselling program.
4   Set out in Commonwealth Royal Commission into Institutional Responses to Child Sexual Abuse, *Redress and Civil Litigation Report* (2015) ('2015 Report').
5   See generally S Degeling and K Barker, 'Private Law and Grave Historical Injustice: The Role of the Common Law' (2015) 41 *Monash University Law Review* 377–413.

claims through the courts have often failed for technical or evidential reasons,[6] this failure should not, we say, be permitted to obscure the fact that private law has a distinctive and particularly powerful normative approach to remedying injustice, which is backed by procedural systems that are transparent, relatively consistent and respectful of individual rights and dignity. Private law has a centuries-old tradition of understanding the types of injustice involved and of appropriate ways of remedying them, and its norms can usefully be brought to bear on domestic reparations system design. One of the most important norms informing private law in this arena, which we argue ought to be permitted more fully to animate reparations design, is the norm of corrective justice.

II. Corrective Justice

There is, we accept, no single conception of corrective justice. The canon is voluminous and we do not attempt to traverse distinctions and differences here.[7] However, it may fairly safely be asserted that corrective justice is distinct from distributive justice and that it has certain, basic, precepts. Corrective justice assumes a bilateral relationship of right and duty between victim and wrongdoer which has been infringed by the wrongdoer. Corrective justice is then done by requiring the wrongdoer to restore the victim as closely as possible to the position he or she would have been in, had the injustice not been done. In doing this, the needs (past and current), relative resources and character of the parties are ignored. In contrast to distributive justice, which contemplates broader political,

---

6   For example, limitation of action or want of a proper defendant to sue. See, for example, *Trustees of the Roman Catholic Church for the Archdiocese of Sydney v Ellis* (2007) 70 NSWLR 565.

7   See generally: Peter Benson, 'The Basis of Corrective Justice and its Relation to Distributive Justice' (1992) 77 *Iowa Law Review* 515; Jules L Coleman, *Risks and Wrongs* (Cambridge University Press, 1992); Jules L Coleman, 'The Practice of Corrective Justice' (1995) 37 *Arizona Law Review* 15; John Gardner, 'What is Tort Law For? Part 1: The Place of Corrective Justice' (2011) 30 *Law & Philosophy* 1; Dennis Klimchuk, 'Unjust Enrichment and Corrective Justice' in Jason W Neyers, Mitchell McInnes and Stephen G A Pitel (eds), *Understanding Unjust Enrichment* (Hart Publishing, 2004) 111; Dennis Klimchuk, 'On the Autonomy of Corrective Justice' (2003) 23 *Oxford Journal of Legal Studies* 49; Anthony T Kronman, 'Contract Law and Distributive Justice' (1980) 89 *Yale Law Journal* 472; Lionel Smith, 'Restitution: The Heart of Corrective Justice' (2001) 79 *Texas Law Review* 2115; Ernest J Weinrib, *The Idea of Private Law* (Harvard University Press, 1995); Ernest J Weinrib, 'Restitutionary Damages as Corrective Justice' (2000) 1 *Theoretical Inquiries in Law* 1; Ernest J Weinrib, 'The Normative Structure of Unjust Enrichment' in Charles Rickett and Ross Grantham (eds), *Structure and Justification in Private Law* (Hart Publishing, 2008) 21; Ernest J Weinrib, *Corrective Justice* (Oxford University Press, 2012); Richard W Wright, 'Right, Justice and Tort Law' in David G Owen (ed), *Philosophical Foundations of Tort Law* (Clarendon, 1997) 159; Richard W Wright, 'Substantive Corrective Justice' (1992) 77 *Iowa Law Review* 625.

social or economic ends and which often distributes resources to victims by reference to criteria of immediate need, the purposes of monetary awards in corrective justice are simply to protect prior rights and restore the parties, as best as can be done, to their original normative positions. Corrective justice is thus wholly backward-looking and fundamentally concerned with eradicating the ills of the past, accepting, of course, that one cannot literally turn back time. When corrective justice is implemented, this may have beneficial side-effects which are distributive, or which create incentives for wrongdoers to alter their future conduct, but such impacts are not the point of doing corrective justice, merely its incidental side-effects. These do not derogate from the fundamentally restorative character of the law's aims, institutions and remedies. Since a corrective justice system must be administered by public courts with legitimating authority, this in turn requires the system that supports corrective justice and its results to be open, accountable, appealable and consistent in its treatment of victims.

The balance of this chapter briefly examines selected aspects of the DART and the Royal Commission Model in the light of private law's ethical commitments as a system of corrective justice, and makes suggestions as to how these schemes may be improved. It is important to remember that, in both instances, institutional responsibility for the relevant abuses is accepted, or is assumed within the terms of the scheme to have been accepted. In relation to abuses in the ADF (as with those in the Catholic Church),[8] public apologies have hence been made by institutional representatives at the highest level.[9] Similarly, in the Royal Commission Model, a person is only eligible for redress if 'he or she was sexually abused

---

8   See, for example, Pope Francis, 'Address to Members of the International Catholic Child Bureau' (Speech delivered on 11 April 2014), w2.vatican.va/content/francesco/en/speeches/2014/april/documents/papa-francesco_20140411_ufficio-cattolico-infanzia.html; Homily of Pope Francis, Holy Mass in the Chapel of the Domus Sanctae Marthae with a Group of Clergy Sex Abuse Victims, 7 July 2014, w2.vatican.va/content/francesco/en/homilies/2014/documents/papa-francesco_20140707_omelia-vittime-abusi.html.

9   Department of Defence (Cth), Statement from General David Hurley, Chief of the Defence Force, 26 November 2012; 'Abuse in Defence' Commonwealth Parliamentary Debates, House of Representatives, 26 November 2012, 13105 (Defence Minister Stephen Smith). See, for example: 'Young men and women have endured sexual, physical or mental abuse from their colleagues, which is not acceptable and does not reflect the values of a modern, diverse, tolerant Australian society … *Acknowledging the past and taking responsibility for it* is only the first step' (Smith, emphasis added).

as a child in an institutional context',[10] which (according to definitions of Recommendation 45) broadly encompasses situations in which an institution is directly or indirectly responsible for the harm.[11]

While we acknowledge that any general assumption of responsibility for the harm is conceptually distinct from a particular victim demonstrating that an institution has infringed his or her rights to the standards normally demanded in a court of law in a private law action (such as a negligence action), this does not, we argue, derogate from the moral force of responsibility having been accepted and from the possibility of more meaningful repair.[12] Despite the fact that some of the traditional requirements of private law actions may not have been demonstrated, it is still valid to characterise the infringement of personal rights which has taken place as a violation of duty and right and to look upon the development of remedial solutions in that light. Both DART and the Royal Commission Model implement a system of payment which, although directed to recognising the suffering of the victim, abandon the commitment to protecting prior entitlements.[13] Contrary to this position, we argue that the norm calling for reparation is not one that is satisfied by discretionary distribution, but one which is founded in the original right–duty relationship between victim and wrongdoer, and which demands the doing of corrective justice when that relationship is violated. Although both schemes are careful to make clear that reparation payments do not of themselves discharge any legal liability,[14] it must be the case that payment under either scheme, which itself rests in part on the funding of that scheme by the implicated institutions,[15] is in substitution for

---

10 2015 Report, Recommendation 43.
11 Ibid. Recommendation 45.
12 Note that while even private law does not assume that the making of a mere apology amounts to an acceptance of legal liability, the apologies that have been made here are of a different order, accepting *responsibility* for the wrong even while denying legal liability.
13 2015 Report, Recommendation 15; DART, *Second Interim Report to the Attorney-General and Minister for Defence* (2013) ('DART Second Report'), Appendix M: 1.5, 1.6 and 2.1.
14 The 2015 Report at page 389 discusses redress as providing an alternative not an addition to civil litigation and in Recommendations 63–65 suggests that as a condition of making a payment a redress scheme should *require* an applicant to release the institution and any government from further liability for institutional child sexual abuse. DART Second Report, Appendix M, 1.6.2, expressly confirms payment does *not affect* any rights of the applicant. Nonetheless, the assumption of both is that mere payment does not discharge liability and conversely (and perversely) that of itself payment *may suggest* some institutional responsibility for the harm.
15 2015 Report, 31–32 and Recommendation 35; DART is funded by the Department of Defence. See, for example, DART, *Seventh Interim Report to the Attorney-General and Minister for Defence* (September 2014) ('DART Seventh Report') 30.

moral obligations generated by wrongdoing. Accepting responsibility for wrongdoing, in our view, means accepting responsibility to do corrective justice, or at least doing something that more approximates corrective justice than distributive schemes of welfare-provision. Accepting responsibility may not mean accepting legal liability, but it still means accepting the responsibility to do corrective justice.

Informed by this norm, reparations schemes should more particularly reflect the circumstances of each victim. Amounts available should be increased to acknowledge the physical, mental, economic and emotional interests infringed, as well as the delay that has been involved in making compensation available. Similarly, the financial caps proposed on reparation amounts could be revised upward, even if they do not reach precisely the same level as would be awarded by a court of law. While we appreciate that neither scheme is intended to effect full compensation,[16] and as such is not a direct analogue for a claim pursued via private law mechanisms in which the individual circumstances of the plaintiff are considered, awards under both DART and the Royal Commission Model could, and should, be more highly individuated out of respect for the personal dignity of every individual involved. Instead, however, DART adopts a stepped approach calibrated to the severity of the abuse, with a fixed award at each step[17] and general factors to guide the decision maker in determining entitlement and level of payment.[18] Similarly, the Royal Commission Model suggests a three-step scale of payment[19] to be assessed and determined by a matrix of the level of abuse, impact of abuse, and additional elements.[20] Neither of these schemes appears to compensate for lost earnings (which conceivably could be a very substantial loss), although it is difficult to tell because the administrative apparatus does not ask about the losses suffered by the particular victim. Instead the schemes focus on the particular events or incidents giving rise to the complaint. In other words, reparation is given for 'abuse' and its broad brush impact; there is no inquiry into loss.

---

16   2015 Report, 220–25; DART Second Report, Appendix M: 1.6.1.

17   DART Second Report, Appendix M: 4.6.

18   DART, *Fourth Interim Report to the Attorney-General and Minister for Defence* (2013) 9 ('Fourth Report').

19   2015 Report, Recommendation 19.

20   Ibid. Recommendations 16 and 17.

Procedural aspects of both schemes also merit consideration. Outcomes and reasons for decisions in relation to individual applicants (suitably anonymised) under DART and the Royal Commission Model have not been (DART) and appear not to be intended to be provided (Royal Commission Model). Apart from the obvious point that greater legitimacy and consistency might be achieved via greater transparency, there is a related point which concerns the right to appeal. The making, or not, of a payment under DART is final and cannot be appealed.[21] The Royal Commission Model specifically contemplates the need for appeal rights, described as 'an internal review process'[22] which, to the extent that the redress scheme is 'established on an administrative basis, should be made subject to oversight by the relevant ombudsman through the ombudsman's complaint mechanism'.[23] In creating an appeal mechanism, we similarly suggest that the lessons of private law be permitted to infuse the drafting process. Appeals should be available on the merits of a particular award, informed, where relevant, by publicly-available, parallel decisions.

The running of time must also be accommodated. Neither scheme contemplates a permanent system of reparation. Indeed, DART is soon to close[24] and the Royal Commission Model envisages a filing deadline and a scheme of finite duration.[25] While we acknowledge the desire for financial certainty on the part of governments and institutions, and the efforts being made to effect institutional change such that historic patterns of abuse are not repeated, the inflexibility of the current system seems unfair. Admittedly, DART has already been extended beyond its initial life.[26] However, the experience of judges awarding damages in parallel cases is that those who suffer psychiatric illness or impairment, itself the product of abuse, may perversely be unable to appreciate their own interest in bringing a claim, and thus delay. In these circumstances,

---

21   DART Second Report, Appendix N. Note, however, in DART Seventh report, 12, there is a procedure for Reconsideration of Decisions 'in reviewing matters previously assessed as out of scope or not plausible on receipt of requests for reconsideration from complainants'.

22   2015 Report, Recommendation 61.

23   Ibid. Recommendation 62.

24   Similarly, DART-funded counselling will not be available after 30 June 2016 and the last date to be referred to counselling is 31 March 2016: Defence Abuse Counselling Program Factsheet (www.defenceabusetaskforce.gov.au/Outcomes/Pages/DefenceAbuseCounsellingProgram.aspx) (accessed 26 February 2016). Similarly it is hoped that the restorative engagement program will conclude by 31 March 2016. See DART Terms of Reference (n 3).

25   2015 Report, Recommendations 46 and 48.

26   Initially required filing by 31 May 2013. Subsequently amended to allow 'complaints from women who experienced sexual abuse at ADFA during the period 1991 and 1998 and registered … by 30 September 2015'. DART Terms of Reference (n 3).

a more permanent and perhaps comprehensive scheme could be established, with the capacity to extend filing deadlines in the same manner as all courts applying limitations statutes. Additionally, we note the Royal Commission Model's advice[27] suggesting removal of limitation periods applying to claims for damages brought by a person, where that claim is founded on personal injury resulting from sexual abuse of that person in an institution when the person is, or was, a child. While this reform to limitation periods in civil litigation may well be a welcome innovation, it also demonstrates the need for some discretion in applying filing deadlines in the reparations mechanism. Equally, we query whether all potential applicants for reparation who fail to file before the deadline will necessarily succeed in litigation (even with an extension of limitation) given the other barriers to success, such as the death of witnesses etc.

Finally, mention must be made of the standard of proof to be applied. DART requires an applicant to demonstrate 'mere plausibility'.[28] The Royal Commission Model proposes 'reasonable likelihood',[29] which is lower than the common law standard of proof. In doing so, the Commission makes the point that it remains:

> sceptical of whether schemes that purport to apply higher standards ... really do [so] ... or if they have any real meaning or any work to do in determining applications where there is no 'witness' other than the applicant and no other 'evidence' against which ... [allegations of abuse] ... can be balanced.[30]

The Commission also noted that its proposed payment levels exceeded those in DART[31] and that, commensurate with this higher level of payment, oral hearings may be required in addition to documentary evidence.[32]

There is obviously a trade-off in the design of both systems in that, at least compared to civil litigation, the amounts available are less, but so is the burden of proof to be met. Notwithstanding this, the Royal Commission Model also requires applicants to release institutions and governments from any civil liability, whereas in DART the right to

---

27   2015 Report, Recommendations 85–88.
28   DART Second Report, Appendix M: 4.5.
29   2015 Report, Recommendation 57.
30   2015 Report, 371.
31   Ibid. 376.
32   Ibid. 363 and Recommendations 51–55.

seek damages in addition is expressly preserved. Given, however, that the decisions of neither system are public, it is simply not possible to know whether or not a higher standard of proof has in any particular case been met (or, in egregious cases of abuse, perhaps conceded). In such instances, it should be open to the decision-maker, we suggest, to award higher amounts than currently proposed, assuming that impacts on the particular circumstances of that victim may be demonstrated.

III. Conclusion

It is possible our parliaments will increasingly have to draft statutes implementing systems of reparation. This discussion has briefly touched on two examples of contemporary relevance, but there are many others. We only have to search the records of parliamentary debate to identify apologies given for past decisions leading to injustice for which civilised societies now express regret and may seek to make redress.[33] The message we have is that, in designing reparation systems, we should not forget that these injustices attract our attention precisely because they infringe our notions of moral right and duty. The norms of corrective justice remind us that the claimant seeks redress as a matter of prior entitlement from institutions which have acknowledged moral responsibility for the wrongdoing in question, even if this has stopped short of conceding legal liability. Reparation in these cases is not, and should not be, drafted along distributive lines that merely seek to meet the most immediate needs of victims, or which compromise their original rights for other social policy objectives.

---

33   For example: United Kingdom, Parliamentary Debates, House of Commons, 24 February 2010, Vol 506, col 301 (Gordon Brown, Prime Minister) (forced child migration); and Julia Gillard, 'National Apology for Forced Adoptions' (Speech delivered at the Great Hall of Parliament House, Canberra, 21 March 2013) (forced adoption).

30

Apologies, Liability and Civil Society: Where to from Here?

Prue Vines[1]

I. Introduction

In this chapter I argue that there is a major need for obligations law to expand its consideration of what amounts to compensation, in order for true corrective justice to operate. For my purposes I will mainly consider the law of negligence for personal injury. There is good reason to think that an excessively legalistic approach to compensation has been problematic, even merely in terms of the monetary amounts that plaintiffs receive, for example, for personal injury. It may be time to abandon the idea of *restitutio in integrum* (putting the injured person in the position they would have been in if the accident had not happened) in respect of damages, so rarely does this actually appear to happen,[2] and replace it with a combination of monetary and other forms of compensation including apologies. In this chapter I consider why an apology might be seen as part of corrective justice, and argue that any reduction or lack of litigation caused by apologies might occur because one of the aims of tort law, that

---

1   Professor, Faculty of Law, University of New South Wales: p.vines@unsw.edu.au.
2   Prue Vines and Matthew Butt, 'Running Out of Compensation Money: Whipping Away the Social Security Blanket?' (2013) 7 *Court of Conscience* 17; Genevieve Grant et al, 'When Lump Sums Run Out: Disputes at the Borderlines of Tort Law, Injury Compensation and Social Security' in Kit Barker et al (eds), *Private Law in the 21st Century* (Hart Publishing, 2016).

of corrective justice, has been met by the apology itself. This requires us to consider the nature of loss as it is felt by the person and as it is recognised by the legal system in tort.

In this chapter I define an apology as a communication between parties expressing regret for harm that has been done by one party to the other, acknowledging fault, and accompanied either by compensation or a promise to ensure the wrong will not happen again.[3] I argue that in the law of torts there is a place for both the spontaneous and the coerced apology.

II. The Needs of Civil Society Go Beyond the Rule of Law

As lawyers we are constantly aware of the rule of law and its importance for civil society. However, how this is considered depends partly on the 'thickness' of the rule of law concept. Where a 'thin' rule of law concept is used, referring to bare legal rules, there may nevertheless be a real lack in the civil society which is facilitated by that rule of law. By this I mean that when bare legal rules are used, a formalistic and less substantive idea of the rule of law is in play. A 'thicker'[4] idea of the rule of law, I argue, sees it embedded in the culture of the society in which it operates, and therefore partakes of a richer sense of what the rules mean. This means, for example, that the purpose of the rule is more likely to be applied than the literal rule because the law can take account of the context within which it operates. Another way of considering this is through an expressive theory of law,[5] that the rules of law operate in a way which goes beyond the minimal verbal content, and in their expression may touch and affect social norms.

---

3   See, *inter alia*, Prue Vines, 'Apologising for Personal Injury in Law: Failing to Take Account of Lessons from Psychology in Blameworthiness and Propensity to Sue' (2014) *16 Psychiatry, Psychology and Law* 42.

4   Drawing on Clifford Geertz, 'Thick Description: Toward an Interpretive theory of Culture' in Clifford Geertz (ed), *The Interpretation of Cultures* (Basic Books, 1973) who saw 'thick' description in ethnography as a way of including the context and often the perspective of the observer.

5   Cass Sunstein, 'On the Expressive Function of Law' (1996) 144(5) *University of Pennsylvania Law Review* 2021; Elisabeth S Anderson and Richard H Pildes, 'Expressive Theories of Law: A General Restatement' (2000) 5 *University of Pennsylvania Law Review* 1503.

As our understanding of both moral reasoning and rationality, along with neuropsychology, develops, it becomes clearer that the emotional life of the human being cannot be severed from reason[6] and has a large part to play in the development of moral and other values. Emotional responses such as disgust, fear, guilt and anger often underlie our 'rational' discourse and help to shape the values articulated in the rational discourse. Law then should reflect an understanding of the emotional life of the people it affects.

The apology is best thought of as a communication of emotion and values: the emotion is remorse or 'sorriness' and the values are those which have been damaged by the wrong which is being apologised for. In this way an apology is an exemplar of the notion that reason and emotion can combine to produce and/or reflect values. Where a wrong has occurred, the best apology occurs where the wrongdoer spontaneously and promptly apologises, acknowledging the wrong and seeking either to prevent it happening again and/or providing compensation. In some cases this reduces the desire to sue or allows for early settlement.[7] But this is not the only possible use of an apology. The fact that the apology recognises values means that in some circumstances even a coerced apology can have value for the victim. This is because where the court or society requires an apology from the wrongdoer the victim feels vindicated. In such a case what matters for the victim is their standing in the community; the fact that the wrongdoer has not (sincerely) acknowledged their wrongfulness does not matter, because the broader community has done so.

III. The Treatment of Apologies in Civil Liability

One recent shift in the legal landscape has been an increasing interest in apologies in transitional justice, and within the legal system. Within the legal system this has been embodied in the move to protect apologies from automatically creating liability by legislation in many countries since 1996.[8] This has been done for two main reasons: to reduce litigation, and

---

6   For example, Martha Nussbaum, *Upheavals of Thought: The Intelligence of Emotions* (Cambridge University Press, 2001); Dylan Evans and Pierre Cruse (eds), *Emotion, Evolution and Rationality* (Oxford University Press, 2004).

7   Prue Vines, 'Apologies and Civil Liability in the UK: A View from Elsewhere' (2008) *12(2) Edinburgh Law Review* 200–30.

8   All Australian jurisdictions, most US States, England and Wales, most Canadian jurisdictions and Scotland all now have various forms of this legislation. See, for example, *Civil Liability Act 2002* (NSW) ss 68–69. The legislation varies considerably in its scope and its definition of apology, but mostly prevents the apology (however defined) from being admissible as evidence of liability or from creating liability.

to ensure that the normal processes of civil society (apologising when one has done something wrong) are not disrupted by an excessively legalistic (one might argue 'thin' or 'non-expressive') view of law. Apologies, although often seen as merely offering sympathy or acknowledgement of fault, may also have a remedial aspect.

Liability in negligence generally results in damages. Damages operate as compensation, as a marker of wrongdoing and as acknowledgment that redress is needed. Apologies do some of the same work. Damages also address needs and many people regard this as the most significant aspect of damages. If damages are only about need, then a no-fault scheme is the best way to deal with loss.[9]

The idea that damages put the person back into the position they were in before the wrong happened[10] has become almost laughable. However, damages are often seen also as the central vehicle of corrective justice in that they operate to redress the balance between the parties by correcting the loss suffered by one party at the expense of the other who caused it. Apologies can be part of this corrective justice process if one considers damages as practical reparation and apology as emotional reparation for the emotional and moral pain suffered by the victim. Some have called this 'symbolic' reparation, but this is only symbolic if one does not regard humiliation or emotional pain as real.

IV. Corrective Justice: Balancing Symbolic, Emotional and Monetary Needs

A. Corrective justice and apologies

Aristotelian notions of corrective justice focus on the dyad where one party hurts the other, and then the balance between the parties must be corrected or equalised. Michael S Moore's definition is as follows:

---

9   See, for example, Harold Luntz, 'Reform of the Law of Negligence: Wrong Questions – Wrong Answers' (2002) 8(2) *UNSWLJ Forum: Reform of the Law of Negligence: Balancing Costs and Community Expectations* 18.
10   See above n 3.

a corrective justice view of tort law asserts that we all have primary moral duties not to hurt others; when we culpably violate such primary moral duties, we then have a secondary moral duty to correct the injustice we have caused. Tort liability rules are no more than the enforcement of these antecedently existing moral duties of corrective justice.[11]

This firmly focuses on the relationship between law and morality. Moore's definition is 'thin' in that it does not take much account of the relationship between law, morality and emotion. I would argue that part of the necessary correction of the injustice includes recognition of the emotional need for vindication[12] which I see as part of corrective justice. Other corrective justice theorists have also generally used a 'thin' view of law. For example, Weinrib,[13] referring to the fact that Aristotle talked about the correlative relationship between the parties in terms of equalising gain and loss, dismisses the fact that in negligence there is no gain apparent. When we look at what is happening, the injured person has a loss, and in paying compensation the wrongdoer in turn suffers loss. Weinrib argues that this is merely a problem of terminology and the loss or gain is only 'normative'. But to say that the correlativity is 'only' normative misses a great deal of the moral richness of tort law. It may be that there *is* a gain when someone negligently inflicts injury on another: that gain is a gain in power,[14] which we mostly pay little attention to, but nevertheless it is a gain which needs to be countered by a loss of power. It can be argued that an apology, which is necessarily humbling, reduces that gain and redresses the wrong and that this is one of its reparative functions.

Apologies focus on the moral wrongfulness of the action taken by the perpetrator. This seems to differ from negligence law which only makes a person liable for a wrong when the wrong has caused a harm (outcome responsibility).[15] However, psychological studies have shown that the more serious the consequences are, the more likely there is to

---

11   'Causation and Responsibility' (1999) 16(2) *Social Philosophy and Policy* 1 at 4.

12   Jason Varuhas, 'The Concept of Vindication in the Law of Torts' (2014) 34 (2) *Oxford Journal of Legal Studies* 253.

13   'The Gains and Losses of Corrective Justice' (1994) 44 *Duke Law Journal* 277.

14   Aquinas suggests that 'a person striking or killing has more of what is evaluated as good, insofar, that is, as he fulfils his will, and so is seen to receive a sort of gain' in James Gordley, 'The Aristotelian Tradition' in David Owen (ed), *Philosophical Foundations of Tort Law* (Oxford University Press, 1995), 138.

15   Steven Perry has argued in 'The Moral Basis of Tort Law' (1992) *77 Iowa Law Review* 449, 497 that the individualised sense of fault which focuses Weinrib's corrective justice theory should be modified by outcome responsibility to better reflect the law of negligence.

be attribution of moral responsibility to the person who caused them.[16] That is, outcome responsibility does seem psychologically to increase people's perception of moral fault. The assignment of responsibility is a very complex part of human behaviour[17] to which the law should respond. The psychological needs of individuals and communities, and the needs of moral communities, are part of the social context in which tort law operates and it is important to have some kind of link between the legal and the moral/psychological universes. Apologies, both spontaneous and as remedies, can do some of this work.[18]

Corrective justice's goal of equality between the parties and co-relativity between the wrong and the righting of the wrong requires proportionality between the wrong, the harm and the compensation. Compensation for negligence may not do this, despite the assumption of corrective justice that the loss is the same as the wrongfulness. In a negligence action the wrong may be small, but the loss very large. The distinction between loss and wrong and the possible disproportion between the wrong and what is seen as redressing the wrong causes major problems in social perceptions of the legitimacy of negligence. The fact that apologies focus on moral wrong, and that they have a healing and reparative function of their own, may be used to redress partially this disproportion in some cases. It is important to be able to avoid a punitive response.[19] In cases where apologies have been ordered, judges have emphasised that such apologies are ordered for redress not punishment.[20]

---

16   Kelly Shaver, 'Redress and Conscientiousness in the Attribution of Responsibility for Accidents' (1970) 6 *Journal of Experimental Social Psychology* 100; Elaine Walster, 'Assignment of Responsibility for Accidents' (1966) 3 *Journal of Personality and Social Psychology* 1973; David Kanouse, 'Language, Labelling and Attribution' in Edward E Jones et al (eds), *Attribution: Perceiving the Causes of Behaviour* (General Learning Press, 1972).

17   The psychological studies of attribution show a number of things of interest to negligence theory, including first that the assignment of moral responsibility is very complex and may be altered by very subtle semantic shifts, second that levels of generality of explanation beget explanations at similar levels of generality, and third that there is indeed a naïve sense of moral responsibility. See, *inter alia*, Sally Lloyd-Bostock, 'Attributions of Cause and Responsibility as Social Phenomena' in Joseph Jaspars, Frank Fincham and Miles Hewstone (eds), *Attribution Theory and Research* (Academic Press, 1983).

18   Prue Vines, 'The Power of Apology: Mercy, Forgiveness or Corrective Justice in the Civil Liability Arena' (2007) 1 *Journal of Public Space* 1–51, epress.lib.uts.edu.au/ojs/index.php/publicspace/home; Robyn Carroll, 'Beyond Compensation: Apology as a Private Law Remedy' in Jeff Berryman and Rick Bigwood (eds), *The Law of Remedies: New Directions in the Common Law* (Irwin Law, 2010) 323.

19   Carroll, above n 18.

20   Carroll (above n 18) refers to *De Simone v Bevacqua* (1994) 7 VAR 246 (a harassment case); *Falun Dafa Association of Victoria Inc v Melbourne City Council* [2004] VCAT 625; *Ma Bik Yung v Ko Chuen* [2002] HKLRD 1.

B. The conception of loss, apologies and compensation

The recognition of loss for the purposes of negligence has developed over time from the purely physical (e.g. personal injury and property damage),[21] to economic loss and mental harm. The latter is still restricted in Australia (but not everywhere else) to psychiatrically recognisable harm and distinguished firmly from 'distress or sorrow'.[22] However, in other domains loss includes injury to personhood, reputational torts being the obvious example. At present when a tort arises, damages are awarded for the recognised losses, but this fails to account for the fact that when a person is harmed a loss may occur which is felt as an injury to personhood, caused by the wrong as well as the harm. This loss, the emotional reaction to the wrong, can be characterised as a normative loss separate from the physical realm. It may well be an experiential loss for the person, but it is also an objective injury to personhood or human dignity which it is important for the legal system to consider in terms of expressive theory or a 'thicker' view of law. It is important to recognise this sort of loss because, if fault is not acknowledged, some litigants will remain unsatisfied, even if they do obtain some form of compensation. It is this type of loss for which an apology may compensate. A damages award coupled with an order to apologise is more likely to vindicate both the physical and emotional loss caused by the harm and give satisfying redress.

V. Conclusion

The distinction and/or the disproportion between wrongfulness and loss in negligence law can be addressed to some extent by apologies. When spontaneous and immediate, apologies may reduce the desire to sue or make it easier to settle early. As remedies, coercive apologies may offer better vindication than damages alone. The law of obligations has taken insufficient care to maintain civil society by failing to adequately recognise the emotional content of the disputes which the law seeks to deal with.

---

21 For example, in *Donoghue v Stevenson* [1932] AC 562, Mrs Donoghue sued for personal injury (gastro-enteritis) and nervous shock (psychiatric harm). It is doubtful whether she could have sued for nervous shock then had she not had the physical injury as well. Until *Hedley Byrne & Co Ltd v Heller & Partners Ltd* [1964] AC 465 it was assumed that pure economic loss was the domain of contract and that one could not sue for it in negligence, and so on.

22 *Mount Isa Mines Ltd v Pusey* (1970) 125 CLR 383 per Windeyer J at 403 and much repeated; *Civil Liability Act 2002* (NSW) s 30 and its equivalents.

The treatment of apologies in civil liability is a case in point. The usual advice not to apologise ignores the needs of civil society and its members for responses other than monetary damages. Reform of the law should move towards the significance of humans' emotional as well as legal life, maintaining the balance of symbolic, emotional and monetary needs in the response to civil wrongs. It is time to order apologies along with damages in such cases. Apologies and damages in various combinations may address both the aims of corrective justice and compensation better and more comprehensively than the declaration of liability in a judgment with damages awarded, as a form of recognition of the fact that the nature of loss is broader than the legal system normally allows. Considering apologies in this way, rather than ignoring them, will allow us more completely to meet the claims of corrective justice; and offers a better chance of the tort process offering real healing than it does at present.

31

Renovating the Concept of Consent in Contract and Property Law

Robyn Honey[1]

I. Introduction

This chapter advocates reform of the concept of consent as it is used in contract and property law. The concept of consent/assent/intent[2] that underpins these laws is outdated and no longer functions as it ought to do. We must reassess the relationship between consent and legal responsibility, which is embedded in the foundations of property and contract law, and recast the legal concept of consent in light of current knowledge and in accordance with 21st century norms and values. These fundamental changes should then drive, and provide direction for, specific reforms of the rules about whether, how and by whom consent must be proven in property and contract claims.

---

1   Murdoch University.
2   In this chapter, no distinction is made between these concepts and 'consent' is used for all of them.

II. The Problem with Consent

A. Underlying issues

Liberal ideology tethers responsibility to consent. In the context of private law, this means that, unless specifically justified (for instance by policy considerations), responsibility and obligation arise only from that which one has freely chosen. Yet, in practice, it often happens that undertakings are enforced and conveyances upheld notwithstanding that they were made in circumstances which suggest an alarmingly poor quality of consent. This is strikingly evident in cases pertaining to contracts and conveyances by elders.[3]

This discrepancy arises from a tension within liberal ideology: between its associated ideas of freedom of the individual (pursuant to which consent is a prerequisite for legal obligation) and the legal formalism which facilitates the rule of law. Although consent is fundamental, it is invisible. Crafting laws about consent necessitates regulating 'the unseeable interior' of the self, the mind. This difficulty is exacerbated by the fact that the most problematic cases occur within contexts traditionally designated as 'private' and so placed outside the purview of the law, that is, inside the home, the family and the marriage. Insofar as lawmakers have tended to see the home as something to be shielded from intrusion, it constitutes another kind of 'unseeable interior'. The same might be said of the institution of marriage.

The challenges presented by the task of maintaining the connection between responsibility and consent raise apprehensions, which have strongly influenced laws about consent. The primary concern is that consent is a matter not amenable to proof, so that challenges going to consent are easily made, but difficult either to substantiate or to refute.[4] Another concern is that, even where consent is compromised, it may be unfair to an 'innocent' party to reverse the transaction or release the subject from their undertaking, especially where that party has given value and/ or relied upon the undertaking. Finally, it is considered that the public interest is not best served by too readily releasing individuals from their undertakings and reversing transactions because this undermines security of receipt, security of title and economic efficiency.

---

3   See, for example, *Johnson v Johnson* [2009] NSWSC 503 and *Anderson v Anderson* [2013] QSC 8.
4   Concern intensifies where the one who seeks to challenge the enforceability of an undertaking on the basis of consent is not the person who gave it, especially where that person is deceased so that direct evidence of her state of mind is unobtainable.

B. Effect on consent law

The concept of consent that emerges from laws skewed by these concerns has been warped in its formation and does not function properly. The most important aspects of this problem are briefly described as follows.

1. Inverted relationship between procedural law and substantive law

Normally substantive law holds primacy over procedural law – rules about *what* must be proven precede a consideration of *how* this ought to be achieved. However, in regulating consent, the issues of first concern have been the location of the onus of proof and the means by which that burden can be discharged.

Foremost among the procedural strategies for dealing with the 'unprovable' nature of consent are the presumption of capacity and the effective 'externalisation' of consent. Both common law and statute provide that every adult person is presumed to have the capacity to manage their own affairs.[5] In addition to this, strong preference has been given[6] to objectively ascertainable acts (over testimony about subjective intentions) as proof of consent. External evidence of consent has come to stand in place of consent itself. Thus, proving consent typically involves no more than establishing that the subject was an adult and that they complied with the pertinent formal requirements or otherwise acted in a manner that 'a reasonable bystander' would take to be an indication of consent. It falls to the party who would challenge on the basis of lack of consent either to prove that the subject lacked capacity or to make out one of the defences grounded in vitiated consent.[7]

This has two consequences: (i) regardless of who brings suit, the risk arising from the difficulties inherent in proving consent is borne by the party who challenges consent, rather than the one who relies on it; and (ii) the constituents and qualities of effective consent are seldom investigated, because the issue tends to be won or lost on allocation of the onus of proof.

---

5   *Attorney General v Parnther* (1792) 3 Bro CC 441, 443; 29 ER 632, 634; *M'Naghten's Case* (1843) 10 Cl&Fin 200, 210; 8 ER 718, 722; *Murphy v Doman* (2003) 58 NSWLR 51, [36]. See also legislative provisions, such as *Guardianship and Administration Act 1990* (WA) s 4(3).
6   By means such as: the statutory imposition of formal requirements (e.g. executed deed, signed written instrument/evidence); the parole evidence rule; and the adoption of objective standards in ascertaining contractual assent or donative intent.
7   Such as *non est factum*, duress or undue influence.

2. No model of consent

Perhaps for want of opportunity therefore, the case law has provided no model to guide the development of laws which better connect responsibility to consent. Instead, consent remains out of focus: hiding in plain sight. It is not as well understood as it might be and mechanisms intended to facilitate it often miss the mark.[8]

3. Vitiated consent is too difficult to establish

An image of consent does emerge from the case law. However, this is no model; it is merely a reflection of the composite effect of laws laid down without the benefit of a blueprint and strongly influenced by concerns about proof. In operation, consent appears to be a binary and morally loaded concept.

(a) Binary

The effect of the presumption of capacity is that consent is either wholly present or absent. To displace the presumption, it must be proven that the subject failed to understand even the 'general nature of the transaction'[9] in question to the extent that they could not have understood it even if it had been explained to them.[10] Conversely, once the presumption has been rebutted, the other party can enforce the undertaking only if they can prove that it took place during a 'lucid interval'.[11] This suggests that persons are either 'lucid' (having full capacity) or wholly incapable. A similar approach is taken in the defences going to consent.[12] There is no contemplation of an 'acceptable level' of consent, nor of 'degrees' of freedom where it pertains to the will.

---

8   For instance, independent legal advice is usually taken to be sufficient to counter a claim of vitiated consent. See, for example, the dictum of Lord Nicholls in *Royal Bank of Scotland v Etridge* [2002] 2 AC 773, [54]. However, while such advice can provide the subject with the prerequisites for an independent decision, no advice can relieve her from the effects of a power imbalance that impinges upon her freedom of choice.

9   *Gibbons v Wright* (1954) 91 CLR 423, 438 citing *Ball v Mannin* (1829) 1 Dow & Cl 380; 6 ER 568.

10   *Gibbons v Wright* (1954) 91 CLR 423, 437–38.

11   *McLaughlin v Daily Telegraph Newspaper Co Ltd [No 2]* (1904) 1 CLR 243, 277; *Edna May Collins by her next friend Glenys Lesley Laraine Poletti v May* [2000] WASC 29, [54]; and *Stone v Registrar of Titles* [2012] WASC 21, 42.

12   See, for example, non est factum, which requires proof that the subject believed the instrument to be radically different from what it actually was (*Petelin v Cullen* (1975) 132 CLR 355, 359) and 'presumed' undue influence, which can be defended only by demonstrating that the undertaking in question was 'the result of the free exercise of the … [subject's] independent will' (*Johnson v Buttress* (1936) 56 CLR 113, 138).

(b) Morally loaded

Even where it has been proven that consent was absent or very badly compromised, this might not suffice. The defence of *non est factum* requires proof of a blameless absence of consent: that the subject's radical misapprehension as to the nature of the instrument was not the result of carelessness or otherwise their own fault.[13] In cases of incapacity falling short of *non est factum* (where consent was very badly compromised), the subject must also prove that the counterparty to the transaction knew or ought to have known of their incapacity.[14] Thus, nothing less than an *absence* of consent will, of itself,[15] suffice to absolve the subject from responsibility.

Taken together and in conjunction with the presumption of capacity, these factors make it very difficult to succeed in making a challenge based on vitiated consent.

4. Legal notion of consent is outdated and unrealistic

The concept of consent which emerges from the cases does not accord with what we now know about choice and decision-making. For instance, its binary character does not operate well in circumstances where cognitive ability fluctuates or declines gradually and unevenly. Consequently, it can prove extremely difficult for persons suffering from dementia or mental illness to access the defence of want of capacity, even when their condition has reached the stage where it is patently unsafe to assume that their consent was of a quality sufficient to form the basis of legal responsibility.[16]

III. Towards a Solution

We need a theoretical model of consent that will provide a schema for reform. This model should be based on an up-to-date understanding of decision-making and choice[17] and a reassessment of the role of consent as a prerequisite for responsibility.[18] At a minimum, it should illuminate the essential attributes of binding consent.

---

13 *Gallie v Lee* (1971) AC 1004, 1019 cited with approval in *Petelin v Cullen* above n 12, 360.

14 *Imperial Loan Company v Stone* (1892) 1 QB 599, 602–3; *Anderson, Stone v Registrar* of *Titles* citing *Collins Edna May Collins by her next friend Glenys Lesley Laraine Poletti v May* [2000] WASC 29, [57] citing *Crago v McIntyre* [1976] 1 NSWLR 729. This is supposedly to justify why 'as between two innocent parties' the law should side with the one who asserts absence of consent. However, it has been insisted upon even in cases where the transaction in question was a gift.

15 That is, without requiring an examination of the other party's knowledge and/or behaviour.

16 See, for example, *Johnson v Johnson* above n 3.

17 Including the conditions and circumstances by which these may be constrained.

18 Autonomy may not be the only value to be considered.

A. Guidelines for change

We can then set about reforming the laws by which this model is given effect. In embarking upon this process, the following guidelines should be observed.

1. Open, not restrictive

The restrictive approach triggered by a preoccupation with the limitations of knowledge should be abandoned. More is to be gained by opening ourselves to the science and scholarship available within and beyond the law to develop our understanding of consent. For instance, lawyers should not be reticent to look to medical science for a better understanding of the processes of cognition. Property and contract lawyers might look beyond the boundaries of their own field to make fullest use of the resources available from legal scholarship. For example, feminist legal theory offers a rich source of scholarship on the impact of imbalance of power on freedom of choice.[19]

2. Substance over procedure

Given the nature of consent, difficulties of proof and a degree of uncertainty are inevitable and this should be reflected in our management of the relationship between procedural and substantive law. Procedural law should not be allowed to 'take over' to the extent that the means of proof dictate the nature of that which is to be proven.

3. Sensitivity to context

Context is critical. Different public policy considerations will apply, depending upon whether the undertaking was made: *inter vivos* or by will; for value or by way of gift; and in a personal or commercial context. It may be that the model will change, or that more than one model is required, depending upon the relational and/or transactional context.

4. Responsibility and human dignity

So strong is the association between personal dignity and notions of autonomy (encompassing both freedom of choice and responsibility for that which has been chosen) that attempts to accommodate the vulnerable are sometimes met with an indignant protest that to do so would infantilise the individual or class that it is sought to assist. This

---

19   See, for instance, Rosemary Hunter and Sharon Cowan (eds), *Choice and Consent: Feminist Engagements with the Law and Subjectivity* (Routledge, 2007).

is understandable; such efforts have sometimes been paternalistic.[20] However, legal responsibility should be disentangled from personal worth and human dignity. It must be possible to delimit personal responsibility without condescension. For instance, surely it would not demean persons who have received a diagnosis of dementia to be relieved of the onus of proving incapacity.

5. Avoid paternalism

As matters stand, those who seek to disclaim liability by challenging consent are usually obliged to cast themselves as incapable or dependant. In renovating these laws, we should not settle for paternalistic 'solutions', which deal with the matter by providing 'protection' for those perceived to be weak or deficient. Disability is not deficiency and vulnerability is not weakness. Dependence is a natural consequence of living in the connected and interdependent way that we are supposed to live. We should rather aim to craft laws that support disability and safeguard the capacity to be vulnerable.

B. Suggestions for change

More specific suggestions for change are as follows.

1. Enabling consent

The legal mechanism by which consent is entrenched as a prerequisite for responsibility should do more than merely withhold support where consent was absent. It should include strategies for creating an environment which facilitates and supports the making of consensual undertakings and transactions.[21] These might include mandating the provision of access to assistance and support appropriate to the nature of the vulnerability, such as:

- assistive technologies to augment communication and cognition;
- assisted decision-making[22] where impaired cognition is the relevant source of vulnerability;

---

20 For example, see *Garcia v National Australia Bank Ltd* (1998) 195 CLR 395, 424 (Kirby J).
21 Property and contract lawyers would do well to look to the scholarship of disability law and policy scholars for assistance with this project. See, for example, Dr Anna Arstein-Kerslake, 'An Empowering Dependency: Exploring Support for the Exercise of Legal Capacity' (2016) 18 *Scandinavian Journal of Disability Research* 77.
22 Whereby the subject may appoint someone to assist or represent her in making the decision in question.

- information and explanation where these are needed; and
- independent advice where vulnerability arises from dependence or difficulty in discerning one's own interests.

2. Relief from responsibility where consent was impaired

Both the law with respect to capacity and the defences going to consent might be enhanced by making relief on the basis of vitiated consent easier to access. However, insofar as these accommodations would be made to enhance autonomy by delimiting the ambit of personal responsibility, they ought only to be available to the subject personally.[23]

(a) Capacity

There are circumstances (such as where the subject had been diagnosed with dementia or mental illness causing serious cognitive disturbance) in which it is appropriate to dispense with the presumption of capacity.

(b) Consent

The law should offer a defence grounded solely on the fact that consent was so badly impaired that the state will not lend its assistance to enforce/ endorse the undertaking or conveyance in question. This would *not* require:

- the other party to have behaved reprehensibly or to have breached any duty;[24] or
- that consent was wholly absent.

Equitable doctrine provides an ideal vehicle for this. Indeed, it is arguable that, in Australia, the doctrine of undue influence[25] and the second limb of *Yerkey v Jones* already go some of the way towards performing this function.[26]

---

23 And not, for instance, to the executor/administrator of her estate. This might go some way towards assuaging the concern described in n 4.

24 It is suggested that this objective would be more cleanly accomplished by means of an action located in unjust enrichment, rather than by casting it as a 'wrong'.

25 *Commercial Bank of Australia Ltd v Amadio* (1983) 151 CLR 447, 474 and *Bridgewater v Leahy* (1998) 194 CLR 471, 478–79.

26 *Yerkey v Jones* 63 CLR 649, 685–86, and affirmed in *Garcia v National Australia Bank Ltd* (1998) 195 CLR 395, 405 and 409.

IV. Conclusion

If consent truly is critical to legal responsibility, then it should not be reduced to a formality or a foregone conclusion. In the absence of a model of consent to guide their development, property and contract law have been too greatly influenced by concerns about proof and fear of uncertainty. This has made relief on the basis of vitiated consent too difficult to access. The state frequently lends its support to the enforcement of undertakings and the endorsement of conveyances notwithstanding that there is a serious danger that the subject's capacity to understand the decision or to exercise a free choice was badly impaired. In such cases, it is clear that the laws of capacity and consent do not serve to promote autonomy. The urgent need to reform the laws about consent presents an opportunity to reassess the relationship between responsibility and consent and to construct a more accurate and effectual model of consent. This model can be used to drive changes in property and contract law that will facilitate the attainment of effective consent and provide better access to relief in cases of vitiated consent. Thus renovated, consent will be better placed to fulfil its purpose of promoting autonomy.

32

Nudging Charities to Balance the Needs of the Present against Those of the Future

Ian Murray[1]

I. Introduction

This chapter explains the need for some temporal rules in charity law. It raises the underexamined issue of the point in time at which charities are expected to produce a public benefit from resources that they hold. Timing is critical to identifying which persons will benefit. Will they be members of the present generation that have provided resources or collectively granted concessions to the charity? Will future generations benefit instead?

The temporal issue will impact in different ways depending upon a charity's purpose and the means it uses to achieve that purpose. The considerations that apply to a bushfire disaster relief charity will diverge from those relevant to a university intended to last in perpetuity.

1   Senior Lecturer, University of Western Australia and PhD candidate, University of Tasmania. This work was supported in part through an Australian Government Research Training Program Scholarship. Particular thanks to Matthew Harding, Pauline Ridge, Gino Dal Pont and Don Chalmers for comments on earlier versions of this research. Any errors remain the author's responsibility.

Nevertheless, to remain relevant to as broad a group of charities as possible, this chapter looks in general terms at the gaps in existing constraints and proposes reforms that would better promote an intergenerational balance.

II. The Need for an Intergenerational Balance

There is a theoretical and practical need for temporal rules. Turning to theory, key charity law goals are to facilitate the pursuit of charitable purposes independently from the state and to incentivise the production of goods for the benefit of the public in pursuing those purposes. This appears from economic theories that explain the production of public and quasi-public goods by the not-for-profit sector (including charities) in place of government production.[2] These goals are also supported by examination of the justification for charity tax concessions[3] and on a doctrinal analysis of charity law's functions.[4] An additional goal is to generate trust and confidence, on the part of those giving to and receiving benefits from charities, that funds received by the charity will be applied to the charitable purpose. This goal is drawn from analysis of the expressive function of charity law[5] and from economic and legal theories that seek to explain why goods are produced by the not-for-profit sector rather than the private sector.[6] Implicit in the goal of incentivising the production of goods is the need for goods to be produced before the end of time. Arguably, the trust and confidence goal also bolsters this conclusion. However, these goals provide limited guidance about the appropriate time.

From a practical perspective, grappling with the issue is critical. While hoarding by Australian charities does not appear systemic at present, there is some potential for accumulation and evidence of significant

---

2   Burton Weisbrod, *The Nonprofit Economy* (Harvard University Press, 1988); Estelle James and Susan Rose-Ackerman, *The Nonprofit Enterprise in Market Economics* (Harwood Academic Publishers, 1986) 20, 27–31.

3   Gino Dal Pont, 'Conceptualising "Charity" in State Taxation' (2015) 44(1) *Australian Tax Review* 48, 50; Evelyn Brody, 'Of Sovereignty and Subsidy: Conceptualizing the Charity Tax Exemption' (1998) 23(4) *Journal of Corporation Law* 585.

4   Matthew Harding, *Charity Law and the Liberal State* (Cambridge University Press, 2014) 38–41, 44; Dal Pont, above n 3, 50.

5   Harding, above n 4, 38–41, 44.

6   By reference to information asymmetries: Henry Hansmann, 'The Role of Non-profit Enterprise' (1980) 89(5) *Yale Law Journal* 835, 843–45. The theories supplement the subsidisation of public goods rationale above.

variation in savings rates across the not-for-profit sector.[7] Further, the level of Australian philanthropy is increasing, as are public expectations of charities. Moreover, concerns have been mooted in Australia and abroad.[8] In addition, research by the Charity Commission for England and Wales indicates that many charities may not have any formal policy for the retention and maintenance of reserved assets, including a significant proportion of charities that hold reserves.[9] This suggests some charity controllers may not be considering the question.

III. Gaps in Existing Constraints

There are various legal rules that apply to restrain the accumulation of assets by charities. These rules provide a mechanism for dealing, at least partially, with governance fears that accumulated funds may be lost or improperly applied. They also enable some limits on the perpetuation of a charity creator's control. However, they are materially deficient in addressing the timing issue.

A. Tax rules

I have discussed elsewhere the tax rules that potentially restrict asset retention by charities.[10] The key rules comprise:

- A minimum annual distribution requirement, generally of 5 per cent or 4 per cent of the market value of a fund's net assets for certain deductible gift recipient charitable ancillary funds.

- To be exempt from income tax a charity must, amongst other requirements, 'apply its income and assets solely for the purpose for which [it] is established'.

---

7   See, for example, Australian Bureau of Statistics, 'Australian National Accounts: Non-Profit Institutions Satellite Account 2012–13' (Cat No 5256, 28 August 2015).

8   'The Native Title Divide', *The West Australian* (Perth), 27 March 2010, 32; Charles Mitchell, 'Saving for a Rainy Day: Charity Reserves' (2002) 8(1) *Charity Law & Practice Review* 35, 41 (fundraising organisations); James Fishman and Stephen Schwarz, *Nonprofit Organizations: Cases and Materials* (Foundation Press, 4th edn, 2010) 7 (US hospitals, universities, museums and religious organisations).

9   Charity Commission, 'Tell it Like it Is: The Extent of Charity Reserves and Reserve Policies' (Research Report No RS13, November 2006) 8–9, 11.

10   Ian Murray, 'Charity Accumulation: Interrogating the Conventional View on Tax Restraints' (2015) 37(4) *Sydney Law Review* 541.

Assuming that recipient organisations use the funds within a reasonable time, the minimum distribution rule promotes some spending for the present. While the income tax exemption rule may discourage material retention of resources in practice, the better view is that the rule does not permit the Australian Taxation Office (ATO) to monitor accumulation beyond ensuring compliance with the charity's governing rules and the law. In this way, the rule acts as a fall-back to trustee and director duties, rather than an additional constraint.

B. Perpetuities rules and general charity supervisory mechanisms

The need to select from sanctioned categories of 'charitable purpose' imposes some constraints upon donor control.[11] Further, the rules against remoteness of vesting and against accumulation potentially apply where there is accumulation in the narrow sense of taking some of the income from a capital sum held by a charity and adding that income to the capital. In contrast, the rule against indestructible trusts does not apply to charities, which may be perpetual. Accordingly, one might have expected that the rules against remoteness and accumulation, which are targeted specifically at balancing current and future generations' interests in the freedom of disposition of property, would partially address the timing issue by limiting mandated accumulation to the perpetuity period. However,[12] the rules against remoteness and accumulation have been abolished for charities in South Australia and potentially Tasmania and the Northern Territory.[13] Further, even in jurisdictions where they apply, the rules do not effect a constraint on accumulation in circumstances where property is expressed to be given on trust for charitable purposes, pursuant to the terms of which the trustees are required (or permitted) to accumulate income.[14]

---

11   See, for example, Rob Atkinson, 'Reforming Cy Pres Reform' (1993) 44(5) *Hastings Law Journal* 1111, 1114–15.

12   Unless an accumulation provision stops a trust from being characterised as having a charitable purpose.

13   Ian Murray, 'Accumulation in Charitable Trusts: Australian Common Law Perpetuities Rules' (2015) 9(1) *Journal of Equity* 30.

14   Ibid; Ian Murray, 'Accumulation in Charitable Trusts: Australian Statutory Perpetuities Rules' (2014) 8(2) *Journal of Equity* 163.

Mechanisms, such as administrative schemes, cy-près schemes, winding-up processes and trustee expediency provisions do permit some degree of change.[15] They therefore limit the charity creator's control over charity property. However, their scope, particularly when applied at the instigation of a regulator, is relatively confined.

C. Governance duties

Charity controllers, be they trustees, company directors or committee members, are subject to a range of common law and statutory duties of care, skill and diligence and of loyalty and good faith. Duties that apply to the exercise of fiduciary powers would require controllers to act upon genuine consideration in exercising powers to retain or accumulate assets.[16] This means that charity controllers must take account of (material) relevant considerations and should not take account of irrelevant considerations.[17] This imposes procedural constraints on accumulation, as charity controllers are likely obliged to conduct a broad survey of the persons who might benefit from pursuit of the relevant charitable purpose, along with the likely relative financial circumstances of these persons in the present and the future.[18] However, as the procedural requirements are not clearly articulated and as judicial review is focused on maintaining the integrity of the process rather than the merits of the ultimate decision, there is significant flexibility. Additionally, the Charity Commission for England and Wales research on reserves policies discussed above suggests that many controllers may not be aware of the duties.

IV. Reform

The timing of charity benefits involves, by definition, matters of distribution. The extent to which charity controllers should be subject to obligations in retaining or distributing charity assets, so as to distribute benefits to different generations, is essentially a matter of ethics.

---

15 Ibid.
16 See, for example, *Karger v Paul* [1984] VR 161, 163–66 (McGarvie J); Rosemary Teele Langford, 'Solving the Fiduciary Puzzle: The Bona Fide and Proper Purposes Duties of Company Directors' (2013) 41(3) *Australian Business Law Review* 127, 130–31, 134.
17 *Scott v National Trust* [1998] 2 All ER 705, 718 (Robert Walker J).
18 Cf *Re Hay's Settlement Trusts* [1982] 1 WLR 202, 209–10 (Megarry VC).

A. Is there a relevant ethical basis?

There are a range of philosophical theories that attempt to articulate what obligations are owed by the present generation in relation to past and future people. While the content and concept of 'intergenerational justice' remain debated, it is often used for such theories, as they typically apply notions of 'justice' from political philosophy to relations between non-contemporaneous persons.[19]

For instance, intergenerational justice may mean that the current generation owes a duty grounded in 'distributive justice' to redistribute resources, to some extent, to persons, whether in the same or in future generations, based on the degree to which this would satisfy their fundamental social and economic needs.[20] The notion of distributive justice inevitably requires attention to Rawls's 'difference principle',[21] being the second condition of the following principle:[22]

> Social and economic inequalities are to satisfy two conditions: first, they are to be attached to offices and positions open to all under conditions of fair equality of opportunity; and second [the difference principle], they are to be to the greatest benefit of the least advantaged members of society.

The difference principle permits differences in socioeconomic status of individuals, but only to the extent that such differences improve the absolute position of the most disadvantaged members of society, for instance because they incentivise greater productivity and hence greater wealth for society. If they do not, then resources should be redistributed to those disadvantaged persons. However, Rawls applied the difference principle to contemporaneous persons, not non-contemporaneous persons. In the intergenerational context, Rawls conceived of intergenerational savings obligations to preserve capital so as to enable the establishment and then

---

19   See, for example, Axel Gosseries and Lukas Meyer (eds), *Intergenerational Justice* (Oxford University Press, 2009) 1–4; Joerg Tremmel (ed), *Handbook of Intergenerational Justice* (Edward Elgar, 2006).

20   See, for example, Frederic Gaspart and Axel Gosseries, 'Are Generational Savings Unjust?' (2007) 6(2) *Politics, Philosophy and Economics* 193, 201–4, 209, 211–12; Dieter Birnbacher, 'Responsibility for Future Generations' in Tremmel, above n 19, 34. Welfare economics adopts this basis when using certain social welfare functions: cf Robin Broadway and Michael Keen, 'Redistribution' in Anthony Atkinson and François Bourguignon (eds), *Handbook of Income Distribution* (North Holland, Vol 1, 2000) 677, 680–83.

21   Many other philosophers also embrace notions of distributive justice based upon a reallocation of resources to satisfy basic social and economic needs.

22   John Rawls, *Justice as Fairness: A Restatement* (Harvard University Press, 2001) 42–43. See also John Rawls, *A Theory of Justice* (Clarendon Press, 1972) 76–83, 302–3.

maintenance of just institutions.[23] These savings obligations acted as a substitute for and constraint on (rather than application of) the difference principle. Subsequent philosophers have, however, demonstrated that distributive principles can be applied to some extent between generations, that cooperation can take place between generations and that it is possible to transfer resources between generations, even if there are difficulties.[24]

Of course, in applying distributive principles across generations, one has to contend with the issue of choosing between those in need in one's own generation and those in need in future generations – who may potentially be better off, overall. In this context, some writers have demonstrated that the principles can discourage both intergenerational 'dissaving' and saving.[25] Therefore, some theorists have favoured Benthamite-type utilitarian approaches to maximising social welfare across generations, which take less account of distributive justice and encourage greater saving.[26]

Intergenerational justice has also been interpreted as requiring that the current generation avoid the pursuit of benefits that would impose costs on future generations, where to do so would result in the world being handed on in a lesser state to future generations, or in a state that fails to meet 'sufficientarian' standards for members of future generations.[27] Such approaches may be based on distributive justice or on notions of sustainability. However, sustainability principles can themselves be conceived of in distributional terms, or otherwise incorporate distributional matters.[28]

Finally, conceptions of intergenerational justice that derive from Rawlsian notions of justice are concerned with the rules for society's basic structure and hence do not directly apply to actions taken by societal associations such as charities. Accordingly, if guidance was to be obtained from

---

23 John Rawls, *A Theory of Justice* (Clarendon Press, 1972) 285, 291–93.

24 Janna Thompson, *Intergenerational Justice: Rights and Responsibilities in an Intergenerational Polity* (Routledge, 2009) 117; Tremmel, above n 19.

25 Gaspart and Gosseries, above n 20, 203–4, 209, 211–12 (once society has accumulated sufficient capital to establish just institutions). Cf Birnbacher, above n 20, 34.

26 See, for example, Birnbacher, above n 20, 32–33.

27 See, for example, Lukas Meyer, 'Intergenerational Justice', in Edward Zalta (ed), *Stanford Encyclopedia of Philosophy* (Summer 2016 edn), plato.stanford.edu/archives/sum2016/entries/justice-intergenerational/ (sufficientarianism relates to whether persons are below a threshold of harm); Peter Laslett, 'Is There a Generational Contract?' in Peter Laslett and James S Fishkin (eds), *Justice Between Age Groups and Generations* (Yale University Press, 1992) 24, 29–30, 44–45.

28 Tremmel, above n 19, 7–9, Chs 1–2.

a Rawlsian notion of justice, then its requirements may need to shape charity law itself – viewed as part of the basic structure.[29] Alternatively, they may inform the principles of 'local justice'[30] that ought to be considered by charity controllers. Certainly, intergenerational justice has been used as a moral guide to the actions of private and governmental actors under a basic structure as well as to the formation of that structure.[31]

B. Implementing obligations

There are significant practical and theoretical impediments to implementing obligations based on theories of intergenerational justice. The practical difficulties include the potential need for charity controllers to take account of other systems for achieving distributive justice, the most significant being the state's role in collecting and redistributing assets. Would intergenerational justice demand that charities be compelled to conserve assets so as to counterbalance insufficient governmental regard for future generations? How would charity controllers determine this?

Equally, charity controllers would have to consider whether future generations might be wealthier and so potentially less deserving of resources, although they must also consider whether the particular benefits they bestow will become comparatively more expensive with time. Charity controllers would also need to compare the costs and benefits, over time, of the alternative courses of action being considered. There are tools that can assist. In particular, while it has limits, welfare economics can provide insights into how to maximise social welfare in pursuit of an intergenerational equity distributional preference. It does so by using a social welfare function that applies to the aggregate utilities of individuals across generations.[32] For instance, this can help account for economic growth by discounting future utilities on the assumption that individuals will derive lower marginal utility from additional consumption enabled by the transfer.

---

29 Cf John Rawls, *Justice as Fairness: A Restatement* (Harvard University Press, 2001) 10–12.
30 See, for example, Jon Elster, 'Local Justice' (1991) 35(2–3) *European Economic Review* 273.
31 See, for example, Thompson, above n 24, 125–27, 150–59; Birnbacher, above n 20, 26; Michael Klausner, 'When Time Isn't Money: Foundation Payout Rates and the Time Value of Money' (2003) 1(1) *Stanford Social Innovation Review* 51.
32 See, for example, Broadway and Keen, above n 20, 680–83.

There is also a key theoretical difficulty. As discussed above, notions of what intergenerational justice requires may legitimately differ. However, there are some commonalities to the theories, such as the implication that neither current nor future persons have a moral priority over the other and the notion that intergenerational justice is concerned with meeting basic social and economic needs of members of society.

In light of the above factors, and cognisant of the charity law goal of pursuing charitable objects independently of government,[33] it seems inappropriate for the state to deal with intergenerational justice by mandating minimum distribution or savings rates. A limit on the duration of charities would also involve state intervention and would operate, at least in the lead up to the termination date, analogously to a minimum distribution requirement. Equally, the state should not delegate the temporal question of how much a particular charity ought to spend or save to a regulator like the ATO. Broadening the circumstances in which cy-près is available to encompass breaches of intergenerational justice would not only be a drastic alteration to those principles, but, because of the breadth of intergenerational justice and of the relevant factors, intergenerational decision-making would likewise be delegated to another arm of government – the courts.

Nevertheless, ensuring that charity controllers consider issues of intergenerational justice, as reasonably understood by the controllers, is consistent with the aims of charity law and with the theories and tools available. This could be achieved by interpreting the existing governance duty to give genuine consideration as requiring this step. Alternatively, the duty could be explicitly incorporated in legislation, perhaps similarly to s 172 of the *Companies Act 2006* (UK) which requires a director to have regard to a range of specified matters in 'act[ing] in the way he considers, in good faith, would be most likely to promote the success of the company'. Either method could be twinned with a requirement to report on the levels of, and reasons for, retained assets, as in England and Wales where most registered charities that prepare accruals-based accounts need to report on reserves and reserves policies.[34]

---

33 This aim would be trumped by principles of justice that delineate the basic structure, if that is how the moral theory is implemented.
34 Charity Commission, *Charity Reserves*, Guidance CC19, January 2016, 9–10.

A further step could be adopted if disclosure proves inadequate in conjunction with the duty identified above. It may prove inadequate if the costs involved in applying principles of intergenerational justice are too high for charity controllers and the regulator. If so, there may be grounds for 'nudging'[35] charity controllers by setting a default rule from which the charity controllers could choose to opt out. For instance, the default rule could involve a safe harbour default minimum distribution rate, such as one that is roughly consistent with generational neutrality for the relevant charity, in that it neither provides for saving nor dissaving. The current ancillary fund minimum distribution rates are likely close to such neutrality.

V. Conclusion

This chapter has highlighted the practical and theoretical need for guidance on the time at which charities are expected to produce a public benefit from resources that they presently hold. In essence, the question is the extent to which the present generation should forego benefits in favour of future generations. Intergenerational justice has been identified as a possible theoretical base upon which decisions can be made, albeit there are impediments, including the range of theories of intergenerational justice.

Accordingly, the reform advocated is a process-focused approach which requires charity controllers to actively consider the interests of current and future generations, applying any reasonably open conception of intergenerational justice. Coupled with disclosure requirements, this reform could be adopted by incorporating it within the duty to exercise powers with genuine consideration, or by explicitly legislating such a duty for charity controllers. If the approach proves inadequate, for instance because it is too costly for charity controllers and regulators, then it could be implemented in conjunction with a safe harbour, such as a default minimum distribution rate.

---

35 Richard Thaler and Cass Sunstein, *Nudge* (Penguin, revised edn, 2009).

Part V. Public Law

33

Voluntary Voting for Referendums in Australia: Old Wine, New Bottle

Graeme Orr[1]

Voter turnout: to compel or not to compel? The question of compulsion in elections has been a perennial in Australia. In the 1960s Professor Joan Rydon said, in opposition to compulsory voting, that where 'the apathetic and ill-informed are forced to the polls by law, it is even more likely that the "scum and dregs" of political life will decide who is to govern the country'.[2] Affirming compulsory voting's hoary status as 'contentious', recent years have witnessed failed attempts to argue that it is unconstitutional,[3] and to legislatively reverse it.[4]

Rydon and the libertarians have not won the day. Compulsory voting – introduced to this country in stages from 1915 – remains the law of the land. Curiously, compulsion first entered at a national level not via elections, but via a kind of referendum, the first conscription plebiscite

---

1   Professor, Law School, University of Queensland.
2   Joan Rydon, 'The Electorate' in John Wilkes (ed), *Forces in Australian Politics* (Angus & Robertson, 1963) 184.
3   *Holmdahl v AEC (No 2)* [2012] SASFC 110. See Anne Twomey, 'Compulsory Voting in a Representative Democracy: Choice, Compulsion and the Maximisation of Participation in Australian Elections' (2014) 13 *Oxford University Commonwealth Law Journal* 283.
4   Josh Butler, 'David Leyonhjelm Proposes Abolishing Compulsory Voting', *Huffington Post*, 2 March 2016 (Leyonhjelm is a libertarian senator).

during World War I.[5] As long as the major parties support it, whether out of democratic principle or because it saves them the cost of 'getting out the vote', compulsion will be a fixture of Australian elections. Reinforcing Australia's reputation as a pragmatic, Benthamite society rather than a rights-oriented one, opinion polls reveal consistent, strong support for electoral compulsion.[6]

Such contented stasis, however, belies a ferment. All is far from well in electoral democracy across the 'advanced democracies'. Symptoms include increased electoral volatility and declining faith in representative government. We might argue about the causes – economic stagnation or social atomisation? We might even argue whether these are problems needing cures, or transitions with positive potential to free-up politics from the two-party system. But the signs are not good.

My argument here is that compulsion, an old wine, is desirable for *elections*. But it doesn't belong in the *referendum* bottle. Compulsion at elections makes sense because:

- Everyone has an interest in day-to-day governance.
- The promise of the ballot is to ensure those interests are heard, through regular elections. There is evidence that, over time, compulsion leads to greater turnout of marginalised groups and that this can generate more egalitarian policy as politicians need to consider a broader range of social interests.[7]
- The ultimate pragmatic purpose of elections, at least in Australia, is to turn over or recall governments and MPs. As tapestries for deliberation, elections are open-ended and cannot be reduced to 'education campaigns', as is the ideal in referendums.[8]

---

5   *Compulsory Voting Act 1915* (Cth). In the end, plebiscites were held in 1916 and again in 1917 under voluntary voting. Earlier in 1915, compulsion had been introduced for Queensland elections: *Elections Act 1915* (Qld) s 63.

6   Between 1998 and 2013, support for compulsory voting ranged from a low of 69.5 per cent in 2010 to a high of 76.7 per cent in 2007 (source, AES exit polls).

7   As postulated by Arend Lijphart, 'Unequal Participation: Democracy's Unresolved Dilemma' (1997) 91 *American Political Science Review* 1. For empirical support, see John M Carey and Yusaku Horiuchi, 'Compulsory Voting and Income Inequality' (2017) 59 *Latin American Politics and Society* 122, a study of effects in Latin America and studies cited there.

8   Graeme Orr, 'Deliberation and Electoral Law' (2013) 12 *Election Law Journal* 421.

- Contrary to Rydon, but echoing the cliché that even a dog knows the difference between being tripped over and kicked, under-informed voters do not undermine the purposes of electoral democracy. Low-information electors act rationally when they adopt heuristics such as 'Are we better off than three years ago?' or 'Do I trust leader X more than Y?'

- As elections are secular rituals which help bind societies, there may be communitarian and symbolic reasons to compel turnout.[9]

These and other arguments about compulsion in elections are well assayed elsewhere.[10] The novel – hence 'law reform' – part of this argument relates to referendums. So referendums will be our focus. In what follows I will briefly outline the reasoning behind changing referendum law to make voting voluntary. To concretise the issue I will also relate a case study, about the most recent constitutional referendum, held in Queensland in March 2016. It shows how compulsion can exacerbate manipulative referendum processes.

I will argue, first, that Australian referendums tend to be on matters of law, especially constitutional law. Constitutional law is meta-law. It is not reasonable to expect everyone to care, let alone have a sensible view about such issues. Second, compulsory voting at such referendums is a conservative, not egalitarian force, helping to stall constitutional amendment. And, finally, there are no 'legitimacy' reasons to compel mass turnout at referendums.

I. The Argument against Compulsion at Referendums

Tracking the summary above, there are three planks to the argument.

First, constitutional law is meta-law. It is unreasonable to expect, let alone demand, that all electors address themselves sensibly to such issues. Elites often respond to this simple insight by bemoaning ignorance of the law

---

9   Graeme Orr, *Ritual and Rhythm in Electoral Systems: A Comparative Legal Account* (Routledge-Ashgate, 2015).

10   For example, Jason Brennan and Lisa Hill, *Compulsory Voting: For and Against* (Cambridge University Press, 2014). Arguments for compulsion in elections are comprehensively made in a body of work by Lisa Hill.

and calling for more 'education'. The road to 'Getting to Yes' is to be paved with more civics education and greater spending on public information before and during referendum campaigns.[11]

There is something valiant, but a little vain, in such calls. Public education on particular referendum proposals may be valuable. But there is a naïve presumption, emanating from a university- and often legally-educated class, that because people like us find public law fascinating and fundamental, all people should. Combined with compulsory turnout, the approach seems to be that institutions and laws can not only lead horses to water, but make them drink it too.

The position might be different if Australia relied on citizens-initiated referendums (CIR) to legislate specific social or policy issues, as do some US jurisdictions. Clearly there are social issues, of such common concern or import, where it is not just reasonable but likely that most electors will have well-reflected, 'values' based responses. But the odd plebiscite on issues like daylight savings – or on marriage equality, as mooted for 2017 – aside, CIR is not part of our tradition. If we governed ourselves through CIR alongside electing representatives, then arguments for compulsion at elections might apply.

Second, compulsory voting at such referendums is a conservative, not egalitarian force. That is, in a stable and well-off jurisdiction like Australia, compulsion is a small-'c' conservative *method*. In election campaigns, outside times of electoral volatility, it tends to dampen swings against incumbents regardless of the party concerned.[12]

In referendums, however, it makes no sense to insist on a conservative method like compulsion. It gives a free-kick to 'No' campaigns to run a 'When in doubt, throw it out' campaign,[13] of the sort Williams and Hume aptly characterise as 'Don't know? Vote "no"'.[14] If the constitutional

---

11   House of Representatives Standing Committee on Legal and Constitutional Affairs, *A Time for Change: 'Yes'/ 'No': Inquiry into the Machinery of Referendums* (Parliament of Australia, 2009) Chs 4–5 illustrate this thinking.

12   I discuss the reasons for this in 'Compulsory Voting: Elections, Not Referendums' (2011) 18 *Pandora's Box* 19.

13   The 'When in doubt ...' slogan was a centerpiece of the anti-Republic campaign in 1999.

14   George Williams and David Hume, *People Power: The History and Future of the Referendum in Australia (UNSW Press, 2010)* 253.

status quo requires protection, this should be explicit, say via some super-majority requirement.[15] Such brakes on constitutional reform should not be introduced unintentionally via compulsion.

Australia suffers constitutional stasis, not constitutional recklessness. Removing compulsion would remove one unnecessary barrier to much needed constitutional modernisation. Former Chief Justice Mason identified 'ignorance of the Constitution, now a well-documented fact' as an inducement to 'no' cases.[16]

But lest it be thought that my conclusions are motivated by 'progressive' bias, I offer the following response. Any presumption that compulsion at Australian elections benefits parties of the left over parties of the right is unproven. Indeed, in its tendency to reinforce the status quo it may simply reinforce exogenous political advantages, such as Labor's at state level (dominated by concerns about service delivery) and the conservative Coalition's at national level (demarked by a focus on national security and public finance). When it comes to policy, history shows that the great waves of progressive reforms in the common law world happened in Australia under compulsion at roughly similar times as they occurred under voluntary voting in New Zealand and the UK. This implies that political culture is more likely to be determinative of policy outcomes than differences in the voting system.

Third, once it is appreciated that referendums are quite different beasts to elections, the claim that compulsory voting 'legitimises' outcomes unravels. Representative government directly impacts everybody's life, every day. Few referendum questions do. It is a category error – as well as an historical and structural misstatement – to assert that because 'constitutional changes can alter Australia's democratic structure, it can be argued that the duty to vote in referendums is greater than the duty to vote in ordinary elections'.[17] Australia's Constitution is largely process oriented and focused on Commonwealth–state powers, without even an explicit separation of powers let alone a focus on democratic rights. As a result, far from embracing momentous questions, referendums have most often concerned attempts to enhance particular Commonwealth powers.

---

15   The double majority rule in the Constitution s 128 is such a rule.

16   Sir Anthony Mason, 'Towards 2001 – Minimalism, Monarchism or Metamorphism' (1995) 21 *Monash University Law Review* 1 at 7.

17   Williams and Hume, above n 14, 49. In similar (muddle-headed) vein, see Sir Isaac Isaacs, *A Stepping Stone to Greater Freedom* (1946) 8–9.

Other referendums have been on issues of legal significance, but of relatively minor import to electors generally, like the 1977 vote on judges' retiring ages. Important machinery questions, on which all sides of politics agree need constitutional reform – such as the sclerotic restrictions on who can be an MP under s 44 of the Constitution – lie marooned like rusting vessels. It is feared that putting their reform to a referendum will encounter voter cynicism about the cost or importance of the question. Similar fears led to the abandonment of the long process to hold a referendum to constitutionally recognise local government. If referendum voting were not compulsory, the argument that 'it's not a bread and butter priority' would have less traction.

Of course a few referendums do profoundly implicate questions of identity, notably referendums about secession.[18] The one true secession referendum, in Western Australia in 1933, was conducted under compulsory voting.[19] But, as the very high turnout at the 1916 conscription plebiscite in Australia and the 2015 Scottish independence referendum demonstrated,[20] the momentous nature of such unusual referendums ensures high participation without legal compulsion.

For their part, state constitutions are largely flexible. Whether a state holds a referendum depends on political strategies and the happenstance of what issues relating to the 'constitution or powers' of state governments and parliaments have been entrenched. Territory constitutions are not even autonomous: they are still merely acts of the Commonwealth Parliament.

A. When referendums go wrong – Queensland 2016

The most recent referendum on these shores was the March 2016 vote on whether to entrench fixed, four-year terms in Queensland's constitution.[21] The proposal was supported by both major parties and three independents, representing 87 of 89 parliamentarians in Queensland's unicameral system. It was also supported by major business and union leaders. Against were the minor parties and various academics, civil libertarians, lawyers and commentators.[22] The 'no' case was not, on the whole, against fixed terms.

---

18 Voting about new states or state boundaries is distinct from s 128. Indeed such votes are really plebiscites as they are not mandated by the Constitution.
19 *Secession Referendum Act 1932* (WA) s 5(2).
20 82.8 per cent and 84.6 per cent of electors respectively.
21 Constitution (Fixed Term Parliament) Amendment Bill 2015 (Qld).
22 Disclosure: I assisted the 'No' case publicly in this referendum.

Rather, it objected to longer terms without any compensating checks or balances in a state with no upper house, no proportional representation, no charter of rights and just one state-wide newspaper. Although the campaign was a Goliath vs David one, the referendum only succeeded 52.8 per cent to 47.2 per cent.

What makes this referendum of interest was its risible process. The Bill was passed in a day, on the final sitting before Christmas. The poll was called, at barely five weeks' notice, to coincide with local government election day. And the 'Yes' case consisted largely of appeals to authority (recommendations by party, business and union leaders) rather than more valid forms of argument.

Part of the gamble of the referendum lay in a hurried process with minimal public education. The only formal voter education was the early-20th century mechanism of 1,000-word 'Yes' and 'No' pamphlets, delivered to households. Electoral Commission staff even reported electors turning up to cast their local government ballot, unaware a referendum was being held.[23]

At the heart of the problem with the process was the bundling of two related but separable issues into a single question. People were not asked whether they wanted 'fixed' terms, and/or 'longer terms'. If they had, the answer would have been clear. Fixed terms provide stability and depoliticise election dates, but shorter terms enhance democratic input and accountability. And so it was that polling, for a public sector union that supported longer terms, showed that a sizeable majority of citizens wanted fixed terms yet a similar majority wanted to keep shorter terms. Electors' democratic instincts and values were keen. But those who framed the question wanted longer terms above all, so an attractive option was bundled with an unattractive option to skew the outcome.

---

23   Graeme Orr and Samara Cassar, 'When Referendums Go Wrong – Queensland's 2016 Fixed Four-Year Term Proposal' (2016) 31 *Australasian Parliamentary Review* 161, 165.

How does this relate to compulsory voting at referendums? A proponent for compulsion might retort that this example shows the importance of a long lead-time and consultative discussion and information, to till the field of public consciousness. And of more debate about how questions are framed, and separated or bundled.[24] But here is the rub.

There was no need for a referendum on fixed terms. Only the length of the parliamentary term was entrenched in Queensland's constitution (and for good historical reason). Yet what amount of public education would it take to explain the nature of 'manner and form entrenchment' in state constitutional practice? Even MPs, highly literate political journalists and otherwise well-read law students were ignorant of the distinction between flexible and entrenched state constitutional issues. What chance regular citizens? On such fine points of constitutional procedure rested the fate of this referendum.

II. Conclusion: Reform

In public law, the dazzle or heft of constitutional issues usually gain more attention than the nitty-gritty of statutory and administrative law.[25] This was the case until relatively recently in the law of politics. Unsurprisingly, it remains especially so in relation to constitutional reform. After all, the machinery of referendums is hardly as interesting as the principles and purposes informing referendums. Of more interest are substantive debates about reform, like the Republic, or Indigenous 'recognition'. Recently there has emerged a burgeoning literature on whether and how referendums might become more deliberatively rich democratic exercises.[26] Intriguingly these deliberative concerns are folding back into machinery questions.[27]

---

24   Some US state constitutions insist that referendums and initiatives 'shall embrace but one subject'. In Queensland the issues were related but separable. They deserved two questions, albeit on the same ballot.

25   Graeme Orr, 'Teaching Public Law: Content, Context and Coherence' (2015) 25 *Legal Education Review* 299 at 307.

26   For example, Paul Kildea 'A Little More Conversation? Assessing the Capacity of Citizens to Deliberate About Constitutional Reform in Australia' (2013) 22 *Griffith Law Review* 291.

27   For example, *Ron Levy,* 'Deliberative Voting: Realising Constitutional Referendum Democracy' [2013] *Public Law* 555; Rodney Smith and Paul Kildea, 'The Challenge of Informed Voting at Constitutional Referendums' (2016) 39 *University of New South Wales Law Journal* 341.

My argument is not about deliberation as such. Voluntary voting would likely affect deliberation for better and for worse. To be implemented seriously, voluntary voting at referendums would have to be accompanied by a rule that referendums not coincide with elections, where compulsion would remain. This would partly disentangle partisan politics from referendum campaigns.

There is also the potential that campaigns under voluntary voting may focus more on turning out the already committed than on 'educating' the broader electorate. If that is a risk at referendums, I would venture to suggest it will only arise in instances of 'big ticket' constitutional reform, where it will be mitigated by the fact that turnout will naturally be higher. In any event, the risk just gives us more reason to strengthen the non-partisan, publicly funded cases at referendum time, as well as learn from overseas, especially UK, experience on the importance of limiting third-party campaigns at constitutional referendums.

My argument also diverges completely from arguments against compulsory voting on libertarian grounds (arguments that reached a bemusing height in an article titled 'It's an Evil Thing to Oblige People to Vote'[28]). Rather, mine is an institutionalist position. Referendums in this country are proposals for a particular type of law reform, and it is neither reasonable nor fair to attempt to require people be concerned about such proposals.

With climate change bearing down upon us, it may not be kosher to perpetuate the metaphor of Australia being 'constitutionally speaking ... the frozen continent'.[29] But voluntary voting at referendums might just melt a little of that rigid ice. It would certainly avoid giving the status quo 'No' case a head-start with 'If in doubt, kick it out' slogans. As the Queensland case study showed, voluntary voting may also take some sting out of manipulative processes by those proposing referendum questions.

The reform advocated here is of the 'suck it and see' variety. Some will try to argue that constitutional reform is on a deeper or more fundamental plane than electing representatives. To which I would ask 'more fundamental

---

28   Derek Chong et al (2005–6) 21(4) *Policy* 10. For a refutation of the libertarian position, see Lisa Hill, 'On the Reasonableness of Compelling Citizens to "Vote": The Australian Case' (2002) *Political Studies* 80. As the scarequotes around 'Vote' in Hill's title imply, in any secret ballot the compulsion is not to vote, but to turn out: see *Faderson v Bridger* (1971) 126 CLR 271 at 272. It would be preferable if ballots said 'you do not have to record a valid vote', a la former *Electoral Act 1985* (SA) s 85(2).
29   Geoffrey Sawer, *Australian Federalism in the Courts* (Melbourne University Press, 1967).

to whom?' Most people live lives in the concrete present. The question of who will wield executive and legislative power in the coming term of government is a pressing question. Constitutional law may or may not indirectly matter to them, but it is too much to demand that everyone participate in its enactment. In any event, if constitutional legitimacy has to be grounded in maximum turnout it is ironic, to say the least, that the creation of a federal Australia was achieved through voluntary voting.[30] That process, for all its racial and class flaws, is valorised today as a rare example of a nation born out of peaceful deliberation rather than violence or neo-colonial struggle. Today's struggle, in contrast, is not to give birth to a new constitution, but to modernise our creaky constitutional structures. Such legal questions require citizen voice and participation, but not mandatory turnout.

---

30   The data is captured in Glenn Rhodes, *Votes for Australia: How Colonials Voted at the 1899–1900 Federation Referendums* (CAPSM, Griffith University, 2002).

34

Reforming Constitutional Reform

Scott Stephenson[1]

I. Introduction

This chapter proposes that Australia's constitutional reform process could be reformed through the use of citizen-led conventions with broad remits to consider a range of constitutional issues. It sets out the case for this reform by answering three questions: why should we think about reforming the constitutional reform process, what is wrong with the current process, and how can it be improved?

II. Why Should We Think about Reforming the Constitutional Reform Process?

There are a number of important issues in contemporary Australian life that have a constitutional dimension and are the subject of discussions that include options for change. Federalism, the protection of fundamental human rights and the recognition of Indigenous persons are three prominent examples where the options for change are an integral part of the conversation. There are also other issues where analysis often takes a normative bent such as the process by which major international treaties are drafted, ratified and implemented (e.g. the Trans-Pacific Partnership

---

1   Senior Lecturer, Melbourne Law School, University of Melbourne.

Agreement) and the mechanisms for holding to account private companies that perform public functions (e.g. the operation of overseas immigration detention facilities). Due to their constitutional dimensions, consideration of the full range of options for change requires putting the possibility of constitutional amendment on the table.

Constitutional amendment will not always be the preferred option for change, but any discussion where the possibility is foreclosed will be partial and, consequently, substandard. An illustration is the National Human Rights Consultation Committee, which was established in 2008 to investigate how Australia could better protect and promote human rights, but was precluded from recommending a constitutionally entrenched bill of rights.[2] Taking constitutional amendment off the table not only eliminated one option from consideration, but also confined the range of other options that could be proposed. The committee's discussion of the different types of statutory bills of rights was limited by the fact that certain models might be precluded by the Constitution's separation of powers doctrine.[3] The protection of fundamental human rights is an issue that has seen a large degree of innovation in recent decades,[4] yet the committee was unable to consider the full range of options and determine which one might be the most appropriate for Australia once the possibility of constitutional amendment was taken off the table. The committee's proposed set of reforms reflected these constraints. The reforms were so modest in scope that the committee and academic commentators found it difficult to identify what, as a practical matter, they would change.[5]

Even when constitutional amendment is put on the table, the difficulty of securing an amendment tends to confine the conversation by focusing on the most modest options for change. More ambitious proposals are dismissed not on their merits, but instead due to the common belief that anything more than the most modest change will be defeated at a referendum. We saw this dynamic emerge in the debate on constitutional recognition of Indigenous persons. Efforts were made to direct the

---

2   National Human Rights Consultation, *Report* (September 2009) Appendix A.

3   Ibid. 373–76.

4   See, for example, Stephen Gardbaum, *The New Commonwealth Model of Constitutionalism: Theory and Practice* (Cambridge University Press, 2013); Scott Stephenson, *From Dialogue to Disagreement in Comparative Rights Constitutionalism* (Federation Press, 2016).

5   Scott Stephenson, 'Constitutional Reengineering: Dialogue's Migration from Canada to Australia' (2013) 11 *International Journal of Constitutional Law* 870, 889–93.

conversation – contrary to the wishes of many Indigenous persons[6] – towards the most modest proposals (e.g. to include a declaration in the Preamble to the Constitution) and away from more ambitious proposals (e.g. to include a legally enforceable non-discrimination provision) on the ground that the latter would not survive the Constitution's difficult amendment procedure.[7]

Therefore, it is arguable that we should reform the constitutional reform process in order (1) to allow the possibility of constitutional amendment to be put on the table when discussing issues that the Constitution affects and (2) to allow the full range of options for change, including ambitious proposals, to be discussed on their merits when constitutional amendment is on the table.

III. What Is Wrong With the Constitutional Reform Process?

It is tempting to attribute the abovementioned trends solely to the difficulty of Australia's constitutional amendment procedure. After all, it is understandable that one would want to keep constitutional amendment off the table or, if it is put on the table, to focus on modest proposals if the likelihood of success is low. And it is beyond doubt that Australia's constitutional amendment procedure is difficult. Prime Minister Robert Menzies' colourful comment captures this widely shared view: 'The truth of the matter is that to get an affirmative vote from the Australian people on a referendum proposal is one of the labours of Hercules'.[8] Comparative constitutional analysis confirms his statement, with Australia having one of the world's most difficult constitutions to amend.[9] However, I argue that the difficulty thesis is too simple. It supplies only part of the picture.

---

6   See, for example, Megan Davis and Marcia Langton (ed), *It's Our Country: Indigenous Arguments for Meaningful Constitutional Recognition and Reform* (Melbourne University Press, 2016).

7   Paul Kelly, 'To Succeed, Indigenous Recognition Must Be Handled Deftly', *The Australian*, 10 September 2014, www.theaustralian.com.au/opinion/columnists/paul-kelly/to-succeed-indigenous-recognition-referendum-must-be-handled-deftly/news-story/cd0fbee39cde82ac00297ecc9fa4bd6d.

8   Quoted in Leslie Finlay Crisp, *Australian National Government* (Longman Cheshire, 5th edn, 1983) 40.

9   George Williams and David Hume, *People Power: The History and Future of the Referendum in Australia* (UNSW Press, 2010) 11.

The other part of the picture is the *ease* of the constitutional amendment procedure. When a constitutional amendment procedure becomes so difficult that it is unworkable in practice, institutional actors will be inclined to start again and install a new procedure – perhaps even in violation of the existing procedure – as has been the case in countries such as Canada and the US.[10] Australia has not reached this point. The country's small number of successful constitutional amendments – eight since 1901 – appears to have convinced most institutional actors and scholars that the reform process is fundamentally sound and that all that is required is better execution. This explains why many proposals for reform of the constitutional reform process are modest suggestions that focus on issues of implementation such as greater education of the public and more bipartisanship.[11] These are valuable suggestions that are worthy of implementation, but they are arguably insufficient to remedy the problem that emerges once we put together both parts of the picture – the ease *and* difficulty theses.

Australia's history of constitutional amendment demonstrates that it is possible to achieve *minor or technical* change (the ease thesis), but also suggests that *major* change is largely beyond the reach of the current process (the difficulty thesis). It has been possible to make a small number of amendments to the Constitution since it came into force in 1901, but most have been minor or technical in character. One possible exception is the 1946 amendment granting Commonwealth Parliament the power to provide a range of social services, an essential component of the welfare state. However, even it was understood as a technical fix to secure a function that parliament was already performing rather than to give parliament power to undertake a new set of functions.[12] Another possible exception is the 1967 amendments concerning the treatment of Aboriginal people. However, it made only minor modifications in

---

10   The US Constitution, including its new amendment procedure, was established in violation of the amendment procedure contained in the Articles of Confederation (see Bruce Ackerman, *We the People: Foundations* (Belknap Press, 1991) 41–42) and in 1980 in Canada the Prime Minister, Pierre Trudeau, threatened to violate the constitutional convention concerning the procedure for amending the Constitution to install a new amendment procedure (see Scott Stephenson, 'When Constitutional Conventions Fail' (2015) 38 *Dublin University Law Journal* 447, 459–63).

11   See, for example, Williams and Hume, *People Power*, above n 9, 239; Graeme Orr, 'Voluntary Voting for Referendums in Australia: Old Wine, New Bottle', Ch 33.

12   The amendment was spurred by a High Court decision that cast doubts on the head of power on which parliament had relied: *Attorney-General (Vic) ex rel Dale v Commonwealth* (1945) 71 CLR 237.

substantive terms,[13] altering which level of government could legislate with respect to Aboriginal people and allowing Aboriginal people to be counted in the census. It did not, for instance, give them the right to vote (already by then granted through ordinary legislation), recognise them as the first inhabitants of Australia or prohibit racial discrimination.

Major amendment is a different form of constitutional change than minor or technical amendment because the former requires public ownership of the amendment process – it is not merely fixing an error or oversight, but changing the nature of the bargain that is struck between the government and the people. If the people do not understand the new bargain to be one that they have authored, there is ample reason for them to use the power given to them by the referendum requirement in s 128 to reject it. Therefore, the referendum requirement is not equivalent to, or a substitute for, public ownership of the amendment process. It ensures that the people get a chance to ratify a proposal, but it does not ensure that they have any say over the *identity* or *content* of the proposal.

When examining the constitutional reform process through the lens of public ownership, Australia has an unimpressive record albeit with some exceptions. The Australian Constitutional Convention convened from 1973 to 1985 exemplifies the historical tendency to adopt an exclusive rather than inclusive process to the authorship of amendment proposals. It was comprised solely of representatives from government and, perhaps unsurprisingly, split along the same party lines that exist in the legislative chambers.[14] The Constitutional Commission established in 1985 was scarcely any better, comprised of a group of unelected and unrepresentative political and legal elites such as former Prime Ministers and Governors-General. However, the commission did take some steps to include the people in the process, conducting public hearings across the country and inviting written submissions.[15] The people nevertheless had no direct role in contributing to the identity or content of the commission's proposals – they were outsiders rather than insiders. The Constitutional Convention commissioned in 1998 to consider whether Australia should become a republic was a significant improvement over prior efforts: half of the delegates were elected by a voluntary postal vote while the other

---

13 This is not to deny the *symbolic* importance of the events in 1967, especially as the proposal received the support of almost 91 per cent of the electorate.
14 Williams and Hume, *People Power*, above n 9, 28.
15 Ibid. 30.

half were appointed by government in consultation with other groups.[16] This format had its shortcomings – in particular, the Convention focused on a single issue and thus most of the elected volunteers were prominent public figures with strong views on the issue of republicanism to the exclusion of ordinary members of the public. But it nevertheless helped generate an unprecedented level of popular interest and involvement in the constitutional amendment process. For instance, large numbers of people watched the Convention's proceedings in person and on television.

IV. How Can the Constitutional Reform Process Be Improved?

The Irish Constitutional Convention held from 2012 to 2014 demonstrates the scope for innovation with respect to the constitutional reform process. My argument is not that Australia should slavishly follow the Irish model, but that it should prompt Australia to reconsider how, and the extent to which, the public can be included in the process of determining the identity and content of proposals for major constitutional amendment. The Irish Constitutional Convention was established to consider eight areas of reform, including the voting age, the electoral system, same-sex marriage and the participation of women in politics, as well as any other relevant constitutional amendments that it recommended. It had 100 members: a chairperson, 33 legislators and 66 citizens of Ireland randomly selected in a manner designed to reflect the age, geographical and gender balance of the electorate. The government did not commit to proceeding with the Convention's recommendations, but did commit to respond formally to each recommendation and to debate it in the legislature.

The Convention met over 10 weekends for a day and a half each time.[17] Sessions included presentations by experts of papers which had been circulated in advance, debates between groups advocating on either side of an issue, and roundtable discussions before votes were taken. The Convention considered two additional subjects (reform of the lower house and the inclusion of economic, social and cultural rights) and issued nine reports, containing a range of recommendations. The government has responded to six of the reports thus far, and put two

---

16   Ibid. 183.
17   Tom Arnold, 'Inside the Convention on the Constitution', *The Irish Times*, 1 April 2014, www.irishtimes.com/news/politics/inside-the-convention-on-the-constitution-1.1744924.

of its recommendations to the people at a referendum held on 22 March 2015. One recommendation, the legalisation of same-sex marriage, was accepted and the other, the reduction in the age of eligibility for the president, was rejected.

The Irish Constitutional Convention contains two principal insights that are relevant to Australia. First, it demonstrates that it is possible to bring the people into the constitutional reform process in a direct and significant way. Ordinary members of the public were given a seat at the table rather than, for example, an invitation to make submissions, and constituted a majority of the Convention, giving their views considerable weight. Second, it demonstrates the potential value of establishing a forum that has a broad remit to consider a range of constitutional issues. Constitutions are interconnected instruments that make it difficult and even problematic to consider issues in isolation. A convention with a wide agenda or a power to investigate (or recommend the investigation of) additional issues can take a holistic approach to reform. For example, the Irish Constitutional Convention used its final report to recommend a second convention to examine, among other things, reform of the legislature's upper house to complement its recommendations for reform of the lower house. Further, this format helps reduce problems associated with participants being strongly committed to a single issue, by requiring compromise and engagement across multiple issues.

Most reflections on the Irish Constitutional Convention have been positive, with commentators suggesting that it demonstrates that ordinary citizens can engage with complex constitutional issues in an enthusiastic and sophisticated manner and that this format can produce real and radical change.[18] While it has not escaped criticism, most of the problems that have been identified relate to the way in which it was set up rather than the concept of citizen-led constitutional reform.[19] For example, some criticisms include that the government was under no obligation to put the Convention's recommendations to the people, that there was a lack of

---

18   Ivana Bacik, 'Can a Constitutional Convention Offer Real and Radical Change?', *LSE Blog*, 15 December 2014, blogs.lse.ac.uk/constitutionuk/2014/12/15/can-a-constitutional-convention-offer-real-and-radical-change/. See also Matthew Wall, 'Change We Can Believe In? Ireland's Constitutional Convention Has Delivered', *TheJournal.ie*, 23 July 2013, www.thejournal.ie/readme/column-change-we-canbelieve-in-ireland%E2%80%99s-constitutional-convention-has-delivered-1003278-Jul2013/; David Farrell, 'The Irish Constitutional Convention Offers a Potential Route-Map for Renewing UK Democracy', *Democratic Audit UK*, 10 October 2014, www.democraticaudit.com/?p=8625.

19   But cf Eoin Carolan, 'Ireland's Constitutional Convention: Behind the Hype about Citizen-Led Constitutional Change' (2015) 13 *International Journal of Constitutional Law* 733.

balance in the 'expert' material put before participants and the insufficient resources allocated to the Convention.[20] These issues point to a final lesson for Australia from the Irish experience: the details matter.

It is not the case that *any* participatory forum – irrespective of its design – will help generate public ownership of the constitutional reform process. Instead, it must be a forum that is established and executed in a way that renders it democratic (i.e. the forum is comprised in a way that represents the people) and deliberative (i.e. the forum is structured in a way that the people's views are heard and influence the outcome of proceedings). A discussion of the full range of considerations that should be taken into account to create such a forum is beyond the scope of this chapter,[21] but the Irish experience does provide a number of helpful points in this regard. For example, the selection process was structured in a way to ensure that a representative group of the population was chosen.[22] Furthermore, the proceedings were structured in a way to minimise the risk that the political participants would dominate discussion and to ensure that exchanges were open, fair, equal, efficient and collegial.[23]

V. Conclusion

A citizen-led convention with a broad remit to consider a range of constitutional issues would be a significant but far from radical development. As the Irish experience illustrates, large swathes of major constitutional reform will not necessarily eventuate. Indeed, the problem that I have identified with the current process is not a lack of major constitutional amendments. The Australian people are entitled to decide that the current arrangements serve them the best. Instead, the problem is a lack of opportunities to deliberate the full range of constitutional options and, in particular, a lack of opportunities for the people to deliberate which options are put on the table – that is, a constitutional reform process that they own. The Irish Constitutional Convention provides a contemporary example of the scope for innovation in establishing such a process.

---

20   Ibid. 745–48.
21   For a more detailed discussion of the issues, see Ron Levy, 'Breaking the Constitutional Deadlock: Lessons from Deliberative Experiments in Constitutional Change' (2010) 34 *Melbourne University Law Review* 805; Paul Kildea, 'A Little More Conversation? Assessing the Capacity of Citizens to Deliberate About Constitutional Reform in Australia' (2013) 22 *Griffith Law Review* 291.
22   The selection process was not, however, without its problems: Carolan, 'Ireland's Constitutional Convention', above n 19, 741–42.
23   Arnold, 'Inside the Convention on the Constitution', above n 17.

35

Does Australia Need a Popular Constitutional Culture?

Lael K Weis[1]

I. Introduction

A distinctive feature of Australian constitutionalism is the absence (or near absence) of popular constitutional culture. There is very little public deliberation about constitutional law. To the extent that issues concerning fundamental legal norms and values are subject to public debate, they are infrequently cast in constitutional terms. But is this a *bad* thing? Does Australia *need* a popular constitutional culture? And if so, how might this be cultivated?

This chapter offers a modest defence of popular constitutional culture as a desirable ingredient of constitutional democracy. In the first place, a constitutionally informed citizenry is required to ensure that the state's exercise of public power falls within the parameters of its legitimate authority. But even more importantly, I argue, popular constitutional culture is required to effectively engage the constitutional amendment process, which is itself necessary to keep the Constitution up to date and in step with contemporary needs and values so that, ultimately, the Constitution can claim authority as our primary source of constitutional law.

---

1   Lecturer, Melbourne Law School.

After outlining this argument and addressing some possible objections, the chapter offers some suggestions for how popular constitutional culture might be cultivated. Here I argue that educative measures are insufficient: reform requires addressing key features of Australian constitutionalism that account for the lack of popular constitutional culture – the absence of a central founding moment, and the character of the Constitution as a charter of government designed for lawyers rather than a constitution of the people.

II. Australian Popular Constitutional Culture (or Lack Thereof)

It is generally accepted that Australia lacks a popular constitutional culture. By 'popular constitutional culture', I mean public deliberation about fundamental legal norms and values that is cast in constitutional terms. By 'constitutional terms', I mean where those norms and values are understood not simply as important or desirable, but as governing the validity of the exercise of public power, as well as the validity of other (ordinary) legal norms. As Elisa Arcioni and Adrienne Stone have recently observed, '[t]o an extent that would surprise many outside observers, the Australian Constitution is not understood to be a repository of shared values, is not thought to contain fundamental principles to which the citizenry agree or aspire and does not frame public debate'.[2]

Why is this so? At the most basic level, it is explained by low levels of public knowledge about constitutional law. In constitutional systems with written constitutions, public deliberation about constitutional law – where it exists – proceeds largely by reference to the written constitution, which serves as the primary source of constitutional law. However, it is also generally accepted that ordinary Australians have poor knowledge about the Constitution, and even low levels of awareness that Australia has a written constitution.[3] Recent civics education studies confirm this, indicating both low levels of constitutional knowledge among school

---

2   See Elisa Arcioni and Adrienne Stone, 'The Small Brown Bird: Values and Aspirations in the Australian Constitution' (2016) 14 *International Journal of Constitutional Law* 60. Arcioni and Stone's thesis is that Australia doesn't lack a constitutional culture altogether, but has a 'modest' constitutional culture, characterised by a 'disinclination of Australians to turn to their Constitution as a source of shared or aspired to values and its consequent reservation to the domain of the specialist': 63.

3   Civics Expert Group, *Whereas the People: Civics and Citizenship Education* (Australian Government Publication Service, 1994).

students and low levels of teacher confidence with constitutional law topics.[4] These studies also indicate that students leave school with only the most basic understanding of constitutional change: although most know that 'a referendum' is a process used to amend the constitution, only 3 per cent understand the significance and implications of amendment.[5]

Although this goes some way toward explaining Australia's lack of a popular constitutional culture, there is a deeper explanation based upon features of the Constitution itself. The first feature concerns the absence of a central founding moment defining fundamental Australian values. Although in comparative terms the use of procedures such as conventions and referendums at the time is noteworthy, the objects of federation were modest. As a result of its genesis as a 'pragmatic exercise in nation building',[6] as well as its historical pedigree as an Act of British Parliament, it is fair to say that the Australian Constitution failed to 'constitute' the Australian people in any meaningful sense.[7] The second feature concerns the character and content of the Constitution, and notably its lack of a bill of rights. The Constitution has been accused of being 'inaccessible',[8] and labelled a 'prosaic document expressed in lawyer's language',[9] in that it concerns topics about powers and structure that have little traction with the kind of views that ordinary members of the public hold about fundamental legal norms and values.[10]

These two features of the Constitution suggest that *even if* there were higher-levels of public knowledge about the Constitution, it would still be unlikely that members of the public would deliberate over matters concerning fundamental legal norms and values in constitutional terms.

---

4   Suzanne Mellor, Kerry Kennedy and Lisa Greenwood, *Citizenship and Democracy: Australian Students' Knowledge and Beliefs: The IEA Civic Education Study of Fourteen Year Olds* (ACER, 2002) xviii, 4, 73, 113, 114 (Table 7.10), 115, 122, 151 (Table BS.2), research.acer.edu.au/civics/1/.

5   Julian Fraillon et al, *National Assessment Program: Civics and Citizenship Years 6 and 10 Report 2013* (ACER, 2014) 43, research.acer.edu.au/civics/22.

6   Lael K Weis, 'What Comparativism Tells Us about Originalism' (2013) 842 *International Journal of Constitutional Law* 842, 850.

7   See Cheryl Saunders, *The Constitution of Australia: A Contextual Analysis* (Hart, 2011) 27 (observing that '[t]he status of Australia at the time of federation … left the idea of its people oddly inchoate').

8   The Hon Justice Ronald Sackville, 'The 2003 Term: The Inaccessible *Constitution*' (2003) 27 *University of New South Wales Law Review* 66.

9   Sir Anthony F Mason, 'The Australian Constitution in Retrospect and Prospect', in Robert French, Geoffrey Lindell and Cheryl Saunders (eds), *Reflections on the Australian Constitution* (2003) 8.

10   But see Arcioni and Stone, above n 2.

Indeed perhaps the reason that civics lessons on constitutional law fall short is that there is too little to inspire interest in the first place: the Constitution is too disconnected from our self-understanding as a people.[11]

III. A Modest Defence of Popular Constitutional Culture

A. The prima facie case

Such is the state of popular constitutionalism in Australia. It is a further question, however, whether this is an undesirable state of affairs. Some might say that Australia gets along fine without a popular constitutional culture. For instance, Jeffrey Goldsworthy has argued that Australian experience shows why it is *not* particularly important that citizens conceive of issues concerning fundamental legal norms and values in constitutional terms.[12] At least when representative democracy functions reasonably well, such matters can be resolved through the ordinary political process – just as they are in systems without written constitutions. Furthermore, popular constitutional culture may well be a cause for concern rather than celebration insofar as it can lead to an undesirable form of constitutional politics.

Putting this concern aside for the moment, why might it be important for citizens to conceive of issues concerning fundamental legal norms and values in *constitutional* terms? One set of reasons concerns accountability. Even a federal constitutional system that consists primarily of structural guarantees cannot rely exclusively on the competition between national and subnational governments to ensure compliance with constitutional requirements. This is particularly so where there is great vertical fiscal imbalance, as is the case in Australia. If citizens do not understand what the constitution requires, then how can we ensure that state institutions operate within the bounds of power allocated to them? The 'Mr Williamses' among us are surely the exception and not the rule[13] (and the 'Mr Papes'

---

11 See Sackville, above n 8, 84.

12 'Constitutional Cultures, Democracy, and Unwritten Principles' (2012) *University of Illinois Law Review* 683, 684–90.

13 The Queensland-based musician and father of six who brought the landmark challenge to the Commonwealth spending power in *Williams v Commonwealth (No 1)* (2012) 248 CLR 156.

the exceptions that prove the rule[14]). Relying on political and legal elites to perform this task seems undesirable as a matter of principle and potentially dangerous as a matter of practice.

So, having a citizenry that is equipped to hold the state accountable is one reason for thinking that popular understanding of the constitution is important. It could be queried, however, whether this really requires popular constitutional culture. This brings us to a second and more significant set of reasons for thinking that it is important for citizens to conceive of issues concerning fundamental legal norms and values in constitutional terms. This has to do with the desirability of having a constitution that reflects contemporary social needs and values.

The authority of constitutional law has traditionally been understood in terms of popular approval: for example, as meriting approval because it reflects a political community's fundamental values, or because it resolves coordination problems that make that political community possible. However, written constitutions that succeed in providing an enduring and stable source of fundamental legal norms and values over time can become out of date, reflecting the needs and values of the past rather than the present. When this happens, constitutions can face a crisis of authority.

The Australian Constitution arguably suffers from such a deficit. It is over 115 years old, and has been amended infrequently (eight times in total). It contains provisions that no longer reflect the needs and values of the Australian people. For instance, it contains provisions that expressly confer legislative power on the Commonwealth Parliament to make racially discriminatory laws, and that tacitly accept that persons may be excluded from a state's voting franchise on the basis of race.[15] Even those who dispute the proposition that the Constitution has little to say about shared Australian values have observed that there is a clamouring for the Constitution to better reflect national identity and contemporary political values.[16]

---

14   The New South Wales-based law lecturer and barrister who brought the landmark challenge to the Commonwealth spending power in *Pape v Commissioner of Taxation* (2009) 238 CLR 1.
15   Australian Constitution ss 51(xxvi), 25. Both provisions are the subject matter of current debates about constitutional amendment.
16   Arcioni and Stone, above n 2, at 16–18.

What does this state of affairs have to do with popular constitutional culture? The connection lies in constitutional amendment. The amendment procedure, section 128, is the primary mechanism for keeping the Constitution up to date. On paper it seems well-designed for that task, prescribing a procedure that is reasonably democratic and practicable. Proposing amendments only requires a majority vote of parliament (either a majority in both houses or twice in one house), as opposed to the supermajority requirements found in many other constitutions. Proposed amendments require approval by a majority of the electorate and a majority of the states at a popular referendum, as opposed to procedures found in many other constitutions that involve no direct popular involvement. In practice, however, constitutional amendment has proven extraordinarily difficult, even where there is evidence that there is broad public support in favour of change.

The trouble, I suggest, is that the amendment process cannot be successfully invoked in the absence of popular constitutional culture. The success of legislative proposal and popular referendum *both* rely on the ability of the citizenry to conceive of issues concerning fundamental legal norms and values in constitutional terms. Yet that is precisely what Australia lacks. As a result of the lack of a popular constitutional culture, there is a fundamental disconnect between the constitutionally prescribed amendment process – the mechanism designed to keep the constitution up to date – and the background conditions needed to engage that process.

This is a significant problem. In the absence of an effective amendment procedure to keep the Constitution up to date, the alternative is progressive judicial interpretation. This occurs where judges 'update' the meaning of constitutional provisions to reflect contemporary social needs and values. Progressive judicial interpretation is both unattractive as a solution to the problem of constitutional change and in practice unlikely to succeed. It is unattractive because it makes judges, not the Australian people, the agents of constitutional change. Even if we are not concerned that judges will simply substitute their own views for the views of the people, we may well doubt whether judges are very good at determining what the views of the people are. Moreover, practically speaking it is a solution that is unlikely to succeed given the well-established formalist (or 'legalist') method of constitutional interpretation used by Australian judges, which favours a modest, text-bound approach.

B. Objections and responses

Prima facie, then, there is a case for cultivating popular constitutional culture on the basis that doing so is necessary to ensure the proper functioning of the constitutional amendment process.[17] However, comparative experience suggests possible grounds for objection. Experience in the United States in particular, where popular constitutional culture is extremely robust, suggests that popular constitutional culture can lead to the politicisation of constitutional law.

The politicisation of constitutional law both blurs the line between constitutional law and other legal and non-legal norms, and has important implications for how the judicial role is conceived. This is undesirable for at least two reasons. In the first place, it undermines public confidence in impartiality of the judiciary. Members of the American public view the United States Supreme Court as a political institution where contentious moral questions of the day are decided based on the ideological preferences of the justices, and the judicial appointments process often looks more like a test of the nominee's political views than an evaluation of the nominee's credentials as a judge and a member of the legal profession. In addition, there are other costs to democracy that come with the politicisation of constitutional law. The sense of inevitability that political and moral disagreements of the day will ultimately be resolved in court as legal questions, to which there purports to be a correct and incorrect answer, may stifle public discourse and lead to polarisation. There is no need for reasoned political deliberation that aims to understand and accommodate different viewpoints if those disagreements will ultimately be resolved by judges.

The modest institutional role currently occupied by the High Court of Australia makes these kinds of concerns seem remote. Nevertheless, it is worth taking them seriously. Here we can note two sets of existing features of the constitutional system that mitigate the possibility that popular constitutional culture would lead to an undesirable constitutional politics. First of all, there are features that lower the stakes for judicial appointments. These include; a mandatory retirement age for federal judges, which prevents strategic retirement to ensure that the appointment

---

17   This is not, importantly, to claim that popular constitutional culture provides *sufficient* conditions for effective engagement of that process.

of a new judge occurs when a particular political party is in power; and an executive appointment process that does not involve heavily politicised legislative procedures, such as interview-style hearings.

Second, the amendment process prescribed by s 128 itself mitigates risk by lowering the stakes of constitutional interpretation. Comparison with the United States is fruitful here. The US Constitution is also very old and has been infrequently amended. This is typically blamed on the onerous amendment procedure prescribed by Art V, which imposes super-majority requirements for proposing and adopting amendments, and which does not prescribe direct involvement by the people. Article V greatly raises the stakes of judicial interpretation of the US Constitution: since the amendment process is not designed to effectively enable the people to amend the constitution, it is largely up to judges to update the constitution to reflect contemporary needs and values. By contrast, when functioning properly, s 128 promises to have the opposite effect. Indeed the amendment procedure it prescribes is frequently cited as a reason in favour of a modest, textualist approach to constitutional interpretation.[18] To the extent that popular constitutional culture would facilitate the proper functioning of the amendment process, then, popular constitutional culture has a built-in safeguard.

IV. Cultivating Popular Constitutional Culture

I conclude with thoughts about the cultivation of popular constitutional culture. Although better civics education could go some way toward improving knowledge about the constitution, given the limited role that the Constitution currently plays in public discourse the potential of educative measures alone seems necessarily limited. What is needed, I suggest, are measures that address the two underlying features of Australian constitutionalism that account for the lack of a popular constitutional culture in the first place.

Starting with the lack of a founding moment, what is needed is a (re)constitution of the Australian people. Opportunities for such a 'constitutional moment' include the movement toward a republic, if and when that gains momentum. They also include the current possibility

---

18   See Lael K Weis, 'Constitutional Amendment Rules and Interpretive Fidelity to Democracy' (2014) 39 *University of Melbourne Law Review* 240.

of Indigenous recognition, but if – and *only* if – recognition takes a form that requires a deeper reconfiguration of the Australian body politic and shared Australian values than most current proposals on the table appear to contemplate.

With respect to the prosaic and lawyerly character of the constitution, the adoption of a bill of rights is the most obvious and most promising prospect for engaging public deliberation on matters of fundamental legal norms and values. It has been suggested that the Constitution's lack of a bill of rights cannot be blamed for the lack of a popular constitutional culture, on the basis that rights provisions and structural provisions are functional equivalents.[19] Even if that is correct, the *subject matter* of the Constitution's structural provisions presents a problem: overwhelmingly, it does not extend to topics that engage the public imagination. Adopting a bill of rights would change that, allowing more accessible, constitutionally-articulated norms and values to serve as anchoring points in public debate.

The modest defence of popular constitutional culture offered in this chapter thus presents a paradox for constitutional reform. The cultivation of popular constitutional culture appears to require engaging the very amendment process that I have just suggested cannot function properly in its absence. Pursuing one of the lines of reform indicated above, then, is essentially an act of constitutional faith: faith that the Australian people will rise to the occasion if and when it is presented.

---

19   Arcioni and Stone, above n 2, 65–67.

36

Constitutional Dimensions of Law Reform

Gabrielle Appleby and Anna Olijnyk[1]

I. Introduction

In Australia, law reform occurs in the shadow of limits imposed by the Constitution. This chapter engages with two aspects of the relationship between law reform and constitutional limits. First, how do constitutional limits influence parliaments' consideration of law reform proposals? Second, what law reforms are needed in order to allow parliaments to engage in proper deliberation about constitutional limits?

Most proposed legislation falls well within constitutional boundaries. In a small (but not negligible) number of cases it will be *unclear* whether proposed legislation falls within the parliament's legislative power. This is most likely when parliaments are asked to pass innovative legislative proposals to address emerging challenges and priorities such as national security, environmental and social issues. For example, when the federal parliament considered in 2012 a proposed amendment to the *Marriage Act 1961* (Cth) that would have allowed same-sex marriage,

---

1   Associate Professor, UNSW Law (Appleby) and Lecturer, Adelaide Law School (Olijnyk). The research in this chapter is supported by Australian Research Council Discovery Project 140101218, 'Law, Order and Federalism'.

there was considerable constitutional uncertainty about whether the Commonwealth's power to make laws with respect to 'marriage' extended that far.[2]

In Part II of this chapter, we explore the way in which Australian parliaments ought to take into account constitutional limits when considering law reform proposals that require legislative development in uncharted constitutional waters. In Part III we consider current parliamentary practice and the ways that practice falls short of our ideal conception. In the final part of the chapter we propose two specific law reforms needed to help parliamentarians meet their obligations to deliberate about constitutionality: the more frequent release of advice provided by the Solicitor-General to the parliament, and the creation of a role for a constitutional law specialist to advise parliament about the constitutional limits of its legislative power.

II. Parliament's Obligation to Deliberate about Constitutionality

What should parliamentarians do when deliberating about a proposed law at the boundaries of established constitutional principles? The option of seeking an advisory opinion from the High Court was foreclosed in 1921.[3] Another option is for parliamentarians to defer to the Executive's assurances that legislation is likely to be constitutionally valid and not consider the issue separately for themselves. While this is often the current practice, we think it is unsatisfactory.

From a purely practical point of view, parliament has an identifiable self-interest in considering questions of constitutional validity because its own legislative goal will be frustrated if legislation is held invalid. But there are more constitutionally fundamental reasons why parliamentarians have a responsibility to consider the constitutionality of proposed legislation. Like all officials in a public institution operating within a constitutional democracy, parliamentarians have obligations under the rule of law.

---

2   For a discussion of the debate about constitutionality on this issue, see Gabrielle Appleby and Adam Webster, 'Parliament's Role in Constitutional Interpretation' (2013) 37 *Melbourne University Law Review* 255.

3   *Re Judiciary and Navigation Acts* (1921) 29 CLR 257.

This obligation is reflected in the parliamentary oath.[4] The responsibility of a parliament to consider the constitutional validity of its legislative actions is underscored by the reality that many enactments will go unchallenged (which might happen for a variety of reasons, from lack of justiciability to lack of a willing plaintiff with standing). If parliament has not seriously considered whether its actions fall within constitutional limits, the rule of law is at risk of being undermined. In Australia, this aspect of parliament's role has not attracted significant academic attention to date.[5]

Constitutionality is not, of course, the only matter parliament should consider when deliberating about proposed legislation. As democratic institutions, parliaments are responsible to the electorate and thus have a strong imperative to pass legislation that responds to the desires, and serves the needs, of the community. We noted previously that constitutional uncertainty often arises when parliament is experimenting with novel legislative approaches to new social and economic conditions and expectations. If parliamentarians only passed legislation when certain it would withstand constitutional challenge, this would rule out many legislative options that might be preferred from a policy point of view. Additionally, challenges to the validity of laws that have been enacted at the edge of constitutional certainty can clarify and develop constitutional principles.[6]

Therefore, we do *not* argue that parliament has an obligation to avoid potential constitutional invalidity of legislative reforms as an absolute or overriding obligation. But nor do we argue that constitutionality is irrelevant. Instead, we argue that when the constitutional position is uncertain, constitutionality should be one of several factors parliamentarians weigh up as part of a holistic deliberative process about

---

4   See, for example, the oath and affirmation for Commonwealth parliamentarians in the Schedule to the Australian Constitution.

5   The exceptions being Daryl Williams, 'The Australian Parliament and the High Court: Determination of Constitutional Questions' in Charles Sampford and Kim Preston (eds), *Interpreting Constitutions: Theories, Principles and Institutions* (Federation Press, 1996) 203; Andrew Lynch and Tessa Meyrick, 'The Constitution and Legislative Responsibility' (2007) 18 *Public Law Review* 153; Gabrielle Appleby and Adam Webster, 'Parliament's Role in Constitutional Interpretation' (2013) 37 *Melbourne University Law Review* 255.

6   Examples of constitutional challenges advancing our understanding of constitutional principles include *Commonwealth v Tasmania* ('*Tasmanian Dam Case*') (1983) 158 CLR 1); *Momcilovic v The Queen* (2011) 245 CLR 1; *Commonwealth v ACT* (2013) 250 CLR 441; and *New South Wales v Commonwealth* ('*Work Choices Case*') (2006) 229 CLR 1.

the merits and risks of the proposal. We emphasise that this applies where there is uncertainty, and ought not to apply where there is consensus among constitutional experts that the proposal is constitutionally invalid.[7] Parliamentarians should evaluate the risk of constitutional invalidity: how certain is the relevant body of constitutional law? How close to the line does the proposed law fall? What will be the consequences if the law is passed and later held invalid? For example, will individuals have suffered non-reversible infringements of their rights? Will significant public expense be incurred in the constitutional challenge? Against this risk, parliamentarians should weigh the importance of the policy objective being pursued. Some policies may be so crucial they can justify a high degree of constitutional risk. Parliamentarians should also examine how the design of a proposed law affects its constitutionality. Can the design be changed to reduce the constitutional risk? If so, will this compromise the policy goal? An important part of the constitutional deliberation will be the consideration and weighing of alternatives by reference to constitutional rules and principles.

Undoubtedly the Executive has its own constitutional obligations to engage with constitutional limits in the development of law reform proposals. But this does not relieve parliament of its obligation. In our conception of parliament's proper role in constitutional interpretation, parliament's contribution is different from that of the Executive. Different parties, and different members of parliament, will have different views about the importance of a given policy goal and the merits of specific legislative design features. Different individuals will be more or less risk averse and may take different views about the constitutional position. In a democracy, it is appropriate that these differences form part of the process of deliberating about proposed legislation. Further, public legislative debate about the constitutionality of proposed legislative action, and a rigorous and detailed consideration of alternative legislative design that might diminish constitutional issues, may prove helpful in subsequent judicial review of the enactment. This is particularly likely when the relevant constitutional principles turn on proportionality-style analyses, in which the availability of viable alternative policy measures is relevant to validity.[8]

---

7 See further discussion in Appleby and Webster, above n 5, 292–94.

8 *McCloy v New South Wales* (2015) 89 ALJR 857; *Betfair Pty Ltd v WA* (2008) 234 CLR 418.

III. Current Practice[9]

When Australian parliamentarians consider the constitutionality of proposed legislation, the debate tends to assume a superficial and binary character. Nuanced weighing of constitutional risk and careful consideration of how legislative design plays into that risk are almost entirely absent. This is at least in part attributable to the lack of constitutional assistance, in the form of professional legal advice, available to parliamentarians, particularly non-government members and backbenchers.

While sometimes acknowledging uncertainty about constitutional limits, government members assure parliament the law is likely to be valid. These assurances will often be provided by reference to legal advice obtained by the government – often by the government's most senior legal adviser, the Solicitor-General – but this advice will not be released to parliament. When parliamentarians simply rely upon the government's assurances that it has received advice relating to constitutional validity, they have insufficient information to engage with the questions that we have asserted are part of robust, responsible constitutional scrutiny. They are unable to gauge the level of risk associated with a proposal, or consider the constitutional risk associated with alternative ways of achieving the policy objective. Nor are the reasons for taking the constitutional risk made public.

Non-government members of parliament will often raise the risk of invalidity, not as a genuine issue that relates to their constitutional responsibilities, but as a reflexively oppositional political manoeuvre. Without a clear conception of parliament's responsibilities to the Constitution and appropriate processes and mechanisms in place to achieve these, the risk is that parliamentarians will employ the Constitution for reasons that have little to do with either constitutional or democratic responsibility. By reference to the 2012 attempt to amend the *Marriage Act 1961* (Cth) to achieve marriage equality and the debates this raised around the scope of the Commonwealth's marriage power, Gabrielle Appleby and Adam Webster identified two fundamental concerns in this respect.[10] The first was that constitutional uncertainty might be

---

9   As there is not scope in this chapter for a detailed explanation of current parliamentary practice around constitutional engagement in the legislative process, we have instead outlined our conclusions from our previous research using case studies of parliamentary deliberation at both state and Commonwealth level. See Appleby and Webster, above n 5.

10   Ibid.

used as a 'shield': parliamentarians not wishing to engage with divisive policy issues that raise difficult moral questions might simply avoid such a political quagmire by claiming constitutional uncertainty as a reason not to act. The second was that constitutional uncertainty might be used as a 'sword' to kill off the proposed reform: parliamentarians might claim that, because of the constitutional uncertainty, parliament should not act but rather the reform should be passed as a constitutional amendment by referendum under s 128 of the Constitution. The difficulties of achieving constitutional change under s 128 are well known. An argument that a reform ought to be sent to referendum is less likely to be an authentic appeal to popular sovereignty than an attempt to ensure the reform's ultimate failure. As both a 'sword' and a 'shield', constitutionality can detract from the quality of the debate about the policy merits of proposed legislation.

The cost of failure to engage in robust constitutional scrutiny is not only the loss of an opportunity for parliament to fulfil its constitutional and democratic obligations as a forum for debate about public policy. It may also lead to the adoption of less-than-optimal policy choices. When non-government parliamentarians become aware of a constitutional issue but lack the expertise or advice to assess the risk, they may urge the parliament to take a constitutionally 'conservative' approach. They are unable to engage with more sophisticated questions such as level of constitutional risk, and possible alternatives that might achieve the same objective. It becomes politically prudent for the government to take a constitutionally safe course. This can mean eschewing options that would better achieve the policy goal, and that *may* be valid, but are less constitutionally certain.[11] Mark Tushnet describes this inappropriate domination of constitutional norms over policy considerations as 'policy distortion'.[12]

Constitutional validity, and the desire to simply implement what are known to be valid constitutional regimes, might undermine the government and parliament's engagement with the policy merits of a proposal: whether it

---

11 Examples include the replication, by several states and territories, of anti-organised crime legislation known to be valid but arguably not best policy: see Gabrielle Appleby, 'The High Court and *Kable*: A Study in Federalism and Rights Protection' (2014) 40 *Monash University Law Review* 673; and amendments made shortly before the passage of the *Australian Citizenship Amendment (Allegiance to Australia) Act 2015* (Cth) (see Commonwealth *Parliamentary Debates*, Senate, 1 December 2015, 9508).

12 Mark Tushnet, 'Policy Distortion and Democratic Debilitation: Comparative Illumination of the Countermajoritarian Difficulty' (1995) 94 *Michigan Law Review* 245.

is responsive and tailored to the needs of the community, whether it is proportionate, whether human rights concerns are addressed, and whether it is likely to be effective.

IV. Two Proposed Reforms

At present, Australian parliamentarians may gain assistance from a number of sources of advice on questions of constitutional validity. But in no Australian jurisdiction is there a dedicated constitutional legal adviser available for parliamentarians or parliamentary committees to access.

Parliamentarians most frequently rely upon the assurances or summaries provided by the government regarding its constitutional advice, often received from the Solicitor-General; and the submissions of constitutional experts to parliamentary committee inquiries. In this part, we identify shortcomings of these sources and propose two reforms to address them.

There is now an established practice that the government will release a summary or assurance about legal advice it has received, but not disclose the full advice. The practice rests not on assertions of legal professional privilege – which is not a valid ground on which to refuse to produce documents to the parliament following *Egan v Chadwick*[13] – but on practice and convention.[14] Pursuant to now established convention, parliament refrains from exercising its powers to require the production of government legal opinions on the basis that there is a strong public interest in maintaining the confidentiality of government legal advice.

It is our view that the adherence to the convention has gone too far, at least insofar as it applies to advice relating to legislative proposals in areas of constitutional uncertainty. In these situations, the government is asking the parliament to be complicit in an action that raises constitutional risk. We argue that, where the proposal raises unresolved and complex constitutional questions, the public interest in disclosing government legal advice on constitutional validity to the parliament outweighs the public interest in maintaining confidentiality in the legal advice. Full disclosure of advice on constitutional risk would allow parliamentarians

---

13   *Egan v Chadwick* (1999) 46 NSWLR 563.
14   See further discussion of the convention in Australia in Anthony Mason, 'The Parliament, the Executive and the Solicitor-General' in Gabrielle Appleby, Patrick Keyzer and John Williams (eds), *Public Sentinels: A Comparative Study of Australian Solicitors-General* (Ashgate, 2014) 49, 65.

to assess the factual assumptions that underpin the advice and understand the subtleties and nuance of the advice and any qualifications contained in it, or degrees of confidence in which it is expressed.[15] This would facilitate (although of course not guarantee) deliberation of the type that we have argued parliamentarians ought to engage in as responsible constitutional actors. Of course, full public disclosure of this advice might be limited sometimes by legitimate public interest claims over certain parts of the advice – for example, parts that might raise national security issues or matters of Cabinet confidentiality. There might also be legitimate reasons that the government wishes to maintain legal professional privilege over the advice, and, as such, arrangements might need to be made to ensure that the release to parliamentarians is done in such a way as to not waive this privilege.

The second source of constitutional advice frequently relied upon by parliamentarians is submissions and evidence from experts – academics, professional legal associations and legal practitioners. Such submissions and evidence will often give rise to a range of different opinions on the same issue. This we actually see as desirable: it gives parliamentarians a sense of the complexity and nuance of particular constitutional issues. It reflects the reality that there is often no easy or single resolution to most constitutional questions.

However, there are a number of shortcomings with parliamentary reliance on such submissions. The first is that the number, spread and quality of submissions will differ depending on who has time, inclination and expertise to make a submission to a committee inquiry. Second, while submissions are often of extremely high quality written by the foremost experts in the field, they are not a direct substitute for legal advice. They are often prepared under extraordinary time pressures. They will often lack the inside factual knowledge that a full legal consideration of the issue requires. The author of the submission, rather than the parliament, will determine which issues to address.

---

15   See similar arguments in Harold Koh, 'Protecting the Office of Legal Counsel from Itself' (1994) 15 *Cardozo Law Review* 513, 51.

We therefore suggest a second reform: the appointment of a dedicated office of 'Counsel to the Parliament', specialising in constitutional and public law, to advise individual parliamentarians and parliamentary committees. The appointee should be a leading constitutional lawyer, with expertise comparable to that of the Solicitor-General.

What is the relationship between the two reform proposals? Is it preferable to implement one or the other, or both? To facilitate and properly equip parliamentarians to engage in best possible practice in relation to legislative deliberation regarding constitutional norms, both reforms ought to be adopted. (Although, we should add, the adoption of only one or the other would still be preferable to the current position.) The government's legal advice is likely to be informed by a more complete factual picture than that which might be provided by Counsel to the Parliament, simply because of the wider factual matrix likely to be available to the government and their advisers. There is also a possibility that the two officers will come to different positions on the constitutional questions, will assess the degree of constitutional risk at different levels, or will formulate and analyse different alternative proposals that might address the identified constitutional risks. Such differences would inform and assist parliamentary deliberation about the questions that we have argued are relevant for responsible constitutional engagement. Finally, we would say it is important that parliament has available to it dedicated constitutional counsel with whom it has a professional lawyer–client relationship because this allows parliamentarians to direct the advice received: to consider, for example, specific provisions or possible alternative formulations to the proposed provisions and do relative constitutional risk assessments.

37

The Parliamentary Joint Committee on Intelligence and Security: A Point of Increasing Influence in Australian Counter-Terrorism Law Reform?

Dominique Dalla-Pozza[1]

I. Introduction

On 12 November 2015, the House of Representatives debated the Australian Citizenship Amendment (Allegiance to Australia) Bill 2015 (Cth). The signature reforms in the Bill (enacted into law that December) are mechanisms for dual citizens to have their citizenship cease if they are involved with terrorist activity.[2] The debate was the first to take place after the Parliamentary Joint Committee on Intelligence and Security

1   Lecturer in Law, The Australian National University. I acknowledge Lachlan Forrester for his research assistance, and The Australian National University College of Law for financial assistance supporting this research.
2   Supplementary Explanatory Memorandum, Australian Citizenship Amendment (Allegiance to Australia) Bill 2015 (Cth), 2–3.

(PJCIS) had handed down its report scrutinising the Bill,[3] and after the government had issued its response to the report.[4] During the debate, Labor MP Michael Danby observed:

> The evolution of this legislation … shows the value of the committee system and *the increasing influence* of the PJCIS … Committees might be seen as too slow for the 24/7 news cycle and the Twitterati, but the result is a pragmatic solution that is best for the Australian people … and it shows that we parliamentarians are doing our job.[5]

In this chapter I examine the claim that PJCIS is wielding 'increasing influence' in the counter-terrorism law reform process. Analysing this claim is relevant to those interested in reform of Australia's counter-terrorism law framework. If we can identify a particular point in the law-making process which is influential, then those interested in shaping the Australian counter-terrorism law framework can focus their efforts on it.

I summarise the extent of PJCIS involvement in 'pre-enactment scrutiny' of the alterations to the Australian counter-terrorism law framework that the Australian Parliament has passed since mid-2014. In this context, pre-enactment scrutiny refers to the processes by which a parliamentary committee examines a Bill before it is enacted into law by the whole parliament. The pre-enactment scrutiny inquiries I am interested in are those where a committee takes evidence from the public (through written submissions or hearings).

I also examine the extent to which the government has accepted recommendations made by the PJCIS. I accept that the question of *how* to assess the influence of parliamentary committees is evolving.[6] Nevertheless, the evidence of the past two years suggests that the PJCIS is capable of making recommendations that require the government to

3   PJCIS, 'Committee Recommends Passage of the Citizenship Bill' (Media Alert, 4 September 2015), www.aph.gov.au/DocumentStore.ashx?id=a178407a-96fd-4400-9781-ecafc142443f.

4   Peter Dutton, Minister for Immigration and George Brandis, Attorney-General, 'Government Responds to Report on the Australian Citizenship Amendment (Allegiance to Australia) Bill 2015' (Joint Media Release, 10 November 2015), www.minister.border.gov.au/peterdutton/2015/Pages/response-citizenship-amendment-bill.aspx.

5   Commonwealth, *Parliamentary Debates*, House of Representatives, 12 November 2015, 13119 (emphasis added).

6   David Monk, 'A Framework for Evaluating the Performance of Committees in Westminster Parliaments' (2010) 16 *Journal of Legislative Studies* 1, 2–5.

adjust the law reform proposals they have put to parliament.[7] Together, these points suggest that the PJCIS now represents a key locus where changes to a counter-terrorism legislative proposal could be advocated and might actually occur.

II. The Extent of PJCIS Pre-enactment Scrutiny of Counter-Terrorism Law Proposals

The PJCIS is the latest parliamentary committee to have oversight over ASIO.[8] The committee was 're-established' in its current form at the end of 2005. The *Intelligence Service Act 2001* (Cth) stipulates that the PJCIS is to consist of six members of the House of Representatives and five Senators.[9] The Act also requires that a 'majority of the Committee's members must be Government members'.[10] The committee has indicated that a 'significant portion of the committee's time during 2014–15 was focussed on examining national security legislation introduced by the Government'.[11]

The PJCIS has conducted pre-enactment scrutiny on six of the major pieces of counter-terrorism legislation introduced between 2014 and 2016.[12] At the time of writing, five of the six pieces of legislation have been enacted. Each inquiry was initiated by the Attorney-General referring the relevant Bill to the PJCIS.[13] This indicates that the government accepted that this form of parliamentary scrutiny was to be part of the law-reform process. It is important to remember that this type of parliamentary scrutiny is

---

7   David Monk, 'Committee Inquiries in the Australian Parliament and Their Influence on Government: Government Acceptance of Recommendations as a Measure of Parliamentary Performance' (2012) 18 *The Journal of Legislative Studies* 143–44.

8   Parliament of Australia, *History of the Intelligence and Security Committee*, www.aph.gov.au/ Parliamentary_Business/Committees/Joint/Intelligence_and_Security/History_of_the_Intelligence_ and_Security_Committee.

9   *Intelligence Services Act 2001* (Cth) s 28(2).

10   *Intelligence Services Act 2001* (Cth) s 28(3).

11   Parliamentary Joint Committee on Intelligence and Security, Parliament of Australia, *Annual Report of Committee Activities 2014–15* (2015) 2.

12   These acts are the *National Security Legislation Amendment Act (No 1) 2014* (Cth); the *Counter-Terrorism Legislation Amendment (Foreign Fighters) Act 2014* (Cth); the *Counter-Terrorism Legislation Amendment Act (No 1) 2014* (Cth); the *Telecommunications (Interception and Access) Amendment (Data Retention) Act 2015* (Cth) (the 'Data Retention Act'); the *Australian Citizenship Amendment (Allegiance to Australia) Act 2015* (Cth); and the Counter-Terrorism Legislation Amendment Bill (No 1) 2015 (Cth).

13   *Annual Report*, above n 11, 5–8 and PJCIS, Parliament of Australia, *Advisory Report on the Counter-Terrorism Legislation Amendment Bill (No 1) 2015* (2016) 1.

not a compulsory feature of the law reform process.[14] The involvement of these types of committees is important, because they provide one structured opportunity for the public, and non-government experts, to provide their opinions about Bills directly to parliamentarians.[15] It also affords parliamentarians the ability to question the departments and agencies which designed the legislation, and that would be responsible for implementing it.[16]

Acknowledging that the government allowed the PJCIS to scrutinise the Bills does not mean that the committee scrutiny process was perfect. One flaw Appleby identifies is that the PJCIS was sometimes required to complete its pre-enactment scrutiny work on a very strict timeframe.[17] On one occasion, the committee pointedly noted that 'it would have been preferable if more time had been available for the inquiry'.[18] I concur that the time constraints placed on committee review were problematic. They made it more difficult for the committee 'to comprehend, question, test [the legislation and] to seek public and expert opinion'[19] to assist them in providing as comprehensive review of the Bills as possible. However, not all of the inquiries of the PJCIS over this period were conducted so quickly. For example, the PJCIS inquiry into the *Data Retention Act 2015* was allowed just under two months to take submissions (albeit over the summer holiday period of December to January). The overall time provided to the committee to complete its report was just over three months.[20]

---

14   The functions of the PJCIS do not *mandate* the type of pre-enactment Bill scrutiny conducted in this period. See *Annual Report*, above n 11, 19–21.

15   Dominique Dalla-Pozza, 'Promoting Deliberative Debate? The Submissions and Oral Evidence Provided to Australian Parliamentary Committees in the Creation of Counter-Terrorism Laws' (2008) 23 *Australasian Parliamentary Review* 39, 56. See also Richard Grant, 'Can We Account for Parliamentary Committees? A Survey of Committee Secretaries' (Parliamentary Studies Paper No 9, Parliamentary Studies Centre, 2009) 6, 8.

16   PJCIS, Parliament of Australia, *Advisory Report on the Counter-Terrorism Legislation Amendment Bill (No 1) 2014* (2014), 11, 13: the Committee recorded evidence received from the Australian Federal Police and the Attorney-General's Department about the proposed changes in that Bill.

17   Gabrielle Appleby, 'The 2014 Counter-Terrorism Reforms in Review' (2015) *Public Law Review* 4, 4–7.

18   PJCIS, Parliament of Australia, *Advisory Report on the Counter-Terrorism Legislation Amendment (Foreign Fighters) Bill 2014* (2014) 3.

19   Appleby, above n 17, 4.

20   See PJCIS, *Advisory Report into the Telecommunications (Interception and Access) Amendment (Data Retention) Bill 2014* (2015), 2, 4.

Despite these problems, the fact remains that the PJCIS was the parliamentary committee most often charged with holding public inquiries examining proposed changes to Australian counter-terrorism law during this period. During 2014–16, only one of the six major counter-terrorism Bills was also referred to a Senate Legislation or References Committee for a separate pre-enactment scrutiny inquiry.[21] That Bill, the Counter-Terrorism Legislation Amendment (Foreign Fighters) Bill, was referred to the Senate Legal and Constitutional Affairs Legislation Committee (SLCALC). However, the SLCALC declined to accept submissions or to call witnesses because the PJCIS was already conducting an inquiry into the Bill.[22] There are two ways to interpret this. The first is to be concerned about the exclusion of the Senate Committee. The decision of the SLCALC not to hold a public inquiry angered some members of the cross-bench because it meant that they were unable to be members of any committee conducting full pre-enactment scrutiny.[23] This is because all members of the PJCIS were members of the major parties.[24] Nevertheless, the SLCALC's deference to the PJCIS can also be interpreted as another indicium of the growing pre-eminence of the PJCIS in the sphere of counter-terrorism law reform. If these trends continue, the PJCIS will be the committee most likely to examine any future substantial proposals for change to the Australian counter-terrorism law framework.

III. Recommendations and 'Strike Rate'

Another key piece of information pointing to the PJCIS playing a crucial role in the Australian counter-terrorism law reform process is the extent to which the government accepted its recommendations. In discussing its pre-enactment scrutiny during the 2014–15 financial year, the committee commented that '[a]cross the four Bills reviewed during the reporting period, the committee made 109 recommendations. *All of these recommendations were accepted* and resulted in 63 amendments to the Bills before the Parliament'.[25]

---

21 Although in their report into the *Data Retention Act* the PJCIS acknowledged that the Senate Legal and Constitutional References Committee was examining broader issues relating to altering the *Telecommunications (Interception and Access) Act 1979* (Cth) as a whole. See 'Advisory Report into the Data Retention Bill', above n 20, 3.
22 Senate Legal and Constitutional Affairs Legislation Committee, Parliament of Australia, *Counter-Terrorism Legislation Amendment (Foreign Fighters) Bill 2014* (2014) 1.
23 For the views of the Australian Greens, see ibid. 6. See also Appleby, above n 17, 5–6 and 10.
24 *Foreign Fighters Bill 2014*, above n 22, 6.
25 *Annual Report*, above n 11, 3 (emphasis added).

Some political scientists refer to this way of assessing influence as assessing a committee's 'strike rate'. The term 'strike rate' means 'the percentage of … [committee] recommendations accepted and implemented by government'.[26] Law reform scholars may be more interested in the extent to which committee recommendations result in concrete amendments to legislation as an indicium of committee influence. By either version of this measure, at least by its own account, the PJCIS has been remarkably influential.

Examining a 2014 PJCIS report on the Counter-Terrorism Legislation Amendment Bill (No 1) 2014 ('2014 CTLA Bill') provides an example of a recommendation from the PJCIS being the acknowledged catalyst for an alteration to the government's proposed amendments to Australia's counter-terrorism laws. The 2014 CTLA Bill proposed amendments to provisions governing when the Australian Federal Police (AFP) can request control orders. Prior to the enactment of the 2014 CTLA Bill, the control order provisions allowed an 'issuing court' to impose an order allowing certain 'conditions' to be placed on 'a person' for the purpose of 'protecting the public from a terrorist act'.[27] The AFP are responsible for applying to the issuing court for the order, but in most cases need to obtain the consent of the Attorney-General before doing so.[28] The conditions that a control order can impose include preventing a person subject to the order from communicating with certain persons, or mandating that they 'wear a tracking device'.[29]

One proposed change in the 2014 CTLA Bill concerned the mechanism by which the AFP could apply for an 'urgent interim control order'. Prior to the late 2014 reforms, a senior AFP officer could apply directly to the issuing court for such an order in certain circumstances. However, the consent of the Attorney-General to the making of the application needed to be granted retrospectively – within four hours of the application being made.[30] The 2014 CTLA Bill proposed to lengthen the amount of time the AFP had to obtain the Attorney-General's consent from four hours to twelve. The PJCIS noted that 'some inquiry participants' did not feel that

---

26   John Halligan, Robin Miller and John Power, *Parliament in the Twenty-First Century* (Melbourne University Press, 2007) 222.

27   *Advisory Report on the Counter-Terrorism Legislation Amendment Bill (No 1) 2014*, above n 16, 6.

28   Ibid. See also *Criminal Code Act 1995* (Cth) s 104.2 (1).

29   *Advisory Report on the Counter-Terrorism Legislation Amendment Bill (No 1) 2014*, above n 16, 6. See also *Criminal Code Act 1995* (Cth) 104.5(3)

30   *Advisory Report on the Counter-Terrorism Legislation Amendment Bill (No 1) 2014*, above n 16, 17.

the 'increase in time' had been 'adequately justified'.[31] The PJCIS agreed, and recommended that the AFP be required to obtain consent within eight hours of the AFP applying for the urgent order. The government accepted this recommendation, and the legislation as enacted reflects it.[32] Indeed, in its response the government mentioned that this change 'reflects the view of the Committee and some witnesses, that 8 hours is sufficient'.[33] The impression that the PJCIS's recommendations are persuasive is bolstered by the fact that the government publicly attributed the making of this amendment specifically to the committee's work.[34]

However, when compared to the overall control order scheme, this change is relatively minor. In its report into the 2014 CTLA Bill the PJCIS noted that 'several submitters' had 'in-principle objections to the existence of control orders'.[35] The committee also noted in passing that another oversight body – the Independent National Security Legislation Monitor – had recommended that the control order powers be completely repealed.[36] Ultimately, the PJCIS concluded that it accepted the justification offered by the AFP that the control order powers were necessary.[37] As such, it did not recommend the complete removal of control orders from Australian law. So at least part of the PJCIS's high success rate may be explained if the recommendations made did not require major changes to the shape and scope of the counter-terrorism law framework. Political scientists who have studied other parliamentary committees have recorded the view of one committee secretary that, to ensure their recommendations are influential, committees can avoid making 'courageous' recommendations.[38] At present, it is unclear how far-reaching the totality of the recommendations made by the PJCIS were. This is an area which would benefit from further academic work.

---

31 Ibid.
32 George Brandis, Attorney-General, 'Government Response to the Committee Report on the Counter-Terrorism Legislation Amendment Bill (No 1) 2014' (Media Release, 25 November 2014) 3, www.attorneygeneral.gov.au/Mediareleases/Documents/GovernmentResponseToCommitteeReportO nTheCounter-TerrorismLegislationAmendmentBillNo1-2014.pdf. See *Criminal Code Act 1995* (Cth) s 104.10.
33 Brandis, above n 32, 3.
34 Monk, 'Evaluating the Performance of Committees', above n 6, 8.
35 *Advisory Report on the Counter-Terrorism Legislation Amendment Bill (No 1) 2014*, above n 16, 9.
36 Ibid. 11.
37 Ibid. 21–22.
38 Halligan, Miller and Power, above n 26, 222–23.

There are two further complications to consider when using committee recommendations to assess the extent of the PJCIS's influence on law reform. The first is the division amongst political scientists about whether using government responses to parliamentary committees is actually a useful way of assessing committee influence.[39] Some argue it is too difficult to accurately quantify the impact of parliamentary committees in isolation, as the process by which policy is formulated contains 'too many players and interactions'.[40] Others think that, while imperfect, the government response 'is the closest approximation ... available' of what the government thinks of a report.[41]

The second caveat concerns the PJCIS's blanket statement that 'all the recommendations were accepted'. Closer examination of the legislative history of the 2014 CTLA Bill demonstrates that not all 'acceptances' are complete. One proposed change in that Bill was to expand the grounds on which a control order could be issued. The changes proposed to expand these grounds to include 'prevent[ing] the provision of support for or the facilitation of a terrorist act' and also the 'provision of support for or the facilitation of the engagement in a hostile activity in a foreign country'.[42] The PJCIS recommended 'that, to the extent possible, the terms "supports" and "facilitates" [in these changes] ... be based on language in the existing Criminal Code' and the Bill *and* explanatory memorandum be altered 'to reflect this'.[43] The PJCIS justified this by arguing the evidence it received 'raised concerns' that it was unclear what was meant by 'the provision of support for' or 'facilitation of a terrorist act'.[44] In response, the government noted that it accepted this recommendation 'in principle'. It agreed to amend the explanatory memorandum but did not propose to alter the Bill.[45]

It is still technically correct to call this an acceptance of the committee's recommendation, but it was not a *complete* acceptance of it.[46] A complete acceptance would have been for the Bill and the explanatory memorandum

---

39 See Monk, 'Government Acceptance', above n 7, 138–39. See also Ian Holland, 'Senate Committees and the Legislative Process' (Parliamentary Studies Paper, No 7, Parliamentary Studies Centre, 2009) 5–6.
40 Halligan, Miller and Power, above n 26, 222.
41 Monk, 'Evaluating the Performance of Committees', above n 6, 8.
42 *Advisory Report on the Counter-Terrorism Legislation Amendment Bill (No 1) 2014*, above n 16, 7.
43 Ibid. 24 (Recommendation 2).
44 Ibid. 14, 24.
45 Brandis, above n 32, 2.
46 See also Monk, 'Government Acceptance', above n 7, 144–45.

to be amended. This suggests that the statement that 'all recommendations were accepted' needs to be carefully unpacked to examine the extent to which the legislation as eventually enacted actually reflects the PJCIS's recommendations.

IV. Conclusion

To return to the question which opened this chapter: is the PJCIS garnering 'increasing influence' in the area of Australian counter-terrorism law reform? On the basis of the study presented here, the answer would be a qualified yes. The fact that the PJCIS has considered the major counter-terrorism law proposals put before parliament over 2014–16 makes it clear this is now the 'committee of choice' to conduct pre-enactment scrutiny. Even if the committee was sometimes rushed, the government seems prepared to have PJCIS scrutiny become a routine element of its counter-terrorism law-making process. If this continues, it will allow the committee to continue to develop its experience and expertise in the issues underpinning counter-terrorism law reform.

The answer to the question is qualified because the recommendations made by the PJCIS are not always in fact translated into amendments which alter counter-terrorism Bills. While on the surface the PJCIS's strike rate seems impressive, the extent to which it reflects actual change to the law is a more complex question. Also worthy of further study is the extent to which the PJCIS recommendations go to the core of the way in which powers such as the control order regime operate. However, despite these qualifications, there are instances where the PJCIS's recommendations have caused changes to Australia's counter-terrorism laws.

That the PJCIS has been given an opportunity to scrutinise counter-terrorism Bills, and that the government seems open to their recommendations, should be recognised. The committee appears to be developing into a key point of influence for those seeking to make the case for law reform of Australia's counter-terrorism law framework. Accordingly, for those seeking change, participating in a future PJCIS inquiry into a counter-terrorism law issue seems a promising place to begin.

38

Rights Dialogue under the Victorian Charter: The Potential and the Pitfalls

Julie Debeljak[1]

I. Introduction

The *Charter of Human Rights and Responsibilities Act 2006* (Vic) was intended to create an inter-institutional dialogue about rights. This chapter outlines the *Charter*'s dialogue mechanisms, and assesses the dialogue in practice. The assessment focuses on examples of institutional dialogue that have involved judicial decisions about rights or with rights implications, and executive and parliamentary reactions thereto. This chapter concludes with reform suggestions for the *Charter*, which can inform debates across Australian jurisdictions.

Committed parliamentary sovereigntists may consider that the *Charter* is operating precisely as intended: bringing rights issues to the fore, and providing a framework for debate, but not substantively hampering the sovereign will of parliament. Those committed to human rights, however, may consider the dialogue in practice demonstrates the need for reform. In decision-making that impacts on rights, the executive retains its dominance: it controls the 'pre-tabling-in-parliament' phase of legislative

---

1   Associate Professor and Deputy Director of the Castan Centre for Human Rights Law, Faculty of Law, Monash University.

development; shapes the rights discussion via extrinsic materials accompanying proposed legislation; and dominates parliament itself. Contributions by members of parliament to rights dialogue on the floor of parliament and through its committees are weak, with little incentive for stronger action. Parliamentary rights culture is nascent at best, and there is no political or legal cost for disregarding rights. The judiciary has the limited power of interpreting laws to be compatible with rights, which leaves the executive and parliament free reign in their responses. Reforms must focus on these elements.

II. Dialogue Mechanisms

There are numerous dialogue mechanisms under the *Charter*. First, the scope of rights, and the legitimacy of limiting rights, are open to debate and reasonable disagreement. The *Charter* recognises this through open-textured rights, and by allowing the imposition of reasonable and demonstrably justifiable limitations on rights under s 7(2) – both of which encourage rights dialogue among the executive, parliament and judiciary.

Second, *Charter* mechanisms regarding the creation and interpretation of legislation are meant to generate dialogue. Under s 28, parliamentarians must issue Statements of Compatibility (SoC) for all proposed laws, which indicate (with reasons) whether proposed laws are rights-compatible or rights-incompatible. Under s 30, the Scrutiny of Acts and Regulations Committee (SARC) must scrutinise all proposed laws and accompanying SoCs against *Charter* rights. SARC reports to parliament, and parliament debates the proposals, deciding whether to enact proposed laws given the rights considerations.

These pre-legislative scrutiny obligations make rights explicit considerations in law-making, creating greater transparency around, and accountability for, decisions that impact on rights. The obligations also create a dialogue between arms of government, allowing each to educate the other about their understanding of relevant rights, whether legislation limits those rights, and whether limits are justified under s 7(2).

Regarding the judiciary, s 32(1) of the *Charter* requires all legislation to be interpreted in a way that is compatible with rights, so far as it is possible to do so consistently with statutory purpose. Where legislation cannot be interpreted rights-compatibly, the judiciary is not empowered to invalidate it; rather, the superior courts may issue an unenforceable 'declaration of inconsistent interpretation' under s 36(2). Under s 37, the responsible minister must table a written response to s 36(2) declarations in parliament within six-months.

The executive and parliament can respond to judicial rulings. They may neutralise an unwanted s 32(1) rights-*compatible* interpretation by legislatively reinstating rights-*incompatible* provisions. They may amend legislation to address rights-*incompatibility* identified in s 36(2) declarations; equally, they may retain the rights-*incompatible* legislation. The dialogue process continues, with executive and parliamentary responses being open to further challenge before the judiciary.

To assess these dialogue mechanisms in practice, Part III considers examples of executive and parliamentary responses to judicial decisions about rights; while Part IV considers examples where judicial decisions *did not* turn on rights, but nevertheless provoked executive and parliamentary responses that *did* impact on rights.

III. Complete Dialogue Cycles

A 'complete dialogue cycle' occurs when each arm of government has contributed to the rights dialogue; particularly, when the executive and parliament respond to judicial decisions about rights. This Part explores two examples where judicial decisions turning on rights have prompted executive and parliamentary responses that have been rights-*unfriendly*.[2]

A. Decisions and responses

First, under the *Serious Sex Offenders Monitoring Act 2005* (Vic), a court may make an extended supervision order in relation to serious sex offenders 'if it is satisfied … that the offender is likely to commit a relevant offence if released in the community on completion of' a custodial sentence. In *RJE*,[3] the court held that the phrase 'is likely to commit a relevant

---

2   See *Taha v Broadmeadows Magistrates' Court* [2011] VSC 642, where the representative response bolsters rights: s 51 of *Sentencing Amendment (Abolition of Suspended Sentences and Other Matters) Act 2013* (Vic).

3   *RJE v Secretary to the Department of Justice* [2008] VSCA 265 ('*RJE*').

offence' had to mean 'more likely than not to commit' an offence,[4] with Maxwell P and Weinberg JA relying on the common law right to liberty, and Nettle JA relying on the s 21 right to liberty and s 32(1) rights-compatible interpretation under the *Charter*.

At the next sitting, parliament responded by overturning the rights-compatible interpretation in *RJE*. The *Serious Sex Offenders Monitoring Amendment Act 2009* (Vic) (*SSOMAA*) inserts s 11(2B), which states that s 11(1) 'permits a determination that an offender is likely to commit a relevant offence on the basis of a lower threshold than a threshold of more likely than not'.

Second, the *Major Crime (Investigative Powers) Act 2004* confers coercive powers for investigating organised crime. Section 39(1) abrogates the privilege against self-incrimination, but s 39(3) provides a residual immunity. In *Das*,[5] according to ordinary interpretation, Warren CJ held that s 39(3) only preserved 'direct use' immunity, which unreasonably and unjustifiably limited *Charter* rights. This was remedied by s 32 rights-compatible interpretation: Warren CJ 'read in' words to s 39(3) additionally preserving 'derivative use' immunity.

Parliament reversed this ruling in the *Criminal Organisations Control and Other Acts Amendments Act 2014* (Vic) (*COCOAAA*). The legislation inserted s 39(4), which provides that nothing in s 39(3) prevents the derivate use of evidence.

B. Executive and parliamentary scrutiny

The rights-scrutiny in the executive's SoC was similar in *RJE-SSOMAA* and *Das-COCOAAA*. In both instances, the minister admitted to reversing the judicial interpretation of legislation and reverting to the legislation's pre-*Charter* understanding. In both, this was justified as a reassertion of the intention of the original parliament when it enacted the original law. Additional arguments about the reasonableness and justifiability of the limitation were also offered.

---

4   *RJE* [2008] VSCA 265 [21], [53] (Maxwell P and Weinberg JA); [97], [107], [113], [117], [119] (Nettle JA).

5   *Re Application under the Major Crime (Investigative Powers Act); Das v Victorian Equal Opportunity and Human Rights Commission 2004* [2009] VSC 381 ('*Das*').

SARC reported on *RJE-SSOMAA* after the amendments passed both houses of parliament. The report criticised the SoC for not explaining how the legislation was rights-compatible. The SARC report on *Das-COCOAAA* highlighted how the SoC limitations analysis differed from the judicial analysis, but acknowledged that parliament was empowered to enact rights-incompatible legislation.

The parliamentary debate on *RJE-SSOMAA* was brief. Parliamentarians acknowledged the legislative reversal of the judicial interpretation, and the gravity of this. Although concern was expressed about the retrospective application of the amendment, debate focused on balancing the rights of the offender against the rights of victims and the broader community; and on legislative safeguards for the offender. The rights aspects of the *Das-COCOAAA* amendments attracted little parliamentary attention – there was no debate about the s 39 amendment potentially violating rights, nor that a judicial ruling was being reversed. Ms Pulford described the amendments as 'minor';[6] while Ms Pennicuik took issue with other rights-related aspects of the legislation, but not the s 39 amendment.

C. Assessing the dialogue

In *RJE-SSOMAA* and *Das-COCOAAA*, dialogue occurred with the executive and parliament reasserting their views on the threshold for issuing extended supervision orders and 'derivative use' immunity. The representative arms utilised dialogue mechanisms. First, the reasonableness and justifiability of limitations were explored, and the rights of competing groups balanced, under s 7(2). Second, the amendment was couched as reasserting parliament's intention, which is an active factor in s 32(1) rights-compatible interpretation.

In *RJE-SSOMAA*, parliament completed debate before SARC reported. Although not unlawful, this undermines the dialogue. That SARC identified issues that the parliamentarians had not considered highlights the importance of SARC reports.

In *Das-COCOAAA*, one interpretation of SARC's commentary on the differing rights analyses of the judiciary and executive is that the Attorney-General should have made a statement of *incompatibility*. This has conceptual implications. If the Attorney-General simply accepted the

---

6   Victoria, *Parliamentary Debates*, Legislative Council, 19 August 2014, 2509 (Ms Pulford).

judiciary's view of the unjustifiability of the limit, this may be considered 'judge-proofing'/'*Charter*-proofing' legislation. '*Charter*-proofing' refers to the practice where the executive and parliament shape their policy and laws to fit judicial interpretations of rights to avoid adverse court rulings, and this more closely resembles a judicial monologue about rights.

However, tensions arise for democratic accountability if the judiciary and executive put forward competing rights analysis. Were the executive to simply assert an alternative narrative of rights, without acknowledging the competing judicial views and offering reasons for departing from those views, the improved rights-transparency in, and greater rights-accountability when, law-making that we hope to gain from dialogue is lost. Moreover, where there is a disagreement between the executive and the judiciary, and this is not acknowledged via a statement of incompatibility, parliament is not properly alerted to the disagreement, as occurred in *Das-COCOAAA*. In that case SARC, the Attorney-General and Ms Pennicuik engaged in rights-dialogue over other amendments, but missed the rights-implications for s 39 and the reversal of *Das*.

Finally, SARC's conclusions in *Das-COCOAAA* were tepid: that the amendments 'may be incompatible' and referral of the issue 'to Parliament for its consideration',[7] despite SARC's analysis suggesting incompatibility.

As examples of *dialogue*, the *Charter* allows the executive and parliament to disagree with the judiciary. As examples of *rights protection*, reasonable people will disagree; but regardless, the *Charter* elevates parliamentary sovereignty over rights protection.

IV. Executive–Parliament Reactions Impacting on Rights

Unlike the complete cycles, some judicial decisions that *did not* turn on *Charter* rights have nevertheless prompted amendments that *did* impact on *Charter* rights. These are explored in this Part.

---

7   SARC, *Alert Digest*, No 9 of 2014, 15.

A. Decisions and responses

In *DPP v Leys*,[8] the court clarified the lawful combination of sentencing options involving community corrections orders, and corrected a drafting error concerning the commencement of interlinked provisions, under the *Sentencing Act 1991* (Vic). Parliament codified the judicial decision via amendments,[9] which were applied retrospectively to ensure that 500 offenders whose sentences may have otherwise been unlawful were deemed to be lawful. Although retrospective application itself is rights-limiting, this was preferred over the rights implications of prospective legislation: being 500 offenders having their rights to liberty, privacy and movement limited because of potentially unlawful sentences.

In *Director of Housing v TK*,[10] the Director issued a notice to vacate under s 250 of the *Residential Tenancies Act 1997* (Vic) *(RTA)* because 'the tenant ha[d] used the rented premises … for any purpose that is illegal'. The notice was *ultra vires* because in two instances the tenant's drug trafficking occurred in common areas (not the rented premises), and in another the tenant's drug trafficking occurred at the front door which was insufficient to establish 'use' of the rented premises. Amendments to the *RTA* ensured that drug trafficking on the rented premises or in a common area triggered the 'notice to vacate' power; expanded the power to cover prescribed indictable offences; and changed the trigger for vacation from a police charge to the Director's reasonable belief.[11] *XFJ* provides another example.[12]

B. Executive–parliamentary scrutiny and dialogue

These examples highlight the representative arms' willingness to respond to judicial decisions by enacting rights-limiting legislation. In discharging pre-legislative rights-scrutiny obligations, the representative arms recognised potential violations of rights in all examples, but reasoned away the violation, or justified the violation referring to the competing rights of others, public safety and the like.

---

8   *DPP v Leys* [2012] VSCA 304 ('*Leys*').
9   *Road Safety and Sentencing Act Amendment Act 2012* (Vic).
10   *Director of Housing v TK (Residential Tenancies)* [2010] VCAT 1839 ('*TK*').
11   *Residential Tenancies Amendment (Public Housing) Act 2011* (Vic).
12   *XFJ v Director of Public Transport* [2008] VCAT 2303 led to the *Transport Legislation Amendments (Driver and Industry Standards) Act 2008* (Vic).

In *Leys* and *XFJ*, SARC reported after the Bill passed both Houses. In *TK*, SARC directly compared the tribunal ruling with the amendments, challenging the rights-compatibility of the executive-led amendments, to no avail in parliament.

Parliamentary contributions were mixed. In *Leys*, debate was truncated, with the amendments enacted within 72 hours, and brief parliamentary debate. Debate in *XFJ* was brief, with the competing rights of the public elevated over individual rights, and parliamentarians lamenting the non-retrospectivity of the amendments (i.e. lamenting the failure to further violate rights). By contrast, debate in *TK* was relatively sophisticated, with the right to housing considered, the competing rights of other tenants balanced, the impact of the reduced evidentiary burden explored, and legislative safeguards recognised.

V. Reforms

These examples demonstrate the need for reform across the dialogue process. During the 'pre-tabling-in-parliament' phase of policy and legislative design, although the executive accounts for rights, this is in secret and there is no guarantee of outside influence. This is problematic because once Cabinet gives 'in-principle' agreement to legislative proposals, it is difficult to secure amendments. If the window for real rights-influence ends at Cabinet, dialogue is nothing more than an executive monologue.

The eight-year *Charter* review recommends that SoCs be issued with exposure drafts.[13] This is an improvement, but the examples highlight that rights-impinging legislation is unlikely to be released in exposure draft and likely to be rushed through parliament. Reforms must include: (a) changes to the political culture surrounding amendments in parliament; and (b) an expansion of voices influencing the pre-Cabinet-approval phase of legislative development, with SARC and the Victorian Equal Opportunity and Human Rights Commission being consulted, in confidence, on draft legislation pre-Cabinet-approval.

---

13   Recommendation 41(b), Michael Brett Young, *From Commitment to Culture: The 2015 Review of the Charter of Human Rights and Responsibilities Act 2006* (Victorian Government Printer, Melbourne, 2015) 188.

SoCs consistently failed to explain 'how' a Bill was (in)compatible. Section 28 must be amended to require consideration of s 7(2) as part of compatibility assessments and evidence-based assessments. Section 28(3) could read: 'A statement of compatibility must state – (a) whether, in the member's opinion, the Bill is compatible with human rights and, if so, how it is compatible *by reference to s 7(2) providing evidence for the assessment*; and (b) if, in the member's opinion, any part of the Bill is incompatible with human rights, the nature and extent of the incompatibility *by reference to s 7(2) providing evidence for the assessment.*'

SARC needs strengthening. First, SARC has two weeks to report on *all* Bills introduced. SARC reports are often not available *before* Bills pass either the lower or both Houses. This mutes SARC's contribution to the dialogue. Parliamentarians have suggested that SARC be convened ad hoc whenever 'urgent Bills' are presented to parliament.[14] In addition, the *Charter* should be amended to prevent a Bill becoming a valid Act until SARC has reported, and parliament has 'properly considered' the report (see below).

Second, although rights-incompatible analysis and ministerial requests for clarification convey SARC's opinion, SARC's recommendations are mild. This may be consistent with the practice of scrutiny committees, but SARC's current practice 'has had little influence over the content of legislation once the Bill has been presented to Parliament'.[15] Were SARC privately consulted on proposed legislation before Cabinet approval, the executive might be induced to present more rights-compatible Bills. SARC's public reports could then be frank rights assessments with (stronger) conclusions (particularly where SARC's private concerns are not addressed).

Parliament must develop and nurture a rights culture, ensuring there is a political cost for not protecting rights and not convincingly justifying limitations on rights. Non-legal methods of cultural change include: (a) developing strong leadership supportive of a rights-respecting culture (top-down approach), and identifying non-senior parliamentarians to act

---

14   Victoria, *Parliamentary Debates*, Legislative Council, 16 August 2012, 3535 (Mr Pakula) and 3541 (Ms Pennicuik).
15   Above n 13, 177, citing the Chair of SARC, Carlo Carli MP.

as change agents among the parliamentary cohort (bottom-up approach);[16] (b) better education about the substance of rights and the proportionality analysis informing limitations to rights, and education about the process of rights-scrutiny and how it feeds into the inter-institutional dialogue; and (c) pressure from constituents.

Legal methods include imposing an obligation on parliament to 'give proper consideration' to SoCs and SARC reports, with a failure to give proper consideration precluding a Bill becoming an Act. In relation to SARC, s 30 should become s 30(1), with: subs (2) preventing parliament enacting laws prior to SARC reporting; subs (3) requiring parliament to give 'proper consideration' to SARC reports; and subs (4) stating 'a failure to comply with sub-sections 30(1), (2) and (3) prevents that bill becoming an act, and any purported act is not valid, has no operation and cannot be enforced'.

Parliament needs costs/consequences for rights-incompatibility, which presents a multifaceted problem. First, unlike the Canadian *Charter*, the Victorian *Charter* is not a constitutional instrument, so the judiciary cannot invalidate rights-incompatible legislation. The latter *Charter* is a statutory instrument similar to Britain's, but unlike Britain – which has a stronger parliamentary rights-culture – there is no oversight by a regional human rights court that issues binding decisions. The threat of constitutional invalidation (Canada) or enforceable regional decision-making (Britain) focuses the mind of parliamentarians.

Second, judicial decision-making under the *Charter* has been weak. Section 32 rights-compatible reinterpretation as a remedy has been undermined and the role of s 7(2) is uncertain;[17] judicial decisions on rights have been timid;[18] and some judges have questioned the dialogue

---

16   Bronwyn Naylor, Julie Debeljak and Anita Mackay, 'A Strategic Framework for Implementing Human Rights in Closed Environments: A Human Rights Regulatory Framework and its Implementation' (2015) 41 *Monash University Law Review* 218, 265–66.

17   Julie Debeljak, 'Who Is Sovereign Now? The *Momcilovic* Court Hands Back Power Over Human Rights That Parliament Intended It To Have' (2011) 22 *Public Law Review* 15–51; Julie Debeljak, 'Proportionality, Rights-Consistent Interpretation and Declarations under the Victorian *Charter of Human Rights and Responsibilities*: The *Momcilovic* Litigation and Beyond' (2014) 40 *Monash University Law Review* 340–88.

18   Julie Debeljak, 'The Rights of Prisoners under the Victorian *Charter*: A Critical Analysis of the Jurisprudence on the Treatment of Prisoners and Conditions of Detention' (2015) 38 *University of New South Wales Law Journal* 1332–85.

conception.[19] Recommendations to strengthen ss 32(1) and 7(2) in the eight-year *Charter* Review, if adopted, should improve the judicial – and thus parliamentary – engagement with rights.[20]

VI. Conclusion

The Victorian executive dominates the debate about rights, both in the pre-tabling and parliamentary phases of law-making. This dominance is not ameliorated by parliament or the judiciary, due to limitations under the *Charter* and cultural approaches to rights. The executive dominance of parliament, at least of the lower house, converts what would be an ideal, three-way 'rights-multilogue' into a two-way rights-dialogue between the executive and judiciary. (Indeed, the debate between constitutional and statutory instruments is better cast as one between judicial versus executive monopolisation of rights.) Without breaking the executive's dominance or adopting a constitutional instrument, an executive-dominated rights-*monologue*, coupled with parliamentary and judicial rights-*heckling*, is what remains.

---

19   *HCA Momcilovic* [2011] HCA 34, [95] (French CJ), [146] (Gummow J, Hayne J concurring), [533–534] (Crennan and Kiefel JJ).
20   Recommendations 28 and 29: above n 13, 137–55.

39

Court Records as Archives: The Need for Law Reform to Ensure Access

Andrew Henderson and Kim Rubenstein[1]

I. Introduction

Since its establishment in 1976, the Federal Court of Australia (the Federal Court) has served as a site for the disputation, negotiation and resolution of issues fundamentally important to Australian society. It does so in the context of Australia's constitutional system that adheres to the rule of law and open justice, in order to enforce the rights of individuals and navigate the boundaries of the powers of the state. As a 'superior court of record',[2] the court's collected case files constitute a permanent record of the proceedings before it.

---

1 Professor Rubenstein, ANU College of Law, is the lead CI on the ARC Discovery Project DP130101954 that this chapter draws upon. Andrew Henderson is a sessional staff member of The Australian National University College of Law and has been employed as a Research Assistant on this project. His co-authorship of this chapter is testament to his own significant contributions to the research output.

2 *Federal Court of Australia Act 1976* (Cth) s 5(2). Superior Courts of Record make decisions that are determinative, and their proceedings must be recorded. The High Court of Australia is also a Superior Court of Record. The High Court's records have been identified for many years as items for 'permanent retention'. This has not occurred until very recently for the Federal Court. Unlike the State Supreme Courts, the Federal Court is a Chapter III court, which gives it a greater degree of prominence with an Australian judiciary. Its statutory jurisdiction, particularly in relation to judicial review, also means that it deals with matters directly connected to the relationship between the individual and the state to an extent that is simply not shared with the Supreme Courts.

The unique role of the Federal Court means that its records speak directly to an individual's relationship with the state and identity as a citizen.[3] When resolving disputes between parties (whether between individual citizens or between a citizen and the state), the Federal Court inevitably has an impact beyond those parties, through the democratic values it espouses and pronounces, the methods of administrative and judicial decision-making undertaken, as well as its engagement as one arm of government in our constitutional make-up. The documents are also rich records of public interest and importance about the relationship between the individual and the state that are not readily accessible elsewhere. However, the public is restricted to accessing only those documents identified as constituting the 'court record'.

The definition of the 'court record' within an Anglo-Australian tradition of precedent[4] is a narrowly defined set of materials and the Federal Court's Rules concerning the public inspection of documents mirror this approach.[5] The importance of the Federal Court's records, however, extends beyond traditional ideas about the 'court record'. We argue that the records constitute a legal, social and cultural archive documenting how individuals and the state have sought to describe and resolve their relationship with one another. The use of the term 'archive' here is not restricted to the common or popular concept of purely historical material or matters simply of historical interest.[6] Over time, the term 'archive' has come to have a range of meanings. Conventionally understood as a collection of records produced by an individual or organisation and housed in a repository, more recently it has been reconceptualised. Today, an archive may be any record that has value as authentic evidence of administrative, corporate, cultural and intellectual activity.[7] In this broader context, we argue that the court's contemporary records, including its

---

3   We are using the term citizen here both in the formal sense of someone who is recognised as a capital 'C' citizen under the *Australian Citizenship Act 2007* (Cth), but also the broader normative small 'c' citizen, being an individual who is a member of the Australian community (i.e. a permanent or temporary resident and not a formal citizen) who has engaged with the State and become an active 'c'itizen in relying on laws to defend his/her rights. For a further discussion about the different meanings of citizenship in Australia, see Kim Rubenstein, *Australian Citizenship Law* (Thomson Reuters, 2nd edn, 2016) Ch 1.

4   The notion of the 'Record' is a complicated legal concept for the purpose of judicial review. See further *Kirk v Industrial Court of NSW* (2010) 239 CLR 531 and *Craig v South Australia* (1995) 184 CLR 163.

5   *Federal Court Rules 2011* (Cth), r 2.32(2).

6   Francis X Blouin Jr and William G Rosenberg, *Processing the Past: Contesting Authority in History and the Archives* (Oxford University Press, 2011), 4.

7   Australian Society of Archivists, *Made, Kept and Used: Celebrating 30 Years of the Australian Society of Archivists* (2005).

records of how it manages its own business, provide an account of how parties, including the state, describe rights and responsibilities today, in the here and now, as well as in the past. These perspectives can inform current debates over our roles and identities as citizens.

This chapter draws on an example from a much larger survey of files held by the National Archive of Australia about the Federal Court and identified as part of the Australian Research Council-funded project, The Court as Archive: Rethinking the Institutional Role of Federal Superior Courts of Record.[8] It argues that the current limits on the court's public access, based on historical concepts of the 'court record', require review and are a potential site of law reform in Australia. This law reform should ensure that the public access principles better reflect deeper understandings of the role and significance of the Federal Court and its records as an archive of value to Australian society.

II. The Federal Court in Context

Proceedings before the Federal Court can hold deep significance for the parties and the wider community. For example, the making of orders under the *Administrative Decisions (Judicial Review) Act 1977* (Cth) may represent protection from unlawful executive action. The making of orders under the *Native Title Act 1993* (Cth) may represent the recognition of deeply held spiritual and cultural connections to the land. For the legal profession in a common law system, judgment might represent a statement of what the law is – with an eye to appeal if the statement is perceived to be wrong. Moreover, Court judgments provide the opportunity to critically assess the performance of the courts and judges in terms of timeliness or even the extent to which they are 'in touch' with the community.[9]

It is this process of determining a dispute between two or more parties that is the basis of the jurisdiction of a Chapter III court[10] and represents the core characteristic of Commonwealth judicial power.[11] However,

---

8   Discovery Project DP130101954, purl.org/au-research/grants/arc/DP130101954. Associate Professor Ann Genovese from the University of Melbourne and Dr Trish Luker from the University of Technology Sydney have been fellow CIs on the project.

9   Murray Gleeson, 'Out of Touch or Out of Reach?' (2006) 7 *The Judicial Review* 241, 241.

10   *In re Judiciary and Navigation Acts* (1921) 29 CLR 257, 266 (Knox CJ, Gavan Duffy, Powers Rich and Starke JJ).

11   *Huddart, Parker & Co Pty Ltd v Moorehead* (1909) 8 CLR 330, 357 (Griffith CJ); see also James Stellios, 'Reconceving The Separation Of Judicial Power' (2011) 22 *Public Law Review* 113, 117.

in a common law system reliant on precedent both as a body of law and a tool of statutory interpretation, the effects of judicial decision-making are not bound in space or time but may be felt well beyond individual disputes.[12] The application of a body of law derived from principles and precedent provides continuity, consistency and certainty in individuals' relationships with one another and with the state.[13] A decision may also reach back in time to either affirm or reject previous interpretations of the law or redefine legal and personal relationships.[14] Through their reasons for decision, Courts reinforce the acceptance of certain ideas while rejecting or disapproving of others.[15] In this sense, Courts play an important role in understanding ideas of identity, belonging, citizenship and rights.

III. The Court as Archive

The focus of lawyers tends to be on the court's record as its end product – orders, reasons and judgment. Reliance on reasons alone is the study of precedent – what has been referred to as 'lawyers' history'.[16] Reasons for decision provide a summary of the facts 'ascertained' by the court and identified as legally significant.[17] In effect, the reasons present a narrow set of facts viewed through a particular lens.[18]

Insistence on a precedential or procedural definition of 'the record' ignores the record's much more significant value as an archive. Materials presented by the parties provide both the canvas and the frame for the decision – they provide the foundation for the decision and describe the broader context within which the decision is made. It is here that Court records arguably hold more value to the researcher as a companion, or even contradictor, to state-run archives.

---

12 Anthony Mason, 'The Use and Abuse of Precedent' (1988) 4 *Australian Bar Review* 93. See also traditional ideas of the common law representing common custom and usage in Rupert Cross and J W Harris, *Precedent in English Law* (Clarendon Press, 1991), 36–37.
13 Ibid. See also *Mirehouse v Rennell* (1833) 1 Cl. & F. 527, 546.
14 Oscar G Chase, '"Supreme" Courts and the Imagination of the Real' (2015) 518 *New York University Public Law and Legal Theory Working Papers*, 14.
15 Ibid.
16 Kinvin Wroth, 'Documents of the Colonial Conflict: Part I – Sources for the Legal History of the American Revolution' (1976) 69 *Law Librarians Journal* 277.
17 Michael McHugh, 'Judicial Method' (1999) 73 *Australian Law Journal* 37.
18 Clifford Geertz, *Local Knowledge: Further Essays in Interpretive Anthropology* (Basic Books, 2008), 173.

Postmodern critiques of archives argue that, to the extent archival institutions are created by, and contain records of, the state, they give primacy to a representation of the community constructed by the state and exclude contradictory voices.[19] Archives are no longer assumed to be an authoritative source of historical knowledge, but are rather understood to create history through the selection, organisation and provision of documents.[20] In the context of the individual's relationship with the state, state-run archives therefore might exclude or explicitly devalue or discredit voices of protest. Within the court's own records, contradictory voices are not just heard but are explicitly required. The evidence and other materials submitted to the court are representative of the voices of those who submitted them. They do not contain just one version of a series of events but may contain two or multiple stories told in different ways and from different perspectives. Within this account are cultural and social assumptions – both explicit and implicit – that provide an insight into those relationships. Perhaps even more crucially these are snapshots of assumptions in conflict – of contested ideas about what is acceptable. This more complete archive begins to explain 'not only what went on in the law's formal processes, but what were the full … effects that law and the life environing the law had on each other'.[21]

The records of one Mrs Law's dispute with the Repatriation Commission provide a specific example of this idea of a more complete archive. The National Archives of Australia (NAA) retains a series of files from various Commonwealth departments[22] and the Cabinet[23] concerning proceedings brought by the Commonwealth challenging the award of a war widow's pension to Mrs Law. James Law, Mrs Law's husband, passed away from lung cancer in late 1976. During World War II he began to smoke heavily – a habit he did not quit until a heart attack three

---

19   Blouin and Rosenberg, above n 6, 159; Ciaran B Trace, 'What is Recorded is Never Simply "What Happened": Record Keeping in Modern Organizational Culture' (2002) 2 *Archival Science* 137. See also s 2A of the *Archives Act 1983* (Cth) and the definition of 'archival resources of the Commonwealth'.

20   Jacques Derrida, *Archive Fever* (University of Chicago Press, 1996); Carolyn Steedman, *Dust: The Archive and Cultural History* (Rutgers University Press, 2002).

21   J Willard Hurst, 'Legal Elements in United States History' in Donald Fleming and Bernard Bailyn (eds), *Perspectives in American History* (Little Brown Books, 1971) Vol 2, 3.

22   National Archives of Australia: Prime Minister's Department – Correspondence files; A1209, Appeals to Federal Court for War Widows Pension 1980–1982, 1980/558 PART 1.

23   National Archives of Australia: Fraser Ministries – Cabinet Memoranda; A12930, Memorandum No 639: *Law v Repatriation Commission* appeal to full court of the Federal Court of Australia – Related to Decision No 11094 1980, 639.

years before his death. After her husband's death, Mrs Law applied for a war widow's pension, arguing her husband had died as a result of an 'occurrence' during his enlistment. The Repatriation Commission did not agree. Mrs Law was successful on appeal before Justice Toohey, then of the Federal Court,[24] and again when the Commission appealed to the Full Court of the Federal Court[25] and the High Court.[26]

The proceedings ultimately affected how the then Repatriation Commission would determine more broadly the claims for death or disability concerning ex-service personnel contracting lung cancer from smoking at the time, and into the future.[27] These files provide some insight into how the state perceived its relationship with its citizens. The files tell a story not apparent from the reasons for decision. Although they opposed Mrs Law's application, Cabinet agreed to meet Mrs Law's costs of the litigation, to continue to pay her pension pending the outcome of the appeal and to investigate other benefits to which she may be entitled.[28] The Commonwealth's agreement to pay Mrs Law's pension creates the impression of magnanimity and generosity – a positive depiction that arguably speaks to larger ideas of how government should be run. A closer reading of the Cabinet Submission recommending the ongoing payment of the pension, however, reveals a discussion of how the government might be perceived, raising a 'general question of whether, as a matter of public policy an appeal against decisions involving a war widow ... should proceed'.[29] Among other factors, Cabinet was invited to consider how the Commonwealth's appeal might affect its relationship with the community, noting that an appeal 'would almost certainly produce a very unfavourable reaction from ex-service organisations from which Government has already criticism over the adoption of policies which eroded repatriation benefits'.[30]

We can review a rich range of material in the NAA due to the agency's choice of materials to be kept, which help us understand the relationship between the individual and the state and indeed more about how the state

---

24   *Law v Repatriation Commission* (1980) 29 ALR 64.
25   *Repatriation Commission v Law* (1980) 31 ALR 140.
26   *Repatriation Commission v Law* (1981) 147 CLR 635.
27   See Judith E Grbich, 'Repatriation Disability Pensions: Reverse Onus of Proof Problems and the Determination and Review System' (1984) 10 *Monash University Law Review* 73.
28   Above n 24.
29   Above n 24.
30   Above n 24.

perceived itself. But these do not necessarily create a complete picture, as they are determined by the agency responsible for the litigation, not the Federal Court itself.

IV. Telling the Whole Story: Court Records and Archives

If we understand the Federal Court's records as an archive, we are immediately presented with a number of inconsistencies and questions, many of which are confronted by this project.

Court records are excluded from the operation of the *Archives Act* unless specific arrangements are made in consultation with the Chief Justice.[31] From the perspective of the constitutional principle of separation of Commonwealth judicial power, this may be appropriate. For the legislature to seek to define and direct a Chapter III court concerning the management of its records – particularly those related to the judicial process – may raise questions of interference.

Commonwealth courts have instead sought to address what constitutes their records through their Rules. The position is approached not from the perspective of preserving important materials, but from the traditional, procedural perspective. It is also done inconsistently between the courts themselves.[32]

Between the NAA and the Federal Court, there are further inconsistencies concerning access to materials and timing that would affect any records of proceedings that might be transferred. Materials accessible today in the Federal Court (e.g. an originating application) may not be accessible at

---

31 *Archives Act 1983* (Cth), ss 19(1), 20(1) and 20(3).

32 At the Commonwealth level, legislation establishing the courts is silent. Consequently, the matter is left to Rules, which are inconsistent across jurisdictions. For example, the *High Court Rules* require the Registrar to maintain the 'records of the Court' and 'documents filed in the registry' as separate things: *High Court Rules 2004* (Cth) rr 4.07.01 and 4.07.02. The *Family Law Rules* use the phrase 'court record' and, while providing no definition, it appears to include documents filed with the registry and may include correspondence and transcript: *Family Law Rules 2004* (Cth) r 24.13 'court document'. The *Federal Court Rules* adopt a similar distinction to the High Court but refer instead to the 'records of the Registry': *Federal Court Rules 2011* (Cth) r 2.31(1). However, a practice note uses 'court file', which extends to all documents filed with the Registry but does not equate it with the record: Federal Court of Australia, *Practice Note CM23 – Electronic Court File and Preparation and Lodgment of Documents*, 10 July 2014, [3.1], [4.4], [4.5], [5.3] and [5.4].

Archives for 21 years.[33] Conversely, materials not available at any time at the Federal Court may become accessible in 21 years time to anyone who applies to the NAA for access.

The records concerning Mrs Law provide an example of this inconsistency and how the state's records influence how it is perceived. To the extent that the records held by the NAA capture the Commonwealth's position, they reflect a particular, and one-sided, understanding of the dispute. Silent in these records are the voices of Mr and Mrs Law or their family. Silent also are the voices of other ex-service personnel and their families who would be affected by the outcome of the appeals. It is here that the Federal Court's records could transcend the procedural to become a unique archive.

Evidence of those involved in litigation, other than the Commonwealth, *may* be held by the NAA, but only where a Commonwealth agency considers it sufficiently important to be kept on their file. These broader materials, developed for the purpose of litigation, form a fundamental element of the judicial process before the Federal Court. Making the materials – which may not exist anywhere else – available begins to tell a more complete story about not only Mr and Mrs Law, but also about individual citizens' expectations of and relationships with the state.

V. Conclusion

Developments within the Federal Court itself, compelled by its discussions with the NAA, reflect a realisation of the importance of the materials it controls. In October 2011, the NAA endorsed the Federal Court's Records Authority for the management and disposal of the court's records.[34]

Certain classes of case file have been identified in the Records Authority as so important that their entire contents are to be permanently retained by NAA, namely, all native title files and 'significant, non-native title files'. While the criteria for determining 'significance' continue to be developed, its inclusion as a basis for identifying records for permanent retention reflects the court's understanding of its role beyond a mechanism for dispute resolution.

---

33 *Archives Act* s 31(1).
34 *Records Authority 2010/00315821 – Federal Court of Australia*, 19 October 2011.

However, the Records Authority applies only to files to be transferred to the NAA. The existing statutory bar on public access to materials held by the NAA will continue to apply, placing those records beyond public access for many years to come. The records that the Federal Court holds are of both historical importance but also of importance today. Limited access places the public in a position of disadvantage in understanding how the state perceives its role and responsibilities. It is also inconsistent with our understanding of open justice and transparency. It is a matter in need of reform.

40

A Positive Freedom of Public Speech? Australian Media Law Reform and Freedom of Political Communication

Andrew T Kenyon[1]

Proposals to reform Australian media law arise frequently; recent examples have included a merger of public broadcasting organisations and changing legislative ownership limits for commercial media. What might such proposals have to do with the idea of free speech, in particular as it relates to public discourse? Here I explore an approach to free speech recognising *positive or structural* aspects of the freedom as well as *negative or liberty* aspects. In short, free speech entails both diversity of voices and absence of censorship, not merely the latter. The outline presented here suggests changes to Australian constitutional interpretation could be warranted, or at least their exploration deserves attention, even if such changes appear unlikely soon.

There are also implications for legislative and executive action – they could take into account positive and structural aspects of free speech which, to date, are rarely acknowledged. That sort of change could more plausibly

1   Professor, and Joint-Director, Centre for Media and Communications Law, University of Melbourne.

happen in the short term, although it also faces challenges. In particular, parliament and executive appear unlikely to achieve adequate protection for free speech if the matter is left entirely open to their choice.

I. Some Introductory Caveats

My interest here lies in public speech or public discourse within democratic contexts. This focus seeks to separate free speech as a constitutive element of democratic government from free speech as a liberal or human right. As with Eric Heinze's recent analysis in the different context of hate speech,[2] my aim is not to suggest that democracy supplies a *complete* approach to free speech; rather, claims to be democratic carry particular necessary implications for free speech. Also by way of caveat, the positive–negative terminology is not meant to suggest that the state is ever *absent* in terms of free speech or state–media relations. The government is always involved; as Victor Pickard states, 'the real question is how the government should be involved'.[3]

Clearly, this approach to free speech involves contested terms, 'democracy' in particular. But the essentially contested nature of democracy offers some support to the approach outlined here. I will take democracy to contain a claim to political self-rule in one form or another. The repeated failure of democracies in practice – the 'internal exclusions and subordinations' of 'class … gender, sexuality, race, religion, ethnicity, and global origin' – does not remove the idea's ambition and appeal. Along with its failures, democracy has also carried 'the language and promise of inclusive and shared political equality, freedom, and popular sovereignty'.[4] The point for present purposes is that forms of self-rule imply a particular approach to free speech and, I would suggest, democratic constitutional arrangements also presuppose it. This is reinforced by the fact that democracies may be reformed. That possibility for reform can be itself seen to require diverse public speech: 'public discourse is the constitution *of* the constitution'.[5]

---

2   Eric Heinze, *Hate Speech and Democratic Citizenship* (Oxford University Press, 2016).
3   Victor Pickard, 'Toward a People's Internet: The Fight for Positive Freedoms in an Age of Corporate Libertarianism' in Maria Edström, Andrew T Kenyon and Eva-Maria Svensson (eds), *Blurring the Lines: Market-driven and Democracy-driven Freedom of Expression* (Nordicom, 2016) 61.
4   Wendy Brown, *Undoing the Demos: Neoliberalism's Stealth Revolution* (MIT Press, 2015) 44.
5   Heinze, above n 2, 6 (emphasis in original).

It is worth noting, however, that completely elite forms of government are excluded from this approach; such forms of government do not require free public speech. But where a democratic polity claims to be *not only* about elite rule, where it claims to temper democracy's tendencies towards elite domination, then wider aspects of free speech are implicated.

II. Positive Freedom of Public Speech

Draconian state restrictions on speech attest to the importance of negative free speech. But to suggest that speech is free whenever the state does not directly restrict it obscures the state's role in public communication. Free speech also has positive aspects. In considering those, there are many intellectual sources that could be drawn on,[6] including:

- legal scholarship about free speech (using ideas broadly consistent with those presented here);

- writing from media studies and media policy, where recent work offers clear engagement with the idea of positive freedom;

- writing about positive liberty or positive freedom, often in political philosophy, although that work has surprisingly little to say directly about free speech or mediated speech;

- human rights law scholarship about positive rights, which again tends to focus on other matters than speech; and

- some formal law, including constitutional courts in France, Germany and other parts of Europe (and perhaps parliamentary processes and legislation in Northern Europe). The legal examples often engage with specific aspects of positive free speech, rather than its wider implications. The German Federal Constitutional Court's analysis of free speech and *broadcasting* is a strong example of that, which is considered further below.

---

6   See, for example, law and media studies literature discussed in Andrew T Kenyon, 'Assuming Free Speech' (2014) 77 *Modern Law Review* 379; Carol C Gould, *Rethinking Democracy: Freedom and Social Cooperation in Politics, Economy, and Society* (Cambridge University Press, 1988); Sandra Fredman, *Human Rights Transformed: Positive Rights and Positive Duties* (Oxford University Press, 2008).

Thus while the concept of positive free speech might appear foreign to Australian law, it is not at all unknown as an idea. Aspects of it can be seen in a host of writing across a range of disciplines, although it has tended to be an idea without powerful friends. Given limited space here, I simply use two short quotes to explore the idea.

Free speech might be considered as a bare liberty that requires only the absence of government restriction. It subjects government action to judicial scrutiny where that action would restrict speech. But free speech need not be seen *only* in such negative terms. Applied philosopher Onora O'Neill observes that the apparent absence of government action does not leave public speech free from influence:

> [L]aissez-faire communications policies merely assign the regulation of communication to nonstate powers. They secure a particular configuration of freedom of expression, which may leave some unable to find their voices and does not guarantee the expression of diverse views.[7]

Similar ideas have been raised by many commentators, but I note the O'Neill example because she then suggests points of relevance here. In short, she argues that, in a *democratic context*, there should be an aim to enable *sustained diverse public communication*, while recognising *the impossibility of complete non-interference* with communication.

Enabling sustained diverse public speech in a democratic context might be thought to lie 'beyond' free speech. But not necessarily, as Judith Lichtenberg explains. The multiple rationales commonly seen to underlie free speech can be grouped into two broad goals:

> These commitments can be described in terms of two basic principles. The first we may call the *noninterference or no censorship principle:* One should not be prevented from thinking, speaking, reading, writing, or listening as one sees fit. The other I call *the multiplicity of voices principle:* The purposes of freedom of speech are realized when expression and diversity of expression flourish.[8]

---

7   Onora O'Neill, 'Practices of Toleration' in Judith Lichtenberg (ed), *Democracy and the Mass Media: A Collection of Essays* (Cambridge University Press, 1990) 155, 178.

8   Judith Lichtenberg, 'Foundations and Limits of Freedom of the Press' in Lichtenberg (ed), *Democracy and the Mass Media: A Collection of Essays* (Cambridge University Press, 1990) 102, 107 (emphasis in original).

She maintains that diverse, multiple voices are needed for free speech interests to be met. More than speech itself, it is debate and diversity of ideas that are required. And such debate and diversity cannot be *assumed* to exist in market-based mass media; theory and practice suggest they require support beyond markets.[9]

III. What Role for Courts?

How might positive aspects of free speech be considered in law? The German Federal Constitutional Court offers a developed example of judgments doing just this. (Although operating within a code-based legal system, the Constitutional Court's decisions have the weight of precedent, binding all actors except itself.) In decisions from 1961 to 2014 the Constitutional Court has set out detailed requirements about television broadcasting, drawing on the free speech protection in Art 5 of the Basic Law and its protection for broadcasting freedom.[10] A contemporary translation of Art 5 reads:

> (1) Everyone has the right freely to express and disseminate their opinions orally, in writing or visually and to obtain information from generally accessible sources without hindrance. *Freedom of the press and freedom of reporting through audiovisual media shall be guaranteed.* There shall be no censorship.[11]

The provision sits within particular constitutional traditions, and the decisions' merits are subject to ongoing domestic debate.[12] My primary interest here, however, lies in particular ideas about free speech seen in the decisions, including: free speech's positive aspects; the broad range of media content covered; the constitutionality of a dual broadcasting system; funding public broadcasting; internal pluralism within public broadcasters; what can be called a 'precautionary' approach; and the contemporary media environment. Here, I mention a little more about

---

9   See, for example, Andrew T Kenyon, 'Assuming Free Speech' (2014) 77 *Modern Law Review* 379.
10   A useful entry point is Donald P Kommers and Russell A Miller, *The Constitutional Jurisprudence of the Federal Republic of Germany* (Duke University Press, 3rd edn, 2012).
11   See, for example, Christian Potschka, *Towards a Market in Broadcasting: Communications Policy in the UK and Germany* (Palgrave Macmillan, 2012) 161 (emphasis added).
12   See, for example, Bernd Grzeszick, 'The "Serving" Freedom to Broadcast: Subjective versus Objective Dimensions of a Fundamental Right' in Hermann Pünder and Christian Waldhoff (eds), *Debates in German Public Law* (Hart, 2014) 75, 85.

four of these areas. Overall, they illustrate the power of the idea that free speech requires efforts be made to provide comprehensive, universally available and diverse information.

A. Free speech has positive aspects

Clearly, free speech is not merely a negative liberty for the Constitutional Court. Article 5's purpose of individual and public opinion formation *requires* state action; it cannot be met merely by a negative duty. Instead, 'a positive order is necessary, which ensures ... the variety of existing opinion is expressed ... as widely and completely as possible'.[13] In this approach to free speech, broadcasting freedom is a state of affairs in which diversity in content is sought along with freedom from state and market control.

In the German context, constitutional rights establish objective principles as well as subjective protections for individuals.[14] The state clearly has a 'protective function'.[15] While acknowledging the German context and history, here I want to flag that a similar result may be reached for free speech rights in other constitutional systems due to the *role of public communication* within a democratic constitutional order.

B. The freedom is broad

Article 5 guarantees a broad freedom. While referring explicitly to freedom of *reporting*, the freedom is not limited to reporting. It serves the wide free speech interests protected by Art 5 as a whole – free individual and public opinion formation – which means it encompasses entertainment content as well as news and commentary. Broadcasting has the constitutional function of providing 'information in the greatest possible breadth and completeness' because 'opinion formation comes about not only in news broadcasts, political commentaries or series on problems of the past, present and future, but also in audio and TV dramas, musical presentations or entertainment broadcasts'.[16] In addition, the requirement is not for 'a minimum provision to which public broadcasting is confined

---

13   BVerfGE 57, 295 (Third broadcasting case).
14   See, for example, Werner Heun, *The Constitution of Germany: A Contextual Analysis* (Hart, 2011) 198–200.
15   See, for example, Dieter Grimm, 'The Protective Function of the State' in Georg Nolte (ed), *European and US Constitutionalism* (Cambridge University Press, 2005) 137.
16   BVerfGE 73, 118 (1986) (Fourth/Lower Saxony broadcasting case).

or could be reduced'.[17] It is for a comprehensive service, available to the entire population, containing substantial diversity of opinion.[18] That is the constitutional mandate of public broadcasting.

C. A dual broadcasting system

The above requirements have led the Constitutional Court to hold that a dual system of public and commercial broadcasting can meet the constitutional requirements, but it is a system in which public broadcasting is primary. Commercial broadcasting has been held constitutionally permissible only where public broadcasting is able to meet the Basic Law's mandate for opinion formation.[19] While that could theoretically change if commercial broadcasting by itself met the constitutional requirements, there is no sign of that in the judicial analysis to date.

D. Speech requires a 'precautionary approach'

The importance of free speech means the Constitutional Court takes what can be called a 'precautionary' approach in seeking to lessen commercial and political pressures on public broadcasting. The quasi-foundational role for speech is seen even in Germany where the right to dignity under Art 1 of the Basic Law takes precedence over, and influences the interpretation of, all other constitutional rights. In its classic *Lüth* decision the Constitutional Court stated:

> The basic right of freedom of opinion is … absolutely basic to a liberal-democratic constitutional order because it alone makes possible the constant intellectual exchange and contest among opinions that form the lifeblood of such an order; it is 'the matrix, the indispensable condition of nearly every other form of freedom'.[20]

The quoted words ending this extract come from US Supreme Court Justice Benjamin Cardozo.[21] Their use underlines the German court's view that the 'primacy' of speech is inherent in any democratic constitutional order. And the court is alive to possible concentration of power over public opinion. Caution against such influence is warranted because 'when

---

17 BVerfGE 74, 297 (1987) (Fifth/Baden-Württemberg broadcasting case).
18 BVerfGE 83, 238 (1991) (Sixth/North Rhine-Westphalia broadcasting case).
19 BVerfGE 90, 60 (1994) (Eighth/Cable Penny broadcasting case).
20 BVerfGE 7, 198 (*Lüth* case).
21 *Palko v Connecticut*, 302 US 319, 327 (1937).

emerging developments prove to be faulty, they can only be rescinded – if at all – to a certain degree and only with considerable difficulty'.[22] That is, speech requires 'prior' protection – protection prior to the institutional political process. The Constitutional Court has continued to apply this reasoning, maintaining that 'precautions for the protection of journalistic diversity' are necessary.[23] There is nothing about the idea that is limited to the German context. And it is worth emphasising that the need for journalistic diversity is not resolved by the internet: the Constitutional Court has continued its approach as recently as 2014, despite the dramatically different context for public communication compared with its first broadcasting decision in the early 1960s.

A point of general interest from this precautionary aspect of the German approach is that neither executive nor legislature can be left to deal with broadcasting merely as a matter of policy entirely separate from free speech requirements. The free speech issues at stake mean the Constitutional Court sets out requirements that the legislature must meet; requirements which, in turn, restrict the executive's room for action. The legislature cannot, for example, limit public broadcasting to its current technological basis.[24] That would breach the requirements of Art 5. The German court acts because it is implausible – and unconstitutional – to leave the structure or architecture of public speech solely to legislative and executive action. If structures affecting public communication also influence political processes – a situation which appears undeniable – there is a sense in which some of the architecture of public speech must be *prior to* public debate and decisions by politicians.

This suggests an approach in which a democratic commitment to free speech implies media of different institutional forms, internal organisation and economic base containing speech of diverse content and style, aimed at different ends, creating different and only partially overlapping publics, and seeking to influence (among other things) political decisions. Public debate and parliamentary or executive action could reshape this style of architecture of public speech to some degree, but the changes could not go beyond the requirements of free speech in terms of non-censorship and diversity.

---

22 BVerfGE 57, 295 (Third case).
23 Fourteenth/ZDF Treaty case (2014) [36].
24 For example, BVerfGE 83, 238 (1991) (Sixth/North Rhine-Westphalia case); BVerfGE 119, 181 (2007) (Twelfth broadcasting case).

The claim being made is not that the German situation fulfils such an approach to free speech, but that it is an example which suggests ways in which a formally democratic system could go some way towards that goal – and go further than is commonly imagined in Australia.

IV. Australian Implications

Free speech in Australia includes a freedom of political communication that is implied in the Constitution. It is said to secure 'what is necessary for the effective operation' of the constitutional system of representative and responsible government.[25] The aim is to give freedom of choice to electors. The overall aim sounds like a plausible vision for democratic free speech: a free and informed choice for voters. Within the realm of political speech, the concept does not appear to be far removed from free speech serving individual and collective opinion formation, as it is said to do under Germany's Basic Law. Beyond that broad similarity, Australia's freedom is said not to be an individual right. Instead it is a limitation on legislative power[26] (and a freedom to which the common law must comply). The first step is understandable, at least in that free speech is not *only* an individual right (when free speech is understood in the terminology of rights at all). Free speech has structural implications; it is not (only) an individual right. But the second step need not follow: free speech need not only be a limitation on legislative power. In Australia, that has been stated more than it has been explained. And the particular reasons that support judicial action, as seen, for example, in the German decisions, have not been addressed.[27]

The Australian approach may well follow from old ideas that freedoms are residual in Australian law, but more could be considered in relation to this particular freedom. In stating that free speech is not an individual right, it appears that the High Court wanted to distinguish freedom of political communication from the US First Amendment. But it may well be that the advocates appearing before it have not provided sufficient examples beyond the US to allow all relevant matters to be considered in terms of

---

25 *Lange v Australian Broadcasting Corporation* (1997) 189 CLR 520.

26 See, for example, *McClure v Australian Electoral Commission* (1999) 163 ALR 734.

27 Even so there are Australian decisions that would be quite consistent with positive free speech: for example, restrictions on political speech that aim to support diversity overall could be upheld as constitutional, as stated from the beginning in *Australian Capital Television v Commonwealth* (1992) 177 CLR 106.

approaches that differ from the US one. That may not change in the short term, in part given the issues of standing and the types of disputes that may come before the High Court. But that situation remains a failing of Australian free speech, in terms of the diversity of speech required by democratic government.

Beyond courts, there are also implications for media policy, such as proposals about the structure or funding of public media or ownership limits for commercial media. Those matters raise positive aspects of free speech, as do issues of appointments to public media boards, statutory missions of media organisations of all types, and so forth. Within the Australian legal system these matters have been left, to date, to parliaments and executives, and to public debate *after* legislative and executive choices have been made relevant to the structures of public speech. The German decisions suggest why the communicative requirements of democracy may be poorly addressed under such an approach. But they also suggest that debate over Australian legislative and executive action could be made explicitly in free speech terms, and their implications support such debate being pursued in those terms. Matters such as the existence and funding of public media and commercial media ownership limits raise questions of free speech that are central to the idea of Australia having a democratic form of government.

41

The Need for Reform of Australia's Birth Registration Systems

Melissa Castan and Paula Gerber[1]

I. Introduction

Having a birth certificate is a key to accessing the rights of citizenship. Most Australians take it for granted that they can prove who they are by producing their birth certificate. But there are a number of Australians – predominantly Indigenous people and those from culturally and linguistically diverse (CALD) communities – who miss out on the rights and benefits of citizenship and struggle to fully participate in society because their birth has never been registered or, if it was, they cannot produce a birth certificate to prove it.

Without a birth certificate it is near impossible to obtain a driver's licence, passport or Tax File Number, or to collect your superannuation.[2] But problems can start much earlier. Schools are not supposed to enrol

1   Senior Lecturer, Monash University Law Faculty, and Deputy Director of the Castan Centre for Human Rights Law (Castan); Professor, Monash University Law Faculty and Deputy Director of the Castan Centre for Human Rights Law (Gerber). This chapter arises out of research funded by the Australian Research Council pursuant to the Linkage Grant 'Closing the Gap on Indigenous Birth Registration' (LP120100160). Further resources resulting from this research can be found in *Proof of Birth* and in the publications set out on the project's website: www.indigenousbirthreg.org.
2   A birth certificate is known as a 'feeder' document, that is, it enables a person to obtain other forms of identification. A person may use their birth certificate to obtain a passport, which could then be used to satisfy ID requirements for other purposes such as obtaining a driver's license or opening a bank account. However, a birth certificate is invariably required to obtain the initial form of ID.

children who do not have a birth certificate, and sports clubs will often ban kids from playing if they cannot produce a birth certificate to prove they are playing in the right age group – for example, the Under 10s soccer team or the Under 14s cricket team.

Lack of a birth certificate can also be a barrier to engaging in the mainstream economy and developing financial literacy because it prevents young people from accessing the keys to economic participation, such as opening a bank account. Thus, the result of a birth not being registered is that vulnerable groups, including Indigenous children and youth, who may already suffer intergenerational disadvantage, find themselves even further behind the eight ball. They may be unable to prove who they are and therefore cannot access the rights of citizenship that most Australians take for granted.[3]

Indeed, not having a birth certificate can lead to a life of isolation and exclusion from society from a very early age.[4] Further problems such as non-recognition as a citizen, increased risk of violence and abuse, and increased risk of separation from family during emergencies, are identified as serious issues of child protection for those whose births have not been registered.[5] Around the world, it is estimated there are approximately 230 million children under five whose births have never been registered. This equates to one in every three children under five.[6] Given the global scale of non-registration of births, the thousands of Australians from Indigenous and CALD communities who have not had their births registered may not seem like a significant problem.[7] However, for the individuals endeavouring to negotiate life without a birth certificate, the problem is very large and very real.

---

3   Paula Gerber and Melissa Castan, 'The Right to Universal Birth Registration in Australia' in Melissa Castan and Paula Gerber (eds), *Proof of Birth* (Future Leaders, 2015), 3 (hereafter *Proof of Birth*).
4   See, for example, Grace Koelma, 'Australian Woman Charmaine Webster Who Legally Doesn't Exist Due to Unregistered Birth, Fights to Prove Her Identity', www.news.com.au/lifestyle/real-life/australian-woman-charmaine-webster-who-legally-doesnt-exist-due-to-unregistered-birth-fights-to-prove-her-identity/news-story/eefbd76d0451458db64c84e6fea0cc06 (viewed 7 July 2014).
5   UN High Commissioner for Refugees (UNHCR), *Child Protection Issue Brief: Birth Registration*, August 2013, www.refworld.org/docid/523fe9214.html (viewed 22 January 2015).
6   UNICEF, *Every Child's Birth Right: Inequities and Trends in Birth Registration* (2013), 14, www.unicef.org/media/files/Embargoed_11_Dec_Birth_Registration_report_low_res.pdf.
7   Will Winter 'The Minimbah Project: Facilitating Birth Registration and Certificates in Rural and Regional Communities' in *Proof of Birth*, 73–74.

This chapter seeks to identify the areas where law reform will provide measurable improvements and contribute to the debate about how best to address the diverse range of issues that prevent Australia achieving truly universal birth registration.

II. Unregistered Births in Australia

Australia can be proud of the fact that around 96 per cent of all births are registered.[8] However, the fact that the vast majority of the unregistered births come from vulnerable populations such as Indigenous and CALD communities is a cause for great concern. While the problem of non-registration is being acknowledged and addressed in developing countries,[9] there is still a reluctance to recognise that a wealthy, OECD country such as Australia has similar problems with under-registration of births within several of its minority groups.

There are two distinct, but related, factors underpinning the lack of birth certificates in Australia, namely:

1. Births are not being registered, so no certificate is available.
2. Births are registered, but a birth certificate was not obtained at the time, and cannot now be obtained because of an inability to (i) satisfy the Registrar of Births, Deaths and Marriages (BDM) ID requirements and/or (ii) pay the fees associated with acquiring a birth certificate.

There are several steps involved in registering a birth and getting a birth certificate, beginning with notification of a birth by the hospital or midwife and concluding with lodgement of a birth registration form by the parents. Notably, the statutes regulating birth registration impose significant *potential* penalties for late registration.[10] Additionally, while registering a birth is free, applying for a birth certificate is not. A fee must be paid at the time of submitting the form.[11]

---

8   A J Lanyon and David John, 'Australia's Civil Registration and Vital Statistics System', in *Proof of Birth*, 53–54.

9   UN High Commissioner for Refugees (UNHCR), *Child Protection Issue Brief: Birth Registration*, August 2013, www.refworld.org/docid/523fe9214.html (viewed 22 January 2015).

10   For example, in Victoria a fine of up to $1,400 can be imposed.

11   The fees range from $31 in Victoria and $53 in New South Wales. Some jurisdictions, such as Victoria, have a fee relief scheme in place for Indigenous Australians.

III. How to Increase Birth Registration Rates within Indigenous Communities

There are a diverse range of factors and issues that underlie non-registration of births by members of Indigenous communities. The multiplicity of causes necessitate an interdisciplinary response that incorporates legal, health, statistical, and community based approaches to the issues. Furthermore, any recommendations and reforms to birth registration, access to birth certificates and changes to identification documents should only be considered after proper consultation with, and the participation of, Indigenous communities and representative organisations. This is consistent with best practice for law reform regarding Indigenous Australians, and adheres to the Free Prior and Informed Consent standard in Art 19 of the Declaration of the Rights of Indigenous Peoples.

The majority of Australians do not experience any significant difficulty registering a birth and obtaining a birth certificate. For this reason, it cannot be said that the entire birth registration system is broken or in need of a major overall.[12] Rather, as Lanyon and John suggest, what is required is 'the development and resourcing of targeted strategies to address the sub-groups of the population more likely to be at risk of not registering the birth of a child'.[13]

With this in mind, there are five areas where improvements could be made that would make a significant difference to how accessible and user-friendly the birth registration system is for disadvantaged sections of the community. These areas are:

A. Education

Although birth registration is recognised as a human right in international law,[14] in Australia it is more often perceived as a responsibility than a right. One of the ways to increase birth registration rates in Indigenous communities would be to increase awareness of birth registration as a human right that every child has, and to highlight the benefits that flow to children from having a birth certificate.

---

12   Melissa Castan and Paula Gerber, 'The Way Forward' in *Proof of Birth*.

13   A J Lanyon and David John, 'Australia's Civil Registration and Vital Statistics System' in *Proof of Birth*, 55.

14   See Art 14 of the International Covenant on Civil and Political Rights and Art 7 of the Convention on the Rights of the Child.

The importance of birth registration to the child needs to be emphasised at a number of key life events, such as at the birth of the child, at baby health check-ups, at school enrolment, and when youths (and others) contemplate getting drivers licences.

Requiring BDM registrars to raise awareness about the importance of birth registration requires legislative reform since the current statutory regime does not include any mandate to provide public education about birth registration.[15] Such legislative reform will need to be accompanied by a budget allocation that provides registrars with the funding necessary to develop and deliver educational programs and to implement more effective communication strategies.

Education about birth registration could also be usefully undertaken by federal agencies. For example, Centrelink and Medicare could help increase birth registration rates by inquiring of parents whether they have registered the child's birth, and providing tangible assistance to obtain a birth certificate, if parents have not yet obtained one. In this way, incidents of non registration could be addressed early in a child's life.

B. Service delivery

In most Australian jurisdictions, birth registration offices are based in the capital cities. Many of the communities and people who have the most difficulties accessing registration processes or certificates live in rural or remote locations, making physical access to the BDM registry facilities a significant burden.

Victoria is a notable exception. It has established approximately 25 regional Justice Centres with trained staff who are able to process applications for birth registration. The cost of running outreach programs is not insignificant. However, the success of community-led 'registration drives'[16] and other efforts to reach communities in remote regions is testament to the value of such initiatives. For example, the Department of Transport, Fines Enforcement, Births, Deaths and Marriages and Centrelink[17]

---

15   The Victorian Law Reform Commission made such a recommendation in relation to the Victorian legislation VLRC *Birth registration and Birth Certificates Report* (2013).
16   See Will Winters, 'The Minimbah Project: Facilitating Birth Registration and Birth Certificates in Rural and Regional Communities', Ch 6 in *Proof of Birth*.
17   See Alice Barter, 'Indigenous Driving Issues in the Pilbara Region', Ch 5 in *Proof of Birth*.

regularly provide a 'one stop shop' for Indigenous communities in remote parts of Western Australia, and this has facilitated the registration of many births from these communities.

Another way of decentralising birth registration and certification processes is to use mobile birth registration units, and train non-registry personnel to assist in birth registration processes. Such initiatives have proven successful in Argentina, which uses mobile units to service the region of Patagonia, and Chile, which has three state-of-the-art vans fitted out with computers and satellite connections to the central registry.[18]

Whether the outreach programs are initiated by community groups, NGOs or government, they always require the cooperation and support of the relevant BDM registries, including making key staff available on site. In terms of law reform, then, registrars should be given specific powers, policies and resources to facilitate outreach programs, in cooperation with community groups or other government agencies, on a continuing basis. A commitment by registrars to regular outreach programs targeting communities where there is evidence of low levels of birth registration would likely see a significant improvement in birth registrations within these communities.

C. Technology

There are two distinct ways in which digital technologies can facilitate birth registration. The first is to increase the accessibility of the systems. At present, birth registration requires the completion of a paper application which must be submitted in person or by post. To make birth registration processes more accessible to all, there is an urgent need to move towards online processes and away from purely paper forms of birth certificate.[19]

There are digital birth registrations systems in place in other countries that Australian governments should be closely examining. There is much we can learn from the innovations being implemented in Uganda and other African nations making use of web-based technologies and smart

---

18   UNICEF, 'Birth Registration: Right from the Start' (2002) 9 *Innocenti Digest* 19, www.childinfo. org/files/birthregistration_Digestenglish.pdf.

19   We note, however, that in areas where there are issues of low literacy, digital technologies of themselves will only address the issues of under-registration when supported by funded case-workers who can assist with the registration process.

phones.[20] Digital technologies make the registration and certification processes far more accessible and have led to a sharp increase in birth registration rates.

The second way that digital technologies can assist with birth registration is to enhance the exchange of information between government departments and agencies in different jurisdictions. Such sharing of information between different registry offices would have been of great assistance to Charmaine Webster, who was repeatedly directed to search the BDM registers in every state in order to establish where she was born.[21] Charmaine's experience is likely to be the experience of many others who have spent years searching for a record of their birth across eight different registries around Australia.

D. Financial assistance

It is well known that having to pay a fee makes it more difficult for people from a low socioeconomic background to obtain a copy of their birth certificate. The fees may also operate as an unintended deterrent to birth registration, due to confusion between the (free) act of registering, and the request for certificates (which currently cost between $31 and $53).[22]

We concur with the view expressed by the UN Committee on the Rights of the Child that BDM registries across Australia should automatically issue the first birth certificate for free upon registration of Indigenous births.[23] There are revenue implications for the registries in issuing free birth certificates. However, given that Indigenous births account for only roughly 5 per cent of all births in NSW each year, this should not represent a significant fiscal barrier. Even in the Northern Territory, where the proportion of Indigenous births is higher, the amount of revenue waived would be only a very small proportion of the registry's overall budget.

---

20 See Jack Regester, Ch 10 in *Proof of Birth*.
21 Grace Koelma, above n 4.
22 Melissa Castan and Paula Gerber, 'The Way Forward' in *Proof of Birth*.
23 Committee on the Rights of the Child, *Concluding Observations on Australia*, 28 August 2012, CRC/C/AUS/CO/4, www.ohchr.org/english/bodies/crc/docs/co/CRC_C_AUS_CO_4.pdf.

All registries should also adopt a policy of a fee waiver for certificates, accompanied by eligibility criteria, as is the case in Victoria. Healthcare, pension and concession cardholders or others receiving Centrelink support (such as Youth Allowance or ABSTUDY) should be eligible for a fee waiver. This should be supported by a change to the relevant BDM Acts. There should also be residual discretion on the part of each registrar to waive fees on a case-by-case basis if an individual does not fall within the abovementioned groups, such as in situations of hardship. Some registrars already have such power under the relevant statute, but may not be exercising their discretion often, if at all. Registrars could consider revising their policies and procedures regarding fees for certificates, to ensure that information about fee waivers is readily accessible to all potential applicants.[24]

Fines and penalty provisions are also in need of reform. They are likely to be the cause of some barriers to registration of births. Many of the documents, forms and websites setting out information on birth registration warn people that failure to register a birth within the prescribed period may result in a fine. In reality such fines are rarely imposed. Registrars recognise that punishing people for registering (even when late) acts as a disincentive to others to submit late registrations. But members of the public have no way of knowing whether they will or will not be subject to a penalty, and are likely to assume that the penalty will be applied. This acts as an unintended disincentive to late registration. It is therefore recommended that all references to fines and penalties be removed from materials provided to the public.[25]

E. Reduce reliance on birth certificate as proof of identity

The perceived heightened risk of identity fraud has led to increased concerns regarding access to birth certificates and improper purposes for which they may be used. While this may be appropriate as a general approach, it has had significant impacts on people without birth certificates. Registrars must balance competing obligations between keeping the BDM registers secure and ensuring that all people have access to vital community services.

---

24 Melissa Castan and Paula Gerber, 'The Way Forward' in *Proof of Birth*.
25 Ibid.

Strict identification procedures have been implemented by BDM registries and numerous other government departments and agencies, as well as private service providers (such as banks and superannuation funds). Reforms should be implemented to facilitate proof of identity without compromising the risk of fraudulent activities.[26] For example, the Department of Transport in Western Australia has a 'Verification of Identity' form to assist participants living in remote areas to apply for a driver's licence where they are unable to meet the standard proof of identity requirements. This is a welcome development that other states and territories should consider.[27]

It would be useful for other licensing authorities and agencies to accept alternate forms of identification, for example, a certificate of Aboriginality,[28] when a person cannot produce a birth certificate.[29] Reducing reliance on birth certificates for proof of identity would help to increase Indigenous people's access to appropriate services and facilitate engagement with mainstream civil society.

IV. Conclusion

This chapter has identified law and policy reform strategies that would facilitate easier access to the birth registration system by Indigenous communities and other vulnerable groups. Given the limited scope of this chapter, there are a number of aspects and issues regarding birth registration and certification that have not been addressed here. For example, it is worth considering whether the demands of the registration or certification processes themselves impact on traditional Indigenous naming practices and associated customs. Those working in law reform and advocacy for birth registration must be mindful of the historical

---

26 There are now Commonwealth ID guidelines that make some proof of identity processes easier, and others harder: see Commonwealth of Australia, *National Identity Proofing Guidelines* (Canberra, 2014), www.ag.gov.au/RightsAndProtections/IdentitySecurity/Documents/NationalIdentityProofing Guidelines.pdf. The suggestion of recognising 'alternative' identity processes is a positive development; see [5.1.3].
27 See www.transport.wa.gov.au/licensing/proof-of-identity.asp.
28 See, for example, the requirement of 'Proof of Aboriginal or Torres Strait Islander Identity' requirements for Centrelink at www.humanservices.gov.au/customer/forms/ra010, and AIATSIS 'Proof of Aboriginality' at aiatsis.gov.au/research/finding-your-family/before-you-start/proof-aboriginality.
29 See, for example, the requirements for proof of identity in order to claim superannuation: Australian Super, 'A Guide to Providing Proof of Your Identity', www.australiansuper.com/-/media/Files/Forms/A%20guide%20to%20providing%20proof%20of%20your%20identity.ashx.

misuse of past systems employed to identify Indigenous people, both in Australia and the rest of the world.[30] When seeking to improve access to the birth registration system for Indigenous birth Australians, we must ensure that the registration processes do no harm to those they seek to aid. As already noted, it is vital that any new law and policy reform only proceed following thorough consultation with Indigenous people themselves.

---

30   See Rod Hagen, 'Traditional Australian Aboriginal Naming Processes', Ch 7 in *Proof of Birth*.

42

Simplifying Government Secrecy?

Daniel Stewart[1]

I. Introduction

There are many legitimate reasons for governments to keep secrets. Exposing the information collected, developed or used by government can undermine a government's effectiveness, inhibiting the provision and creation of new information. Exposure can adversely affect private individuals and businesses. However, public disclosure can also subject government action to scrutiny, enhance trust, or provide a resource to be utilised for private or collective gain. Balancing the costs and benefits associated with disclosure of government information is difficult, and has led in Australia – including at the Commonwealth level – to an increasingly complex array of regulation and restriction.

This chapter demonstrates that complexity through two recent cases involving the disclosure of Commonwealth Government information by individuals working within government. The first looks at attempts to protect witnesses to conditions in Australian immigration detention centres. The second looks to the ramifications of engagement by public servants with social media. Both suggest that the possible benefits of disclosure of government information can be obscured by the risk of more immediate adverse consequences. The complexity and uncertainty of the

1 Senior Lecturer, ANU College of Law, The Australian National University.

various forms of regulation in this area itself acts as a disincentive for government disclosure. A common framework for assessing the balance of public interests is needed.

II. Restrictions on Government Disclosure

Unauthorised disclosure of information that is not already publicly accessible, when relayed in circumstances implying limitations on the use or disclosure of that information, is protected by the courts through the equitable action for breach of confidence.[2] However, breach of confidence applies differently when government is involved. In *Commonwealth v John Fairfax & Sons*[3] the Commonwealth Government was not able to rely on confidentiality to prevent further distribution and partial newspaper serialisation of a series of diplomatic briefings and cables. Mason J declined to accept the cables were confidential, despite their classified status:

> The court will not prevent the publication of information which merely throws light on the past workings of government, even if it be not public property, so long as it does not prejudice the community in other respects. Then disclosure will itself serve the public interest in keeping the community informed and in promoting discussion of public affairs. If, however, it appears that disclosure will be inimical to the public interest because national security, relations with foreign countries or the ordinary business of government will be prejudiced, disclosure will be restrained. There will be cases in which the conflicting considerations will be finely balanced, where it is difficult to decide whether the public's interest in knowing and in expressing its opinion, outweighs the need to protect confidentiality.[4]

The concern over public disclosure of the cables was not with their content but what the fact of release might mean for the relationship between Australia and the countries concerned. As the Secretary of the Department of Foreign Affairs at the time suggested: '[i]t is much more likely to facilitate our future relations if the government has been seen to try its utmost to prevent that [disclosure] happening'.[5]

---

2   *Corrs Pavey Whiting & Byrne v Collector of Customs (Vic)* (1987) 14 FCR 434, 443.
3   (1980) 147 CLR 39 ('*Fairfax*').
4   Ibid. 52.
5   Ibid. 46.

Mason J was not persuaded that 'the degree of embarrassment to Australia's foreign relations which flow from disclosure is enough to justify interim protection of confidential information'.[6] Confidentiality of government information depended on the possible effect on a recognised government interest outweighing the public interest in disclosure. Striking that balance continues to define the limits of government secrecy, both in terms of how it is struck, and who gets to decide.

III. Role of Legislation

In various ways *Fairfax* is a high-water mark for openness in government. The case came at a time when the traditional view of the need for government secrecy, based on the Westminster system's reliance on responsible government and a politically neutral public service, was starting to be questioned. The process of law reform in this area has meant that inherent limitations on the executive's capacity to generate and maintain secrecy have been largely overtaken by reliance on legislative authority to collect, and disclose, information.[7]

By the time *Fairfax* was decided, freedom of information legislation had already been introduced into the Commonwealth Parliament, though it would take until 1982 to be enacted. The *Freedom of Information Act 1982 (Cth)* (*FOI Act*) was meant to shift the emphasis away from executive discretion towards establishing a right of access subject only to listed categories of exceptions. In doing so it set out a range of government interests which could be used by the executive to justify withholding disclosure, expanding upon those interests considered legitimate in common law conceptions of confidentiality.[8]

The *FOI Act* was closely followed by the *Archives Act 1983* (Cth), providing for the preservation and future public use of government records. A recognition of the need to maintain public trust in the way government collects, uses and stores private information also led to the

---

6   Ibid. 54.

7   See Daniel Stewart, 'Assessing Access to Information in Australia: The Impact of Freedom of Information Laws on the Scrutiny and Operation of the Commonwealth Government' in John Wanna, Evert Lindquist and Penelope Marshall (eds), *New Accountabilities, New Challenges* (ANU Press, 2015).

8   Stewart, above n 7.

Privacy Act 1988 (Cth). Much more recently, the *Public Interest Disclosure Act 2013* (Cth) (*PID Act*) was introduced to augment the protection for whistleblowers to disclose wrongdoing and maladministration.[9]

Each of these pieces of legislation was introduced in recognition of the benefits of government disclosure of information but takes a very different approach to regulating the different interests involved. There are also a wide range of general policies, standards and guidance that impact how government agencies handle information. The National Archives of Australia has identified some 72 such instruments which, directly or indirectly, need to be considered by Commonwealth agencies and, in some cases, non-government bodies, including those that contract with government to provide services to the public.[10]

Subject matter specific legislation providing for the collection or use of information also plays an important role. In *Re Smith Kline & French Laboratories (Australia) Ltd and Secretary, Department of Community Services and Health*,[11] for example, information supplied to the government for the purposes of regulatory approval of a pharmaceutical product could be used for approval of a competitor's version of the same substance. Confidentiality was limited by the legislative objective of enhancing public health and safety.

In other circumstances the legislative context may place limits on the use and disclosure of information. In *Johns v Australian Securities Commission*[12] the High Court stated:

> A statute which confers a power to obtain information for a purpose defines, expressly or impliedly, the purpose for which the information when obtained can be used or disclosed. The statute imposes on the person who obtains information in exercise of the power a duty not to disclose the information obtained except for that purpose.

---

9   Note that external public interest disclosures can be made under the *PID Act* only in a narrow range of circumstances and usually only after an internal disclosure has been made: see Philip Moss, *Independent Review of the Public Interest Disclosure Act 2013*, www.dpmc.gov.au/resource-centre/government/review-public-interest-disclosure-act-2013 (viewed 20 April 2017).

10   National Archives of Australia, *Legislation, Policies, Standards and Advice and Your Agency's Accountability*, August 2015, www.naa.gov.au/information-management/information-governance/legislation-standards/index.aspx (viewed 17 May 2016).

11   (1991) 28 FCR 291.

12   (1993) 178 CLR 408.

Identifying the purposes for which information was obtained, and the subsequent limits on further use or disclosure of that information, is therefore a statute-by-statute proposition. Even interpreting the limits of explicit provision in legislation for disclosure or, more usually, preventing disclosure, involves assessing the intended role of information disclosure in light of the context and purpose of the statute as a whole.

It is the complexity of the interaction between these multiple sources regulating disclosure of government information which gives rise to the need for reform. The effect is often to leave disclosure to the discretion of the executive. A common framework would allow more explicit reference to the public interest in government disclosure when balanced against the interests protected through individual statutes.

IV. Court Sanctioned Disclosure

AS v Minister for Immigration and Border Protection (Ruling No. 3)[13] is one of a number of class action cases relating to the conditions in immigration detention centres with which Australia is involved. This case concerned a negligence claim arising from medical treatment available on Christmas Island. An interim application was brought to protect the ability of witnesses to speak to lawyers for the plaintiffs without facing possible prosecution.

Section 42 of the *Border Force Act 2015* (Cth) makes it a criminal offence for an entrusted person to record or disclose protected information. Entrusted persons include Immigration and Border Protection employees as well as a variety of persons who provide services to the department, including state, territory and foreign government employees, and government contractors and consultants. This includes medical staff at the centre. Protected information is information obtained by entrusted persons in that capacity. Under s 42(2) an offence is not committed where the record or disclosure is: authorised under various explicit circumstances, including where it is necessary to prevent or lessen serious threat to the life or health of an individual; made in the course of employment or service; required or authorised by law; or required by an order or direction of a court or tribunal.

---

13   [2015] VSC 642.

While s 42 has been the subject of considerable criticism, the explicit reference in that section to the making of a court order or direction enabled that court to protect voluntary disclosure by witnesses. The main concern of the Victorian Supreme Court in this matter then became how the obligations under s 42 related to other legislative and common law duties. Ultimately s 42 was held not to enable the court to release witnesses from other obligations or potential liabilities.

For example, s 70 of the *Crimes Act 1914* (Cth) makes it an offence for Commonwealth officers, including persons performing services for or on behalf of the Commonwealth, to publish or communicate, without authority, any fact or document which they know or possess by virtue of being a Commonwealth officer and which is their duty not to disclose. Section 70 does not in itself create a duty not to disclose. That duty may arise under the *Public Service Act 1999* (Cth), for example, or potentially under contractual or equitable obligations of confidentiality. It is not clear if s 70 applies to oral opinions or advice; the breadth of publication or communication seems limited only by intention; and there appears no need to demonstrate harm to any public or private interest, whether anticipated or actual.[14]

The uncertainty over what information might be disclosed by witnesses and which relevant duty of non-disclosure might be in issue meant that the court in *AS* was not willing to make an order protecting witnesses from s 70. Similarly, while the court was willing to set aside any obligations of confidentiality which involve 'an interference with the administration of justice', the nature of the obligation and extent of that interference had to be identified with precision. Many future court hearings might be required to consider how obligations of confidentiality might arise, and be overcome.

---

14   Justice Susan Kenny, 'Secrecy Provisions: Policy and Practice' (Address to the National Information Law Conference in Canberra, 24 March 2011), www.alrc.gov.au/news-media/2011/secrecy-provisions-policy-and-practice#_ftn48.

V. Engagement With the Public through Social Media

Starr v Department of Human Services[15] considered the fairness of the dismissal of a departmental employee after he had made several comments on public discussion forums including Whirlpool and Sportal. The comments were made over nearly a three year period, on his own time and on his own computer. They had come to the department's attention after several comments in which he had corrected some information posted by the department's social media unit. The department investigated and discovered earlier comments which, together with departmental records, enabled the employee to be identified. The investigation also revealed several comments where the employee had expressed his frustration at having to deal with 'junkies' and 'spastics' and 'deadbeat leeches', that a large proportion of clients were not genuine, and that processing times were disgraceful.

The Fair Work Commission found these later comments to be in breach of the APS Code of Conduct[16] and various departmental policies and guidelines.[17] These included obligations to avoid conflicts of interest;[18] not use information or one's position to cause a detriment to the government;[19] uphold APS values of ethical, respectful, accountable and impartial service and the integrity and good reputation of the Australian Public Service;[20] and not disclose information obtained in connection with employment as a public servant under the Public Service Regulations 1999.[21]

However, the Commission also found that the penalty of dismissal was disproportionate to the gravity of Mr Starr's misconduct, having regard to all the circumstances including that his conduct did not affect his actual

---

15   [2016] FWC 1460.

16   *Public Service Act* s 13.

17   For example, Department of Human Services, *Social Media Policy for Departmental Staff*, www.humanservices.gov.au/corporate/media/social-media-department/social-media-policy-departmental-staff (viewed 20 April 2017). See also the recently revised Australian Public Service Commission, *APS Values and Code of Conduct in Practice*, ss 4 and 6, www.apsc.gov.au/publications-and-media/current-publications/values-and-conduct (viewed 20 April 2017).

18   s 13(7).

19   s 13(10).

20   s 13(11) and s 10.

21   Which includes non-disclosure of such information 'if it is reasonably foreseeable that the disclosure could be prejudicial to the effective working of government', or communicated or received in confidence, unless otherwise authorised or already in the public domain: r 2.1.

work performance, caused no demonstrated detriment to the department, was engaged in impulsively rather than with deliberation, and consisted of a small number of widely interspersed comments over a period of years.[22]

In doing so the Commissioner interpreted the APS Values and Code of Conduct through the lens of the Constitutionally implied freedom of political communication:

> which, to the extent necessary to maintain the effective operation of the system of representative and responsible government provided for by the Constitution, operates to preclude the exercise of legislative power to curtail the freedom.[23]

That meant the need for a public servant to be apolitical only restricted political comments which could compromise the ability of public servants to carry out their functions, in this case taking into account the administrative rather than political nature of their particular role. It also meant that some harm to the department would have to be demonstrated. Damaging the department's reputation for treating people with respect and impartially and fairly was such a harm. Correcting erroneous information was not.

VI. Further Reform

The secrecy provision discussed in the case studies above are arguably relatively limited in their scope. The Australian Law Reform Commission, in its *Secrecy Laws and Open Government in Australia* report,[24] examined some 506 secrecy provisions in 176 pieces of legislation, including 358 distinct criminal offences. The ALRC recommended repeal of s 70 along with the even more complex s 79 of the *Crimes Act*, and replacing them with a general secrecy offence for unauthorised disclosures that have a demonstrated adverse effect on the public interest through:

- harming security, defence or international relations;
- interfering with an investigation of criminal offences;
- endangering life or physical safety; or
- prejudicing public safety.

---

22   [2016] FWC 1460 at [93].
23   [2016] FWC 1460 at [72], citing *Lange v Australian Broadcasting Corporation* (1997) 189 CLR 520 at 559–62.
24   Report No 112, 2010.

In those circumstances disclosure would have to be: in the course of an officer's functions or duties; authorised by an agency head or minister by declaring that the disclosure would, on balance, be in accordance with the public interest; or already in the public domain.[25]

The ALRC considered more specific secrecy protection should only be enacted where necessary, and generally through an express requirement that the disclosure has caused, or was likely or intended to cause, harm to a specified public interest. A blanket protection against disclosure would be warranted only for limited categories of information, such as national security or where a relationship of trust between the government and individuals is integral for an effective regulatory system but not able to be proved in a criminal prosecution.[26]

The ALRC's recommendations recognise the need for a common framework in which eroding the public interest in government disclosure could be justified. Such a framework was recently discussed in *McCloy v State of New South Wales*,[27] where the protection of the implied freedom of political communication was held to involve three questions:

1. Does the law effectively burden the freedom of political communication in its terms, operation or effect?
2. Are the purposes of the law and the means adopted legitimate, in the sense they are compatible with the maintenance of the constitutionally prescribed system of representative government?
3. Is the law reasonably appropriate and adapted to advancing that legitimate purpose? In other words, is it proportional?

Proportionality in turn requires that there be no suitable and reasonably practicable alternative means of achieving the same purpose, and the importance of that purpose outweighs the extent of the restriction on communication.

As a general framework, assessing the proportionality of any legislative restriction on disclosure of government information involves a value judgement of whether the particular harm caused by the disclosure in question outweighs the public benefit in disclosure. Legislation still has

---

25   ALRC Report 112, Recommendations 5–7.
26   Ibid. Recommendations 8–9.
27   [2015] HCA 34.

a legitimate role in setting out the range of interests that might need protecting, but more than merely speculative evidence of the harm should be required before any particular disclosure is prevented.[28]

VII. Conclusion

As the case studies set out in this paper suggest, identifying the limitations on disclosure of government information is a complex task. The uncertain operation and interaction of the various legislative and other restrictions can only act to further deter disclosure. Despite the long history or reform in this area, government disclosure often remains a matter of government discretion.

However, the general approach to government confidentiality of Mason J in *Fairfax,* reflected more recently in the approach of the ALRC and the emerging approach to proportionality in the implied freedom of political communication, suggests that a common framework is possible. Few government interests in themselves justify limiting disclosure. Other interests require identifying both the nature and extent of any adverse effect caused by the disclosure in question and considering alternative, less restrictive means to achieve government purposes. Any remaining harm has to be balanced against the benefits of disclosure. By making more explicit the values involved in that balancing of the effects of disclosure, a more developed and accepted understanding of the benefits of disclosure, now and in the future, might be realised.

---

28   See *Gaynor v Chief of the Defence Force (No 3)* [2015] FCA 1370.

Part VI. Legal Practice and Legal Education

43

Australian Legal Practice: Ethical Climate and Ethical Climate Change

Vivien Holmes, Stephen Tang, Tony Foley
and Margie Rowe[1]

I. Introduction

This chapter discusses new research into the ethical climate of Australian legal workplaces. Our research confirms that ethics are perceived as a lived culture in legal practice. We know from other research that appropriate regulation can encourage senior management to create organisational cultures which support ethical behaviour. Unfortunately, the new *Legal Profession Uniform Law* (*LPUL*), in force in NSW and Victoria,[2] takes a step backwards in this regulatory space. We join calls for reforms that will see the promise of such regulation renewed.

---

1   All of ANU College of Law, The Australian National University.
2   The *Legal Profession Uniform Law* (*LPUL*) was enacted in NSW in 2014 and then adopted in Victoria by the *Legal Profession Uniform Law Application Act 2014*. The *LPUL* came into force in both jurisdictions in July 2015 and replaced the NSW and Victorian *Legal Profession Acts* (2004).

II. Research into Workplace Ethical Culture[3]

The past 25 years has seen considerable research on the impact of the organisational environment on employees' behaviour.[4] The idea that a person's workplace environment might influence them toward (un)ethical behaviours is now well accepted. One significant stream of research in this field has been research into the 'ethical climate' of workplaces, 'ethical climate' being defined as 'the shared perception of what is correct behaviour, and how ethical situations should be handled in an organization'.[5] The most commonly used instrument of measurement in such research is Victor and Cullen's Ethical Climate Questionnaire (ECQ), a questionnaire designed to 'tap respondents' perceptions of how the members of an organization typically make decisions concerning "events, practices, and procedures" requiring ethical criteria'.[6] In 2010, in light of further research into ethical decision-making, Arnaud revised the ECQ and came up with a further questionnaire, the Ethical Climate Index (ECI),[7] which we used in our research (see below).

Significantly, in a meta-analysis of research into sources of unethical decisions at work, Kish-Gephart[8] found that the most significant dimensions of ethical climate for predicting (un)ethical behaviour were as follows:

- 'Principled', where there is a focus on following rules that protect the company and others;

---

3   'Ethical culture' and 'ethical climate' are defined differently in the literature, but the concepts overlap. This chapter uses ethical culture in the sense of it being a subset of organisational culture, 'representing a multidimensional interplay among various "formal" and "informal" systems of behavioural control that are capable of promoting either ethical or unethical behaviour'. Linda Klebe Treviño, Kenneth D Butterfield and Donald L McCabe, 'The Ethical Context in Organizations: Influences on Employee Attitudes and Behaviors' 8 *Business Ethics Quarterly* 447, 451.

4   Jennifer J Kish-Gephart, David A Harrison and Linda Klebe Treviño, 'Bad Apples, Bad Cases, and Bad Barrels: Meta-Analytic Evidence About Sources of Unethical Decisions at Work' (2010) 95 *Journal of Applied Psychology* 1; David M Mayer, 'A Review of the Literature on Ethical Climate and Culture' in *Oxford Handbook of Organizational Climate and Culture* (Oxford University Press, 2014).

5   Bart Victor and John B Cullen, 'A Theory and Measure of Ethical Climates in Organizations' (1987) 9 *Research in Corporate Social Performance and Policy* 51.

6   John D Cullen, Bart Victor and James W Bronson, 'The Ethical Climate Questionnaire: An Assessment of Its Development and Validity' (1993) 73 *Psychological Reports* 667, 669.

7   Anke Arnaud, 'Conceptualizing and Measuring Ethical Work Climate: Development and Validation of the Ethical Climate Index' (2010) 49 *Business and Society* 345.

8   Kish-Gephart, Harrison and Treviño, above n 4, 21.

- 'Benevolent', which 'focuses employee's attention on the well-being of multiple stakeholders, such as employees, customers and the community';
- 'Egoistic', which promotes 'an "everyone for himself" atmosphere'.

According to Kish-Gephart, the stronger the 'principled' and 'benevolent' climate dimensions, and the stronger the communication of 'the range of acceptable and unacceptable behaviour', the 'fewer unethical decisions in the workplace'.[9] Conversely, the stronger the egoistic dimension, the more likely is unethical behaviour.[10]

III. The Ethical Climate of Australian Legal Practices

Our research explored the ethical climate of Australian legal workplaces, as perceived by new lawyers. Our target population was lawyers within 3–12 months of entering the profession. We surveyed 325 new lawyers across all Australian jurisdictions and across all practice types: Private 63.6 per cent (Small: 32.6 per cent, Medium: 12.3 per cent, Large: 13.8 per cent, In-House: 4.9 per cent); Government 22.8 per cent; Community 8.9 per cent; Other 3.1 per cent. Respondents' median age was 26 years. Most were full-time employees (91.5 per cent) and nearly two-thirds were female (62.3 per cent).

Using Arnaud's ECI and other validated instruments, we constructed an online survey to measure respondents' perceptions of the ethical climate of their workplace, as well as the following factors:

- Organisational Learning;
- Perceived Professionalism/Professional Identity;
- Meeting of Basic Psychological Needs;
- Job Satisfaction & Career Satisfaction;
- Psychological Distress & Optimism;
- Work Environment: employer type, practice area, etc.;
- Demographics & Legal Education Background.

---

9   Ibid.
10   Ibid.

IV. Respondents' Perceptions of Ethical Climate

We used Exploratory Factor Analysis (EFA) to test whether the 17 ECI survey items could be reduced into a smaller number of identifiable ethical climate dimensions. The results suggested that there were three such dimensions.[11] Two are essentially positive:

- Integrity and Responsibility, representing a sensitivity to ethical behaviour and formal ethical rules, and an inclination to be compliant, conscientious and accountable;
- Ethic of Care, indicative of a culture in which people express empathy and understanding to each other and strive, as professionals, to develop positive and respectful relationships.

The other is principally negative:

- Power and Self-Interest, signifying that power, control and instrumental outcomes are more important than principles such as honesty, ethical rules or relationships; that people would be willing to break rules to obtain personal benefit.

Each dimension is an independent contributing factor to how ethical climate is perceived. That is, participants perceive that their workplace climate contains *more* or *less* of each one of these qualities. Figure 43.1 shows that the distribution of these dimensions is quite wide. We note that these three ethical climate dimensions are very similar to the three noted by Kish-Gephart as being predictive of (un)ethical behaviour.

---

11   This is not to say that there are not other ethical climate dimensions existing in law firms, simply that we have been able to distil three independent ingredients of ethical climate as measured on the ECI for newly admitted lawyers.

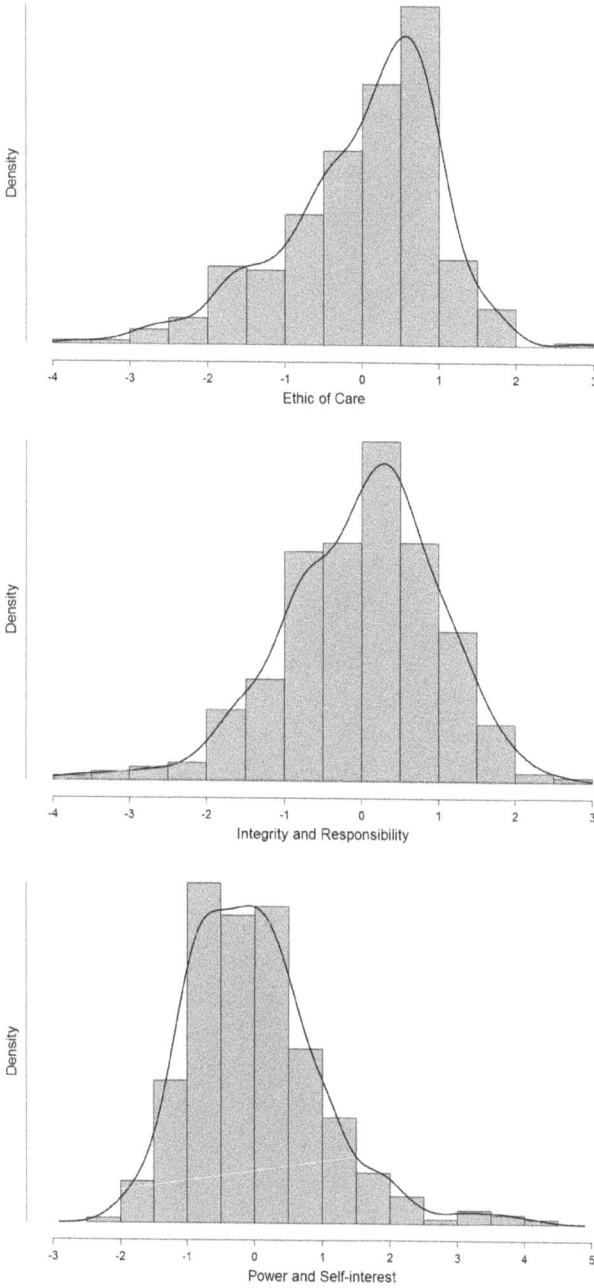

Figure 43.1: Density plot showing the distribution of each ethical climate factor

Source: The authors

V. Predictors of Ethical Climate

We investigated a set of factors as possible predictors of the ethical climate in participants' workplaces. As a preliminary we controlled for age and gender, and found no significant effects for either of these factors.

A. Practice type

We investigated the extent to which the ethical dimensions identified by respondents depended on the *type* of practice – 'private practice' (small, medium, large), 'in-house', 'government' or 'community' – in which respondents were employed. We found perceptions of the integrity/ responsibility ethical dimension were dependent to a small degree on practice type: lawyers in private practice overall (including in-house) had lower perceptions of this dimension than those working in government or community practice.

We then compared differences between 'private practice' (small/ medium/large practices as a whole) and in-house lawyers. We found nothing additional to the above about the integrity/responsibility ethical dimension. But we found that lawyers in in-house practice had higher perceptions of the power/self-interest dimension (large law firms were also trending in the same direction) when compared with lawyers in medium and small law firms. It seems that on the whole, in-house lawyers (even allowing for the relatively small number of responses obtained) seemed to perceive their workplace as characterised by a preparedness to break rules when necessary.

Combining these analyses we looked at whether working in a particular practice type produced particularly weak perceptions of any of the dimensions. We found that lawyers in small/medium firms gave low ratings to the (positive) integrity/responsibility dimension, and at the same time, low ratings to the (negative) self-interested dimension. This suggests almost an ethical vacuum or apathy, the absence of an ethical consciousness, an indication that these young lawyers had entered a world of practice where ethics were invisible (at least to them).

Surprisingly, we found that other structural features, such as working in a litigious/non-litigious practice, or serving a certain kind of client (personal, corporate, government), were not predictive of particular ethical dimensions. Our conclusion is that overt structural characteristics of the lawyers' practices (specifically, practice type) do have a small effect on perceptions of a firm's ethical culture.

B. Organisational learning culture

In addition to structural factors, we analysed the lawyers' perceptions about the learning culture of the practice in which they worked. An organisational learning culture (OLC) is evidenced by a high sense of trust, by high regard for initiative, by reward and encouragement for participation in learning, by flexibility and adaptability to challenge and change.[12] We found that high perceptions of an OLC were predictive of much higher levels of the integrity/responsibility ethical dimension. They were also predictive of the ethic of care dimension. Conversely, we found that high perceptions of an OLC were predictive of lower levels of the self-interest ethical dimension.

This result reinforces the importance of looking beyond mere structural characteristics of practices (size, practice type, client base) to also consider non-structural 'qualities' (such as learning culture), which are significantly more predictive of a practice's ethical climate and which can override the influence of structural factors.

VI. Job Satisfaction and Wellbeing

Importantly, our analysis showed direct relationships between ethical climate dimensions and job satisfaction. A strong power and self-interest climate dimension correlated with *lower* job satisfaction, while strong integrity and responsibility, and (especially) ethic of care climate dimensions, correlated with *greater* job satisfaction.

These findings are consistent with Kish-Gephard's findings, that higher job satisfaction is related to a lower level of unethical behaviour in organisations.[13]

---

12 Catherine L Wang and Pervaiz K Ahmed, 'Organisational Learning: A Critical Review' (2003)
10 *The Learning Organization* 8.
13 Kish-Gephart, Harrison and Treviño, above n 4, 12.

467

We know from our previous research with these same new lawyers that basic psychological needs (autonomy, competence and relatedness) are very good predictors of wellbeing and satisfaction in newly-admitted lawyers.[14] Analysis of survey data shows direct relationships between ethical climate and the meeting of these needs. In particular, a strong power and self-interest dimension has a (small) negative effect on autonomy, competence and relatedness, while a strong ethic of care dimension is predictive of greater autonomy and relatedness.

VII. Being Professional

Respondents were asked to choose, from a list of 24 factors, the 10 factors most definitive of 'professional'. For the purposes of analysis, we grouped the 24 factors into six categories: *Communication* (e.g. 'communicating openly, courteously and respectfully with clients and colleagues (including opponents)'); *Ethics* (e.g. 'being honest and trustworthy, including with the court'); *Justice* (e.g. 'having a commitment to improving society through your participation in the law'); *Skills* (e.g. 'having a good, up to date knowledge of legal content and processes'); *Work* (e.g. 'taking responsibility for your own work'); and *Problem* (e.g. 'ensuring that you never appear weak to your colleagues or clients'). Respondents then ranked their 10 factors in order of importance. For example, a respondent might rank an item in the communications category at positions 1, 5 and 9 in their 'definition' of 'professional'.

We correlated a respondent's perception of the ethical climate of their workplace and the importance (ranking) they gave to the 'professionalism' factors. We found (from ordinal regression analysis) that, the higher a person rated their ethical climate on the *ethic of care* dimension, the more frequently they included *communication* and *justice* items in their top 10, but the less frequently they included *work* and *problem* items. The higher a person rated their ethical climate on the *integrity/ responsibility* dimension, the more frequently they included *ethics* items in their top 10, but the less frequently they included *work* items. Further, higher perceptions of a *power/self-interest* climate were associated with more frequent ranking of *work* and *problem* items in the top 10. Inclusion of *skills* items was not

---

14   Tony Foley et al, 'Helping Junior Lawyers Thrive' (2015) 89 *Law Institute Journal* 44.

predicted by any ethical climate dimension. These results suggest that, not surprisingly, the ethical climate of a new lawyer's workplace influences their understanding of what it means to be a professional.

VIII. Influencing the Ethical Culture of Australian Legal Practices

Our study is the first ethical climate analysis of Australian legal practice. But the broad ethical culture of Australian legal practices has come under scrutiny in other ways. In 2008, Parker and colleagues applied the concept of 'ethical infrastructure' to Australian large law firms. They used a broad conceptualisation of 'ethical infrastructure' to denote formal and informal management policies and the promotion of ethical dialogue and values.[15] The authors contend that large law firms should consciously design and implement 'ethical infrastructures' to both counteract pressures for misbehaviour and positively promote ethical behaviour and discussions. We note there is no reason why this call should be confined to large law firms.

Alongside this research, a new regulatory regime was targeting ethical infrastructure. Reforms in 2001 to the NSW *Legal Profession Act 1987* (replicated in the *Legal Profession Act 2004* (*LPA*)) allowed law firms to incorporate, but required incorporated legal practices (ILPs) to have a legal practitioner director. That director's task was to ensure, through the development of 'appropriate management systems' (AMS), ILP compliance with the *LPA*.[16] Collaboration between the NSW Office of the Legal Services Commissioner and the legal profession resulted in an 'education toward compliance' strategy in relation to the AMS requirements. ILPs were required to complete a self-assessment process (SAP) which evaluated compliance with 10 specific objectives of sound legal practice.[17] Those objectives were 'intended to help ILPs work out how to professionalize ethical conduct, rather than [prescribe] detailed

---

15   Christine Parker et al, 'The Ethical Infrastructure of Legal Practice in Larger Law Firms: Values, Policy and Behaviour' (2008) 31 *UNSW Law Journal* 158, 160, n 6.

16   NSW *LPA* s 140.

17   Susan Fortney and Tahlia Gordon, 'Adopting Law Firm Management Systems to Survive and Thrive: A Study of the Australian Approach to Management-Based Regulation' (2012) 10 *University of St Thomas Law Journal* 152, 153.

management systems and processes'.[18] Importantly, the regulator was authorised to conduct a compliance audit of an ILP *whether or not a complaint* had been made in relation to the practice. So, audits could be done proactively, as a preventative measure. Queensland, WA, Northern Territory and the ACT eventually adopted a similar statutory and regulatory approach.[19]

Evaluation of NSW's 'light touch' approach to regulation of the profession has shown it had a significant impact. Parker and colleagues conducted a preliminary evaluation based on an analysis of complaint rates. They concluded that the SAP 'may well be guiding, encouraging, and requiring many practitioners consciously and systematically to think through practice management issues, including ethics management, for the very first time'.[20] Other scholars describe the implementation of the AMS requirement as 'a watershed event in the regulation of law firms'.[21] Fortney evaluated the process in 2012 by surveying legal practitioner directors. The majority of respondents reported that the SAP 'had a positive effect on different aspects of firm practice, most notably firm management, supervision and risk management, followed by a positive impact on client services'.[22] It is not hard to see a link between 'the process of learning and changes'[23] prompted by the SAP, and an improved organisational learning culture (and, by inference, stronger integrity/responsibility and ethic of care climate dimensions). Further, Schenyer credits the NSW program for giving content to the concept of 'ethical infrastructure' by 'identifying the ten types of recurring problems that infrastructure should be designed to prevent or at least mitigate'.[24] It is clear that the *LPA* requirement of AMS was a powerful regulatory tool for improving the ethical culture of law firms.

---

18   Christine Parker, Tahlia Gordon and Steve Mark, 'Regulating Law Firm Management: An Empricial Assessment of an Innovation in Regulation of the Legal Profession in New South Wales' (2010) 37 *Journal of Law and Society* 466, 471.

19   Steve Mark and Tahlia Gordon, 'Innovations in Regulation – Responding to a Changing Legal Services Market' (2009) 22 *Georgetown Journal of Legal Ethics* 501, 511; John Briton and Scott Mclean, 'Incorporated Legal Practices: Dragging the Regulation of the Profession into the Modern Era' 11 *Legal Ethics* 241.

20   Parker, Gordon and Mark, above n 18, 495.

21   Fortney and Gordon, above n 17, 154.

22   Ibid. 181.

23   Ibid. 167.

24   Ted Schneyer, 'On Further Reflection: How "Professional Self-Regulation" Should Promote Compliance with Broad Ethical Duties of Law Firm Management' (2011) 53 *Arizona Law Review* 577, 585.

Unfortunately, the *Legal Profession Uniform Law* (*LPUL*), in force in NSW and Victoria since July 2015, has taken a backward step in this regulatory space. The requirement (on ILPs) under the LPAs to implement and maintain AMS has been discarded. There is now no positive obligation placed upon an ILP, or any other type of law practice, to implement AMS. Instead, a law practice may be given a 'management systems direction' by a relevant regulatory authority to ensure that AMS are 'implemented and maintained'.[25] However, such a direction can only be made if the authority considers it reasonable to do so after an examination/ investigation into a law practice, or a compliance audit.[26] As the former NSW Legal Services Commissioner (Steve Mark) has noted, this means that 'a law practice will only know what standard it is expected to comply with AFTER being audited and found wanting'.[27] This contrasts with the *LPA* scheme which so successfully used AMS as a proactive tool to encourage compliance. Mark and Briton, the former Queensland Legal Services Commissioner, have both called for a return to the proactive use of AMS.[28]

IX. Conclusion: Needed Reform

Our research clearly shows that ethics is perceived by new lawyers as a lived culture in legal practice, and not simply or primarily as a personal disposition. The ethical climate in which a new lawyer works influences them towards, or away from, ethical behaviour. It moulds their perceptions of what it means to be a professional and what is appropriate professional behaviour. It affects their job satisfaction and their wellbeing. We know that the ethical culture of legal practices can be shaped through regulatory tools such as AMS, which help to improve organisational learning culture and ethical infrastructure. Our research shows that a significant number of legal practices in Australia would benefit from such improvements, and adds to the force of calls for a return to the proactive use of AMS in the regulation of the legal profession.

---

25 *LPUL*, above n 2, s 257.

26 Ibid.

27 Steve Mark and Tahlia Gordon, 'Vale Appropriate Management Systems' (2015) *Creative Consequences*, creativeconsequences.com.au/vale-appropriate-management-systems (viewed 18 November 2015).

28 Ibid.; John Briton, 'Between the Idea and the Reality Falls the Shadow' (2015), www.monash. edu/law/research/centres/clars/news-events/anzlec5-sustainable-legal-ethics (viewed 17 May 2017).

Strengthening Australian Legal Ethics and Professionalism

Adrian Evans[1]

I. Introduction

Initiatives designed to reform and strengthen legal professional ethics are obviously needed. While we are constantly exposed to courageous, justice-centred lawyers and judges, these individual examples of good lawyering are not the everyday reality of many peoples' encounters with the legal profession.

Consider other lawyers' continuing moral silence and diverse misconduct in the theft of client funds and habitual overcharging leading to constant appearances in courts and disciplinary tribunals; of in-house counsel with insufficient courage who overlook insider corruption in the Reserve Bank or AWB; of litigation lawyers who advise delay and obstruction as the preferred strategy of those Catholic bishops who have covered up priests' paedophilia; of over-zealous commercial lawyering which actively facilitates socially and environmentally destructive development in Queensland and PNG, not to mention routinely callous and discourteous lawyer-to-lawyer behaviours across the country. To cap it all off, the global controversy erupting from the millions of Panama Papers, leaked from a single law firm, clarifies that the international legal profession differs

---

1   Faculty of Law, Monash University.

little from the local in its attempts to dignify tax evasion as tax avoidance.[2] All of these point to an ethically challenged legal profession which (most unfortunately) established law associations (all voluntary groupings) can ill-afford to sufficiently acknowledge. And government is mostly silent on these problems, because there are very few attorneys-general or investigative commissioners who come from outside the profession. So the potential for institutional law reform designed to reduce misconduct and strengthen individual morality is very limited.

Nevertheless, if coincidentally there were a media campaign emerging from an egregious scandal, appropriate judicial or maverick politician leadership and some level of educational and professional consensus about the extent of current de-professionalism, then change might occur. Here are three achievable initiatives that might be pursued.

II. Legal Ethics and Professionalism Education

Addressing stronger legal ethics at the regulatory level will remain superficial and transitory without longer-term changes to legal education that strengthen wellbeing and develop justice-focused values in new graduates,[3] especially in those who aspire to commercial legal practice. How can a new lawyer who, over four years or more, is consistently educated to maximise the short-term interests of corporate clients regardless of justice – and who is paid and offered promotion according to the energy of their immediate billing of those same clients – hope to avoid developing a fractured psychology? And how can they be reasonably expected to suddenly develop a concern for those adversely impacted by their clients' operations, be they aggressively growth-focused rather than sustainable, tax evading rather than tax paying, or even corrupt?

To undermine and, I suggest, appropriately subvert such ego-driven lawyering, there is an effective and achievable educational pedagogy, one which operates on law students' psyche before materialism can completely dominate. In-house, live client, poverty-law clinical legal education (CLE)

---

2   Mossack Fonseca may now be the most widely known law firm of all, for the wrong reasons. See *ABC News*, 5 April 2016, www.abc.net.au/news/2016-04-05/why-the-panama-papers-mossack-fonseca-leaks-really-matters/7300262.

3   See Vivien Holmes, '"Giving Voice to Values": Enhancing Students' Capacity to Cope with Ethical Challenges in Legal Practice' (2015) 18(2) *Legal Ethics* 115.

– which explicitly articulates a virtue ethics approach, rather than the normally dominant role morality or consequentialism – can become a mandatory part of every law degree, in the interests of redirecting law graduates towards the essential social value of legal professionalism – a concern for justice. CLE is not some variant of scientology for lawyers. It is a powerful, globally accepted pedagogy that lacks only some law deans' political courage.

A. In-house, live client, poverty law experience – not just simulation

Legal clinics come in many sizes and shapes, but not all purported clinics will achieve for students a heartfelt desire for justice. The best of clinical legal education involves an in-house experience, in the sense that the law school rather than an external agency operates the clinical site. Law schools can generally focus on conscious teaching of a justice agenda more deliberately than an agency such as a law firm or government department. Similarly, clients need to be real ('live'), if their everyday hopes and predicaments are to affect students emotionally. And those predicaments are most acute when clients are truly in need, as opposed to small businesses seeking advice on for example, GST compliance. Simulation is important and can encourage identification with clients despairing of a lack of access to justice, but it excels at teaching skills, not the development of a deep and life-changing empathy.

B. Virtue ethics – not dominant role morality or consequentialism

The intellectual base to justice is often assumed in law schools, rather than analysed and taught. Justice is a quintessential moral concept, and in particular a virtue in the Aristotelian sense. Justice is one of a number of virtues that sit inside the framework of virtue ethics, as opposed to the other two much better known and competing frameworks of consequentialism and Kantianism. But legal ethics education typically concentrates on the latter two methodologies, in particular role morality or zealous advocacy, which is an applied Kantian category that is not directly concerned for justice except to the extent that it coincidentally aligns with a client's needs.

Teaching of legal ethics with a justice focus must redirect its energy towards virtue ethics, if overall justice is to mean something more to future lawyers than what an individual client may desire or need.

III. Enhancing Ethical Infrastructure

The *Uniform Law* regulatory initiative covering NSW and Victoria is limping along towards a hoped-for national uniformity, but it is going so slowly that it risks attracting national disability insurance support. There are no real signs of a national leadership vision emerging from the Uniform Legal Services Council; no sense of urgency about, for example, reforming the profoundly inadequate continuing professional development system, the highly partisan conduct rules which allow a single law firm to act against a former client in the face of that client's utter objections, and no embarrassment about the way in which our law societies and regulators use clients' funds without their effective knowledge.

A. Mickey-Mouse CPD

Continuing Professional Development (CPD) when first introduced in the 1980s was deliberately minimal, in order to build a degree of practitioner confidence in the concept: 10 hours per annum per practitioner, no assessment, no requirement for or monitoring of competent delivery, no face-to-face attendance requirements and minimal enforcement. Only one hour per annum is required for legal ethics.[4] Such a basic structure no longer represents a quality-driven framework, if the objective is to build a credible ethical infrastructure.

B. Entrenching successive conflicts of interest

There have been many criticisms of the *Australian Solicitors Conduct Rules*,[5] but the most important concern the egregious sanctification of the practice of some major law firms when it comes to dealing with prior clients. The *Rules*, specifically r 10.2, were heavily influenced by the large law firms' group (i.e. the 10–12 very large Australian law firms, many

---

4   See, for example, the *Legal Profession Uniform Continuing Professional Development (Solicitors) Rules 2015*, rr 8 and 9, www.legislation.nsw.gov.au/sessionalview/sessional/sr/2015-242.pdf.

5   See *Legal Profession Uniform Law Australian Solicitors' Conduct Rules 2015*, www.legislation.nsw.gov.au/viewtop/inforce/subordleg+244+2015+cd+0+N.

of which are now global players) to permit a firm to ignore the loyalty those prior clients might have thought they were owed and allow them to act for a new client against them, regardless of the prior client's protest.[6] This single provision does more than almost any other regulatory rule to establish that the real priority of the largest firms is one of business rather than fidelity, and that the justice agenda is not inherently a compelling call on their partners' time.

C. Unconscionable use of interest earned on clients' trust moneys distorts the moral funding of regulation

Unlike most other countries, Australia in effect forces many clients to unwittingly contribute from their trust moneys to the various activities which financially support the legal profession. Known generically as Interest on Lawyers Trust Accounts (IOLTA), each of legal regulation, legal aid, lawyers' own education and, ironically (given this conference), lawyers' systemic advocacy of law reform, are regular beneficiaries of such money. Clients can avoid this leakage if they know to insist that they be paid their interest, but if they are ignorant, as most are, the transfer happens silently in the background. Between $50–100 million is diverted annually around Australia in this manner.

Efforts have been made in the past to propose a national conduct rule requiring practitioners to assess whether clients could obtain a net interest benefit from their own funds, but have been met with professional silence, presumably because of the significant conflict of interest faced by the law societies and regulators should they pursue such a conduct rule. In particular, societies and legal services commissioners would have to fund a greater proportion of regulatory expenses from lawyer levies, which is in fact what occurs in most other countries.[7]

It is time to redress a fundamentally unethical funding structure and establish a regulatory funding model that links percentage contributions by lawyers to the gross revenue (not taxable profit) of the firm, and eschews any connection to subsidies from IOLTA funds. And the question

---

6   The requirement for an Information Barrier in such situations is beside the point: the prior client is effectively told that its earlier relationship was a business deal only, not that of a fiduciary or confidant.

7   The only major exception is South Africa, which has long operated a trust account interest transfer scheme similar to Australian jurisdictions.

remains: how is it ethical – and the act of a genuine fiduciary – to not advise and warn clients of this clandestine subsidy, or at least to give them the option of keeping what is already their own money?[8]

D. The courage to regulate lawyers

But this clear need for a stronger local ethical culture and uniform infrastructure across Australia is, to many eyes, of little significance in the face of legal practice globalisation, with its *Uber*-like 'new law' models that subcontract to lawyers everywhere and hide moral accountability for individual lawyers' performance inside global firms' corporate structures, if not cyberspace; structures into which regulators only hesitantly venture, and then only in response to the rare complaint that is not resolved quietly and internally by managing partners who will do almost anything to preserve those corporate reputations. Think of George Clooney in *Michael Clayton*, but do not think such a scenario is incredible.

Though they ought to do so, it will not be enough for the current non-*Uniform Law* jurisdictions to simply adopt the apparently impressive compliance audit provisions of NSW and Victoria. Former Queensland Legal Services Commissioner (LSC) John Briton has provided a powerful analysis of the compliance audit powers, which only permit an LSC to audit where he or she has 'reasonable grounds' to do so.[9] This seemingly innocuous limitation keeps the LSC relatively impotent,[10] because he/she can rarely if ever enter a firm to check out a mere rumour or to explore an intuition; they will first need a formal complaint or a whistleblower.

Currently, regulators encountering exceptional circumstances, but who lack witnesses, must have the courage to decide that there are reasonable grounds for a compliance audit and go into the largest firms. Even then, there is no requirement for the existence of the audit to be made public. But that courage and that transparency are not yet on display. Transparency International or another well-regarded public interest or consumer guardian would have much to contribute in strengthening the Uniform Legal Services Council if invited to join by someone in authority.

---

8   See Adrian Evans, *The History and Control of the Solicitors Guarantee Fund (Vic) and its Ethical Implications for the Legal Profession* (LLM, by major thesis, Monash University, 1997).

9   *Legal Profession Uniform Law Application Act 2014* (Vic) s 256.

10   John Briton, 'Between the Idea and the Reality Falls the Shadow', www.monash.edu/law/centres/clars/news-events/anzlec5-sustainable-legal-ethics.

Consider for instance the huge meltdown in the share price of our largest listed lawyer: Slater and Gordon. The firm lost $958 million in market capitalisation in just six months,[11] as a result of incorrect financial projections and perhaps bad luck, maintaining throughout that clients' interests were at no time compromised.[12] The firm had only until the end of April 2016 to convince its bankers that it has sufficient cash flow from completed clients' files to fund, regardless of salaries, a net debt of $741m within 12 months.[13] It could easily be that the firms' clients were or are suffering even though debt repayments have now been successfully delayed, in the sense that major and continuing negative publicity about share price falls and unresolved class actions against the firm are prejudicing some clients' confidence in their individual lawyers and/or causing them to query case management decisions, particularly those concerning case settlements.[14]

Is there a link between Slater and Gordon's firm-wide financial decisions about projected earnings and its case management policy? We don't know, but the published accounts for the six months to December 2015 are enough of a public indicator that a compliance audit is needed, and we do not know that that has happened. If it has occurred, there has been no public announcement that the audit is complete and that the firm is in the clear. Suffice to say, law reform in ethical infrastructure is needed and, in the case of listed corporations that also want to be law firms, will need to provide for much greater investigative capacity and transparency than is currently permitted by the *Uniform Law*.

IV. Personal Ethical Accountability

If ethical infrastructure can easily go further, then why not individual ethical accountability? It would be a central mistake to think it is enough to move on the institutional or systemic front, but not on the personal. I have suggested that the assessment of an individual lawyer's general morality –

---

11   Jonathan Shapiro, 'Slater and Gordon Recruit Jumps Ship as Stock Sinks to New Low', *The Age*, Business News, 29 March 2016, 21.

12   Ibid.

13   Ibid.

14   News Limited reported on 2 May 2016 that the firm had avoided corporate shame and restructured (delayed) its debt repayments by 2–3 years under a deal with its lead banker, Westpac, www.news.com.au/finance/business/breaking-news/slatergordon-lenders-nod-for-restructure/news-story/b3ad8a69956a636359aa24895d24cd42.

involving not just their understanding of 'lawyer types' and general moral methodologies, but also the strength of desirable psychological traits and attitudes such as the virtues of honesty, courage and integrity – ought to become mainstream as a part of strengthening the CPD process, not to mention the fundamental purpose of improving personal conduct.[15]

More specifically, what appears to be needed is the recognition that character-strengthening is likely to be the new parameter in enhancing professional ethics. Accordingly, *general morality* personal ethics education and qualitative assessment of character at set intervals after admission is called for.

These reforms are technically achievable, either voluntarily at the behest of individual law associations – who might take the view that it is better to get in first and manage the process from inside the profession – or compulsorily as a condition of annual licensing, at the direction of a future Uniform Legal Services Council.

The various technical options for assessing these qualities were recently canvassed in the UK,[16] but no one inside the profession or within an Attorney-General's office has yet bitten the reform bullet. Why the hesitation? There remains a considerable and primitive suspicion among practising lawyers that psychology is essentially an occult enterprise, or has at least the potential to substantially impact on their decision-making. The former fear is regrettable, but the latter is partially correct. A lawyer who is assessed psychologically as part of their routine annual licensing, not because of some perceived mental health problem, but to measure for reasonable levels of integrity and social empathy, is arguably more likely to understand and connect with clients who are deserving of more justice than their bank accounts will run to. Such positive attitudes are likely to impact favourably on the decisions they make to run cases and increase access to justice. They may also begin to improve public perceptions of legal professional reputations. There are well-accepted psychological

---

15   See generally Adrian Evans, *Assessing Lawyers' Ethics* (Cambridge University Press, Melbourne, 2011).

16   Richard Moorhead, Victoria Hinchly, Christine Parker, David Kershaw and Soren Holm, *Designing Ethics Indicators for Legal Services Provision*, UCL Centre for Ethics and Law, Working Paper No. 1, 2012, papers.ssrn.com/sol3/papers.cfm?abstract_id=2159296.

scales (personal attribute inventories and psychological inventory questionnaires) that have been developed to measure, among many other things, an individual's degree of honesty and integrity.[17]

Professional integrity is a key social good that the legal profession can use not just to improve overall conduct and reputation, but to sustain lawyers' relevance in a modern technologically-infatuated business world. There is in fact no in-principle reason why a lawyer's measured levels of or capacity for integrity would not attract professional acceptance as a value-add mechanism, if some of the latest predictions for removing lawyers from lucrative transactional work altogether came to fruition. Think for example, of the emerging Blockchain technology, which the major banks at least consider capable of establishing (among several other lawyer-excluding apps) an encrypted binary equivalent of the old 'chain of title' so important in the conveyance of general law land.[18]

In the face of continuing major ethics failures among lawyers, there is a tangible prospect of improved conduct as a result of heightened awareness by practitioners of their own 'integrity ranking', and of the marketing opportunity offered by such rankings. There will be fears about privacy and state control of lawyers, but these are arguments that are already essentially lost in the Australian context, and becoming historical only.[19]

V. Conclusion

I suggest that each of the above suggestions in legal professional regulation be undertaken as a matter of urgency by government in the interests of a reimagined ethical role for lawyers in contributing to a sustainable 21st century society.

---

17   A well-known example of such an instrument is the Minnesota Multiphasic Personality Inventory. See www.verywell.com/what-is-the-minnesota-multiphasic-personality-inventory-2795582.

18   See Fabian Horton, 'Chain Reaction' (2016) 90(4) *Law Institute Journal* 69. If the true 'value add' of a lawyer to a standardised contract is his/her integrity, and that integrity is measured, then the active insertion of the lawyer into that transaction, despite the purported Blockchain guarantee, could add to the client's overall satisfaction by offering an additional level of safety, in the face of what will be inevitable efforts to hack the chains of code and expose the transaction to fraud.

19   *WikiLeaks* and its investigative imitators have established that broad scale electronic surveillance of all sorts is pervasive. In relation to State control of lawyers, the Uniform Legal Services Council is undoubtedly a creature of government, albeit comprising a majority of lawyers among its members.

45

Since Lawyers Work in Teams, We Must Focus on Team Ethics

Justine Rogers[1]

I. Introduction

James Hardie, AWB, McCabe, Foreman and the Catholic Church cases have revealed how ethical misconduct occurs within and by lawyers' teams. They have made clear that ethical decision-making and behaviour are beset by group dynamics and that individual morality corrodes without the right sort of consultation. This chapter presents team ethics as due for action, being a decisive but under-recognised part of lawyers' practice and morality.

Lawyers today need to know how to rely on and support each other in teams. People working in teams to pursue shared objectives is a basic fact of organisational functioning.[2] Due to client demands, the complexity of issues and changing practice conditions, teamwork constitutes an increasing proportion of legal activity.[3] This is particularly so in large law

---

1   Lecturer, University of New South Wales Law School.
2   Christopher P Neck and Charles C Manz, 'From Groupthink to Teamthink: Toward the Creation of Constructive Thought Patterns in Self-managing Work Teams' (1994) 47(8) *Human Relations* 929; Janet Weinstein and Linda H Morton, 'Collaboration and Teamwork' (2015) *Faculty Scholarship Paper* 163, 1.
3   H Gardner and M A Valentine, 'Collaboration Among Highly Autonomous Professionals: Costs, Benefits and Future Research Directions' in Shane Thyre and Edward J Lawler (eds), *Advances in Group Processes* (Emerald Group Publishing, 2015) 209; Weinstein and Morton, above n 2, 2.

firms, and government and in-house departments. However, teams are also found in and cut across multiple legal entities and disciplines.[4] Teams can be hierarchical or collaborative,[5] and vary in their degrees of formality, stability and self-consciousness.[6]

Most importantly for this chapter, the team is a central mediator of ethics. All of us develop morally as members of social groups, including of our workplaces, which are now the central sites for lawyers' identities. More and more, lawyers recognise and resolve ethics issues within a team structure. Teams acquire strong or weak ethics cultures and voice climates. An 'ethics culture' consists of the organisation's formal structures and informal, shared and learned stories, attitudes and behaviour relevant to ethics.[7] Culture to the organisation is what personality is to the individual: a hidden, yet unifying theme that provides meaning, direction and mobilisation. An 'ethics voice climate' gets at whether speaking up about ethics issues is encouraged,[8] or whether, at the other end, there is a 'climate of silence'.[9] Within a single organisation, the teams' ethics cultures and climates can vary, and/or diverge from those of the organisation. These deviations can act as destabilising forces,[10] though they also offer the possibility for new, positive ideas and routines to develop, for potential diffusion then throughout the organisation.

However, despite the expansion of team activity, legal practice is marked out, and typically perceived, as self-reliant and competitive.[11] 'Lawyers often think about their own ethical behaviour as a matter of individual, independent judgment in the specific context of their own clients in their own situation'.[12] The disciplinary architecture fortifies these beliefs.[13] The conduct rules, for instance, attend to certain features of a lawyer's relationship with their colleagues, as people they may consult with on

---

4   Weinstein and Morton, above n 2, 2–3.

5   Gardner and Valentine, above n 3, 213–14.

6   Alex Steel, Anna Huggins and Julian Laurens, 'Valuable Learning, Unwelcome Assessment: What LLB and JD Students really think about Group Work' (2014) 36 *Sydney Law Review* 291.

7   Lei Huang and Ted A Paterson, 'Group Ethical Voice: Influence of Ethical Leadership and Impact on Ethical Performance' (2014) 43 *Journal of Management* 1157.

8   Ibid. 3–4.

9   Elizabeth Wolfe Morrison and Frances J Milliken, 'Speaking Up, Remaining Silent: The Dynamics of Voice and Silence in Organizations' (2003) 40(6) *Journal of Management Studies* 1353.

10   Christine Parker et al, 'The Ethical Infrastructure of Legal Practice in Larger Law Firms: Values, Policy and Behaviour' (2008) 31 *UNSW Law Journal* 158, 173–74.

11   Weinstein and Morton, above n 2, 2.

12   Parker et al, above n 10, 166.

13   Ibid.

ethical matters, but not as team-members working together, clarifying and defending ideas with one another, and whose behaviour affects that of others.

This chapter examines the scholarship and draws on the author's own (2014) study of UNSW law students' ethics capacities, to chart some of what we know about the influences of the team on ethics, both general and specific to law. The aim is to convey its sweeping significance to initiate change.

Part II outlines some of the negative potential impacts of the team on ethics. Part III examines the positive. The chapter uses Rest's model of ethical decision-making, developed between the 1980s and 1990s, to delineate these influences. Rest and his colleagues understood moral behaviour as involving at least four interlinked and necessary psychological components. The processes are:

1. *Moral sensitivity* or interpreting a situation as having ethical dimensions and imagining those affected and cause–effect chains of events.
2. *Moral judgment* or judging which action would be morally justified.
3. *Moral motivation* or giving priority to moral values over others, and taking personal responsibility for moral outcomes.
4. *Moral character* or having the courage to persist with moral action, overcoming fatigue, temptation and countervailing pressures.[14]

Rest's model recognised the affective and non-linear qualities inherent in moral behaviour. Nevertheless, his theory has been extensively criticised for its rationalist foundations, including by 'social intuitionist' scholars who have uncovered that moral judgment, one of Rest's components, is primarily made rapidly, emotionally and intuitively, and that any analysis is largely used to justify initial reactions.[15] It is also regarded as too focused on the individual and not enough on their social and collective situations. Indeed, the primary content of this chapter comes from behavioural ethics

---

14   J R Rest, *Moral Development: Advances in Research and Theory* (Praeger, 1986); J R Rest, 'Background: Theory and Research' in J R Rest and D Narvaez (eds), *Moral Development in the Professions: Psychology and Applied Ethics* (LEA, 1994) (Postconventional Moral Thinking, 101–2; see page 10 for citations).

15   Jonathan Haidt, *The Righteous Mind: Why Good People are Divided by Politics and Religion* (Vintage, 2012); see, for example, list of sources in Robert A Prentice, 'Behavioral Ethics: Can it Help Lawyers (and Others) Be Their Best Selves' (2015) 29 *Notre Dame Journal of Law, Ethics & Public Policy* 35, fn 124.

research, a separate strand concerned with how people actually behave in moral contexts, and how the situation, specifically of being in a team, can nudge them towards or away from an ethical direction.[16] Rest's framework is used here, notwithstanding, as a helpful way of breaking up the research, which was in fact its original function. Further, with its ultimate focus on improving outwardly observable behaviour by delineating at least some of the major prerequisites for ethical behaviour, it also suggests valuable lines of action for legal education and training, and organisational and regulatory change. Certain implications of this second, intuitive approach are addressed towards the chapter's end, which offer cautions for team-based ethics.

The conclusion is a set of recommendations for education, practice, regulation and scholarship. This proposal should be positioned within a wider reform movement that advocates for concepts of ethical conduct and accountability to be expanded to address their collective dimensions.[17]

II. Negative Impacts of the Team on Ethics

A. Moral sensitivity

- Fragmentation: teamwork separates people from the complete task, each other, the client, and others affected by their decisions, limiting the possibility for ethical awareness.[18]

- Self-confidence bias: teams assume their inherent morality and may, then, perceive moral questioning as unnecessary or even threatening.[19]

- Moral exclusion: teamwork can encourage beliefs that only members, or powerful members within it, are entitled to moral considerations.[20]

---

16   Max H Bazerman and Francesco Gino, 'Behavioral Ethics: Towards a Deeper Understanding of Moral Judgment and Dishonesty', *Annual Review of Law & Social Science* (forthcoming) 9.

17   Kimberly Kirkland, 'Ethics in Large Law Firms: The Principle of Pragmatism' (2005) 35 *University of Memphis Law Review* 631; Parker et al, above n 10; Milton C Regan Jr, 'Nested Ethics: A Tale of Two Cultures' (2013) 42 *Hofstra Law Review* 143.

18   Parker et al, above n 10, 163–65.

19   Irving L Janis, *Groupthink: Psychological Studies of Policy Decisions and Fiascoes* (Houghton Mifflin, 2nd edn, 1982) 256–57.

20   Parker et al, above n 10, 165.

B. Moral judgment

- Groupthink: cohesive groups tend to strive for consensus and make assumptions about unanimity. Their members self-censor, ignore alternatives, and dehumanise outsiders,[21] or at least polarise their views to accord with those of the leader or majority.[22]

- Conformity bias: the inclination to coordinate or comply is stronger if members have identified with the group or if they risk exclusion or shame.[23]

- In-group bias: outside voices tend to be restrained since they represent interruptions to valued relationships within the team.[24] As a pertinent, though less obvious example, the legal academic-teacher is, to some extent, an outside voice in their students' analyses of legal ethical issues. The students have already begun to forge relationships, real and imagined, with the legal profession. A student in my research told me: 'I want to hear from law firms and lawyers that being ethical is in their best interests, not just from academics'.

C. Moral motivation

- Diffusion of obligation: team members can believe that responsibility for ethical issues lies with someone else.[25]

- Myth of invisibility: a team can give individuals a sense of protection from outside scrutiny.[26]

- In general, group work encourages learned passivity.[27]

---

21 Janis, above n 19.
22 Cass R Sunstein and Reid Hastie, *Wiser: Getting beyond Groupthink to Make Groups Smarter* (Harvard Business Press, 2015).
23 Janis, above n 19, 5–8; Patricia H Werhane et al, *Obstacles to Ethical Decision-making: Mental Models, Milgram and the Problem of Obedience* (Cambridge University Press, 2013) 102–3.
24 Ibid. 106.
25 Jennifer K Robbennolt and Jean R Sternlight, 'Behavioral Legal Ethics' 45(3) (2013) *Arizona State Law Journal* 1107, 1149.
26 Werhane et al, above n 23, 116.
27 Ibid. 119.

D. Moral action

An individual in a group may decide not to speak up or otherwise persist in unethical behaviour if the costs outweigh the benefits.[28] These assessments can be inaccurate both ways; that moral action would or would not be worthwhile.[29] There are three risk factors:

1. Safety

Raising an ethics issue can upset relationships within the group,[30] and risks, or is seen to risk,[31] labelling, exclusion and retaliation.[32] To make this assessment, team members use social information about culture and climate, primarily the leader's informal conduct, including any undermining behaviours,[33] as well as the leader's routine attitudes towards uncertainty and mistakes.[34] A climate of silence is related to a punitive culture, or a workplace in which it is not safe for employees to raise and learn from their mistakes.

2. Likely impact

Individuals assess their likely ability to initiate change in relation to their level of autonomy in their job.[35] They also evaluate whether past wrongdoers were disciplined[36] and systemic problems corrected,[37] or whether raising the issue was, or seemed, futile.[38] A student reported: 'I would need evidence that something was done about complaints to bother reporting anything'.

---

28 Jeffrey A LePine and Linn Van Dyne, 'Predicting Voice Behavior in Work Groups' (1998) 83(6) *Journal of Applied Psychology* 853.

29 Ethan R Burris, 'The Risks and Rewards of Speaking Up: Managerial Responses to Employee Voice' (2012) 55(4) *Academy of Management Journal* 851.

30 Shahidul Hassan, 'The Importance of Ethical Leadership and Personal Control in Promoting Improvement-Centered Voice among Government Employees' (2015) 25(3) *Journal of Public Administration Research and Theory* 697.

31 Gardner and Valentine, above n 3.

32 James R Detert and Ethan R Burris, 'Leadership Behavior and Employee Voice: Is the Door really Open?' (2007) 50(4) *Academy of Management Journal* 869.

33 M Lance Frazier and Wm Matthew Bowler, 'Voice Climate, Supervisor Undermining, and Work Outcomes: A Group-Level Examination' (2015) 41(3) *Journal of Management* 841.

34 Detert and Burris, above n 32.

35 Hassan, above n 30, 703; Robbennolt and Sternlight, above n 25, 1180.

36 Linda K Treviño, Gary R Weaver and Scott J Reynolds, 'Behavioral Ethics in Organizations: A Review' (2006) 32(6) *Journal of Management* 951.

37 Robbennolt and Sternlight, above n 25, 1179.

38 Prentice, above n 15, 40; Huang and Paterson, above n 7, 7–8.

3. Harm to other interests

The benefits of collaboration appear to accrue at the collective.[39] This appears wasteful within a 'stars culture' in which the individual's expertise and client relationships generate status.[40] Further, the team itself can act as the centre of patronage networks needed for advancement as well as a mechanism of evaluation. Research into government professionals shows a negative relationship between performance monitoring and 'improvement-centred employee voice', or the propensity to make suggestions to improve the organisation, including its ethical culture.[41] One student said: 'To be ethical, I'd need to see support for the person voicing the concern, proof that you won't be condemned or bullied or overlooked for promotion'.

The strain of group dynamics has an upsetting, diminishing influence on each of these components. Teamwork can deplete time and cognitive resources as energy is diverted to impression management, and the logistics of organising and integrating expertise.[42] Lawyers tend to be more self-protective, less interpersonally sensitive and less steady in the face of pressure than the general population.[43] Teamwork can create extra feelings of exposure and incompetence.[44] Shame tends to lead to turning inward and away from others,[45] and fear of exclusion can result in contempt towards the team.[46] Though not a typical response, one student reported that teamwork in my course was 'bad for wellbeing and reminded me of high school'. Nonetheless, there is potential for team-based ethics to be highly beneficial and productive.

---

39   Gardner and Valentine, above n 3, 215.
40   Gardner and Valentine, above n 3.
41   Hassan, above n 30, 714.
42   Gardner and Valentine, above n 3, 215.
43   L Richard and L Rohrer, 'A Breed Apart?' (2011) *The American Lawyer* 43.
44   Elisabeth Dunne and Mike Rawlins, 'Bridging the Gap between Industry and Higher Education: Training Academics to Promote Student Teamwork' (2000) 37 *Innovations in Education and Teaching International* 361; Steel, Huggins and Laurens, above n 6, 318–19.
45   Treviño, Weaver and Reynolds, above n 36.
46   Madan M Pillutla and Stefan Thau, 'Actual and Potential Exclusion as Determinants of Individuals' Unethical Behaviour in Groups' in David DeCremer (ed), *Psychological Perspectives on Ethical Behaviour and Decision-Making* (IAP, 2009) 107.

III. Positive Impacts of the Team on Ethics

A. and B. Moral sensitivity and moral judgment

A team has the potential to enhance ethical sensitivity and judgment by increasing the chance that someone will detect the ethics issue in the first place, and then by offering the opportunity to examine a wider survey of beliefs about the problem and the objectives for addressing it. Further, a team presents the possibility for an analytical process in which stereotyping about stakeholders is reduced and the range of harms likely to be considered is extended.[47]

C. Moral motivation

A team identity grounded in ethics is a powerful, intrinsic motivator if it is meaningful for members[48] within their specific context. A team with a salient ethical identity is more likely to foster a collective confidence in which ethical issues are regarded as opportunities not threats.[49] Indeed, members come to regard unethical conduct as a form of harm to their team, which must be managed and prevented.[50]

D. Moral action

Ethics leadership is arguably the most determinative of whether or not a member or members of a team are likely to seek to resolve an ethics issue, at all or at least by seeking advice from within the team. An ethical leader is an ethical role model who treats people fairly and actively gives the team the context to prepare for and engage in critical, ethical thinking, including by having a discussion without the leader's presence if that is likely to improve ethical dialogue.[51] Ethical leaders recognise their colleagues' uniqueness, ask extra questions to encourage deeper conversation, follow up on ethical decisions,[52] and adopt a change-

---

47 Werhane et al, above n 23, 104.
48 Robbennolt and Sternlight, above n 25, 1181.
49 Marlene E Turner et al, 'Threat, Cohesion, and Group Effectiveness: Testing a Social Identity Maintenance Perspective on Groupthink' (1992) 63(5) *Journal of Personality and Social Psychology* 781.
50 Treviño, Weaver and Reynolds, above n 36, 969; Robbennholt and Sternlight, above n 25, 1177.
51 Hassan, above n 30, 701–2.
52 LePine and Van Dyne, above n 28.

oriented style.[53] The types of conversations they guide advance ethics-as-deliberation and ethics-as-possibility.[54] The phenomenon becomes, then, 'teamthink', not groupthink.[55]

The relevant leader here is someone with whom the team regularly interacts. In more collaborative, ad hoc groups, with potentially shifting memberships, these issues are more challenging since much of the value of teams of which we know rests on time and trust.

IV. A Couple of Cautions

A. The deliberative ethics problem

A rational, reflective approach would seem to be vital in reducing the harmful psychological drives induced by the team and the non-conscious emotions that can bedevil our responses to ethics issues when left on our own. However, putting aside here an important debate about the ultimate power of emotion and intuition over reason, in certain circumstances, automatic responses are more ethically appropriate.[56] Deliberation can disrupt these responses by strengthening attachments to rule-guided criteria and/or by increasing the chances of non-moral factors being considered.[57]

B. The team ethics problem

The necessity for outsider input to the team to help reduce the risks of ethical parochialism and fading has already been implied in the discussion so far. In addition to this external contribution, individual team members must retain the 'identity space'[58] for their own, independent reflection. Where needed, lawyers must be able to make disclosures about or otherwise exercise dissent against the team and the client, separate from team processes.

---

53 Detert and Burris, above n 32.
54 Neck and Manz, above n 2; Mark G Edwards and Nin Kirkham, 'Situating "Giving Voice to Values": A Metatheoretical Evaluation of a New Approach to Business Ethics' (2014) 121(3) *Journal of Business Ethics* 477.
55 Neck and Manz, above n 2.
56 Chen-Bo Zhong, 'The Ethical Dangers of Deliberative Decision Making' (2011) 56.1 *Administrative Science Quarterly* 1.
57 Ibid.
58 G R Weaver, 'Virtue in Organizations: Moral Identity as a Foundation for Moral Agency' (2006) 27(3) *Organization Studies* 341.

V. Implications

A. Legal education and training

National university regulations and the 'Threshold Learning Outcomes' for law now stipulate that law students acquire and be able to demonstrate skills in collaboration.[59] Meanwhile, a growing body of research is establishing the positive links between teamwork, and achievement, critical thinking, problem-solving ability, creativity and wellbeing.[60] Nonetheless, teamwork remains a fringe part of the law degree, and there is, unfortunately, scant pedagogical material to use to teach teamwork and its relationship to lawyers' ethics.

Until this material is developed, at the very least, educators need to make law students and lawyers aware of the ways in which teams impact ethical decision-making and behaviour. More helpful also would be to inculcate in students skills to deliver and receive ethics information within a team.[61] In light of the cautions above, the emphases here should be on dialogue, possibility and action.[62]

B. Legal practice

Managers and other professional leaders should support the educational suggestions above. Moreover, they need to recognise, develop and reward ethical lawyers at each level and across each team-type. Research shows that those in a team with higher moral reasoning are not more likely than others to emerge as leaders. Firms need to consider actively identifying these individuals for leadership programs.[63]

They also need to contemplate how ethical behaviour is to be reinforced within and across teams. Valuable starting questions might be: 'What sorts of conversations do we need to engage in to help bring our core

---

59   Australian Learning & Teaching Council, *Resources to Assist Discipline Communities to Define Threshold Learning Outcomes (TLOs): An Outcome of the ALTC's Learning and Teaching Academic Standards (LTAS) Project* (Australian Government Department of Education, Employment and Workplace Relations, Canberra, 2011) 5. See Steel, Huggins and Laurens, above n 6, 297–98.
60   Ibid. 295.
61   An excellent base is Mary Gentile's *Giving Voice to Values* program, currently used at ANU College of Law and UNSW Law.
62   Edwards and Kirkham, above n 54.
63   Treviño, Weaver and Reynolds, above n 36, 957.

ethical concerns [and obligations] and those of others into the open?'[64] Are these conversations likely to happen in light of the rest of our firm culture and climate? These may need to be considered for intra-firm, inter-disciplinary, cross-jurisdictional and global teams as well.[65]

C. Professional regulation

Team-based ethics should be a part of the profession's Continuing Professional Development (and assessment?). More contestable is the tacit case for team-based regulation and discipline.

D. Legal scholarship

Writers have called for more research on the team as an ethical decision-making unit and on team-level ethical phenomena.[66] Some lines of inquiry that would be fruitful are:

- Types of ethical cultures and climates within hierarchical and collaborative teams, and within and across legal practices.

- What kinds of ethical discussion currently take place and among whom?[67]

- What types of ethics issues are addressed and which are off-limits?[68] Are discussions in terms of rules or do they include values behind rules?[69] Whose behaviour or objectives are (allowed to be) questioned?

- When might unethical conduct of a team require team discipline?

- Is the client part of the team? Is it possible to say, in certain situations, that the client is the leader of the team? What does this mean for lawyers' ethics?

- Finally, does teamwork in law firms improve, or have potential to improve, ethical outcomes?

---

64   M G Edwards et al, 'Voicing Possibilities: A Performative Approach to the Theory and Practice of Ethics in a Globalised World' in D E Palmer (ed), *Handbook of Research on Business Ethics and Corporate Responsibilities* (InfoSci-Books, 2015) 249.

65   Ibid.

66   Treviño, Weaver and Reynolds, above n 36, 968.

67   Burris, above n 29, 870.

68   Huang and Paterson, above n 7, 2.

69   Parker et al, above n 10.

46

The Legal Roots of a Sustainable and Resilient Economy: New Kinds of Legal Entities, New Kinds of Lawyers?

Bronwen Morgan,[1] Joanne McNeill[2] and Isobel Blomfield[3]

This chapter seeks to persuade professional lawyers and ecologically-minded social entrepreneurs that a significant gap in legal professional services currently exists in the ecosystem of support for small-scale sustainable economy initiatives. The chapter has four parts. Part I makes a general case for the proposition that legal reforms facilitating the growth of small-scale sustainable economy initiatives (SSEIs) are an important dimension of facilitative environmental law. Part II identifies existing patterns of support. Part III draws on the limitations of these existing patterns, when understood in the context of the distinctive needs of SSEIs, to sketch an outline of four possible responses to this gap. These are: cultivating a vital yet elusive sense of what we call 'the touch'; introducing novel hybrid legal forms for the conduct of SSEI activity; developing and adapting specific technical skill sets to the SSEI context; and improving the cost, accessibility and relevance of legal support.

---

1   Faculty of Law, UNSW.
2   Institute for Culture & Society, Western Sydney University.
3   Faculty of Law, UNSW.

I. Addressing Environmental Challenges 'From the Inside Out'

A key challenge facing environmental law in the near-to-medium-term future is the degree to which its effectiveness is constrained by its structural relationship to commercial law, and the related implications for legal professional services. In responding to environmental challenges through the medium of law, regulatory responses are limited by their secondary relationship to the internal structure of economic exchange: they effectively bolt environmental goals onto the edifice of commercial exchange as a protective afterthought. A more productive approach lies in reworking the tacit legal underpinnings of commercial activities. Creative use of commercial and transactional legal strategies has the potential to weave social and ecological values into the heart of exchange, and thus to address environmental law goals 'from the inside out'.

The primary genesis of this chapter is grounded in data collected between 2013 and 2015 in the Activism and Enterprise Project (the 'A&E Project'[4]) which was funded to explore the basic insight stated above. The A&E project carried out primary empirical research into community-based sustainability initiatives and grassroots innovations responding to climate change challenges, across a continuum from social activism to social enterprise. The purpose of the research was to explore the legal and regulatory frameworks that helped or hindered these innovative initiatives, a subset of which we are now calling SSEIs. The social significance of these initiatives was that they reconfigured economies and established alternatives to unsustainable practices. The capacity of SSEIs to make a positive contribution to the overall social fabric and to the building of resilient communities is related to how they negotiate life-cycle shifts: from vision to early experimentation and then to stable operation. These shifts are shaped in important ways by law and regulation.

A brief example of an SSEI can illustrate what is at stake. The Open Food Network (OFN), based in Melbourne, provides a digital platform and related services that link producers and consumers of local ethical food, enabling, as its website states 'farmers, eaters and independent food

---

4   Short-form for Australian Future Fellowship Award FT110100483 held by Professor Morgan for 'Between Social Enterprise and Social Movement: Responses to Climate Change at the Intersection of Rights and Regulation'. The support of the ARC for this work is gratefully acknowledged.

enterprises to connect, trade, manage Food Hubs and coordinate logistics'. As a web-based platform that curtails the power of the middleman, OFN emphasises its desire to create positive social change of a systemic kind, one that will disrupt the existing dominance of large-scale commercial provision of food or housing. It has open-source principles at the centre of both its software and its human relations, designed to support small community groups anywhere in the world in setting up local initiatives easily and at low cost. However, OFN has struggled to source legal advice that helps it build an income stream flowing through its provision of a software platform while simultaneously protecting the inbuilt sociality and affordability of the practices of like-minded groups around the world in a collaborative community. Clear and affordable legal advice would greatly assist projects such as OFN to replicate horizontally, rather than scale up, and thus to expand the SSEI sector in a sustainable manner.

The growth of SSEIs is not easily defined as the emergence of a 'sector'. Drawing on the A&E project as well as data from the International Comparative Social Enterprise Models (ICSEM) research project,[5] we can say that SSEIs prioritise social relationships, some degree of economic democracy, interdependency and values other than economic efficiency and low costs, including but not limited to ecological values. They are a subset of social enterprise, and overlap with some aspects of the sharing economy: not the turbo-sharing economy of Airbnb and Uber, but smaller-scale, more socially-oriented versions of these technologically innovative enterprises. But it is fair to say that the definition of an identifiable sector in this context remains diffuse. This is, in part, precisely because the legal, financial and organisational structures of our current economy do not sit comfortably with these types of initiatives. Therefore the very 'gap' that underpins the discussion presented here undermines their visibility. The suggestions for reform in this chapter are therefore intended to draw out the institutional potential of SSEIs and to improve the 'fit' between them and their larger ecosystem.

---

5   See emes.net/research-projects/social-enterprise/icsem-project/. Australia has a team participating in this international project, including two of the authors of this chapter.

II. Existing Pathways of Legal Support for SSEIs

There are three main sources of existing support.

A) First, some law firms provide advice to social enterprises, but most focus on not-for-profit and limited pro bono advice. Generally, law firms that provide professional legal services to the social enterprise sector in Australia are not easily identified as such without prior knowledge of personal contacts. Legal practitioners, particularly those in large urban areas, draw primarily on their existing commercial experience to provide advice on legal matters to social enterprises generally, and therefore to the SSEI subgroup also. This expertise tends to divide into not-for-profit and for-profit specialisms and experience. Most of these firms also offer pro bono services; however, the majority require the entity to be not-for-profit to be eligible to access these.

The recent advent of technology-enabled clearing houses designed to assist small businesses and start-ups to find relatively low-cost legal advice is potentially relevant to some SSEIs. These are being heralded as 'disruptive services'[6] for their potential to make access to professional legal services easier and more affordable for small businesses. They typically use standard commercial documentation and the underlying assumptions of for-profit business models and legal structures.

Some smaller firms with more of a creative and hybrid focus are recently emerging. Clearpoint Counsel[7] is one example with a core focus on SSEI-relevant services. Branded as 'Legal Services. Reimagined. Simply', it offers 'holistic, collaborative and entrepreneurial services', stressing that 'we believe law should be a tool to empower you'. In addition to a variety of more traditional commercial advice, it offers specialist advice on 'social enterprise and sustainable economies law' as well as 'B Corporation Training and Certification'.

---

6   In Australia, examples include LawPath, LegalVision, LegalZoom, AdventBalance: see www.lawyersweekly.com.au/opinion/16286-legal-market-ripe-for-disruptive-innovation and the recent establishment of the Law Society project on the Future of Law and Innovation in the Profession (FLIP): www.law.unsw.edu.au/sites/law.unsw.edu.au/files/images/lib/future_of_legal_profession.pdf.
7   www.clearpointcounsel.com.

B) Second, cognate initiatives have emerged to service social enterprise specifically and in some cases SSEIs. Some, such as Business Enterprise Centres, Justice Connect and Get Mutual provide services predominantly tied to specific legal forms (for-profit, not-for-profit and cooperatives respectively). These have limited use for SSEIs that seek to establish hybrid business models that draw on both profit and not-for-profit dimensions. Others, such as the Expert Advice Exchange of the NSW Government, a sub-initiative of the NSW Environmental Defenders' Office, Lex Mundi Pro Bono Foundation and the University of Melbourne Law School Sustainable Business Clinic, do serve hybrid initiatives but are all very small, specialised and embryonic. Overall, they privilege not-for-profit structures as the primary eligibility criterion, while more than half the social enterprises responding to two recent surveys in Australia had chosen for-profit or cooperative structures.[8]

C) Finally, social enterprise capacity-building programs broker select initiatives to access legal advice, sometimes at 'low-bono' fee levels, when needed.[9] These usually provide fairly general 'legal matters' style workshops or other material to groups of participants in a standard format, or 'template' style advice (e.g. on purchaser agreements, insurance arrangements or volunteer contracts). They sometimes also secure individualised legal support. But such support is only available to entities admitted to the program after a lengthy application process, and is often vulnerable to dispensing untimely or overly standard advice ill-suited to bespoke and/or complex arrangements.

In short, many of the existing avenues of support are shaped by assumptions of a divide between not-for-profit and for-profit legal structures which maps onto a related gulf between pro bono advice and expensive commercial advice. Moreover, while pro bono legal practitioners generally have access to well-developed networks, for those attempting to build their expertise and skills around working with social enterprises and SSEIs, there is no way, other than word of mouth, for them to identify each other or to expand opportunities to share knowledge and expertise.

---

8   ICSEM project, above n 5 and Stephen Bennett et al, *Legal Models Working Group Report* (Social Innovation, Enterprise and Entrepreneurship Alliance, July 2014), www.employeeownership.com.au/wp-content/uploads/2015/02/Legal-Models-Working-Group-Draft-Final-Report.pdf.
9   See, for example, National Pro Bono Resource Centre, *Review of Parramatta City Council's Social Enterprise Pro Bono Legal Panel* (2011), on file with second author.

III. Four Dimensions of an Effective Ecosystem of Professional Legal Support

A. Supporting legal practitioners to cultivate 'the touch'

There is, then, a felt demand for a more extensive and effective ecosystem of professional legal support for small-scale initiatives that confound traditional distinctions between for-profit and not-for-profit economic activity. The key limitation of the existing pathways is an overarching unmet need that is challenging to convey succinctly. It can perhaps best be described as a culture fit with values prominent in the social enterprise sector and the SSEI subgroup, a 'contextual sensitivity' or, as described by one interviewee, 'the touch'. 'The touch' is grounded in a mix of shared values, especially economic democracy, community development, a holistic worldview and an understanding of how to meld social relationality with practical governance. It is partly experiential, embedded in tacit craft knowledge, and partly normative, linked to a set of ethical and political commitments, though not to any particular ideology.

By virtue of this elusive status, it is likely something that is best fostered in experiential peer to peer settings, particularly ones that link a network of both legal and non-legal professionals who are committed to the ethos involved. Such a network might have considerable value for legal professionals in both large firms and small firm or solo practice settings. For the former, it would provide professional development channels to help legitimise social enterprise generally and SSEI specifically as viable 'market segments'. For the latter, there is evidence that some working in this area identify themselves as 'corporate refugees' from 'war-torn law firms, battered and wanting to … move away from negative, adversarial, competitive and risk-averse models of practising'.[10] There may also be opportunities to tap into technology-based networks that 'reduce the impediment of geographical distances' and create a 'virtual legal practice' which allows for small firms to aggregate work while simultaneously

---

10   Bronwen Morgan and Declan Kuch, *The Sharing Economy: More than the Sum of its Parts? Implications for Legal Services* (2014), Summary Report of Janelle Orsi Australia Workshop Series, UNSW Law School, www.activismandenterprise.weebly.com/uploads/2/2/3/2/22323902/140317_-_orsi_aus_tour_unsw_writeup_-_final.pdf.

allowing them to stay competitive in the marketplace.[11] These can connect and support sole practitioners, such as Lawyer Mums Australia[12] or clusters of 'dormant' legal practitioners, such as in Northern NSW,[13] potentially interested in developing new and different practice streams.

B. Introducing hybrid legal models for economic enterprises

Legal forms matter too, however. SSEIs face intractable problems here in falling between traditional classifications of not-for-profit and for-profit. For the former, SSEIs typically generate and distribute earned income in ways quite different from standard charities. The latter may find the generic corporations template used by standard for-profit companies do not typically integrate SSEI-specific characteristics into the 'DNA' of the entity, nor protect them over the long term. Either way, a simplified choice of legal form that would allow trading, investment and income flows to supplement grant-based support and without adding undue organisational complexity, especially in relation to reporting, governance and tax status, would benefit SSEIs. It would also assist them in protecting their purpose and preventing private extraction of their assets as a result of changes of form, buy-outs or winding-up.

A range of innovations around hybrid legal structures are emerging that help to address these issues.[14] Some of these are statutory legal models, such as the Community Interest Company in the UK that melds shareholder investment with an asset lock and capped dividends; or the Benefit Corporation structure in the US that enables directors to pursue a general public benefit without fear of shareholder retaliation. Other innovations offer special clauses such as the use of 'golden shares' to protect social mission;[15] or model rules, adopted by voluntary choice of the entity, for modifying the constitution of a standard corporation,

---

11   Caroline Hart, 'Sustainable Regional, Rural and Remote Legal Practice in Queensland: The Importance of Innovation in Alliances and the Use of Information Technology' (2011) 16(1) *Deakin Law Review* 225, 252.

12   A Facebook group: see www.facebook.com/LawyerMumsAustralia/.

13   Morgan and Kuch, above n 10.

14   Bronwen Morgan, 'Transcending the Corporation: Social Enterprise, Cooperatives and Commons-Based Governance' in Thomas Clarke and Justin O'Brien (eds), *The Oxford Handbook on the Corporation* (Oxford University Press, in press).

15   Nick O'Donohoe and Simon Rowell, 'Going for Gold' (Big Society Capital, 2015), www. bigsocietycapital.com/sites/default/files/pdf/Golden%20Share%20Report.pdf.

such as the Fair Shares model[16] (which securely embeds social purpose and integrates founders, producers, employees, customers, service users and investors equally into core governance processes), and a voluntary certification version of the Benefit Corporation approach, a 'B-Corp' brand, in essence, that validates governance, transparency, environmental and social impact through third-party certification. However, none of these are in widespread use in Australia, although the B-Corp brand is gaining some traction.

C. Adapting specific technical skill sets to the SSEI context

While the existence of a hybrid legal form would assist in defining a distinctive legal site for SSEIs, they often encounter ongoing regulatory grey areas in trying to secure operational stability. Advice better suited to large-scale commercial operation tends to convey a reported 'fixation with legal impediments'[17] and to fit poorly with SSEI culture. Pro bono advice is all too often 'off-the-shelf', overly complex and unwieldy for SSEI purposes and adds layers of unnecessary complexity to operations. While a sense of 'the touch' helps here, there are also technically distinctive aspects to SSEI operations. For example, ownership arrangements may include designing flat governance structures, protecting commitments to economic democracy, recognising 'sweat equity' returns, and structuring 'end of life' distributions that mix grant and investment income. Intellectual property issues may require expertise in open source and other commons-based forms of licensing, while employee contracts may systematically blur lines between staff and volunteers, and novel forms of land use, leasing and insurance relations often predominate.

This range of technical knowledge provides positive opportunities for the professional network suggested above to develop targeted seminars and training, potentially linked to continuing professional education and/or the development of new curricula in university degrees.

---

16   See www.fairshares.coop/.
17   Morgan and Kuch, above n 10.

D. Improving access

The inaccessibility of legal advice is a centuries-old problem, but of bittersweet intensity here, given the potentially transformative ideals of SSEIs. Access can be improved both by enhancing relevance and reducing cost. A publicly available database of SSEI professionals from the network could encourage user-driven rankings and reviews to animate referrals and relevance. To stem the problem of one-size-fits all, overly didactic template advice, purpose-focused clusters within the network could deliver group-based training sessions to assist with the customisation of template advice. One-stop shops for particular sectors (e.g. food, energy) could develop referrals and partnerships between and beyond the legal profession. Clusters could also be geographically based, especially in regional areas, running local clinics covering a wide range of issues.

Since cluster-based strategies essentially allow 'bulk purchasing' of legal advice, they will help to reduce cost, opening up the possibility of widespread availability of 'low bono' services. These can be underpinned by, for example, transparency of costs charged on network sites, fee caps for particular types of advice, or retainers that include access to a specified quantity of advice within a given period. A broader cultural shift in expectations about what a typical private lawyer is entitled to earn is also part of this:[18] perhaps 'community enterprise lawyer' could complement 'community legal centre' legal identities.

IV. Conclusion

Overall two key reforms would assist in closing the gap in professional legal services for SSEIs in Australia: the establishment and promotion of hybrid legal models, whether statutory or self-regulatory, for enterprise activity; and the establishment and coordination of an SSEI-specific professional development network for legal practitioners and other key service providers. An effective professional network would prioritise 'the touch', break down divisions between not-for-profit/for-profit/cooperative legal status, facilitate 'trusted' partnering and/or referral between legal practitioners, widen access to and reduce the cost of legal services, and

---

18   RMIT Centre for Innovative Justice, *Affordable Justice* (2013) 48, mams.rmit.edu.au/qr7u4uejwols1.pdf.

develop clusters based on purpose and geography. While acknowledging the limits of purely legal reform in this area, we hope this discussion will catalyse a broader interest in cross-sectoral and multidisciplinary collaboration in the service of seeing the emerging Australian SSEI sector thrive.

47

Wearing Two Hats: Lawyers Acting as Mediators

Mary Anne Noone[1]

I. Introduction

Professional legal bodies promote the use of lawyers as mediators because of their specialist skills, and claim that 'with their skills, training and experience solicitors are ideally placed to be mediators'.[2] Many lawyers train to be mediators. However, they face a challenge; how to reconcile their various professional responsibilities while wearing two distinct hats: officer of the court and neutral third party.[3]

In this chapter, I discuss issues facing lawyers acting as mediators including clash of values, identification of systemic injustice, parties' access to information and advice and dubiousness of mediators' immunity against legal liability. Initially, I outline models of mediation, the accreditation system of mediators and detail the numbers of lawyers who offer mediation services. In conclusion, three reforms are proposed.

---

1   Professor, Law School, La Trobe University.

2   'Soliciting the Right Kind of Mediator' (2005) 79(4) *Law Institute Journal* 22 (News section).

3   The wearing two hats analogy is also used for lawyers who act as advocates and negotiators (see Bobette Wolski, *Skills, Ethics and Values for Legal Practice* (Lawbook Co, 2nd edn, 2009) 116) and in-house counsel who are also the company secretary (Emilios Kyrou, 'Legal Professional Privilege for General Counsel Wearing Two Hats' (2000) 5 *Law Society Journal* 42).

II. Mediation and Accreditation

Courts and tribunals require disputing parties to use alternative dispute resolution (ADR) processes often as a condition precedent to accessing these forums. This integration is reinforced in legislation; for example, an objective of the *Civil Dispute Resolution Act 2011* (Cth) is to ensure people take genuine steps to resolve disputes before instituting civil proceedings. Mediation is the most common form of ADR utilised in all forms of litigation.

In practice, there is significant variation in the context and process of mediations. There are at least four models of mediation: facilitative, evaluative, settlement and transformative. The facilitative model underpinned early developments in community mediation; however, with the increased use of court-related mediation, the settlement and evaluative models are commonly used in practice. The models are not necessarily distinct alternative forms of practice but rather 'tendencies in practice'. Within any one mediation, different modes might be adopted at different times.[4]

With the exponential growth in numbers of mediators in the 1990s, the desire to ensure quality and accountability in mediation practice led to the development of accreditation and practice standards for Australian mediators. The National Mediator Accreditation Scheme (NMAS) became operative in January 2008. In 2017 there were 3,216 mediators accredited by Recognised Mediation Accreditation Bodies (RMABs).[5]

Mediators who are (voluntarily) accredited must comply with the Approval Standards as well as the Practice Standards. The standards specify practice and competency requirements for mediators; inform participants and others about what they can expect of the mediation process and mediators; set out minimum practice requirements and allows mediators to develop or comply with additional standards if they so wish.[6] The standards provide that where a mediator practices under a legislative framework,

---

4   Laurence Boulle, *Mediation: Principles, Process and Practice* (LexisNexis, 3rd edn, 2011) 43–45.

5   A list of accredited mediators is available on the Mediator Standards Board website: www.msb.org.au/.

6   National Mediator Accreditation System, Part III, *Practice Standards* (2015).

this prevails over any inconsistency with the standards. Additionally, the standards state a mediator must adhere to the ethical code prescribed by the professional organisation of which they are a member.[7]

III. Lawyers as Mediators

The legal profession was initially sceptical of the expansion in ADR which was in part a response to critiques of the traditional adversarial legal dispute system, including criticism of the dominant and controlling role of lawyers. Some lawyers, however, quickly embraced mediation within the scope of their professional services. For instance, in 1989, Lawyers Engaged in Alternative Dispute Resolution (LEADR) was formed to promote the use of alternative dispute resolution instead of litigation.[8]

Since that time, many lawyers, both barristers and solicitors, have trained in mediation. Lawyers' professional organisations (including Law Societies in Victoria, South Australia, Western Australia, Queensland and New South Wales, and Bar Associations in Queensland South Australia and Victoria) accredit lawyers to be mediators and also have a responsibility to monitor the standards. The legal professional associations actively promote the benefits of engaging a mediator with lawyers' skills. In court-annexed mediations, the mediator chosen will invariably be a legal practitioner. Lawyers' professional indemnity insurance policies now consider mediation to be a 'legal service' and lawyers acting as mediators are insured against liability in this work.[9]

The professional bodies for both solicitors and barristers have dedicated directories for the public to identify lawyers who are also mediators. An indication of numbers of lawyers who also mediate is that 10.58 per cent (213) of barristers[10] and 1 per cent (101) of solicitors are accredited mediators in Victoria. Law firms are also promoting a specific focus on providing dispute resolution services. For example, in Victoria:

---

7   Ibid. cll 1.3 and 8.3.

8   LEADR opened its organisation to non-lawyers in 1990s and recently amalgamated with the Institute of Arbitrators and Mediators to form the Resolution Institute: www.resolution.institute/.

9   For example, see Law Society of New South Wales, *Guidelines for Mediators Who Act as Mediators*, www.lawsociety.com.au/resources/adr/MediatorsPanel/index.htm.

10   Victoria Bar, *Barrister's Directory*, www.vicbar.com.au/barrister-directory/mediator-arbitrator-search/search-for-a-mediator and Law Institute of Victoria, www.liv.asn.au/Mediators (viewed 21 April 2017).

McFarlane Legal: Dispute Resolution is a law firm that practises solely in the area of resolving disputes using alternative dispute resolution techniques – predominantly mediation, arbitration and facilitation. 'We are experts in the area and we have an enviable track record of resolving the great majority of disputes that come before us'.[11]

There are separate codes of conduct for lawyers and accredited mediators but, as the National Mediator Standards indicate, the lawyer's professional obligations prevail over any conflicting mediator standards. The lawyers' code of professional conduct is designed 'to assist solicitors to act ethically and in accordance with the principles of professional conduct established by the common law and these rules'.[12] In this code the definition of 'court' includes 'an arbitration or mediation or any other form of dispute resolution'.

Some state law societies have adopted specific guidelines for solicitors who act as mediators.[13] Similarly, the Law Council of Australia has approved *Ethical Standards for Mediators* that are intended to serve as a guide for the conduct of mediators, to inform the mediating parties of what they should expect, and to promote public confidence in mediation as a process for resolving disputes.[14]

IV. Issues for Lawyers Who Act as Mediators

Comparing the usual practice of lawyering with mediation practice, there is a fundamental variance between a rights versus interests-based approach. 'Interest-based processes are concerned with finding solutions that meet the needs and interests of the parties involved. Rights-based processes are concerned with determining outcomes based on rights, rules and law.'[15] The National Alternative Dispute Resolution Advisory Council (NADRAC) noted the 'alternative' in ADR sometimes refers to 'interest-based' dispute resolution processes as an alternative to 'rights-

---

11   www.mcfarlanelegal.com.au/.

12   *Legal Profession Uniform Law Australian Solicitors' Conduct Rules 2015*, cl 3.1.

13   For example, Law Society of NSW, above n 9.

14   Law Council of Australia, *Ethical Standards for Mediators*, Updated Version, August 2011, learnedfriends.com.au/getmedia/b72ee6c5-cbf4-4c8f-b170-cd7bc66fd5cf/Walker_Ethical-Guidelines.aspx.

15   National Alternative Dispute Resolution Advisory Council, *ADR Terminology: A Discussion Paper* (2002) 10. The interest-based approach to negotiation was popularised in Roger Fisher and William L Ury, *Getting to Yes: Negotiating Agreement Without Giving In* (Penguin Press, 1981).

based' processes. Additionally, the core values underpinning mediation – neutrality, self-determination, voluntariness and confidentiality – can pose challenges for the mediations lawyers are often involved in. For example, with the increased use of court-directed mediation, parties' 'voluntary' participation is compromised. Similarly strict adherence to concepts of confidentiality, neutrality and self-determination are the focus of critical analysis.[16]

Lawyer–mediators face ethical challenges when they have to choose between competing values.[17] In a qualitative research project exploring ethical and practical issues in mediation, mediators provided examples of ethical issues from their own experience:

- confidentiality of settlement in a mediation involving an abuse survivor and a church organisation raising questions about the preservation of the victim's legal rights;
- tension between the mediator's obligations to the parties and larger public interest questions, e.g. if there's a point of law that needs clarifying;
- parties about to enter an agreement that is outside the law;
- lack of good faith and deceptive conduct by one party;
- capacity of parties (e.g. one party had an intellectual disability and the proposed agreement was significantly different from a likely hearing outcome); workplace bullying dispute and victim was too stressed to be in the same room as the other party;
- inequality and power differentials, particularly where one party is uninformed or misinformed;
- information received in private session about potential bankruptcy of the party.[18]

The examples illustrate how mediators have to grapple with complex ethical conundrums.

---

16   Mary Anne Noone and Lola Akin Ojelabi, 'Ethical Challenges for Mediators: An Australian Perspective' (2014) 45 *Washington University Journal of Law and Policy* 145.

17   Boulle, above n 4; Julie MacFarlane, 'Mediating Ethically: The Limits of Codes of Conduct and the Potential of a Reflective Practice Model' (2002) 40 *Osgoode Hall Law Journal* 49; Patricia Marshall 'The "Partial" Mediator: Balancing Ideology and the Reality' (2010) 11(8) *ADR Bulletin* 176; Rachel Field, 'Mediation Ethics in Australia: A Case for Rethinking the Foundational Paradigm' (2012) 19 *James Cook University Law Review* 41.

18   Noone and Akin Ojelabi, above n 16.

Professional standards for lawyers and mediators are designed to assist an individual practitioner in resolving and avoiding ethical dilemmas. However, these do not address all ethical issues and they sometimes contain competing or conflicting provisions and values. Additionally the mediators' standards can clash with lawyers' codes of conduct.[19] The lawyer's duty that is most challenged, when lawyers act as mediators, is their duty to the court.

When an individual is admitted to legal practice in Australia they become an officer of the court. Consequent duties include not engaging in abuse of process or bringing the administration of justice into disrepute.[20] The conduct of lawyers who act as mediators might be called into question when the outcomes of mediations are seen to be unjust, unfair, and illegal or expose systemic issues.

For lawyers acting as mediators, the following issues are accentuated by their officer of the court status:

- Does a lawyer–mediator have a greater responsibility to ensure just and lawful outcomes?
- What responsibility does the lawyer–mediator have for ensuring parties are well informed, especially about rights they may be foregoing?
- Should lawyer–mediators breach confidentiality when it is in the public interest or there is systemic abuse?[21]
- Can lawyer–mediators seek immunity in their Agreements to Mediate?

Lawyers acting as mediators should be exemplars, guaranteeing their mediation practice facilitates access to justice rather than impedes it. A requirement that lawyer–mediators ensure parties, who are foregoing legal entitlements or rights, are aware this is the case, and are encouraged to seek information and legal advice, is needed. The duty to administration of justice should prevail and, when lawyer–mediators recognise that

---

19   Ellen Waldman (ed), *Mediation Ethics: Cases and Commentaries* (Jossey-Bass, 2011); Noone and Akin Ojelabi, above n 16.

20   *Legal Profession Uniform Law 2014* s 2.2.25; Gino Dal Pont, *Lawyers' Professional Responsibility* (Thomson Reuters, 2013) 536.

21   Dominik Leimguber, 'Confidentiality, Public Interest and the Mediator's Ethical Dilemma' (2013) 24 *Australasian Dispute Resolution Journal* 187; Mary Anne Noone, 'ADR, Public Interest Law and Access to Justice: The Need for Vigilance' (2011) 37(1) *Monash University Law Review* 57.

the agreement available to the parties is unfair, they have an ethical responsibility not to be complicit in the acceptance of the injustice without taking some action.[22]

In 2000, the Australian Law Reform Commission (ALRC) noted several factors that may indicate when ADR processes are unsuitable for resolving a dispute and court adjudication is more suitable. They were:

- when a definitive or authoritative resolution of the matter is required for precedential value;
- when the matter significantly affects persons or organisations who are not parties to the ADR process;
- when there is a need for public sanctioning of conduct or where repetitive violations of statutes and regulations need to be dealt with collectively and uniformly;
- when parties are unable to negotiate effectively themselves or with the assistance of a lawyer;
- in family law matters, where there is a history of family violence.[23]

The Victorian Parliament Inquiry into Alternative Dispute Resolution recommended ADR providers publish, in a de-identified form, regular case studies and reports on systemic issues and any other issues of public interest that arise as part of their ADR processes.[24] Recommendations aimed at improving the 'appropriateness' of ADR services included training for ADR practitioners on cross-cultural differences and power imbalances, recognition of the difficulties of people with language difficulties and limited literacy, as well as the provision of information and legal advice prior to involvement in ADR.

Another challenging area for lawyers acting as mediators is conducting the process in a way which is fair, even-handed, objective and unbiased. Lawyers normally work in a partisan way where they seek to advance the interests of only one party in a dispute. Additionally lawyers may be chosen as mediators by parties, with the expectation, based on promotional

---

22   Hilary Astor and Christine Chinkin, Dispute *Resolution in Australia* (Butterworths, 2nd edn, 2002) 230.
23   Australian Law Reform Commission, *Managing Justice: A Review of the Federal Civil Justice System* (ALRC, 2000) [6.62].
24   Parliament of Victoria, Law Reform Committee, *Inquiry into Alternative Dispute Resolution and Restorative Justice: Final Report of the Victorian Parliament Law Reform Committee* (Victorian Government Printer, 2009) 84.

material, that they bring their expertise to the process and will perform an evaluative function of liability and other issues.[25] NADRAC has suggested that practitioners' responsibilities include identification and disclosure of 'any existing or prior relationship between the practitioner and the parties; any interest in the outcome of the dispute; any present or future conflicts of interest; any values, experience or knowledge that may prevent a practitioner from acting impartially'.[26] When lawyers act as mediators, the concern for impartiality and neutrality is accentuated. It is generally accepted that legal practitioners should not act as a mediator in a case involving their own client although this is not specifically prohibited.[27] Certainly they should be experts in identifying conflicts of interests but until recently their broad knowledge and skills have been embedded in an adversarial approach.[28] These skills do not easily transfer to mediation and additional training is required. The legal profession has recognised this concern with impartiality and sought to address it in the codes of conduct for lawyer–mediators in both New South Wales and Queensland.[29]

The promotion of lawyers as mediators by their professional organisations for 'their special skills, training and experience' implies a level of knowledge and expertise above that of other mediators. Lawyer–mediators are likely to be held to a higher standard of care than non-lawyer–mediators.[30] Anecdotally, many barristers undertake evaluative or settlement-focused mediations. A series of cases, recently summarised by Spencer, 'disclose an apparent lack of clarity by parties, lawyers and mediators as to the status of the parties' intentions to be bound by an agreement that is subject to the execution of formal contract'.[31] In summarising these cases Spencer raises the spectre of mediator liability as he argues that in all the cases the lawyers and the presiding mediator should 'have anticipated the issues that ultimately arose for adjudication by the courts'. It seems likely that in

---

25 Boulle, above n 4, 221.
26 National Alternative Dispute Resolution Advisory Council, *Maintaining and Enhancing the Integrity of ADR Processes: From Principles to Practice Through People* (NADRAC, 2011).
27 Law Council of Australia, above n 14, cl 3.
28 Christine Parker and Adrian Evans, *Inside Lawyers' Ethics* (Cambridge University Press, 2nd edn, 2014) 228–36.
29 Boulle, above n 4, 490: *Queensland Law Society Standards of Conduct for Solicitor Mediators*, s 4.1 and *NSW Law Society Guidelines for Solicitors who Act as Mediators*, s 5.1.
30 Boulle, above n 4, 723.
31 David Spencer, 'Landing in the Right Class of Subject to Contract Agreements' (2015) 26 *Australasian Dispute Resolution Journal* 75.

the near future, particularly if the mediator is a lawyer who should know about the need to be clear about the intention to be bound, that person may also be joined as a third party to litigation:

> It seems that the eagerness to conclude mediation caused critical matters not to be negotiated and therefore left the intention of parties immediately bound in doubt ... Some mediators, many of whom in court-annexed mediation schemes are legally trained, fail to establish the parties' intentions to be immediately bound. Parties can be forgiven, since they are not legally trained; however, lawyers and mediators should know better.[32]

A related issue for lawyer–mediators is the use of immunity clauses in agreements to mediate. This practice by lawyers is questionable both legally and ethically.[33] It is common practice for mediators to get the parties to sign an Agreement to Mediate, especially when it is not court-related mediation. Lawyers' professional associations provide precedent Agreements to Mediate to their members. These agreements routinely contain a clause where the parties grant immunity from liability to the mediator. For example:

> The mediator will not be liable to a party for any act or omission in the performance of the mediator's obligations under this agreement unless the act or omission is fraudulent.[34]

When the mediator is a legal practitioner, there is real doubt about the appropriateness and lawfulness of such exclusion clauses. At common law, lawyers cannot, by means of an exclusion clause in the retainer agreement, reduce their standard of care or exempt themselves from liability for default in the performance of their professional responsibilities.[35] In Victoria, lawyers were, until recently, also legislatively prohibited from contracting out of liability to their clients unless this is permitted by other legislation such as the professional standards scheme.[36] If a lawyer does enter into such an agreement, it is said to be void.[37]

---

32 Ibid. 84.
33 Mary Anne Noone, 'Liability Matters for Lawyer Mediators' (2007) 81(10) *Law Institute Journal* 52.
34 Law Society of NSW, *Agreement to Mediate*, cl 25.
35 Dal Pont, above n 20, [5.180]; see also *Wilkinson v Feldworth Financial Services Pty Ltd* (1998) 29 ACSR 642.
36 *Legal Profession Act 2004* (Vic) s 7.2.11 (2).
37 Ibid. s 7.2.11 (3).

Three policy reasons for prohibiting lawyers from limiting their liability are: public confidence in lawyers and the justice system would be diminished if lawyers could avoid actions for negligence by having a broadly worded exclusion clause in the retainer agreement; the public service aspect of professionalism is inconsistent with the notion that lawyers can exclude liability to their clients; and by including an exclusion clause in the retainer, the lawyer is putting their own interests above their clients and this is a conflict of interest and duty.[38] Given that mediation is accepted as one of the services lawyers can provide, these same reasons should apply to the Agreement to Mediate used by lawyers.

Mediation is a legal service offered by many lawyers and the relevant legal professional indemnity insurance schemes provide cover for mediations conducted by lawyers if they form part of the normal work of the legal practice.[39] There is a major contradiction between the required unlimited liability of legal practitioners and the limited liability lawyers seek when they work as mediators. It is illogical for lawyers simultaneously to be permitted to sign agreements containing exclusion clauses. The public policy reasons prohibiting exclusions clauses generally in a lawyer's retainer apply equally in the context of a lawyer acting as mediator signing an agreement with the parties. This is the case especially if one or more of the parties are not legally represented.

Lawyers who act as mediators should be concerned about the lawfulness of exclusion clauses in Agreements to Mediate. Lawyers acting as mediators must fulfil their professional responsibilities and not seek immunity in mediation. In the context of the general critique of mediators' immunities, lawyers should be enhancing the administration of justice by leading the way and removing exclusion of liability clauses from their Agreements to Mediate.

V. Conclusion

Lawyers who act as mediators face challenges when wearing the two distinct hats of lawyer and mediator. As officers of the court, lawyers do have additional responsibilities which cannot be put aside when they act as mediators. Lawyers who are mediators should be exemplars of ethical

---

38   Dal Pont, above n 20.
39   Confirmed by representative of Victoria's Legal Practitioners Liability Committee, June 2015.

and appropriate mediation practice. They should be impartial, treat the parties fairly without bias, ensure the parties have access to information and advice to realistically assess the proposed mediated agreement and avoid all conflicts of interest. Additionally, lawyer–mediators should not seek to limit their liability by the use of exclusion clauses in Agreements to Mediate.

To address some of the concerns raised in this chapter, three specific suggestions for inclusion in the various codes of conduct for lawyer–mediators are:

- a requirement to ensure parties are aware of legal rights (access to information and/or advice) before agreeing to forego them in the negotiated settlement;
- procedures established for mediators to report systemic issues that they identify in disputes they mediate; and
- prohibition on immunity from liability in mediations.

48

Enabling Marginalised Voices to Be Heard: The Challenge to Law Reform Bodies

Liz Curran[1]

I. Introduction

Often the processes for law reform enable only certain voices to be heard, facilitating involvement by the most well-resourced pressure groups or lobbyists, the articulate and well educated. Yet laws affect us all. For some people, especially in lower socioeconomic contexts, government policies and laws affect every element of life from income security to the habitable condition of public housing to access to health services and pensions. People with poor literacy and numeracy have unequal access to opportunity and rarely have a voice or a way to provide feedback. The current structures for seeking input from these groups into law reform are problematic. They assume knowledge of the processes and of the law and legal rights, and the confidence to take action which is often absent for these groups.[2]

---

1   Senior Lecturer, The Australian National University, Legal Workshop.
2   Christine Coumarelos et al, *Access to Justice and Legal Needs: Legal Australia Wide Survey: Legal Need in Australia* (Law and Justice Foundation of New South Wales, 2012); Liz Curran and Maryanne Noone, 'Access to Justice: A New Approach Using Human Rights Standards' (2008) 15(3) *International Journal of the Legal Profession*, 195.

As a result, laws that deeply affect these communities are made in isolation with little input from those with direct experience. It is left to community agencies and peak bodies to try to relay experiences of their clients. This second-hand input is valuable, but does not give voice to the affected communities and their direct lived experience. If law reform is disconnected from lived experience, it is consequently blunt and less effective.

This chapter highlights why the current approach to law reform is problematic in the context of participatory democracy. It explores the obligations of lawyers and identifies innovative ways that law reform can occur beyond traditional avenues for law reform. It presents three case studies which have had a significant impact in changing laws, regulation and behaviours and demonstrate different law reform processes that can be timely and responsive to the immediate need of individuals. Some suggestions for inclusive law reform are also offered.

II. The Role of Lawyers in Law Reform

Lawyers have an obligation to uphold the rule of law and maintain the integrity of the legal system.

The following principles which underpin the rule of law[3] are relevant to this discussion:

- The law is made by representatives of the people in an open and transparent way;
- The law and its administration is subject to open and free criticism by the people ...;
- The law is capable of being known to everyone, so that everyone can comply.

As noted, sections of the community often do not know the law, or know where to turn, nor do they have the confidence to action their rights.[4] They seldom have resources to enable their voices to be heard as to how the laws that affect them are shaped. As Davis notes, this sits in a context of often professional lobbyists and well-resourced groups

---

3   See Rule of Law Institute of Australia, *Principles*, www.ruleoflaw.org.au/principles/.
4   Curran and Noone, above n 2.

that provide input.[5] This scenario has implications for the rule of law. Furthermore, executive governments in Australia have extended their own powers[6] limiting court review. This practice has affected human rights cases by limiting court scrutiny of executive action.[7]

Under the *Australian Solicitor's Conduct Rules* (Vic, NSW) rr 3 and 4, lawyers have duties to the administration of justice.[8] Accordingly, legal professionals have a role in identifying systemic problems because of their explicit obligations to ensure confidence in and integrity of the legal system. Being a lawyer is not limited just to the delivery of legal services as part of an industry. Lawyers as officers of the court have a deeper ethical obligation to identify and respond to systemic problems that impede confidence in the legal system and undermine its integrity. The advocacy by lawyers for clients through law reform and campaigns for change to policy administration[9] are core to the lawyers' ethical duties where laws are unjust and unfair.

---

5   Ian Davis, 'Targeted Consultations' in Brian Opeskin and David Weisbrot (eds), *The Promise of Law Reform* (The Federation Press, 2005) Ch 10, 148–59, 154.

6   See ABC Radio National, 'Gillian Triggs Criticises "Executive Overreach" in Defiant Speech', *AM*, 6 June 2015 (Simon Lauder), www.abc.net.au/am/content/2015/s4250111.htm.

7   See *Children, Youth and Families Amendment (Permanent Care and Other Matters) Act* (2014) (Vic); Office of the Public Advocate, 'Legal and Child Welfare Groups Call for Reinstatement of Child Protection Powers for Children's Court' (28 February 2017) www.publicadvocate.vic.gov.au/childrens-matters-media-release; Michael Chaaya, 'Proposed Changes to the Review of Migration Decisions: Sensible Reform Agenda or Political Expediency?' (1996) 19(4) *Sydney Law Review* 547.

8   See Frederick Ellison on the obligations of legal professionals to seek the social good, in Michael Davis and Frederick A Ellison (eds), *Ethics and the Legal Profession* (Prometheus Books, 1986) 18; Simon Longstaff, *The Lawyer's Duty to the Community* (The Ethics Centre, 1 March 1995), www.ethics.org.au/on-ethics/our-articles/before-2014/the-lawyers-duty-to-the-community. Former Chief Justice the Hon Murray Gleeson has also noted the obligation of the legal professions to ensure the public welfare and maintain confidence in the legal system – see Murray Gleeson, *Are the Professions Worth Keeping?* (Speech delivered at the Greek-Australian International Legal and Medical Conference, 31 May 1999), www.hcourt.gov.au/assets/publications/speeches/former-justices/gleesoncj/cj_areprofe.htm; Murray Gleeson, *Public Confidence in the Courts* (Speech delivered at the National Judicial College of Australia, Canberra, 9 February 2007) 6-7, www.hcourt.gov.au/assets/publications/speeches/former-justices/gleesoncj/cj_9feb07.pdf; Carl T Bogus, 'The Death of an Honourable Profession' (1996) 71(4) *Indiana Law Journal* 911.

9   Liz Curran, 'Attorney General George Brandis Set to Silence CLCs', *The Saturday Paper* (online), 14 June 2014, www.thesaturdaypaper.com.au/opinion/topic/2014/06/14/attorney-general-george-brandis-set-silence-clcs/1402668000.

III. Why Evidence- and Practice-Based Research Are Critical for Good Law Reform

Evidence- and practice-based experience and research that are linked to and not remote from day-to-day experience of laws can inform effectiveness, efficiency and positive outcomes. In 2007 the author wrote '[i]f governments of any political persuasion want to remain connected with the public and stay in power, they need to listen to their public. On many occasions, politicians claim to be connected to their communities. Often in reality, this is not the case'.[10]

Effective service programs (or laws that have been evaluated as effective) are often under-resourced or disbanded by government without empirical basis. The Productivity Commission made this point and called for research into this situation to inform government policy in Recommendation 24.[11]

The author further noted in 2007, 'The process of law reform is very slow to reap results as it often involves a sustained and persistent effort to raise awareness and change often entrenched cultures'.[12] At that time the author struggled to find literature related to the process of law reform that focused on engaging with public experience. Then, in 2013, the author was again commissioned to examine seven law reform projects.[13] Since the author's report in 2007, the conduct of law reform had changed, and was more creative, strategic and responsive to community, and less reactive.

The author's 2013 study revealed multiple strategies to overcome problems with people's experience of the law. The author was able to identify successful and impactful law reform initiatives of community legal centres (CLCs) (often conducted in collaboration with the people affected or other agencies). The processes used showed a strategic and

---

10   Liz Curran, *Making the Legal System More Responsive to Community: A Report on the Impact of Victorian Community Legal Centre (CLC) Law Reform Initiatives*, 2007, 4.

11   Productivity Commission, *Commission Inquiry into Access to Justice Arrangements Report: Volume 1*, Inquiry Report 72, 2014, 37, 43, 75–76.

12   Curran, above n 9.

13   See Liz Curran, *Solving Problems – A Strategic Approach: Examples, Processes & Strategies* (Legal Workshop, The Australian National University College of Law, 13 May 2013), law.anu.edu.au/sites/all/files/legalworkshop/final_report_solving_legal_problems_curran_calc_13_march_2013.pdf.

multipronged approach to law reform using innovative approaches that directly engaged client experiences of the impact of the law and developed solutions to problems.[14] Some are discussed below.

IV. Case Studies

The following two case studies, 'National Bulk Debt Negotiation' and the 'Do Not Knock Sticker', were initiated by CLCs. A third case study is about direct community advocacy to a Parliamentary Inquiry. All of these case studies demonstrate ways lawyers can have a more direct role in empowering communities with the skills they might need to make arguments (something lawyers consider as part of their own professional toolkit) and enable community members to present their case first-hand to lawmakers.

A. Case study one: Bulk debt negotiation

The National Bulk Debt Project (the Project) which is still ongoing, aims to protect the income of those experiencing long-term financial hardship. It has not only led to a decision by creditors to desist in pursuing loans against the most vulnerable or disadvantaged but to changes in practice, codes of conduct and hardship provisions.

The project used unconventional approaches to bring about law reform and changes in predatory and poor practice.[15] It aims to assist judgment-proof debtors struggling to repay. 'Judgment-proof' means there is no real likelihood that debtors can pay, that is, because they need all their income just to pay for food, rent and utilities or, as in Victoria, they have legislative protection from being sued. Instead of negotiations taking place for each client separately (which takes time and resources), they were bundled together into a 'bulk negotiation'. All cases involved clients on a low income. In the author's report of 2013, the examination of the project noted that many clients had multiple debts. Most clients experienced disadvantage including mental illness, disability, ill health or were full-time carers. Cases were collected en masse by financial counsellors and CLC

---

14   Ibid. 8.
15   A project of the West Heidelberg Community Legal Service, the Victoria Law Foundation, NSW and Victoria Legal Aid and Footscray Community Legal Service. The author discloses that she was Director of the West Heidelberg Community Legal Service at that time and secured the project's initial funding.

lawyers and the clients' circumstances were documented by a volunteer and taken in bulk to each bank by the project lawyer. The project has since been extended to other industries. In many instances, the client either did not owe the debt in the first place, proceedings were prohibited by law or it was unrealistic to pursue them due to their personal circumstances (e.g. cancer or disability), which served to highlight problems in debt collection practice. Few of the complainants previously could have actioned their legal rights due to a lack of knowledge, resources or access to legal assistance on an individual case-by-case basis.

1. Impact

This project has made the banks see that their pursuit is harmful and often costly and inefficient. The debts taken in bulk have avoided costly individual court processes, poor recovery, harmful practices and waste of corporate resources.

The author's 2013 report revealed that the project has directly assisted over 2,500 debtors and negotiated waiver or closure of debts worth more than $15 million.[16] Updated on 12 April 2016, additional impacts of the project include:

- 70 per cent of debts were waived.
- A National Hardship Register introduced in January 2014 is directly traceable to the work of the project.
- Criteria and processes developed via bulk debt negotiations have been specifically incorporated into some of the major banks' business practices.
- The Code of Banking Practice has been updated with minimum standards for signatories.[17]

The project in this case study has led to the reform of banking practices. It has saved money, not just for the banks in wasted processes, but also in reduced court proceedings (previously undertaken as individual matters in courts on a case-by-case basis). It has also reduced stress and anxiety

---

16   Curran, above n 13, 26–34; Denis Nelthorpe and Kate Digney, *The Bulk Negotiation Project: Client Profiles and Client Outcomes* (West Heidelberg Community Legal Service and Victoria Law Foundation, 2011) 3.

17   J Holland, *Negotiating Bulk Debt: Outcomes from the Bulk Debt Negotiation Project* (unpublished report for Victoria Legal Aid, West Heidelberg Community Legal Service, Legal Aid NSW, Good Shepherd Australia & New Zealand, 2016). The author thanks Denis Nelthorpe for sharing this report.

for those with debts. Moreover, it has revealed many debts were not being lawfully pursued, giving rise to other systemic issues for the regulators. Poor laws affect lives; they can do harm, cause stress and lead to poor health.[18]

B. Case study two: 'Do Not Knock' becomes law of trespass

The Consumer Action Law Centre (CALC) in Melbourne was receiving complaints about door-to-door sales including high-pressure techniques to get people to sign contracts; misleading and deceptive conduct; faulty goods and services; the targeting of vulnerable groups; and the use of fraudulent contracts and conduct.

A novel and practical sticker affixed to the front door of a person's home saying 'Do Not Knock' served to deflect aggressive predatory sales practices (which targeted public housing estates with concentrations of new arrivals, elderly and people with a disability and poor literacy skills) while leading to a change in precedent. Law reform was achieved with a community awareness campaign; a sticker to protect people day-to-day; the compilation of complaints and provision of data to the regulator; media exposure; collaboration between council, the regulator and community agencies, legal and non-legal; and court action.

1. Impact

The sticker is used on doorways across Australia and is distributed by CALC, local councils and governments.

CALC collected complaints from consumers about continued 'door knocking' despite having the sticker on their door. These complaints were logged in bulk with the Australian Competition and Consumer Commission (ACCC). The ACCC then lodged a case in the Federal Court against a utility company. The court ruled that ignoring a sticker risks

---

18 Pascoe Pleasence, Nigel J Balmer and Alexy Buck, 'The Health Cost of Civil-Law Problems: Further Evidence of Links between Civil-law Problems and Morbidity, and the Consequential Use of Health Services' (2008) 5(2) *Journal of Empirical Legal Studies* 351.

a fine of $50,000.[19] The case before a single judge of the Federal Court was upheld on appeal. If the sticker is ignored, it constitutes trespass. Changes have also been made to industry codes.

This case study goes to show how a creative idea such as a 'Do Not Knock' sticker can have a significant impact in changing laws. The case illustrates how clients can be included and empowered to participate directly in law reform through a trusted intermediary (in this case CALC). It involved a collaboration of financial counsellors and social workers alongside affected clients. Further details about the approaches and processes are available in the 2013 report.[20]

C. Case study three: Enabling community voice

Community members in a public housing Residents' Group (RG) in West Heidelberg (one of the poorest locations in Australia) were empowered to make their own submission. They had consistently reported poor housing for over a decade with no response.

The Victorian Government called a Parliamentary Inquiry into Public Housing in Victoria. The inquiry was called with a very limited lead-time at Christmas. The author (then Director of the West Heidelberg Legal Service) saw an inquiry advertisement and brought it to the residents' attention. The residents wanted to participate in an inquiry but had no idea how or what to do. They felt no one would listen to them. A plan of action and training was developed identifying what skills would be needed to participate in the inquiry. Enabling RG participation involved intensive sequential building-block training that was responsive to needs and gaps in skills, as very few members of the RG knew anything about decision-makers and processes. Many were fearful of departmental reprisals and so systems were developed to protect community members such as using numbers rather than names in the Focus Groups residents conducted with public housing residents. This underlines why people feel discouraged from participation in law reform processes.

---

19   *Australian Competition and Consumer Commission v Neighbourhood Energy Pty Ltd* [2012] FCA 1357.
20   Curran, above n 13, 29–34.

These Focus Groups were recorded and transcribed by a pro bono law firm and formed into a written submission. The RG were called to 'give evidence' before the Parliamentary Inquiry. At first the parliamentarians directed questions to the author who had to firmly defer to the RG. Once the parliamentarians listened to the RG, the often brutal reality of life on a public housing estate led the parliamentarians to conclude it was 'the most powerful and compelling submission' and later adopted some recommendations of the RG. One politician noted at the hearing it was 'a most significant moment in democratic participation'.

V. Suggestions for Inclusive Law Reform

The author recognises that in a context of limited resources and funding for law reform bodies[21] it is hard to think about non-traditional approaches to law reform. The ALRC,[22] Victorian Law Reform Commission[23] and other bodies have tried to increase public participation.[24] Many of these processes rely on computer access, which is effectively a form of social exclusion for those without internet access or computer literacy. Community agencies are also under significant resource constraints, as noted by the Productivity Commission (PC) in its Final Report on Access to Justice Arrangements.[25] The author's 2013 report[26] shows that this has not prevented innovations in law reform practice occurring. Many initiatives derive from a need to find better ways of responding due to a lack of capacity for one-on-one cases, identifying the systemic causes in multiple cases and working collectively to address problems at the source.

---

21   Michael Kirby, Plenary Address delivered at the Inaugural National Law Reform Conference, Canberra, 14 April 2016.
22   See Australian Law Reform Commission, *Talk to Us* (24 September 2015), www.alrc.gov.au/talk-us.
23   See Victorian Law Reform Commission, *About Community Law Reform* (26 May 2016), www.lawreform.vic.gov.au/all-projects/about-community-law-reform.
24   Ian Davis, 'Targeted Consultations' and Roslyn Atkinson, 'Law Reform and Community Participation' in Brian Opeskin and David Weisbrot (eds), *The Promise of Law Reform* (The Federation Press, 2005) Ch 10, 148–59; Ch 11, 160–74.
25   Productivity Commission, *Commission Inquiry into Access to Justice Arrangements Report: Volume 2,* Inquiry Report 72, 2014, 696–700.
26   Curran, above n 13.

Law reform agencies and regulators can learn from these case studies. Scarce resources need not be an inhibitor. Initiatives can include:

- facilitated Focus Groups instead of written submissions where targeted participants are de-identified, enabled, and supported in a safe space (Case Study Three);

- submissions developed through community lunches and conversations with people directly affected by policies. These gatherings could be facilitated by community agency linkages to bring together affected communities;

- training and working with communities through their trusted intermediaries, be they 'peer-to-peer' learning or skilled-up, supported by legal and non-legal professionals, which the case studies above demonstrate can enable civil participation;

- anonymous input (for those who fear reprisals or are embarrassed or do not want public attention);

- advice telephone lines set up to help people navigate having their views heard through either direct support in making oral or written submissions;

- closer liaison with community groups and organisations about their trend identification of systemic issues (Case Studies One and Two);

- problem-solving of individual complaints by collective complaints (e.g. National Bulk Debt Negotiation).

VI. Conclusion

The author has argued that it is possible for law reform processes to engage better with the people often marginalised by society who are deeply affected by laws and their administration through innovative approaches.[27] Law Reform bodies with their expertise can bring about a reality check by facilitating connected and realistic, practical policy responses that capture and channel voices into evidence-based research.

---

27   Catholic Commission for Justice, Development and Peace, "*It's Not Easy Walkin' in There*": *Aboriginal Reconciliation: Towards Practical and Culturally Respectful Solutions* (Catholic Commission for Justice, Development and Peace, 1999).

There is a role for lawyers, consistent with their professional duties to the rule of law, to ensure confidence in and integrity of the legal system, and to empower and upskill communities. Lawyers have a significant role to play in demystifying the political and legislative processes and enabling participation and in advocacy and empowering communities to ensure the law protects them and is fair and just.

In its Final Report on Access to Justice Arrangements,[28] the Productivity Commission stressed that there is a 'disconnect between legal need and government funding'[29] and a need for innovative holistic approaches to problem solving.[30] It endorsed the systemic work done by agencies.[31] This view contrasts notably with government actions actively discouraging such systemic work.[32] The PC encourages regulators to respond to such systemic issues and be more proactive in stopping problems at their core and preventing additional costs.[33]

This view might be considered a 'call to action' to law reform bodies. Given the significant obstacles many people have to having their voices heard in law-making, the public is increasingly disengaged. If we truly inhabit a participatory democracy, we need to find ways for people who are often hindered by personal circumstances to have a direct voice. Arming community service agencies (so often stretched in terms of resources and demands of service delivery) with the ability to build capacity within communities to engage directly with law reform can lead to greater input and change. If this occurs, policy will be more relevant, responsive, timely, comprehensive and effective. This is needed at times of increasing worldwide public alienation from legislative and political systems.

---

28 Productivity Commission, *Commission Inquiry into Access to Justice Arrangements Report: Overview*, Inquiry Report 72, 2014, 28.
29 Ibid.
30 Productivity Commission, above n 11 (Vol 1), 171–176; n 21 (Vol 2), 713; *Overview*, above n 28, 43.
31 Productivity Commission, *Overview*, above n 28, 12, 11, 31; n 21 (Vol 2), 708–713.
32 See new cl 5 inserted by federal government funding agreements with legal aid commissions and community legal centres. See also Curran, above n 9.
33 Productivity Commission, *Overview*, above n 28, 30–31.

49

The End of Ramism: And the Shape of Things To Come

Craig Collins[1]

I. Introduction

In his opening address to the National Law Reform conference, Michael Kirby, from his vantage point spanning several decades and by reciting a few lines from W B Yeats's *Sailing to Byzantium*, perfectly captured the conference theme as:

> set upon a golden bough to sing
> To lords and ladies of Byzantium
> Of what is past, or passing, or to come.[2]

From the vantage point of a golden bough set high above the terrain bounded by 500 years of Western university and legal education, this chapter speaks of Ramism as something past and something passing. It also postulates what, in the digital age, is still to come. As Kirby observed, all of this is pretty fundamental to what legal academics do and how we do it.[3]

---

1   Senior Lecturer, Legal Workshop, The Australian National University; craig.collins@anu.edu.au.
2   William Butler Yeats, *Sailing to Byzantium* (Poetry Foundation, 15 April 2016), www.poetryfoundation.org/poem/172063; recited by Michael Kirby, 'Plenary Address' (Speech delivered at The National Law Reform Conference, Canberra, 14 April 2016).
3   Kirby, above n 2.

Ramism was a Renaissance movement which, by harnessing the power of letterpress printing, transformed university education. The Ramists introduced a new method which, by becoming so deeply entrenched over centuries, has sunk beneath our consciousness. The point in talking about the ending of something so seemingly obscure as Ramism is to raise awareness that our current method of university education does indeed have a beginning. Further, this method was born out of past technological innovation. And, with this technology becoming superseded, some quite profound implications follow for future method in university education.

Specifically, this chapter identifies three challenges to which legal education should be geared in the near-to-medium-term future:

1. becoming self-aware of, and detaching from, our Ramist imprinting;
2. reimagining and reshaping law curricula for a post-Ramist world; and
3. riding the wave of new media.

Given the extent of the technological shift which has already occurred, none of the above challenges are matters of choice, so much as challenges to our adaptive capacity. This chapter focuses on proposed legal and policy responses to these challenges, including recalibrating the requirements for admission to practice as an Australian lawyer. More particularly, the chapter argues for reducing the weighting attached to the 'academic requirements' – and expanding the 'professional legal education requirements' – as our single best policy response to the larger forces confronting legal education in Australia today.

To begin, it is useful for us to grasp how the last great wave of technological innovation transformed method in university education.

II. The Renaissance Ramists

Petrus Ramus was a Professor at the University of Paris from 1551 until about 1568. His book, *Professio Regia*, published posthumously in 1576, carries the first use of the Latin word 'curriculum' ('race' or 'racecourse') in an educational context. For all that, as Adrian Johns says, '[a]mong the heroes of intellectual history, few can be less heroic' than Ramus.[4] Walter

---

4   Adrian Johns, 'Foreword' in Walter Ong, *Ramus: Method and the Decay of Dialogue* (University of Chicago Press, first published 1958, 2004 edn) v.

Ong describes Ramus as a 'shoddy scholar'. Johns refers to him 'at best ... as an inveterate intellectual opportunist. At worst ... his ideas seem "close to the view of a madman"'.[5] At one time, the French King Francis I banned Ramus from teaching or publishing any philosophy due to his incompetence.[6]

Much to the chagrin of the scholarly elite, Ramus still succeeded in destroying the established Aristotelian-dialogical method of university education. His method harnessed the power of letterpress printing, reducing and simplifying knowledge as 'schema' and 'content' on the printed page and moving deductively and hierarchically from the general to the particular. Accordingly, 'in making logic spatial [the Ramists] in effect bound reason and memory to the kind of page that the press made. They turned books into containers of knowledge'.[7] It now 'became possible for the ... university lecturer to focus the whole pedagogical economy on the spatial arrangement of material before his pupils'.[8] But this was a 'dry as dust' approach to curriculum which applied a crude logic and was 'orientated entirely to sight, not to sound':[9]

> As a movement, it was by and large anti-dialogic, anti-dramatic, anti-poetic, and anti-symbolic ... Dynamic, face-to-face interaction as the source of knowledge was 'eclipsed' ... by the viewing of pages. This amounted to the inculcation of a new set of 'mental habits', prior to almost all reasoning, and upon which modern thought would rest.[10]

While there was a transitional struggle and rearguard action by traditionalists, within 'two generations, Ramism was becoming less evident, not because it ceased to exist, but because it had been incorporated into the standard organisational protocol for books themselves'.[11] As a concept, Ramism soon fell into obscurity because 'nobody argued about it any more. It had become second nature'.[12] And, of course, just as printing press technology proliferated, textbooks spread like wildfire – changing the shape of university education for centuries to come.

---

5   Ong, above n 4, 24.
6   Johns, above n 4, viii.
7   Ibid. vii.
8   Ibid.
9   Ibid. ix.
10 Ong, above n 4, 318.
11 Johns, above n 4, ix.
12 Ibid.

III. Challenge of the Common Law

Ramists maintained that their pedagogy could be applied to '[a]ny conceivable subject – rhetoric, politics, law, history, biography, medicine, physics, mathematics' and so on.[13] As Johns notes, '[t]heir ambition was to use this so-called 'method' to supplant university teaching in its entirety. And, remarkably enough, they more or less succeeded'.[14]

The kind of university law contemplated by Ramists was Roman and Canon law. Both presented a neat fit with Ramism, with deductive processes flowing down from higher, binding legal propositions and with the precision of Latin drawing sharp conceptual lines upon the page. English common law was rather different. For one thing, it was not the subject of university education until some two centuries after Ramus – when Sir William Blackstone assumed the first Chair in Common Law at Oxford in 1757. Customary law followed a more inductive approach, flowing from the ground up. This was 'unwritten law' based upon a form of collective, social-habit memory. The role of lawyers was mainly confined to process and remedy, not so much reasoning about substantive law from first principles. Verdict and liability reposed within the hands of juries, which determined disputes without reasons. This kind of law would prove to be a very bad fit with Ramist pedagogy – and remains so to this day.

Blackstone was the first to try fitting the square peg of the common law into the round hole of a Ramist structure, eventually producing *Blackstone's Commentaries on the Laws of England*. In the absence of having any other schema to hand, he adopted the structure of Roman law texts. In doing so, Blackstone famously offered an architectural metaphor: comparing Roman Law with the fine symmetry and proportions of the classical style, and the common law inheritance with the rambling 'old Gothic castle', 'erected in the days of chivalry, but fitted up for the modern inhabitant'.[15]

Recognising the limitations of his own achievement, Blackstone said 'it is impracticable to comprehend many rules of modern law, in a scholarlike scientifical manner, without recourse to the antient'. Lawyers, too, regarded Blackstone's book as a crude and simplistic attempt to capture

---

13   Ibid. vii.
14   Ibid.
15   Carol Matthews, 'A "Model of the Old House": Architecture in Blackstone's Life and Commentaries', in Wilfred Prest (ed), *Blackstone and His Commentaries* (Hart Publishing, 2014) 33.

the art and mystery of common law. Indeed, Michael Lobban has argued persuasively that attempts by Blackstone and Bentham to impose system and coherence upon the common law – by delineating positivist rules and narrow sources of law – were 'outside the mainstream of what lawyers thought the law was about'.[16] Propelled further by John Austin, Professor of Jurisprudence at the University of London from 1826, legal positivism was an academic construct. Here was a tool for making the common law fit the square hole of a Ramist framework.

Ramism was further entrenched by the casebook method developed at the Harvard Law School by Professor Christopher Langdell in the 1870s. This approach was 'based upon generalisations – principles and categories of classification – from the data of reported cases'.[17] The notion of legal science arose from applying Aristotelian logic to bounded casebook 'content', skewing learning towards the projected ruminations of appellate judges while marginalising the more practical, lawyerly preoccupations with process and remedy. This new method 'demanded a new cadre of academic specialists',[18] as '[o]nly full time scientists can pursue legal science'[19] within 'an autonomous field of knowledge'.[20] In the United States, 'Harvardism – which by 1900 meant primarily the case method taught by a full time faculty … spread to law schools everywhere'.[21]

IV. Late Ramists: Australian Legal Academics

In Australia, until the 1960s, the predominant mode of legal education remained the apprenticeship model, through articles of clerkship. From then, with full-time law students and a new cadre of full-time legal academics growing in significant numbers, the Langdellian casebook method was adopted as the model of curriculum. The notion of law so framed was 'law as science'. As Nick James notes:

---

16   Michael Lobban, *The Common Law and English Jurisprudence 1760–1850* (Clarendon Press, 1991) 13.
17   Robert Gordon, 'The Case For (and Against) Harvard' (1995) 93 *Michigan Law Review* 1231.
18   Ibid. 1234.
19   William La Piana, *Logic & Experience: The Origin of Modern American Legal Education* (Oxford University Press, 1994) 57.
20   Gordon, above n 17, 1234.
21   Ibid. 1235.

This approach to teaching law deemphasized the connections with legal practice and, at the same time maintained the separation of law from other disciplines in the university ... Legal scientism thus served to enhance and protect the discipline's new found academic credibility.[22]

Surveying the landscape in 2000, David Weisbrot suspected 'that if Professor Langdell walked into a contemporary law school in the United States or Australia ... he would feel right at home ... the nature of the core curriculum, the dominance of doctrine, and the basic approach to pedagogy have changed very little'.[23]

This also reflected the approach taken to prescribing the 'academic requirements' for admission to legal practice. This approach embodied a Ramist framework listing 11 categories of legal knowledge, with each category further subdivided from left to right across the page. Known as the 'Priestley 11', this would define textbook 'content' – as it continues to do so today. While the range of elective courses proliferated around this compulsory core, these were still shaped and delivered by the casebook method and Ramist pedagogy.

And so, with the Ramist notion of curriculum dating from the 1570s, it was only from the 1960s that Ramism strongly took hold in Australian legal education. As it happened, this was right at the tail end of the Ramist wave, just as the seeds of its own destruction were sparking into life. For, in 1969, the infant internet first 'spoke'.[24]

V. The Internet Ends Ramism

By the 1990s, John Perry Barlow, an early prophet of the digital age, was highlighting how the 'new wine' of information was rapidly being detached from the 'old bottles' of physical containment, such as books.

---

22   Nickolas James, 'A Brief History of Critique in Australian Legal Education' (2000) 24 *Melbourne University Law Review* 965, 968.
23   David Wiesbrot, 'What Lawyers Need to Know, What Lawyers Need to be Able to Do: An Australian Experience' (2000) *Journal of the Association of Legal Writing Directors* 21.
24   Agence-France Press, 'Internet Is 40 Years Young', *The Sydney Morning Herald* (online), 30 October 2009, www.smh.com.au/technology/technology-news/internet-is-40-years-young-20091030-hp5d.html.

'With the advent of digitization', he said, it became 'possible to replace all previous information storage forms with one meta-bottle: complex – and highly liquid – patterns of ones and zeros'.[25]

By 2000, while campaigning against copyright law's futile protection of 'old bottles', Barlow proclaimed that 'the great cultural war has broken out at last. Long awaited by some and a nasty surprise to others, the conflict between the industrial age and the virtual age is now being fought out in earnest'.[26] In the face of this contest, the age of letterpress printing remains, to evoke Yeats, something passing – and virtually lost.

While the early phase of this cultural war is the tangible decline of books and the transfer of content online, this still presupposes a Ramist mental framework and traditional university curricula. But as digital natives grow in number across our teaching and learning spaces, a larger, more fundamental conceptual shift is emerging. Indeed, looking ahead, Microsoft founder Bill Gates has predicted as one of his four 'big bets' for the next 15 years that 'better software will revolutionise learning' and that 'online education will flourish'.[27]

VI. The Shape of Things to Come

Marshall McLuhan described Ramus as 'the first man in history to "surf" on a wave of information launched by new media'.[28] This same opportunity is now presenting itself. If Ramism reflects a mentality made possible by letterpress printing, then what reconfigurations might cyberspace permit? McLuhan and Ong studied Renaissance Ramism with a view to better understanding the present. What can we learn from the past about the shape of things to come? From what direction will this new shape emerge?

Answering the first question invites reflection about all of those things left out by Ramism: the dialogic, dramatic, poetic and symbolic. Some balance needs to be restored towards sound and voice, including the value of dynamic, face-to-face interaction as a source of knowledge – now

25   John Perry Barlow, 'The Economy of Ideas' (1994) 2.03 *Wired* 1, archive.wired.com/wired/archive/8.10/download.html.
26   Ibid.
27   Bill and Melinda Gates, *2015 Gates Annual Letter*, www.gatesnotes.com/2015-annual-letter?WT.mc_id=01_21_2015_DO_com_domain_0_00&page=0&lang=en.
28   Johns, above n 4, ix.

through synchronous interactions online. 'Interaction' is the key word, but of a kind different from eyeballing the page. New media permits multimedia engagement.

Reimagining the shape of law curricula requires some measure of self-awareness of, and detachment from, our Ramist imprinting. The bodily form of Ramism is not just the printed page, nor the Priestley 11. It is also carried by the biological wiring of our brains. In this way, Ramism might be understood as the imprint left upon our minds by so much learning and teaching from books and from the conventional shape of university curricula. Accordingly, modern academics are all Ramists. Indeed, there is probably no segment of humanity which is more invested in Ramism – and less interested in seeing learning in any other way – than university academics.

If the Renaissance is any guide, then the shape of new law curricula will be imagined and designed by 'inveterate intellectual opportunist(s)', much like Ramus himself. It is unlikely that innovation will be driven by elite professors and established academics, having built their success and reputations upon the foundations of a Ramist worldview. Even so, following the pattern of the past, it is a pretty sure thing that, within a generation or two, there will be few (if any) Ramists left.

VII. Initiation into the Discipline

In Australia, we face a widening gulf between our system of university legal education and a legal profession necessarily driven by market responsiveness, global competition and rapid technological change. And yet reform debates still seem stuck within existing frameworks. By lifting our gaze to the horizon, arguing about the actual content of the Priestley 11, and whether we should have a Priestley 12 and so on, seems almost as trivial as fighting over flapping fish stranded on a retreating shoreline – just as a tsunami is gathering force out at sea.

For the profession, the opportunity is presented to reconceptualise accredited legal education in a manner which is far less 'Ramist remote' from the actual experience of entry-level lawyers. While tapping into the latest global developments in technology, education and learning psychology, the profession has a large role to play in reconstructing the entry pathway from the ground up. Rather than confining attention to the bounded terrain of 'content coverage', the real question is this: what qualities and capabilities are both necessary and desirable for human initiation into the discipline of law?

VIII. Conclusion

The above historical account has sought to situate Australian university legal education within the larger context of Ramist pedagogy and text-book method. It has also sought to present a case that we are, indeed, facing the end of Ramism. If this last proposition is accepted, then three particular challenges for university legal education seem to follow for the near-to-medium term future:

1. becoming self-aware of, and detaching from, our Ramist imprinting;
2. reimagining and reshaping law curricula for a post-Ramist world; and
3. riding the wave of new media.

In historic terms, the academic requirements for admission to practice as an Australian lawyer (the Priestley 11) were only recently devised and entrenched, reflecting a Ramist conception of knowledge and pedagogy. If the above account and identified challenges are accepted, then it is hard to imagine the validity and relevance of those academic requirements surviving the end of Ramism.

By contrast, the practical legal education requirements for admission to practice are far less shaped by Ramist pedagogy. Practical skill and knowledge, combined with professional values, have always been inculcated in other ways. The academic trajectory from Blackstone to the university law curricula of today, via the Langdellian casebook method, has only ever occurred in parallel with the more deeply-rooted community of discourse – the kind of mind and talk – by which lawyers themselves achieve mastery within the profession itself. New media offers opportunities for replicating online the kinds of interactions and support which propels this model of development. Indeed, with the vacuum left by the end of Ramism, the solution presenting itself is more akin to the way that lawyers have been learning and developing all along without it.

Accordingly, this chapter calls for recalibrating the regulatory balance in legal education – proposing that less weight be attached to the academic requirements and more weight to the practical legal education component – for the purposes of admission to practice as an Australian lawyer.

Practical legal education, which seeks to replicate the nature of learning within the profession itself, remains a less encumbered, more grounded, innovative and adaptive space. And it is from this direction that law students will be much better placed to surf the wave of new media into the legal profession of the future.

50

Shared Space and the Regulation of Legal Education

Paul Maharg[1]

I. Introduction

Rebecca is a new member of staff in the new University of Kioloa Law School. She is an environmental lawyer, loves teaching and learning and thinks the subject of her research so important that, in the words of Naomi Klein, this changes everything. She wants to design an entirely new law curriculum for students and structure it thematically in environmental law. Every subject will be taught in part through the lens of the environment – environmental regulation and the part it can play in many subjects within the legal curriculum; the history of environmental concern, and the history of indigenous cultures' sustainable use of land and sea; the history and science of climate change, the place of policy and role of governmental intervention, the rise of consumer movements resisting commercial exploitation of the world's resources, and much else. It will have options in law, literature and the environment, re-wilding nature, the future of sustainable cities, and the like. And it will be entirely online. It's designed not just for students interested in environmental law, but for anyone doing any job linked to the environment in, for example, regulation, policy, innovation, bioscience, medscience, enforcement and

1   Professor, The Australian National University College of Law.

much else. Professional accreditation in law might be integrated, possibly in other disciplines too, as optional streams. It will include a Masters option as well which, being offered online, will be available internationally.

Her Dean can see the idea working financially and supports it politically at the Law School Management Group, and staff are interested, all the more so in that the small group of environmental lawyers in the Law School, all equally interested in the idea, will be doing most of the design work on the curriculum and will be fronting-up the proposal for accreditation.

But what's required of accreditation? She begins to map it out. First there's the Law School Teaching and Learning Committee that has to approve the general curriculum design and the individual subjects; and since this is a new curriculum, it will want to see marketing reports and staff resource reports (to ensure the Law School can resource the proposal) and much else. Then the proposal goes to the University Education Committee which is far from a rubber-stamp job, and will look at how the curriculum affects the university brand, amongst other issues. Then NSW accreditation is sought. There is liaison with the profession, with environmental groups, and many others.

Next she begins to think about how the curriculum will be judged at the various stages. She looks at the current (2016) regulatory guidelines for higher education (HE) programs in Law in Australia, which include the following:

1. Council of Australian Law Deans (CALD) Standards;
2. Australian Qualifications Framework (AQF);
3. TEQSA HE Standards Framework (Threshold Standards) 2015 (with a new framework that came into force 1 January 2017);
4. Learning and Teaching Academic Standards Statement;
5. Generic Framework on Internationalising the Law Curriculum;
6. National PLT Competences.[2]

---

2   CALD Standards are available at www.cald.asn.au/docs/CALD%20-%20standards%20project%20 -%20final%20-%20adopted%2017%20November%202009.pdf. Australian Qualifications Framework; see www.aqf.edu.au. The TEQSA provides an overview of the new HE Standards Framework, www.teqsa. gov.au/teqsa-contextual-overview-hes-framework. The Academic Standards Statement is available at www. cald.asn.au/assets/lists/ALSSC%20Resources/KiftetalLTASStandardsStatement2010.pdf.   The   CALD Internationalising Framework is set out at curriculum.cald.asn.au/generic-framework/.

She is dismayed by the cascade of standards, competences, statements, guidelines, outcomes, many of them overlapping, sometimes contradictory, expressed in vague lexis that gives little real indication of actual educational standards. There is no meta-document that guides her through all this, or the maze of accreditation process across Australia's states and territories. How is her innovation going to survive such weight of regulatory command and admonition? On closer inspection, each code bears the marks of its makers, their interpretation of what legal education has been, their present anxieties, their attempt to prescribe the future and to close down and command. But these are not her anxieties or her hopes. She, not they, will be designing the innovative program and helping students learn. But already she can feel her excitement fading at the sheer scale of this task. She puts the project to one side. Maybe next year.

II. Regulation and the Anxiety of Influence

What Rebecca faces is the result of 'decentred regulation' which, as Black describes it, is characterised by five factors: complexity, fragmentation, interdependence, overlapping public and private interests, and ungovernability.[3] Extensive regulation begets more regulation, in spite of best practice codes arguing for the opposite, which increases tension and competition between the regulatory actors and further destabilises the field.[4] There is almost no empirical evidence to support the concept that educational quality will be improved by greater competition accompanied by less regulation. On the other hand, it is well known that a greater volume of regulation does not necessarily lead to better education. This was recognised by the then DIICCSRTE (Department of Industry, Innovation, Climate Change, Science, Research and Tertiary Education) which commissioned a report to reduce regulatory burden on Australian HE generally. The aim was laudable, but could only mitigate against an ungovernable system that will inevitably grow in size and complexity.[5]

---

3   Julia Black, 'Decentring Regulation: Understanding the Role of Regulation and Self-Regulation in a "Post-Regulatory" World' (2001) 54 *Current Legal Problems* 103.
4   See Judith Healy and Paul Dugdale, 'Regulatory Strategies in Safer Patient Health Care' in Judith Healy and Paul Dugdale (eds), *Patient Safety First: Responsive Regulation in Health Care* (Allen & Unwin, 2009) 1.
5   See Kwong Lee Dow and Valerie Braithwaite, *Review of Higher Education Regulation* (Commonwealth of Australia, 2013) Appendix A, 'Assuring Quality While Reducing the Higher Education Regulatory Burden'.

This is by no means limited to Australian legal education. In recent decades legal education regulation internationally has accelerated in volume, pace and intensity.[6] In the last decade we can cite seven such movements. In 2006–9 the Law Society of Scotland laid aside a small-scale review of the primary program in professional training, to review, nationally, the entire legal educational process, from day one of law school through to point of qualification after traineeship (and there was also consideration of Continuing Professional Development, CPD).[7] In Canada, the Federation of the Law Societies of Canada carried out, like the Law Society of Scotland, two years of national consultation relating to criteria for approving common law degrees for the purpose of entry into bar admission programmes in Canada.[8]

Meanwhile in England the three leading regulators of professional education, CILEx (Legal Executives), the Bar Standards Board (BSB) and the Solicitors Regulation Authority (SRA) began the lengthy process of reviewing professional legal education in what eventually became known as the Legal Education and Training Review (2011–13). The context for the review included the effects of liberalisation of the legal services market, implemented by the *Legal Services Act 2007*, and the report was published in 2013.[9]

The US has seen considerable upheaval in legal education since the onset of the global financial crisis, which has resulted in significant downturn in the numbers of positions for young lawyers, and subsequently the numbers of students entering law schools. This, together with dissatisfaction regarding many issues of regulation of legal education, led to the formation of the American Bar Association (ABA) Task Force which took a little over a year to report on the situation in US law schools.[10] Concurrently, the

---

6   Julian Webb et al, 'Setting Standards. The Future of Legal Services Education and Training Regulation in England and Wales' (SRA, BSB, IPS, 2013), letr.org.uk. The authors summarised this in their Literature Review, and brought up to date earlier analyses of the reform movement. Numerous articles confirm this; for example, Andrew Boone and Julian Webb, 'Legal Education and Training in England and Wales: Back to the Future?' (2008) 58 *Journal of Legal Education* 79.

7   See www.lawscot.org.uk/education-and-careers/education-and-training-policy/.

8   See flsc.ca/national-initiatives/canadian-law-school-programs/.

9   See letr.org.uk for the report and associated Literature Review.

10   Two reports were produced: one on the future of American law schools (see www.americanbar.org/groups/professional_responsibility/taskforceonthefuturelegaleducation.html) and another on the future of the financing of legal education (see www.americanbar.org/groups/legal_education/committees/aba-task-force-on-the-financing-of-legal-education-.html). For commentary, see Richard L Abel, '"You Never Want a Serious Crisis to Go to Waste": Reflections on the Reform of Legal Education in the US, UK, and Australia' (2015) 22 *International Journal of the Legal Profession* 3.

Canadian Bar Associations began the first comprehensive study of the state of the Canadian legal market, called the Legal Futures Initiative, which culminated in a report completed in 2014 called *Futures: Transforming the Delivery of Legal Services in Canada.*[11] Significantly, the report and the initiative went hand-in-hand with another called the Equal Justice Initiative, both of them having implications for the future of Canadian legal education.

In Australia meanwhile the Law Admissions Consultative Committee began to review legal educational processes and standards in a Review of Academic Requirements. In their initial report (completed in 2015) they noted the great variety of standards, codes and outcomes populating the regulatory space in Australia, and cited the LETR Report as follows:

> the [LETR] report notes the lack of an overall and coherent legal education system as such. That being so, and in order to avoid a tournament of regulators as to who will regulate whom, the regulators are encouraged to consider greater collaboration …

The report also identifies a number of overarching issues for the regulators, designed to promote common learning outcomes and consistency.[12]

Most recently, the Law Society of Hong Kong has instructed a review of legal education, reporting in late 2016, following an earlier report that was prepared on the subject of a common entry examination, but which has not yet been released by the Law Society.

All this activity denotes what the literary critic Harold Bloom has termed the anxiety of influence. There are complex relations between regulators internationally as they watch each other and the actors around them. Strong regulators struggle with their predecessors and their peers, in much the same way as writers do with other strong writers; and such leading regulators give models of action for regulators in other jurisdictions. As Bloom observes, '[t]o deconstruct a poem is to indicate the precise location of its figuration of doubt, its uncertain notice of that limit where

---

11   See www.cba.org/CBA-Legal-Futures-Initiative/Home/ for information on the Initiative. The report cited above is available at www.cba.org/CBA-Legal-Futures-Initiative/Reports/Futures-Transforming-the-Delivery-of-Legal-Service.

12   The report is entitled *Review of Academic Requirements for Admission to the Legal Profession*, www.lawcouncil.asn.au/LACC/images/pdfs/01.12.14_-_Review_of_Academic_Requirements_for_Admission.pdf.

persuasion yields to a dance or interplay of tropes'.[13] For Bloom, there were two broad categories of poetic tropes: 'tropes of action and tropes of desire'.[14] Replace the word 'poem' with that of 'report', and we have a precise description of many legal education regulators, caught between a deepening anxiety of influence and the need to persuade, and the tropes of desire and of action that lead them to attempt to regulate and command.

III. Disintermediation and Regulation

But is such regulation best for legal education? Could it be that we have, fundamentally, the wrong mode of regulatory activity? Let us think about the meta-activities that law schools are engaged in, the activities that Rebecca will engage in, should her program ever see the light of day. At the heart of law schools, and this is true of the earliest in 1088 at Bologna as it is of the most recently-formed law school such as the University of Kioloa, lies a highly complex process of *mediation*. Such mediation includes the activities of curation, of innovation and of learning knowledge, skill and value, all processes highly intertwined with each other. We preserve the past in order to transmit it to the future. But we also have a duty to critique, interpret and innovate, through analysis of myriad legal cultures, their performativities and their fields and habitus.[15] We also learn, and we help our students to learn, how to curate, interpret, reason, practise skill, and learn value. Above all, legal scholars mediate the past and prepare students for the future; and how we do that is as much a domain of jurisprudential activity as any other sub-domain of that area of law. It is also essentially an interdisciplinary activity.

---

13   Harold Bloom, *The Anxiety of Influence. A Theory of Poetry* (Oxford University Press, 1974) 308. 'Tropes' is a key term for Bloom. It refers, generally, less to the rhetorical sense of a figure or device (i.e. a static collection of terms such as metaphor, metonymy, and the like), and more to the psychological moves a writer makes within a precise historical context to persuade a reader.
14   Ibid. 401.
15   Arising from linguistics and the philosophy of language, a performativity is not simply an utterance or performance, but an act that effects or affects identity and action. A judge pronouncing a judgment is a typical example; a promise is another, particularly when treated legally as actionable, as in the construct of *pollicitatio* under Roman Law. The concept of a field or *habitus* derives of course from Bourdieu. See, for example, Pierre Bourdieu and Jean Passeron, *Reproduction in Education, Society and Culture* (Sage, 1977). The idea of the 'habitus' has been highly influential in education, describing as it does the enduring and transferable dispositions in society that affect individuals, as embodied for example in the notion of 'cultural capital'. For a critique of the latter concept based upon empirical educational research carried out at Oxford University, see Anna Zimdars, Alice Sullivan and Anthony Heath, 'Elite Higher Education Admissions in the Arts and Sciences: Is Cultural Capital the Key?' (2009) *Sociology* 43, 648.

Such mediation, however, is subject to intermediation by technologies, by economic and political forces, by social and institutional agents and by innovation. And it is subject to disintermediation – to the disruption in the process by which established intermediaries (other processes, workflows, technologies, agents) are removed or replaced, or the process itself is reconfigured. Disintermediation is an essential element of historical change in law school mediation, present most strikingly in the digital revolution of the past few decades, but present in all legal education.[16]

Regulators and their codes rarely acknowledge the constant process of disintermediation. Their reports and codes are often the result of a set of social pressures upon legal education or higher education, but, caught in tropes of desire and action, they often seek the autopoiesis of closure.[17] They attempt to close down or remediate the effects of those pressures through the design and enforcement of a code or a set of recommendations. Meanwhile social pressures such as those brought on by disintermediation have already morphed and produced new, often unforeseen and rarely intended educational and social consequences around the new code or recommendations. We need an approach to regulation that eschews the hierarchical command of much regulatory practice in the field and instead seeks to understand the effects of disintermediation and other social processes within law school assemblages and networks.

IV. The Shared Space: A Portrait of the Regulator as Collaborator

Much of the architecture of regulation in Australian HE is built upon the regulatory principles of risk, necessity and proportionality – principles that have been derived from other systems of regulation but which I would argue are of themselves insufficient to provide ethical and effective regulation for higher education. What may be required is:

---

16   Paul Maharg, 'Disintermediation' (2016) 50 *The Law Teacher* 114.

17   As many commentators have pointed out, the self-reproductive power of a system such as a legal system lies in its ability to be at once open and closed: it is autopoietic. Teubner described how, 'unlike neo-liberal and structuralist theories', autopoiesis emphasises 'the complex, the local, the closed and the unstable against global, coherent, artificing and equilibrating mechanisms': Gunther Teubner (ed), *Autopoietic Law: A New Approach to Law and Society* (Walter de Gruyter, 1988) 9. For regulators, the concept of closure is a dominant one, where the dynamic play of agents and the creative power of collaborative action are seen as a threat to the command model of regulation, which seeks the stasis of control.

1. A new attitude to Open Education and Open Research, and the encouragement of co-production and of communities of practice across educational institutions and across disciplines and professions.

2. A view of regulation as comprising not just quality assurance but quality enhancement, where responsibility is given to the actors in the regulated field to regulate their own behaviour according to their own aims, subject to monitoring.

In the Legal Education and Training Review Report we advocated, *inter alia*, an approach to regulation that we called the 'shared space'. It was summarised in the report as the sustained development of 'a community of educators, regulators, policy-makers and professionals working in provision of legal services, drawing information from other jurisdictions, other professions and other regulators to identify best practices in [legal education] and its regulation' (para 6.158). The approach was outlined in more detail in Ch 3 of the LETR Literature Review, where we investigated the role that design played in the shared space, contrasting it with role played by hierarchical regulation, and the potential it had to shape regulated activity:

> Design can be used to enhance responsibility and accountability, and extend agency ...; indeed it can do so by clearing a space, as it were, in hierarchy so that self-governance, often according to extra-legal norms, is possible in ways that it would not otherwise be within communities of practice.[18]

We recommended that the frontline regulators of legal education form a Legal Council to provide the neutral space for regulators, providers and many others to meet and plan this new approach. In their report, Lee Dow and Braithwaite similarly recommended the formation of an Advisory Council and a collaborative approach to co-regulation and self-regulation which describes regulators and institutions working in partnership. As Raban and Cairns describe it, citing Lee Dow and Braithwaite:

> They would need to 'share the same objective (excellence in teaching, learning and research, for example)' and 'the purpose of the regulatory encounter' should be 'to raise concerns about risks and obstructions to achieving (these) objectives and to work through problems to find a satisfactory solution'.[19]

---

18   Ibid. Ch 3, para 45.
19   Colin Raban and David Cairns, 'How Did It Come to This?' (2014) 18 *Perspectives: Policy and Practice in Higher Education* 112, 117.

But excellence in teaching and learning is, as an aim, so high-level that in practice it means little. And under the top-down model of regulation, which still is the essence of this regulatory relationship, the hidden agendas of what constitutes excellence threaten to silence the shared conversation. Institutions will try to second-guess what constitutes excellence in the eyes of the regulator. The regulator will point to market devices (e.g. student choice) as proxies for excellence, an argument advanced by the Browne Report in the UK, and by Universities Australia, and dismissed by many academics.[20]

In the shared space by contrast, HE institutions would have much more agency and work closely with others, including regulators. The Scottish model of QE or Quality Enhancement is one model for a partial shared space. Regulators learn as much as institutions do from the process – arms-length measurement of quality is not the point of the exercise, where institutions lead the review of themselves, and where both regulation and its processes are streamlined and much more focused. Students there play a key role in the enhancement process. Land and Gordon describe aspects of it thus:

> There has been a strong concern to create a sense of ownership and legitimation among all those with a vested interest. In particular, considerable emphasis has been placed on paying attention to the voice(s) of students and encouraging their participation not just as consumers of a service but, after appropriate training, as genuine partners in the review of quality. It has been characterised generally by a shift from audit to improvement, to a more developmental approach, with a focus on teaching and learning themes, and strong emphasis on evaluation and subsequent responsiveness to feedback.[21]

In shared spaces such as this there is the possibility that innovation can be encouraged, disintermediation better understood, and that open cultures can be developed. Along with harmonisation and streamlining of codes in Australian legal education regulation, there is the potential that it could significantly improve legal education regulation. There is even the possibility that, under such a regulatory regime, Rebecca's program might become reality.

---

20   E J P Browne, 'Securing a Sustainable Future for Higher Education: An Independent Review of Higher Education Funding and Student Finance' (2010), www.independent.gov.uk/browne-report; 'Universities Australia Submission to the Review of Higher Education Regulation' (Universities Australia, 2013).

21   George Gordon and Ray Land, '"To See Ourselves as Others See Us": The Scottish Approach to Quality Enhancement' in George Gordon and Ray Land (eds), *Enhancing Quality in Higher Education: International Perspectives* (Routledge, 2016) 82.

51

Dreaming of Diversity in Legal Education

Margaret Thornton[1]

I. Introduction

The compulsory core of legal education has not changed markedly since law was first taught in the university in the 19th century, despite extensive social change. Most recently, we have witnessed the transformation of the legal profession, state disinvestment in public universities, a proliferation of law students and a raft of new law schools. Against this backdrop, I question the wisdom of continuing to adhere to a standardised 'core' curriculum and uniform admission rules when less than 50 per cent of law graduates go into private practice and remain there.

I outline the trajectory of change and make some suggestions as to the way forward. I argue that the case for diversity of the law curriculum should be placed squarely on the legal education agenda. I recommend that the Priestley 11 be abandoned, allowing law schools to focus on their individual strengths. Specialisation in the context of a broad liberal education would not only be academically desirable, it would also better equip graduates for a diverse range of destinations.

---

1   Professor of Law, The Australian National University.

II. The Production of Law Graduates

Australian higher education was radically transformed when all colleges of advanced education (CAEs) were incorporated into a unified higher education system in 1989, which led to the creation of 16 new universities in four years.[2] Despite the orchestrated transition from an elite to a mass system, there was not a commensurate increase in public funding, which led to a shift from free higher education to a user-pays regime. The number of Australian law schools then rapidly increased as the new vice-chancellors believed that law could be taught cheaply and the income would help to subsidise the more resource-intensive parts of the university. Differential rates for HECS were introduced in 1997, with law at the top rate,[3] but this had no discernible effect on the demand for law places.

In 25 years, the number of law schools has more than tripled – from 12 to 40 across 47 campuses, including Australia's first for-profit law school.[4] Government disinvestment in higher education also encouraged established law schools to increase their intakes, which were boosted by the lifting of the cap on Commonwealth-funded places and the introduction of the Juris Doctor (JD). The increase in law graduation rates has been phenomenal:

Year	No of Graduates
1984	1,932
2001	6,149
2014	14,600 (all u/grad & p/grad law programs)

Source: Edmund Tadros and Katie Walsh, 'Too Many Law Graduates and Not Enough Jobs', *Financial Review*, 22 October 2015, www.afr.com/business/legal/too-many-law-graduates-and-not-enough-jobs-20151020-gkdbyx. The collection of precise disaggregated data is difficult and confusing because of the varied approaches adopted by the federal, state and territory authorities. The Australian Council of Law Deans settled on a total of 7,583 LLB and JD graduates in 2015. See Melissa Coade, 'Counting the So-called 'Glut' of Law Grads', *Lawyers Weekly*, 25 November 2016, www.lawyersweekly.com.au/news/20080-counting-the-so-called-glut-of-law-grads. This figure did not include other sources of graduate lawyers, such as the Legal Profession Admission Board of NSW, which produced 166 graduates in 2015–16 (NSW Department of Justice, *Annual Report 2015–16*, www.lpab.justice.nsw.gov.au/Documents/Annual%20Report%202015-16.pdf).

---

2   Simon Marginson and Mark Considine, *The Enterprise University: Power, Governance and Reinvention in Australia* (Cambridge University Press, 2000) 29.
3   Along with medicine, dentistry and veterinary science, www.aph.gov.au/About_Parliament/Parliamentary_Departments/Parliamentary_Library/Publications_Archive/archive/hecs.
4   TOP Education Institute, *Sydney City School of Law: Australia's Newest Law School* (2016), www.top.edu.au/home/school-of-law.

III. Sameness or Difference?

One would have thought that the proliferation of so many new law schools presented an ideal opportunity for diversifying the law curriculum. However, it had the opposite effect. Because the admitting authorities were suspicious of the new schools, they favoured uniformity. Indeed, the adoption of uniform admission rules (the 'Priestley 11'[5]) coincided with the establishment of the first wave of new schools in the early 1990s.

Theoretically, completion of the Priestley 11 was not necessary for a student to graduate with an LLB but, out of deference to the profession, the 11 prescribed areas of knowledge were incorporated into each university's compulsory curriculum. Indeed, no Australian law school was brave enough to bypass Priestley and specify an alternate set of requirements, except one, although the attempt was short-lived. When La Trobe began its LLB program in 1992, only two subjects were specified as compulsory: Legal Reasoning and Socio-legal Research Methods. However, within two years and before the first cohort had even graduated, the newly-ratified Priestley 11 was made compulsory for the award of the LLB, although most students had chosen to include the specified areas of knowledge in their course of study anyway – 'just in case' they decided to take out a practising certificate.[6]

It is notable that the Priestley Committee ignored the broadening of the curriculum that had been occurring in law schools since the 1970s, choosing to prioritise doctrinal and technical competence over context and critique. The Victorian Council of Legal Education (the rules for which became the model for the Australian Uniform Admission Rules) rejected family law in favour of company law in 1990 on the basis that 'the building block components of family law were covered by "contract, property and trusts"';[7] gender, affectivity and family relations were deemed dispensable.

---

5   After Justice Priestley who chaired the Law Admissions Consultative Committee of State and Territory Law Admitting Authorities in 1992. The specified areas of knowledge are Criminal Law and Procedure, Torts, Contracts, Property, Equity (including Trusts), Company Law, Administrative Law, Federal and State Constitutional Law, Civil Procedure, Evidence, Ethics and Professional Responsibility.

6   Margaret Thornton, *Quinquennial Professorial Report to University Council* (La Trobe University, Melbourne, 1995), on file with the author.

7   Council of Legal Education Victoria, *Report of Academic Course Appraisal Committee on Legal Knowledge Required for Admission to Practise* (Council of Legal Education Victoria, 1990).

As in Canada, Priestley accorded short shrift to non-doctrinal subjects with a long academic tradition, such as legal theory and legal history.[8] The centripetal pull of technocratic business-oriented law and the imprimatur of the admitting authorities determined what was important, underscored by the credentialism and vocationalism that accompanied the user-pays mentality.[9] Even the fact that the Pearce Report had recognised the generalist nature of the law degree only a few years earlier was accorded short shrift.

The deference towards the admitting authorities underscores not only the subordination of law schools to the legal profession but also the failure of law to develop as an independent discipline within the academy.[10] The expansion of law schools would have been an ideal time to argue for diversity but there is an absence of unanimity among academics as to just what the primary role of a law school should be – a site for the training of practitioners or an independent academic discipline. In recent years, the scales have tipped away from a liberal legal education in favour of vocationalism, entailing deference to known knowledge. Even from a functional perspective, however, one would have to query whether having 40 virtually identical programs is economically rational. The uniformity of the curriculum arises from what Thomasset and Leperrièrre refer to as the infeudation of law schools to the profession.[11] They suggest that the domination of the profession is such that there would need to be a revolution to slough it off.

IV. Challenging Priestley

The Priestley 11 has been subject to criticism over the years, not only from those seeking a more liberal orientation to legal education, but also from legal practitioners themselves who have felt that inadequate attention was being paid to what lawyers actually do.[12] The response led to the

---

8   Cf Harry Arthurs, '"Valour Rather than Prudence": Hard Times and Hard Choices for Canada's Legal Academy' (2013) 76 *Saskatchewan Law Review* 73, 86.

9   Margaret Thornton, *Privatising the Public University: The Case of Law* (Routledge, 2012) 59–109.

10   Cf Mary Keyes and Richard Johnstone, 'Changing Legal Education: Rhetoric, Reality, and Prospects for the Future' (2004) 26 *Sydney Law Review* 537, 542.

11   Claude Thomasett and René Leperrièrre, 'Faculties under Influence: The Infeudation of Law Schools to the Legal Professions' in Fiona Cownie (ed), *The Law School: Global Issues, Local Questions* (Ashgate, 1999).

12   Australian Law Reform Commission, *Managing Justice: A Review of the Federal Civil Justice System* (Report No 89) (2000), 123–27.

incorporation of more practice-related skills into the curriculum,[13] but the effect was to induce not only a less liberal orientation to the law degree but also an instantiation of the idea that traditional legal practice is the logical destination for all law graduates.

In 2015, the Law Admissions Consultative Committee (LACC) proposed a limited review of the academic requirements for admission, influenced by the Legal Education and Training Review conducted in England and Wales in 2013.[14] LACC wanted to know whether civil procedure, company law and evidence, together with ethics and professional responsibility, should continue to be prescribed areas of knowledge and whether statutory interpretation should be included as a new academic requirement.[15]

The key question is whether a designated area of knowledge is foundational to a law degree, not whether it is a useful addition. It is suggested that civil procedure, company law and evidence could all be omitted as they are included in the PLT Competency Standards, but ethics and professional responsibility should be retained. To focus on legal doctrine, or law as it is, is to teach frozen knowledge that is likely to be out of date by the time the student graduates. The focus should be on principles and transferable knowledge. Ethics and professional responsibility are foundational, not only to legal practice, but to most areas of employment. The inclusion of statutory interpretation is also supported. Not only do we live in an age of statutes, but the principles and techniques of interpretation are poorly understood. As with ethics, interpretative skills possess a high degree of transferability, for they are central to all linguistic and text-based disciplines, including law and public policy.

I also note that the Priestley 11 remains resolutely domestic in its orientation, despite the reality of globalisation, although a report commissioned by the Australian Government Office for Learning and Teaching in 2012 recommended that the law degree be internationalised,

---

13   Thornton, above n 9, 81–84.
14   Legal Education and Training Review (LETR) of England and Wales (viewed 21 March 2016), letr.org.uk/wp-content/uploads/LETR-Report.pdf.
15   LACC had not reported at the time of writing.

favouring a 'light-handed' approach by the admitting authorities.[16] Some stakeholders nevertheless expressed strong support for making private international law compulsory within the Priestley 11,[17] which reflects law firms' emphasis on profit maximisation.

V. Towards Diversity in Legal Education

Less than 50 per cent of law graduates embark on a career in private law firms,[18] while the remainder pursue a diverse range of careers in the public service and the non-profit sector, business and finance, international institutions such as the United Nations, as well as journalism, research and teaching positions. Why, then, should they be compelled to undertake an expensive legal education predicated on the assumption that they will embark on private practice and earn substantial salaries on the corporate track?[19] In any case, as the total number of solicitors in Australian law firms is just over 66,000,[20] it would be impossible to place the majority of graduates in law firms. Of course, law schools are not responsible for ensuring that their graduates find employment and they are unlikely to be sued if graduates are unsuccessful, as has occurred in the US.[21] However, vocationalism is a dimension of government policy that law schools cannot afford to ignore.

---

16   Office for Learning and Teaching, Department of Industry, Innovation, Science, Research and Tertiary Education (Australian Government), *Internationalising the Australian Law Curriculum for Enhanced Global Legal Practice* (Australian Government Office for Learning and Teaching, 2012) 86, www.olt.gov.au/resource-internationalising-australian-law-curriculum-enhanced-global-legal-practice-2012.

17   Ibid. 69.

18   A 2010 survey by Graduate Careers Australia revealed that only 43.7 per cent of graduates started work in law firms (a drop from 49.1 per cent five years earlier). See Nicola Berkovic, 'Fewer Law Graduates are Choosing Practice as a Career', *The Australian* (online), 1 July 2011, www.theaustralian.com.au/business/legal-affairs/fewer-law-graduates-are-choosing-practice-as-a-career/story-e6frg97x-1226085138499. In the US, 55 per cent of law graduates were employed in full-time, bar passage-required employment nine months after graduation in 2011. See William Henderson, 'A Blueprint for Change' (2013) 40 *Pepperdine Law Review* 461, 475.

19   In 2016, the cost of a Commonwealth-supported place for Law was $44,000 and set to rise to $58,000 according to predictions of the Australian Scholarships Group. See *Australian HES* online, 1 March 2016, www.theaustralian.com.au/higher-education.

20   Law Council of Australia, www.lawcouncil.asn.au/lawcouncil/index.php/12-resources/231-how-many-lawyers-are-there-in-australia.

21   Elizabeth Olson, 'Law Graduate Gets Her Day in Court, Suing Law School', *New York Times*, 7 March 2016, www.cnbc.com/2016/03/07/law-graduate-gets-her-day-in-court-suing-law-school.html.

In 2011–12, most of the top-tier Australian corporate law firms became globalised as a result of amalgamation with London-based 'Magic Circle' firms.[22] The aim was to maximise profits. Efficiencies were also introduced, such as resorting to companies specialising in document review, discovery and predictive coding in order to undertake more cheaply work traditionally performed by associates. The emphasis on profit maximisation has meant that law firms may no longer be prepared to assume responsibility for training substantial numbers of new graduates, who could find themselves vying with cheaper paralegals for entry-level positions.

Contrary to the uniformity of destination anticipated by the admitting authorities, there is increasing pressure on law firms to diversify[23] and there is criticism from within the profession that students have not had sufficient exposure to alternative forms of employment, such as corporate in-house roles.[24] Social justice advocates are also critical of the notable shortages of lawyers in regional, rural and remote areas and the fact that ordinary citizens cannot afford access to legal services.[25] Despite such needs, traditional legal practice, particularly corporate practice, continues to be regarded as the raison d'être of legal education.

Even if graduates enter traditional legal practice initially, they are unlikely to remain on a single career trajectory. A recent study of Millennials (those born after 1982) found that 46 per cent expect to leave their current employer within the next two years.[26] The Pearce Report noted 30 years ago that more than 50 per cent of law graduates were entering diverse destinations, but the curriculum has failed to take adequate cognisance of this reality, despite the explosion in numbers. It is therefore time that we thought more creatively about the inclusion of transferable skills in the law curriculum with an eye not only to actual student destinations but also to

22 Margaret Thornton, 'Hypercompetitiveness or a Balanced Life? Gendered Discourses in the Globalisation of Australian Law Firms' (2014) 17(2) *Legal Ethics* 153.
23 Stefanie Garber, 'Firms Urged to Push into Non-legal Sectors', *Lawyers Weekly*, 17 February 2016, www.lawyersweekly.com.au/news/17993-firms-urged-to-push-into-non-legal-sectors.
24 Stefanie Garber, 'Students Underexposed to In-house Roles', *Lawyers Weekly*, 17 February 2016, www.lawyersweekly.com.au/news/17998-students-underexposed-to-in-house-roles.
25 Productivity Commission (Australian Government), *Access to Justice Arrangements: Productivity Commission Inquiry Report* (Productivity Commission, 2014).
26 Felicity Nelson, 'Young Lawyers View Staying Put as "Career Suicide"', *Lawyers Weekly*, 10 February 2016, www.lawyersweekly.com.au/careers/17953-young-lawyers-view-staying-put-as-career-suicide.

their educational benefits. Attention should be paid to problem solving, leadership, ethics, values, project management and creative thinking, as well as sociolegal research methods and interdisciplinary perspectives.[27]

The issue of diversity in destination begs the question of whether difference rather than sameness should be addressed by the admitting authorities, although the signs are not propitious. When Alfred Reed suggested in 1921 that different 'bars' be created in the US, this was regarded as heretical.[28] Would it be possible to develop varying gradations of admission in Australia today? Should we effect a divorce from Priestley in the interests of a more diverse and dynamic curriculum?

The divorce could entail separating the admission and the academic requirements, with a national exam to follow practical legal training for those who wished to be admitted. Although the administration of such an exam would be cumbersome, it could be managed by state and territory admitting authorities or the Law Council. However, as Thomasett and Leperrière make clear, a separate exam would not necessarily overcome the problem of infeudation, as whatever subjects are specified by the admitting authorities tend to influence the content of the law curriculum, even if no longer compulsory.[29]

I believe that it should be made clear to students at the outset that legal practice is only one of many possible destinations for them. Accordingly, law schools should be free to design their own curricula. Each school could designate as compulsory certain basic areas of knowledge, such as contract and constitutional law, followed by specialisation in a cluster of cognate subjects, comparable to a major in the BA. Specialist streams could be devoted to human rights, gender, race, crime, international law, comparative law, environmental law, public law, commercial law, etc., in addition to more general offerings. I particularly want to exhort a shift away from an obsession with doctrine to a focus on transferable skills, as suggested, including negotiation, conflict resolution and an ethical consciousness appropriate for a dynamic global environment. This is where the role of collaboration rather than adversarialism, as advocated

---

27 Cf Keyes and Johnstone, above n 10, 541.
28 Richard W Bourne, 'The Coming Crash in Legal Education: How We Got Here, and Where We Go Now' (2011/2012) 45 *Creighton Law Review* 651, 696.
29 Thomasett and Leperrière, above n 11, 198.

by Pauline Collins,[30] would come into its own. In reimagining the curriculum, I am not ignoring vocationalism, for a broad liberal education would better prepare students for a wide array of destinations in which a law degree would be advantageous.

VI. Conclusion

I suggest taking a leaf out of the report of the Ontario Higher Education Quality Council regarding differentiation among universities in Ontario in 2013,[31] which argued that the funding formula should be amended to ensure that the province's 20 universities have the resources to enable them to pursue a policy of achieving what each one does best. How much more sensible it would be for the Australian Government to do the same in respect of 40-plus law schools rather than accept that they all should be pale copies of one another.

Elements of diversity of a socioeconomic nature can be discerned as new schools struggle to compete with those possessing significant positional goods arising from age, wealth and metropolitan location. However, is entrenching class differences between the 'haves' and the 'have nots' the type of diversity that we wish to promote? A liberal legal education that focuses on critical thinking, values, principles and ethics in the context of diverse curricula offerings undoubtedly provides a superior education for law students, as well as constituting better preparation for a range of positions in a context of dynamic and uncertain social change.

---

30   Pauline Collins, 'Australian Legal Education at a Cross Roads' (2016) 58(1) *Australian Universities' Review* 30.
31   Higher Education Quality Council of Ontario, *The Diversity of Ontario's Universities: A Data Set to Inform the Differentiation Discussion* (Higher Education Quality Council of Ontario, 2013), www.heqco.ca/SiteCollectionDocuments/HEQCO%20Diversity_ENG.pdf.

Bibliography

A. Books and Journals

Abel, Richard L, '"You Never Want a Serious Crisis to Go to Waste"': Reflections on the Reform of Legal Education in the US, UK, and Australia' (2015) 22 *International Journal of the Legal Profession* 3

Ackerman, Bruce, *We the People: Foundations* (Belknap Press, 1991)

Adjei, Patricia and Natalie P Stoianoff, 'The World Intellectual Property Organization (WIPO) and the Intergovernmental Committee: Developments on Traditional Knowledge and Cultural Expressions' (2013) 92 *Intellectual Property Forum* 37

Aloisi, Antonio, 'Commoditized Workers: Case Study Research on Labour Law Issues Arising from a Set of "On-demand/Gig Economy" Platforms' (2016) 37(3) *Comparative Labor Law and Policy Journal* (forthcoming)

Anand, Vikas, Blake Ashforth and Mahendra Joshi, 'Business as Usual: The Acceptance and Perpetuation of Corruption in Organizations' (2004) 18 *Academy of Management Executive* 39

Anderson, Elisabeth S and Richard H Pildes, 'Expressive Theories of Law: A General Restatement' (2000) 5 *University of Pennsylvania Law Review* 1503

Anderson, Robert T, 'Water Rights, Water Quality, and Regulatory Jurisdiction in Indian Country' (2015) 34(2) *Stanford Environmental Law Journal* 195

Appleby, Gabrielle and Adam Webster, 'Parliament's Role in Constitutional Interpretation' (2013) 37 *Melbourne University Law Review* 255

Appleby, Gabrielle, 'The High Court and *Kable*: A Study in Federalism and Rights Protection' (2014) 40 *Monash University Law Review* 673

Appleby, Gabrielle, 'The 2014 Counter-Terrorism Reforms in Review' (2015) *Public Law Review* 4

Arcioni, Elisa and Adrienne Stone, 'The Small Brown Bird: Values and Aspirations in the Australian Constitution' (2016) 14 *International Journal of Constitutional Law* 60

Arnaud, Anke, 'Conceptualizing and Measuring Ethical Work Climate: Development and Validation of the Ethical Climate Index' (2010) 49 *Business and Society* 345

Arnold, Craig and Lance Gunderson, 'Adaptive Law and Resilience' (2013) 43 *Environmental Law Reporter* 10436

Arstein-Kerslake, Anna, 'An Empowering Dependency: Exploring Support for the Exercise of Legal Capacity' (2016) 18 *Scandinavian Journal of Disability Research* 77. doi.org/10.1080/15017419.2014.941926

Arthurs, Harry, '"Valour Rather than Prudence": Hard Times and Hard Choices for Canada's Legal Academy' (2013) 76 *Saskatchewan Law Review* 73

Asch, Solomon, 'Studies of Independence and Conformity: A Minority of One Against a Unanimous Majority' (1956) 70 *Psychological Monographs* 1

Ashworth, Andrew, 'Is the Criminal Law a Lost Cause?' (2000) 116 *Law Quarterly Review* 225

Astor, Hilary and Christine Chinkin, *Dispute Resolution in Australia* (Butterworths, 2nd edn, 2002)

Atkinson, Rob, 'Reforming Cy Pres Reform' (1993) 44(5) *Hastings Law Journal* 1111

Baldwin, Claudia and Mark Hamstead, *Integrated Water Resource Planning* (Earthscan, 2015)

Banks, Gary, *Structural Reform Australian-Style: Lessons for Others?* Presentation to the IMF and World Bank (Washington DC, 26–27 May 2005) and OECD (Paris, 31 May 2005)

Bant, Elise, 'Statute and Common Law: Interaction and Influence in Light of the Principle of Coherence' (2015) 38(1) *UNSW Law Journal* 362

Bant, Elise, 'Rescission, Restitution and Compensation', in Simone Degeling and Jason Varuhas (eds), *Equitable Compensation and Disgorgement* (Hart Publishing, 2017)

Bant, Elise and Jeannie Paterson, 'Limitations on Defendant Liability for Misleading or Deceptive Conduct under Statute: Some Insights from Negligent Misstatement', in Kit Barker, Ross Grantham and Warren Swan (eds), *The Law of Misstatements: 50 Years on from Hedley Byrne v Heller* (Bloomsbury, 2015)

Barnett, Tim, Ken Bass and Gene Brown, 'Religiosity, Ethical Ideology, and Intentions to Report a Peer's Wrongdoing' (1996) 15 *Journal of Business Ethics* 1161

Bartels, Lorana, 'The ACT Prison: Human Rights Rhetoric Versus Crowded and Bored Reality' (2015) 9 *Court of Conscience* 21

Bartels, Lorana, 'Sentencing Review 2014–15' (2015) 39 *Criminal Law Journal* 326

Bartels, Lorana and Jeremy Boland, 'Human rights and Prison: A Case Study from the Australian Capital Territory', in Elaine Fishwick, Marinella Marmo and Leanne Weber (eds), *Routledge International Handbook of Criminology and Human Rights* (Routledge, forthcoming)

Bartels, Lorana and Rick Sarre, 'Law Reform Targeting Crime and Disorder', in Rick Sarre and Antje Deckert (eds), *Australian and New Zealand Handbook of Criminology, Crime and Justice* (Palgrave, forthcoming)

Barter, Alice, 'Indigenous Driving Issues in the Pilbara Region', in Melissa Castan and Paula Gerber (eds), *Proof of Birth* (Future Leaders, 2015)

Bazemore, Gordon, 'Restorative Justice and Earned Redemption: Communities, Victims, and Offender Reintegration' (1998) 41(6) *American Behavioral Scientist* 768

Bazerman, Max H and Francesco Gino, 'Behavioral Ethics: Towards a Deeper Understanding of Moral Judgment and Dishonesty' *Annual Review of Law & Social Science* (forthcoming)

Beatson, Jack, 'Has the Common Law a Future?' (1997) 56 *Cambridge Law Journal* 300

Bell, Stephen and Alex Park, 'The Problematic Metagovernance of Networks: Water Reform in New South Wales' (2006) 26(1) *Journal of Public Policy* 63

Benson, Peter, 'The Basis of Corrective Justice and its Relation to Distributive Justice' (1992) 77 *Iowa Law Review* 515

Benzanson, Randall P, 'The Libel Suit in Retrospect: What Plaintiffs Want and What Plaintiffs Get' (1986) 74 *California Law Review* 789

Berg, Janine, 'Income Security in the On-demand Economy: Findings and Policy Lessons for a Survey of Crowdworkers' (2016) 37(3) *Comparative Labor Law and Policy Journal* 543

Berkes, Fikret, Johan Colding and Carl Folke (eds), *Navigating Social Ecological Systems: Building Resilience for Complexity and Change* (Cambridge University Press, 2003)

Biber, Eric and J Ruhl, 'The Permit Power Revisited: The Theory and Practice of Regulatory Permits in the Administrative State' (2014) 64 *Duke Law Journal* 133

Biber-Klemm, Susette and Danuta Szymura Berglas, 'Problems and Goals', in Susette Biber-Klemm, Thomas Cottier and Danuta Szymura Berglas (eds), *Rights to Plant Genetic Resources and Traditional Knowledge: Basic Issues and Perspectives* (CAB International, 2006)

Black, Julia, 'Proceduralizing Regulation: Part I' (2000) 20 *Oxford Journal of Legal Studies* 597

Black, Julia, 'Proceduralizing Regulation: Part II' (2001) 21 *Oxford Journal of Legal Studies* 33

Black, Julia, 'Decentring Regulation: Understanding the Role of Regulation and Self-Regulation in a "Post-Regulatory" World' (2001) 54 *Current Legal Problems* 103

Blenkinsopp, Jon and Marissa Edwards, 'On Not Blowing the Whistle: Quiescent Silence as an Emotion Episode', in Neal Ashkanasy, Wilfred Zerbe and Charmine Härtel (eds), *Emotions, Ethics and Decision-Making* (Emerald Publishing, 2008)

Bloom, Harold, *The Anxiety of Influence. A Theory of Poetry* (Oxford University Press, 1974) 308

Blouin, Francis X Jr, and William G Rosenberg, *Processing the Past: Contesting Authority in History and the Archives* (Oxford University Press, 2011)

Blumm, Michael C, 'Federal Reserved Water Rights as a Rule of Law' (2016) 52 *Idaho Law Review* 369

Bogus, Carl T, 'The Death of an Honourable Profession' (1996) 71(4) *Indiana Law Journal* 911

Bojczenko, Mickael N and Diane Sivasubramaniam, 'A Psychological Perspective on Preventive Detention Decisions' (2016) *Psychiatry, Psychology and Law* 1

Bok, Sissela, *Secrets: On the Ethics of Concealment and Revelation* (Vintage Books, 1989)

Boone, Andrew and Julian Webb, 'Legal Education and Training in England and Wales: Back to the Future?' (2008) 58 *Journal of Legal Education* 79

Bornstein, Brian H and Edie Greene, 'Jury Decision Making: Implications for and from Psychology' (2011) 20(1) *Current Directions in Psychological Science* 63

Boulle, Laurence, *Mediation: Principles, Process and Practice* (LexisNexis, 3rd edn, 2011)

Bourdieu, Pierre and Jean Passeron, *Reproduction in Education, Society and Culture* (Sage, 1977)

Bourne, Richard W 'The Coming Crash in Legal Education: How We Got Here, and Where We Go Now' (2011/2012) 45 *Creighton Law Review* 651

Braithwaite, John, *Restorative Justice and Responsive Regulation* (Oxford University Press, 2002)

Brennan, Jason and Lisa Hill, *Compulsory Voting: For and Against* (Cambridge University Press, 2014)

Briton, John and Scott Mclean, 'Incorporated Legal Practices: Dragging the Regulation of the Profession into the Modern Era' 11 *Legal Ethics* 241

Broadway, Robin and Michael Keen, 'Redistribution', in Anthony Atkinson and François Bourguignon (eds), *Handbook of Income Distribution* (North Holland, Vol 1, 2000)

Brody, Evelyn, 'Of Sovereignty and Subsidy: Conceptualizing the Charity Tax Exemption' (1998) 23(4) *Journal of Corporation Law* 585

Bronitt, Simon, 'Towards A Universal Theory of Criminal Law: Rethinking the Comparative and International Project' (2008) 27 *Criminal Justice Ethics* 53

Bronitt, Simon and Miriam Gani, 'Criminal Codes in the 21st Century: The Paradox of the Liberal Promise', in Bernadette McSherry, Alan Norrie and Simon Bronitt (eds), *Regulating Deviance: The Redirection of Criminalisation and the Futures of Criminal Law* (Hart Publishing, 2009)

Bronitt, Simon and Bernadette McSherry, *Principles of Criminal Law* (Lawbook Co, 4th edn, 2017)

Brooks, Neil, 'Taxing the Wealthy', in Chris Evans, Richard Krever and Peter Mellor (eds), *Australia's Future Tax System: The Prospects after Henry* (Thomson Reuters, 2010)

Brown, A J, Evalynn Mazurski and Jane Olsen, 'The Incidence and Significance of Whistleblowing', in A J Brown (ed), *Whistleblowing in the Public Sector* (ANU E Press, 2008)

Brown, Wendy, *Undoing the Demos: Neoliberalism's Stealth Revolution* (Zone Books, 2015)

Burgman, Mark, et al, 'Designing Regulation for Conservation and Biosecurity' (2009) 13(1) *Australasian Journal of Natural Resources Law and Policy* 93

Burris, Ethan R, 'The Risks and Rewards of Speaking Up: Managerial Responses to Employee Voice' (2012) 55(4) *Academy of Management Journal* 851

Cameron, Camille, 'Case Note. Hired Guns and Smoking Guns: *McCabe v British American Tobacco Australia Ltd*' (2002) 25(3) *UNSW Law Journal* 768

Campbell, Tom, *The Legal Theory of Ethical Positivism* (Dartmouth, 1996)

Carlsmith, Kevin M and John M Darley, 'Psychological Aspects of Retributive Justice' (2008) 40 *Advances in Experimental Social Psychology* 193

Carlsmith, Kevin M, John M Darley and Paul H Robinson, 'Why Do We Punish? Deterrence and Just Deserts as Motives For Punishment' (2002) 83(2) *Journal Of Personality and Social Psychology* 284

Carlsmith, Kevin M, John Monahan and Alison Evans, 'The Function of Punishment in the "Civil" Commitment of Sexually Violent Predators' (2007) 25(4) *Behavioral Sciences & the Law* 437

Carolan, Eoin, 'Ireland's Constitutional Convention: Behind the Hype about Citizen-Led Constitutional Change' (2015) 13 *International Journal of Constitutional Law* 733

Carroll, Robyn, 'Beyond Compensation: Apology as a Private Law Remedy', in Jeffrey Berryman and Rick Bigwood (eds), *The Law of Remedies: New Directions in the Common Law* (Irwin Law, 2010)

Carroll, Robyn and Jeffrey Berryman, 'Making Amends by Apologising for Defamatory Publications – Developments in the 21st Century', in Kit Barker, Ross Grantham and Karen Fairweather (eds), *Private Law in the 21st Century* (Hart Publishing, 2017)

Castan, Melissa and Paula Gerber, 'The Way Forward', in Melissa Castan and Paula Gerber (eds), *Proof of Birth* (Future Leaders, 2015)

Chaaya, Michael, 'Proposed Changes to the Review of Migration Decisions: Sensible Reform Agenda or Political Expediency?' (1996) 19(4) *Sydney Law Review* 547

Chaiken, Shelly, 'Heuristic Versus Systematic Information Processing and the Use of Source Versus Message Cues in Persuasion' (1980) 39(5) *Journal of Personality and Social Psychology* 752

Chaiken, Shelly and Yaacov Trope, *Dual-process Theories in Social Psychology* (Guilford Press, 1999)

Chase, Oscar G, '"Supreme" Courts and the Imagination of the Real' (2015) 518 *New York University Public Law and Legal Theory Working Papers* 14

Chinkin, Christine, 'Women's International Tribunal on Japanese Military Sexual Slavery' (2001) 95 *American Journal of International Law* 335

Clark, Haley, 'What is the Justice System Willing to Offer? Understanding Sexual Assault Victim/Survivors' Criminal Justice Needs' *Family Matters* No 85 (Australian Institute of Family Studies, 2010)

Clear, Todd, *Imprisoning Communities: How Mass Incarceration Makes Disadvantaged Neighborhoods Worse* (Oxford University Press, 2007)

Clough, Jonathan and Carmel Mulhern, *The Prosecution of Corporations* (Oxford University Press, 2002)

Clough, Jonathan, 'A Glaring Omission? Corporate Liability for Negligent Manslaughter' (2007) 20 *Australian Journal of Labour Law* 29

Coase, Ronald, 'The Problem of Social Cost' (1960) 3 *Journal of Law and Economics* 1

Coffee, John C Jr, 'Can Lawyers Wear Blinders? Gatekeepers and Third Party Opinions' (2005) 84 *Texas Law Review* 59

Coffee, John C Jr, *Gatekeepers: The Professions and Corporate Governance* (Oxford University Press, 2006)

Coleman, Jules L, *Risks and Wrongs* (Cambridge University Press, 1992)

Coleman, Jules L, 'The Practice of Corrective Justice' (1995) 37 *Arizona Law Review* 15

Collins, Hugh, 'Introduction', in Gunter Teubner, *Networks as Connected Contracts* (Hart, 2011)

Collins, Matthew, 'Five Years On: A Report Card on Australia's National Scheme Defamation Laws' (2011) 16 *Media and Arts Law Review* 317

Collins, Pauline, 'Australian Legal Education at a Cross Roads' (2016) 58(1) *Australian Universities' Review* 30

Colson, Charles, Taskforce on Corrections, *Transforming Prisons, Restoring Lives: Final Recommendations of the Charles Colson Task Force on Federal Corrections* (Urban Institute, 2016)

Cooper, Davina, *Everyday Utopias: The Conceptual Life of Promising Spaces* (Duke University Press, 2014)

Cooper, Joel, Elizabeth A Bennett, and Holly L Sukel, 'Complex Scientific Testimony: How Do Jurors Make Decisions?' (1996) 20(4) *Law & Human Behavior* 379

Cosens, Barbara, Lance Gunderson and Brian Chaffin, 'The Adaptive Water Governance Project: Assessing Law, Resilience and Governance in Regional Socio-Ecological Water Systems Facing a Changing Climate' (2014) 51 *Idaho Law Review* 1

Cossins, Annie, 'The Behaviour of Serial Child Sex Offenders; Implications for the Prosecution of Child Sex Offences in Joint Trials' (2011) 35(3) *Melbourne University Law Review* 821

Cover, Robert, 'Nomos and Narrative' (1983) 97 *Harvard Law Review* 4

Cowdery, Nicholas, *Getting Justice Wrong: Myths, Media and Crime* (Allen and Unwin, 2001)

Craig, Robin, 'Stationarity is Dead – Long Live Transformation: Five Principles for Climate Change Adaptation Law' (2010) 34 *Harvard Environmental Law Review* 9

Craig, Robin and J Ruhl, 'Designing Administrative Law for Adaptive Management' (2014) 67 *Vanderbilt Law Review* 1

Craig, Robin K and Melinda Benson, 'Replacing Sustainability' (2013) 46 *Akron Law Review* 841

Creighton, Peter and Elise Bant, 'Recipient Liability in Western Australia' (2000) 29 *Western Australian Law Review* 205

Crisp, Leslie Finlay, *Australian National Government* (Longman Cheshire, 5th edn, 1983)

Cross, Rupert and J W Harris, *Precedent in English Law* (Clarendon Press, 1991)

Cullen, John D, Bart Victor and James W Bronson, 'The Ethical Climate Questionnaire: An Assessment of Its Development and Validity' (1993) 73 *Psychological Reports* 667

Curran, Liz and Maryanne Noone, 'Access to Justice: A New Approach Using Human Rights Standards' (2008) 15(3) *International Journal of the Legal Profession* 195

Cush, Rachael and Jane Goodman-Delahunty, 'The Influence of Limiting Instructions on Processing and Judgments of Emotionally Evocative Evidence' (2006) 13(1) *Psychiatry, Psychology and Law* 110

Czaykowska-Higgins, Ewa, 'Research Models, Community Engagement, and Linguistic Fieldwork: Reflections on Working within Canadian Indigenous Communities, Language Documentation and Conservation' (2009) 3(1) *Language Documentation & Conservation* 15

Dal Pont, Gino, *Lawyers' Professional Responsibility* (Thomson Reuters, 5th edn, 2012)

Dal Pont, Gino, *Lawyers' Professional Responsibility* (Thomson Reuters, 2013)

Dal Pont, Gino, 'Conceptualising "Charity" in State Taxation' (2015) 44(1) *Australian Tax Review* 48

Dalla-Pozza, Dominique, 'Promoting Deliberative Debate? The Submissions and Oral Evidence Provided to Australian Parliamentary Committees in the Creation of Counter-Terrorism Laws' (2008) 23 *Australasian Parliamentary Review* 39

Daly, Kathleen and Brigitte Bouhours, 'Rape and Attrition in the Legal Process: A Comparative Analysis of Five Countries', in M Tonry (ed), *Crime and Justice: An Annual Review of Research* (University of Chicago Press, 2010)

Daly, Kathleen and Brigitte Bouhours, 'Rape and Attrition in the Legal Process: A Comparative Analysis of Five Countries' (2010) 39 *Crime and Justice* 565. doi.org/10.1086/653101

Darley, John, 'Just Punishments: Research on Retributional Justice', in M Ross and D T Miller (eds), *The Justice Motive in Everyday Life* (Cambridge University Press, 2002) 314

Darley, John M, Kevin M Carlsmith and Paul H Robinson, 'Incapacitation and Just Deserts as Motives For Punishment' (2000) 24(6) *Law and Human Behavior* 659

Davidov, Guy, 'The Enforcement Crisis in Labour Law and the Fallacy of Voluntarist Solutions' (2010) 26 *International Journal of Comparative Labour Law and Industrial Relations* 61

Davidov, Guy, 'Indirect Employment: Should Lead Companies Be Liable?' (2015) 37 *Comparative Labor Law & Policy Journal* 5

Davies, Margaret, 'The Law Becomes Us: Rediscovering Judgment' (2012) 20 *Feminist Legal Studies* 167

Davies, Margaret, *Law Unlimited: Materialism, Pluralism, and Legal Theory* (Routledge, 2017)

Davis, Brent and Kym Dossetor, '(Mis)perceptions of Crime in Australia' (Trends and Issues in Crime and Criminal Justice No 396, Australian Institute of Criminology, 2010)

Davis, Ian, 'Targeted Consultations', in Brian Opeskin and David Weisbrot (eds), *The Promise of Law Reform* (The Federation Press, 2005)

Davis, Megan and Marcia Langton (ed), *It's Our Country: Indigenous Arguments for Meaningful Constitutional Recognition and Reform* (Melbourne University Press, 2016)

Davis, Michael, and Frederick A Ellison (eds), *Ethics and the Legal Profession* (Prometheus Books, 1986)

Dawson, Sir Daryl, 'Legal Services Market' (1996) 5 *Journal of Judicial Administration* 147

De Stefano, Valerio, 'Crowdsourcing, the Gig-Economy and the Law' (2016) 37(3) *Comparative Labor Law and Policy Journal* 1

Debeljak, Julie, 'Who Is Sovereign Now? The *Momcilovic* Court Hands Back Power Over Human Rights That Parliament Intended It To Have' (2011) 22 *Public Law Review* 15

Debeljak, Julie, 'Proportionality, Rights-Consistent Interpretation and Declarations under the Victorian *Charter of Human Rights and Responsibilities*: The *Momcilovic* Litigation and Beyond' (2014) 40 *Monash University Law Review* 340

Debeljak, Julie, 'The Rights of Prisoners under the Victorian *Charter*: A Critical Analysis of the Jurisprudence on the Treatment of Prisoners and Conditions of Detention' (2015) 38 *University of New South Wales Law Journal* 1332

Degeling, Simone and Kit Barker, 'Private Law and Grave Historical Injustice: The Role of the Common Law' (2015) 41 *Monash University Law Review* 377

Delaney, David, *The Spatial, the Legal and the Pragmatics of World-Making: Nomospheric Investigations* (Routledge, 2010)

Denning, Alfred Thomson (Baron), 'The Universities and Law Reform' (1949) 1 *Journal of the Society of Public Teachers of Law* 258

Derrida, Jacques, *Archive Fever* (University of Chicago Press, 1996)

Detert, James R and Ethan R Burris, 'Leadership Behavior and Employee Voice: Is the Door really Open?' (2007) 50(4) *Academy of Management Journal* 869

Dietrich, Joachim, 'Minors and the Exclusion of Liability for Negligence' (2007) 15 *Torts Law Journal* 87

Dietrich, Joachim, 'Liability for Personal Injuries from Recreational Services and the New Australian Consumer Law' (2011) 19 *Torts Law Journal* 55

Dietrich, Joachim, 'Service Guarantees and Consequential Loss under the ACL: The illusion of uniformity' (2012) 20 *Competition & Consumer Law Journal* 43

Dolgopol, Ustinia, 'Redressing Partial Justice – A Possible Role for Civil Society', in Ustina Dolgopol and Judith Gardam (eds), *The Challenge of Conflict: International Law Responds* (Martinus Nihjoff, 2006)

Donahue, John, 'Assessing the Relative Benefits of Incarceration: Overall Changes and the Benefits on the Margin', in Steven Raphael and Michael Stoll (eds), *Do Prisons Make Us Safer? The Benefits and Costs of the Prison Boom* (Russell Sage Federation Press, 2009)

Doob, Tony and Julian Roberts, *An Analysis of the Public's View of Sentencing: A Report to the Department of Justice, Canada* (Dept of Justice, 1983)

Doremus, Holly, 'Adapting to Climate Change with Law that Bends without Breaking' (2010) 2 *San Diego Journal of Climate Energy Law* 45

Douglas, Heather, Francesca Bartlett, Trish Luker and Rosemary Hunter (eds), *Australian Feminist Judgments: Righting and Rewriting Law* (Hart, 2014)

Douglas, Richard J, G R Mullins and S R Grant, *The Annotated Civil Liability Act 2003 (Qld)* (LexisNexis, 3rd edn, 2012)

Dunne, Elisabeth and Mike Rawlins, 'Bridging the Gap between Industry and Higher Education: Training Academics to Promote Student Teamwork' (2000) 37 *Innovations in Education and Teaching International* 361

Eades, Diana, 'Judicial Understandings of Aboriginality and Language Use in Criminal Cases', in Peter Toner (ed), *Strings of Connectedness: Essays in Honour of Ian Keen* (ANU Press, 2015)

Edmond, Gary and M San Roque, 'Quasi-Justice: Ad Hoc Expertise and Identification Evidence' (2009) 33 *Criminal Law Journal* 8

Edwards, Mark G and Nin Kirkham, 'Situating "Giving Voice to Values": A Metatheoretical Evaluation of a New Approach to Business Ethics' (2014) 121(3) *Journal of Business Ethics* 477

Edwards, Mark G, et al, 'Voicing Possibilities: A Performative Approach to the Theory and Practice of Ethics in a Globalised World', in D E Palmer (ed), *Handbook of Research on Business Ethics and Corporate Responsibilities* (InfoSci-Books, 2015)

Ellison, Louise, 'Closing the Credibility Gap: The Prosecutorial Use of Expert Witness Testimony in Sexual Assault Cases' (2005) 9 *International Journal of Evidence and Proof* 239

Ellison, Louise and Vanessa E Munro, 'A Stranger in the Bushes, or an Elephant in the Room? Critical Reflections upon Received Rape Myth Wisdom in the Context of a Mock Jury Study' (2010) 13(4) *New Criminal Law Review: An International and Interdisciplinary Journal* 781

Elster, Jon, 'Local Justice' (1991) 35(2–3) *European Economic Review* 273

Esqueda, Cynthia W, Russ K E Espinoza and Scott E Culhane, 'The Effects of Ethnicity, SES, and Crime Status on Juror Decision Making: A Cross-Cultural Examination of European American and Mexican American Mock Jurors' (2008) 30(2) *Hispanic Journal of Behavioral Sciences* 181

Estlund, Cynthia, 'Who Mops the Floor at the Fortune 500? Corporate Self-Regulation and the Low Wage Workplace' (2008) 12(3) *Lewis & Clark Law Review* 671

Estrich, Susan, *Real Rape* (Harvard University Press, 1987)

Evans, Adrian, *Assessing Lawyers' Ethics* (Cambridge University Press, Melbourne, 2011)

Evans, Dylan and Pierre Cruse (eds), *Emotion, Evolution and Rationality* (Oxford University Press, 2004)

Ewick, Patricia and Susan Silbey, 'Conformity, Contestation, and Resistance: An Account of Legal Consciousness' (1992) 26 *New England Law Review* 731

Farmer, Lindsay, 'The Obsession with Definition: The Nature of Crime and Critical Legal Theory' (1996) 5 *Social and Legal Studies* 57

Farmer, Lindsay, *Criminal Law, Tradition and Legal Order* (Cambridge University Press, 1997)

Feather, Norman T, *Values, Achievement, and Justice: Studies in the Psychology of Deservingness* (Springer Science & Business Media, 2006)

Fehr, Ernst and Simon Gächter, 'Altruistic Punishment in Humans' (Pt Nature Publishing Group) (2002) 415(6868) *Nature* 137

Fehr, Ernst and Urs Fischbacher, 'Third-party Punishment and Social Norms' (Pt Elsevier Science) (2004) 25(2) *Evolution and Human Behavior* 63

Field, Rachel, 'Mediation Ethics in Australia: A Case for Rethinking the Foundational Paradigm' (2012) 19 *James Cook University Law Review* 41

Finkel, Norman, *Commonsense Justice: Jurors' Notions of the Law* (Cambridge, MA: Harvard University Press, 2001)

Finn, Paul, 'Statutes and the Common Law' (1992) 22 *University of Western Australia Law Review* 7

Finn, Paul, 'Statutes and the Common Law: The Continuing Story', in Suzanne Corcoran and Stephen Bottomley (eds), *Interpreting Statutes* (Federation Press, 2005)

Fisher, Roger and William L Ury, *Getting to Yes: Negotiating Agreement Without Giving In* (Penguin Press, 1981)

Fishman, James and Stephen Schwarz, *Nonprofit Organizations: Cases and Materials* (Foundation Press, 4th edn, 2010)

Fiske, Susan T and Shelley E Taylor, *Social Cognition: Topics in Social Psychology* (New York: Random House, 1984)

Fleming, John, 'Retraction and Reply: Alternative Remedies for Defamation' (1978) 12 *University of British Columbia Law Review* 15

Foerster, Anita, Andrew Macintosh and Jan McDonald, 'Trade-offs in Adaptation Planning: Protecting Public Interest Environmental Values' (2015) 17 *Journal of Environmental Law* 1

Foley, Tony, et al, 'Helping Junior Lawyers Thrive' (2015) 89 *Law Institute Journal* 44

Folke, Carl, 'Resilience: The Emergence of a Perspective for Social-Ecological Systems' (2006) 16(3) *Global Environmental Change* 2253

Folke, Carl, et al, 'Adaptive Governance of Social-Ecological Systems' (2005) 30 *Annual Review Environment & Resources* 441

Ford, Harold, Arthur John and W A Lee, *Principles of the Law of Trusts* (Thomson Reuters, Sydney, 4th edn, 2010)

Fortney, Susan and Tahlia Gordon, 'Adopting Law Firm Management Systems to Survive and Thrive: A Study of the Australian Approach to Management-Based Regulation' (2012) 10 *University of St Thomas Law Journal* 152

Fraser, Helen, 'Issues in Transcription: Factors Affecting the Reliability of Transcripts as Evidence in Legal Cases' (2003) 10 *International Journal of Speech Language and the Law* 203

Fraser, Helen, 'Transcription of Indistinct Forensic Recordings: Problems and Solutions from the Perspective of Phonetic Science' (2014) 1 *Language and Law/Linguagem e Direito* 5

Fraser, Helen, 'Transcription of Indistinct Covert Recordings Used as Evidence in Criminal Trials', in Hugh Selby and Ian Freckelton (eds), *Expert Evidence* (Thomson Reuters, 2015)

Fraser, Helen and Bruce Stevenson, 'The Power and Persistence of Contextual Priming: More Risks in Using Police Transcripts to Aid Jurors' Perception of Poor Quality Covert Recordings' (2014) 18 *International Journal of Evidence and Proof* 205

Frazier, M Lance and Wm Matthew Bowler, 'Voice Climate, Supervisor Undermining, and Work Outcomes: A Group-Level Examination' (2015) 41(3) *Journal of Management* 841

Freckelton, Ian, et al, *Expert Evidence and Criminal Jury Trials* (Oxford University Press, 2016)

Fredman, Sandra, *Human Rights Transformed: Positive Rights and Positive Duties* (Oxford University Press, 2008). doi.org/10.1093/acprof:oso/9780199272761.001.0001

Fricker, Miranda, *Epistemic Injustice: Power and the Ethics of Knowing* (Oxford University Press, 2007)

Fuller, Lon L and William R Perdue Jr, 'The Reliance Interest in Contract Damages: 1' (1936) 46 *Yale Law Journal* 52

Gardbaum, Stephen, *The New Commonwealth Model of Constitutionalism: Theory and Practice* (Cambridge University Press, 2013)

Gardner, H and M A Valentine, 'Collaboration Among Highly Autonomous Professionals: Costs, Benefits and Future Research Directions', in Shane Thyre and Edward J Lawler (eds), *Advances in Group Processes* (Emerald Group Publishing, 2015)

Gardner, John, 'What is Tort Law For? Part 1: The Place of Corrective Justice' (2011) 30 *Law & Philosophy* 1

Garland, David, *Punishment and Modern Society: A Study in Social Theory* (Oxford University Press, 1990). doi.org/10.7208/chicago/9780226922508.001.0001

Garland, David, *Mass Imprisonment: Social Causes and Consequences* (Sage, 2001)

Garland, David, *The Culture of Control: Crime and Social Order in Contemporary Society* (Oxford University Press, 2001)

Garmestani, Ahjond and Craig Allen, *Social-ecological Resilience and Law* (Columbia University Press, 2013)

Gaspart, Frederic and Axel Gosseries, 'Are Generational Savings Unjust?' (2007) 6(2) *Politics, Philosophy and Economics* 193

Gava, John, 'The Rise of the Hero Judge' (2001) 24 *UNSW Law Review* 747

Geertz, Clifford, 'Thick Description: Toward an Interpretive theory of Culture', in Clifford Geertz (ed), *The Interpretation of Cultures* (Basic Books, 1973)

Geertz, Clifford, *Local Knowledge: Further Essays in Interpretive Anthropology* (Basic Books, 2008)

Gelb, Karen, *More Myths and Misconceptions* (Victorian Sentencing Advisory Council, 2008)

Gelb, Karen, *Understanding Family Violence Court Proceedings: The Impact of Family Violence on the Magistrates Court of Victoria* (March 2016)

Genn, Hazel, *Judging Civil Justice* (Hamlyn Lectures 2008, CUP, 2009)

George, Patrick, *Defamation Law in Australia* (LexisNexis Butterworths, 2nd edn, 2012)

Gerber, Monica M and Jonathan Jackson, 'Authority and Punishment: On the Ideological Basis of Punitive Attitudes towards Criminals' (2016) 23(1) *Psychiatry, Psychology and Law* 113

Gerber, Paula and Melissa Castan, 'The Right to Universal Birth Registration in Australia', in Melissa Castan and Paula Gerber (eds), *Proof of Birth* (Future Leaders, 2015)

Getzler, Joshua, *A History of Water Rights at Common Law* (Oxford University Press, 2006). doi.org/10.1093/acprof:oso/9780199207602.001.0001

Getzler, Joshua, '*Morice v Bishop of Durham* (1805)', in Charles Mitchell and Paul Mitchell (eds), *Landmark Cases in Equity* (Hart, 2012)

GHD, Hamstead Consulting and Vanessa O'Keefe, *A Framework for Managing and Developing Groundwater Trading* (National Water Commission, 2011)

Gilbert, Daniel T and J Gregory Hixon, 'The Trouble of Thinking: Activation and Application of Stereotypic Beliefs' (1991) 60(4) *Journal of Personality and Social Psychology* 509

Glantz, Stanton, et al (eds), *The Cigarette Papers* (University of California Press, 1998)

Gleeson, Murray, 'Out of Touch or Out of Reach?' (2006) 7 *The Judicial Review* 241

Glister, Jamie, 'Breach of trust and consequential loss' (2014) 8 *Journal of Equity* 235

Godden, Lee and Anita Foerster, 'Introduction: Institutional Transitions and Water Law Governance' (2011) 22(2/3) *The Journal of Water Law* 53

Goldsworthy, Jeffrey, 'Constitutional Cultures, Democracy, and Unwritten Principles' (2012) *University of Illinois Law Review* 683

Goode, Matthew, 'Codification of the Australian Criminal Law' (1992) 16 *Criminal Law Journal* 5

Goode, Matthew, 'Constructing Criminal Law Reform and the Model Criminal Code' (2002) 26 *Criminal Law Journal* 152

Goode, Matthew, 'Codification of the Criminal Law' (2004) 28 *Criminal Law Journal* 226

Gordley, James, 'The Aristotelian Tradition', in David Owen (ed), *Philosophical Foundations of Tort Law* (Oxford University Press, 1995)

Gordon, George and Ray Land, '"To See Ourselves as Others See Us": The Scottish Approach to Quality Enhancement', in George Gordon and Ray Land (eds), *Enhancing Quality in Higher Education: International Perspectives* (Routledge, 2016)

Gordon, Robert, 'The Case For (and Against) Harvard' (1995) 93 *Michigan Law Review* 1231

Gordon, Robert A, et al, 'Perceptions of Blue-Collar and White-Collar Crime: The Effect of Defendant Race on Simulated Juror Decisions' (1988) 128(2) *The Journal of Social Psychology* 191

Gosseries, Axel and Lukas Meyer (eds), *Intergenerational Justice* (Oxford University Press, 2009)

Gould, Carol C, *Rethinking Democracy: Freedom and Social Cooperation in Politics, Economy, and Society* (Cambridge, 1988)

Gould, Jon B, et al, *Predicting Erroneous Convictions: A Social Science Approach to Miscarriages of Justice* (National Institute of Justice, 2012)

Graham, Mary, 'Some Thoughts about the Philosophical Underpinnings of Aboriginal Worldviews' (2008) 45 *Australian Humanities Review* 181

Grant, Genevieve, et al, 'When Lump Sums Run Out: Disputes at the Borderlines of Tort Law, Injury Compensation and Social Security', in Kit Barker et al (eds), *Private Law in the 21st Century* (Hart Publishing, 2016)

Grantham, Ross, 'The Proceduralisation of Australian Corporate Law' (2015) 43 *Federal Law Review* 233

Grantham, Ross, 'The Legitimacy of the Company as a Source of (Private) Power', in Kit Barker, Simone Degeling, Karen Fairweather and Ross Grantham (eds), *Private Law and Power* (Oxford, Hart, 2016)

Grantham, Ross B and Charles E F Rickett, 'Property Rights as a Legally Significant Event' (2003) 62 *Cambridge Law Journal* 717

Grbich, Judith, 'The Body in Legal Theory' (1992) 11 *University of Tasmania Law Review* 26

Grbich, Judith E, 'Repatriation Disability Pensions: Reverse Onus of Proof Problems and the Determination and Review System' (1984) 10 *Monash University Law Review* 73

Green, Odom, et al, 'Barriers and Bridges to the Integration of Social-Ecological Resilience and Law' (2015) 13(6) *Frontiers in Ecology and Environment* 332

Grimm, Dieter, 'The Protective Function of the State', in Georg Nolte (ed), *European and US Constitutionalism* (Cambridge University Press, 2005)

Gromet, Dena M and John M Darley, 'Restoration and Retribution: How Including Retributive Components Affects the Acceptability of Restorative Justice Procedures' (2006) 19(4) *Social Justice Research* 395

Groves, Matthew, 'The Implied Undertaking Restricting the Use of Material Obtained during Legal Proceedings' (2003) 23(3) *Australian Bar Review* 314

Grzeszick, Bernd, 'The "Serving" Freedom to Broadcast: Subjective versus Objective Dimensions of a Fundamental Right', in Hermann Pünder and Christian Waldhoff (eds), *Debates in German Public Law* (Hart, 2014)

Gunderson, Lance H and C S Holling (eds), *Panarchy: Understanding Transformations in Human and Natural Systems* (Island Press, 2002)

Gunderson, Lance H, Craig R Allen and C S Holling (eds), *Foundations of Ecological Resilience* (Island Press, 2009)

Gundlach Michael J, Scott C Douglas and Mark J Martinko, 'The Decision to Blow the Whistle: A Social Information Processing Framework' (2003) 28 *Academy of Management Review* 107

Gunningham, Neil, Peter Grabosky and Darren Sinclair, *Smart Regulation* (Oxford University Press, 1998)

Gunningham, Neil and Cameron Holley, 'Next Generation Environmental Regulation' (2016) 12 *Annual Review of Law and Social Science* 273

Habermas, Jurgen, *Theory of Communicative Action* Vol 2 (Beacon Press, 1987)

Hagen, Rod, 'Traditional Australian Aboriginal Naming Processes', in Melissa Castan and Paula Gerber (eds), *Proof of Birth* (Future Leaders, 2015)

Haidt, Jonathan, *The Righteous Mind: Why Good People are Divided by Politics and Religion* (Vintage, 2012)

Halligan, John, Robin Miller and John Power, *Parliament in the Twenty-First Century* (Melbourne University Press, 2007)

Hamer, David A, 'Proof of Serial Child Sexual Abuse: Case-law Developments and Recidivism Data', in Thomas Crofts and Arlie Loughnan (eds), *Criminalisation and Criminal Responsibility in Australia* (Oxford University Press, 2015)

Hamer, David A, 'Tendency Evidence in *Hughes v The Queen*: Similarity, Probative Value and Admissibility' (2016) 38 *Sydney Law Review* 391

Hamstead, Mark, Claudia Baldwin and Vanessa O'Keefe, 'Water Allocation Planning in Australia', *Waterlines (6)* (National Water Commission, 2008)

Hannaford, John, 'The Changing Face of Law Reform' (1999) 73 *Australian Law Journal* 503

Hannan, Ewin, 'Old School, New School' (2016) 17 *AFR Boss* 23

Hansmann, Henry, 'The Role of Non-profit Enterprise' (1980) 89(5) *Yale Law Journal* 835

Harding, Matthew, *Charity Law and the Liberal State* (Cambridge University Press, 2014). doi.org/10.1017/CBO9781139136358

Harding, Matthew, 'Equity and Statute in Charity Law' (2015) 9 *Journal of Equity* 167

Hardy, Tess, 'Who Should Be Held Liable for Workplace Contraventions and on What Basis?' (2016) 29 *Australian Journal of Labour Law* 78

Hargreaves, Emma, 'The Nature of Beneficiaries' Rights under Trusts' (2011) 25 *Trust Law International* 163

Hart, Caroline, 'Sustainable Regional, Rural and Remote Legal Practice in Queensland: The Importance of Innovation in Alliances and the Use of Information Technology' (2011) 16(1) *Deakin Law Review* 225

Hart, Herbert Lionel Adolphus, 'Positivism and the Separation of Law and Morality' (1958) 71 *Harvard Law Review* 593

Hassan, Shahidul, 'The Importance of Ethical Leadership and Personal Control in Promoting Improvement-Centered Voice among Government Employees' (2015) 25(3) *Journal of Public Administration Research and Theory* 697

Healy, Judith and Paul Dugdale, 'Regulatory Strategies in Safer Patient Health Care', in Judith Healy and Paul Dugdale (eds), *Patient Safety First: Responsive Regulation in Health Care* (Allen & Unwin, 2009)

Heinze, Eric, *Hate Speech and Democratic Citizenship* (Oxford University Press, 2016)

Hekman, Susan, 'Backgrounds and Riverbeds: Feminist Reflections' (1999) 25 *Feminist Studies* 427

Hemming, Andrew, 'When Is a Code a Code?' (2010) 15(1) *Deakin Law Review* 65

Henderson, William, 'A Blueprint for Change' (2013) 40 *Pepperdine Law Review* 461

Heron, John, *Co-operative Inquiry: Research into the Human Condition* (Sage, London, 1996)

Heun, Werner, *The Constitution of Germany: A Contextual Analysis* (Oxford, 2011)

Heydon, John Dyson, 'Judicial Activism and the Death of the Rule of Law' (2004) 10 *Otago Law Review* 493

Higgins, Vaughan and Stewart Lockie, 'Re-discovering the Social: Neo-Liberalism and Hybrid Practices of Governing in Rural Natural Resource Management' (2002) 18(4) *Journal of Rural Studies* 419

Hill, Lisa, 'On the Reasonableness of Compelling Citizens to "Vote": The Australian Case' (2002) *Political Studies* 80

Hobday, Alistair J, et al, 'Dynamic Ocean Management: Integrating Scientific and Technological Capacity with Law, Policy, and Management' (2014) 33 *Stanford Environmental Law Journal* 122

Hogg, Russell and David Brown, *Rethinking Law and Order* (Pluto Press, 1998)

Hoitink, David and Anthony Hopkins, 'Divergent Approaches to the Admissibility of Tendency Evidence in New South Wales and Victoria: The Risk of Adopting a More Permissive Approach' (2015) 39 *Criminal Law Journal* 303

Holdsworth, William, *A History of English Law* (Sweet & Maxwell, 7th edn, 1971)

Holley, Cameron and Darren Sinclair, 'Compliance and Enforcement of Water Licences in NSW: Limitations in Law, Policy and Institutions' (2013) 15 *Australasian Journal of National Resources Law and Policy* 149

Holley, Cameron and Darren Sinclair, 'Deliberative Participation, Environmental Law and Collaborative Governance: Insights from Surface and Groundwater Studies' (2013) 30(1) *Environmental and Planning Law Journal* 32

Holley, Cameron and Darren Sinclair, 'A New Water Policy Option for Australia? Collaborative Water Governance, Compliance and Enforcement and Audited Self-Management' (2014) 17(2) *Australasian Journal of National Resources Law and Policy* 189

Holley, Cameron and Darren Sinclair, 'Governing Water Markets – Achievements, Limitations and the Need for Regulatory Reform' (2016) 33(4) *Environmental and Planning Law Journal* 301

Holley, Cameron and Darren Sinclair, 'Rethinking Australian Water Governance: Successes, Challenges and Future Directions' (2016) 33(4) *Environmental and Planning Law Journal* 275

Holmes, Vivien, '"Giving Voice to Values": Enhancing Students' Capacity to Cope with Ethical Challenges in Legal Practice' (2015) 18(2) *Legal Ethics* 115

Horton, Fabian, 'Chain Reaction' (2016) 90(4) *Law Institute Journal* 69

Howe, John, and Richard Mitchell, 'The Evolution of the Contract of Employment in Australia: A Discussion' (1999) 12 *Australian Journal of Labour Law* 113

Huang, Lei and Ted A Paterson, 'Group Ethical Voice: Influence of Ethical Leadership and Impact on Ethical Performance' (2014) 43 *Journal of Management* 1157

Huesmann, L Rowell and Cheryl-Lynn Podolski, 'Punishment: A Psychological Perspective', in McConville and Devon (eds), *The Use of Punishment* (Willan Publishing, 2003)

Hunter, Rosemary and Sharon Cowan (eds), *Choice and Consent: Feminist Engagements with the Law and Subjectivity* (Routledge, 2007)

Hunter, Rosemary, Clare McGlynn and Erika Rackley (eds), *Feminist Judgments: From Theory to Practice* (Hart, 2010)

Hurst, J Willard, 'Legal Elements in United States History', in Donald Fleming and Bernard Bailyn (eds), *Perspectives in American History* (Little Brown Books, 1971)

Hurst, James Willard, *The Legitimacy of the Business Corporation* (Charlottesville, University Press of Virginia, 1970)

Hussey, Karen, Jamie Pittock and Stephen Dovers, 'Justifying, Extending and Applying "Nexus" Thinking in the Quest for Sustainable Development', in J Pittock, K Hussey and S Dovers (eds), *Climate, Energy and Water* (CUP, 2015). doi.org/10.1017/CBO9781139248792.001

Isaacs, Sir Isaac, *A Stepping Stone to Greater Freedom* (1946)

Jackson, Sue, et al, 'Meeting Indigenous peoples' Objectives in Environmental Flow Assessments: Case Studies from an Australian Multi-Jurisdictional Water Sharing Initiative' (2015) 522 *Journal of Hydrology* 141

Jacobs, P A, 'A Plea for Law Reform' (1940) 13 *Australian Law Journal* 398

James, Estelle and Susan Rose-Ackerman, *The Nonprofit Enterprise in Market Economics* (Harwood Academic Publishers, 1986)

James, Nickolas, 'A Brief History of Critique in Australian Legal Education' (2000) 24 *Melbourne University Law Review* 965

Janis, Irving L, *Groupthink: Psychological Studies of Policy Decisions and Fiascoes* (Houghton Mifflin, 2nd edn, 1982)

Jessop, Bob, 'The Rise of Governance and the Risk of Failure: The Case of Economic Development' (1998) 50(155) *International Social Science Journal* 29

Johns, Adrian, 'Foreword', in Walter Ong, *Ramus: Method and the Decay of Dialogue* (University of Chicago Press, first published 1958, 2004 edn)

Jonathan Adler, 'Dynamic Environmentalism and Adaptive Management: Legal Obstacles and Opportunities' (2015) 11 *Journal of Law, Economics & Policy* 133

Jordan, Cally, 'Unlovely and Unloved: Corporate Law Reform's Progeny' (2009) 33 *Melbourne University Law Review* 626

Jubb, Peter, 'Whistleblowing: A Restrictive Definition and Interpretation' (1999) 21 *Journal of Business Ethics* 77

Kahneman, Daniel, *Thinking, Fast and Slow* (Macmillan, 2011)

Kanouse, David, 'Language, Labelling and Attribution', in Edward E Jones et al (eds), *Attribution: Perceiving the Causes of Behaviour* (General Learning Press, 1972)

Kaptein, Muel, 'From Inaction to External Whistleblowing: The Influence of the Ethical Culture of Organizations on Employee Responses to Observed Wrongdoing' (2011) 98 *Journal of Business Ethics* 513

Karkkainen, Bradley Archon Fung and Charles Sabel, 'After Backyard Environmentalism' (2000) 44 *American Behavioural Scientist* 692

Kebbell, Mark R and Nina J Westera, 'Promoting Pre-recorded Complainant Evidence in Rape Trials: Psychology and Practice Perspectives' (2011) 35 *Criminal Law Journal* 376

Kenyon, Andrew, 'Six Years of Australian Uniform Defamation Law: Damages, Opinion and Defence Meanings' (2012) 35 *University of New South Wales Law Journal* 31

Kenyon, Andrew T, 'Assuming Free Speech' (2014) 77 *Modern Law Review* 379

Keyes, Mary and Richard Johnstone, 'Changing Legal Education: Rhetoric, Reality, and Prospects for the Future' (2004) 26 *Sydney Law Review* 537

Kildea, Paul, 'A Little More Conversation? Assessing the Capacity of Citizens to Deliberate About Constitutional Reform in Australia' (2013) 22 *Griffith Law Review* 291

King, Michael, et al, *Non-Adversarial Justice* (The Federation Press, 2nd edn, 2014)

Kirby, Michael, '"Judicial Activism"? A Riposte to the Counter-Reformation' (2005) 11 *Otago Law Review* 1

Kirby, Michael, 'The Rule of Law beyond the Law of Rules' (2010) 33(3) *Australian Bar Review* 197

Kirby, Michael D, 'Law Reform, Why?' (1976) 50 *Australian Law Journal* 459

Kirkland, Kimberly, 'Ethics in Large Law Firms: The Principle of Pragmatism' (2005) 35 *University of Memphis Law Review* 631

Kish-Gephart, Jennifer J, David A Harrison and Linda Klebe Treviño, 'Bad Apples, Bad Cases, and Bad Barrels: Meta-Analytic Evidence About Sources of Unethical Decisions at Work' (2010) 95 *Journal of Applied Psychology* 1

Klausner, Michael, 'When Time Isn't Money: Foundation Payout Rates and the Time Value of Money' (2003) 1(1) *Stanford Social Innovation Review* 51

Kleiman, Mark, *When Brute Force Fails: How to Have Less Crime and Less Punishment* (Princeton University Press, 2009). doi.org/10.1515/9781400831265

Klimchuk, Dennis, 'On the Autonomy of Corrective Justice' (2003) 23 *Oxford Journal of Legal Studies* 49

Klimchuk, Dennis, 'Unjust Enrichment and Corrective Justice', in Jason W Neyers, Mitchell McInnes and Stephen G A Pitel (eds), *Understanding Unjust Enrichment* (Hart Publishing, 2004)

Koh, Harold, 'Protecting the Office of Legal Counsel from Itself' (1994) 15 *Cardozo Law Review* 513

Kommers, Donald P and Russell A Miller, *The Constitutional Jurisprudence of the Federal Republic of Germany* (Duke University Press, 3rd edn, 2012)

Kooiman, Jan and Svein Jentoft, 'Meta-governance: Values, Norms and Principles, and the Making of Hard Choices' (2009) 87(4) *Public Administration* 818

Koomen, Kaaren, 'Breach of Confidence and the Public Interest Defence: Is it in the Public Interest? A Review of the English Public Interest Defence and the Options for Australia' (1994) 10 *Queensland University of Technology Law Journal* 56

Krasnostein, Sarah and Arie Freiberg, 'Pursuing Consistency in an Individualistic Sentencing Framework: If You Know Where You're Going, How Do You Know When You've Got There' (2013) 76 *Law & Contemporary Problems* 265

Kronman, Anthony T, 'Contract Law and Distributive Justice' (1980) 89 *Yale Law Journal* 472

Kropotkin, Peter, *Law and Authority: An Anarchist Essay* (Open Socialist Publishing, 2006)

Kyrou, Emilios, 'Legal Professional Privilege for General Counsel Wearing Two Hats' (2000) 5 *Law Society Journal* 42

La Piana, William, *Logic & Experience: The Origin of Modern American Legal Education* (Oxford University Press, 1994)

Lacey, Nicola, 'Legal Constructions of Crime', in Mike Maguire, Rod Morgan and Robert Reiner (eds), *The Oxford Handbook of Criminology* (Oxford University Press, 4th edn, 2007)

Lacey, Nicola, *The Prisoners' Dilemma: Political Economy and Punishment in Contemporary Democracies* (Cambridge University Press, 2008). doi.org/10.1017/CBO9780511819247

Langford, Rosemary Teele, 'Solving the Fiduciary Puzzle: The Bona Fide and Proper Purposes Duties of Company Directors' (2013) 41(3) *Australian Business Law Review* 127

Lanyon, A J and David John, 'Australia's Civil Registration and Vital Statistics System', in Melissa Castan and Paula Gerber (eds), *Proof of Birth* (Future Leaders, 2015)

Larcombe, Wendy, 'The Ideal Victim v Successful Rape Complainants: Not What You Might Expect' (2002) 10(2) *Feminist Legal Studies* 131

Larcombe, Wendy, 'Falling Rape Conviction Rates: (Some) Feminist Aims and Measures for Rape Law' (2011) 19(1) *Feminist Legal Studies* 27

Larcombe, Wendy, 'Sex Offender Risk Assessment: The Need to Place Recidivism Research in the Context of Attrition in the Criminal Justice System' (2012) 18(4) *Violence Against Women* 482

Larcombe, Wendy and Mary Heath, 'Developing the Common Law and Rewriting the History of Rape in Marriage in Australia: *PGA v The Queen*' (2012) 34 *Sydney Law Review* 785

Larcombe, Wendy, et al, '"I Think It's Rape and I Think He Would Be Found Not Guilty": Focus Group Perceptions of (un)Reasonable Belief in Consent in Rape Law' (2016) 25(5) *Social & Legal Studies* 611–629.

Laslett, Peter, 'Is There a Generational Contract?', in Peter Laslett and James S Fishkin (eds), *Justice Between Age Groups and Generations* (Yale University Press, 1992)

Latimer, Paul and A J Brown, 'Whistleblower Laws: International Best Practice' (2008) 31 *University of New South Wales Law Journal* 766

Lawson, Andrew, *Farmers, Voluntary Stewardship Programs, and Collaborative Natural Resource Governance in Rural Australia* (PhD thesis, University of New England, 2016)

Le Mire, Suzanne, 'Document Destruction and Corporate Culture: A Victorian Initiative' (2006) 19 *Australian Journal of Corporate Law* 304

Leeming, Mark, 'Theories and Principles Underlying the Development of the Common Law – The Statutory Elephant in the Room' (2013) 36(3) *UNSW Law Journal* 1002

Leigh, Andrew, *Battlers and Billionaires: The Story of Inequality in Australia* (Redback Press 2013)

Leimguber, Dominik, 'Confidentiality, Public Interest and the Mediator's Ethical Dilemma' (2013) 24 *Australasian Dispute Resolution Journal* 187

LePine, Jeffrey A and Linn Van Dyne, 'Predicting Voice Behavior in Work Groups' (1998) 83(6) *Journal of Applied Psychology* 853

Lerner, Melvin J, 'The Justice Motive: Where Social Psychologists Found It, How They Lost It, and Why They May Not Find It Again' (2003) 7(4) *Personality and Social Psychology Review* 388

Leveson, Sir Brian, *Review of Efficiency in Criminal Proceedings* (Judiciary of England and Wales, January 2015)

Levy, Ron, 'Breaking the Constitutional Deadlock: Lessons from Deliberative Experiments in Constitutional Change' (2010) 34 *Melbourne University Law Review* 805

Levy, Ron, 'Deliberative Voting: Realising Constitutional Referendum Democracy' (2013) *Public Law* 555

Lichtenberg, Judith, 'Foundations and Limits of Freedom of the Press', in Judith Lichtenberg (ed), *Democracy and the Mass Media: A Collection of Essays* (Cambridge University Press, 1990)

Lievore, Denise, *Non-reporting and Hidden Recording of Sexual Assault: An International Literature Review* (Australian Institute of Criminology for the Commonwealth Office of the Status of Women, 2003)

Lijphart, Arend, 'Unequal Participation: Democracy's Unresolved Dilemma' (1997) 91 *American Political Science Review* 1

Lindsay, Bruce, 'Public Participation, Litigation and Adjudicative Procedure in Water Resources Management' (2016) 33(4) *Environmental and Planning Law Journal* 325

Lloyd-Bostock, Sally, 'Attributions of Cause and Responsibility as Social Phenomena', in Joseph Jaspars, Frank Fincham and Miles Hewstone (eds), *Attribution Theory and Research* (Academic Press, 1983)

Lloyd-Bostock, Sally, 'The Effects on Juries of Hearing about the Defendant's Previous Criminal Record: A Simulation Study' (2000) *Criminal Law Review* 734

Lobban, Michael, *The Common Law and English Jurisprudence 1760–1850* (Clarendon Press, 1991)

Lockwood, Michael, et al, 'Multi-level Environmental Governance: Lessons from Australian Natural Resource Management' (2009) 40(2) *Australian Geographer* 169

Lombard, Sulette and Vivienne Brand, 'Corporate Whistleblowing: Public Lessons for Private Disclosure' (2014) 42 *Australian Business Law Review* 351

Loughnan, Arlie, 'Drink Spiking and Rock Throwing: The Creation and Construction of Criminal Offences in the Current Era' (2010) 35 *Alternative Law Journal* 18

Luntz, Harold, 'Reform of the Law of Negligence: Wrong Questions – Wrong Answers' (2002) 8(2) *UNSWLJ Forum: Reform of the Law of Negligence: Balancing Costs and Community Expectations* 18

Lynch, Andrew and Tessa Meyrick, 'The Constitution and Legislative Responsibility' (2007) 18 *Public Law Review* 153

MacCoun, Robert J, 'Drugs and the Law: A Psychological Analysis of Drug Prohibition' (1993) 113(3) *Psychological Bulletin* 497

MacFarlane, Julie, 'Mediating Ethically: The Limits of Codes of Conduct and the Potential of a Reflective Practice Model' (2002) 40 *Osgoode Hall Law Journal* 49

Macintosh, Andrew, Anita Foerster and Jan McDonald, 'Policy Design, Spatial Planning and Climate Change Adaptation: A Case Study from Australia' (2014) 57 *Journal of Environmental Planning and Management* 1

Mack, Kathy, Anne Wallace and Sharyn Roach Anleu, *Judicial Workload: Time, Tasks and Work Organisation* (Australasian Institute of Judicial Administration, 2013)

Macrae, C Neil, et al, 'Stereotypes as Energy-Saving Devices: A Peek Inside the Cognitive Toolbox' (1994) 66(1) *Journal of Personality and Social Psychology* 37

Maharg, Paul, 'Disintermediation' (2016) 50 *The Law Teacher* 114

Marginson, Simon and Mark Considine, *The Enterprise University: Power, Governance and Reinvention in Australia* (Cambridge University Press, 2000)

Mark, Steve and Tahlia Gordon, 'Innovations in Regulation – Responding to a Changing Legal Services Market' (2009) 22 *Georgetown Journal of Legal Ethics* 501

Marshall, Patricia, 'The "Partial" Mediator: Balancing Ideology and the Reality' (2010) 11(8) *ADR Bulletin* 176

Marshall, Virginia, 'The Progress of Aboriginal Water Rights and Interests in the Murray–Darling Basin in NSW: An Essential Element of Culture' (2015) *Australian Environment Review* 158

Marshall, Virginia, 'Deconstructing Aqua Nullius: Reclaiming Aboriginal Water Rights and Communal Identity in Australia' (2016) 8(26) *Indigenous Law Bulletin*

Marshall, Virginia, *Overturning Aqua Nullius: Securing Aboriginal Water Rights* (Aboriginal Studies Press, 2017)

Martin, Paul and Donna Craig, 'Accelerating the Evolution of Environmental Law through Continuous Learning from Applied Experience', in Paul Martin and Amanda Kennedy (eds), *Implementing Environmental Law* (Edward Elgar, 2015)

Martin, Paul and Neil Gunningham, 'Improving Regulatory Arrangements for Sustainable Agriculture: Groundwater as an Illustration' (2014) 1(1) *Australian Journal of Environmental Law* 5

Martin, Paul and Kip Werren, 'The Use of Taxation Incentives to Create New Eco-Service Markets: Critical Issues', in Lin-Heng Lye and Janet E Milne (eds), *Critical Issues in Environmental Taxation* (Oxford University Press, 2009)

Martin, Paul and Jacqueline Williams, 'Next Generation Rural Natural Resource Governance: A Careful Diagnosis', in Volker Mauerhofer (ed), *Legal Aspects of Sustainable Development* (Springer International Publishing, 2016)

Martin, Paul, et al, *Developing a Good Regulatory Practice Model for Environmental Regulations Impacting on Farmers* (Australian Farm Institute and Land and Water Australia, 2007)

Mason, Anthony, 'The Use and Abuse of Precedent' (1988) 4 *Australian Bar Review* 93

Mason, Anthony, 'The Parliament, the Executive and the Solicitor-General', in Gabrielle Appleby, Patrick Keyzer and John Williams (eds), *Public Sentinels: A Comparative Study of Australian Solicitors-General* (Ashgate, 2014)

Mason, Sir Anthony, 'Towards 2001 – Minimalism, Monarchism or Metamorphism' (1995) 21 *Monash University Law Review* 1

Mason, Sir Anthony F, 'The Australian Constitution in Retrospect and Prospect', in Robert French, Geoffrey Lindell and Cheryl Saunders (eds), *Reflections on the Australian Constitution* (Federation Press, 2003)

Matsuda, Mari, 'When the First Quail Calls: Multiple Consciousness as Jurisprudential Method' (1988) 11 *Women's Rights Law Reporter* 7

Matthews, Carol, 'A "Model of the Old House": Architecture in Blackstone's Life and Commentaries', in Wilfred Prest (ed), *Blackstone and His Commentaries* (Hart Publishing, 2014)

Mayer, David M, 'A Review of the Literature on Ethical Climate and Culture', in *Oxford Handbook of Organizational Climate and Culture* (Oxford University Press, 2014)

Mazzella, Ronald and Alan Feingold, 'The Effects of Physical Attractiveness, Race, Socioeconomic Status, and Gender of Defendants and Victims on Judgments of Mock Jurors: A Meta-Analysis' (1994) 24(15) *Journal of Applied Social Psychology* 1315

McCrystal, Shae, 'Organising Independent Contractors: The Impact of Competition Law', in Judy Fudge, Shae McCrystal and Kamala Sankaran, *Challenging the Legal Boundaries of Work Regulation* (Hart, Oxford, 2012)

McDonald, Jan, 'The Role of Law in Adapting to Climate Change' (2011) 2(2) *WIREs: Climate Change* 283

McDonald, Jan and Megan C Styles, 'Legal Strategies for Adaptive Management under Climate Change' (2014) 17 *Journal of Environmental Law* 1

McDonald, Jan, et al, 'Rethinking Legal Objectives for Climate-Adaptive Conservation' (2016) *Ecology and Society* (forthcoming)

Mcfatter, Robert M, 'Purposes Of Punishment: Effects of Utilities of Criminal Sanctions on Perceived Appropriateness' (1982) 67(3) *Journal of Applied Psychology* 255

McHugh, Michael, 'Judicial Method' (1999) 73 *Australian Law Journal* 37

McKay, Carolyn, 'Video Links from Prison: Permeability and the Carceral World' (2016) 5(1) *International Journal for Crime, Justice and Social Democracy* 21

McKimmie, Blake M, Barbara M Masser and Renata Bongiorno, 'What Counts as Rape? The Effect of Offence Prototypes, Victim Stereotypes and Participant Gender on How the Complainant and Defendant Are Perceived' (2014) 29(1) *Journal of Interpersonal Violence* 2273

McKimmie, Blake M, Jillian M Hays and David Tait, 'Just Spaces: Does Courtroom Design Affect How the Defendant is Perceived? (2016) 23 *Psychiatry, Psychology and Law* 865. doi.org/10.1080/13218719.2016 .1174054

McKimmie, Blake M, et al, 'Jurors' Responses to Expert Witness Testimony: The Effects of Gender Stereotypes' (2004) 7(2) *Group Processes and Intergroup Relations* 131

McKimmie, Blake M, et al, 'Stereotypical and Counterstereotypical Defendants: Who Is He and What Was the Case Against Her?' (2013) 19(3) *Psychology, Public Policy and Law* 343

McLean, Bethany and Peter Elkind, *The Smartest Guys in the Room* (Penguin Books, 2004)

McSherry, Bernadette, *Managing Fear: The Law and Ethics of Preventive Detention and Risk Assessment* (Routledge, 2013)

Megarry, Robert E, 'Administrative Quasi-Legislation' (1944) 60 *Law Quarterly Review* 125

Meuleman, Louis, *Public Management and the Metagovernance of Hierarchies, Networks and Markets: The Feasibility of Designing and Managing Governance Style Combinations* (Springer Science & Business Media, 2008)

Meuleman, Louis and Ingeborg Niestroy, 'Common but Differentiated Governance: A Metagovernance Approach to Make the SDGs Work' (2015) 7(9) *Sustainability* 12295

Miceli, Marcia and Janet Near, *Blowing the Whistle: The Organizational and Legal Implications for Companies and Employees* (Lexington Press, 1992)

Michelini, Ronald L and Stephan R Snodgrass, 'Defendant Characteristics and Juridic Decisions' (1980) 14(3) *Journal of Research in Personality* 340

Milgram, Stanley 'Behavioral Study of Obedience' (1963) 67 *Journal of Abnormal and Social Psychology* 371

Miller, Russell, *Annotated Trade Practices Act – Australian Competition and Consumer Law* (Thomson Reuters 31st edn, 2010)

Miller, Russell, *Miller's Australian Competition Law and Policy* (Thomson Reuters, 2nd edn, 2012)

Miller, Russell, *Miller's Australian Competition and Consumer Law Annotated* (Thomson Reuters 38th edn, 2016)

Milliken, Frances J, Elizabeth W Morrison and Patricia F Hewlin, 'An Exploratory Study of Employee Silence: Issues that Employees don't Communicate Upward and Why' (2003) 40 *Journal of Management Studies* 1453

Milo, Dario, *Defamation and Freedom of Speech* (Oxford University Press, 2008). doi.org/10.1093/acprof:oso/9780199204922.001.0001

Mitchell, Barry, 'Public Perceptions of Homicide and Criminal Justice' (1998) 38(3) *British Journal of Criminology* 453

Mitchell, Barry, 'Further Evidence of the Relationship between Legal and Public Opinion on the Law of Homicide' (2000) *Criminal Law Review* 814

Mitchell, Charles, 'Saving for a Rainy Day: Charity Reserves' (2002) 8(1) *Charity Law & Practice Review* 35

Monk, David, 'A Framework for Evaluating the Performance of Committees in Westminster Parliaments' (2010) 16 *Journal of Legislative Studies* 1

Monk, David, 'Committee Inquiries in the Australian Parliament and Their Influence on Government: Government Acceptance of Recommendations as a Measure of Parliamentary Performance' (2012) 18 *The Journal of Legislative Studies* 143

Moore, Michael S, 'Causation and Responsibility' (1999) 16(2) *Social Philosophy and Policy* 1

Morgan, Bronwen, 'Transcending the Corporation: Social Enterprise, Cooperatives and Commons-Based Governance', in Thomas Clarke and Justin O'Brien (eds), *The Oxford Handbook on the Corporation* (Oxford University Press, in press)

Morrison, Wayne, *Jurisprudence: From the Greeks to Post-modernism* (Cavendish, 1997)

Murphy, Jeffrie G and Jean Hampton, *Forgiveness and Mercy* (Cambridge University Press, 1990)

Murray, Ian, 'Accumulation in Charitable Trusts: Australian Statutory Perpetuities Rules' (2014) 8(2) *Journal of Equity* 163

Murray, Ian, 'Accumulation in Charitable Trusts: Australian Common Law Perpetuities Rules' (2015) 9(1) *Journal of Equity* 30

Murray, Ian, 'Charity Accumulation: Interrogating the Conventional View on Tax Restraints' (2015) 37(4) *Sydney Law Review* 541

Naylor, Bronwyn, Julie Debeljak and Anita Mackay, 'A Strategic Framework for Implementing Human Rights in Closed Environments: A Human Rights Regulatory Framework and its Implementation' (2015) 41 *Monash University Law Review* 218

Near, Janet and Marcia Miceli, 'Organizational Dissidence: The Case of Whistle-Blowing' (1985) 4 *Journal of Business Ethics* 1

Near, Janet and Marcia Miceli, 'Effective Whistleblowing' (1995) 20 *Academy of Management Review* 679

Neck, Christopher P and Charles C Manz, 'From Groupthink to Teamthink: Toward the Creation of Constructive Thought Patterns in Self-managing Work Teams' (1994) 47(8) *Human Relations* 929

Nelson, Donald R, W Neil Adger and Katrina Brown, 'Adaptation to Environmental Change: Contributions of a Resilience Framework' (2009) 32 *Annual Review of Environment & Resources* 395

Nelthorpe, Denis and Kate Digney, *The Bulk Negotiation Project: Client Profiles and Client Outcomes* (West Heidelberg Community Legal Service and Victoria Law Foundation, 2011)

News, 'Soliciting the Right Kind of Mediator' (2005) 79(4) *Law Institute Journal* 22

Nicholls, Lord, 'Knowing Receipt: The Need for a New Landmark', in W R Cornish, Richard Nolan, Janet O'Sullivan and Graham Virgo (eds), *Restitution Past, Present and Future: Essays in Honour of Gareth Jones* (Hart Publishing, 1998)

Noelle-Neumann, Elisabeth, 'The Spiral of Silence: A Theory of Public Opinion' (1974) 24 *Journal of Communication* 24

Noone, Mary Anne, 'Liability Matters for Lawyer Mediators' (2007) 81(10) *Law Institute Journal* 52

Noone, Mary Anne, 'ADR, Public Interest Law and Access to Justice: The Need for Vigilance' (2011) 37(1) *Monash University Law Review* 57

Noone, Mary Anne and Lola Akin Ojelabi, 'Ethical Challenges for Mediators: An Australian Perspective' (2014) 45 *Washington University Journal of Law and Policy* 145

Norrie, Alan, *Crime, Reason and History: A Critical Introduction to Criminal Law* (Cambridge University Press, 2nd edn, 2001)

North, Gill, 'Regulation Governing the Provision of Credit Assistance and Financial Advice in Australia: A Consumer's Perspective' (2015) 43 *Federal Law Review* 369

Nussbaum, Martha, *Upheavals of Thought: The Intelligence of Emotions* (Cambridge University Press, 2001). doi.org/10.1017/CBO9780511840715

O'Donovan, Katherine, *Sexual Divisions in Law* (Weidenfeld and Nicholson, 1985)

O'Higgins, Paul, '"Labour is not a Commodity"– an Irish Contribution to International Labour Law' (1997) 26 *Industrial Law Journal* 225

O'Neill, Onora, 'Practices of Toleration', in Judith Lichtenberg (ed), *Democracy and the Mass Media: A Collection of Essays* (Cambridge University Press, 1990)

O'Regan, Robin S, 'Sir Samuel Griffith's Criminal Code' (1991) 7(2) *Australian Bar Review* 141

Oguaman, Chidi, *International Law and Indigenous Knowledge: Intellectual Property, Plant Biodiversity and Traditional Medicine* (University of Toronto Press, Toronto, 2006). doi.org/10.3138/9781442676244

Olsen, Frances, 'The Family and the Market: A Study of Ideology and Legal Reform' (1983) 96 *Harvard Law Review* 1497

Opeskin, Brian and David Weisbrot (eds), *The Promise of Law Reform* (Federation Press, 2005)

Opeskin, Brian, 'The State of the Judicature: A Statistical Profile of Australian Courts and Judges' (2013) 35(3) *Sydney Law Review* 489

Orr, Graeme, 'Compulsory Voting: Elections, Not Referendums' (2011) 18 *Pandora's Box* 19

Orr, Graeme, 'Deliberation and Electoral Law' (2013) 12 *Election Law Journal* 421

Orr, Graeme, *Ritual and Rhythm in Electoral Systems: A Comparative Legal Account* (Routledge-Ashgate, 2015)

Orr, Graeme, 'Teaching Public Law: Content, Context and Coherence' (2015) 25 *Legal Education Review* 299

Orr, Graeme and Samara Cassar, 'When Referendums Go Wrong – Queensland's 2016 Fixed Four-Year Term Proposal' (2016) 31 *Australasian Parliamentary Review* 161

Ostrom, Elinor, *Governing the Commons: The Evolution of Institutions for Collective Action* (Cambridge University Press, 1990). doi.org/10.1017/CBO9780511807763

Overington, Caroline, *Kickback: Inside the Australian Wheat Board Scandal* (Allen and Unwin, 2007)

Parachin, Adam, 'Legal Privilege as a Defining Characteristic of Charity' (2009) 48 *Canadian Business Law Journal* 36

Parker, Christine and Adrian Evans, *Inside Lawyers' Ethics* (Cambridge University Press, 2nd edn, 2014)

Parker, Christine, Suzanne Le Mire and Anita Mackay, 'Lawyers, Confidentiality and Whistleblowing: Lessons from the McCabe Tobacco Litigation' (2017) 40(3) *Melbourne University Law Review*

Parker, Christine, Tahlia Gordon and Steve Mark, 'Regulating Law Firm Management: An Empricial Assessment of an Innovation in Regulation of the Legal Profession in New South Wales' (2010) 37 *Journal of Law and Society* 466

Parker, Christine, et al, 'The Ethical Infrastructure of Legal Practice in Larger Law Firms: Values, Policy and Behaviour' (2008) 31 *UNSW Law Journal* 158

Parker, Stephen, *Courts and the Public* (Australian Institute of Judicial Administration, 1998)

Pascoe, Janine and Michelle Welsh, 'Whistleblowing, Ethics and Corporate Culture: Theory and Practice in Australia' (2011) 40 *Common Law World Review* 144

Passant, John, 'Neoliberalism in Australia and the Henry Tax Review' (2013) 8(1) *The Journal of the Australasian Tax Teachers Association* 117

Pearce, Dennis C and R S Geddes, *Statutory Interpretation in Australia* (LexisNexis, 8th edn, 2014)

Pennington, Nancy and Reid Hastie, 'Explaining the Evidence: Tests of the Story Model for Juror Decision Making' (1992) 62(2) *Journal of Personality and Social Psychology* 189

Perry, Steven, 'The Moral Basis of Tort Law' (1992) *77 Iowa Law Review* 449

Petty, Richard E and John T Cacioppo, 'The Elaboration Likelihood Model of Persuasion' (1986) 19 *Advances in Experimental Social Psychology* 123

Pickard, Victor, 'Toward a People's Internet: The Fight for Positive Freedoms in an Age of Corporate Libertarianism', in Maria Edström, Andrew T Kenyon and Eva-Maria Svensson (eds), *Blurring the Lines: Market-driven and Democracy-driven Freedom of Expression* (Nordicom, 2016)

Piketty, Thomas, *Capital in the Twenty-First Century* (The Belknap Press of Harvard University Press, 2014). doi.org/10.4159/9780674369542

Pillutla, Madan M and Stefan Thau, 'Actual and Potential Exclusion as Determinants of Individuals' Unethical Behaviour in Groups', in David DeCremer (ed), *Psychological Perspectives on Ethical Behaviour and Decision-Making* (IAP, 2009)

Pleasence, Pascoe, Nigel J Balmer and Alexy Buck, 'The Health Cost of Civil-Law Problems: Further Evidence of Links between Civil-law Problems and Morbidity, and the Consequential Use of Health Services' (2008) 5(2) *Journal of Empirical Legal Studies* 351

Post, Robert, 'Who's Afraid of Jurispathic Courts: Violence and Public Reason in Nomos and Narrative' (2005) 17 *Yale Law Journal of Law and the Humanities* 9

Potschka, Christian, *Towards a Market in Broadcasting: Communications Policy in the UK and Germany* (Palgrave MacMillan, 2012). doi.org/10.1057/9780230370197

Pound, Roscoe, 'Law in Books and Law in Action' (1910) 44 *American Law Reports* 12

Prassl, Jeremias, *The Concept of the Employer* (Oxford University Press, 2015)

Prentice, Robert A, 'Behavioral Ethics: Can it Help Lawyers (and Others) Be Their Best Selves?' (2015) 29 *Notre Dame Journal of Law, Ethics & Public Policy* 35

Pritchard, Bill, *Land of Discontent: The Dynamics of Change in Rural and Regional Australia* (UNSW Press, 2000)

Quilty, Simon, 'The Magnitude of Experience of Parental Incarceration in Australia' (2005) 12(1), *Psychiatry, Psychology and Law* 256

Raban, Colin and David Cairns, 'How Did It Come to This?' (2014) 18 *Perspectives: Policy and Practice in Higher Education* 112

Rachlinski, Jeffrey J, et al, 'Does Unconscious Racial Bias Affect Trial Judges?' (2008) 84 *Notre Dame Law Review* 1195

Ramsay, Ian, 'Company Law and the Economics of Federalism' (1990) 19 *Federal Law Review* 169

Rawls, John, *A Theory of Justice* (Clarendon Press, 1972)

Rawls, John, *Justice as Fairness: A Restatement* (Harvard University Press, 2001)

Reason, Peter and Hilary Bradbury, *Handbook of Action Research* (Sage, London, 2nd edn, 2007)

Regan, Milton C Jr, 'Nested Ethics: A Tale of Two Cultures' (2013) 42 *Hofstra Law Review* 143

Reid, Nick and Patrick Nunn, 'Aboriginal Memories of Inundation of the Australian Coast Dating from More than 7000 Years Ago' (2016) 47 *Australian Geographer* 11

Rest, J R, *Moral Development: Advances in Research and Theory* (Praeger, 1986)

Rest, J R, 'Background: Theory and Research', in J R Rest and D Narvaez (eds), *Moral Development in the Professions: Psychology and Applied Ethics* (LEA, 1994)

Rhodes, Glenn, *Votes for Australia: How Colonials Voted at the 1899–1900 Federation Referendums* (CAPSM, Griffith University, 2002)

Richard, Larry and Lisa Rohrer, 'A Breed Apart?' (2011) *The American Lawyer* 43

Richards, Neil and Jonathan King, 'Three Paradoxes of Big Data' (2013) 66 *Stanford Law Review Online* 41

Richetin, Juliette, et al, 'The Moderator Role of Intuitive Versus Deliberative Decision Making For the Predictive Validity of Implicit and Explicit Measures' (2007) 21(4) *European Journal of Personality* 529

Ridley, A M, F Gabbert and D J La Rooy, *Suggestibility in Legal Contexts* (Wiley-Blackwell, 2013)

Riley, Joellen, 'The Definition of the Contract of Employment and its Differentiation from Other Contracts and Other Work Relations', in Mark Freedland, Alan Bogg, David Cabrelli et al (eds), *The Contract of Employment* (Oxford University Press, United Kingdom, 2016)

Riley, Joellen, 'Regulating Work in the "Gig" Economy', in Mia Ronnmar and Jenny Julen Votinius, *Festskrift Till Ann Numhauser-Henning* (Jurisforlaget I Lund, Sweden, 2017)

Ritchie, Euan, et al, 'Continental-Scale Governance Failure Will Hasten Loss of Australia's Biodiversity' (2013) 27(6) *Conservation Biology* 1133

Robbennolt, Jennifer K and Jean R Sternlight, 'Behavioral Legal Ethics' 45(3) (2013) *Arizona State Law Journal* 1107

Roberts, Lynne, et al, 'A Country Not Divided: A Comparison of Public Punitiveness and Confidence in Sentencing across Australia' (2011) 44 *Australian and New Zealand Journal of Criminology* 370

Roberts, Paul, 'Philosophy, Feinberg, Codification, and Consent: A Progress Report on English Experiences of Criminal Law Reform' (2001) 5 *Buffalo Criminal Law Review* 173

Rockström, J, et al, 'Planetary Boundaries: Exploring the Safe Operating Space for Humanity' (2009) 14(2) *Ecology and Society* 32

Rogers, Brishen, 'Toward Third-Party Liability for Wage Theft' (2010) *Berkeley Journal of Employment and Labour Law* 1

Rolph, David, *Defamation Law* (Lawbook Co, 2016)

Roma, Antonio, 'Energy, Money and Pollution' (2006) 56 *Ecological Economics* 534

Romzek, Barbara and Melvin Dubnick, 'Accountability in the Public Sector: Lessons from the Challenger Tragedy' (1987) 47 *Public Administration Review* 227

Rowden, Emma, et al, *Gateways to Justice: Design and Operational Guidelines for Remote Participation in Court Proceedings* (University of Western Sydney, 2013)

Rubenstein, Kim, *Australian Citizenship Law* (Thomson Reuters, 2nd edn, 2016)

Ruhl, J B, 'Regulation by Adaptive Management – Is It Possible?' (2005–2006) 7 *Minnesota Journal of Law, Science, & Technology* 72

Ruhl, J B, 'Climate Change Adaptation and the Structural Transformation of Environmental Law' (2010) 40 *Environmental Law* 363

Rydon, Joan, 'The Electorate', in John Wilkes (ed), *Forces in Australian Politics* (Angus & Robertson, 1963)

Sackville, Justice Ronald, 'The 2003 Term: The Inaccessible *Constitution*' (2003) 27 *University of New South Wales Law Review* 66

Sackville, Ronald, 'Law Reform Agencies and Royal Commissions: Toiling in the Same Field?', in Brian Opeskin and David Weisbrot (eds), *The Promise of Law Reform* (Federation Press, 2005)

Sammon, Marty and Mark Thomson, *Land Stewardship: Private Investor Needs for Land Stewardship Investment* (Department of Sustainability and Environment, State Government of Victoria, 2003)

Sansbury, Tauto, 'State and Territory Implementation of the Recommendations of the Royal Commission' (2001) 5(8) *Indigenous Law Bulletin* 6

Santos, Boaventura de Sousa, *Epistemologies of the South: Justice against Epistemicide* (Paradigm Publishers, 2014)

Sarat, Austin, '"The Law is All Over": Power, Resistance, and the Legal Consciousness of the Welfare Poor' (1990) 2 *Yale Journal of Law and the Humanities* 343

Saulnier, Alana and Diane Sivasubramaniam, 'Restorative Justice: Underlying Mechanisms and Future Directions' (2015) 18(4) *New Criminal Law Review* 510

Saunders, Cheryl, *The Constitution of Australia: A Contextual Analysis* (Hart, 2011)

Sawer, Geoffrey, *Australian Federalism in the Courts* (Melbourne University Press, 1967)

Schaefer and Hansen, 'Similar Fact Evidence and Limited Use Instructions: An Empirical Investigation' (1990) 14 *Criminal Law Journal* 157

Schauer, Frederick, 'The Path-Dependence of Legal Positivism' (2015) 101 *Virginia Law Review* 957

Schneyer, Ted, 'On Further Reflection: How "Professional Self-Regulation" Should Promote Compliance with Broad Ethical Duties of Law Firm Management' (2011) 53 *Arizona Law Review* 577

Schuller, Regina A, Deborah J Terry, and Blake M McKimmie, 'The Impact of an Expert's Gender on Jurors' Decisions' (2001) 25 *Law and Psychology Review* 59

Schuller, Regina A, Deborah J Terry, and Blake M McKimmie, 'The Impact of Expert Testimony on Jurors' Decisions: Gender of the Expert and Testimony Complexity' (2005) 35(6) *Journal of Applied Social Psychology* 1266

Scully, Maureen and Mary Rowe, 'Bystander Training Within Organizations' (2009) 2 *Journal of the International Ombudsman Association* 1

Senate Standing Committee on Legal and Constitutional Affairs, *Value of a Justice Reinvestment Approach to Criminal Justice in Australia* (Commonwealth of Australia, 2013)

Shaver, Kelly, 'Redress and Conscientiousness in the Attribution of Responsibility for Accidents' (1970) 6 *Journal of Experimental Social Psychology* 100

Sherman, Jeffrey W, Frederica R Conrey, and Carla J Groom, 'Encoding Flexibility Revisited: Evidence for Enhanced Encoding of Stereotype-Inconsistent Information Under Cognitive Load' (2004) 22(2) *Social Cognition* 214

Smith, Lionel, 'Constructive Trusts and Constructive Trustees' (1999) 58 *Cambridge Law Journal* 294

Smith, Lionel, 'Restitution: The Heart of Corrective Justice' (2001) 79 *Texas Law Review* 2115

Smith, Rodney and Paul Kildea, 'The Challenge of Informed Voting at Constitutional Referendums' (2016) 39 *UNSW Law Journal* 341

Sourdin, Tania, Elizabeth Richardson and Nerida Wallace, *Self-represented Litigants: Literature Review* (Monash University, 2012)

Spencer, David, 'Landing in the Right Class of Subject to Contract Agreements' (2015) 26 *Australasian Dispute Resolution Journal* 75

Spigelman, James, 'Measuring Court Performance' (2006) 16(2) *Journal of Judicial Administration* 69

Stafford Smith, Mark, et al, 'Rethinking Adaptation for a 4 Degree Centigrade World' (2011) 369 *Philosophical Transactions of the Royal Society* 196

Steedman, Carolyn, *Dust: The Archive and Cultural History* (Rutgers University Press, 2002)

Steel, Alex, Anna Huggins and Julian Laurens, 'Valuable Learning, Unwelcome Assessment: What LLB and JD Students really think about Group Work' (2014) 36 *Sydney Law Review* 291

Stellios, James, 'Reconceving The Separation of Judicial Power' (2011) 22 *Public Law Review* 113

Stephenson, Scott, 'Constitutional Reengineering: Dialogue's Migration from Canada to Australia' (2013) 11 *International Journal of Constitutional Law* 870

Stephenson, Scott, 'When Constitutional Conventions Fail' (2015) 38 *Dublin University Law Journal* 447

Stephenson, Scott, *From Dialogue to Disagreement in Comparative Rights Constitutionalism* (Federation Press, 2016)

Stern, L D, et al, 'Processing Time and the Recall of Inconsistent and Consistent Behaviors of Individuals and Groups' (1984) 47(2) *Journal of Personality and Social Psychology* 253

Stewart, Daniel, 'Assessing Access to Information in Australia: The Impact of Freedom of Information Laws on the Scrutiny and Operation of the Commonwealth Government', in John Wanna, Evert Lindquist and Penelope Marshall (eds), *New Accountabilities, New Challenges* (ANU Press, 2015)

Stiglitz, Joseph E, *The Price of Inequality* (Penguin Books Ltd, London, 2012)

Stoianoff, Natalie and Alpana Roy, 'Indigenous Knowledge and Culture in Australia – The Case for Sui Generis Legislation' (2015) 41(3) *Monash University Law Review*

Styles, Bridgette, 'The Power of a Timely Apology' (2013) 51(7) *Law Society Journal* 24

Sunstein, Cass, 'On the Expressive Function of Law' (1996) 144(5) *University of Pennsylvania Law Review* 2021

Sunstein, Cass R and Reid Hastie, *Wiser: Getting beyond Groupthink to Make Groups Smarter* (Harvard Business Press, 2015)

Tan, Po-Ling, Kathleen Bowmer and Claudia Baldwin, 'Continued Challenges in the Policy and Legal Framework for Collaborative Water Planning' (2012) 474 *Journal of Hydrology* 84

Tan, Poh-Ling, Kathleen Bowmer and John Mackenzie, 'Deliberative Tools for Meeting the Challenges of Water Planning in Australia' (2012) 474 *Journal of Hydrology* 2

Tan, Poh-Ling, David George and Maria Comino, 'Cumulative Risk Management, Coal Seam Gas, Sustainable Water, and Agriculture in Australia' (2015) 31(4) *International Journal of Water Resources Development* 682

Tarrant, Stella, 'Building Bridges in Australian Criminal Law: Codification and the Common Law' (2013) 39(3) *Monash University Law Review* 838

Teubner, Gunther (ed), *Autopoietic Law: A New Approach to Law and Society* (Walter de Gruyter, 1988)

Thaler, Richard and Cass Sunstein, *Nudge* (Penguin, revised edn, 2009)

Thomasett, Claude and René Leperrièrre, 'Faculties under Influence: The Infeudation of Law Schools to the Legal Professions', in Fiona Cownie (ed), *The Law School: Global Issues, Local Questions* (Ashgate, 1999)

Thompson, Janna, *Intergenerational Justice: Rights and Responsibilities in an Intergenerational Polity* (Routledge, 2009)

Thornton, Margaret, 'The Cartography of Public and Private', in Margaret Thornton (ed), *Public and Private: Feminist Legal Debates* (Oxford University Press, 1995)

Thornton, Margaret, *Quinquennial Professorial Report to University Council* (La Trobe University, 1995, unpublished)

Thornton, Margaret, *Privatising the Public University: The Case of Law* (Routledge, 2012)

Thornton, Margaret, 'Hypercompetitiveness or a Balanced Life? Gendered Discourses in the Globalisation of Australian Law Firms' (2014) 17(2) *Legal Ethics* 153

Tilbury, Michael, Simon N M Young and Ludwig Ng, 'Law Reform Today', in Michael Tilbury, Simon N M Young and Ludwig Ng (eds), *Reforming Law Reform: Perspectives from Hong Kong and Beyond* (Hong Kong University Press, 2014)

Trace, Ciaran B, 'What is Recorded is Never Simply "What Happened": Record Keeping in Modern Organizational Culture' (2002) 2 *Archival Science* 137

Tremmel, Joerg (ed), *Handbook of Intergenerational Justice* (Edward Elgar, 2006)

Treviño, Linda K, Gary R Weaver and Scott J Reynolds, 'Behavioral Ethics in Organizations: A Review' (2006) 32(6) *Journal of Management* 951

Treviño, Linda Klebe, Kenneth D Butterfield and Donald L McCabe, 'The Ethical Context in Organizations: Influences on Employee Attitudes and Behaviors' 8 *Business Ethics Quarterly* 447

Trimboli, Lily, 'Juror Understanding of Judicial Instructions in Criminal Trials' (2008) 119 *NSW BOCSAR Crime and Justice Bulletin*

Tullock, Gordon, 'Public Choice', in Steven Durlauf and Lawrence Blume (eds), *The New Palgrave Dictionary of Economics* (London, Palgrave Macmillan, 2nd edn, 1987)

Turner, Marlene E, et al, 'Threat, Cohesion, and Group Effectiveness: Testing a Social Identity Maintenance Perspective on Groupthink' (1992) 63(5) *Journal of Personality and Social Psychology* 781

Tushnet, Mark, 'Policy Distortion and Democratic Debilitation: Comparative Illumination of the Countermajoritarian Difficulty' (1995) 94 *Michigan Law Review* 245

Twomey, Anne, 'Compulsory Voting in a Representative Democracy: Choice, Compulsion and the Maximisation of Participation in Australian Elections' (2014) 13 *Oxford University Commonwealth Law Journal* 283

Tyler, Tom, *Readings in Procedural Justice* (Ashgate, 2005)

Tyler, Tom R, *Why People Obey the Law* (Princeton University Press, 2006)

Van Dyne, Linn, Soon Ang and Isabel Botero, 'Conceptualizing Employee Silence and Employee Voice as Multidimensional Constructs' (2003) 40 *Journal of Management Studies* 1359

Vandekerckhove, Wim, 'The Perception of Whistleblowing Worldwide', in Richard Calland and Guy Dehn (eds), *Whistleblowing Around the World: Law, Culture and Practice* (ODAC and PCaW in partnership with the British Council, 2004)

Vandekerckhove, Wim, and David Crowther, *Whistleblowing and Organisational Social Responsibility* (Ashgate e-Books, 2006)

Varuhas, Jason, 'The Concept of Vindication in the Law of Torts' (2014) 34 (2) *Oxford Journal of Legal Studies* 253

Victor, Bart and John B Cullen, 'A Theory and Measure of Ethical Climates in Organizations' (1987) 9 *Research in Corporate Social Performance and Policy* 51

Vidmar, Neil and Dale T Miller, 'Social Psychological Processes Underlying Attitudes toward Legal Punishment' (1980) *Law and Society Review* 565

Vines, Prue, 'The Power of Apology: Mercy, Forgiveness or Corrective Justice in the Civil Liability Arena' (2007) 1 *Journal of Public Space* 1

Vines, Prue, 'Apologies and Civil Liability in the UK: A View from Elsewhere' (2008) 12(2) *Edinburgh Law Review* 200

Vines, Prue, 'Apologising for Personal Injury in Law: Failing to Take Account of Lessons from Psychology in Blameworthiness and Propensity to Sue' (2014) 16 *Psychiatry, Psychology and Law* 42

Vines, Prue and Matthew Butt, 'Running Out of Compensation Money: Whipping Away the Social Security Blanket?' (2013) 7 *Court of Conscience* 17

Waldman, Ellen (ed), *Mediation Ethics: Cases and Commentaries* (Jossey-Bass, 2011)

Wallace, Anne, Kathy Mack and Sharyn Roach Anleu, 'Judicial Caseload Allocation and Specialisation: Finding the "Right Judge"?' (December 2012) *International Journal for Court Administration* 68

Wallace, Anne, *Australia's Indigenous People – A Curriculum Framework for Professional Development Programs for Australian Judicial Officers* (National Judicial College of Australia, 2013)

Walster, Elaine, 'Assignment of Responsibility for Accidents' (1966) 3 *Journal of Personality and Social Psychology* 1973

Wan, Wai-Yin, et al, 'The Effect of Arrest and Imprisonment on Crime' (Crime and Justice Bulletin No 158, NSW Bureau of Crime Statistics and Research, 2012)

Wang, Catherine L and Pervaiz K Ahmed, 'Organisational Learning: A Critical Review' (2003) 10 *The Learning Organization* 8

Ward, Tony, 'Usurping the Role of the Jury? Expert Evidence and Witness Credibility in English Trials' (2009) 13 *International Journal of Evidence and Proof* 83

Waters, David, 'The Wisdom of Whistleblowing: The Sarbanes-Oxley Act of 2002 and the "Noisy Withdrawal" Provision' (2010) 34 *Journal of the Legal Profession* 411

Watson, Irene, 'Sovereign Spaces, Caring for Country and the Homeless Position of Aboriginal Peoples' (2009) 108 *South Atlantic Quarterly* 27

Watson, Irene, 'First Nations Stories, Grandmother's Law: Too Many Stories to Tell', in Heather Douglas, Francesca Bartlett, Trish Luker and Rosemary Hunter (eds), *Australian Feminist Judgments: Righting and Rewriting Law* (Hart, 2014)

Watson, Irene, *Aboriginal Peoples, Colonialism and International Law: Raw Law* (Routledge, 2015)

Weatherburn, Don, *Law and Order in Australia: Rhetoric and Reality* (Federation Press, 2004)

Weatherburn, Don, '"Rack 'Em, Pack 'Em and Stack 'Em": Decarceration in an Age of Zero Tolerance' (2016) 28 *Current Issues in Criminal Justice* 137

Weaver, Gary R, 'Virtue in Organizations: Moral Identity as a Foundation for Moral Agency' (2006) 27(3) *Organization Studies* 341

Weeks, Greg, 'The Use and Enforcement of Soft Law by Australian Public Authorities' (2014) 42 *Federal Law Review* 181

Weil, David, *The Fissured Workplace: Why Work Became So Bad for So Many and What Can Be Done to Improve It* (Harvard University Press, 2014). doi.org/10.4159/9780674726123

Weinrib, Ernest, 'The Gains and Losses of Corrective Justice' (1994) 44 *Duke Law Journal* 277

Weinrib, Ernest J, *The Idea of Private Law* (Harvard University Press, 1995)

Weinrib, Ernest J, 'Restitutionary Damages as Corrective Justice' (2000) 1 *Theoretical Inquiries in Law* 1

Weinrib, Ernest J, 'The Normative Structure of Unjust Enrichment', in Charles Rickett and Ross Grantham (eds), *Structure and Justification in Private Law* (Hart Publishing, 2008)

Weinrib, Ernest J, *Corrective Justice* (Oxford University Press, 2012)

Weinstein, Janet and Linda H Morton, 'Collaboration and Teamwork' (2015) *Faculty Scholarship Paper* 163

Weis, Lael K, 'What Comparativism Tells Us about Originalism' (2013) 842 *International Journal of Constitutional Law* 842

Weis, Lael K, 'Constitutional Amendment Rules and Interpretive Fidelity to Democracy' (2014) 39 *University of Melbourne Law Review* 240

Weisbrod, Burton, *The Nonprofit Economy* (Harvard University Press, 1988)

Weisbrot, David, 'What Lawyers Need to Know, What Lawyers Need to be Able to Do: An Australian Experience' (2000) *Journal of the Association of Legal Writing Directors* 21

Weisbrot, David, 'The Future for Institutional Law Reform', in Brian Opeskin and David Weisbrot (eds), *The Promise of Law Reform* (Federation Press, 2005)

Wells, D, '"The Griffith Code" – Then and Now' (1994) 3(2) *Griffith Law Review* 205

Wentworth Group of Concerned Scientists, *Blueprint for a Healthy Environment and a Productive Economy* (Wentworth Group, 2014)

Wenzel, Michael, et al, 'Retributive and Restorative Justice' (2008) 32(5) *Law and Human Behavior* 375

Werhane, Patricia H, et al, *Obstacles to Ethical Decision-making: Mental Models, Milgram and the Problem of Obedience* (Cambridge University Press, 2013)

Werren, Kip, *Utilising Taxation Incentives to Promote Private Sector Funded Conservation* (PhD Thesis, University of Western Sydney, 2015)

Wheeler, Sarah, et al, 'Reviewing the Adoption and Impact of Water Markets in the Murray–Darling Basin, Australia' (2014) 518 *Journal of Hydrology* 28

Wheeler, Sarah, Alec Zuo and Neal Hughes, 'The Impact of Water Ownership and Water Market Trade Strategy on Australian Irrigators' Farm Viability' (2014) 129 *Agricultural Systems* 81

Whincop, Michael J, 'The Political Economy of Corporate Law Reform in Australia' (1999) 27 *Federal Law Review* 77

Wiersema, Annecoos, 'A Train without Tracks: Rethinking the Place of Law and Goals in Environmental Law and Natural Resources Law' (2008) 38 *Environmental Law Journal* 1239

Wilkinson, Richard, and Kate Pickett, *The Spirit Level: Why Greater Equality Makes Societies Stronger* (2009, Bloomsbury Press, New York)

Williams, Daryl, 'The Australian Parliament and the High Court: Determination of Constitutional Questions', in Charles Sampford and Kim Preston (eds), *Interpreting Constitutions: Theories, Principles and Institutions* (Federation Press, 1996)

Williams, George and David Hume, *People Power: The History and Future of the Referendum in Australia* (UNSW Press, 2010)

Williams, John, Tim Stubbs and Ann Milligan, *An Analysis of Coal Seam Gas Production and NRM in Australia* (JWSS, 2012)

Wilson, C E, Tiffany H Morrison and J-A Everingham, 'Linking the "Meta-Governance" Imperative to Regional Governance in Resource Communities' (2017) 50 *Journal of Rural Studies* 188

Winter, Will, 'The Minimbah Project: Facilitating Birth Registration and Certificates in Rural and Regional Communities', in *Proof of Birth* (Future Leaders, 2015)

Wissler, Roselle L and Michael J Saks, 'On the Inefficacy of Limiting Instructions' (1985) 9 *Law and Human Behaviour* 37

Wistrich, Andrew J, Chris Guthrie, and Jeffrey J Rachlinski, 'Can Judges Ignore Inadmissible Information? The Difficulty of Deliberately Disregarding' (2005) 153(4) *University of Pennsylvania Law Review* 1251

Wittgenstein, Ludwig, *On Certainty* (Blackwell, 1969)

Woinarski, John, Andrew Burbidge and Peter Harrison, 'Ongoing Unravelling of a Continental Fauna: Decline and Extinction of Australian Mammals since European Settlement' (2015) 112 *Proceedings of the National Academy of Sciences* 4531

Wolfe Morrison, Elizabeth, and Frances J Milliken, 'Speaking Up, Remaining Silent: The Dynamics of Voice and Silence in Organizations' (2003) 40(6) *Journal of Management Studies* 1353

Wolski, Bobette, *Skills, Ethics and Values for Legal Practice* (Lawbook Co, 2nd edn, 2009)

Wright, Richard W, 'Substantive Corrective Justice' (1992) 77 *Iowa Law Review* 625

Wright, Richard W, 'Right, Justice and Tort Law', in David G Owen (ed), *Philosophical Foundations of Tort Law* (Clarendon, 1997)

Wroth, Kinvin, 'Documents of the Colonial Conflict: Part I – Sources for the Legal History of the American Revolution' (1976) 69 *Law Librarians Journal* 277

Young, Michael Brett, *From Commitment to Culture: The 2015 Review of the Charter of Human Rights and Responsibilities Act 2006* (Melbourne, 2015)

Zehr, Howard, Harry Mika and Mark Umbreit, 'Restorative Justice: The Concept' (1997) 59 *Corrections Today* 68

Zhong, Chen-Bo, 'The Ethical Dangers of Deliberative Decision Making' (2011) 56.1 *Administrative Science Quarterly* 1

Zimdars, Anna, Alice Sullivan and Anthony Heath, 'Elite Higher Education Admissions in the Arts and Sciences: Is Cultural Capital the Key?' (2009) *Sociology* 43

B. Cases

ABC Developmental Learning Centres Pty Ltd v Wallace [2007] VSCA 138

ACCC v Pfizer Australia Pty Ltd [2015] FCA 113

ACCC v Real Estate Institute of Western Australia Inc [1999] FCA 18

Akron Securities Ltd v Iliffe (1997) 41 NSWLR 353

Alpha Wealth Financial Services Pty Ltd v Frankland River Olive Company Limited [2008] WASC 119

Anderson v Anderson [2013] QSC 8

AS v Minister for Immigration and Border Protection (Ruling No. 3) [2015] VSC 642

ASIC v Somerville [2009] NSWSC 934

Aslam, Farrer v Uber BV, Uber London and Uber Britannia Ltd, Case Nos 2202551/2015 (12 October 2016)

Attorney General v Parnther (1792) 3 Bro CC 441

Attorney-General (NT) v Kearney (1985) 158 CLR 510

Attorney-General (Vic) ex rel Dale v Commonwealth (1945) 71 CLR 237

Australian Capital Television v Commonwealth (1992) 177 CLR 106

Australian Competition and Consumer Commission v Neighbourhood Energy Pty Ltd [2012] FCA 1357

Australian Financial Services and Leasing Pty Limited v Hills Industries Limited [2014] HCA 14

Australian Financial Services and Leasing Pty Ltd v Hills Industries Ltd (2014) 253 CLR 560

AYSA Amateur Youth Soccer Association v Canada (Revenue Agency) [2007] 3 SCR 217

Baker v Campbell (1983) 153 CLR 52

Ball v Mannin (1829) 1 Dow & Cl 380; 6 ER 568

Barnes v Addy (1874) LR 9 Ch App 244

Benson v The Queen [2014] VSCA 51

Betfair Pty Ltd v WA (2008) 234 CLR 418

Boulton v The Queen [2014] VSCA 342

Bridgewater v Leahy (1998) 194 CLR 471

British American Tobacco Australia Limited v Peter Gordon [2009] VSC 619

British American Tobacco Australia Ltd v Fairfax [2006] NSWSC 1328

British American Tobacco Australia Ltd v Peter Gordon [2006] NSWSC 1473

British American Tobacco Australia Ltd v Peter Gordon [2007] NSWSC 109

British American Tobacco Australia Ltd v Peter Gordon [2007] NSWSC 230

British American Tobacco Australia Ltd v Peter Gordon [2009] VSC 619

British American Tobacco Australia Ltd v Peter Gordon [2009] VSC 77

British American Tobacco Australia Ltd v Peter Gordon [2007] NSWSC 292

British American Tobacco Australia Services Limited v Cowell [2002] VSCA 197

British American Tobacco Australia Services Limited v Slater & Gordon Ltd and Roxanne Joy Cowell [2009] VSC 619

British American Tobacco Australia Services Ltd v Cowell (as representing the estate of Rolah Ann McCabe, deceased) [2003] VSCA 43

British American Tobacco Australia Services Ltd v John Fairfax Publications [2006] NSWSC 1175

British American Tobacco Australia Services Ltd v John Fairfax Publications [2006] NSWSC 1197

Butera v Director of Public Prosecutions (1987) 164 CLR 180

BVerfGE 119 (2007) (Twelfth broadcasting case)

BVerfGE 57, 295 (Third broadcasting case)

BVerfGE 7, 198 (Lüth case)

BVerfGE 73, 188 (1986) (Fourth/Lower Saxony broadcasting case)

BVerfGE 74, 297 (1987) (Fifth/Baden-Württemberg broadcasting case)

BVerfGE 83, 238 (1991) (Sixth/North Rhine-Westphalia broadcasting case)

BVerfGE 90, 60 (1994) (Eighth/Cable Penny broadcasting case)

C G Maloney Pty Ltd v Hutton-Potts [2006] NSWCA 136

Caffey v Leatt-hayter [No 3] [2013] WASC 348 (20 September 2013)

Central Bayside General Practice Association Ltd v Commissioner of State Revenue (2006) 228 CLR 168

Chamber of Commerce and Industry of Western Australia Inc v Commissioner of State Revenue [2012] WASAT 146

Chesterman v Federal Commissioner of Taxation (1923) 32 CLR 362

Christopher Anthony Dale v Clayton Utz (No 2) [2013] VSC 54

Clark v Macourt (2013) 88 ALJR 190

Commercial Bank of Australia Ltd v Amadio (1983) 151 CLR 447

Commissioners for Special Purposes of Income Tax v Pemsel [1891] AC 534

Commonwealth v ACT (2013) 250 CLR 441

Commonwealth v Fairfax (1980) 147 CLR 39

Commonwealth v Tasmania (1983) 158 CLR 1

Corporate Systems Publishing v Lingard (No 4) [2008] WASC 21

Corrs Pavey Whiting & Byrne v Collector of Customs (Vic) (1987) 14 FCR 434

Cowell v British American Tobacco Australia Services Ltd [2007] VSCA 301

R v Cox & Railton (1884) 10 QBD 153

Crago v McIntyre [1976] 1 NSWLR 729

Craig v South Australia (1995) 184 CLR 163

Crystal Palace Trustees v Minister of Town and Country Planning [1950] 2 Ch 857

Dale v Clayton Utz (No 2) [2013] VSC 54

David Securities Pty Ltd v Commonwealth Bank of Australia (1992) 175 CLR 353

De Simone v Bevacqua (1994) 7 VAR 246

Demagogue Pty Ltd v Ramensky (1992) 39 FCR 31

Director of Housing v TK (Residential Tenancies) [2010] VCAT 1839

Director of Public Prosecutions v Leys [2012] VSCA 304

DJV v The Queen [2008] NSWCCA 272

Doe v Unocal, 395 F3d 932 (9th Cir, 2002)

Donoghue v Stevenson [1932] AC 562

Downing v Federal Commissioner of Taxation (1971) 125 CLR 185

Edna May Collins by her next friend Glenys Lesley Laraine Poletti v May [2000] WASC 29

Egan v Chadwick (1999) 46 NSWLR 563

Ell v Milne (No 9) [2014] NSWSC 489 (11 April 2014)

Equuscorp Pty Ltd v Haxton (2012) 246 CLR 498

Evans v European Bank Ltd (2004) 61 NSWLR 75

Faderson v Bridger (1971) 126 CLR 271

Fair Work Ombudsman v Haider Pty Ltd [2015] FCCA 2113 (30 July 2015)

Fair Work Ombudsman v Liquid Fuel Pty Ltd [2015] FCCA 2694

Fair Work Ombudsman v South Jin Pty Ltd [2015] FCA 1456

Falun Dafa Association of Victoria Inc v Melbourne City Council [2004] VCAT 625

Falvo v Australian Oztag Sports Association (2006) Aust Torts Reps 81-831

FH v The Queen [2014] NSWCCA 231

Foskett v McKeown [2001] 1 AC 102

Fourteenth/ZDF Treaty case (2014)

FWO v Devine Marine [2015] FCA 370

Gallie v Lee (1971) AC 1004

Garcia v National Australia Bank Ltd (1998) 195 CLR 395

Gaynor v Chief of the Defence Force (No 3) [2015] FCA 1370

Gibbons v Wright (1954) 91 CLR 423

Giorgianni v The Queen (1985) 156 CLR 473

Hedley Byrne & Co Ltd v Heller & Partners Ltd [1964] AC

Henville v Walker (2001) 206 CLR 459

HML v The Queen (2008) 235 CLR 334

Holmdahl v AEC (No 2) [2012] SASFC 110

Huddart, Parker & Co Pty Ltd v Moorehead (1909) 8 CLR 330

Hughes v The Queen [2015] NSWCCA 330

Hughes v The Queen [2017] HCATrans 016

Hunt v Radio 2SM Pty Ltd (No. 2) [2010] NSWDC 43

IMM v The Queen [2016] HCA 14

Imperial Loan Company v Stone (1892) 1 QB 599

Initial Services v Putterill [1968] 1 QB 396

Inland Revenue Commissioners v City of Glasgow Police Athletics Association [1953] AC 380 (HL)

Insight Vacations Pty Ltd v Young (2011) 243 CLR 149

Jaber v Rockdale City Council (2008) Aust Tort Reps 81-952

McCabe v British American Tobacco Australia Services Ltd [2007] VSC 216

McCloy v New South Wales (2015) 89 ALJR 857

McClure v Australian Electoral Commission (1999) 163 ALR 734

McGovern v Attorney-General [1982] 1 Ch 321

McLaughlin v Daily Telegraph Newspaper Co Ltd [No 2] (1904) 1 CLR 243

Melway Publishing Pty Ltd v Robert Hicks Pty Ltd [2001] HCA13; (2001) 205 CLR 1

Mikronis v Adams [2004] 1 DCLR (NSW) 369

Miller v Miller (2002) 242 CLR 446

Ministry of Health v Simpson [1951] AC 251

Mirehouse v Rennell (1833) 1 Cl. & F. 527

Momcilovic v The Queen [2011] HCA 34

Momcilovic v The Queen (2011) 245 CLR 1

Morice v Bishop of Durham (1804) 9 Ves Jun 399; (1805) 10 Ves Jun 522

Motorcycling Events Group Australia Pty Ltd v Kelly [2013] NSWCA 361

Mount Isa Mines Ltd v Pusey (1970) 125 CLR 383

Munchies Management Pty Ltd v Belperio (1988) 58 FCR 274

Murdoch v The Queen [2013] VSCA 272

Murphy v Doman (2003) 58 NSWLR 51

Murphy v Overton Investments Pty Ltd (2004) 216 CLR 388

Nail v News Group Newspapers Ltd [2004] EMLR 362

New South Wales Lotteries Corporation Pty Ltd v Kuzmanovski (2011) 195 FCR 234

New South Wales v Commonwealth (2006) 229 CLR 1

Novel Inc v Microsoft Corporation [2013-2] Trade Cases 78,523

Palko v Connecticut, 302 US 319 (1937)

Pape v Commissioner of Taxation (2009) 238 CLR 1

Pedavoli v Fairfax Media Publications Pty Ltd (2014) 324 ALR 166

Petelin v Cullen (1975) 132 CLR 355

PGA v The Queen [2012] 245 CLR 355

Philip Morris Asia v Australia PCA Case no. 2012-12

Pingel v Toowoomba Newspapers Pty Ltd [2010] QCA 175 (16 July 2010)

Port of Brisbane Corporation v ANZ Securities Limited [2002] QCA 158

Potter v Fair Work Ombudsman [2014] FCA 187

Project Blue Sky Inc v Australian Broadcasting Authority (1998) 194 CLR 355

Qualtieri v The Queen (2006) 171 A Crim R 463

R v AC Hatrick Chemicals Pty Ltd (1995) 140 IR 243

R v AH (1997) 42 NSWLR 702

R v Apostilides (1984) 154 CLR 563

R v Bell; Ex parte Lees (1980) 146 CLR 141

R v Beserick (1993) 30 NSWLR 510

R v Birmingham & Gloucester Railway Co (1842) 3 QB 223

R v C, CN [2013] SASCFC 44

R v DG [2010] VSCA 173

R v F, AD [2015] SASCFC 130

R v Flynn [2008] 2 Cr App R 266

R v Landmeter [2015] SASCFC 3

R v Lisoff [1999] NSWCCA 364

R v Maiolo (No 2) (2013) 117 SASR 1

R v Wagar, 2015 ABCA 327 (CanLII)

R v WJT [2001] NSWCCA 405

R v WR (No 3) [2010] ACTSC 89

R v Zappavigna [2015] SASCFC 8

Re Application under the Major Crime (Investigative Powers Act) 2004
    [2009] VSC 381

Re Dawson [1966] 2 NSWR 211

Re Diplock [1948] Ch 465

Re Hay's Settlement Trusts [1982] 1 WLR 202

Re Judiciary and Navigation Acts (1921) 29 CLR 257

Re Mowbray; Brambles Australia Ltd v British American Tobacco Australia
    Services Ltd [2006] NSWDDT 15

Re Smith Kline & French Laboratories (Australia) Ltd and Secretary,
    Department of Community Services and Health (1991) 28 FCR 291

Repatriation Commission v Law (1980) 31 ALR 140

Repatriation Commission v Law (1981) 147 CLR 635

RJE v Secretary, Department of Justice [2008] VSCA 265

Roberts v Gill & Co [2010] UKSC 22

Rodden v The Queen [2008] NSWCCA 53

Ron Kingham Real Estate Pty Ltd v Edgar [1999] 2 QdR 439

Royal Bank of Scotland v Etridge [2002] 2 AC 773

Royal College of Surgeons of England v National Provincial Bank Ltd
    [1952] AC 681 (HL)

Rural Press Ltd v ACCC [2003] HCA 75; 216 CLR 53

RWC v The Queen [2010] NSWCCA 332

Scott v National Trust [1998] 2 All ER 705

Scott v Scott (1963) 109 CLR 649

Selangor United Rubber Estates Limited v Cradock (No 3) [1968] 1 WLR 1555,

Sleeman v Tuloch Pty Ltd (No 4) [2013] NSWDC 111

Smith v Perese [2006] NSWSC 288

Starr v Department of Human Services [2016] FWC 1460

Steadman v The Queen (No 2) [2013] NSWCCA 56

Stone v Registrar of Titles [2012] WASC 21

Summertime Holdings Pty Ltd v Environmental Defender's Office Ltd (1998) 45 NSWLR 291

Szanto v Melville [2011] VSC 574 (4 November 2011)

Taha v Broadmeadows Magistrates' Court [2011] VSC 642

Tasmanian Electronic Commerce Centre Pty Ltd v Federal Commissioner of Taxation (2005) 142 FCR 371

Tenji v Henneberry & Associates Pty Ltd (2000) 98 FCR 324

Tesco Supermarkets Ltd v Nattrass [1972] AC 153

The Solicitor-General v Miss Alice [2007] 2 NZLR 783

Trustees of the Roman Catholic Church for the Archdiocese of Sydney v Ellis (2007) 70 NSWLR 565

Universal Music Australia Pty Ltd v ACCC [2003] FCAFC 193; (2003) ATPR 41-947

Vadasz v Pioneer Concrete (1995) 184 CLR 102

Velkoski v The Queen [2014] VSCA 121

Vreman and Morris v Albury City Council [2011] NSWSC 39

Wilkinson v Feldworth Financial Services Pty Ltd (1998) 29 ACSR 642

Williams v Commonwealth (No 1) (2012) 248 CLR 156

Wingecarribee Shire Council v Lehman Brothers Australia Ltd (in liq) [2012] FCA 1028

XFJ v Director of Public Transport [2008] VCAT 2303

Yerkey v Jones 63 CLR 649

Young Investments Group Pty Ltd v Mann (2012) 293 ALR 537

C. Legislative Materials

Aboriginal and Torres Strait Islander Heritage Protection Act 1984 (Cth)

Aboriginal Heritage Amendment Act 2016 (Vic)

Access and Benefits Sharing of Genetic Resources and Associated Traditional Knowledge, Law No 13.123 of May 20, 2015 (Brazil)

Advisory Report on the Counter-Terrorism Legislation Amendment Bill (No 1) 2014 (Cth)

Age Discrimination in Employment Act (USC)

Archives Act 1983 (Cth)

Australian Citizenship Act 2007 (Cth)

Australian Citizenship Amendment (Allegiance to Australia) Act 2015 (Cth)

Australian Law Reform Commission Act 1996 (Cth)

Australian Securities and Investments Commission Act 2001 (Cth)

Australian Solicitors Conduct Rules, Law Council of Australia, www.lawcouncil.asn.au/policy-agenda/regulation-of-the-profession-and-ethics/australian-solicitors-conduct-rules

Biodiscovery Act 2004 (Qld)

Bribery Act 2010 (UK)

Charities Act 2013 (Cth)

Children, Youth and Families Amendment (Permanent Care and Other Matters) Act (2014) (Vic)

Civil Law (Wrongs) Act 2002 (ACT)

Civil Liability Act 2002 (NSW)

Competition and Consumer (Industry Codes – Franchising) Regulation 2014 (Cth)

Competition and Consumer Act 2010 (Cth)

Competition and Consumer Amendment (Competition Policy Review) Bill 2017 (Cth)

Competition and Consumer Amendment (Misuse of Market Power) Bill 2016 (Cth)

Competition Policy Reform (New South Wales) Act 1995

Compulsory Voting Act 1915 (Cth)

Constitution (Fixed Term Parliament) Amendment Bill 2015 (Qld)

Consumer Credit and Corporations Legislation Amendment (Enhancements) Act 2012 (Cth)

Contracts Review Act 1980 (NSW)

Corporations Act 2001 (Cth)

Counter-Terrorism Legislation Amendment (Foreign Fighters) Act 2014 (Cth)

Counter-Terrorism Legislation Amendment Act (No 1) 2014 (Cth)

Counter-Terrorism Legislation Amendment Bill (No 1) 2015 (Cth)

Crimes (Document Destruction) Act 2006 (Vic)

Crimes (Industrial Manslaughter) Amendment Act 2003 (ACT)

Crimes Act 1900 (ACT)

Criminal Code Act 1995 (Cth)

Criminal Code Amendment Act 1997 (Tas)

Defamation Act 1996 (UK)

Defamation Act 2005 (NSW)

Defamation Act 2005 (Qld)

Defamation Act 2005 (SA)

Defamation Act 2005 (Tas)

Defamation Act 2005 (Vic)

Defamation Act 2005 (WA)

Defamation Act 2006 (NT)

Defamation Act 2009 (Ire)

Duties Act 2008 (WA)

Elections Act 1915 (Qld)

Electoral Act 1985 (SA)

Employment Rights Act 1996 (UK)

Environment Protection and Biodiversity Conservation Act 1999 (Cth)

Evidence (Discreditable Conduct) Amendment Act 2011 (SA)

Evidence (Document Unavailability) Act 2006 (Vic)

Evidence Regulation 2007 (NZ)

Explanatory Memorandum, Fair Work Amendment (Protecting Vulnerable Workers) Bill 2017 (Cth)

Explanatory Memorandum, Trade Practices Amendment (Australian Consumer Law) Bill No 2 (2010) (Cth)

Extension of Charitable Purposes Act 2004 (Cth)

Fair Trading Act 1985 (Victoria)

Fair Trading Act 1987 (NSW)

Fair Trading Amendment (Australian Consumer Law) Act 2010 (NSW)

Fair Work Act 2009 (Cth)

Fair Work Amendment (Protecting Vulnerable Workers) Bill 2017 (Cth)

Family Law Rules 2004 (Cth)

Federal Court of Australia Act 1976 (Cth)

Federal Court of Australia, *Practice Note CM23 – Electronic Court File and Preparation and Lodgment of Documents*, 10 July 2014

Federal Court Rules 2011 (Cth)

Foreign Fighters Bill 2014 (Cth)

Guardianship and Administration Act 1990 (WA)

High Court Rules 2004 (Cth)

Indigenous Peoples Rights Act of 1997 (Philippines)

Industrial Relations Act 1996 (NSW)

Intelligence Services Act 2001 (Cth)

Introducing a Protection Regime for the Collective Knowledge of Indigenous People Derived from Biological Resources, Law No 27,811 of 2002 (Peru)

Jury Directions Act 2015 (Vic)

Land Tax Assessment Act 2002 (WA)

Law Commission of Canada Act 1996 (Canada)

Law Commissions Act 1965 (UK)

Law Reform Commission Act 1973 (Cth)

Legal Profession Act 2004 (Vic)

Legal Profession Act 2004 (NSW)

Legal Profession Uniform Continuing Professional Development (Solicitors) Rules 2015

Legal Profession Uniform Law 2014 (NSW)

Legal Profession Uniform Law Application Act 2014 (Vic)

Legal Profession Uniform Law Australian Solicitors' Conduct Rules 2015 (NSW)

National Consumer Credit Protection Act 2009 (Cth)

National Security Legislation Amendment Act (No 1) 2014 (Cth)

Native Title Act 1993 (Cth)

Native Title Amendment Act 1998 (Cth)

NSW Law Society Guidelines for Solicitors who Act as Mediators

Owner Drivers and Forestry Contractors Act 2005 (Vic)

Partnership Act 1891 (SA)

Payroll Tax Act (NT)

Pay-Roll Tax Assessment Act 2002 (WA)

Queensland Biotechnology Code of Ethics 2006

Queensland Code of Ethical Practice for Biotechnology 2001

Queensland Law Society Standards of Conduct for Solicitor Mediators

Registered Organisations (Fair Work) Amendment Act 2016 (Cth)

Residential Tenancies Amendment (Public Housing) Act 2011 (Vic)

Road Safety and Sentencing Act Amendment Act 2012 (Vic)

Road Transport (Public Passenger Services) Act 2001 (ACT)

Secession Referendum Act 1932 (WA)

Sentencing Amendment (Abolition of Suspended Sentences and Other Matters) Act 2013 (Vic)

Serious Sex Offenders (Detention and Supervision) Act 2009 (Victoria)

Special System for the Collective Intellectual Property Rights of Indigenous Peoples for the Protection and Defense of their Cultural Identity and their Traditional Knowledge, Law No 20 of June 26, 2000 (Panama)

Supplementary Explanatory Memorandum, Australian Citizenship Amendment (Allegiance to Australia) Bill 2015 (Cth)

Taxation Administration Act (NT)

Taxation Administration Act 2003 (WA)

Telecommunications (Interception and Access) Act 1979 (Cth)

Telecommunications (Interception and Access) Amendment (Data Retention) Act 2015 (Cth)

Trade Practices Act 1974 (Cth)

Trade Practices Amendment (Liability for Recreational Services) Bill 2002 (Cth)

Trustees Act 1962 (WA)

Trusts Act 1973 (Qld)

Water Act 2007 (Cth)

Water Management Act 2000 (NSW)

Wrongs Act 1958 (Vic)

D. Reports

Attorney-General (ACT), *Defamation Report in the ACT* (1998)

Attorney-General's Department, *Revised Outline of a Possible National Defamation Law* (2004)

Attorney-General's Department, *Proposed Amendments to the Foreign Bribery Offence in the Criminal Code Act 1995,* Public Consultation Paper (2017)

Attorney-General's Task Force for Defamation Law Reform (NSW), *Defamation Law Proposals for Reform in NSW* (2002)

Australian Bureau of Statistics, *Water Account Australia 2012–13* (2014)

Australian Bureau of Statistics, 'Australian National Accounts: Non-Profit Institutions Satellite Account 2012–13' (Cat No 5256, 28 August 2015)

Australian Capital Territory Community Law Reform Committee, *Defamation Report*, Report No 10 (1995)

Australian Capital Territory Justice and Community Safety Directorate, *Justice Reinvestment Strategy* (2015)

Australian Government Department of the Environment, *State of the Environment Report 2011* (2011)

Australian Government Department of the Environment, *Australia's Fifth National Report under the Convention on Biological Diversity* (2014)

Australian Government Department of Sustainability, Environment, Water, Population and Communities, *National Framework for Compliance and Enforcement Systems for Water Resource Management* (2012)

Australian Government, 'Our North, Our Future: White Paper on Developing Northern Australia' (White Paper, Australian Government, 2015)

Australian Law Reform Commission, *Unfair Publication: Defamation and Privacy*, Report No 11 (1979)

Australian Law Reform Commission, *Managing Justice: A Review of the Federal Civil Justice System,* Report No 89 (2000)

Australian Law Reform Commission, *Uniform Evidence Law*, Report No 102 (2005)

Australian Law Reform Commission, *Making Inquiries – A New Statutory Framework*, Report No 111 (2009)

Australian Law Reform Commission, *Family Violence*, Report No 114 (2009)

Australian Law Reform Commission, *Secrecy Laws and Open Government in Australia*, Report No 112 (2010)

Australian Law Reform Commission, *Family Violence: A National Legal Response*, Report No 114 (2010)

Australian Law Reform Commission, *Connection to Country: Review of the Native Title Act 1993 (Cth)*, Report No 126 (2015)

Australian Securities Investment Commission, *Interest-Only Home Loan Review*, Report No 445 (August 2015)

Australian Society of Archivists, *Made, Kept and Used: Celebrating 30 Years of the Australian Society of Archivists* (2005)

Catholic Commission for Justice, Development and Peace, '*It's Not Easy Walkin' in There': Aboriginal Reconciliation: Towards Practical and Culturally Respectful Solutions* (1999)

Charity Commission, 'Tell it Like it is: The Extent of Charity Reserves and Reserve Policies', Research Report No RS13 (2006)

Commonwealth of Australia, *Caring for Our Country – Outcomes 2008–2013* (National Landcare Program, 2013)

Commonwealth of Australia, *Financial Service Inquiry Interim Report* (2014)

Commonwealth of Australia, *Financial System Inquiry Final Report* (2014)

Commonwealth of Australia, Defence Abuse Response Taskforce, *Second Interim Report to the Attorney-General and Minister for Defence* (2013)

Commonwealth of Australia, Defence Abuse Response Taskforce, *Fourth Interim Report to the Attorney-General and Minister for Defence* (2013)

Commonwealth of Australia, Defence Abuse Response Taskforce, *Seventh Interim Report to the Attorney-General and Minister for Defence* (2014)

Commonwealth of Australia, Royal Commission into Institutional Responses to Child Sexual Abuse, *Redress and Civil Litigation Report* (2015)

Cossins, Annie, National Child Sexual Assault Reform Committee, *Alternative Models for Prosecuting Child Sex Offences in Australia* (2010)

Coumarelos, Christine, et al, *Access to Justice and Legal Needs: Legal Australia Wide Survey Legal Need in Australia*, Law and Justice Foundation of New South Wales (2012)

Council of Legal Education Victoria, *Report of Academic Course Appraisal Committee on Legal Knowledge Required for Admission to Practise* (1990)

Court Services Victoria, *Court Services Victoria Annual Report 2015–16,* Report No 22 (2016)

Curran, Liz, *Making the Legal System More Responsive to Community: A Report on the Impact of Victorian Community Legal Centre (CLC) Law Reform Initiatives* (2007). dx.doi.org/10.2139/ssrn.2395076

Gardini, R, *Review of the Franchising Code of Practice: Report to the Minister for Small Business, Customs and Construction* (1994)

Gibbs, Harry, Ray Watson and Andrew Menzies, *Review of Commonwealth Criminal Law: Final Report* (1991)

Holland, J, *Negotiating Bulk Debt: Outcomes from the Bulk Debt Negotiation Project* (unpublished report for Victoria Legal Aid, West Heidelberg Community Legal Service, Legal Aid NSW, Good Shepherd Australia & New Zealand, 2016)

Judicial Council on Cultural Diversity, *The Path to Justice: Aboriginal and Torres Strait Islander Women's Experience of the Courts: A Report Prepared for the Judicial Council on Cultural Diversity* (2016)

Judicial Council on Cultural Diversity, *The Path to Justice: Migrant and Refugee Women's Experience of the Courts: A Report Prepared for the Judicial Council on Cultural Diversity* (2016)

Law Council of Australia, Submission to the Senate Economics Reference Committee, *Inquiry into Foreign Bribery*, 24 August 2015

Law Society of NSW, *The Future of Law and Innovation in the Profession,* Law Society of NSW Report (2017)

Martin, Paul and Jacqueline Williams, 'Policy Risk Assessment' (CRC for Irrigation Futures Technical Report Series No 03/10, 2010)

Martin, Paul, Jacqueline Williams and Christopher Stone, 'Transaction Costs and Water Reform: The Devils Hiding in the Details' (Cooperative Research Centre for Irrigation Futures Technical Report No 08/08, 2008)

National Alternative Dispute Resolution Advisory Council, *ADR Terminology: A Discussion Paper* (2002)

National Alternative Dispute Resolution Advisory Council, *Maintaining and Enhancing the Integrity of ADR Processes: From Principles to Practice through People* (2011)

National Biodiversity Strategy Review Task Group, *Australia's Biodiversity Conservation Strategy 2010–2030* (2010)

National Human Rights Consultation, *Report* (2009)

National Water Commission, *Australian Water Reform 2009: Second Biennial Assessment of Progress in Implementation of the National Water Initiative* (Australian Government, 2010)

National Water Commission, *Sustainable Levels of Extraction: National Water Commission Position* (2010)

National Water Commission, *The NWI – Securing Australia's Water Future: 2011 Assessment* (2011)

National Water Commission, *Water Markets in Australia: A Short History* (2011)

National Water Commission, *Coal Seam Gas and Water Position Statement* (2012)

National Water Commission, *Monitoring and Evaluation for Adaptive Water Management: Issues Paper* (2013)

National Water Commission, *The National Water Planning Report Card 2013* (2013)

National Water Commission, *Australia's Water Blueprint: National Reform Assessment 2014* (2014)

National Water Commission, *Water for Mining and Unconventional Gas under the National Water Initiative* (2014)

New South Wales Law Reform Commission, *Defamation*, Report No 11 (1971)

New South Wales Law Reform Commission, *Defamation*, Report 75 (1995)

New South Wales Law Reform Commission, *Jury Directions*, Report 136 (2012)

Office for Learning and Teaching, Department of Industry, Innovation, Science, Research and Tertiary Education, *Internationalising the Australian Law Curriculum for Enhanced Global Legal Practice* (2012)

Office of the Fair Work Ombudsman, *A Report of the Fair Work Ombudsman's Inquiry into 7-Eleven* (2016)

Parker, Seamus and Robert Speed, 'Agricultural Water Pricing: Australia' (Background Report to OECD Study 'Sustainable Management of Water Resources', OECD, 2010)

Parliamentary Joint Committee on Corporations and Financial Services, Parliament of Australia, *Inquiry into Whistleblower Protections in the Corporate, Public and Not-For-Profit Sectors* (2017)

Parliamentary Joint Committee on Intelligence and Security, Parliament of Australia, *Advisory Report on the Counter-Terrorism Legislation Amendment (Foreign Fighters) Bill 2014* (2014)

Parliamentary Joint Committee on Intelligence and Security, Parliament of Australia, *Annual Report of Committee Activities 2014–15* (2015)

Parliamentary Joint Committee on Intelligence and Security, Parliament of Australia, *Advisory Report on the Counter-Terrorism Legislation Amendment Bill (No 1) 2015* (2016)

Productivity Commission, *Review of National Competition Policy Reforms*, Report No 33 (2005)

Productivity Commission, *Review of Australia's Consumer Policy Framework*, Inquiry Report No 45 (2008)

Productivity Commission, *Access to Justice Arrangements: Productivity Commission Inquiry Report* (2014)

Productivity Commission, *Commission Inquiry into Access to Justice Arrangements Report: Volume 1,* Inquiry Report 72 (2014)

Productivity Commission, *Report on Government Services 2016* (2016)

Productivity Commission, *Inquiry into Progress with the Reform of Australia's Water Resources Sector* (2017)

Queensland Law Reform Commission, *Report on the Law relating to Trusts, Trustees, Settled Land and Charities,* QLRC Report 8 (1971)

Queensland Law Reform Commission, *Review of the Trusts Act 1973*, QLRC Report 71 (2013)

Saddoff, Claudia W, et al, 'Securing Water, Sustaining Growth: Report of the GWP/OECD Task Force on Water Security and Sustainable Growth' (2015)

Senate Economics Legislation Committee, Senate, *Competition and Consumer Amendment (Misuse of Market Power) Bill 2016 Report* (2017)

Senate Education and Employment References Committee, *Inquiry into the Impact of Australia's Temporary Work Visa Programs on the Australian Labour Market and on the Temporary Work Visa Holders Final Report* (2016)

Senate Legal and Constitutional Affairs Legislation Committee, Parliament of Australia, *Counter-Terrorism Legislation Amendment (Foreign Fighters) Bill 2014* (2014)

Standing Committee of Attorneys-General Working Group of State and Territory Officers, Senate, *Proposal for Uniform Defamation Laws* (July 2004)

Standing Committee on Industry, Science and Technology, House of Representatives, *Finding a Balance towards Fair Trading in Australia* (1997)

Standing Committee on Legal and Constitutional Affairs, House of Representatives, *A Time for Change: 'Yes'/'No': Inquiry into the Machinery of Referendums* (2009)

Swanson Trade Practices Act Review Committee, Parliament of Australia, *Report to the Minister for Business and Consumer Affairs* (1976)

The Law Commission, *A Criminal Code for England and Wales*, Consultation Paper No 177 (1989)

The Law Commission, *Consent in the Criminal Law: A Consultation Paper*, Consultation Paper No 139 (1995)

The Virtual Consulting Group and Griffin NRM Pty Ltd, *National Investment in Rural Landscapes: An Investment Scenario for NFF and ACF with the Assistance of LWRRDC* (Australian Conservation Foundation and National Farmers Federation with assistance from Land & Water Resources Research & Development Corporation, 2000)

Trade Practices Act Review Committee, *Review of the Competition Provisions of the Trade Practices Act* (2003)

Victoria, Royal Commission into Family Violence, *Report and Recommendations Volume III* (2016)

Victorian Government, *Inquiry into Alternative Dispute Resolution and Restorative Justice: Final Report of the Victorian Parliament Law Reform Committee* (2009)

Victorian Law Reform Commission, *Birth registration and Birth Certificates Report* (2013)

Warner, Kate, et al, 'Public Judgement on Sentencing: Final Results from the Tasmanian Jury Sentencing Study' (Trends and Issues in Crime and Criminal Justice No 407, Australian Institute of Criminology, 2011)

Watson, Irene and Kungari Aboriginal Heritage Association, Submission No 103 to Parliament of South Australia Natural Resources Committee, *Inquiry into Unconventional Gas (Fracking) in the South East of South Australia*, 29 January 2015

Watson, Irene and Kungari Aboriginal Heritage Association, Submission to Nora Creina Golf Course and Tourism Resort, *Major Project Public Environmental Report* (January 2016)

Weatherburn, Don and David Indermaur, 'Public Perceptions of Crime Trends in New South Wales and Western Australia' (Crime and Justice Bulletin No 80, BOCSAR, 2004)

Weatherburn, Don, Jiuzhao Hua and Steve Moffatt, 'How Much Crime Does Prison Stop? The Incapacitation Effect of Prison on Burglary' (Crime and Justice Bulletin No 93, BOCSAR, 2006)

Weil, David, 'Improving Workplace Conditions through Strategic Enforcement' (Report to the Wage and Hour Division, United States Department of Labor, 2010)

Wood, James Roland T, *Royal Commission into the New South Wales Police Service*, (Report Volume 1: Corruption, Government of NSW, 1997)

E. Treaties

ASEAN Framework Agreement on Access to Biological and Genetic Resources, 24 February 2000 (draft)

Common Regime on Access to Genetic Resources, Andean Pact, Decision 391, 2 July 1996, Official Gazette 17 July 1996

Convention on Biological Diversity, opened for signature 5 June 1992, 1760 UNTS 79 (entered into force 29 December 1993)

Convention on Biological Diversity (COP), Decision V/16 (15–26 May 2006), Fifth Ordinary Meeting, www.cbd.int/decision/cop/default.shtml?id=7158

Convention on the Rights of the Child, 20 November 1989, UNTS 1577 (entered into force 2 September 1990)

International Covenant on Civil and Political Rights, opened for signature 16 December 1966, UNTS 999 (entered into force 23 March 1976)

Matters Concerning Intellectual Property and Genetic Resources, Traditional Knowledge and Folklore WIPO, WO/GA/26/6, WIPO General Assembly, Twenty-Sixth (12th Extraordinary) Session, Geneva, (September 25 to October 3, 2000)

Model Legislation for the Protection of the Rights of Local Communities, Farmers and Breeders, and for the Regulation of Access to Biological Resources, Organisation of African Unity (2000)

Model Provisions for National Laws on the Protection of Expressions of Folklore Against Illicit Exploitation and Other Prejudicial Action (UNESCO and WIPO, 1982)

Nagoya Protocol on Access to Genetic Resources and the Fair and Equitable Sharing of Benefits Arising from their Utilization to the Convention on Biological Diversity, opened for signature 2 February 2011 (entered into force 12 October 2014)

Swakopmund Protocol on the Protection of Traditional Knowledge and Expressions of Folklore within the framework of the African Regional Intellectual Property Organization (ARIPO, 2010)

United Nations Convention against Corruption, GA Res A/58/422, UNTS Vol 2349 (31 October 2003)

United Nations Declaration on the Rights of Indigenous People, GA Res 61/295, UN GAOR, 61st sess, 107th plen mtg, Agenda Item 68, Supp No 49, UN Doc A/RES/61/295 (13 September 2007)

F. Other

3AW, 'Daughter of Hit-run Victim Criticises "Lenient" Jail Sentence Handed to Driver', 1 December 2015, www.3aw.com.au/news/daughter-of-hitrun-victim-criticises-lenient-jail-sentence-handed-to-driver-20151201-glc8a1.html

Ackland, Richard, 'McCabe Litigation Took 10 Years in Two States', *Justinian*, 2 April 2011

Ackland, Richard, 'A Sully Serve for Sullied Media, Law Reformers', *The Sydney Morning Herald* (online), 30 March 2017, www.smh.com.au/news/opinion/a-sully-serve-for-sullied-media-law-reformers/2007/03/29/1174761664005.html

Ackman, Dan, 'Sherron Watkins Had Whistle, But Blew it', 14 February 2002, *Forbes*, www.forbes.com/2002/02/14/0214watkins.html

Agence-France Press, 'Internet Is 40 Years Young', 30 October 2009, *The Sydney Morning Herald,* www.smh.com.au/technology/technology-news/internet-is-40-years-young-20091030-hp5d. html

American Bar Association, *ABA Presidential Task Force on the Financing of Legal Education* (2017), www.americanbar.org/groups/legal_education/committees/aba-task-force-on-the-financing-of-legal-education-.html

AMP.NATSEM, *Buy Now Pay Later: Household Debt in Australia*, Income and Wealth (Report Issue 38, December 2015)

Arnold, Tom, 'Inside the Convention on the Constitution', *The Irish Times* (online), 1 April 2014, www.irishtimes.com/news/politics/inside-the-convention-on-the-constitution-1.1744924

Australian Broadcasting Corporation, 'Fact Check: Does Australia Have One of the Highest Loss of Species Anywhere in the World?' *ABC News* (online), 4 March 2016, www.abc.net.au/news/2015-08-19/fact-check-does-australia-have-one-of-the-highest-extinction/6691026

Australian Broadcasting Corporation, 'Mornings with Steve Austin', 612 ABC Radio, 21 March 2016, blogs.abc.net.au/queensland/2016/03/technical-issues-with-electoral-roll-polling-station-workers.html

Australian Bureau of Statistics, *Corrective Services, Australia – December 2001 Quarter* (Cat No 4512.0, ABS, 2002)

Australian Bureau of Statistics, *Corrective Services, Australia – December 2005 Quarter* (Cat No 4512.0, ABS, 2006)

Australian Bureau of Statistics, *1301.0 – Year Book Australia, 2009–10: Australia's Biodiversity* (2010) ABS, www.abs.gov.au/ausstats/abs@.nsf/Previousproducts/1301.0Feature%20Article12009%E2%80%9310?opendocument&tabname=Summary&prodno=1301.0&issue=2009%9610&num=&view=

Australian Bureau of Statistics, *Corrective Services, Australia – December 2010 Quarter* (Cat No 4512.0, ABS, 2011)

Australian Bureau of Statistics, *Personal Safety Survey: 4906.0* (2012)

Australian Bureau of Statistics, *Corrective Services, Australia – December 2012 Quarter* (Cat No 4512.0, ABS, 2013)

Australian Bureau of Statistics, *Residential Property Price Indexes: Eight Capital Cities* (2015)

Australian Bureau of Statistics, *Income at Current Prices, December Quarter 2015* (December 2015), www.abs.gov.au/ausstats/abs@.nsf/Latestproducts/5206.0Main%20Features4Dec%202015?opendocument&tabname=Summary&prodno=5206.0&issue=Dec%202015&num=&view=

Australian Bureau of Statistics, *Corrective Services, Australia – December 2015 Quarter* (Cat No 4512.0, ABS, 2016)

Australian Consumer Law, *Competition Policy Review Final Report* (March 2015), competitionpolicyreview.gov.au/final-report/

Australian Council of Social Service (ACOSS), *Inequality in Australia 2015: A Nation Divided* (2015), www.acoss.org.au/wp-content/uploads/2015/06/Inequality_in_Australia_FINAL.pdf

Australian Government, *Australia's Future Tax System: Report to the Treasurer, Part Two: Detailed Analysis, Vol 1* (AGPS, 2009)

Australian Government, *Consultations and Reviews* (2015) Treasury, www.treasury.gov.au/ConsultationsandReviews/Consultations/2015/Options-to-strengthen-the-misuse-of-market-power-law/Submissions

Australian Government, *Defence Abuse Response Taskforce: Amended Terms of Reference* (November 2015) DART, www.defenceabusetaskforce.gov.au/Aboutus/Documents/Amended-Terms-of-Reference.pdf

Australian Government, *Options to Strengthen the Misuse of Market Power Law*, (December 2015) Discussion Paper, www.treasury.gov.au/~/media/Treasury/Consultations%20and%20Reviews/Consultations/2015/Options%20to%20strengthen%20the%20misuse%20of%20market%20power%20law/Key%20Documents/PDF/dpoptions_marketpowerlaw.ashx

Australian Government, *Our North Our Future: White Paper on Developing Northern Australia* (2015), Department of Industry, industry.gov.au/ONA/whitePaper/Paper/index.html

Australian Government, *The Nagoya Protocol in Australia* (2015), Department of Environment, www.environment.gov.au/system/files/pages/9fc06ac0-f5af-4b47-a80f-d9378088d743/files/nagoya-factsheet_1.pdf

Australian Government Department of the Environment and Energy, *EPBC Act List of Threatened Flora* (2017), www.environment.gov.au/cgi-bin/sprat/public/publicthreatenedlist.pl?wanted=flora

Australian Greens, *Buffett Rule: A High-Income Tax Guarantee* (2016), greens.org.au/buffett-rule

Australian Greens, *Justice Policy* (16 April 2016), Greens Policies, greens.org.au/policies/justice

637

Australian Institute of Aborignal and Torres Strait Islander Studies, *Proof of Aboriginality*, AITSIS, aiatsis.gov.au/research/finding-your-family/before-you-start/proof-aboriginality

Australian Institute of Health and Welfare (AIHW), *Youth Detention Population in Australia* (2015)

Australian Law Reform Commission, *Talk to Us* (24 September 2015), www.alrc.gov.au/talk-us

Australian Law Reform Commission, *Incarceration Rates of Aboriginal and Torres Strait Islander Peoples* (1 December 2016), www.alrc.gov.au/inquiries/indigenous-incarceration

Australian Learning and Teaching Council, *Learning and Teaching Academic Standards Statement,* 2010, www.cald.asn.au/assets/lists/ALSSC%20Resources/KiftetalLTASStandardsStatement2010.pdf

Australian Prudential Regulation Authority, *Residential Mortgage Lending* (Prudential Practice Guide APG 223, APRA, 5 November 2014)

Australian Prudential Regulatory Authority, 'APRA Outlines Further Steps to Reinforce Sound Residential Mortgage Lending Practices' (Media Release, 9 December 2014)

Australian Prudential Regulatory Authority, *Quarterly Authorised Deposit-taking Institution Property Exposures – December 2015* (Report, APRA, 23 February 2016)

Australian Prudential Regulation Authority, *Insight*, Issue 1, 2016

Australian Public Service Commission, *APS Values and Code of Conduct in Practice* (20 April 2017), www.apsc.gov.au/publications-and-media/current-publications/values-and-conduct

Australian Red Cross, *Vulnerability Report 2016: Rethinking Justice* (2016), www.redcross.org.au/files/VulnerabilityReport2016.pdf

Australian Securities Investment Commission, 'Lenders to Improve Standards Following Interest-Only Loan Review' (Media release 15-220MR, 20 August 2015)

Australian Super, *A Guide to Providing Proof of Your Identity* (August 2016), www.australiansuper.com/~/media/Files/Forms/A%20guide%20 to%20providing%20proof%20of%20your%20identity.ashx

Australian Taxation Office, *Corporate Tax Transparency Report for the 2013– 14 Income Year* (2016), www.ato.gov.au/Business/Large-business/In-detail/Tax-transparency/Corporate-tax-transparency-report-for-the-2013-14-income-year/

Australian Taxation Office, *Corporate Tax Transparency Report for the 2014–15 Income Year* (2017), www.ato.gov.au/business/large-business/ in-detail/tax-transparency/corporate-tax-transparency-report-for-the-2014-15-income-year/?page=5#Net_losses_and_nil_tax_payable

Bacik, Ivana, 'Can a Constitutional Convention Offer Real and Radical Change?', *LSE Blog* (online), 15 December 2014, blogs.lse.ac.uk/ constitutionuk/2014/12/15/can-a-constitutional-convention-offer-real-and-radical-change/

Back, Alexandra, 'Attorney-General Simon Corbell Stands Firm On One-punch Laws', *Canberra Times,* 1 February 2016, www.canberratimes. com.au/act-news/attorneygeneral-simon-corbell-stands-firm-on-onepunch-laws-20160131-gmieeu.html

Bagaric, Mirko, 'Prisons Policy is Turning Australia into the Second Nation of Captives' (10 April 2015), *The Conversation*, theconversation. com/prisons-policy-is-turning-australia-into-the-second-nation-of-captives-38842

Barlow, John Perry, 'The Economy of Ideas' (1994) 2.03 *Wired* 1, archive. wired.com/wired/ archive/8.10/download.html

Bartels, Lorana, 'The State of Imprisonment in Australia: Can the ACT Achieve a "Human Rights" Prison?' (17 April 2015) *The Conversation*, theconversation.com/state-of-imprisonment-can-act-achieve-a-human-rights-prison-39119

Bennett, Stephen, et al, *Legal Models Working Group Report* (Social Innovation, Enterprise and Entrepreneurship Alliance, July 2014), www.employeeownership.com.au/wp-content/uploads/2015/02/ Legal-Models-Working-Group-Draft-Final-Report.pdf

Berg, Chris, 'Policy without Parliament: The Growth of Regulation in Australia' (2007) 19(3) *Institute of Public Affairs: IPA Backgrounder*

Berkovic, Nicola, 'Fewer Law Graduates are Choosing Practice as a Career', *The Australian* (online), 1 July 2011, www.theaustralian.com.au/business/legal-affairs/fewer-law-graduates-are-choosing-practice-as-a-career/story-e6frg97x-1226085138499

Billson, Bruce, 'Government Names Competition Review Panel' (27 March 2015) Media Release, bfb.ministers.treasury.gov.au/media-release/014-2014/

Birnbauer, William, 'Cheated by the Law. Exclusive – Exposed: Dirty Tricks behind Top Lawyers' Plot to Deny Justice to Cancer Victims' *The Age* (online), 29 October 2006, www.theage.com.au/news/national/cheated-by-the-law/2006/12/22/1166290725873.html

Birnbauer, William, 'Lawyer Revealed as Smoking Source', *The Age*, 28 January 2007

Birnbauer, William, 'Thrust, Parry as Law Firm Slams Ex-partner', *The Age*, 4 February 2007

Boisjoly, Roger, 'Telecon Meeting', in *Ethical Decisions – Morton Thiokol and the Challenger Disaster* (15 May 2006), www.onlineethics.org/Topics/ProfPractice/PPEssays/thiokolshuttle/shuttle_telecon.aspx

Bornstein, Josh, *The Great Uber Fairness Fallacy* (5 April 2017), joshbornstein.com.au/writing/the-great-uber-fairness-fallacy-as-a-driver-how-do-you-bargain-with-an-app/

Brandis, George, Attorney-General, 'Government Response to the Committee Report on the Counter-Terrorism Legislation Amendment Bill (No 1) 2014' (Media Release, 25 November 2014), www.attorneygeneral.gov.au/Mediareleases/Documents/GovernmentResponseToCommitteeReportOnTheCounter-TerrorismLegislationAmendmentBillNo1-2014.pdf

Briton, John, *Between the Idea and the Reality Falls the Shadow* (2015), Monash University, www.monash.edu/law/centres/clars/news-events/anzlec5-sustainable-legal-ethics

Brown, David, 'Is Rational Law Reform Still Possible in a Shock-jock Tabloid World?', *The Conversation*, 15 August 2014, theconversation. com/is-rational-law-reform-still-possible-in-a-shock-jock-tabloid-world-30416

Brown, David, 'State of Imprisonment: Prisoners of NSW Politics and Perceptions', *The Conversation*, 21 April 2015, theconversation. com/state-of-imprisonment-prisoners-of-nsw-politics-and-perceptions -38985

Browne, E J P, *Securing a Sustainable Future for Higher Education: An Independent Review of Higher Education Funding and Student Finance* (2010), www.independent.gov.uk/browne-report

Butler, Josh, 'David Leyonhjelm Proposes Abolishing Compulsory Voting', *Huffington Post*, 2 March 2016

Byres, Wayne, 'Sound Lending Standards and Adequate Capital: Preconditions for Long Term Success' (Speech delivered at COBA and CEO & Director Forum, Sydney, 13 May 2015)

CALD, *Internationalising Framework* (2017), curriculum.cald.asn.au/ generic-framework/

Cameron, David, *Cameron Prison Reform Speech in Full* (8 February 2016), www.politics.co.uk/comment-analysis/2016/02/08/cameron-prison-reform-speech-in-full

Canadian Bar Association, *Legal Futures Initiative* (2017), www.cba.org/ CBA-Legal-Futures-Initiative/Home/

Carey, John M and Yusaku Horiuchi, *Compulsory Voting and Income Inequality* (2014), papers.ssrn.com/sol3/papers.cfm?abstract_id=237 4092

Carroll, Lauren, 'Federal Prison Population Drops for First Time in 3 Decades, Eric Holder Says', *Politifact*, 23 February 2015, www.politifact.com/truth-o-meter/statements/2015/feb/23/eric-holder/federal-prison-population-drops-first-time-3-decad/

Charity Commission, *Charity Reserves* (Guidance CC19, Charity Commission, January 2016)

Chen, Adrian, 'An Uber Labor Movement born in a LaGuardia Parking Lot', *New Yorker*, 8 February 2016, www.newyorker.com/business/currency/an-uber-labor-movement-born-in-a-laguardia-parking-lot

Cherry, Kendra, *Minnesota Multiphasic Personality Inventory* (22 June 2016), Very Well, www.verywell.com/what-is-the-minnesota-multiphasic-personality-inventory-2795582

Civics Expert Group, *Whereas the People: Civics and Citizenship Education* (Report, Civics Expert Group, 1994)

Clennell, Andrew, 'How DPP Greg Smith Went from Rambo to Cream Puff With Stance of Sentencing in NSW', *Daily Telegraph*, 24 January 2014, www.dailytelegraph.com.au/how-dpp-greg-smith-went-from-rambo-to-cream-puff-with-stance-of-sentencing-in-nsw/story-e6freuy9-1226251663461

Clough, Jonathan, 'The Role of Question Trails in Assisting Juror Comprehension' (Speech delivered at the 10th Annual Jury Research and Practice Conference, Australian National University, 8 February 2013)

Coade, Melissa, 'Counting the So-called "Glut" of Law Grads', *Lawyers Weekly*, 25 November 2016, www.lawyersweekly.com.au/news/20080-counting-the-so-called-glut-of-law-grads

Committee on the Rights of the Child, *Concluding Observations on Australia* (28 August 2012), CRC/C/AUS/CO/4, www2.ohchr.org/english/bodies/crc/docs/co/CRC_C_AUS_CO_4.pdf

Commonwealth of Australia, *National Competition Policy: Report by the Independent Committee of Inquiry* (1993)

Commonwealth of Australia, *Parliamentary Debates*, House of Representatives, 26 November 2012

Commonwealth of Australia, *National Identity Proofing Guidelines* (2014), Rights and Protections, www.ag.gov.au/RightsAndProtections/IdentitySecurity/Documents/NationalIdentityProofingGuidelines.pdf

Commonwealth of Australia, *Parliamentary Debates*, House of Representatives, 12 November 2015

Commonwealth of Australia, *Parliamentary Debates*, Senate, 1 December 2015

Commonwealth of Australia, *Australian Consumer Law Fact Sheet 2* (2016), Consumer Law, consumerlaw.gov.au/files/2016/03/ACL_Review_FS2.pdf

Corporations Law Simplification Program, *Task Force – Plan of Action* (Attorney-General's Department, December 1993)

Cowra Guardian, 'Justice Reinvestment Program Reaches New Milestone', *Cowra Guardian*, 8 January 2016, www.cowraguardian.com.au/story/3649006/justice-reinvestment-program-reaches-new-milestone/?cs=593

Curran, Liz, 'Attorney General George Brandis Set to Silence CLCs', *The Saturday Paper* (online), 14 June 2014, www.thesaturdaypaper.com.au/opinion/topic/2014/06/14/attorney-general-george-brandis-set-silence-clcs/1402668000

Curran, Liz, *Solving Problems – A Strategic Approach: Examples, Processes & Strategies* (Legal Workshop Report, Australian National University College of Law, 13 May 2013), law.anu.edu.au/sites/all/files/legalworkshop/final_report_solving_legal_problems_curran_calc_13_march_2013.pdf

Curwen, Lesley, 'The Corporate Conscience', *The Guardian* (online), 21 June 2003, www.theguardian.com/business/2003/jun/21/corporatefraud.enron

Department of Defence (Cth), *Statement from General David Hurley, Chief of the Defence Force* (Department of Defence, 26 November 2012)

Department of Human Services, *Proof of Aboriginal or Torres Strait Islander Identity* (13 October 2016), Centrelink, www.humanservices.gov.au/customer/forms/ra010

Department of Human Services, *Social Media Policy for Departmental Staff* (20 April 2017), Social Media Department, www.humanservices.gov.au/corporate/media/social-media-department/social-media-policy-departmental-staff

Department of Police and Justice, Government of New South Wales, *Department of Police and Justice 2013–14 Annual Report* (2014), www.justice.nsw.gov.au/Documents/Annual%20Reports/2013-14_Annual_Report.pdf

Department of the Attorney-General, *Videolinks* (11 March 2016), Court and Tribunal Services, www.courts.dotag.wa.gov.au/V/video_link.aspx?uid=3226-3984-5962-8567

Digital Finance Analytics, *The Stressed Finance Landscape Data Analysis* (2015)

Douglas, Bob, et al, *Advance Australia Fair? What to Do About Growing Inequality in Australia* (2014), MailChimp, gallery.mailchimp.com/d2331cf87fedd353f6dada8de/files/1b2c7f48-928f-4298-81db-cf053a224320.pdf

Dow, Kwong Lee and Valerie Braithwaite, *Review of Higher Education Regulation* (Department of Education and Training, Australian Government, 2013)

Dutton, Peter, Minister for Immigration and George Brandis, Attorney-General, 'Government Responds to Report on the Australian Citizenship Amendment (Allegiance to Australia) Bill 2015' (Joint Media Release, 10 November 2015), www.minister.border.gov.au/peterdutton/2015/Pages/response-citizenship-amendment-bill.aspx

Edmund Tadros and Katie Walsh, 'Too Many Law Graduates and Not Enough Jobs', *Financial Review* (online), 22 October 2015, www.afr.com/business/legal/too-many-law-graduates-and-not-enough-jobs-20151020-gkdbyx

Environmental Justice Australia, 'Aboriginal Water Rights: Legal analysis of Submissions to the Review of the Commonwealth Water Act' (Submission, Environmental Justice Australia, 20 November 2014)

European Commission, 'Agreement on Commission's EU Data Protection Reform Will Boost Digital Single Market' (Press Release, IP/15/6321, 15 December 2015)

Evans, Adrian, *The History and Control of the Solicitors Guarantee Fund (Vic) and its Ethical Implications for the Legal Profession* (LLM Thesis, Monash University, 1997)

Evidence to Parliamentary Joint Committee on the Australian Commission for Law Enforcement Integrity, *Integrity of Overseas Commonwealth Law Enforcement Operations*, 4 October 2012

Eyers, James, 'The Man Who Blew the Whistle on CBA', *Financial Review* (online), 28 June 2014, www.afr.com/business/banking-and-finance/financial-services/the-man-who-blew-the-whistle-on-cba-20140627-je1mp

Fair Work Ombudsman, *Annual Report 2014–15* (2015)

Fair Work Ombudsman, Submission to the Senate Education and Employment Legislation Committee, *Inquiry into the Fair Work Amendment (Protecting Vulnerable Workers) Bill 2017*, 6 April 2017

Farrell, David, 'The Irish Constitutional Convention Offers a Potential Route-Map for Renewing UK Democracy', *Democratic Audit UK*, 10 October 2014, www.democraticaudit.com/?p=8625

Ferguson, Adele and Klaus Toft, '7-Eleven: The Price of Convenience', *Four Corners*, 31 August 2015

Ferguson, Adele and Sarah Danckert, '7-Eleven Kills Independent Wage Panel', *The Sydney Morning Herald*, 11 May 2016

Finder.com, *100% Home Loans: Borrow 100% of the Property Value* (2017), www.finder.com.au/100-percent-home-loans

Fraillon, Julian, et al, *National Assessment Program: Civics and Citizenship Years 6 and 10 Report 2013* (2014), ACER Research, research.acer.edu.au/civics/22

Fraser, Helen, 'Covert Recordings as Evidence in Court: The Return of Police "Verballing"?' *The Conversation,* 23 March 2013, theconversation.com/covert-recordings-as-evidence-in-court-the-return-of-police-verballing-14072

G20, *Anti-Corruption Action Plan (2013–2014)* (2012), G20 Mexico, www.oecd.org/g20/topics/anti-corruption/G20_AntiCorruption_Action_Plan_%282013-2014%29.pdf

Garber, Stefanie, 'Firms Urged to Push into Non-legal Sectors', *Lawyers Weekly* (online), 17 February 2016, www.lawyersweekly.com.au/news/17993-firms-urged-to-push-into-non-legal-sectors

Garber, Stefanie, 'Students Underexposed to In-house Roles', *Lawyers Weekly* (online), 17 February 2016, www.lawyersweekly.com.au/news/17998-students-underexposed-to-in-house-roles

Gates, Bill and Melinda Gates, *2015 Gates Annual Letter* (2015), www.gatesnotes.com/2015-annual-letter?WT.mc_id=01_21_2015_DO_com_domain_0_00&page=0&lang=en

Gillard, Julia, *National Apology for Forced Adoptions* (Speech delivered at the Great Hall of Parliament House, Canberra, 21 March 2013)

Glaze, Lauren, et al, *Correctional Populations in the United States* (NCJ 249513, US Bureau of Justice Statistics, 2015)

Gleeson, Murray, *Are the Professions Worth Keeping?* (Speech delivered at the Greek-Australian International Legal and Medical Conference, 31 May 1999)

Gleeson, Murray, *Public Confidence in the Courts* (Speech delivered at the National Judicial College of Australia, Canberra, 9 February 2007)

Godfrey, Nick, *Why is Competition Important for Growth and Poverty Reduction?* (Global Forum on Investment Report, OECD, March 2008)

Good, Erica, 'US Prison Populations Decline, Reflecting New Approach to Crime', *New York Times*, 25 July 2013, www.nytimes.com/2013/07/26/us/us-prison-populations-decline-reflecting-new-approach-to-crime.html

Gordon, Michael, 'Patrick Dodson Makes Impassioned Plea for "a Smarter Form of Justice"', *The Sydney Morning Herald*, 13 April 2016, www.smh.com.au/federal-politics/political-news/patrick-dodson-makes-emotional-plea-for-action-on-aboriginal-incarceration-20160413-go52vi.html

Gorrey, Megan and Alexandra Back, 'Man Charged Over Alleged One-punch Attack in Civic', *Canberra Times*, 8 January 2016, www.canberratimes.com.au/act-news/canberra-victim-of-new-years-one-punch-attack-in-civic-surprised-hes-alive-20160108-gm1x8e.html

Gorrey, Megan, 'Attorney-General Gordon Ramsay Says Legal Aid Critical to "Inclusive" Judiciary', *Canberra Times*, 4 February 2017, www.canberratimes.com.au/act-news/attorneygeneral-gordon-ramsay -says-legal-aid-critical-to-inclusive-judiciary-20170131-gu2d8j.html

Grant, Richard, 'Can We Account for Parliamentary Committees? A Survey of Committee Secretaries' (Parliamentary Studies Paper No 9, 2009)

Graycar, Adam, *Crime in Twentieth Century Australia* (Cat No 1301.1, ABS, 2001)

Green, Jonathan, 'Back to Prison', *ABC Background Briefing*, 18 May 2014, www.abc.net.au/radionational/programs/backgroundbriefing/2014- 05-18/5452044

Hannam, Peter, 'Parched NSW Seeks Help as National Water Commission Axed', *The Sydney Morning Herald* (online), 13 May 2015, www.smh. com.au/environment/parched-nsw-seeks-help-as-national-water- commission-axed-20150513-gh0ork.html

Harding, Luke, 'Panama Papers Source Breaks Silence over "Scale of Injustices"', *The Guardian*, 7 May 2016

Hardy, Tess and Joo-Cheong Tham, *Submission to the Senate Education and Employment Legislation Committee, Inquiry into the Fair Work Amendment (Protecting Vulnerable Workers) Bill 2017* (10 April 2017)

Hardy, Tess, 'Brandishing the Brand: Enhancing Employer Compliance through the Regulatory Enrolment of Franchisors' (Paper presented at the Labour Law Research Network Conference, Amsterdam, 25–27 June 2015)

Henderson, Anna, 'Bill Shorten Pledges to End "National Shame" By Reviving Indigenous Imprisonment Reduction Targets', *ABC News*, 19 November 2015, www.abc.net.au/news/2015-11-19/labor- pledges-to-revive-indigenous-justice-targets/6953032

Higher Education Quality Council of Ontario, *The Diversity of Ontario's Universities: A Data Set to Inform the Differentiation Discussion* (2013) HECQO, www.heqco.ca/SiteCollectionDocuments/HEQCO %20Diversity_ENG.pdf

Higher Education Standards Framework, *Tertiary Education Quality and Standards Agency*, Australian Government, www.teqsa.gov.au/teqsa-contextual-overview-hes-framework

Holland, Ian, *Senate Committees and the Legislative Process*, Parliamentary Studies Paper No 7 (2009)

Holley, Cameron and Darren Sinclair, *Water Extraction in NSW: Stakeholder Views and Experience of Compliance and Enforcement* (UNSW Report, CWI, 2015), www.connectedwaters.unsw.edu.au/sites/all/files/Water-extraction-in-NSW-stakeholder-views-of-compliance-and-enforcement-survey-report.pdf

Hopkins, Sarah, 'Justice Reinvestment Saves Huge Costs of Law-and-Order Auctions', *The Conversation*, 20 October 2014, theconversation.com/justice-reinvestment-saves-huge-costs-of-law-and-order-auctions-33018

IISD Reporting Services, 'OAS, UNEP Increase Cooperation on Environmental Rule of Law' (19 November 2014), Sustainable Development and Policy Practice, sd.iisd.org/news/oas-unep-increase-cooperation-on-environmental-rule-of-law/

Indigenous Knowledge Forum, *Indigenous Knowledge Forum Report*, Ninti One, Innovation for Remote Australia (2012), www.indigenousknowledgeforum.org/images/ikf-report.pdf

Inman, Michael, 'No One Punch Laws in ACT, Says Corbell', *Canberra Times* (online), 4 February 2014, www.canberratimes.com.au/act-news/no-onepunch-laws-in-act-says-corbell-20140203-31xpn.html

Inman, Michael, 'Suspended Sentence for Shoe Store Manager Who Stole More Than $70,000', *Canberra Times* (online), 12 November 2015, www.canberratimes.com.au/act-news/suspended-sentence-for-shoe-store-manager-who-stole-more-than-70000-20151112-gkx06r.html

Inman, Michael, 'Devout Christian Brenton Honeyman Gets Suspended Jail Sentence for Child Porn Possession', *Canberra Times* (online), 6 January 2016, www.canberratimes.com.au/act-news/devout-christian-gets-suspended-jail-sentence-for-child-porn-possession-20160106-gm08h1.html

Intergovernmental Committee on Intellectual Property and Genetic Resources, Traditional Knowledge and Folklore, *Glossary of Key Terms Related to Intellectual Property and Genetic Resources, Traditional Knowledge and Traditional Cultural Expressions* (Report of Twenty-Second Session, Geneva, July 9–13 2012)

International Consortium of Investigative Journalists and Elise Worthington, 'Why the Panama Papers Mossack Fonseca Leaks 'Really Matters' (5 April 2016), ABC News, www.abc.net.au/news/2016-04-05/why-the-panama-papers-mossack-fonseca-leaks-really-matters/7300262

Jeffrey Morris, Submission No 421 to the Senate Economics Reference Inquiry, *The Performance of the Australian Securities and Investments Commission* (21 October 2013)

Judcom NSW, *Purposes of Sentencing* (14 May 2017), Sentencing Bench Book, www.judcom.nsw.gov.au/publications/benchbks/sentencing/purposes_of_sentencing.html

Judicial College of Victoria, *Sentencing Purposes Generally,* (10 April 2015), Victorian Sentencing Manual, www.judicialcollege.vic.edu.au/eManuals/VSM/index.htm#15298.htm

Judicial Council on Cultural Diversity, *Cultural Diversity within the Judicial Context: Existing Court Resources* (15 February 2016, Judicial Council on Cultural Diversity), www.jccd.org.au/publications/

Kelly, David, 'Legal Market Ripe for Disruptive Innovation' *Lawyers Weekly,* 19 March 2016, www.lawyersweekly.com.au/opinion/16286-legal-market-ripe-for-disruptive-innovation

Kelly, Paul, 'To Succeed, Indigenous Recognition Must Be Handled Deftly', *The Australian* (online), 10 September 2014, www.theaustralian.com.au/opinion/columnists/paul-kelly/to-succeed-indigenous-recognition-referendum-must-be-handled-deftly/news-story/cd0fbee39cde82ac00297ecc9fa4bd6d

Kenny, Justice Susan, *Secrecy Provisions: Policy and Practice* (Speech delivered to the National Information Law Conference, Canberra, 24 March 2011), www.alrc.gov.au/news-media/2011/secrecy-provisions-policy-and-practice#_ftn48

Khadem, Nassim, and Craig Butt, 'Which of Australia's Biggest Companies Are Not Paying Tax', *The Sydney Morning Herald* (online), 17 December 2015, www.smh.com.au/business/the-economy/which-of-australias-biggest-companies-are-not-paying-tax-20151216-glpl3a.html

Kirby, Michael, *Plenary Address* (Speech delivered at the Inaugural National Law Reform Conference, Canberra, 14 April 2016)

Koelma, Grace, 'Australian Woman Charmaine Webster Who Legally Doesn't Exist Due to Unregistered Birth, Fights to Prove Her Identity' *News Limited*, 7 July 2014, www.news.com.au/lifestyle/real-life/australian-woman-charmaine-webster-who-legally-doesnt-exist-due-to-unregistered-birth-fights-to-prove-her-identity/news-story/eefbd76d0451458db64c84e6fea0cc06

Lauder, Simon, 'Gillian Triggs Criticises "Executive Overreach" in Defiant Speech', 6 June 2015, ABC Radio National, *AM*, www.abc.net.au/am/content/2015/s4250111.htm

Law Commission of Canada, *Policies* (22 December 2004), Library and Archives of Canada, epe.lac-bac.gc.ca/100/206/301/law_commission_of_canada-ef/2006-12-06/www.lcc.gc.ca/about/mandate-en.asp

Law Council of Australia, *Ethical Standards for Mediators* (August 2011), www.lawcouncil.asn.au/lawcouncil/images/LCA-PDF/a-z-docs/EthicalGuidelinesforMediators.pdf

Law Council of Australia, *How Many Lawyers are There in Australia?* (22 November 2016), FAQ, www.lawcouncil.asn.au/lawcouncil/index.php/12-resources/231-how-many-lawyers-are-there-in-australia

Law Council of Australia, *Review of Academic Requirements for Admission to the Legal Profession*, www.lawcouncil.asn.au/LACC/images/pdfs/01.12.14_-_Review_of_Academic_Requirements_for_Admission.pdf

Law Institute of Victoria, *Mediators* (2015), Find a Lawyer and Other Professional, www.liv.asn.au/Mediators

Law Society of NSW, *Agreement to Mediate*, www.lawsociety.com.au/cs/groups/public/documents/internetcontent/675691.pdf

Law Society of NSW, *Guidelines for Mediators Who Act as Mediators* (2017), www.lawsociety.com.au/resources/adr/MediatorsPanel/index.htm

Law Society of Scotland, *Education and Training Policy*, www.lawscot.org.uk/education-and-careers/education-and-training-policy/

Legal Education and Training Review (LETR) of England and Wales, *Setting Standards: The Future of Legal Services Education and Training Regulation in England and Wales* (June 2013), letr.org.uk/wp-content/uploads/LETR-Report.pdf

Leigh, Andrew, 'Prisons Dilemma: An Economist's Perspective on Incarceration' (Paper presented at the Justice Connections 4 Symposium, Canberra, November 2015)

Liberal Party of Australia, 'The Coalition's Policy to Protect Vulnerable Workers', 19 May 2016

Longstaff, Simon, *The Lawyer's Duty to the Community* (The Ethics Centre, 1 March 1995), www.ethics.org.au/on-ethics/our-articles/before-2014/the-lawyers-duty-to-the-community

Lowe, Philip, *National Wealth, Land Values and Monetary Policy* (Speech delivered to the 54th Shann Memorial Lecture, Perth, 12 August 2015), www.bis.org/review/r150812f.pdf

Mark, Steve and Tahlia Gordon, *Vale Appropriate Management Systems* (2015), Creative Consequences, creativeconsequences.com.au/vale-appropriate-management-systems/

Marks, Russell, 'Taking Victims Seriously', *The Monthly* (online), 14 March 2015, www.themonthly.com.au/blog/russell-marks/2015/14/2015/1426288245/taking-victims-seriously

Marshall, Virginia, *A Web of Aboriginal Water Rights: Examining the Competing Aboriginal Claim for Water Property Rights and Interests in Australia* (PhD Thesis, Macquarie University, 2014)

Martin, Douglas, 'Roger Boisjoly, 73, Dies; Warned of Shuttle Danger', *The New York Times* (online), 3 February 2012, www.nytimes.com/2012/02/04/us/roger-boisjoly-73-dies-warned-of-shuttle-danger.html?_r=0

Martin, Paul and Kip Werren, 'Discussion Paper: An Industry Plan for the Victorian Environment?' (Department of Sustainability and Environment, State Government of Victoria, 2009)

Meldrum-Hanna, Caro and Ali Russell, 'Slaving Away', *Four Corners*, 4 May 2015

Mellor, Suzanne, Kerry Kennedy and Lisa Greenwood, *Citizenship and Democracy: Australian Students' Knowledge and Beliefs: The IEA Civic Education Study of Fourteen Year Olds* (ACER, 2002)

Meyer, Lukas, 'Intergenerational Justice', in Edward Zalta (ed), *Stanford Encyclopedia of Philosophy* (2016), plato.stanford.edu/archives/sum 2016/entries/justice-intergenerational/

Milliken, Robert, 'Ending Sydney's Law-and-Order Auction', *Inside Story*, 3 April 2012, insidestory.org.au/ending-sydneys-law-and-order-auction

Moore, Elizabeth, *Crime and Justice Statistics: Bureau Brief*, Report No 77 (NSW Bureau of Crime Statistics and Research (February, 2012)

Moorhead, Richard, et al, *Designing Ethics Indicators for Legal Services Provision* (2012), papers.ssrn.com/sol3/papers.cfm?abstract_id=2159296

Moran, Susannah, 'Cloaks of Privilege and Smoking Guns', *The Australian Financial Review*, 19 May 2006

Morgan, Bronwen, and Declan Kuch, *The Sharing Economy: More than the Sum of its Parts? Implications for Legal Services* (Summary Report of Janelle Orsi Australia Workshop Series, UNSW Law School, 2014), www.activismandenterprise.weebly.com/uploads/2/2/3/2/22323902/140317_-_orsi_aus_tour_unsw_writeup_-_final.pdf

Morris, Jeffrey, *The Performance of the Australian Securities and Investments Commission* (Submission No 421 to the Senate Economics Reference Inquiry, October 21, 2013)

Morrison, Lisa, 'Twenty-year Domestic Violence Victim Attacks "Lenient" Sentence for Ex-Partner', *The West Australian* (online), 31 July 2015, au.news.yahoo.com/thewest/regional/great-southern/a/29150713/twenty-year-domestic-violence-victim-attacks-lenient-sentence-for-ex-partner/

Moss, Philip, *Independent Review of the Public Interest Disclosure Act 2013* (20 October 2016), Department of Prime Minister and Cabinet, www.dpmc.gov.au/resource-centre/government/review-public-interest-disclosure-act-2013

Murphy, Katherine, 'Labor Faces Internal Wrangle Over "Buffett rule" to Stop Wealthy Avoiding Tax', *The Guardian Australia* (online), 4 April 2017, www.theguardian.com/australia-news/2017/apr/04/labor-faces-internal-wrangle-over-buffett-rule-to-stop-wealthy-avoiding-tax

National Archives of Australia, *Legislation, Policies, Standards and Advice and Your Agency's Accountability* (August 2015), www.naa.gov.au/records-management/publications/legislation-policies-standards-advice-and-your-agencys-accountability.aspx

National Archives of Australia, Fraser Ministries – Cabinet Memoranda; A12930, Memorandum No 639: *Law v Repatriation Commission* appeal to Full Court of the Federal Court of Australia – Related to Decision No 11094 1980

National Archives of Australia: Prime Minister's Department – Correspondence files; A1209, Appeals to Federal Court for War Widows Pension 1980–1982, 1980/558 Part 1

National Economic Council, *The Buffett Rule: A Basic Principle of Tax Fairness* (April 2012), www.whitehouse.gov/sites/default/files/Buffett_Rule_Report_Final.pdf

National Mediator Accreditation System, Part III, *Practice Standards* (National Mediator Accreditation System, 2015)

National Pro Bono Resource Centre, *Review of Parramatta City Council's Social Enterprise Pro Bono Legal Panel* (2011)

National Water Commission, *Australian Water Markets: Trends and Drivers 2007–08 to 2012–13* (2013), www.nwc.gov.au/publications/topic/water-industry/trends-and-drivers-2012-13

Naylor, Bronwyn, 'The Evidence Is In: You Can't Link Imprisonment to Crime Rates', *The Conversation*, 23 April 2015, theconversation.com/the-evidence-is-in-you-cant-link-imprisonment-to-crime-rates-40074

Nelson, Felicity, 'New Law School May Leave Grads Stranded', *Lawyers Weekly* (online), 29 September 2015, www.lawyersweekly.com.au/news/17221-new-law-school-may-leave-grads-stranded

Nelson, Felicity, 'Young Lawyers View Staying Put as "Career Suicide"', *Lawyers Weekly* (online), 10 February 2016, www.lawyersweekly.com.au/careers/17953-young-lawyers-view-staying-put-as-career-suicide

NSW Bar Association, Submission to the New South Wales Department of Attorney-General and Justice, *Review of Defamation Act 2005*, undated

NSW Department of Attorney-General and Justice, 'Submission to the Review of the Defamation Act 2005' (16 February 2011), Statutory Reviews, www.justice.nsw.gov.au/justicepolicy/Pages/lpclrd/lpclrd_consultation/lpclrd_stat_reviews.aspx#ReviewofDefamationAct2005

NSW Department of Finance, Services and Innovation, *The Collaborative Economy in NSW – A Position Paper* (November 2015), www.finance.nsw.gov.au/publication-and-resources/collaborative-economy

NSW Department of Justice, *Annual Report 2015–16* (2016), www.lpab.justice.nsw.gov.au/Documents/Annual%20Report%202015-16.pdf

NSW Office of Water, 'Compliance Policy' (NSW DPI, May 2015), www.water.nsw.gov.au/__data/assets/pdf_file/0005/560192/compliance_policy_2015.pdf

O'Brien, Richard, 'Turnbull & Morrison Tax Consultants', *The Australian Independent Media Network* (online), 11 December 2016, theaimn.com/turnbull-morrison-tax-consultants/

O'Donohoe, Nick and Simon Rowell, *Going for Gold* (Big Society Capital, 2015), www.bigsocietycapital.com/sites/default/files/pdf/Golden%20Share%20Report.pdf

O'Dwyer, Kelly, 'Have Your Say on the Australian Consumer Law' (Media Release, 31 March 2016), kmo.ministers.treasury.gov.au/media-release/029-2016/

OECD Centre for Tax Policy and Administration, *Revenue Statistics 2015 – Australia* (2015), www.oecd.org/tax/revenue-statistics-australia.pdf

Office of the Public Advocate, *Legal and Child Welfare Groups Call for Reinstatement of Child Protection Powers for Children's Court* (28 February 2017), Public Advocate Victoria, www.publicadvocate.vic.gov.au/childrens-matters-media-release

Olding, Rachel, 'BOCSAR Crime Stats Boss Don Weatherburn Calls for Lighter Prison Sentences', *The Sydney Morning Herald* (online), 17 February 2016, www.smh.com.au/nsw/weatherburn-comes-out-swinging-20160216-gmvavn.html

Olson, Elizabeth, 'Law Graduate Gets Her Day in Court, Suing Law School', *New York Times* (online), 7 March 2016, www.cnbc.com/2016/03/07/law-graduate-gets-her-day-in-court-suing-law-school.html

Organisation for Economic Cooperation and Development, *Divided We Stand: Why Inequality Keeps Rising – Country Note: Australia* (2011), www.oecd.org/australia/49177643.pdf

Pannell, David, *Public Benefits, Private Benefits: The Final Framework* (Pannell Discussions No 80, 19 June 2006), www.pannelldiscussions.net/2006/06/80-public-benefits-private-benefits-the-final-framework/

Parliament of Australia, *The Higher Education Contribution Scheme* (12 August 2003), Parliamentary Library, www.aph.gov.au/About_Parliament/Parliamentary_Departments/Parliamentary_Library/Publications_Archive/archive/hecs

Parliament of Australia, *History of the Intelligence and Security Committee* (2017), Parliamentary Joint Committee on Intelligence and Security, www.aph.gov.au/Parliamentary_Business/Committees/Joint/Intelligence_and_Security/History_of_the_Intelligence_and_Security_Committee

Parliamentary Joint Committee on Intelligence and Security, 'Committee Recommends Passage of the Citizenship Bill' (Media Alert, 4 September 2015), www.aph.gov.au/Parliamentary_Business/Committees/Joint/Intelligence_and_Security/Citizenship_Bill/Media_Releases

Parliamentary Joint Committee on Intelligence and Security, Parliament of Australia, *Advisory Report into the Telecommunications (Interception and Access) Amendment (Data Retention) Bill 2014* (2015)

Passant, John, 'Taxing Resource Rents in Australia – What a Capital Idea' (Working Paper, 2016), www.researchgate.net/publication/292149294_Taxing_resource_rents_in_Australia_-_what_a_capital_idea

Phillips, Matthew, 'The World's Debt is Alarmingly High. But is it Contagious?' *The Sydney Morning Herald* (online) 25 February 2016, www.smh.com.au/business/the-economy/the-worlds-debt-is-alarmingly-high-but-is-it-contagious-20160224-gn2baj.html

Pope Francis, 'Address to Members of the International Catholic Child Bureau' (Speech delivered to International Catholic Child Bureau, Vatican, 11 April 2014), w2.vatican.va/content/francesco/en/speeches/2014/april/documents/papa-francesco_20140411_ufficio-cattolico-infanzia.html

Pope Francis, *Holy Mass in the Chapel of the Domus Sanctae Marthae with a Group of Clergy Sex Abuse Victims* (7 July 2014), w2.vatican.va/content/francesco/en/homilies/2014/documents/papa-francesco_20140707_omelia-vittime-abusi.html

Pratt, Timothy, 'Obama: "Drug Addiction Is a Health Problem, Not a Criminal Problem"', *The Guardian* (online), 30 March 2016, www.theguardian.com/us-news/2016/mar/29/barack-obama-drug-addiction-health-problem-not-criminal-problem

PricewaterhouseCoopers, *Fighting Fraud in the Public Sector* (Research Report, PWC, 2010)

Proactive Compliance Deed between the Commonwealth of Australia (as represented by the Office of the Fair Work Ombudsman) and 7-Eleven Stores Pty Ltd (6 December 2016)

Records Authority 2010/00315821 – Federal Court of Australia, 19 October 2011, www.naa.gov.au/information-management/records-authorities/types-of-records-authorities/Agency-RA/2010/00315821/

Reserve Bank of Australia, *Financial Aggregates March 2016* (RBA, 29 April 2016)

Reserve Bank of Australia, *Monthly D2 Lending and Credit Aggregates March 2016* (RBA, 29 April 2016)

Reserve Bank of Australia, *Statement on Monetary Policy* (May 2016)

Reserve Bank of New Zealand, *Summary of Submissions and Final Policy Position on the Review of the Asset Class Treatment of Residential Property Investment Loans in BS2A and BS2B* (RBNZ, 29 May 2015)

Reserve Bank of New Zealand, *Bulletin*, Vol 79(12), July 2016

Richardson, David, *Surprise Me When I'm Dead: Revisiting the Case for Estate Duties* (2016), The Australia Institute, www.tai.org.au/sites/defualt/files/Revisiting%20the%20Case%20for%20Estate%20Duties.pdf

RMIT Centre for Innovative Justice, *Affordable Justice* (2013), mams.rmit.edu.au/qr7u4uejwols1.pdf

Rosalky, David, *COAG Review of the National Water Commission* (2011)

Rose, Sally, and James Eyers, 'Australia's Banks Are "Too Big to Get Sick": APRA', *The Sydney Morning Herald* (online), 4 April 2016, www.smh.com.au/business/banking-and-finance/australias-banks-are-too-big-to-get-sick-apra-20160403-gnwztl.html#ixzz44ndw9ZLl

Royal Commission into Institutional Responses to Child Sexual Abuse, *Terms of Reference* (13 November 2014), www.childabuse royalcommission.gov.au/about-us/terms-of-reference

Rule of Law Institute of Australia, *Principles*, www.ruleoflaw.org.au/principles/

Sarre, Rick, 'Social Innovation, Law and Justice' (Paper presented at the History and Future of Social Innovation Conference, Adelaide, June 2008)

Scrutiny of Acts and Regulations Committee, Parliament of Victoria, *Alert Digest* (Alert Digest No 9, Parliament of Victoria, 2014), www.parliament.vic.gov.au/images/stories/committees/sarc/Alert_Digests/Alert_Digest_No_9_of_2014.pdf

Senate Standing Committee on Economics, *Report: Competition and Consumer Amendment (Misuse of Market Power) Bill 2016 [Provisions]*, Parliament of Australia, 16 February 2017, www.aph.gov.au/Parliamentary_Business/Committees/Senate/Economics/Misuseof marketpower16/Report

Shapiro, Jonathan, 'Exploring Australia's "Wealth Effect"', *The Sydney Morning Herald*, 19 November 2014

Shapiro, Jonathan, 'Slater and Gordon Recruit Jumps Ship as Stock Sinks to New Low', *The Age*, 29 March 2016

Sheil, Christopher, and Stilwell, Frank, *The Wealth of the Nation: Current Data on the Distribution of Wealth in Australia* (2016), Evatt Foundation, evatt.org.au/files/files/The%20Wealth%20of%20the%20Nation.pdf

Social Policy Research Centre and ACOSS, *Poverty in Australia 2016* (2014)

Standing Committee on Industry Science and Technology, House of Representatives, *Small Business in Australia: Challenges, Problems and Opportunities* (Commonwealth of Australia, 1990)

Tait, David, et al, 'Towards a Distributed Courtroom' (Consultation Document, Court of the Future Network, 2015)

Taylor, Ingmar and Larissa Andelman, 'Accessorial Liability under the *Fair Work Act*' (Paper presented at the Australian Labour Law Association, Sydney, 14–15 November 2014)

Toki, Valmaine, *Study on the Relationship between Indigenous Peoples and the Pacific Ocean* (UN ESC Permanent Forum on Indigenous Issues, Agenda Item 3 E/C.19/2016/3, 19 February 2016)

Tomlin, Sam, 'Locking Bad People Up "Works": Minister for Justice Rejects Calls for Prison Overhaul', *ABC News*, 31 March 2016, www.abc.net.au/news/2016-03-31/federal-justice-minister-rejects-prison-criticism/7289038

TOP Education Institute, *Sydney City School of Law: Australia's Newest Law School* (2016), www.top.edu.au/home/school-of-law

Trade Practices Consultative Committee, *Small Business and the Trade Practices Act* (Report Vol 1, Commonwealth of Australia, 1979)

Treasury, *Tax Expenditure Statement 2015* (Commonwealth, 2016), www.treasury.gov.au/-/media/Treasury/Publications%20and%20Media/Publications/2016/Tax%20Expenditures%20Statement%202015/Downloads/PDF/2015_TES.ashx

Treasury, *Tax Expenditure Statement 2015* (Commonwealth, January 2016), www.treasury.gov.au/PublicationsAndMedia/Publications/2016/TES-2015

Tucker, Eric, 'A Bipartisan Task Force is Suggesting a Policy Shift That Could Save the Federal Government $5 Billion', *Business Insider* (online), 26 January 2016, www.businessinsider.com/ap-task-force-recommends-how-to-cut-us-prisoner-count-by-60000-2016-1?IR=T

Turnbull, Malcolm, 'Fixing Competition Policy Drive Economic Growth and Jobs' (16 March 2016), Media Releases, www.pm.gov.au/media/2016-03-16/joint-media-statement-fixing-competition-policy-drive-economic-growth-and-jobs

UK Department for Business Innovation and Skills, *Guidance on the Consumer Protection (Amendment) Regulations* (UK Department for Business Innovation and Skills, 2014)

UN High Commissioner for Refugees (UNHCR), *Child Protection Issue Brief: Birth Registration* (August 2013), www.refworld.org/docid/523fe9214.html

UN Sustainable Development Knowledge Platform, Sustainable Goal 6, www.un.org/sustainabledevelopment/water-and-sanitation

UNICEF, 'Birth Registration: Right from the Start' (2002) 9 *Innocenti Digest* 19, www.childinfo.org/files/birthregistration_Digestenglish.pdf

UNICEF, *Every Child's Birth Right: Inequities and Trends in Birth Registration* (2013) www.unicef.org/media/files/Embargoed_11_Dec_Birth_Registration_report_low_res.pdf

United Kingdom, *Parliamentary Debates*, House of Commons, 24 February 2010

United Nations Convention against Corruption, *Resource Guide on Good Practices in the Protection of Reporting Persons* (August 2015), United Nations, www.unodc.org/documents/corruption/Publications/2015/15-04741_Person_Guide_eBook.pdf

United States Sentencing Commission, *2016 Guidelines Manual* (2016), www.ussc.gov/guidelines

United Voice and the Tax Justice Network, *Who Pays for Our Common Wealth? Tax Practices of the ASX 200* (Melbourne, 2014), www.united voice.org.au/news/who-pays-our-common-wealth

Universities Australia, Submission to the *Review of Higher Education Regulation* (2013)

US Department of Justice and US Securities and Exchange Commission, *A Resource Guide to the US Foreign Corrupt Practices Act* (US Department of Justice and US Securities and Exchange Commission, 2012)

US Department of Justice, 'Siemens AG and Three Subsidiaries Plead Guilty to Foreign Corrupt Practices Act Violations and Agree to Pay $450 Million in Combined Criminal Fines' (Press Release, 15 December 2008)

UTS Indigenous Knowledge Forum and North West Local Land Services, *Recognising and Protecting Aboriginal Knowledge Associated with Natural Resource Management*, (White Paper, Office of Environment and Heritage NSW, 2014), indigenousknowledgeforum.org/components/com_content/models/forms/white_paper.pdf

Vera Institute of Justice, *The Price of Prisons: What Incarceration Costs Taxpayers* (Vera Institute of Justice, 2012)

Victoria Bar, *Barrister's Directory* (2017), www.vicbar.com.au/barrister-directory/mediator-arbitrator-search/search-for-a-mediator

Victoria, *Parliamentary Debates*, Legislative Council, 16 August 2012

Victoria, *Parliamentary Debates*, Legislative Council, 19 August 2014

Victorian Law Reform Commission, *About Community Law Reform* (26 May 2016), www.lawreform.vic.gov.au/all-projects/about-community-law-reform

Wahlquist, Calla, 'Nigel Scullion Scoffs at Proposed National Target on Indigenous Jail Rates', *The Guardian*, 12 February 2016, www.theguardian.com/australia-news/2016/feb/12/nigel-scullion-scoffs-at-proposed-national-target-on-indigenous-jail-rates

Wall, Matthew, 'Change We Can Believe In? Ireland's Constitutional Convention Has Delivered', *Thejournal.ie*, 23 July 2013, www.thejournal.ie/readme/column-change-we-canbelieve-in-ireland%E2%80%99s-constitutional-convention-has-delivered-1003278-Jul2013

Walmsley, Roy, *World Prison Population List* (ICPR, 11ᵗʰ edn, 2016)

Waters, Cara, 'Outsourcing Jobs Frees Up Entrepreneurs', *The Sydney Morning Herald*, 4 April 2016

Webb, Julian, et al, 'Setting Standards. The Future of Legal Services Education and Training Regulation in England and Wales' (SRA, BSB, IPS, 2013), letr.org.uk

Weisbrot, David, Submission No 16 to Senate Legal and Constitutional Committee, *Inquiry into the Australian Law Reform Commission*, 28 January 2011

West Australian, 'The Native Title Divide', *The West Australian* (Perth), 27 March 2010

Wilkins, Georgia, 'Driver Sues Uber after termination', *Australian Financial Review*, 19 May 2016

Williams, Timothy, 'Police Leaders Join Call to Cut Prison Rosters', *New York Times* (online), 20 October 2015, www.nytimes.com/2015/10/21/us/police-leaders-join-call-to-cut-prison-rosters.html

Willits, Will, 'Australia Vulnerable to Debt Crisis, Says Forbes', *The Sydney Morning Herald* (online), 28 March 2016, www.smh.com.au/business/the-economy/australia-vulnerable-to-debt-crisis-says-forbes-20160328-gns1jn.html

World Health Organization (WHO), *Tobacco Fact Sheet No 339* (Fact Sheet No 339, WHO, 6 July 2015)

Yeates, Clancy, 'Mortgage Brokers to Remain in Spotlight after ASIC Review', *The Sydney Morning Herald* (online), 8 May 2016, www.smh.com.au/business/banking-and-finance/mortgage-brokers-to-remain-in-spotlight-after-asic-review-20160506-goo666

Yeats, William Butler, 'Sailing to Byzantium' (15 April 2016), Poetry Foundation, www.poetryfoundation.org/poem/172063